Knowledge of interpersonal communication is essential to maintaining healthy relationships. This book will help you better understand your communication and improve your skills. Check out the list of common interpersonal communication issues below and use the guide to find some (but not all!) of the relevant content in the book. After reading the text coverage, try the feature activities and watch the videos in VideoCentral* at **bedfordstmartins.com/reflectrelate**. *See the inside back cover for information on how to access VideoCentral.

TRY THESE FEATURES . . .

AND WATCH THESE VIDEOS . . .

Skills Practice	Self-Reflection	Focus on Culture	Self-Quiz	VideoCentral
Learn how to be a competent online communicator on page 27	Think about ethical obligations when communicating online on page 24			Watch *self-monitoring* and consider how to adjust your communication
Practice overcoming negative self-fulfilling prophecies on page 41	Ponder how others' impressions of you influence your sense of self on page 41	Read about appearance cultures and self-esteem on page 44	Test your self-esteem on page 45	View how *social comparison* and *self-fulfilling prophecies* affect your self-esteem
Learn how to better express empathy on page 100		Think about how your race affects your perception of others on page 87	Find out how to empathize with others on page 100	Review *empathy* to analyze how well you express empathy
Respond effectively to someone who needs emotional support on page 137	Consider the links among feedback, empathy, and emotional expression on page 129			Look at *supportive communication* and think about how you help friends in need
Improve your responding abilities during online encounters on page 155	Examine how negative feedback can influence an interaction on page 153	Learn why perceived differences can influence your ability to listen on page 156	Gauge how multitasking online can divide your attention on page 150	
Discover how to use cooperative language online on page 195	Ponder whether always being as informative as possible is the best choice on page 193		Test your level of deception acceptance on page 204	View *"you" language,* *"I" language,* and *"we" language* for pointers on speaking competently
		Consider how the use of touch varies in different cultures on page 224		
Create conflict resolutions through collaboration on page 259	Consider the consequences for using reactivity in response to conflict on page 258	Learn about radical pacifism as a way to approach conflict on page 261	Learn how you approach conflict on page 256	Look at *collaboration,* *accommodation,* *competition,* and *avoidance* to learn about conflict approaches
Practice communicating more competently when jealous on page 311	Assess your views on types of betrayal on page 308	Read about infidelity around the world on page 310	Think about how often you betray romantic partners on page 307	View *relational maintenance* and consider if the relationship is worth saving
Improve your use of technology to communicate with family on page 336	Think about the role of family stories on page 327	Think about the balance of autonomy and connection on page 338	Find out what type of family communication pattern you have on page 331	
Practice online interactions with long-distance friends on page 376			Test how durable your friendships are on page 375	Watch *agentic friendships* and *communal friendships* to better understand friendship types
Learn how to sharpen your advocacy skills on page 402	Assess the communication behaviors of successful people at work on page 402	Confront the model minority myth on page 403	Test your peer relationship maintenance on page 398	Review *upward communication* and *advocacy* for insight on workplace messages

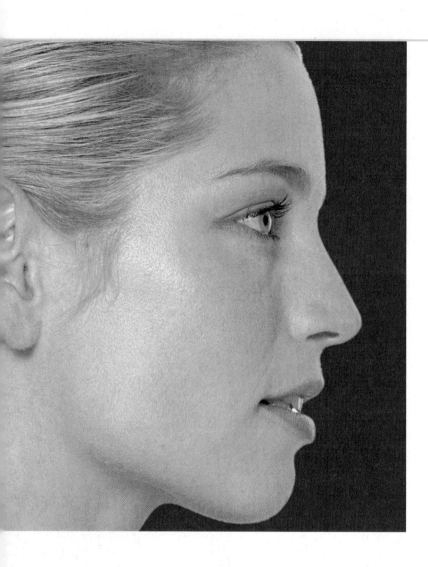

Reflect & Relate

AN INTRODUCTION TO INTERPERSONAL COMMUNICATION

Steven McCornack

Michigan State University

THIRD EDITION

Bedford/St. Martin's

Boston • New York

For Bedford/St. Martin's

Publisher for Communication: Erika Gutierrez
Senior Developmental Editor: Noel Hohnstine
Editorial Assistant: Alexis Smith
Production Editor: Jessica Gould
Assistant Production Manager: Joe Ford
Senior Market Development Manager: Sally Constable
Marketing Manager: Stacey Propps
Copy Editor: Virginia Perrin
Indexer: Melanie Belkin
Photo Researcher: Susan McDermott Barlow
Permissions Manager: Kalina K. Ingham
Art Director: Lucy Krikorian
Text Design: Jerilyn Bockorick
Cover Design: Billy Boardman
Cover Photos: Young woman, profile © Getty Images; Man, profile © Ron Krisel/Getty Images
Composition: Cenveo Publisher Services
Printing and Binding: RR Donnelley and Sons

President, Bedford/St. Martin's: Denise B. Wydra
Presidents, Macmillan Higher Education: Joan E. Feinberg and Tom Scotty
Director of Development: Erica T. Appel
Director of Marketing: Karen R. Soeltz
Production Director: Susan W. Brown
Associate Production Director: Elise S. Kaiser
Managing Editor: Shuli Traub

Library of Congress Control Number: 2012943458

Manufactured in the United States of America.

7 6 5 4 3
f e d c b

For information, write: Bedford/St. Martin's, 75 Arlington Street, Boston, MA 02116 (617-399-4000)

ISBN 978-0-312-56459-9   ISBN 978-1-4576-0468-3 (Loose-leaf Edition)
ISBN 978-1-4576-0461-4 (Instructor's Annotated Edition)

At the time of publication, all Internet URLs published in this text were found to accurately link to their intended Web sites. If you do find a broken link, please forward the information to asmith@bedfordstmartins.com so that it can be corrected for the next printing.

"Have a relationship with a person that goes on for years, well that's completely unpredictable. You've cut off all your ties to the land and you're sailing into the unknown; into uncharted seas. People hold onto these images—father, mother, husband, wife— because they seem to provide some firm ground. But there's no wife there. What does that mean, a wife? A husband? A son? A baby holds your hands, and then suddenly there's this huge man lifting you off the ground, and then he's gone. Where's that son?"

—*My Dinner with Andre* (1981)

One of the things I love most about teaching interpersonal communication is the connections I forge with my students. Spending time with smart, interesting, and diverse young people who are curious about ideas and hungry for knowledge is an honor, a privilege, and a delight. In class and during office hours, we discuss how course content can solve perplexing real-life communication challenges. During these conversations, I can't help but notice how different my students today are from their predecessors. Hairstyle and clothing variations are obvious. So, too, are the differences in pop culture referents; current students grew up with *Arthur*, *South Park*, and *Glee* rather than *Sesame Street*, *Friends*, and *Cosby*. But the biggest difference is the students' degree of technological immersion. When teaching, I see row after row of laptops, tablets, and smartphones. Before class begins or while standing outside my office door, students seamlessly transition between talking directly with one another to communicating online—texting, checking Facebook, watching and commenting on YouTube, or posting to Twitter.

Yet despite these differences, my current students and their predecessors share the same motivations for taking the class: they want to communicate more skillfully; they want to know how to better handle jealousy, anger, betrayal, and grief; and—more than anything else—*they want to improve their relationships*. It is an enduring joy for me to help them master material that can achieve such goals. When they complete the course, they may still be tethered to their technology, but they'll also carry with them the latest theory and research on social media, interpersonal relationships, and communication competence, empowering them to make wise communicative decisions both online and off.

My students and my experiences teaching them are what originally motivated me to write *Reflect & Relate*. I wanted to provide my fellow interpersonal teachers, and their students, with a textbook that is at once welcoming, friendly, personal, trustworthy, and practical. A book that is rock solid in content, represents the finest of new and classic scholarship in our discipline, and provides a clear sense of the field as a domain of scientific endeavor, not just "common sense." A book that doesn't read like a typical textbook, but instead is so engaging that students might "accidentally" read through entire chapters before they realize they have done so! A book featuring examples that hook students' interest, clearly illustrate the concepts being discussed, and help students relate theory and research to real-life situations. And, of course, my core mission: a book that doesn't just tell students what to do, but teaches students *how* to systematically reason through interpersonal communication challenges. Thus, students walk away from reading it knowing how to solve their own problems and flexibly adapt to dynamic changes in contexts and relationships. Everything in *Reflect & Relate* is designed to achieve these objectives.

When it came time to revise *Reflect & Relate* for the third edition, I drew upon suggestions given by instructors and students during my conversations with them, and the wisdom so graciously offered by many of you in your detailed reviews. From this rich knowledge base, I built a revision that radically boosts the book's utility for teachers and increases its relevance for today's tech-savvy student population. My first step was to reach students where they already spend most of their time: online. In addition to providing the latest scholarship on online communication, I want students to take advantage of the Web's interactivity while reading *Reflect & Relate*. The new VideoCentral feature is one way to do just that. By prompting students to watch and respond to online videos, Video-Central merges online and book resources to help students better understand key concepts. Even more, the new *InterpersonalClass* provides students and teachers with a robust online course space where they can access the e-book, watch videos, take quizzes, and interact through discussion forums and message boards, giving students a chance to practice all the online interpersonal skills *Reflect & Relate* teaches!

The third edition also contains a ton of new and recent research representing the very best of interpersonal scholarship, including the impact of the Internet on listening and attention, long-distance romantic relationship maintenance, supportive communication, and much more. Two new chapters on family relationships and friendships, respectively, provide students with in-depth coverage of these important relationship types, while scores of new examples—*The Hunger Games*, *How I Met Your Mother*, Walter Mischel's famous "marshmallow experiment," and even the NFL, to name just a few—will resonate with students and illustrate key concepts for them. In addition, interpersonal communication competence now appears throughout the book—including a special section on online competence in Chapter 1—so students will be thinking about interpersonal skills from the very start of the book. Meanwhile, the new Instructor's Annotated Edition offers more instructional support than ever before.

I'm thrilled about all that *Reflect & Relate* has to offer you and your students, and I would love to hear what you think about it. Please feel free to drop me a line at **mccornac@msu.edu** or on Facebook so we can chat about the book and the course, or just "talk shop" about teaching interpersonal communication.

Features

Reflect & Relate Offers an Accessible, New Look at the Discipline

- ***Reflect & Relate* presents a fresh perspective on interpersonal communication.** *Reflect & Relate* weaves together discussions of classic and cutting-edge scholarship from interpersonal communication, psychology, sociology, philosophy, and linguistics. But unlike other texts, the focus remains on how these concepts are linked to interpersonal communication and how communication skills can be improved.

- *Reflect & Relate* **balances new topics of growing interest along with classic coverage.** The text integrates coverage of social media, workplace bullying, multitasking online, and other new topics alongside familiar topics like self-awareness, conflict approaches, and nonverbal communication codes.

- **Integrated discussions on culture and gender appear in every chapter.** *Reflect & Relate* treats individual and cultural influences as integral parts of the story by tackling in every chapter the myths and realities of how race, gender, ethnicity, sexual orientation, religion, and age shape communication. In the third edition, new examples and updated coverage include the differences between high- and low-context cultures and how gender (in)equality around the world influences power.

- *Reflect & Relate* **offers clear explanations, engaging examples, and a stunning art program.** The text is truly a page-turner, engaging students' interest with clear and compelling writing. Nearly every major concept is illustrated with examples drawn from pop culture, history, current events, and everyday life—examples that reflect the diversity of students themselves in terms of age, gender, lifestyle, occupations, and culture. Meanwhile, the smart, lavish art program works with the examples to grab students' attention and focus them on the subject at hand.

Reflect & Relate Helps Students Look More Deeply at Themselves—and Develop Skills for a Lifetime

- *Self-Reflection* **questions foster critical self-awareness.** Self-awareness is essential for effective communication, and carefully placed *Self-Reflection* questions teach students how to examine their own experiences and communication in light of theory and research. As a result, students gain a better understanding of concepts—such as emotional intelligence, stereotyping, and relationship ethics—and of themselves. They also learn the habit of ongoing critical self-reflection, which leads to better communication outcomes.

- *Skills Practice* **exercises strengthen students' abilities.** Every chapter contains three skills exercises—one devoted to online communication—that give step-by-step instruction on practical skills such as appropriately self-disclosing and interpreting nonverbal codes. *Skills Practice* activities are specifically designed to be easily and practically implemented by students in their everyday lives.

- *Focus on Culture* **boxes and** *Self-Quiz* **tests help students gain knowledge about their own communication.** *Focus on Culture* boxes challenge students to think about how the influence of their own cultures shapes their communication. Rooted in research, *Self-Quiz* exercises help students analyze their strengths and weaknesses so they can focus on how to improve their communication.

Reflect & Relate Helps Students Improve Their Relationships

- **Romantic, family, friend, and workplace relationships are addressed individually.** Tailoring communication strategies to particular relationships is both essential and challenging, so *Reflect & Relate* devotes four full chapters to these key communication contexts, giving students in-depth knowledge along with practical strategies for using communication to improve relationships. Special emphasis is given to relationship maintenance—a key relational concern many students bring to the classroom.

- **Unique *Making Relationship Choices* case studies take application to a new level.** These activities challenge students to draw on all their knowledge when facing difficult relationship issues and create their own solutions. Instead of just asking students "What would you do?" or offering them solutions, *Making Relationship Choices* teaches students how to systematically reason through problems to generate their own constructive solutions. Students walk step-by-step through realistic scenarios—critically self-reflecting, considering others' perspectives, determining best outcomes, and identifying potential roadblocks—to make informed communication decisions.

What's New in the Third Edition?

Reflect & Relate has the latest on communicating online and uses the Internet to reach students

- **Cutting-edge coverage of online communication.** Whether social networking sites or Twitter, text messages or IMs, *Reflect & Relate* encourages students to reflect on their own online communication behavior. The entire book is thoroughly updated with the absolute latest research, such as online impression management and online jealousy. By pairing current scholarship with practical advice on how to improve skills, the book gives students all the tools they need to immediately make more informed choices. The text also features "hot off the press" research from two of the top scholars in online communication—Malcolm Parks (University of Washington) and Joe Walther (Michigan State University)—as well as unique content provided by Dr. Parks regarding online competence in Chapter 1.

- **Newly integrated VideoCentral helps students *see* concepts in action and encourages self-reflection.** The new VideoCentral feature merges *Reflect & Relate* with the Web by connecting theories in the text with online video illustrations that help students *really* understand interpersonal communication. A fully interactive feature, each video activity includes two reflection questions that encourage students to consider how the concepts may impact their own relationships and lives. With more than 70 videos in the collection, there are multiple opportunities in each chapter to assign the videos as the basis for journal entries or to start class discussions. For ideas on how to integrate VideoCentral into your course, see the Instructor's Annotated Edition and the Instructor's Resource Manual. To access the videos and for a complete list of available clips, see the inside back cover or visit **bedfordstmartins.com/reflectrelate**.

- *InterpersonalClass* **makes going digital easy.** Bringing together content and tools that help you manage your course materials, classes, and students, this online course space is preloaded with the *e-Book for Reflect & Relate*, more than 70 videos (from *VideoCentral: Interpersonal Communication*), abundant quiz and test questions, and more. You can easily customize the site by adding notes, readings, links, and video (your own or embedded from sites like YouTube). You can also create assignments around any of the content in *InterpersonalClass*, including sections from the e-book, chapter summaries, quizzes, and *VideoCentral*. The Video tab makes it easy to upload, embed, and comment on video as well as create video assignments for the individual student, for groups, and for the whole class. Finally, you can stay on top of individual and classroom performance with powerful testing, tracking, grading, and organizing tools. Learn more at **yourinterpersonalclass.com**.

Reflect & Relate provides a new structure that offers flexibility and in-depth coverage

- **New, full chapters on family relationships and friendships.** To help students better understand these important relationship types and to allow instructors flexibility in covering relationships in their courses, these two new chapters provide in-depth and up-to-date discussions:
  - Chapter 10, "Relationships with Family Members," delves into the communication that defines families, like family stories and maintenance tactics, while also exploring challenges like stepfamily transitions, conflict, and parental favoritism.
  - Chapter 11, "Relationships with Friends," explains how and why we make friends, how friendships change over our lifetime, types of friendships, and even friendship rules. It also includes communication strategies for keeping up with long-distance friends and handling friendship betrayal.

- **Integrated coverage of interpersonal communication competence.** To help reinforce the importance of communication competence in all interactions, *Reflect & Relate* now integrates this essential content throughout the entire book. Starting in Chapter 1, students are introduced to the principles of competence, both online and off. Then in subsequent chapters, students will learn about how competence influences all areas of interpersonal communication, including online self-presentation, verbal aggression, defensiveness, communication apprehension, and ethnocentrism.

Reflect & Relate offers lots of new content in areas that interest students the most

- **New, cutting-edge scholarship in hot areas.** Topics like multitasking online, workplace bullying, conflict approaches, social media, and supportive communication can be found in every chapter. This new content reflects issues of concern for today's students and represents the very best of scholarship within the field of interpersonal communication.

- **Current, powerful stories and images hook students' interest.** *Reflect & Relate* is full of new, hip, and relatable examples that students will want to read.

  - *The text and photo program* pulls from pop culture—everything from *The Hunger Games* to *Modern Family*—as well as current events and real stories from the author and his students to provide content that resonates with students and is easy to show and discuss in class.

  - *New chapter openers* feature a diverse group of contributors who share amazing, real, and compelling stories about the impact of interpersonal communication in everyday life. Whether dealing with a long-distance partner (Chapter 1), coping with difficult emotions (Chapter 4), or understanding family relationships (Chapter 10), these are stories that students can look to, learn from, and use to transform their own lives and relationships.

Reflect & Relate now has even more instructor support with an Instructor's Annotated Edition

Developed by Alicia Alexander (Southern Illinois University Edwardsville), the Instructor's Annotated Edition (IAE) offers more than 120 activity ideas, assignment tips, in-class discussion topics, and media suggestions, as well as ways to incorporate clips from *VideoCentral: Interpersonal Communication* into your class. Additionally, the IAE provides an Activity Guide full of classroom exercise ideas culled from interpersonal instructors around the country and a special introduction from author Steve McCornack called "Teaching with *Reflect & Relate*." See the Resources for Instructors section on pages xii–xiii for more details about this and other available supplements.

Digital Options

For more information on these resources, please visit the online catalog at **bedfordstmartins.com/reflectrelate/catalog**.

New! *InterpersonalClass for Reflect & Relate*. *InterpersonalClass* is designed to support students in all aspects of the introduction to interpersonal communication course. It's fully loaded with the *e-Book for Reflect & Relate*, clips from

VideoCentral: Interpersonal Communication, and multiple opportunities for students to assess their learning. Even better, new functionality makes it easy to upload and annotate video, embed YouTube clips, and create video assignments for individual students, groups, or the whole class. Adopt *InterpersonalClass* and get all the premium content and tools in one fully customizable course space; then assign, rearrange, and mix our resources with your own. **Learn more at yourinterpersonalclass.com.**

Student site at bedfordstmartins.com/reflectrelate. Students will find an abundance of online and free study tools to help them excel in class, including expanded chapter quizzes with more questions than ever, chapter summaries, vocabulary flash cards, and a glossary. In addition, students can access other online resources such as *VideoCentral: Interpersonal Communication* and the *e-Book for Reflect & Relate*.

Reflect & Relate **e-books and digital options.** The *e-Book for Reflect & Relate* includes the same content as the print book and allows students to add their own notes and highlight important information. Instructors can customize the e-book by adding their own content and deleting or rearranging the chapters. Another option is the *Bedford e-Book to Go*, a PDF-style e-book downloadable to your laptop or tablet. Digital versions of *Reflect & Relate* are also available through our publishing partners' sites: CourseSmart, Barnes & Noble Nook-Study, Kno, CafeScribe, or Chegg. For more information, see **bedfordstmartins .com/ebooks**.

Resources for Students and Instructors

For more information on these resources or to learn about package options, please visit the online catalog at **bedfordstmartins.com/reflectrelate/catalog**.

Resources for Students

Student Workbook for Reflect & Relate, **Third Edition,** by Jennifer Samonte Valencia (Design Institute of San Diego). This workbook provides interactive study outlines built around key terms and concepts to help students develop a stronger grasp of the material. In addition, vocabulary activities reinforce terminology, communication and relationship exercises allow students to practice their skills, and practice quizzes help them prepare for examinations.

The Essential Guide to Intercultural Communication, by Jennifer Willis-Rivera (University of Wisconsin, River Falls). This brief and useful guide offers an overview of key communication areas, including perception, verbal and nonverbal communication, interpersonal relationships, and organizations, from a uniquely intercultural perspective. Enhancing the discussion are contemporary and fun examples drawn from real life, as well as an entire chapter devoted to intercultural communication in popular culture.

The Essential Guide to Group Communication, **Second Edition,** by Dan O'Hair (University of Kentucky) and Mary Wiemann (Santa Barbara City College). This concise and incisive print text explains the role of group communication within organizations and other settings and contains useful guidelines for acting as an effective leader, avoiding groupthink, and achieving optimal results.

The Essential Guide to Rhetoric by William M. Keith (University of Wisconsin, Milwaukee) and Christian O. Lundberg (University of North Carolina, Chapel Hill). Written by two leaders in the field, this concise guide combines concrete, relevant examples with jargon-free language to provide an accessible and balanced overview of key historical and contemporary rhetorical theories.

Media Career Guide: Preparing for Jobs in the 21st Century, by Sherri Hope Culver (Temple University) and James Seguin (Robert Morris College). Practical, student-friendly, and revised with recent statistics on the job market, this guide includes a comprehensive directory of media jobs, practical tips, and career guidance for students considering a major in the media industries.

Resources for Instructors

For more information or to order or download the Instructor Resources, please visit the online catalog at **bedfordstmartins.com/reflectrelate/catalog**.

New! *Instructor's Annotated Edition for Reflect & Relate,* **Third Edition,** edited by Alicia Alexander (Southern Illinois University Edwardsville). A valuable resource for instructors with any level of experience, the comprehensive Instructor's Annotated Edition provides more than 120 suggestions for activities and assignments, recommendations for videos and Web sites that illustrate course concepts, and tips for starting in-class discussions. In addition, a special introduction from author Steven McCornack at the front of the Instructor's Annotated Edition provides insight into how the book works, while the Activity Guide—a collection of classroom activities submitted by interpersonal instructors around the country—is sure to spark a new idea for an activity in your class.

Instructor's Resource Manual for Reflect & Relate, **Third Edition,** by Joseph Ortiz (Scottsdale Community College), Marion Boyer (Kalamazoo Valley Community College, Emeritus), and Curt VanGeison (St. Charles Community College). The extensive Instructor's Resource Manual includes teaching notes on managing an interpersonal communication course, organization, and assessment; sample syllabi; advice on addressing ESL and intercultural issues; and tips for using the pedagogical features of *Reflect & Relate*. In addition, a teaching guide provides suggestions for implementing the book's thorough coverage of cultural issues, and a **new** section offers guidance on getting into VideoCentral and getting the most out of it. Every chapter also includes lecture outlines and class discussion starters, class and group exercises, assignment suggestions, video and music recommendations, and Web site links.

Test Bank for Reflect & Relate, **Third Edition,** by Charles J. Korn (Northern Virginia Community College). Available both in print and as software formatted for Windows and Macintosh, the Test Bank is one of the largest for the introductory interpersonal communication course, with more than 100 multiple-choice, true/false, short-answer, and essay questions for every chapter. This easy-to-use Test Bank also identifies the level of difficulty for each question, includes the book page the answer is found on, and connects every question to a learning objective.

Teaching Interpersonal Communication: Resources and Readings by Elizabeth J. Natalle (University of North Carolina, Greensboro). The first professional resource written specifically for the introductory interpersonal communication course, *Teaching Interpersonal Communication* provides instructors with practical advice on course logistics ranging from how to develop a teaching approach to how to manage a classroom, including constructing a syllabus, administering tests, and integrating theory and skills into a course. The book covers scholarly issues and includes excerpts from five foundational readings in the field and an annotated bibliography of more than 75 primary sources.

The Interpersonal Communication e-Newsletter is a teaching and research e-newsletter for instructors of the introductory interpersonal communication course. Sign up by e-mailing ipc@bedfordstmartins.com. You can also access an archive of the e-newsletters in the Instructor Resources tab at **bedfordstmartins.com/reflectrelate/catalog.**

PowerPoint slides for *Reflect & Relate* provide support for important concepts addressed in each chapter, including graphics of key figures and questions for class discussion. The slides are available for download from the Instructor Resources tab at **bedfordstmartins.com/reflectrelate/catalog.**

VideoCentral: Interpersonal Communication DVD. The instructor DVD for *VideoCentral: Interpersonal Communication* gives you another convenient way to access the collection of more than 70 clips. The DVD is available upon adoption of *Reflect & Relate*; please contact your local publisher's representative.

Content for Course Management Systems. Plug our content into your course management system. Whatever you teach—whether you use Blackboard, WebCT, Desire2Learn, Angel, Sakai, or Moodle—adopters can download cartridges containing content specifically designed for *Reflect & Relate* with no strings attached. Visit **bedfordstmartins.com/coursepacks** for more information and to download coursepacks.

The Bedford/St. Martin's Video Resource Library. A wide selection of interpersonal communication-related movies is available. Qualified instructors are eligible to select videos from the resource library upon adoption of the text. Please contact your local publisher's representative for more information.

Acknowledgments

I would like to thank everyone at Bedford/St. Martin's who was involved in this project and whose support made it possible, especially Macmillan Higher Education Presidents Joan Feinberg and Tom Scotty, Bedford/St. Martin's President Denise Wydra, Director of Development Erica Appel, and Production Director Sue Brown. Thanks to the editorial team who worked with me throughout the process: Publisher Erika Gutierrez and Editorial Assistant Alexis Smith. A very special thanks to the person most intimately involved in this revision, Senior Editor Noel Hohnstine. Without your brilliant editing, dedication to artistic integrity, creative insights, patience, humor, kindness, unwavering optimism, and unfailing support, this third edition would never have come to fruition. This book is *yours*. The book also would not have come together without the efforts of Managing Editor Shuli Traub and Project Editor Jessica Gould, who oversaw the book's tight schedule; the watchful eyes of Assistant Production Manager Joe Ford; and the beautiful new design by Jerilyn Bockorick and stunning photo research by Susan McDermott Barlow. The enthusiasm and support from the marketing team is particularly appreciated: Director of Marketing Karen Melton Soeltz, Marketing Manager Stacey Propps, Senior Marketing Development Manager Sally Constable, Marketing Assistants Allyson Russell and Kate George, and the entire sales force of Bedford/St. Martin's.

On a more personal level, I want to thank all those who assisted me personally with the book during its development, and those who collaborated with me in contributing their extraordinary stories to the text: Melissa Seligman, Vy Higginsen, Brenda Villa, Eric Staib, Leigh-Anne Goins, Vivian Derr, and Silvia Amaro. I would like to thank my undergraduate and graduate mentors, Malcolm Parks and Barbara O'Keefe, for instilling within me a fierce love of our discipline and deep respect for the sacred endeavor that is undergraduate teaching. Thanks to my parents, Connie and Bruce McCornack, for raising me to value reading, books, and the unparalleled power of engaging human narrative—both spoken and written. Thanks to my boys—Kyle, Colin, and Conor—who have blessed and enriched my life more than words on a page could ever express. And most of all, I want to thank my unfailing source for relevant and interesting examples, Kelly Morrison. Your exceptional skill in the classroom, and the broad and deep generosity that marks your interactions with others in the world at large, are a constant source of inspiration for me as teacher, spouse, parent, and human being.

Throughout the development of this textbook, hundreds of interpersonal communication instructors voiced their opinion through surveys, focus groups, and reviews of the manuscript, and I thank them all.

For the third edition: Ashley Fitch Blair, *Union University*; Angela Blais, *University of Minnesota, Duluth*; Deborah Brunson, *University of North Carolina, Wilmington*; Cassandra Carlson, *University of Wisconsin, Madison*; Kristin Carlson, *University of Minnesota, Duluth*; Janet Colvin, *Utah Valley University*; Andrew Cuneo, *University of Wisconsin, Milwaukee*; Melissa Curtin, *University of California, Santa Barbara*; Paige Davis, *Cy-Fair College*; Sherry Dewald, *Red Rocks Community College*; Marcia D. Dixson, *Indiana University–Purdue University, Fort Wayne*; Jean Farrell, *University of Maryland*; David Gaer, *Laramie County Community College*; Jodi Gaete, *Suffolk County Community College*; Carla Gesell-Streeter, *Cincinnati State Technical and Community College*; Neva Gronert, *Arapahoe Community College*; Katherine Gronewold, *North Dakota State University*; Virginia Hamilton, *University of California, Davis*; Kristin Haun, *University of Tennessee, Knoxville*; Doug Hurst, *St. Louis Community College, Meramec*; Nicole Juranek, *Iowa Western Community College*; Janice Krieger, *Ohio State University*; Gary Kuhn, *Chemekata Community College*; Melanie Lea-Birck, *Bossier Parish Community College*; Myra Luna Lucero, *University of New Mexico*; Valerie Manno Giroux, *University of Miami*; Sorin Nastasia, *Southern Illinois University Edwardsville*; David Naze, *Prairie State College*; Gretchen Norling, *University of West Florida*; Laura Oliver, *University of Texas, San Antonio*; Lance Rintamaki, *University at Buffalo*; Jeanette Ruiz, *University of California, Davis*; Rebecca Sailor, *Aims Community College*; Alan H. Shiller, *Southern Illinois University Edwardsville*; Mara Singer, *Red Rocks Community College*; Jamie Stech, *Iowa Western Community College*; Deborah Stieneker, *Arapahoe Community College*; Kevin Stoller, *Indiana University–Purdue University, Fort Wayne*; Renee Strom, *St. Cloud State University*; Deatra Sullivan-Morgan, *Elmhurst College*; Marcilene Thompson-Hayes, *Arkansas State University*; Lindsay Timmerman, *University of Wisconsin, Milwaukee*; Curt VanGeison, *St. Charles Community College*; Charles Veenstra, *Dordt College*; Jamie Vega, *Full Sail University*; Judith Vogel, *Des Moines Area Community College*; Thomas Wagner, *Xavier University*.

For the second edition: Michael Laurie Bishow, *San Francisco State University*; Angela Blais, *University of Minnesota, Duluth*; Judy DeBoer, *Inver Hills Community College*; Greg Gardner, *Rollins College*; Jill Gibson, *Amarillo College*; Betsy Gordon, *McKendree University*; Robert Harrison, *Gallaudet University*; Brian Heisterkamp, *California State University, San Bernardino*; Eileen Hemenway, *North Carolina State University*; Yanan Ju, *Connecticut State University*; Beverly Kelly, *California Lutheran University*; Howard Kerner, *Polk Community College*; Karen Krumrey-Fulks, *Lane Community College*; Karen Krupar, *Metro State College of Denver*; Gary Kuhn, *Chemeketa Community College*; Victoria Leonard, *College of the Canyons*; Annie McKinlay, *North Idaho College*; Michaela Meyer, *Christopher Newport University*; Maureen Olguin, *Eastern New Mexico University, Roswell*; James Patterson, *Miami University*; Evelyn Plummer, *Seton Hall University*; Laurie Pratt, *Chaffey College*; Narissra M. Punyanunt-Carter, *Texas Tech University*; Thomas Sabetta, *Jefferson Community College*; Bridget Sampson, *California State University, Northridge*; Cami Sanderson, *Ferris State University*; Rhonda Sprague, *University of Wisconsin, Stevens Point*; Robert Steinmiller,

Henderson State University; Deborah Stieneker, *Arapahoe Community College*; Anita J. Turpin, *Roanoke College*; Inci Ozum Ucok, *Hofstra University*; Paula Usrey, *Umpqua Community College*; Charles Veenstra, *Dordt College*; Sylvia Walters, *Davidson Community College*; Michael Xenos, *University of Wisconsin, Madison*; Phyllis Zrzavy, *Franklin Pierce University*.

For the first edition: A special thank you goes to the dedicated members of the editorial board, whose commitment to the project was surpassed only by their help in shaping the book: Kathy Adams, *California State University, Fresno*; Stuart Bonnington, *Austin Peay State University*; Marion Boyer, *Kalamazoo Valley Community College*; Tamala Bulger, *University of North Carolina*; Stephanie Coopman, *San Jose State University*; Susan Drucker, *Hofstra University*; Greg Gardner, *Rollins College*; Kathleen Henning, *Gateway Technical College*; Sarah Kays, *DeVry Institute*; Charles J. Korn, *Northern Virginia Community College*; Karen Krumrey-Fulks, *Lane Community College*; Gary Kuhn, *Chemeketa Community College*; Anna Martinez, *Reedley College*; Elizabeth J. Natalle, *University of North Carolina, Greensboro*; Randall Pugh, *Montana State University*; Marta Walz, *Elgin Community College*; and Cherie White, *Muskingum Area Technical College*.

I would also like to thank everyone else who participated in this process: **Alabama:** Robert Agne, *Auburn University*; Jonathan Amsbary, *University of Alabama*; Bill Huddleston, *University of North Alabama*; James Vickrey, *Troy State University*; Angela Gibson Wible, *Shelton State Community College*. **Arizona:** Anneliese Harper, *Scottsdale Community College*; Douglas Kelley, *Arizona State University, West*; Fred Kester, *Yavapai College, Prescott*; Mark Lewis, *Phoenix College*; Joseph Ortiz, *Scottsdale Community College*. **Arkansas:** Patricia Amason, *University of Arkansas*; Jason Hough, *John Brown University*; Robert Steinmiller, *Henderson State University*. **California:** Katherine Adams, *California State University, Fresno*; Susan Childress, *Santa Rosa Junior College*; Stephanie J. Coopman, *San Jose State University*; Kristin Gatto Correia, *San Francisco State University*; Eve-Anne Doohan, *University of San Francisco*; Jeannette Duarte, *Rio Hondo College*; Anne Duran, *California State University, Bakersfield*; William Eadie, *San Diego State University*; Allison Evans, *California State University, Bakersfield*; G. L. Forward, *Point Loma Nazarene University*; Kimberly Hubbert, *Cerritos College*; Annika Hylmö, *Loyola Marymount University*; Cynthia Johnson, *College of the Sequoias*; Beverly Kelley, *California Lutheran University*; William Kelly, *University of California, Los Angeles*; Randall Koper, *University of the Pacific*; Victoria Leonard, *College of the Canyons*; Ben Martin, *Santa Monica College*; Anna Martinez, *Reedley College*; Lawrence Jerome McGill, *Pasadena City College*; William F. Owen, *California State University, Sacramento*; Laurie Pratt, *Fullerton College*; Catherine Puckering, *University of California, Davis*; Jose Rodriguez, *California State University, Long Beach*; Teresa Turner, *Shasta College*; Jennifer Valencia, *San Diego Miramar College*; Richard Wiseman, *California State University, Fullerton*. **Colorado:** Eric Aoki, *Colorado State University*; Diane Blomberg, *Metropolitan State College of Denver*; Cheryl McFarren, *Arapahoe Community College*; Susan

Pendell, *Colorado State University*; Dwight Podgurski, *Colorado Christian University*. **Connecticut:** Yanan Ju, *Central Connecticut State University*; Hugh McCarney, *Western Connecticut State University*; William Petkanas, *Western Connecticut State University*; Terri Toles-Patkin, *Eastern Connecticut State University*; C. Arthur VanLear, *University of Connecticut*; Kathryn Wiss, *Western Connecticut State University*. **Florida:** Kenneth Cissna, *University of South Florida*; Ed Coursey, *Palm Beach Community College*; Susan S. Easton, *Rollins College*; Greg Gardner, *Rollins College*; Katherine Nelson, *Barry University*; Maria Roca, *Florida Gulf Coast University*; Ann Scroggie, *Santa Fe Community College*. **Georgia:** Allison Ainsworth, *Gainesville College*; Marybeth Callison, *University of Georgia*; Michael H. Eaves, *Valdosta State University*; Pamela Hayward, *Augusta State University*; Gail Reid, *University of West Georgia*; Jennifer Samp, *University of Georgia*. **Hawaii:** Chiung Chen, *Brigham Young University, Hawaii*; Cailin Kulp O'Riordan, *University of Hawaii, Manoa*; Alan Ragains, *Windward Community College*. **Idaho:** Robyn Bergstrom, *Brigham Young University, Idaho*; Marcy Horne, *Lewis-Clark State College*; Annie McKinlay, *North Idaho College*. **Illinois:** Leah Bryant, *De Paul University*; Tim Cole, *De Paul University*; James Dittus, *Elgin Community College*; Katy Fonner, *Northwestern University*; Daena Goldsmith, *University of Illinois, Urbana-Champaign*; Sarah Strom Kays, *DeVry Institute*; Betty Jane Lawrence, *Bradley University*; Jody Littleton, *Parkland College*; Jay Martinson, *Nazarene University*; Lisa Miczo, *Western Illinois University*; Willona Olison, *Northwestern University*; Michael Purdy, *Governors State University*; Lesa Stern, *Southern Illinois University, Edwardsville*; Marta Walz, *Elgin Community College*. **Indiana:** Austin Babrow, *Purdue University*; Rebecca Bailey, *Valparaiso University*; Alexandra Corning, *University of Notre Dame*; John Greene, *Purdue University*; Krista Hoffmann-Longtin, *Indiana University–Purdue University, Indianapolis*; Irwin Mallin, *Indiana University–Purdue University, Fort Wayne*; Janet Morrison, *Ivy Tech State College*; James H. Tolhuizen, *Indiana University Northwest*; Ralph Webb, *Purdue University*. **Iowa:** Julie Simanski, *Des Moines Area Community College*; Erik Stroner, *Iowa Central Community College*; Charles Veenstra, *Dordt College*. **Kansas:** David Sherlock, *Independence Community College*; Richard Stine, *Johnson County Community College*. **Kentucky:** Chuck Bryant, *University of Kentucky*; Joy Hart, *University of Louisville*; Mona Leonard, *Jefferson Community College*; Tracy Letcher, *University of Kentucky*; Gregory Rickert, *Bluegrass Community and Technical College*; Kandi L. Walker, *University of Louisville*. **Louisiana:** Terry M. Cunconan, *Louisiana Tech University*; Karen Fontenot, *Southeastern Louisiana University*; Loretta L. Pecchioni, *Louisiana State University*. **Maine:** Julie Zink, *University of Southern Maine*. **Maryland:** Laura Drake, *University of Maryland*; Linda Heil, *Harford Community College*; Audra McMullen, *Towson University*; Susan Ondercin, *Carroll Community College*. **Massachusetts:** Linda Albright, *Westfield State College*; Clea Andreadis, *Middlesex Community College*; Jonathan Bowman, *Boston College*; Elise Dallimore, *Northeastern University*; Joe Klimavich, *Worcester State College*; Michael Milburn, *University of Massachusetts, Boston*; Derrick TePaske, *Framingham State College*; Nancy Willets, *Cape Cod Community College*. **Michigan:** Patricia Amason, *Ferris State University*; Isolde Anderson, *Hope College*; Julie Apker, *Western Michigan University*; Steve

Bennett, *Washtenaw Community College*; Marion Boyer, *Kalamazoo Valley Community College*; James Cantrill, *Northern Michigan University*; Robert Loesch, *Ferris State University*; Jennifer Hubbell Ott, *Kalamazoo Valley Community College*; Dennis Patrick, *Eastern Michigan University*; Cami Sanderson-Harris, *Ferris State University*; Sandi Smith, *Michigan State University*; Patricia Sotirin, *Michigan Technical University*. **Minnesota:** Angela Lynn Blais, *University of Minnesota, Duluth*; Christa Brown, *Minnesota State University, Mankato*; Kari Frisch, *Central Lakes College*; Lori Halverson-Wente, *Rochester Community and Technical College*; Ascan Koerner, *University of Minnesota, Twin Cities*; Mariangela Maguire, *Gustavus Adolphus College*; Minda Orina, *University of Minnesota, Twin Cities*; Patricia Palmerton, *Hamline University*; Daniel Paulnock, *Saint Paul College*; Karri Pearson, *Normandale Community College*; R. Jeffrey Ringer, *St. Cloud State University*; Dan West, *Rochester Community and Technical College*. **Missouri:** Leigh Heisel, *University of Missouri, St. Louis*; Lynette Jachowicz, *Maple Woods Community College*; Virgil Norris, *Park University*; Jennifer Summary, *Southeast Missouri State University*. **Montana:** Randall Pugh, *Montana State University, Billings*; Julie Robinson, *Montana State University, Billings*. **Nebraska:** Karla Jensen, *Nebraska Wesleyan University*; Chad M. McBride, *Creighton University*; Lisa Schreiber, *Dana College*. **New Hampshire:** Phyllis Zrzavy, *Franklin Pierce College*. **New Jersey:** Keith Forrest, *Atlantic Cape Community College*; Rebecca Sanford, *Monmouth University*; Madeline Santoro, *Union County College*. **New Mexico:** Candace Maher, *University of New Mexico*; Virginia McDermott, *University of New Mexico*; Kevin Mitchell, *Eastern New Mexico University*; Pamela Stovall, *University of New Mexico, Gallup*. **New York:** Priya Banerjee, *State University of New York, Brockport*; Rex Butt, *Bronx Community College*; Joseph S. Coppolino, *Nassau Community College*; Susan Drucker, *Hofstra University*; Diane Ferrero-Paluzzi, *Iona College*; Douglas Gaerte, *Houghton College*; Andrew Herman, *State University of New York, Geneseo*; Patricia Iacobazzo, *John Jay College*; Anastacia Kurylo, *Manhattan Marymount College*; Michael Lecesse, *State University of New York, New Paltz*; Linda Reese, *College of Staten Island*; Gordon Young, *Kingsborough Community College*. **North Carolina:** Melissa Atkinson, *Surry Community College*; Alessandra Beasley, *Wake Forest University*; Tamala Bulger, *University of North Carolina, Wilmington*; Allison Carr, *Davidson County Community College*; James Manning, *Western Carolina State University*; Nina-Jo Moore, *Appalachian State University*; Elizabeth J. Natalle, *University of North Carolina, Greensboro*; Chris Poulos, *University of North Carolina, Greensboro*; Melinda Sopher, *North Carolina State University*. **Ohio:** Yemi Akande, *John Carroll University*; Carolyn Anderson, *University of Akron*; Christina S. Beck, *Ohio University*; Kathleen Clark, *University of Akron*; Rozell Duncan, *Kent State University*; David Foster, *University of Findlay*; Stephen Haas, *University of Cincinnati*; William Harpine, *University of Akron*; Kathryn C. Maguire, *Cleveland State University*; Lisa Murray-Johnson, *Ohio State University*; Artemio Ramirez, *Ohio State University*; Deleasa Randall-Griffiths, *Ashland University*; Teresa Sabourin, *University of Cincinnati*; Teresa Thompson, *University of Dayton*; John Warren, *Bowling Green State University*; Cherie White, *Muskingum Area Technical College (now Zane State*

College). **Oklahoma:** Penny Eubank, *Oklahoma Christian University*; Billy Wolfe Jr., *University of Oklahoma*. **Oregon:** Nick Backus, *Western Oregon University*; Cynthia Golledge, *Portland Community College, Sylvania*; Karen Krumrey-Fulks, *Lane Community College*; Gary Kuhn, *Chemeketa Community College*; Paula Usrey, *Umpqua Community College*. **Pennsylvania:** Mary Badami, *Bloomsburg University of Pennsylvania*; Janet Bodenman, *Bloomsburg University of Pennsylvania*; Denise Danford, *Delaware County Community College*; Joseph Donato, *Harrisburg Area Community College, Lebanon*; Karen Lada, *Delaware County Community College*; David Paterno, *Delaware County Community College*; Elaine Zelley, *La Salle University*. **South Carolina:** Merissa Ferrara, *College of Charleston*; Charmaine Wilson, *University of South Carolina, Aiken*. **Tennessee:** Stuart Bonnington, *Austin Peay State University*; Katherine Hendrix, *University of Memphis*. **Texas:** Shae Adkins, *North Harris College*; Richard Bello, *Sam Houston State University*; Ceilidh Charleson-Jennings, *Collin County Community College*; Karen Daas, *St. Mary's University*; Jill Gibson, *Amarillo College*; Marian Houser, *Texas State University, San Marcos*; Shelly D. Lane, *Collin County Community College*; Laurie Metcalf, *Texas A&M University*; Mark Morman, *Baylor University*; John Nicholson, *Angelo State University*; James Pauff, *Tarleton State University*; Frank G. Pérez, *University of Texas, El Paso*; Lori Peterson, *St. Edward's University*; Narissra Punyanunt-Carter, *Texas Tech University*; Juliann Scholl, *Texas Tech University*; Susan Selk, *El Paso Community College*; Barbara Yancy-Tooks, *El Paso Community College*. **Utah:** Matthew Barton, *Southern Utah University*; Brian Heuett, *Southern Utah University*. **Vermont:** Genevieve Jacobs, *Champlain College*. **Virginia:** Melissa Aleman, *James Madison University*; Jill Jurgens, *Old Dominion University*; Charles J. Korn, *Northern Virginia Community College, Manassas*; Melanie Laliker, *Bridgewater College*; Michaela Meyer, *Christopher Newport University*; Thomas Morra, *Northern Virginia Community College, Annandale*; Nan Peck, *Northern Virginia Community College, Annandale*; Jeffrey Pierson, *Bridgewater College*; James Roux, *Lynchburg College*. **Washington:** Mara Adelman, *Seattle University*; Margaret Kreiner, *Spokane Community College*; Mark Murphy, *Everett Community College*; Roxane Sutherland, *Clark College*. **Washington, D.C.:** Robert Harrison, *Gallaudet University*; Clay Warren, *George Washington University*. **West Virginia:** Robert Bookwalter, *Marshall University*; Matthew Martin, *West Virginia University*. **Wisconsin:** Cheri Campbell, *University of Wisconsin, Waukesha*; Valerie Hennen, *Gateway Technical College*; Craig Hullett, *University of Wisconsin, Madison*; Rebecca Imes, *Carroll College*; Carol Knudson, *Gateway Technical College*; Lindsay Timmerman, *University of Wisconsin, Milwaukee*.

Finally, no textbook is created by one person. Thank you to the interpersonal communication discipline and its students.

brief contents

part one / Interpersonal Essentials

4

Experiencing and Expressing Emotions 108

part two / Interpersonal Skills

5

Listening Actively   144

6
Communicating Verbally   174

7
Communicating Nonverbally   208

8
Managing Conflict and Power   242

part three / Interpersonal Relationships

9
Relationships with Romantic Partners   278

10
Relationships with Family Members   320

11
Relationships with Friends   352

VideoCentral Ⓒ Go to **bedfordstmartins.com/reflectrelate** for videos on agentic friendships and communal friendships.

12
Relationships in the Workplace   384

Reflect & Relate is a very thorough, engaging, clearly written, visually interesting, and pedagogically brilliant textbook.

Virginia Hamilton
University of California, Davis

Reflect & Relate is an exceptional text. Its clear and concise explanations, exercises and activities, and case studies engage and excite students, and it allows them to adopt helpful information into their personal lives.

James Patterson
Miami University

Reflect & Relate takes on the tough topics that most authors are hesitant to discuss. If you want your students to take interpersonal communication into the real world, this is the textbook for you!

Victoria Leonard
College of the Canyons

Students find *Reflect & Relate* engaging, which makes them more likely to actually READ the assignments.

Neva Gronert
Arapahoe Community College

I love *Reflect & Relate*'s continued focus on the student, I love the currency of both the concepts and the examples, and I love that this textbook will make a difference in students' relationships.

Marta Walz
Elgin Community College

I believe that the most important thing a textbook can teach students is how to make better communication decisions so that they can build happier and healthier interpersonal relationships.

Steven McCornack grew up in Seattle, Washington, in the years before Microsoft and grunge music. For as long as he can remember, he has been fascinated with how people create, maintain, and disband close relationships, especially the challenges confronting romantic couples. As an undergraduate at the University of Washington, he pursued this passion by studying with Malcolm "Mac" Parks, who inspired within Steve the desire to devote his life to interpersonal communication teaching and research.

Steve moved to the Midwest in 1984, pursuing his graduate studies under the tutelage of Barbara O'Keefe at the University of Illinois, where he received his master's and PhD. Hired in 1988 to teach in the Department of Communication at Michigan State University, Steve has remained there ever since and now serves as associate professor, coordinator of the undergraduate program, and faculty adviser to the Undergraduate Communication Association. He has published more than 20 articles in leading communication journals and has received several prestigious awards and fellowships related to undergraduate teaching, including the Lilly Endowment Teaching Fellowship, the Amoco Foundation Excellence-in-Teaching Award, the MSU All-University Teacher/Scholar Award, and the Michigan State University Alumni Association Teaching Award.

To Steve, authoring *Reflect & Relate* represents the culmination of more than 25 years of devout interest in how best to share knowledge of interpersonal communication theory and research with undergraduate students. His courses are some of the most popular on campus. Other than his love of teaching, Steve's principal passions are his family (wife Kelly and three redheaded sons, Kyle, Colin, and Conor), his music (he plays drums and piano), his yoga practice, and karate training.

Reflect & Relate

AN INTRODUCTION TO INTERPERSONAL COMMUNICATION

1

Introducing Interpersonal Communication

She is home with the kids,

who are alternating between angry and clingy.[1] She's trying to cook dinner, but the smoke detector keeps blaring, causing the dog to bark. Sure enough, it's at this moment the phone rings. Glancing at the caller ID, she sees it is the caller she hoped for. She answers, because despite the chaos around her, this could be their last conversation. He says, "I've been waiting in line for two hours to talk and I only have ten minutes. I've had a really bad day and miss you all." What should she say? Choice #1: *Lie*. Tell him everything's fine, and mask her frustration with coolness. But he'll sense her aloofness and leave the conversation worrying about why she is distracted. Is she angry with him? Having an affair? Choice #2: *Be honest*. Tell him that things are chaotic, and ask whether he can talk to the kids for a minute while she clears her head.

Military wife, author, and *New York Times* columnist Melissa Seligman has lived this scene many times during her husband's combat deployments. She has learned to choose the second path because of the inescapable connection between communication choices and relationship outcomes. As she describes, "When a family member is gone for *a year* at a time, how can you sustain closeness? How do you maintain a three-dimensional marriage in a two-dimensional state? The only way is through open, honest, and loving communication."

Interpersonal communication is the bridge that connects us to others

[1]All information that follows is adapted from a personal interview with the author, July 2011. Published with permission from Melissa Seligman.

The Seligmans use multiple media to maintain intimacy, including webcams, and exchanging videos, e-mails, phone calls, and letters. Melissa notes, "This way, we have a rounded communication relationship. We even send care packages of leaves, sand, pine needles, or pieces of fabric with cologne or perfume, to awaken the senses and cement the memories we have of each other." They also journal, then read each other's writings when they are reunited. The journals "have the dates, circumstances, and what went unsaid in the day-to-day minutiae of our lives. They are our way of staying connected when ripped apart."

Melissa Seligman uses similarly diverse communication in her professional work with military support groups. "In my working life, I am on Facebook, Skype, and Web conference calls all the time. Texting. Instant-messaging. All of these are essential." But she also is mindful of the limits of technology, recognizing the importance of tailoring the medium to the task. "Technology cannot sustain a relationship, and relying on it to do so will create chaos. Rather, choosing the technology that best suits an individual's relationship is the key."

Across years of experience, Melissa Seligman and her family have learned to cope with intense versions of the same challenges we *all* face in our relationships. How can I better manage my anger and frustration? What can I do to maintain closeness with those I love? How can I communicate in a way that's both honest *and* kind? In 2010, she and co-author Christina Piper released a children's book, *A Heart Apart*, which helps young children cope with the absence of military parents. When she is asked to reflect on the importance of communication, Melissa thinks of the next generation: "Children need to know and understand that anger and sadness go along with missing someone. They must be taught the importance of communication, and how to communicate well. This sets them up for success when their emotions begin to flow. Feelings are not right or wrong—it's what you choose to do with them that counts. Teaching our children to communicate well is the best gift we can give them."

My life, like yours, is filled with interpersonal communication, in all its varied forms. While I'm sitting in the kitchen, writing on my laptop, the sound of Radiohead's "Lotus Flower" suddenly splits the silence. It's a text from my son Kyle, who's attending a music festival: "fleet foxes were awesome!" A few minutes later I get an e-mail alert: it's a Facebook message from Kyle's girlfriend Margot, who's in France visiting relatives: "Just wanted to say hi to everyone!" While I'm reading Margot's message, a chat message pops up from Franki, my friend in California: "Check out the photos of my new beagle puppies!" While I'm surfing her puppy photo album, my wife Kelly and sons Colin and Conor walk in and ask, "Dad, do you want to order pizza tonight?"

Interpersonal communication is the bridge that connects us to others. Through interpersonal communication, we build, maintain, and even end relationships with romantic partners, family members, friends, coworkers, and others. We do this through texting, instant-messaging, social networking site posts and chat, e-mail, face-to-face interactions, and phone calls. And we switch back and forth between these various forms fluidly, effortlessly.

But regardless of how we're communicating, or with whom, one fact inescapably binds us: *the communication choices we make determine the personal, interpersonal, and relationship outcomes that follow.* When we communicate well, we create desirable outcomes, such as positive emotions and satisfying relationships. When we communicate poorly, we generate negative outcomes, such as interpersonal conflict or dissatisfaction with a relationship. By studying interpersonal communication, you can acquire knowledge and skills to boost your interpersonal competence. This, in turn, will help you to build and maintain satisfying relationships, and ultimately, improve your quality of life.

In this chapter, we begin our study of interpersonal communication. You'll learn:

- What communication is and the different models for communication
- The nature of interpersonal communication, the role it plays in relationships, and the needs and goals it helps us fulfill
- How to improve your interpersonal communication competence, both online and off
- Major issues related to the study of interpersonal communication

What Is Communication?

How we create and exchange messages with others

We think about communication constantly—everything from thought-provoking course lectures to the meaning of warm smiles displayed by attractive new coworkers. But taking a class on communication is different from personally pondering it. When you're formally educated about communication, you gain knowledge that goes far beyond your intuition, allowing you to broaden and deepen your skills as a communicator. The process of learning about communication begins by answering a basic question: what *is* communication?

◗ Whether we are watching a movie, going to school, visiting with friends, or starting a new romance, communication plays a significant role in our every-day experiences.

DEFINING COMMUNICATION

The National Communication Association, a professional organization representing communication teachers and scholars in the United States, defines **communication** as the process through which people use messages to generate meanings within and across contexts, cultures, channels, and media (NCA, n.d.). This definition highlights the five features that characterize communication.

First, communication is a *process* that unfolds over time through a series of interconnected actions carried out by the participants. For example, your friend texts you asking if you want to go to a movie, you call her back to say yes and to make the arrangements, and so forth. Because communication is a process, everything you say and do affects what is said and done in the present and the future.

Second, those engaged in communication (*communicators*) use *messages* to convey meaning. A **message** is the "package" of information that is transported during communication. When people exchange a series of messages, whether face-to-face or online, the result is called an **interaction** (Watzlawick, Beavin, & Jackson, 1967).

Third, communication occurs in a seemingly endless variety of **contexts**, or situations. We communicate with others at ball games, while at work, and in household kitchens. In each context, a host of factors influences how we communicate, such as how much time we have, how many people are in the vicinity, and whether the setting is personal or professional. Think about it: you probably communicate differently with your romantic partner when you're in class than when you're watching a movie at home and snuggling on the couch.

Fourth, people communicate through various *channels*. A **channel** is the sensory dimension along which communicators transmit information. Channels can be auditory (sound), visual (sight), tactile (touch), olfactory (scent), or oral (taste). For example, your manager at work smiles at you and says, "I'm very impressed with your job performance" (visual and auditory channels). A visually impaired friend "reads" a message you left her, touching the Braille letters with her fingertips (tactile). Your romantic partner shows up at your house exuding an alluring scent and carrying delicious takeout, which you then share together (olfactory and oral).

Fifth, to transmit information, communicators use a broad range of **media**—tools for exchanging messages. Consider the various media used by Melissa Seligman and her husband, described in our chapter opener. Webcams, cell phones, texting, e-mail, letters, face-to-face interaction, all of these media and more, can be used to communicate. And we often use multiple media channels simultaneously—for example, texting while checking our Facebook, or calling someone while scrolling through our e-mail. (See Figure 1.1 for common media forms.)

○ The context of an interaction—whether it is a formal or casual setting, with a good friend or a romantic interest—will influence how we communicate.

self-
reflection

What communication media do you use most often? Why do you rely more on these than others? How does the type of message you need to communicate—casual, professionally important, deeply personal—influence your choice of media?

| Text-messaging (SMS) | Face-to-face interaction | Social networking sites | E-mail | Talking on the phone |

figure 1.1 **Five Most Common Forms of Communication Media Used by College Students**

Sources: Dean (2011) and Lenhart, Purcell, Smith, and Zickuhr (2010).

UNDERSTANDING COMMUNICATION MODELS

Think about all the different ways you communicate each day. You text-message your sister, excitedly announcing that you got the job you wanted. You give a speech in your communication class, acting more animated when you see your audience's attention start to wane. You exchange a knowing glance with your best friend when a person you both dislike boasts about his latest romantic conquest. Now reflect on how these forms of communication differ from each other. Sometimes (like when text-messaging), you create messages and send them to receivers, the messages flowing in a single direction from origin to destination. In other instances (like when speaking in front of your class), you present messages to recipients, and the recipients signal to you that they've received and understood them. Still other times (like when you and your best friend exchange a glance), you mutually construct meanings with others, with no one serving as "sender" or "receiver." These different ways of experiencing communication are reflected in three models that have evolved to describe the communication process: the linear model, the interactive model, and the transactional model. As you will see, each of these models has both strengths and weaknesses. Yet each also captures something unique and useful about the ways you communicate in your daily life.

Linear Communication Model   According to the **linear communication model**, communication is an activity in which information flows in one direction, from a starting point to an end point (see Figure 1.2). The linear model contains several components (Lasswell, 1948; Shannon & Weaver, 1949). In addition to a *message* and a *channel*, there must be a **sender** (or senders) of the message—the individual(s) who generates the information to be communicated, packages it into a message, and chooses the channel(s) for sending it. There also is **noise**—factors in the environment that impede messages from reaching their destination. Noise includes anything that causes our attention to drift from messages—such as poor reception during a cell-phone call or the smell of fresh coffee nearby. Last, there must be a **receiver**: the person for whom a message is intended and to whom the message is delivered.

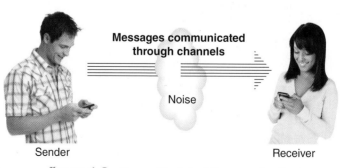

Sender   Receiver

Messages communicated through channels

Noise

figure 1.2   **Linear Model of Communication**

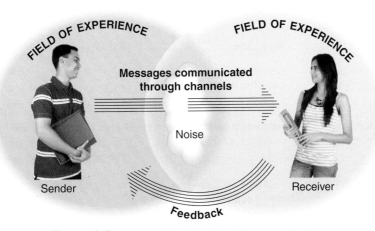

figure 1.3 **Interactive Model of Communication**

Interactive Communication Model   The **interactive communication model** also views communication as a process involving senders and receivers (see Figure 1.3). However, according to this model, transmission is influenced by two additional factors: feedback and fields of experience (Schramm, 1954). **Feedback** is comprised of the verbal and nonverbal messages that recipients convey to indicate their reaction to communication. Whether it's eye contact, utterances such as "uh-huh" and "that's right," or nodding, receivers deliver feedback to let senders know they've received and understood the message and to indicate their approval or disapproval. **Fields of experience** consist of the beliefs, attitudes, values, and experiences that each participant brings to a communication event. People with similar fields of experience are more likely to understand each other while communicating than are individuals with dissimilar fields of experience.

Transactional Communication Model   The **transactional communication model** (see Figure 1.4) suggests that communication is fundamentally multi-directional. That is, each participant equally influences the communication

VideoCentral ▣

bedfordstmartins.com /reflectrelate

Transactional Communication Model
Watch this clip online to answer the questions below.

Can you think of situations where you jointly created meaning with another person? How did this happen? In what ways are these situations different from ones that follow the interactive communication model?

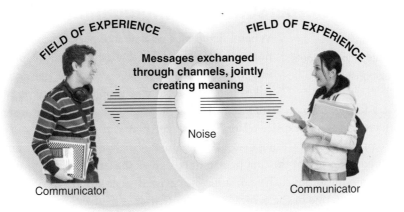

figure 1.4 **Transactional Model of Communication**

table 1.1 **Communication Models**

Model	Examples	Strength	Weakness
Linear	Text and instant-messaging, e-mail, wall posts, scripted public speeches	Simple and straightforward	Doesn't adequately describe most face-to-face or phone conversations
Interactive	Classroom instruction, group presentations, team/coworker meetings	Captures a broad variety of communication forms	Neglects the active role that receivers often play in constructing meanings
Transactional	Any encounter (most commonly face-to-face) in which you and others jointly create communication meaning	Intuitively captures what most people think of as interpersonal communication	Doesn't apply to many forms of online communication, such as e-mail, Facebook posts, and text-messaging

behavior of the other participants (Miller & Steinberg, 1975). From the transactional perspective, there are no "senders" or "receivers." Instead, all the parties constantly exchange verbal and nonverbal messages and feedback, *collaboratively* creating meanings (Streek, 1980). This may be something as simple as a shared look between friends, or it may be an animated conversation among close family members in which the people involved seem to know what the others are going to say before it's said.

These three models represent an evolution of thought regarding the nature of communication, from a relatively simplistic depiction of communication as a linear process to one that views communication as a complicated process that is mutually crafted. However, these models don't necessarily represent "good" or "bad" ways of thinking about communication. Instead, each of them is useful for thinking about different forms of communication. See Table 1.1 above for more on each model.

What Is Interpersonal Communication?

Interpersonal communication impacts our relationships

When I first took a class on interpersonal communication as an undergraduate, I was amazed at the practical importance of the information we were learning. We talked about how and why people communicate when they are falling in (and out of) love, fighting, forming friendships, and fostering healthy family and workplace relationships. I'd go home after every class and drive my roommates crazy by using material from class to analyze their relationships!

Of course, I'm not the first person to recognize the significance of interpersonal communication; such realization has existed since the dawn of recorded history. In fact, one of the earliest texts ever written—the maxims of the Egyptian sage Ptah Hotep (2200 B.C.E.)—was essentially a guidebook for enhancing interpersonal skills (Horne, 1917). Ptah Hotep encouraged people to be truthful, kind, and tolerant in their communication. He urged active listening, especially for situations in which people lack experience, because "to not do so is to embrace ignorance." He also emphasized mindfulness in word choice, noting that "good words are more difficult to find than emeralds."

DEFINING INTERPERSONAL COMMUNICATION

Why has learning about interpersonal communication always been considered so valuable? Because knowledge of interpersonal skills is essential for maintaining healthy interpersonal *relationships*. For most people, having happy relationships with romantic partners, friends, family members, and coworkers is of the utmost importance (Myers, 2002).

The link that exists between relationships and interpersonal communication is clearly illustrated by our definition: **interpersonal communication** is a dynamic form of communication between two (or more) people in which the messages exchanged significantly influence their thoughts, emotions, behaviors, and relationships. This definition has four important implications. First, interpersonal communication differs from some other forms of communication—such as office memos, e-mail spam, and formal lectures or speeches—because it's *dynamic*. Dynamic means that interpersonal communication is constantly in motion and changing over time. Most interpersonal communication is spontaneously created—arising from our thoughts, moods, and emotions of the moment—unlike the carefully planned messages that dominate advertisements, professional journalism, and formal public speeches. For example, consider a Skype interaction you have with a sibling who lives overseas. The first few moments may be awkward or tense as you strive to reconnect with one another. This tension is reflected in long pauses between short sentences. Then one of you cracks a joke, and the whole exchange suddenly feels warmer. Just a few minutes later, as you realize you have to end the encounter, the conversation slows, and the mood shifts yet again to sadness and regret, as each of you tries to delay the inevitable disconnection.

Second, most interpersonal communication is *transactional*; both parties contribute to the meaning. For example, you and a romantic partner share an intimate dinner, jointly reminiscing about past times together and exchanging expressions of affection fluidly back and forth. But some interpersonal communication isn't transactional. You know that your sibling is feeling depressed over a breakup, so you send her a consoling text message in the middle of her workday. You don't expect her to respond, and she doesn't because she's busy. There's no feedback and no interplay between you and your sister. Instead, there is a sender (you), a message (your expression of support), and a receiver (your sister), making it a linear encounter, albeit an interpersonal one.

Third, interpersonal communication is primarily **dyadic**—it involves pairs of people, or dyads. You chat with your daughter while driving her to school, or you exchange a series of Facebook messages with a long-distance friend. Of

self-reflection

How do *you* define interpersonal communication? Can interpersonal communication happen between more than two people? Can it happen through text or e-mail? Or is it the content of what is discussed that makes communication interpersonal? What types of communication are *not* interpersonal?

When we interpersonally communicate, we forge meaningful bonds with others

course, some interpersonal communication may involve more than just two people. For instance, several family members converse at once while sitting around the dinner table, or a group of friends talk while enjoying an evening out. The dyadic nature of interpersonal communication allows us to distinguish it from **intrapersonal communication**—communication involving only one person, in the form of talking out loud to oneself or having a mental "conversation" inside one's head.

Finally, and perhaps most importantly, interpersonal communication creates *impact*: it changes participants' thoughts, emotions, behaviors, and relationships. The impact on relationships is one of the most profound and unique effects created through interpersonal communication. When we interpersonally communicate, we forge meaningful bonds with others—easing the distance that naturally arises from differences between people. Philosopher Martin Buber (1965) argued that we can make that distance seem "thinner" through our communication. Specifically, Buber suggests, when we embrace the fundamental similarities that connect us with others, strive to see things from others' points of view, and communicate in ways that emphasize honesty and kindness, we feel closer to others. We don't have to agree with everything another person says and does, but to communicate competently with others, we need to approach them with an open mind and welcoming heart, affording them the same attention and respect we expect for ourselves. According to Buber, we then perceive our relationship with that person as **I-Thou**.

In contrast, when we focus on our differences, refuse to accept or even acknowledge rival viewpoints as legitimate, and communicate in ways that emphasize our own supposed superiority over others, the distance between us and others "thickens" to the point where it becomes impenetrable. As a consequence, we increasingly perceive our relationships as **I-It**: we regard other people as "objects which we observe, that are there for our use and exploitation" (Buber, 1965, p. 24). The more we view others as objects, the greater is the likelihood that we'll communicate with them in disrespectful, manipulative, or exploitative ways. When we treat others this way, our relationships deteriorate.

Interpersonal communication contrasts sharply with **impersonal communication**—exchanges that have a negligible perceived impact on our thoughts, emotions, behaviors, and relationships. For example, you're watching TV with your lover, and one of you casually comments on an advertisement that is annoying. Within most close relationships, at least some communication has this impersonal quality. But we can shift to interpersonal at a moment's notice. A while after the ad commentary, you snuggle up to your partner and murmur, "I love you." You're rewarded by warm eye contact, a tender smile, and a gentle hug—all signs that your message has had a significant impact on your partner.

Highlighting the mental, emotional, behavioral, and relational impact of interpersonal communication reinforces the central theme of this text: *the communication choices we make determine the personal, interpersonal, and relationship outcomes that follow.* Through communicating interpersonally with others, you can change your own feelings and thoughts about both yourself and others; alter others' opinions of you; cause heartbreak or happiness; incite hugs or hostility;

skills practice

I-Thou Communication
Shifting your communication from I-It to I-Thou

❶ Think of someone you have to interact with regularly, but with whom you have an I-It relationship.

❷ Identify the qualities that cause you to see this person as different from or inferior to you.

❸ Analyze these differences. Are they really a cause for concern?

❹ Identify similarities you have in common with this person.

❺ Develop a plan for communicating with this person in ways that accept and respect differences while appreciating and emphasizing similarities.

▷ Whether an encounter is considered interpersonal depends on those people participating in the encounter. Some only consider an encounter interpersonal if they gain new knowledge, make different decisions, or forge an I-Thou connection. Others consider an encounter interpersonal if information is conveyed. When do you think an encounter is interpersonal?

and create, maintain, or dissolve relationships. This power makes your interpersonal communication choices critically important.

PRINCIPLES OF INTERPERSONAL COMMUNICATION

Now that you know the definition of interpersonal communication, we can expand our understanding of how it functions in our daily lives by looking at several principles suggested by scholars, based on decades of research and theory development. These principles are affirmed repeatedly throughout our text, and each one suggests practical insights into how you can improve your interpersonal communication choices, skills, and relationships.

Interpersonal Communication Conveys Both Content and Relationship Information   During every interpersonal encounter, people simultaneously exchange two types of information (Watzlawick et al., 1967). *Content information* is the actual meaning of the words you utter. *Relationship information* consists of signals indicating how each of you views your relationship. These signals may indicate whether you consider yourself superior, equal, or inferior to the other person and whether you see the relationship as intimate, acquainted, or estranged.

You convey content information directly through spoken or written words, but you communicate relationship information primarily through nonverbal cues. These cues can include vocal tone, pitch, and volume; facial expression and eye contact; hand gestures; position in relation to the listener; and posture. For instance, suppose your housemate hasn't been doing his fair share of kitchen cleanup. One evening, after he leaves his dirty dishes in the sink (again!), you walk into the living room where he's watching TV. You sit down next to him, smile, and say in a friendly tone of voice, "Do you think you could rinse your dishes off and put them in the dishwasher when you're done with them?" Now imagine the exact same situation—except this time you stand between him and the TV, scowl, point your finger at him, and shout, "Do you think you could rinse your dishes off and put them in the dishwasher when you're done with them?!" In both scenarios, the content information is identical—you use exactly the same words—but you communicate very different relationship information. In the first scene, you indicate that you like and respect your housemate, and consider him an equal. In the second, you communicate anger and dislike, and imply that you see yourself as superior or more powerful.

Relationship information strongly influences how people interpret content information (Watzlawick et al., 1967). In the example above, your housemate will look much more to your actions than your words to decide how you feel about him and the relationship. During most interpersonal encounters, however, people aren't consciously aware of the relationship information being delivered. You don't usually sit there thinking, "Gee, what's this person trying to convey to me about how she sees our relationship?" Relationship information becomes most obvious when it's unexpected or when it suggests that the sender's view of the relationship is different from the receiver's. For example, a new acquaintance says something overly intimate to you, or a coworker starts ordering you around as if he's your manager. When such events occur, we often experience annoyance or anxiety ("Who does he think he is?!"). That's why it's important to communicate relationship information in ways that are sensitive to and respectful of others' impressions of the relationship, while at the same time staying true to your own relationship feelings.

◖ In the movie *Crazy, Stupid, Love,* a conversation between estranged couple Cal and Emily Weaver changes from distant to intimate to hostile. What experience have you had in handling changing relationship information within a single encounter? How has it influenced your communication choices?

Because relationship information influences how people interpret content information, it can be considered a specific form of **meta-communication**—communication about communication (Watzlawick, Beavin, & Jackson, 1967). Meta-communication includes any message, verbal or nonverbal, that has as its central focus the meaning of communication—everything from discussion of previous comments ("I actually was joking when I sent you that text message") to exchanged glances between friends questioning how a message should be interpreted ("What did he mean when he said that?"). During interpersonal encounters, meta-communication helps us to understand each other's communication, giving us additional guidance regarding how messages should be perceived.

Interpersonal Communication Can Be Intentional or Unintentional

During interpersonal encounters, people attach meaning to nearly everything you say and do—whether you intend to send a message or not. Scholars express this as the axiom, "One cannot not communicate" (Watzlawick et al., 1967, p. 51). In most situations, you intend certain meanings, and people understand you. Sometimes, however, people read meanings into behaviors that you didn't intend as communicative. In such instances, interpersonal communication *has* occurred, even though it was unintentional. For example, imagine that you greet a friend of yours, "Hey, how's it going?" She greets you back, "Hi—good to see you!" So far so good—both messages were intentional, and both were interpreted correctly. But then, as your friend tells you about her new boyfriend, your contact lens gets displaced. It's the third time it's happened today, so you sigh loudly in frustration, and move your eyes to try and get it back in position. Your friend, seeing this, thinks you're sighing and rolling your eyes *as a message* about her boyfriend, and gets angry, "Oh, so you disapprove of him? Why!?" Whether you like it or not, interpersonal communication *has* occurred, even though it was unintentional. To avoid such misunderstandings, keep this simple rule in mind: when you're interacting with others, most of what you say and do will be perceived as communication.

Interpersonal Communication Is Irreversible

Every time you communicate interpersonally, you and the other person affect your future communication and the quality of your relationship. Take the way you answer your cell phone. The ring tone prompts you to look at the incoming number. Your identification of the caller influences how you answer—a warm and enthusiastic "Hi!" or a terse "Yeah?"—depending on how you feel about the caller. Your answer in turn influences how the caller responds. And his or her response further affects your next comment.

This interconnectedness of action makes all interpersonal communication irreversible. By posting a message on someone's Facebook wall, sending a text, leaving a voicemail message, or expressing a thought out loud during a face-to-face encounter, you set in motion the series of outcomes that follow. Simply, once you've said something, you can't take it back. When it comes to interpersonal communication and relationships, there are no "freebies" or "get out of jail free" cards. This is why it's important to think carefully before you communicate. Ask

self-reflection

Consider an instance in which you didn't intend to communicate a message but someone saw your behavior as communication. How did this person misinterpret your behavior? What were the consequences? What did you say and do to correct the individual's misperception?

self-reflection

Think of an encounter in which you said something and then immediately regretted it. What effects did your error have on you? On the other person or people involved? On your relationship? How could you have expressed the same information differently to avoid negative outcomes?

○ Each interpersonal interaction we have shapes our future communication. Before expressing a potentially hurtful thought, consider what outcomes you're setting in motion.

yourself, "Is what I'm about to say going to lead to outcomes I want?" If the answer is no, revise your message accordingly.

Interpersonal Communication Is Dynamic   When you interact with others, your communication and all that influences it—perceptions, thoughts, feelings, and emotions—are constantly in flux. This has several practical implications. First, no two interactions with the same person will ever be identical. People with whom we once interacted effortlessly and joyfully can seem difficult to talk with during our next encounter. Those we once felt awkward around may become our closest confidants.

Second, no two moments within the *same* interaction will ever be identical. The complex combination of perceptions, thoughts, moods, and emotions that fuels our interpersonal communication choices is constantly changing. For instance, you meet your long-distance romantic partner at the airport, and for the first few minutes after he or she debarks from the plane you both feel joyous. But half an hour later, while driving home, you suddenly find yourselves at a loss for things to talk about. As the minutes pass, the tension increases as you both silently ponder, "What happened?"

MOTIVES FOR INTERPERSONAL COMMUNICATION

At 19 months of age, Helen Keller fell ill with a severe fever that destroyed her sight and hearing (Dash, 2001). Helen had learned to speak quite early and had a substantial vocabulary (for a toddler), but when she stopped hearing she

self-
reflection

Recall an interaction that took a sudden turn for the worse. How did each person's communication contribute to the change in the interaction's quality? What did you say or do to deal with the problem?

Helen Keller

stopped trying to talk. In the years that followed, she created primitive messages through pulling, shoving, pinching, and shivering, but she had lost the knowledge of how to *interpersonally* communicate.

With no ability to connect with others through communication, she became filled with hatred and an all-encompassing sense of isolation. She called the resulting sense of self "The Phantom." The Phantom routinely flew into screaming tantrums that ceased only when utter exhaustion set in. In one of her early lessons with Annie Sullivan—the woman who eventually taught Helen how to communicate through hand signals— The Phantom became so enraged that she punched Annie in the mouth, knocking out one of her front teeth.

But when Annie finally taught Helen how to communicate through sign language, The Phantom was slain. As Helen explained years later, "It seemed that something of the mystery of communication was revealed to me . . . and suddenly I felt a misty consciousness as of something remembered— a thrill of returning thought." Helen Keller went on to master sign language, Braille, and spoken language and graduated magna cum laude from Radcliffe College.

As the Helen Keller story powerfully illustrates, when we communicate interpersonally, we connect with others—fulfilling a profound human need. We also achieve important personal and professional goals. When these outcomes are denied us, we lapse into isolation and loneliness or, worse yet, have a violent "Phantom" emerge from within, as did Helen Keller.

Interpersonal Communication and Human Needs   Psychologist Abraham Maslow (1970) suggested that we seek to fulfill a hierarchy of needs in our daily lives. Only when the most basic needs (at the bottom of the hierarchy) are fulfilled do we turn our attention to pursuing higher-level ones. Interpersonal communication allows us to develop and foster the interactions and relationships that help us fulfill these needs. At the foundational level are *physical needs* such as air, food, water, sleep, and shelter. If we can't satisfy these needs, we prioritize them over all others. Once physical needs are met, we concern ourselves with *safety needs*—such as job stability and protection from violence.

Then we seek to address *social needs*: forming satisfying and healthy emotional bonds with friends, family members, and romantic partners. Next are *self-esteem* needs, the desire to have others' respect and admiration. We fulfill these needs by contributing something of value to the world. Finally, we strive to satisfy *self-actualization needs* by articulating our unique abilities and giving our best in our work, family, and personal life.

Interpersonal Communication and Specific Goals   In addition to enabling us to meet fundamental needs, interpersonal communication helps us meet three types of goals (Clark & Delia, 1979). During interpersonal interactions, you may pursue one or a combination of these goals. The first—**self-presentation goals**— are desires you have to present yourself in certain ways so that others perceive you as being a particular type of person. For example, you're conversing with a roommate who's just been fired. You want him to know that you're a supportive friend, so you ask what happened, commiserate, and offer to help him find a new job.

You also have **instrumental goals**—practical aims you want to achieve or tasks you want to accomplish through a particular interpersonal encounter. If you want to borrow your best friend's prized Porsche for the weekend, you might remind her of your solid driving record and your sense of responsibility to persuade her to lend you the car.

Finally, you use interpersonal communication to achieve **relationship goals**—building, maintaining, or terminating bonds with others. For example, if you succeed in borrowing your friend's car for the weekend and accidentally drive it into a nearby lake, you will likely apologize profusely and offer to pay for repairs to save your friendship.

RESEARCH IN INTERPERSONAL COMMUNICATION

The goal of this textbook is to provide you with knowledge regarding interpersonal communication that will help you improve your communication choices, skills, and relationships. But to be useful, knowledge has to be trustworthy. That means it must be based on solid research and theory. How does this come about?

When you conduct *research*, you formulate a question, then try to answer it through careful observation or the creation of a controlled "test" or experiment. When you develop *theory*, you formulate propositions (statements) about your interests, then identify factors relevant to them and how those factors interrelate (Chaffee & Berger, 1987).

To illustrate how research and theory give rise to interpersonal communication knowledge, let's walk through an example. Imagine that you post a message

CLOSE TO HOME © 2001 John McPherson. Reprinted with permission of UNIVERSAL UCLICK. All rights reserved.

in one of your favorite online discussion groups. Within hours, you find a couple of nasty responses or *flames*—inappropriately aggressive online messages that most people wouldn't communicate face-to-face. You're shocked and confused. But more than anything else, you want to know why this happened. So you decide to do some research and develop a theory.

Communication scholars typically take one of two approaches when conducting research and developing theory. Through *qualitative approaches*, they make careful observations, identify patterns in what they're seeing, and try to determine the principles behind their observations (Znaniecki, 1934). If you opted to study flaming qualitatively, you would follow several steps (Katz, 1983). First, you would carefully define what you meant by "flaming," based on observation of various flame messages. You would consider questions such as: What characteristics of an online message make it a "flame"? How is flaming different from other negative messages? Once you had a clear definition of flaming, you would formulate tentative *hypotheses*—predictions that describe the relationship between your phenomenon of interest and other related factors. For example, you might hypothesize that flaming is more likely to occur in certain discussion forums than in others or that certain types of messages are especially likely to trigger flames. Then you would test your hypotheses by observing multiple instances of flaming in online discussion groups. If your observations consistently confirmed your hypotheses, you would conclude that your hypotheses were likely correct. If your observations disconfirmed your hypotheses, you would revise your hypotheses until they matched your observations. Then you would create a set of propositions describing the nature of flaming and the factors that influence it. These propositions would constitute your "Flame Theory."

Whereas qualitative approaches begin with observation and description and then move to development of theory, *quantitative approaches* follow the opposite order. Researchers first propose a theory, then they formulate hypotheses based on that theory, and finally they test those hypotheses by conducting an experiment. For example, to study flaming from a quantitative perspective, you might first read previous research on flaming. You then would select an existing theory or create your own. From this theory, you would choose specific hypotheses and design and conduct a controlled test of them. For example, you might hypothesize that anonymity boosts flaming frequency and conduct a study in which people are provided with either anonymous or identifiable accounts. If the results from the controlled test support your hypothesis, you would consider your theory plausible. If the results do not match the hypothesis, you would reject the hypothesis and view your theory as suspect.

Many people view qualitative and quantitative approaches as opposites or even rivals, but both are equally valid for the study of interpersonal communication. They both generate valuable and trustworthy knowledge. For example, qualitative approaches are especially well suited for learning the details, nuances, and richness of real-life communication patterns. Quantitative approaches are excellent for determining the frequency of various communication behaviors, as well as systematically testing the influence of various factors on such behaviors (Pomerantz, 1990).

skills practice

Using Research Methods Online

How to analyze online communication challenges with research

❶ Think of a problem you commonly face when communicating with others online—such as encountering someone whose messages are constantly rude or vague.

❷ Identify the factors that seem to cause the problem and formulate a hypothesis.

❸ Carefully observe encounters in which the problem arises, testing if the factors in your hypothesis are really the causes.

❹ Identify ways you can change, control, or improve the factors that cause the problem.

❺ Implement these changes; then see if the problem is resolved. If not, repeat the process until a solution is found.

What Is Interpersonal Communication Competence?

For nine seasons of *South Park*, Jerome "Chef" McElroy was the only adult trusted and respected by the show's central characters: Kyle, Stan, Kenny, and Cartman. Voiced by the late, great R&B singer Isaac Hayes (1942–2008), Chef was friend, confidante, and advice-giver to the children. In a routine interaction, the boys—while waiting in the school's lunch line—would be greeted by Chef with a warm "Hello children!" They then would share their concerns and seek his counsel. Chef would do his best to provide appropriate, effective, and ethical advice, often bursting into song. Of course, given his reputation as a "ladies' man," the boys frequently asked him for advice regarding relationships and sex. Chef would stammer, dodge, or scold the children for asking. Sometimes he would answer in vague and allusive ways, trying to remain child-appropriate, but ending up completely unintelligible. In other instances he'd get carried away, singing about his sexual exploits before remembering his audience. But despite occasional lapses in effectiveness and appropriateness, Chef consistently was the most ethical, kind, and compassionate adult in a show populated by insecure, self-absorbed, and outright offensive characters.

⬤ Jerome "Chef" McElroy's style may have been unconventional, but he strived for competence in his communication with the boys of *South Park*.

Many of us can think of a Chef character in our own lives—someone who, even if he or she occasionally errs, always *strives* to communicate competently. Often, this person's efforts pay off; competent communicators report more relational satisfaction (including happier marriages), better psychological and physical health, and higher levels of educational and professional achievement than others (Spitzberg & Cupach, 2002).

Although people who communicate competently report positive outcomes, they don't all communicate in the same ways. No one recipe for competence exists. Communicating competently will help you achieve more of your interpersonal goals, but it doesn't guarantee that all of your relationship problems will be solved.

Throughout this text, you will learn the knowledge and skills necessary for strengthening your interpersonal competence. In this chapter, we explore what competence means and how to improve your competence online. Throughout later chapters, we examine how you can communicate more competently across various situations, and within romantic, family, friendship, and workplace relationships.

UNDERSTANDING COMPETENCE

Interpersonal communication competence means consistently communicating in ways that are *appropriate* (your communication follows accepted norms),

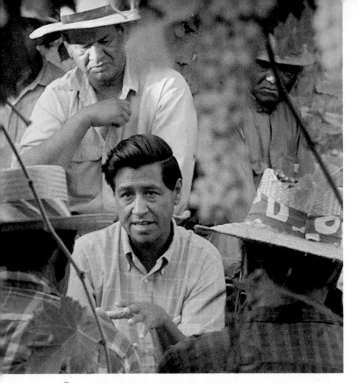

Labor leader César Chávez spent most of his life speaking out for America's poorest farm laborers. Whether speaking with union volunteers or powerful politicians, Chávez's interpersonal communication competence allowed him to translate his personal intentions into actions that changed the world.

effective (your communication enables you to achieve your goals), and *ethical* (your communication treats people fairly) (Spitzberg & Cupach, 1984; Wiemann, 1977). Acquiring knowledge of what it means to communicate competently is the first step in developing interpersonal communication competence (Spitzberg, 1997).

The second step is learning how to translate this knowledge into **communication skills**, repeatable goal-directed behaviors and behavioral patterns that you routinely practice in your interpersonal encounters and relationships (Spitzberg & Cupach, 2002). Both steps require *motivation* to improve your communication. If you do not believe your communication needs improvement, or if you believe that competence is unimportant or no more than common sense, your competence will be difficult, if not impossible, to refine. But, if you are strongly motivated to improve your interpersonal communication, you can master the knowledge and skills necessary to develop competence.

Appropriateness The first characteristic of competent interpersonal communication is **appropriateness**—the degree to which your communication matches situational, relational, and cultural expectations regarding how people should communicate. In any interpersonal encounter, norms exist regarding what people should and shouldn't say, and how they should and shouldn't act. For example, in *South Park*, Chef commonly struggled when the boys asked him to talk about topics that aren't considered appropriate for children. Part of developing your communication competence is refining your sensitivity to norms and adapting your communication accordingly. People who fail to adapt their communication to situational norms are perceived by others as incompetent communicators.

We judge how appropriate our communication is through **self-monitoring**: the process of observing our own communication and the norms of the situation in order to make appropriate communication choices. Some individuals closely monitor their own communication to ensure they're acting in accordance with situational expectations (Giles & Street, 1994). Known as *high self-monitors,* they prefer situations in which clear expectations exist regarding how they're supposed to communicate. In contrast, *low self-monitors* don't assess their own communication or the situation. They prefer encounters in which they can "act like themselves" rather than having to abide by norms (Snyder, 1974).

While communicating appropriately is a key part of competence, *over-emphasizing* appropriateness can backfire. If you focus exclusively on appropriateness and always adapt your communication to what others want, you may end up forfeiting your freedom of communicative choice to peer pressure or fears of

self-reflection

Think of an interpersonal encounter in which different people expected very different things from you in your communication. How did you choose which expectations to honor? What were the consequences of your decision? How could you have communicated in a way perceived as appropriate by everyone in the encounter?

Test Your Self-Disclosure

Place a check mark next to the statements you agree with. Then count the total number of statements you checked to see if you're a high or low self-monitor.

——— I find it easy to imitate others' behavior.

——— When I'm uncertain how to act during an interpersonal encounter, I look to others' behaviors for cues.

——— I would probably make a good actor.

——— In different situations and with different people, I often act like very different persons.

——— Even if I'm not enjoying myself, I often behave as if I'm having a good time.

——— I find it easy to change my behavior to suit different people and situations.

——— I sometimes appear to others to be experiencing deeper emotions than I really am.

——— I'm pretty good at making other people like me.

——— I'm not always the person I appear to be.

Note: This *Self-Quiz* is adapted from the self-monitoring scale provided by Snyder (1974).

Scoring: 0–4 indicates you're probably a low self-monitor; 5–9 suggests you're a high self-monitor.

being perceived negatively (Burgoon, 1995). For example, think of a person who always gives in to what others want and never advocates for his or her own goals. Is this individual a competent communicator? How about the friend who always tells people only what they want to hear rather than the truth? As these examples suggest, exclusive attention to appropriateness can hurt both the communicator and those around him or her.

Effectiveness   The second characteristic of competent interpersonal communication is **effectiveness**: the ability to use communication to accomplish the three types of interpersonal goals discussed earlier (self-presentational, instrumental, and relational). There's rarely a single communicative path for achieving all of these goals, and sometimes you must make trade-offs. For example, a critical part of maintaining satisfying close relationships is the willingness to occasionally sacrifice instrumental goals to achieve important relational goals. Suppose you badly want to see a movie tonight, but your romantic partner needs your emotional support to handle a serious family problem. Would you say, "I'm sorry you're feeling bad—I'll call you after I get home from the movie" (emphasizing your instrumental goals)? Or would you say, "I can see the movie some other time—tonight I'll hang out with you" (emphasizing your relational goals)? The latter approach, which facilitates relationship health and happiness, is obviously more competent.

Ethics   The final defining characteristic of competent interpersonal communication is **ethics**, the set of moral principles that guide our behavior toward others (Spitzberg & Cupach, 2002). At a minimum, we are ethically obligated to

VideoCentral ▣

bedfordstmartins.com /reflectrelate

Self-Monitoring
Watch this clip online to answer the questions below.

Does this video show a low self-monitor or a high self-monitor? Please explain your reasoning. Have you ever changed your behavior after self-monitoring? If so, under what circumstances?

avoid intentionally hurting others through our communication. By this standard, communication that's intended to erode a person's self-esteem, that expresses intolerance or hatred, that intimidates or threatens others' physical well-being, or that expresses violence is unethical and therefore incompetent (Parks, 1994).

To truly be an ethical communicator, however, we must go beyond simply not doing harm. During every interpersonal encounter, we need to strive to treat others with respect, and communicate with them honestly, kindly, and positively (Englehardt, 2001). For additional guidelines on ethical communication, review the "Credo for Ethical Communication" below.

We all are capable of competence in contexts that demand little of us—situations where it's easy to behave appropriately, effectively, and ethically. True competence is developed when we consistently communicate competently across *all* situations that we face—contexts that are uncertain, complex, and unpleasant, as well as those that are simple, comfortable, and pleasant. One of the goals of this book is to arm you with the knowledge and skills you need to meet challenges to your competence with confidence.

IMPROVING YOUR COMPETENCE ONLINE

Much of our interpersonal communication occurs online, through e-mail, text, instant-messaging, and posting on social networking sites such as Facebook.

self-reflection

Is the obligation to communicate ethically absolute or situation-dependent? That is, are there circumstances in which it's ethical to communicate in a way that hurts someone else's feelings? Can one be disrespectful or dishonest, and still ethical? If so, when?

Credo of the National Communication Association

The National Communication Association (NCA) is the largest professional organization representing communication instructors, researchers, practitioners, and students in the United States. In 1999, the NCA Legislative Council adopted this "Credo for Ethical Communication" (National Communication Association, 1999).

- We advocate truthfulness, accuracy, honesty, and reason as essential to the integrity of communication.

- We endorse freedom of expression, diversity of perspective, and tolerance of dissent to achieve informed and responsible decision making.

- We strive to understand and respect other communicators before evaluating and responding to their messages.

- We promote communication climates of caring and mutual understanding that respect the unique needs and characteristics of individual communicators.

- We condemn communication that degrades people through distortion, intimidation, coercion, and violence, or expression of intolerance and hatred.

- We are committed to the courageous expression of personal convictions in pursuit of fairness and justice.

- We advocate sharing information, opinions, and feelings when facing significant choices while also respecting privacy and confidentiality.

- We accept responsibility for the short- and long-term consequences for our own communication and expect the same of others.

Signs of the social networking times.

This provides enormous benefits. It enables us to meet and form friendships and romances with people we wouldn't encounter otherwise, and it helps us maintain established relationships (Howard, Rainie, & Jones, 2001). It also bolsters our sense of community. Whereas people used to gather around the proverbial watercooler to chat, now social networking sites, discussion groups, and blogs are gathering places (Shedletsky & Aitken, 2004). In our study of interpersonal communication, we use **online communication** to refer to any interaction by means of social networking sites (such as Facebook), e-mail, text- or instant-messaging, Skype, chatrooms, and even massively multiplayer video games like *World of Warcraft* (Walther & Parks, 2002).

Given how often we use technology to interpersonally communicate, building online competence becomes extremely important. Based on years of research, scholar Malcolm Parks offers five suggestions for improving your online communication competence (see Table 1.2 on page 26).[2]

1. *Match the gravity of your message to your communication medium.* An essential part of online competence is knowing when to communicate online versus offline. For many interpersonal goals, online communication is more effective. Text-messaging a friend to remind her of a coffee date makes more sense than dropping by her workplace, and it's probably quicker and less disruptive than calling her. E-mail may be best when dealing with problematic people or certain types of conflicts. That's because you can take

---

[2]Personal communication with author, May 13, 2008. This material was developed specifically for this text and published with permission of Dr. Malcolm Parks; may not be reproduced without written consent of Dr. Parks and the author.

time to think and carefully draft and revise responses before sending them—something that isn't possible during face-to-face interactions.

But online communication is not the best medium for giving in-depth, lengthy, and detailed explanations of professional or personal dilemmas, or for conveying weighty relationship decisions. Despite the ubiquity of online communication, many people still expect important news to be shared in person. Most of us would be surprised if a spouse revealed a long-awaited pregnancy through e-mail, or if a friend disclosed a cancer relapse through a text message.

2. *Don't assume that online communication is always more efficient.* Matters of relational significance or issues that evoke strong emotional overtones are more effectively and ethically handled in person or over the phone. But so too are many simple things—like deciding when to meet and where to go to lunch. Many times, a one-minute phone call or quick, face-to-face exchange can save several minutes of texting.

3. *Presume that your posts are public.* You may be thinking of the laugh you'll get from friends when you post the funny picture of you drunkenly hugging the houseplant on Facebook. But what about family members, future in-laws, or potential employers who see the picture? That clever joke you made about friend A in an e-mail to friend B—what if B forwards it to C who then forwards it to A? Even if you have "privacy settings" on your

table 1.2 **Online Communication Competence**

Online Competence Suggestion	Best Practices Suggestion
1. Match the gravity of your message to your communication medium.	*Online* is best for quick reminders, linear messages, or messages that require time and thought to craft. *Offline* is best for important information: engagements, health issues, etc.
2. Don't assume that online communication is always more efficient.	If your message needs a quick decision or answer, a phone call or face-to-face conversation may be best. Use online communication if you want the person to have time to respond.
3. Presume that your posts are public.	If you wouldn't want a message published for public consumption, don't post/send it online.
4. Remember that your posts are permanent.	Even after you delete something, it still exists on servers and may be accessible.
5. Practice the art of creating drafts.	Don't succumb to the pressure to respond to e-mails immediately. Taking your time will result in a more competent message.

personal page, what's to stop authorized-access friends from downloading your photos and posts and distributing them to others? Keep this rule in mind: anything you've sent or posted online can potentially be seen by anyone.

4. *Remember that your posts are permanent.* The things you say online are like old TV shows: they hang around as reruns forever. Old e-mails, photographs, videos, and blogs—all of these may still be accessible years later. As just one example, everything you have ever posted on Facebook is stored on their server, whether you delete it from your profile or not. And Facebook legally reserves the right to sell your content, as long as they delete personally identifying information (such as your name) from it. One of my students learned this the hard way, when he saw a personal family photo he had uploaded to Facebook packaged as the "sample photo" in a gift frame at a local store. Think before you post.

5. *Practice the art of creating drafts.* Get into the habit of saving text and e-mail messages as "drafts," then revisiting them later and editing them as needed for appropriateness, effectiveness, and ethics. Because online communication makes it easy to flame, many of us impetuously fire off messages that we later regret. Sometimes the most competent online communication is none at all—the result of a process in which you compose a text, save it as a draft, but delete it after reviewing it and realizing it's incompetent.

Issues in Interpersonal Communication

Adapting to influences on interpersonal communication

As we move through the twenty-first century, scholars and students alike are increasingly appreciating how important interpersonal communication is in our daily lives and relationships. Moreover, they're recognizing the impact of societal changes such as diversity and technological innovation. To ensure that the field stays current with social trends, communication scholars have begun exploring the issues of culture, gender and sexual orientation, online communication, and the dark side of interpersonal relationships.

CULTURE

In this text, we define **culture** broadly and inclusively, as an established, coherent set of beliefs, attitudes, values, and practices shared by a large group of people (Keesing, 1974). Culture includes many different types of large-group influences such as nationality, ethnicity, religion, gender, sexual orientation, physical and mental abilities, and even age. We learn our cultural beliefs, attitudes, and values from parents, teachers, religious leaders, peers, and the mass media (Gudykunst & Kim, 2003). As our world gets more diverse, scholars and students must consider cultural differences when discussing interpersonal communication theory and research and how communication skills can be improved.

skills practice

Online Competence
Become a more competent online communicator.

❶ Before communicating online, ask yourself: is the information important or complicated; or does it require a negotiated decision? If so, call or communicate face-to-face instead.

❷ Don't share content you consider private. Anything you text, e-mail, or post can be exported elsewhere by anyone who has access to it.

❸ Save messages as drafts, then revisit them later, checking appropriateness, effectiveness, and ethics.

❹ When in doubt, delete, don't send!

⬤ Understanding how culture, gender, and sexual orientation can influence interpersonal communication will help you communicate more effectively.

Throughout this book, we examine differences and similarities across cultures and consider their implications for interpersonal communication. As we cover this material, critically examine the role that culture plays in your own interpersonal communication and relationships.

GENDER AND SEXUAL ORIENTATION

Gender consists of social, psychological, and cultural traits generally associated with one sex or the other (Canary, Emmers-Sommer, & Faulkner, 1997). Unlike biological sex, which we're born with, gender is largely learned. Gender influences how people communicate interpersonally, but scholars disagree about how. For example, you may have read in popular magazines or heard on TV that women are more "open" communicators than men, and that men "have difficulty

Intercultural Competence

When Pepsi first began selling in China, their advertising slogan, "Come alive—You're the Pepsi Generation!" was mistranslated as, "Resurrect! Your body will be made of Pepsi!" Clairol's "Mist Stick" curling iron had great sales around the world except in Germany, where "mist" is slang for manure (the company was unwittingly marketing a "poop stick").

Intercultural communication challenges aren't limited to language. Gestures in the United States and Canada such as the "OK" sign (thumb and index finger touching) and "thumbs-up" are considered obscenities in many countries.

Throughout this text, we discuss cultural differences in communication and how you can best adapt to them. Such skills are essential, given that hundreds of thousands of college students choose to pursue their studies overseas, international travel is increasingly common, and technology continues to connect people worldwide. As a starting point for building your intercultural competence, consider these suggestions:

1. Think globally. If the world's population was reduced in scale to 1,000 people, only 56 would be from Canada, Mexico, and the United States.

2. Learn appropriateness. Take the time to learn the practices of other cultures before interacting with people from them.

3. Be respectfully inquisitive. When you're unsure about how to communicate, politely ask. People will view you as competent—even if you make mistakes—when you sincerely try to learn and abide by their cultural expectations.

4. Use simple language. Avoid slang and jargon. A phrase like "Let's cut to the chase" may make sense if you're originally from Canada or the United States, but won't necessarily be understood elsewhere.

5. Be patient with yourself, and others. Becoming interculturally competent is a lifelong journey, not a short-term achievement.

discussion questions

- How has *your* cultural background shaped how you communicate with people from other cultures?
- What's the biggest barrier that keeps people of different cultures from communicating competently with each other?

---

communicating their feelings." But when these beliefs are compared with research and theory on gender and interpersonal communication, it turns out that differences (and similarities) between men and women are more complicated than the popular stereotypes suggest. Throughout this book, we discuss such stereotypes and look at scholarly research on the impact of gender on interpersonal communication.

Each of us also possesses a **sexual orientation**: an enduring emotional, romantic, sexual, or affectionate attraction to others that exists along a continuum ranging from exclusive homosexuality to exclusive heterosexuality and that includes various forms of bisexuality (APA Online, n.d.). You may have heard that gays and lesbians communicate in ways different from "straights" or that each group builds, maintains, and ends relationships in distinct ways. But as with common beliefs about gender, research shows that same-gender and opposite-gender relationships are formed, maintained, and dissolved in similar ways. We also discuss these assumptions about sexual orientations throughout this text.

Dealing with a Difficult Friend

1 BACKGROUND

Communicating competently is challenging, especially when close relationship partners say and do things that provoke us. When problematic encounters happen online, it makes dealing with them even more difficult. Read the case study; then, drawing upon all you know about interpersonal communication thus far, work through the problem-solving model at the end of the exercise—a model designed to help you make more systematic and better relationship decisions in your life.

2 CASE STUDY

Kaitlyn, Cort, and you have been best friends for years. The three of you are inseparable, and people joke that you're more like triplets than a trio of friends. After high school, you and Cort become college housemates. Kaitlyn can't afford tuition yet, so she stays in your hometown to work and save money. Despite the distance, the three of you stay in daily contact.

Recently, however, things have changed. Kaitlyn has been hanging out with people you consider shady. She's been drinking heavily, and boasting about her all-night binges. You try to be supportive, but you're worried about her.

You awake one Sunday to find a Facebook photo album posted by Kaitlyn, documenting her latest party adventure. Her description reads, "A new low is reached—I *LUV* it!!" Surfing through the slideshow, you see Kaitlyn drinking until she passes out. Several photos show her friends laughing and posing with her while she's unconscious. In one image, they've drawn a smiley face on her forehead with a Sharpie. Looking at these photos, you're heartsick with humiliation for your friend. Why would Kaitlyn hang with people who would treat her like that? But you also can't understand why she would post these pictures. What if her family saw them? Or her employers? You e-mail her, telling her she should delete the album, and saying that you're worried about her behavior and her choice of new friends. You await her response for the rest of the day, but she doesn't call, text, or write.

That night your computer crashes, so you borrow Cort's laptop. While you're working, a message alert sounds. It's an e-mail from Kaitlyn to Cort. You know you shouldn't read it, but then you see your name mentioned. It's a rage message, in which Kaitlyn blasts you for prying into her business, for judging her, for thinking you're better than her, and for telling her what to do. It's personal, profane, and *very* insulting.

You feel sick to your stomach with shock. You love Kaitlyn, but you're also furious with her. How could she say such horrible things when all you were trying to do was help? Just at that moment, a Facebook chat message pops up. It's from Kaitlyn to Cort: "So glad u r finally online! I want to talk with u about our nosy, o-so-perfect friend!"

③ YOUR TURN

Think about the ideas and insights regarding interpersonal communication you've learned while reading this chapter. Keep them in mind while working through the following five steps. These steps constitute a process that can help you make more competent interpersonal communication choices in important relationships. Remember, there are no right answers to the questions posed here. So think hard about what choice you will make! (P.S. Need help? See the *Helpful Concepts* listed below.)

● step 1

Reflect on yourself. What are your thoughts and feelings in this situation? What assumptions are you making about Kaitlyn and her interpersonal communication? Are your assumptions accurate? Why or why not?

● step 2

Reflect on your partners. Put yourself in Kaitlyn's shoes. Consider how she is thinking and feeling. Are her views valid?

● step 3

Identify the optimal outcome. Think about what's happened. Consider your own feelings as well as those of Kaitlyn. Given all these factors, what's the best, most constructive relationship outcome possible here? Be sure to consider not just what's best for you, but what's best for Kaitlyn as well.

● step 4

Locate the roadblocks. Taking into consideration your own thoughts and feelings, those of Kaitlyn, and all that has happened in this situation, what's preventing you from achieving the optimal outcome you identified in Step 3?

● step 5

Chart your course. What can you say and do to overcome the roadblocks you identified in Step 4 and to achieve your optimal relationship outcome?

HELPFUL CONCEPTS

I-Thou and I-It, **13**

Relationship information, **14**

The irreversibility of interpersonal communication, **16**

Ethics, **23**

Improving your online competence, **24**

ONLINE COMMUNICATION

Radical changes in communication technology have had a profound effect on our ability to interpersonally communicate. Cell phones keep us in almost constant contact with friends, family members, colleagues, and romantic partners. Our ability to communicate easily and frequently, even when separated by geographic distance, is further enhanced through *online communication*. In this book, we treat such technologies as tools for connecting people interpersonally—tools that are now thoroughly integrated into our lives. In every chapter, you'll find frequent mention of these technologies as they relate to the chapter's specific topics.

THE DARK SIDE OF INTERPERSONAL RELATIONSHIPS

Interpersonal communication strongly influences the quality of our interpersonal relationships, and the quality of those relationships in turn affects how we feel about our lives. When our involvements with lovers, family, friends, and coworkers are satisfying and healthy, we typically feel happier in general (Myers, 2002). But the fact that relationships can bring us joy obscures the fact that relationships, and the interpersonal communication that occurs within them, can often be destructive.

In studying interpersonal communication, you can learn much by looking beyond constructive encounters to the types of damaging exchanges that occur all too frequently in life. *The greatest challenges to your interpersonal communication skills lie not in communicating competently when it is easy to do so but in practicing*

self-QUIZ   The Dark Side of Interpersonal Relationships

Read the following phrases describing relationship challenges. Place a check mark next to each challenge that you believe you could address by improving your interpersonal communication skills. Then read the instructions below to interpret your score.

———— Feeling plagued by the sense that you're not the kind of person you should be or that others expect you to be

———— Thinking of and treating others in a negative, stereotypical fashion

———— Dealing with unwanted anger in ways that avoid chronic hostility and aggression

———— Managing grief related to the loss of a loved one

———— Feeling extreme fear and anxiety when interacting with others

———— Managing people who are verbally and physically aggressive toward you

———— Reducing the likelihood of violence during interpersonal conflicts

———— Managing romantic jealousy in yourself and your partners

———— Dealing with betrayal in friendship relationships

———— Coping with parental favoritism shown toward a sibling

———— Responding effectively to abuse from a coworker or supervisor

Scoring: You can better manage *all* of these relationship challenges by improving your interpersonal communication, as you'll discover throughout this text.

competent interpersonal communication when doing so is difficult. Throughout the text, we will discuss many of the negative situations that you may experience, as well as recommendations for how to deal with them.

The Journey Ahead

Studying communication is the first step to improving it

Interpersonal communication is our primary vehicle for exchanging meaning, connecting emotionally, and building relationships with others. This makes it essential that we base our interpersonal decisions on the best knowledge to which we have access. No one would consider making choices about collegiate majors, future careers, or monetary interests without first gathering the most trustworthy information available. Interpersonal communication should be no different.

This chapter—which introduces key definitions and important principles—will start you on your journey into the study of interpersonal communication. As we travel together through interpersonal essentials, skills, and relationships, the transformative potential of your interpersonal communication will become apparent.

We began this chapter with a military wife struggling to juggle the competing demands of raising her children and maintaining her marriage. Melissa Seligman uses multiple media to stay connected with her husband during his combat deployments. At the same time, she has learned that computers, phones, and care packages are merely tools. The most important thing is open, honest, and loving communication.

How do you stay close with loved ones who are distant? What tough communication choices have you faced in these relationships?

The story of Melissa Seligman's struggle reminds us of an inescapable truth that forms the foundation for this book. Our close relationships are *the* most important things in our lives, and it's our choices regarding how we communicate that determine

POSTSCRIPT

whether these relationships survive and thrive, or fade away.

chapter review

key terms

▶ You can watch brief, illustrative videos of these terms and test your understanding of the concepts online in *VideoCentral: Interpersonal Communication* at **bedfordstmartins .com/reflectrelate**.

key concepts

What Is Communication?

- Scholars have studied **communication** for thousands of years. The **message** is the basic unit of communication, and we exchange messages during **interactions** with others. During communication, **contexts** shape how we create and interpret messages, and messages are conveyed through a variety of **channels** and **media**.

- The **linear communication model** describes the basic set of components necessary for communication to occur, including a **sender**, a message, a channel, **noise**, and a **receiver**. The **interactive communication model** builds on the linear model, adding both **feedback** and **fields of experience**. The **transactional communication model** presents the notion that communication participants collaboratively create meaning.

What Is Interpersonal Communication?

- When most people think of **interpersonal communication**, they think of **dyadic** communication. This allows us to distinguish it from **intrapersonal communication**.

- Interpersonal communication differs from other types of communication in that it changes (and is changed by) participants' emotions, thoughts, behavior, and relationships. One way to understand interpersonal communication is the difference between **I-Thou** and **I-It**. Interpersonal communication also enables us to connect with others in ways that are more meaningful and profound than through **impersonal communication**.

- Whenever we interpersonally communicate with others, we exchange both content and relationship information. Because relationship information influences how others interpret the content of what we have said, it can be considered a form of **meta-communication**.

- Interpersonal communication is characterized by four principles: it has content and relationship information, it can be intentional or unintentional, it's irreversible, and it's dynamic.

- We use interpersonal communication for a broad range of purposes, including fulfilling a hierarchy of needs and pursuing **self-presentation**, **instrumental**, and **relationship goals**.

- Scholars conduct *research* and create *theory* to better understand how people communicate interpersonally. Both *qualitative* approaches and *quantitative* approaches to research and theory involve the creation and testing of hypotheses, although the manner in which such tests are conducted is quite different.

What Is Interpersonal Communication Competence?

- While there is not one way for achieving it, **interpersonal communication competence** means consistently communicating with others in ways that are appropriate, effective, and ethical. To strengthen your interpersonal competence, you must translate this understanding into action in the form of **communication skills**, and consistently strive for excellence in your communication.

- Competent interpersonal communicators are sensitive to norms of **appropriateness**. People use **self-monitoring** to observe and judge how appropriate (or not) their communication is to norms. To be truly competent, you must strike a balance among appropriateness, effectiveness, and attention to ethics in your communication. Too much concern for appropriateness can render your communication ineffective.

- We often consider people who demonstrate **effectiveness** in achieving their interpersonal goals as being interpersonally competent. But people can be exceptionally effective communicators and still be unethical or inappropriate. In such cases, their communication is incompetent.

- The final component of competence is **ethics**. Although a minimum standard for ethical communication is "do no harm to others," many people feel that true competence can be achieved only through consistent demonstration of respect toward others.

- For competent **online communication**, adhere to these five suggestions: match your message to your medium, don't assume online communication is always more efficient, presume your posts are public, remember that your posts are permanent, and practice the art of creating drafts.

Issues in Interpersonal Communication

- Certain topics are becoming increasingly relevant for students and teachers of interpersonal communication: **culture**, **gender** and **sexual orientation**, online communication, and the dark side of interpersonal relationships.

key skills

- What is the definition of interpersonal communication? Find the answer on pages 11–14.

- How might you shift your communication from I-It to I-Thou? Try the *Skills Practice* on page 13 to find out.

- What is the fundamental connection between communication knowledge, communication choices, and relationship outcomes? Review the answer on pages 13–14.

- What are the two practical implications of viewing interpersonal communication as dynamic? Review the answer on page 17.

- How can you use research methods to analyze online communication challenges? Try the *Skills Practice* on page 20.

- Interested in becoming a more competent interpersonal communicator? Learn about the characteristics of competence on pages 21–24.

- How sensitive and adaptive are you to situational appropriateness norms? Discover the answer by taking the *Self-Quiz* on page 23.

- Curious about how to incorporate ethics into your interpersonal communication? Review the National Communication Association's "Credo for Ethical Communication" on page 24.

- Have you had difficulty communicating competently online? Discover suggestions for improvement on pages 24–27. Then complete the *Skills Practice* on page 27 to put these principles into action.

- What challenges from the dark side of interpersonal communication can be better managed through building your interpersonal skills? Find the answer by taking the *Self-Quiz* on page 32.

- How would you deal with the ethics surrounding a changing friendship and communication you weren't supposed to see? Complete the *Making Relationship Choices* exercise on pages 30–31 to find out.

2 Considering Self

Artist Eric Staib describes his 2002 painting *labeled* (left) as a self-portrait. "It depicts my feelings about how my peers saw me when I was growing up. The hands pointing, words said under people's breath. You can tell what they're thinking: you're an idiot, you're stupid, you're a joke."[1]

By the time Eric was in third grade, he knew he was different. Whereas his classmates progressed rapidly in reading and writing, Eric couldn't make sense of words on the written page. But it wasn't until fifth grade that Eric finally was given a label for his difference: learning disabled, or "LD." The LD label stained Eric's sense of self, making him feel ashamed. His low self-esteem spread outward, constraining his communication and relationships. "My whole approach was *Don't get noticed!* I'd slouch down in class, hide in my seat. And I would never open up to people. I let nobody in."

Frustrated with the seemingly insurmountable challenges of reading and writing, Eric channeled intense energy into art. By eleventh grade, Eric had the reading and writing abilities of a fifth grader but managed to pass his classes through hard work and artistic ability. He graduated from high school with a D average.

> By deepening your self-understanding, you can begin to clarify your thoughts and feelings about your self.

[1]All information presented regarding artist Eric Staib was provided with his permission, from an interview conducted by the author in February 2005.

2 / Considering Self

the first time in my life, I had a label for myself other than 'learning disabled.' To me, the LD label meant I couldn't learn. But dyslexia was different. It could be overcome.

The specialist taught me strategies for working with my dyslexia, and gave me my most important tool—my Franklin Spellchecker—to check spellings. But most importantly, I was taught that it was okay to be dyslexic."

Many of Eric's LD peers turned to substance abuse and dropped out of school, but Eric pursued his education further, taking classes at a local community college. There, something happened that transformed his view of his self, his self-esteem, and the entire course of his life. While taking his first written exam of the semester, Eric knew the answers, but he couldn't write them down. No matter how hard he focused, he couldn't convert the knowledge in his head into written words. Rather than complete the exam, he wrote the story of his disability on the answer sheet, including his struggles with reading and writing and the pain associated with being labeled LD. He turned in his exam and left. Eric's professor took his exam to the college dean, and the two of them called Eric to the dean's office. They told him, "You need help, and we're going to help you." Their compassion changed Eric's life. Eric's professor arranged for Eric to meet with a learning specialist, who immediately diagnosed him as dyslexic. As Eric explains, "For

Armed with an improving sense of self, Eric went from hiding to asserting himself, "from low self-esteem to being comfortable voicing my opinion, from fear to confidence." That confidence led him to transfer to a Big 10 university, where he graduated with a degree in studio arts, percussion, and horticulture. He subsequently earned a postgraduate degree in K–12 art education, graduating with a straight-A average.

Eric Staib is now an art instructor in the Midwest and was a 2006 recipient of the Robert Rauschenberg Foundation Power of Art Award, given to the top arts educators in the country each year. He also teaches instructors how to use art to engage learning-disabled students. What means the most to him is the opportunity to pass down the legacy of his personal transformation. "When I think about my dyslexia, it's really incredible. What was my greatest personal punishment is now the most profound gift I have to offer to others."

Every word you've ever spoken during an encounter, every act of kindness or malevolence you've committed, has the same root source—your self. When you look inward to your self, you are peering into the wellspring from which all of your interpersonal actions flow. But even as your self influences your interpersonal communication, it is shaped by your communication as well. Through communicating with others, we learn who we are, what we're worth, and how we should act. This means that the starting point for improving your communication is to understand your self. By deepening your self-understanding, you can begin to clarify your thoughts and feelings about your self; comprehend how these are linked to your interpersonal communication; and develop strategies for enhancing your sense of self, your communication skills, and your interpersonal relationships.

In this chapter, we explore the source of all interpersonal communication: the self. You'll learn:

- The components of self, as well as how critical self-reflection can be used to improve your communication skills and your self-esteem
- The ways in which gender, family, and culture shape your sense of self
- How to present and maintain a positive self when interacting with others
- The importance of online self-presentation
- The challenges of managing selves in relationships, including suggestions for successful self-disclosure

The Components of Self

Your self is the driving force of your communication

At Delphi in ancient Greece, the temple of the sun-god Apollo was adorned with the inscription *Gnothi se auton*—"Know thyself." According to legend, when one of the seven sages of Greece, Chilon of Sparta, asked Apollo, "What is best for people?" the deity responded with that simple admonition. More than 2,500 years later, these words still ring true, especially in the realm of interpersonal communication and relationships. To understand our interactions with others and the bonds we forge, we must first comprehend ourselves. But what exactly is "thyself" that we need to know?

The **self** is an evolving composite of self-awareness, self-concept, and self-esteem. Although each of us experiences the self as singular ("*This* is who I am"), it actually is made up of three distinct, yet integrated, components that evolve continually over time, based on your life experiences.

SELF-AWARENESS

Self-awareness is the ability to step outside yourself (so to speak); view yourself as a unique person distinct from your surrounding environment; and reflect on your thoughts, feelings, and behaviors. According to sociologist George Herbert Mead (1934), self-awareness helps you to have a strong sense of your self because

◯ Our self-concept is influenced by our beliefs about how others view us.

Social Comparison
Watch this clip online to answer the questions below.

What aspects of your self are you more likely to compare with others? How does this impact your self-awareness?
  Want to see more? Check out VideoCentral for a clip on **self-fulfilling prophecies**.

during interpersonal encounters you monitor your own behaviors and form impressions of who you are from such observations. For example, your best friend texts you that she has failed an important exam. You feel bad for her, so you immediately text her a sympathetic and comforting response. Your self-awareness of your compassion, coupled with your observation of your kindhearted message, lead you to think about yourself: "I'm a caring and supportive friend."

As we're watching and evaluating our own actions, we also engage in **social comparison**: observing and assigning meaning to others' behavior and then comparing it against ours. Social comparison has a particularly potent effect on self when we compare ourselves against people we admire and wish to emulate. When we compare favorably against respected others, we think well of ourselves ("I'm as hardworking and successful as the best employees in this company"). When we don't compare favorably, we think less of ourselves ("I wish I could be as open and outgoing as my friends").

You can greatly enhance your interpersonal communication by practicing a targeted kind of self-awareness known as *critical self-reflection*. To engage in critical self-reflection, ask yourself the following questions:

- What am I thinking and feeling?
- Why am I thinking and feeling the way I am?
- How am I communicating?
- How are my thoughts and feelings affecting my communication?
- How can I improve my thoughts, feelings, and communication?

The ultimate goal of critical self-reflection is embodied in the last question: How can I *improve?* Improving your interpersonal communication is possible only when you accurately understand how your self drives your communication behavior. In the remainder of this chapter, and in the marginal *Self-Reflection* exercises you'll find throughout this book, we help you make links between your self and your communication.

SELF-CONCEPT

Self-concept is your overall perception of who you are ("On the whole, I'm a _____ person"). Your self-concept is based on the beliefs, attitudes, and values you have about yourself. *Beliefs* are convictions that certain things are true—for example, "I'm an excellent student." *Attitudes* are evaluative appraisals, such as "I'm happy with my appearance." *Values* represent enduring principles that guide your interpersonal actions—for example, "I think it's wrong to . . . ."

Your self-concept is shaped by a host of factors, including your gender, family, friends, and culture (Vallacher, Nowak, Froehlich, & Rockloff, 2002). As we saw in the opening story about Eric Staib, one of the biggest influences on your self-concept is the labels others put on you. How do others' impressions of you shape your self-concept? Sociologist Charles Horton Cooley (1902) argued that it's like looking at yourself in the mirror, or "looking glass" as it was known in his era. When you stand in front of a mirror, you consider your physical appearance through the eyes of others, including lovers, friends, family, and even the media. Do others see you as attractive? Overweight? Too tall or too short? Do you possess "desirable" eye, skin, and hair colors, according to others? Seeing yourself in this fashion—and thinking about how others must see you—has a powerful effect on how you think about your physical self. Cooley noted that the same process shapes our broader self-concept: it is based in part on your beliefs about how others see you. This includes their perceptions and evaluations of you ("People think I'm talented, and they like me") as well as your emotional response to those beliefs ("I feel good/bad about how others see me"). Cooley called the idea of defining our self-concepts through thinking about how others see us the **looking-glass self**.

In considering your self-concept and its impact on your interpersonal communication, keep two implications in mind. First, because your self-concept consists of deeply held beliefs, attitudes, and values, changing it is difficult. Once you've decided you're a compassionate person, for example, you'll likely perceive yourself that way for a long time (Fiske & Taylor, 1991).

Second, our self-concepts often lead us to make **self-fulfilling prophecies**, predictions about future interactions that lead us to behave in ways that ensure the interaction unfolds as we predicted. Some self-fulfilling prophecies set positive events in motion. For instance, you may see yourself as professionally capable and highly skilled at communicating. This view leads you to predict job interview success. During the actual interview, your prophecy of success leads you to communicate in a calm, confident, and impressive fashion, which consequently creates success; the interviewers like and are impressed by you, and their reaction confirms your prophecy.

Other self-fulfilling prophecies set negative events in motion. I once had a friend who believed he was unattractive and undesirable. Whenever we went out to parties or clubs, his self-concept would lead him to predict interpersonal failure: "What's the point; no one will talk to me anyway." He would then spend the entire time sitting at our table, scowling and staring morosely into his drink. Needless to say, no one would approach him or try to talk to him. At the end of the evening, he'd say, "See, I told you no one would want to talk to me!"

SELF-ESTEEM

Self-esteem is the overall value, positive or negative, that we assign to ourselves. Whereas self-awareness prompts us to ask "Who am I?" and self-concept is the answer to that question, self-esteem is the answer to the follow-up question, "Given who I am, what's my evaluation of my self?" When your overall estimation of self is negative, you'll have a meager sense of self-worth and suffer from low self-esteem. When your evaluation of self is positive, you'll enjoy high self-esteem.

Your self-esteem strongly shapes your interpersonal communication, relationships, and physical and mental health (Pyszczynski, Greenberg, Solomon, Arndt, & Schimel, 2004). In simple terms, when you're happy with yourself, this happiness

self-reflection

Consider your looking-glass self. What kinds of labels do your friends use to describe you? Your family? How do you feel about others' impressions of you? In what ways do these feelings shape your interpersonal communication and relationships?

skills practice

Self-Fulfilling Prophecies
Overcoming negative self-fulfilling prophecies

❶ Identify a communication problem you experience often (e.g., social anxiety).

❷ Describe situations when it occurs, including what you think, say, and do.

❸ Use critical self-reflection to identify how your thoughts and feelings shape your communication.

❹ List things you could say and do that would generate positive results.

❺ In similar situations, block negative thoughts and feelings that arise, and focus your attention on practicing your listed positive behaviors.

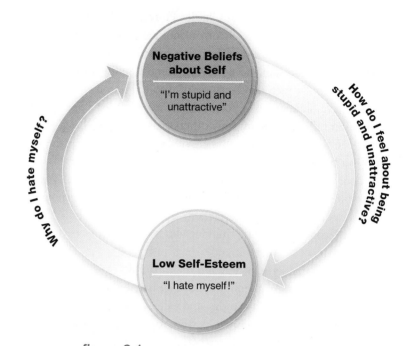

figure 2.1 Low Self-Esteem: A Vicious Cycle

radiates inward and outward. People with high self-esteem report greater life satisfaction, communicate more positively with others, and experience more happiness in their relationships than do people with low self-esteem (Fox, 1997). People with high self-esteem also exhibit greater leadership ability, athleticism, and academic performance (Fox, 1992). High self-esteem helps insulate people from stress and anxiety: people with high esteem report fewer anxiety-related disorders, and are better able to cope with stress (Pyszczynski et al., 2004). By contrast, low self-esteem can spawn a destructive feedback loop, as depicted in Figure 2.1.

Measuring Up to Your Own Standards   The key to bolstering your self-esteem is understanding its roots. **Self-discrepancy theory** suggests that your self-esteem is determined by how you compare to two mental standards (Higgins, 1987). The first is your *ideal self*, the characteristics you want to possess based on your desires. This is the "perfect you"—the embodiment of all the attributes you consider admirable. These characteristics may be mental, physical, emotional, material, and even spiritual. The second standard is your *ought self*, the person others wish and expect you to be. This stems from expectations of your family, friends, colleagues, and romantic partners as well as cultural norms. According to self-discrepancy theory, you feel happy and content when your perception of your self matches both your ideal and ought selves: "I'm the kind of person I want to be" and "I'm the kind of person others wish me to be" (Katz & Farrow, 2000). However, when you perceive your self to be inferior to both your ideal and ought selves, you experience a discrepancy between your self and these standards and are likely to suffer low self-esteem (Veale, Kinderman, Riley, & Lambrou, 2003).

◀ People who experience a discrepancy between themselves and their ideal self often wonder: "Why can't I be the person I want to be?" Those who experience a discrepancy between themselves and their ought self often wonder: "Why can't I be the person others want me to be?" What experiences have you had with these questions?

Improving Your Self-Esteem   Your self-esteem can start to improve only when you reduce discrepancies between your self and your ideal and ought selves. How can you do this? Begin by assessing your self-concept. Make a list of the beliefs, attitudes, and values that make up your self-concept. Be sure to include both positive and negative attributes. Then think about your self-esteem. In reviewing the list you've made, do you see yourself positively or negatively?

Next, analyze your ideal self. Who do you wish you were? Be sure to consider the physical, mental, emotional, material, and spiritual aspects of your desired self. Is this ideal attainable, or is it unrealistic? If it is attainable, what would you have to change to become this person? If you made these changes, would you be satisfied with yourself, or would your expectations for yourself simply escalate further?

How Does the Media Shape Your Self-Esteem?

focus
on CULTURE

Korean American comedian Margaret Cho describes herself as a "trash-talkin' girl comic." In this excerpt from her one-woman show *The Notorious C.H.O.,* she offers her thoughts on self-esteem:

You know when you look in the mirror and think, "Oh, I'm so fat, I'm so old, I'm so ugly"? That is not your authentic self speaking. That is billions upon billions of dollars of advertising—magazines, movies, billboards—all geared to make you feel bad about yourself so that you'll take your hard-earned money and spend it at the mall. When you don't have self-esteem, you will hesitate before you do anything. You will hesitate to go for the job you really want. You will hesitate to ask for a raise. You will hesitate to defend yourself when you're discriminated against. You will hesitate to vote. You will hesitate to dream. For those of us plagued with low self-esteem, improving [it] is truly an act of revolution! (Custudio, 2002)

Cho is right. We live in an "appearance culture," a society that values and reinforces extreme, unrealistic ideals of beauty and body shape (Thompson, Heinberg, Altabe, & Tantleff-Dunn, 1999). In an appearance culture, standards for appearance are defined through digitally enhanced images of bodily perfection produced by the mass media (Field et al., 1999). When we internalize media standards of perfect body and perfect beauty, we end up despising our own bodies and craving unattainable perfection (Jones, Vigfusdottir, & Lee, 2004). This results in low self-esteem, depression, and, in some cases, self-destructive behaviors such as eating disorders (Harrison, 2001).

discussion questions

- Consider your own body. How have images of ideal beauty in magazines and on TV influenced your ideas about what constitutes an attractive body?
- How do your feelings about your body affect your self-esteem? How do they affect your interpersonal communication and relationships?

Third, analyze your ought self. Who do others want you to be? Can you ever become the person others expect? What would you have to do to become this person? If you did all of these things, would others be satisfied with you, or would their expectations escalate?

Fourth, revisit and redefine your standards. This step requires intense, concentrated effort over a long period of time. If you find that your ideal and ought selves are realistic and attainable, move to the final step described below. If you decide that your ideal and ought selves are unrealistic and unattainable, redefine these standards so that each can be attainable through sustained work. If you find yourself unable to abandon unrealistic and unattainable standards, don't be afraid to consult with a professional therapist or other trusted resource for assistance.

Finally, create an action plan for resolving any self-discrepancies. Map out the specific actions necessary to eventually attain your ideal and ought selves. Frame your new standards as a list of goals, and post them in your planner, cell phone, personal Web page, bedroom, or kitchen to remind yourself of these goals. Since self-esteem can't be changed in a day, a week, or even a month, establish a realistic time line. Then implement this action plan in your daily life, checking your progress as you go.

Test Your Self-Esteem

This quiz can help you gauge your self-esteem. Read each statement and assign it a score depending on how much you agree with it. If you strongly agree, give it a 3; if you agree, give it a 2; if you disagree, give it a 1; and if you strongly disagree, give it a 0. Then total your score and see how it compares to the Scoring section below.

_____ On the whole, I am satisfied with myself.

_____ I feel that I have a number of good qualities.

_____ I am able to do things as well as most other people.

_____ I feel that I am a person of worth, at least on an equal plane with others.

_____ I have a positive attitude toward myself.

Note: This *Self-Quiz* is adapted from the self-esteem scale developed by Rosenburg (1965).

Scoring: Scores of 7 and below indicate low self-esteem; scores of 8 and above represent high self-esteem.

The Sources of Self

Outside forces influence your view of self

For most of us, critical self-reflection isn't a new activity. After all, we spend much of our daily lives looking inward, so we feel that we know our selves. But imagine for a moment that you don't. You wake up in your bed, and although you recognize your surroundings, you have no memory of self. Nothing. How will you find out who you are?

You might first examine your own body. Knowing whether you are male or female would immediately give you a wealth of useful knowledge about your self, such as which clothes you should wear and how you should talk and act. Second, you would likely venture downstairs to talk with family members, gathering as much information from them as you could. You would also watch how they respond to you. Do they seem intimate and caring toward you? Distant and aloof? Unpredictable and uncertain? Last, you would probably turn on the computer and surf the Internet, watch TV, or even take a walk into town, looking for clues about how people communicate with each other in public, how they dress, and how they behave. From these observations, you might begin to form ideas about where you fit in this culture.

Of course, at the end of the day, you still would have huge holes in your self-knowledge. Biologists and psychologists agree that roughly half of what makes us who we are is determined by our biological heritage (Rothbart, Ahadi, & Evans, 2000). But this doesn't mean that our self-awareness, self-concept, and self-esteem are 50 percent identical to those of our parents and other ancestors. Instead, our selves are shaped by the powerful outside forces of gender, family, and culture.

GENDER AND SELF

Arguably the most profound outside force shaping our sense of self is our **gender**— the composite of social, psychological, and cultural attributes that characterize us as

⬤ The sources of self include your biological sex, your family, and your culture.

male or female (Canary, Emmers-Sommer, & Faulkner, 1997). It may strike you as strange to see gender described as an "outside force." Gender is innate, something you're born with, right? Actually, scholars distinguish gender, which is largely learned, from *biological sex*, which we're born with. Each of us is born with biological sex organs that distinguish us anatomically as male or female. However, our gender is shaped over time through our interactions with others.

Immediately after birth, we begin a lifelong process of gender socialization, learning from others what it means personally, interpersonally, and culturally to be "male" or "female." Girls are typically taught feminine behaviors, such as sensitivity to one's own and others' emotions, nurturance, and compassion (Lippa, 2002). Boys are usually taught masculine behaviors, learning about assertiveness, competitiveness, and independence from others. As a result of gender socialization, men and women often end up forming comparatively different self-concepts (Cross & Madson, 1997). For example, women are more likely than men to perceive themselves as connected to others and to assess themselves based on the quality of these interpersonal connections. Men are more likely than women to think of themselves as a composite of their individual achievements, abilities, and beliefs—viewing themselves as separate from other people. At the same time, just because these differences exist doesn't mean that all men and all women think of themselves in identical ways. Many men and women appreciate and embrace both feminine and masculine characteristics in their self-concepts.

FAMILY AND SELF

When we're born, we have no self-awareness, self-concept, or self-esteem. As we mature, we slowly become aware of ourselves as unique and separate from our environments and begin developing self-concepts. Our caregivers play a crucial role in this process, providing us with ready-made sets of beliefs, attitudes, and values from which we construct our fledgling selves. We also forge emotional bonds with our caregivers, attachments that form the foundation for all of our future interpersonal connections (Bowlby, 1969). Our communication and interactions with caregivers powerfully shape our beliefs regarding the functions, rewards, and dependability of interpersonal relationships (Domingue & Mollen, 2009).

self-reflection

What lessons about gender did you learn from your family when you were growing up? From your friends? Based on these lessons, what aspects of your self did you bolster—or bury—given what others deemed appropriate for your gender? How did these lessons affect how you interpersonally communicate?

These beliefs, in turn, help shape two dimensions of our thoughts, feelings, and behavior: attachment anxiety and attachment avoidance (Collins & Feeney, 2004). *Attachment anxiety* is the degree to which a person fears rejection by relationship partners. If you experience high attachment anxiety, you perceive yourself as unlovable and unworthy—thoughts that may result from being ignored or even abused during youth. Consequently, in close relationships you experience chronic fear of abandonment. If you have low attachment anxiety, you feel lovable

47

and worthy of attention—reflections of a supportive and affectionate upbringing. As a result, you feel comfortable and confident in your intimate involvements.

Attachment avoidance is the degree to which someone desires close interpersonal ties. If you have high attachment avoidance, you'll likely experience little interest in intimacy, preferring solitude instead. Such feelings may stem from childhood neglect or an upbringing that encouraged autonomy. If you experience low attachment avoidance, you seek intimacy and interdependence with others, having learned in youth that such connections are essential for happiness and well-being.

Four attachment styles derive from these two dimensions (Collins & Feeney, 2004; Domingue & Mollen, 2009). **Secure attachment** individuals are low on both anxiety and avoidance: they're comfortable with intimacy and seek close ties with others. Secure individuals report warm and supportive relationships, high self-esteem, and confidence in their ability to communicate. When relationship problems arise, they move to resolve them ("We can work this out"), and are willing to solicit support from others—for example, asking a friend for advice on how to handle an argument with a spouse. In addition, they are comfortable with sexual intimacy, and unlikely to engage in risky sexual behavior.

Preoccupied attachment adults are high in anxiety and low in avoidance: they desire closeness, but are plagued with fear of rejection. They may use sexual contact to satisfy their compulsive need to feel loved. When faced with relationship challenges, preoccupied individuals react with extreme negative emotion and a lack of trust ("I know you don't love me!"). Their constant worrying and demands for attention and reassurance can drive relationship partners away, so these individuals often have difficulty maintaining long-term involvements.

People with low anxiety but high avoidance have a **dismissive attachment** style. They view close relationships as comparatively unimportant, instead prizing and prioritizing self-reliance. Relationship crises evoke hasty exits ("I don't need this kind of hassle!"), and they are more likely than other attachment styles to engage in casual sexual relationships and to endorse the view that sex without love is positive.

Finally, **fearful attachment** adults are high in both attachment anxiety *and* avoidance. They fear rejection and tend to shun relationships, preferring to avoid the pain they believe is an inevitable part of intimacy. Fearful individuals can develop close ties if the relationship seems to guarantee a lack of rejection, such as when a partner is disabled or otherwise dependent on them. But even then, they suffer from a chronic lack of faith in themselves, their partners, and the relationship's viability.

CULTURE AND SELF

At the 1968 Summer Olympics, U.S. sprinter Tommie Smith won the men's 200-meter gold medal, and teammate John Carlos won the bronze. During the medal ceremony, as the American flag was raised and "The Star-Spangled Banner" played, both runners closed their eyes, lowered their heads, and raised black-gloved fists. Smith's right fist represented black power, and Carlos's left fist represented black unity (Gettings, 2005). The two fists, raised next to each other, created an

▶ Tommie Smith and John Carlos's protest at the 1968 Summer Olympics showed how they identified with the African American culture of the time.

arch of black unity and power. Smith wore a black scarf around his neck for black pride, and both men wore black socks with no shoes, representing African American poverty. These symbols and gestures, taken together, clearly spoke of the runners' allegiance to black culture and their protest of the poor treatment of African Americans in the United States (see the photo on page 49).

Many Euro-Americans viewed Smith's and Carlos's behavior at the ceremony as a betrayal of "American" culture. Both men were suspended from the U.S. team and thrown out of the Olympic Village, the athletes' home during the games. They and their families began receiving death threats. Over time, however, people of all American ethnicities began to sympathize with their protest. Thirty years later, in 1998, Smith and Carlos were commemorated in an anniversary celebration of their protest.

In addition to gender and family, our culture is a powerful source of self. But what exactly is "culture"? Although we've all heard and used the word before, *culture* means different things to different people (Martin & Nakayama, 1997). In this book, we define culture broadly and inclusively. **Culture** is an established, coherent set of beliefs, attitudes, values, and practices shared by a large group of people (Keesing, 1974). If this strikes you as similar to our definition of self-concept, you're right; culture is like a collective sense of self shared by a large group of people.

Thinking of culture in this way has three important implications. First, culture includes many different types of large-group influences. Culture may include your nationality as well as your ethnicity, religion, gender, sexual orientation, physical abilities, and even age. We learn our cultural beliefs, attitudes, and values from parents, teachers, religious leaders, peers, and the mass media (Gudykunst & Kim, 2003). Second, most of us belong to more than one culture simultaneously—possessing the beliefs, attitudes, and values of each. Third, the various cultures to which we belong sometimes clash. When they do, we often have to choose the culture to which we pledge our primary allegiance.

Numerous distinctions exist between cultures, everything from food and religion to communication differences such as verbal expression and views on power and social status. A cultural difference that especially shapes our view of self is whether our culture of origin is individualistic or collectivistic. If you were raised in an **individualistic culture**, you likely were taught that individual goals are more important than group or societal goals. People in individualistic cultures are encouraged to focus on themselves and their immediate family (Hofstede, 1998), and individual achievement is praised as the highest good (Waterman, 1984). Examples of individualistic countries include the United States, Canada, New Zealand, and Sweden (Hofstede, 2001). If you were raised in a **collectivis-**

self-
reflection

When you consider your own cultural background, to which culture do you "pledge allegiance"? How do you communicate this allegiance to others? Have you ever suffered consequences for openly communicating your allegiance to your culture? If so, how?

50

◁ Cultural identity is part of a sophisticated definition of self, as Professor Alfred Guillaume Jr. passionately describes: "I am a 50-year-old American. I am black, Roman Catholic, and Creole. . . . The segregated South wanted me to believe that I was inferior. The Catholic Church taught me that all of God's people were equal. My French Creole heritage gave me a special bond to Native Americans, to Europeans, and to Africans. This is the composite portrait of who I am. I like who I am and can imagine being no other."

tic culture, you likely were taught the importance of belonging to groups or "collectives" that look after you in exchange for your loyalty. In collectivistic cultures, the goals, needs, and views of groups are emphasized over those of individuals, and the highest good is cooperation with others rather than individual achievement. Collectivistic countries include Guatemala, Pakistan, and Taiwan (Hofstede, 2001).

Presenting Your Self

Managing your self both online and off

Rick Welts is one of the most influential people in professional basketball.[2] He created the NBA All-Star Weekend and is cofounder of the women's professional league, the WNBA. For years he served as the NBA's executive vice president and chief marketing officer, and he now is president of the Phoenix Suns. But throughout his entire sports career—40 years of ascension from ball boy to executive—he lived a self-described "shadow life," publicly playing the role of a straight male, while privately being gay. The lowest point came when his longtime partner died and Welts couldn't publicly acknowledge his loss. Instead, he took only two days off from work—telling colleagues that a friend had passed—and for months compartmentalized his grief. Finally, following his mother's death, he decided to reconcile his public and private selves. In early 2011, he "came out" publicly. As Welts describes, "I want to pierce the silence that envelops the subject of being gay in men's team sports. I want to mentor gays who harbor doubts about a sports career, whether on the court or in the front office. But most of all, I want to feel whole, authentic."

In addition to our private selves, the composite of our self-awareness, self-concept, and self-esteem, each of us also has a public self—the self we present to others, the person we want others to see (Fenigstein, Scheier, & Buss, 1975). We actively create our public selves through our interpersonal communication and behavior.

In many encounters, our private and public selves mirror each other. At other times, they seem disconnected. In extreme instances, like that of Rick Welts, we may intentionally craft an inauthentic public self to hide something about our private self we don't want others to know. But regardless of the nature of your private self, it is your public self that your friends, family members, and romantic partners hold dear. Most (if not all) of others' impressions of you are based on

---

[2]All of the information that follows regarding Welts is adapted from Barry (2011).

▶ Rick Welts was ultimately able to reconcile his private self with his public self. What parts of your private self do you keep hidden from public view?

their appraisals of your public self. Simply, people know and judge the "you" who communicates with them—not the "you" you keep inside. Thus, managing your public self is a crucial part of competent interpersonal communication.

MAINTAINING YOUR PUBLIC SELF

Renowned sociologist Erving Goffman (1955) noted that whenever you communicate with others, you present a public self—your **face**—that you want others to see and know. Face doesn't just happen; you actively create and present it through your communication. Your face can be anything you want it to be— "perky and upbeat," "cool and level-headed," or "tough as nails." We create different faces for different moments and relationships in our lives, such as our face as a parent, college student, coworker, or homeless-shelter volunteer.

Sometimes your face is a **mask**, a public self designed to strategically veil your private self (Goffman, 1959). Masks can be dramatic, such as when Rick Welts hid his grief over the loss of his longtime partner. Or, masks can be subtle— for example, the parent who acts calm in front of an injured child so the youngster doesn't become frightened. Some masks are designed to inflate one's estimation in the eyes of others. One study found that 90 percent of college students surveyed admitted telling at least one lie to impress a person they were romantically interested in (Rowatt, Cunningham, & Druen, 1998). Other masks are crafted so people underestimate us and our abilities (Gibson & Sachau, 2000). For instance, you might act sad and lethargic around a future opponent during a racquetball tournament, letting it slip "how bad" you've been playing all day (even though you've actually won all your games). Your hope is that your opponent won't adequately prepare, and you will gain a competitive advantage.

Regardless of the form our face takes—a genuine representation of our private self, or a mask designed to hide this self from others—Goffman argued that

VideoCentral ◉

bedfordstmartins.com /reflectrelate

Mask
Watch this clip online to answer the questions below.

When, if ever, have you chosen to use a mask to veil your private self or emotions? What motivates you to use a mask? Do you think others use masks for similar reasons?

Want to see more? Check out VideoCentral for a clip on **face**.

we often form a strong emotional attachment to our face because it represents the person we most want others to see when they communicate with and relate to us.

Sometimes after we've created a certain face, information is revealed that contradicts it, causing us to lose face (Goffman, 1955). Losing face provokes feelings of shame, humiliation, and sadness—in a word, **embarrassment**. For example, in October 2004, singer Ashlee Simpson performed live on NBC's *Saturday Night Live.* Or did she? Simpson and her band performed her first song, "Pieces of Me," without a hitch. Later, when they began playing their second song, the music for "Pieces of Me" began playing over the loudspeakers, complete with Simpson's vocal track. The faux pas revealed to viewers that Simpson and her band had lip-synched their first song. Embarrassed, Simpson ran off the stage. At the end of the show, she came back onstage with host Jude Law and tried to alleviate her embarrassment by blaming her band, telling audience members, "My band started playing the wrong song, and I didn't know what to do."

While losing face can cause intense embarrassment, this is not the only cost. When others see us lose face, they may begin to question whether the public self with which they're familiar is a genuine reflection of our private self. For example, suppose your workplace face is "dedicated, hardworking employee." Everything you say and do at the office bolsters this image. You ask your boss if there's extra work to be done, help fellow coworkers, show up early, stay late, and so forth. But if you tell your manager that you need your afternoon schedule cleared to work on an urgent report and then she sees you playing *World of Warcraft* on your computer, she'll undoubtedly view your actions as inconsistent with your communication. Your face as the "hardworking employee" will be called into question, as will your credibility.

Because losing face can damage others' impressions of you, maintaining face during interpersonal interactions is extremely important. How can you effectively maintain face?[3] Use words and actions consistent with the face you're trying to craft. From one moment to the next and from one behavior to the next, your interpersonal communication and behaviors must complement your face, rather than clash with it. Also, make sure your communication and behaviors mesh with the knowledge that others already have about you. If you say or do things that contradict what others know is true about you, they'll see your face as false. For example, if your neighbor knows you don't like him because a friend of yours told him so, he's likely to be skeptical the next time you adopt the face of "friendly, caring neighbor" by warmly greeting him.

Finally, for your face to be maintained, your communication and behavior must be reinforced by objects and events in the surrounding environment— things over which you have only limited control. You can communicate in a consistent fashion and have everyone believe you, but if a contradictory event occurs, you will lose face. For example, imagine that your romantic partner is overseas for the summer, and you agree to video chat regularly. Your first scheduled chat is Friday at 5 p.m. But when 5 p.m. Friday rolls around, your server is down, preventing you from Internet access. By the time the server is up again,

self-reflection

Recall an embarrassing interpersonal encounter. How did you try to restore your lost face? Were you successful? If you could relive the encounter, what would you say and do differently?

---

[3]All of the information that follows regarding how to successfully maintain face is adapted from Goffman (1955).

skills
practice

Apologizing
Creating a skillful apology

❶ Watch for instances in which you offend or disappoint someone.

❷ Face-to-face (if possible) or by phone, acknowledge the incident and admit your responsibility.

❸ Apologize for any harm you have caused.

❹ Avoid pseudo-apologies that minimize the event or shift accountability, like "I'm sorry you overreacted" or "I'm sorry you think I'm to blame."

❺ If the person accepts your apology, express gratitude for their understanding.

your partner has already signed off, leaving a perplexed message regarding your "neglect." To restore face, you'll need to explain what happened.

Of course, all of us fall from grace on occasion, whether it's getting caught gaming when we should be working, failing to be available when we've promised, or lip-synching when we should be singing. But remember, most people want you to be able to maintain face, because your face is the positive, public "you" with whom they're most familiar. So when something happens that causes you to lose face, promptly acknowledge that the event happened, admit responsibility for any of your actions that contributed to the event, apologize for your actions and for disappointing others, and move to maintain your face again. Apologies are fairly successful at reducing people's negative impressions and the anger that may have been triggered—especially when such apologies avoid excuses that contradict what people know really happened (Ohbuchi & Sato, 1994). People who deny their inconsistencies or who blame others for their lapses (like Ashlee Simpson) are judged much more harshly.

THE IMPORTANCE OF ONLINE SELF-PRESENTATION

One of the most powerful vehicles for presenting your self online is your profile photo. Whether it's on Facebook, LinkedIn, Google, Tumblr, Flickr, Foursquare, or any other site, this image, more than any other, represents who you are to others. It is attached to pretty much everything you do: status updates, messages, wall posts, links, photo and video uploads, and so forth. Of course, you can store many profile

▶ The freedom to create an online identity can cause discord if people think it doesn't match your offline persona. In the top inset is the photo I first posted to Facebook. In the bottom inset is the "happier" one that I replaced the first with.

photos, but at any given time you can only display one—making your profile photo *the* defining image representing your online self. When I first built my Facebook profile, the photo I chose was one taken at a club, right before my band went onstage. For me, it depicted the "melancholy artist" that I consider part of my self-concept. But presenting my self online in this fashion was a disaster. Within hours of posting it, I was flooded with messages from students, colleagues, and even long-lost friends: "Are you OK?" "Did someone die?" I quickly pulled the photo and replaced it with a more positive one—a sunny image of me and my boys taken atop a mountain near Sun Valley. Now I use the melancholy photo only rarely, as accompaniment to a sad or angry status update.

Presenting the Self Online   Online communication provides us with unique benefits and challenges for self-presentation. When you talk with others face-to-face, people judge your public self not just on what you're saying but also what you look like—your age, gender, clothing, facial expressions, and so forth. Each of these cues provides others with information about who you are, independent from anything you might say. Similarly, during a phone call, vocal cues such as tone, pitch, and volume help you and your conversation partner draw conclusions about each other. But during online interactions, the amount of information communi-

Celebrities are notorious for making poor online communication choices for which they must later apologize. In 2011, Ashton Kutcher even had to give up control of his own Twitter account after a misguided post created severe backlash. How would your online profile and posts be judged if reported in the mainstream media?

cated—visual, verbal, and nonverbal—is radically restricted and more easily controlled. We carefully choose our photos and edit our text messages, e-mail, instant messages, and profile descriptions. We selectively self-present in ways that make us look good, without having to worry about verbal slipups, uncontrollable nervous habits, or physical disabilities that might make people judge us (Parks, 2007).

People routinely present themselves online (through photos and written descriptions) in ways that amplify positive personality characteristics such as warmth, friendliness, and extraversion (Vazire & Gosling, 2004). For instance, photos posted on social networking sites typically show groups of friends, fostering the impression that the person in the profile is likable, fun, and popular (Ellison, Steinfield, & Lampe, 2007). These positive and highly selective depictions of self generally work as intended. Viewers of online profiles tend to form impressions of a profile's subject that match the subject's intended self-presentation (Gosling, Gaddis, & Vazire, 2007). So, for example, if you post profile photos and descriptions in an attempt to portray your self as "wild" and "hard partying," this is the self that others will likely perceive.

The freedom that online communication allows us in flexibly crafting our selves comes with an associated cost: unless you have met someone in person, you

self-reflection

Have you ever distorted your self-presentation online to make yourself appear more attractive and appealing? If so, was this ethical? What were the consequences—for yourself and others—of creating this online mask?

will have difficulty determining whether their online self is authentic or a mask. Through misleading profile descriptions, fake photos, and phony screen names, people communicating online can assume identities that would be impossible for them to maintain in offline encounters (Rintel & Pittam, 1997). On online dating sites, for example, people routinely distort their self-presentations in ways designed to make them more attractive (Ellison, Heino, & Gibbs, 2006). Some people may also "gender swap" online, portraying themselves as female when they're male, or vice versa—often by posting fake photos (Turkle, 1995). For this reason, scholars suggest that you should never presume the gender of someone you interact with online if you haven't met the person face-to-face, even if he or she has provided photos (Savicki, Kelley, & Oesterreich, 1999).

Evaluating the Self Online   Because of the pervasiveness of online masks, people often question the truthfulness of online self-presentations, especially overly positive or flattering ones. *Warranting theory* (Walther & Parks, 2002) suggests that when assessing someone's online self-descriptions, we consider the **warranting value** of the information presented—that is, the degree to which the information is supported by other people and outside evidence (Walther, Van Der Heide, Hamel, & Schulman, 2008). Information that was obviously crafted by the person, that isn't supported by others, and that can't be verified offline has *low warranting value*, and most people wouldn't trust it. Information that's created or supported by others and that can be readily verified through alternative sources on- and offline has *high warranting value*, and consequently is perceived as valid. So, for example, news about a professional accomplishment that you post on your Facebook page will have low warranting value. But if the same information is also featured on your employer's Web site, its warranting value will increase (Walther et al., 2008). Profile photos and albums are also assessed in terms of warranting value. Photos you take and post of yourself will have less warranting value than similar photos of you taken and posted by others, especially if the photos are perceived as having been taken without your knowledge, such as "candid" shots (Walther et al., 2008).

Not surprisingly, the warranting value of online self-descriptions plummets when they are directly contradicted by others. Imagine that Jane, a student in your communication class, friends you on Facebook. Though you don't know her especially well, you accept and, later, check out her page. In the content that Jane has provided, she presents herself as quiet, thoughtful, and reserved. But messages from her friends on her Facebook wall contradict this, saying things like: "You were a MANIAC last night!" and "U R A wild child!" Based on this information, you'll likely disregard Jane's online self-presentation and judge her instead as sociable and outgoing, perhaps even "crazy" and "wild."

Research shows that when friends, family members, coworkers, or romantic partners post information on your page, their messages shape others' perceptions of you more powerfully than your own postings do—especially when their postings contradict your self-description (Walther et al., 2008). This holds true not just for personality characteristics such as extraversion (how "outgoing" you are), but also physical attractiveness. One study of Facebook profiles found that when friends posted things like "If only I was as hot as you" or (alternatively) "Don't pay any attention to those jerks at the bar last night; beauty is on the inside," such comments influenced others' perceptions of the person's attractiveness more than the person's own description of his or her physical appeal (Walther et al., 2008).

IMPROVING YOUR ONLINE SELF-PRESENTATION

Taken as a whole, the research and theory about online self-presentation suggests three practices for improving your online self-presentation. First, keep in mind that online communication is dominated by visual information such as text, photos, and videos. Make wise choices in the words and images you select to present yourself to others. For example, many women managers know they're more likely than their male peers to be judged solely on appearance, so they post photos of themselves that convey professionalism (Miller & Arnold, 2001).

Second, always remember the important role that warranting value plays in shaping others' impressions of you. The simple rule is *what others say about you online is more important than what you say about yourself*. Consequently, be wary of allowing messages and wall postings on your personal Web pages that contradict the self you want to present, or that cast you in a negative light—even if you think such messages and postings are cute, funny, or provocative. If you want to track what others are posting about you away from your personal pages, set up a Google Alert or regularly search for your name and other identifying keywords. This will allow you to see what information, including photos, others are posting about you online. When friends, family members, coworkers, or romantic partners post information about you that disagrees with how you wish to be seen, you can (politely) ask them to delete it.

Finally, subject your online self-presentation to what I call *the interview test*: ask yourself, "Would I feel comfortable sharing all elements of this presentation—photos, personal profiles, videos, blogs—in a job interview?" If your answer is no, modify your current online self-presentation immediately. In a survey of 1,200 human resources professionals and recruiters, 78 percent reported using search engines to screen candidates while 63 percent reported perusing social networking sites (Balderrama, 2010).

It's not just potential future employers who will investigate you—it's your current one as well, as Seattle resident Peter Whitney discovered. Whitney never thought anyone at work would read his blog. "It was for my friends and family," he said. "Why or how would anyone at work stumble across it?" (Wallack, 2005). Whitney used his blog to share personal thoughts, feelings, and frustrations about everyday life with those he considered close to him. As it turns out, his coworkers and managers also were reading his entries, and the information on the site got him fired. In one online rant, Whitney complained about being pressured to contribute money toward buying a birthday gift card for a manager he didn't consider a friend. Shortly after, that same manager confronted him. "She said that her feelings had been hurt by my comments," noted Whitney. He subsequently was fired. "I was shocked," he noted later. "I thought it would just merit a warning, not get me terminated."

skills practice

Your Online Self
Maintaining your desired online face

❶ Describe your desired online face (e.g., "I want to be seen as popular, adventurous, and attractive").

❷ Critically compare this description with your profiles, photos, and posts. Do they match?

❸ Revise or delete content that doesn't match your desired face.

❹ Repeat this process for friends' postings on your personal pages.

❺ In your future online communication—texting, e-mailing, and posting—present yourself only in ways that mesh with your desired face.

The Relational Self

Sharing your self can foster intimacy

One of the reasons we carefully craft the presentation of our self is to create interpersonal relationships. We present our self to acquaintances, coworkers, friends, family members, and romantic partners, and through our interpersonal communication, relationships are fostered, maintained, and sometimes ended. Within each of these relationships, how close we feel to one another is defined largely by how much of our self we reveal to others and vice versa.

Managing the self in interpersonal relationships isn't easy. Exposing our self to others can make us feel vulnerable, provoking tension between how much to reveal versus how much to veil. Even in the closest of relationships certain aspects of the self remain hidden, from our partners as well as ourselves.

OPENING YOUR SELF TO OTHERS

In the movie *Shrek*, the ogre Shrek forges a friendship with a likable but occasionally irksome donkey (Adamson & Jenson, 2001). As their acquaintanceship deepens to friendship, Shrek tries to explain the nature of his inner self to his companion:

SHREK: For your information, there's a lot more to ogres than people think!
DONKEY: Example . . . ?
SHREK: Example . . . Ok . . . Um . . . Ogres . . . are like onions.
DONKEY: They stink?
SHREK: Yes . . . NO!
DONKEY: Or they make you cry?
SHREK: No!
DONKEY: Oh . . . You leave 'em out in the sun and they get all brown and start sprouting little white hairs!

SHREK: No! Layers! Onions have layers—OGRES have layers! Onions have layers! You get it!? We both have layers!

DONKEY: Ooohhhh . . . you both have layers . . . oh. You know, not everybody likes onions . . . CAKE! Everybody loves cakes! Cakes have layers!

Shrek was not the first to use the onion as a metaphor for self. In fact, the idea that revealing the self to others involves peeling back or penetrating layers was first suggested by psychologists Irwin Altman and Dalmas Taylor (1973) in their **social penetration theory**. Like Shrek, Altman and Taylor envisioned the self as an "onion-skin structure," consisting of sets of layers.[4]

At the *outermost, peripheral layers* of your self are demographic characteristics such as birthplace, age, gender, and ethnicity (see Figure 2.2). Discussion of these characteristics dominates first conversations with new acquaintances: What's your name? What's your major? Where are you from? In the *intermediate layers* reside your attitudes and opinions about music, politics, food, entertainment, and other such matters. Deep within the "onion" are the *central layers* of your self—core characteristics such as self-awareness, self-concept, self-esteem, personal values, fears, and distinctive personality traits. We'll discuss these in more detail in Chapter 3.

The notion of layers of self helps explain the development of interpersonal relationships, as well as how we distinguish between casual and close involvements. As relationships progress, partners communicate increasingly personal information to each other. This allows them to mutually penetrate one another's peripheral, then intermediate, and finally central selves. Relationship development, therefore, is like slowly pushing a pin into an onion: it proceeds layer by layer, without skipping layers.

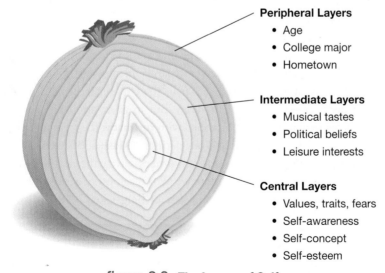

Peripheral Layers
- Age
- College major
- Hometown

Intermediate Layers
- Musical tastes
- Political beliefs
- Leisure interests

Central Layers
- Values, traits, fears
- Self-awareness
- Self-concept
- Self-esteem

figure 2.2 **The Layers of Self**

---

[4]Although Altman and Taylor use *personality* to describe the self, they define personality in terms of self-concept and self-esteem, and use the terms *personality* and *self* interchangeably throughout their text (for example, see 1973, pp. 17–19).

◗ The ability to share our selves with someone else feels like a rare experience, but when the opportunity arises, information flows more freely and greater relational intimacy develops.

The revealing of selves that occurs during relationship development involves both breadth and depth. *Breadth* is the number of different aspects of self each partner reveals at each layer—the insertion of more and more pins into the onion, so to speak. *Depth* involves how deeply into one another's self the partners have penetrated: have you revealed only your peripheral self, or have you given the other person access into your intermediate or central selves as well?

Although social penetration occurs in all relationships, the rate at which it occurs isn't consistent. For example, some people let others in quickly, while others never grant access to certain elements of their selves no matter how long they know a person. The speed with which people grant one another access to the broader and deeper aspects of their selves depends on a variety of factors, including the attachment styles discussed earlier in the chapter (see the *Self-Quiz* on page 61 to discover *your* attachment style). But in all relationships, depth and breadth of social penetration is intertwined with **intimacy**: the feeling of closeness and "union" that exists between us and our partners (Mashek & Aron, 2004). The deeper and broader we penetrate into each other's selves, the more intimacy we feel; the more intimacy we feel, the more we allow each other access to broad and deep aspects of our selves (Shelton, Trail, West, & Bergsieker, 2010).

YOUR HIDDEN AND REVEALED SELF

The image of self and relationship development offered by social penetration theory suggests a relatively straightforward evolution of intimacy, with partners gradually penetrating broadly and deeply into each other's selves over time. But in thinking about our selves and our relationships with others, two important questions arise: First, are we really aware of all aspects of ourselves? Second, are we willing to grant others access to all aspects of ourselves?

Discover Your Attachment Style

self-
QUIZ

One determinant of how quickly you'll reveal yourself to others and form intimate relationships is your *attachment style* (discussed on pages 47–48 in this chapter): secure, preoccupied, dismissive, or fearful. To gauge your attachment style, select the set of beliefs that best represents your view of intimacy. Then match your choice to the key below.

_____ Attachment Style A

- I am comfortable without close emotional relationships.
- It is very important to me to feel independent and self-sufficient, and I prefer not to depend on others or have others depend on me.

_____ Attachment Style B

- It is easy for me to become emotionally close to others.
- I am comfortable depending on others and having others depend on me.

_____ Attachment Style C

- I want to be emotionally intimate with others, but I often find that others are reluctant to get as close as I would like.
- I am uncomfortable being without close relationships, but I worry that others don't value me as much as I value them.

_____ Attachment Style D

- I am uncomfortable getting close to others.
- I worry that I will be hurt if I allow myself to become intimate with others.

Note: The material provided in this *Self-Quiz* is adapted from Bartholomew and Horowitz (1991, p. 244).

Key: A = Dismissive (individuals who have little need for closeness; they allow others to get to know them slowly, if at all); B = Secure (people who reveal themselves at a steady pace, as they enjoy intimacy); C = Preoccupied (those who unveil themselves hurriedly, because of their compulsive need to feel loved); D = Fearful (persons who often shut people out completely, as intimacy makes them feel vulnerable)

We can explore possible answers to these questions by looking at the model of the relational self called the Johari Window, named after the psychologists who developed it, Joe Luft and Harry Ingham (Luft, 1970). The Johari Window (see Figure 2.3 on page 62) suggests that some "quadrants" of our selves are open to self-reflection and sharing with other people, while others remain hidden—to both ourselves and others.

During the early stages of an interpersonal relationship and especially during first encounters, our *public area* of self is much smaller than our *hidden area*. As relationships progress, partners gain access to broader and deeper information about their selves; consequently, the public area expands and the hidden area diminishes. The Johari Window thus provides us with a useful alternative metaphor to social penetration. As relationships develop, we don't just let people "penetrate inward" to our central selves; we let them "peer into" more parts of our selves by revealing information that we previously hid from them.

Importantly, as our interpersonal relationships develop and we increasingly share previously hidden information with our partners, our *unknown* and *blind* quadrants remain fairly stable. By their very nature, our unknown areas remain unknown throughout much of our lives. And for most of us, the blind area remains imperceptible. That's because our blind areas are defined by our deepest-rooted

<table>
<tr>
<td>

Quadrant I

Public Area
Aspects of your self that you and others are aware of. Includes everything you openly disclose—from music and food preferences to religious beliefs and moral values.

</td>
<td>

Quadrant II

Blind Area
Facets of your self that are readily apparent to others through your interpersonal communication but that you're not aware of. Includes strengths that you may not see in yourself or character flaws that don't mesh with your self-concept.

</td>
</tr>
<tr>
<td>

Quadrant III

Hidden Area
Parts of your self that you're aware of but that you hide from most others. These include destructive thoughts, impulses, and fantasies, and disturbing life experiences that don't fit comfortably with your public self or your own self-concept.

</td>
<td>

Quadrant IV

Unknown Area
Aspects of your self that you and others aren't aware of, such as unconscious motives and impulses that strongly influence your interpersonal communication and relationships. While you can't gain access to your unknown area through critical self-reflection, you can indirectly infer aspects of your unknown area by observing consistent patterns in your own behavior.

</td>
</tr>
</table>

figure 2.3 **The Johari Window**

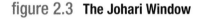

self-reflection

Consider your "blind area" of self. What strengths might you possess that you don't recognize? What character flaws might exist that don't mesh with your self-concept? How can you capitalize on these strengths and mend your flaws so that your interpersonal communication and relationships improve?

beliefs about ourselves—those beliefs that make up our self-concepts. Consequently, when others challenge us to open our eyes to our blind areas, we resist.

To improve our interpersonal communication, we must be able to see into our blind areas and then change the aspects within them that lead to incompetent communication and relationship challenges. But this isn't easy. After all, how can you correct misperceptions about yourself that you don't even know exist or flaws that you consider your greatest strengths? Delving into your blind area means challenging fundamental beliefs about yourself—subjecting your self-concept to hard scrutiny. Your goal is to overturn your most treasured personal misconceptions. Most people accomplish this only over a long period of time and with the assistance of trustworthy and willing relationship partners.

DISCLOSING YOUR SELF TO OTHERS

In his 2008 memoir *Rock On*, humorist Dan Kennedy details his experiences as a marketing executive for Atlantic Records. While recording a public-service announcement with the band the Donnas, Dan shared private information with them—a decision he quickly regretted:

> "So, do you like your job?" one of them asks me. "Yeah, you know. Whatever. I guess it's pretty cool as far as jobs go. Pretty, you know, chill." When I hear it

come out of my mouth, it sounds like one of those cheesy modern dads trying to get his daughters to think he's cool so they'll admit to drinking beer on the weekends and then he can lecture them. "I kinda do whatever I need to do and nobody really asks me any questions. Yesterday I took a two-and-a-half-hour lunch with a friend. What are they gonna say?" Just then, the product manager and the vice president for radio come in from the control room. "Okay, this shouldn't take long, we should have you out of here pretty quick. I see you've already met Dan." And that's when it happened. To this day I can't remember which one started it. "Yeah we met. He was telling us how he takes two-and-a-half-hour lunches with his friend and nobody says anything." Then the other girls start laughing and chiming in. "Yeah, he's all, What are they gonna say?" I give them a look while biting my lip, bulging my eyes, and barely shaking my head "no" in hopes of discreetly stopping this. But there's no way to get them to turn back. "Yeah, we asked him if he likes his job and he was like, 'I guess, if you gotta have a job.' I stand there with a terrified polite smile frozen on my face avoiding eye contact with the product manager and vice president, waiting for the moment when the three of us would start laughing. After five or six seconds of silence, it becomes apparent this isn't one of those moments (Kennedy, 2008).

We all can think of situations in which we've revealed private information about ourselves to others. This is known as **self-disclosure** (Wheeless, 1978), and it plays a critical role in interpersonal communication and relationship development. According to the **interpersonal process model of intimacy**, the closeness we feel toward others in our relationships is created through two things: self-disclosure and responsiveness of listeners to disclosure (Reis & Patrick, 1996). Relationships are intimate when both partners share private information with each other *and* each partner responds to the other's disclosures with understanding, caring, and support (Reis & Shaver, 1988). One practical implication of this is *just because you share your thoughts and feelings with someone doesn't mean that you have an intimate relationship*. For example, if you regularly chat with a classmate, both online and off, and tell her all of your secrets—but she never does the same in return—your relationship isn't intimate, it's one-sided. In a similar fashion, tweeting or posting personal thoughts and feelings and having people read them online doesn't create intimate relationships. Intimacy only exists when both people are sharing with and supporting each other.

On the other hand, as the Dan Kennedy example illustrates, when listeners are nonsupportive in response to disclosures, or people disclose information that's perceived as problematic, intimacy can be undermined. Think about an instance in which you shared something deeply personal with a friend, but he or she responded by ridiculing or judging you: "That's the stupidest thing I've ever heard—I can't *believe* you think that!" How did this reaction make you feel? Chances are, it widened, rather than narrowed, the emotional distance between you and your friend. Research suggests that one of the most damaging events that can happen in interpersonal relationships is a partner's sharing information that the other person finds inappropriate and perplexing (Planalp & Honeycutt, 1985). This is especially

Self-Disclosure
Watch this clip online to answer the questions below.

Do you ever find it easier to self-disclose to a stranger? Why or why not? How much self-disclosure do you expect from a close friend, and when, if ever, is it too much?

▶ On the television show *How I Met Your Mother*, Ted and Robin's relationship gets off to an awkward start when Ted tells her he loves her on their first date. Throughout their relationship, their conflicting ideas of self-disclosure cause discomfort and ultimately create distance between them.

true in relationships where the partners are already struggling with challenging problems or experiencing painful transitions. For example, during divorce proceedings, parents commonly disclose negative and demeaning information about each other to their children. The parents may see this sharing as stress-relieving or "cathartic" (Afifi, McManus, Hutchinson, & Baker, 2007). But these disclosures only intensify the children's mental and physical distress and make them feel caught between the two parents (Koerner, Wallace, Lehman, & Raymond, 2002)—something we'll discuss more in Chapter 10 on family relationships.

Differences in Disclosure   Researchers have conducted thousands of self-disclosure studies over the past 40 years (Tardy & Dindia, 1997). These studies suggest five important facts regarding how people self-disclose.

First, in any culture, people vary widely in the degree to which they self-disclose. Some people are naturally transparent, others are more opaque (Jourard, 1964). Trying to force someone who has a different idea of self-disclosure than yours to open up or be more discreet is not only presumptuous but can damage the relationship (Luft, 1970).

Second, people across cultures differ in their self-disclosure. For instance, people of Asian descent tend to disclose less than do people of European ancestry. Japanese disclose substantially less than Americans in both friendships and romantic relationships, and they view self-disclosure as a less important aspect of intimacy development than do Americans (Barnlund, 1975). Researchers found similar tendencies among people of Chinese heritage. In general, Euro-Americans tend to disclose more frequently than just about any other cultural group, including Asians, Hispanics, and African Americans (Klopf, 2001).

Third, people disclose more quickly, broadly, and deeply when interacting online than face-to-face. One reason for this is that during online encounters, people can't see those with whom they are interacting, and so the consequences of such disclosure seem less noticeable (Joinson, 2001). Additionally, because much of online communication lacks nonverbal cues, words take on more importance and intensity than those exchanged during face-to-face interactions. The consequence of all this is that we often overestimate the intimacy of online interactions and relationships.

To help ensure competent online disclosure, scholar Malcolm Parks offers the following advice: *Be wary of the emotionally seductive qualities of online interaction.*[5] Disclose information slowly and with caution. Remember that online communication is both public and permanent; hence, *secrets that you post, text, or e-mail are no longer secrets*. Few experiences in the interpersonal realm are more uncomfortable than "post-cyber-disclosure panic"—that awful moment when you wonder who else might be reading the innermost thoughts you just revealed in an e-mail or a text message to a friend (Barnes, 2001).

Fourth, self-disclosure appears to promote mental health and relieve stress (Tardy, 2000). Especially when the information is troubling, keeping it inside can escalate your stress levels substantially, resulting in immune system breakdown, ulcers, and high blood pressure (Pennebaker, 1997). Keeping troubling information trapped inside can also lead it to dominate your thoughts because you must constantly monitor what you say to avoid disclosing the secret (Kelly & McKillop, 1996). Of course, the flip side of disclosing troubling secrets to others is that people might react negatively and you might be more vulnerable.

Finally, little evidence exists that supports the stereotype that men can't disclose their feelings in relationships. In close same-sex friendships, for example, both men and women disclose deeply and broadly (Shelton et al., 2010). And in cross-sex romantic involvements, men often disclose at levels equal to or greater than their female partners (Canary et al., 1997). As just one example, husbands in dual-career marriages disclose more than their wives (Rosenfeld & Welsh, 1985). This has led gender and communication scholars to agree, "It is time to stop perpetuating the myth that there are large sex differences in men's and women's self-disclosure" (Dindia & Allen, 1992, p. 118). At the same time, however, both men and women feel more comfortable disclosing to female than to male recipients (Dindia & Allen, 1992). Teenagers are more likely to disclose to mothers and best female friends than to fathers and best male friends—suggesting that adolescents may perceive females as more empathic and understanding than males (Garcia & Geisler, 1988).

Competently Disclosing Your Self   Based on all we know about self-disclosure, how can you improve your disclosure skills? Consider these recommendations for competent self-disclosure:

- **Follow the advice of Apollo: know your self.** Before disclosing, make sure that the aspects of your self you reveal to others are aspects that you want to

self-reflection

During your childhood, to which family member did you feel most comfortable disclosing? Why? Of your friends and family right now, do you disclose more to women or men, or is there no difference? What does this tell you about how gender has guided your disclosure decisions?

---

[5]Personal communication with author, May 13, 2008. This material was developed specifically for this text and published with permission of Dr. Malcolm Parks; may not be reproduced without written consent of Dr. Parks and the author.

Ethics and Self-Disclosure

1 BACKGROUND

Self-disclosure is the primary vehicle people use to communicate their private selves to others in interpersonal relationships. Yet choosing when and how to self-disclose or ask for self-disclosure can be tricky, particularly when ethical considerations are involved. Read the following Case Study, and work through the five steps under Your Turn to learn how you can ethically self-disclose.

2 CASE STUDY

You work for Jaime, a longtime family friend who owns a small but thriving business. Before you started the job, Jaime made a deal with you: she would pay your college tuition if you promised to work for her for three years following graduation. Her generosity made it possible for you to get your BA—something you never could have afforded otherwise. Needless to say, you feel very loyal to Jaime.

A few months ago, Jaime hired Jonathan, whom you've known since grade school. Jonathan's public self is impressive: he's funny, charming, and intelligent. He manages to cheer you up no matter what's happening in your life. But you've always wondered whether his public self is really just a mask. Jonathan doesn't let people into his central self; he keeps everyone, including you, at a distance. Whenever conversations get too personal, he cracks a joke. Over the years, no matter what the situation—a group project, dinner out, or weekend trips with friends—things always seem to miraculously work out so that Jonathan contributes the least and benefits the

most. You can't help but wonder whether he's a nice guy with incredible luck or someone who constantly manipulates situations to his advantage.

One day, you learn that Jaime has just made the same tuition offer to Jonathan, and he has accepted. You and Jonathan go out to celebrate. But when you toast Jaime's generosity, Jonathan laughs and says, "To the suckers of the world!" When you tell him how excited you are that you'll be working together for several more years, Jonathan says, "We'll see." You suddenly have the uncomfortable feeling that he's planning to renege on his end of the deal. You decide to press him: "You're not planning on bailing on Jaime after she pays your tuition, are you?" Jonathan hesitates for a moment, then suddenly smiles and shifts into joke mode. "Do you have a *wiretap* on you or something? Are you *Jaime's little spy*?"

You realize you can't press Jonathan further without disclosing your long-term suspicions about his hidden self or forcing him to disclose something he obviously doesn't want to discuss. At the same time, your loyalty to Jaime compels you to discover the truth about his motives.

3 YOUR TURN

Think about the interpersonal communication skills and insights you gained while reading this chapter. Work through the following five steps, which will give you practice making thoughtful interpersonal communication choices in your relationships. Remember, there is no one right answer, so think hard about what choice you will make!

● step 1

Reflect on yourself. What are your thoughts and feelings about Jonathan? Is your impression of him and his motives accurate, or could you be mistaken? Do you feel more loyal to Jonathan or to Jaime? What role should loyalty play in shaping your relationship choice?

● step 2

Reflect on your partner. Put yourself in Jonathan's shoes. What is he thinking and feeling about you? What is his perspective on Jaime's tuition offer? Is his viewpoint legitimate?

● step 3

Identify the optimal outcome. What's the most constructive relationship outcome for you and Jonathan? Can you maintain your relationship with Jonathan and your loyalty to Jaime? Consider what's best not only for you but for all those involved as well.

● step 4

Locate the roadblocks. Taking into consideration your own thoughts and feelings, those of Jonathan, and all that has happened in this situation, what is keeping you from achieving the optimal outcome you defined in Step 3?

● step 5

Chart your course. What might you say to Jonathan to overcome the roadblocks and achieve your optimal relationship outcome?

HELPFUL CONCEPTS

Face and masks, **52**

Maintaining face, **53**

Recommendations for competent self-disclosure, **65**

A key aspect to understanding your self is to practice critical self-reflection by analyzing what you are thinking and feeling, why, and how this is influencing your communication. This can help you improve your communication and your relationships. Even John F. Kennedy took time for reflection in the Oval Office during his presidency.

reveal and that you feel certain about. This is especially important when disclosing intimate feelings, such as romantic interest. When you disclose feelings about others directly to them, you affect their lives and relationship decisions. Consequently, you're ethically obligated to be certain about the truth of your own feelings before sharing them with others.

- **Know your audience.** Whether it's a wall post or an intimate conversation with a friend, think carefully about how others will perceive your disclosure and how it will impact their thoughts and feelings about you. If you're unsure of the appropriateness of a disclosure, don't disclose. This holds equally true for online and face-to-face encounters. Instead of disclosing, talk more generally about the issue or topic first, gauging the person's level of comfort with the conversation before revealing deeper information.

- **Don't force others to self-disclose.** We often presume it's good for people to "open up" and share their secrets, particularly those that are troubling them. Although it's perfectly appropriate to let someone know you're available to listen, it's unethical and destructive to force or cajole others into sharing information against their will. People have reasons for not wanting to tell you things—just as you have reasons for protecting your own privacy.

- **Don't presume gender preferences.** Don't fall into the trap of thinking that because someone is a woman, she will disclose freely; or that because he's a man, he's incapable of discussing his feelings. Men and women are more similar than different when it comes to disclosure. At the same time, be mindful of the tendency to feel more comfortable disclosing to women. Don't presume that because you're talking with a woman it's appropriate for you to freely disclose.

- **Be sensitive to cultural differences.** When interacting with people from different backgrounds, disclose gradually. As with gender, don't presume disclosure patterns based on ethnicity. Just because someone is of European descent doesn't mean he or she will want to openly share intimate thoughts and feelings, and just because someone is Asian doesn't mean he or she will be comparatively reluctant to disclose.

- **Go slowly.** Share intermediate and central aspects of your self gradually and only after thorough discussion of peripheral information. Moving too quickly to discussion of your deepest fears, self-esteem concerns, and personal values not only increases your sense of vulnerability, but it may make others uncomfortable enough to avoid you.

Improving Your Self

The self constantly evolves

One of the greatest gifts we possess is our capacity for self-awareness. Through self-awareness, we can ponder the kind of person we are, what we're worth, where we come from, and how we can improve. We can craft face and strive to maintain it. We can openly disclose some aspects of our selves and protect other aspects. And all the while, we can stand apart from our selves, critically reflecting on our interpersonal communication and relationship decisions: was I right or was I wrong?

At the same time, we're often hampered by the beliefs, attitudes, and values we hold about our selves. Our self-concepts can trap us in destructive self-fulfilling prophecies. Whether imposed by gender, culture, or family, the standards we embrace suggesting who we should be are often unattainable. When we inevitably fall short of these standards, we condemn our selves, destroying our own self-esteem.

But our selves are not static. We constantly evolve, so we always have the opportunity to improve our selves and enhance our interpersonal communication and relationships. Through dedicated and focused effort, we can learn to avoid destructive self-fulfilling prophecies and resolve discrepancies between our self-concepts and standards that damage our self-esteem. We can also maintain face and disclose our selves competently to others. The starting point for improving our selves is the same as it ever was: the advice mythically offered to Chilon by Apollo. Know thyself.

ook again at the painting *labeled*. Note that this work of art isn't simply a portrait of the pain and isolation felt by one artist suffering from dyslexia. It embraces all of us. We've all had fingers pointed and names hurled at us.

What metaphorical fingers point at you? Are some of those fingers your own? What names go with them? How do these shape the ways in which you communicate with others and make choices in your relationships?

This chapter began with a self-portrait of suffering—an artist stigmatized in youth by labels. But we can all draw inspiration from Eric Staib's story. Each of us possesses the uniquely human capacity to turn our personal punishments into profound gifts, just as Eric did.

POSTSCRIPT

chapter review

key terms

◉ You can watch brief, illustrative videos of these terms and test your understanding of the concepts online in *VideoCentral: Interpersonal Communication* at **bedfordstmartins .com/reflectrelate**.

key concepts

The Components of Self

- The root source of all interpersonal communication is the **self**; thus, understanding the self and its connection to communication is critical for improving interpersonal skills. The self is an evolving composite of **self-awareness**, *self-concept*, and *self-esteem*.

- During interpersonal encounters, we make sense of our selves and our communication in part by comparing our behaviors with those of others. **Social comparison** has a particularly pronounced impact on our sense of self when the people to whom we're comparing ourselves are those we admire.

- When most of us think of our selves, what comes to mind is our **self-concept**. Our self-concept is defined at least in part through our **looking-glass self**. Our self-concept can sometimes trap us in **self-fulfilling prophecies**, although we can overcome these by analyzing our underlying beliefs about self.

- It is a daunting challenge to have positive **self-esteem** while living in an appearance culture dominated by images of bodily and facial perfection. Many of us have unnatural and unrealistic appearance standards. **Self-discrepancy theory** explains the link between these standards and our feelings about our selves, as well as ways in which we can overcome low self-esteem.

The Sources of Self

- Our self-concept and self-esteem come from many sources, one of which is **gender**. At the same time that our families teach us gender lessons, they also create emotional bonds with us that form the foundation for various attachment styles, including **secure attachment**, **preoccupied attachment**, **dismissive attachment**, and **fearful attachment**. These attachment styles influence our adult interpersonal relationships.

- Many of us identify with more than one **culture**. As a consequence, we're occasionally thrust into situations in which we must choose a primary cultural allegiance. Depending on whether we're raised in a primarily **individualistic culture** or **collectivistic culture**, we learn values and beliefs about effective interpersonal communication that may differ from those of people raised in different cultures.

Presenting Your Self

- The **face** we present to others is the self others perceive and evaluate. Sometimes our face reflects our inner selves, and sometimes we adopt **masks**. When we lose face, **embarrassment** results.
- When online, information posted about you from others has higher **warranting value** than what you post directly.
- Use *the interview test* to help you determine how to present your self online.

The Relational Self

- According to **social penetration theory**, we develop relationships by gradually delving deeper and more broadly into different layers of self. The more we reveal, the more **intimacy** we feel with others.
- Revealing private information about our selves to others is **self-disclosure** and it, along with the responsiveness of listeners to such disclosure, makes up the **interpersonal process model of intimacy**.

key skills

- Want to refine your critical self-reflection ability? Learn how by reviewing the steps of critical self-reflection on page 40.
- Interested in overcoming self-fulfilling prophecies that plague your communication? Try the *Skills Practice* on page 41.
- Ever feel as if you're not the person you wish you could be or the person others want you to be? Find out why on pages 41–42.
- How can you improve your self-esteem and consequently your communication and relationships? Learn how by reviewing the information on pages 43–44 and completing the *Self-Quiz* on page 45.
- How can you effectively maintain face during interpersonal encounters? Follow the recommendations on pages 52–54 and try the *Skills Practice* on page 54 for advice on making a skillful apology when you lose face.
- What can you do to maintain your desired face online? Review the suggestions described on pages 54–57; then complete the *Skills Practice* on page 57.
- How can you improve your self-disclosure skills? Review pages 62–69, complete the *Self-Quiz* on page 61, and then put your skills to the test by working through the *Making Relationship Choices* exercise on pages 66–67.

3 Perceiving Others

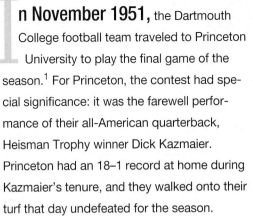

In **November 1951,** the Dartmouth College football team traveled to Princeton University to play the final game of the season.[1] For Princeton, the contest had special significance: it was the farewell performance of their all-American quarterback, Heisman Trophy winner Dick Kazmaier. Princeton had an 18–1 record at home during Kazmaier's tenure, and they walked onto their turf that day undefeated for the season.

From the opening kickoff, it was a brutal affair. Kazmaier suffered a late hit in the second quarter that broke his nose, caused a concussion, and forced him from the field. In retaliation, Princeton defenders knocked two consecutive Dartmouth quarterbacks out of the game, one of them with a broken leg. Several fights erupted, and referees' flags filled the afternoon air, most of them signaling "roughing." Although Princeton prevailed, both sides left the stadium bitter about the on-field violence.

In the days that followed, perceptions of the game diverged wildly, depending on scholastic allegiance. Princeton supporters denounced Dartmouth's "dirty play," and the *Daily Princetonian* decried Dartmouth for "deliberately attempting to cripple Kazmaier." The Dartmouth student paper countered, accusing Princeton's coach of urging his players to "get" the Dartmouth quarterbacks.

We rely on perception constantly to make sense of everything and everyone in our environment.

[1]The information that follows is adapted from Hastorf & Cantril (1954) and Palmer Stadium (2008).

3 / Perceiving Others

Perceptual differences weren't limited to players and attendees. A Dartmouth alumnus in the Midwest heard reports of his team's "disgusting" play and requested a copy of the game film. After viewing it, he sent a telegram to the university: "Viewing of the film indicates considerable cutting of important parts. Please airmail the missing excerpts." Why did he believe that the film had been edited? Because when he watched it, he didn't perceive *any* cheap shots by his team.

Intrigued by the perceptual gulf between Princeton and Dartmouth devotees, two psychologists—Albert Hastorf from Dartmouth and Hadley Cantril from Princeton—teamed up to study reactions to the game. What they found was striking. After viewing the game film, students from both schools were asked, "Who instigated the rough play?" Princeton students overwhelmingly blamed Dartmouth, while Dartmouth students attributed the violence to both sides. When questioned about whether Dartmouth had intentionally injured

Kazmaier, Princeton students said yes; Dartmouth students said no. And when asked about penalties, Dartmouth students perceived both teams as committing the same number. Princeton students said Dartmouth committed twice as many as Princeton. Though the two groups saw the same film, they perceived two very different games.

Although Hastorf and Cantril examined rival perceptions of a historic college football game, their results tell us much about the challenges we face in responsibly perceiving other people. Each of us perceives the "games," "cheap shots," and "fights" that fill our lives in ways skewed to match our own beliefs and desires. All too often we fail to consider that others feel just as strongly about the "truth" of their viewpoints as we do about ours. Every time we perceive our own behavior as beyond reproach and others' as deficient, see others as exclusively to blame for conflicts, or neglect to consider alternative perspectives and feelings, we are exactly like the Dartmouth and Princeton fans who could perceive only the transgressions of the *other* team.

But competent interpersonal communication and healthy relationships are not built upon belief in perceptual infallibility. Instead, they are founded upon recognition of our perceptual limitations, constant striving to correct perceptual errors, and sincere effort invested in considering others' viewpoints.

Perception is our window to the world. Everything we experience while interacting with others is filtered through our perception. While information seems to enter our conscious minds without bias, our perception is not an objective lens. Instead, it's a product of our own mental creation. When we perceive, we actively create the meanings we assign to people, their communication, and our relationships, and we look to our perception—not reality itself—to guide our interpersonal communication and relationship decisions. This is why it's essential to understand how perception works. By honing our awareness of the perception process, we can improve our interpersonal communication and forge better relationships.

In this chapter, we explore how you can improve your perception to become a better interpersonal communicator. You'll learn:

- How the perception process unfolds and which perceptual errors you need to watch for
- The influence that culture, gender, and personality have in shaping your perception of others and your interpersonal communication
- How you form impressions of others, and the benefits and limitations of the methods you use
- Strategies for improving your perceptual accuracy

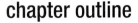
Perception as a Process

Perception helps
us understand
our world

In the movie *Inception*, Dom Cobb—played by Leonardo DiCaprio—is a master at extraction, the art of entering others' unconscious minds while they're asleep and stealing their thoughts. Since living inside others' dreams can lead one to confuse dream states with reality, Cobb has a "totem" that he keeps with him always, a simple tool that allows him to tell quickly whether he's dreaming or awake. Cobb's totem is a top: when he is within a dream state, it will spin smoothly and endlessly, whereas when he is awake, it will spin for a few moments, then wobble and fall.

Like Dom Cobb, each of us has a totem we trust to tell us what's real and what isn't: *our perception*. **Perception** is the process of selecting, organizing, and interpreting information from our senses. We rely on perception constantly to make sense of everything and everyone in our environment. Perception begins when we select information on which to focus our attention. We then organize the information into an understandable pattern inside our minds and interpret its meaning. Each activity influences the other: our mental organization of information shapes how we interpret it, and our interpretation of information influences how we mentally organize it. (See Figure 3.1 on page 76.) Let's take a closer look at the perception process.

In the movie *Inception*, Dom Cobb's totem helps him distinguish what is real and what is not.

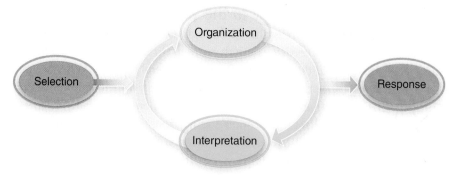

figure 3.1 **The Process of Perception**

SELECTING INFORMATION

It's finals week, and you're in your room studying for a difficult exam. Exhausted, you decide to take a break and listen to some music. You don your headphones, press play, and close your eyes. Suddenly you hear a noise. Startled, you open your eyes and remove your headphones, to find that your housemate has just yanked open your bedroom door. "I've been yelling at you to pick up your phone for the last five minutes," she snaps. "What's going on?!"

The first step of perception, **selection**, involves focusing attention on certain sights, sounds, tastes, touches, or smells in our environment. Consider the housemate example. Once you hear her enter, you would likely select her communication as the focus of your attention. The moment you do this, the process of perception begins: you watch and listen, trying to organize what she is saying into a coherent mental image and to make sense of its meaning. You might even select a more narrow aspect of her verbal or nonverbal communication as your attention focus: her loud and angry voice or a certain phrase that she uses.

The degree to which particular people or aspects of their communication attract our attention is known as **salience** (Fiske & Taylor, 1991). When something is salient, it seems especially noticeable and significant. We view aspects of interpersonal communication as salient under three conditions (Fiske & Taylor, 1991). First, communication is salient if the communicator behaves in a visually and audibly stimulating fashion. A yelling and energetically gesturing housemate is more salient than a housemate standing motionless and quietly informing us about a phone call. Second, communication becomes salient if our goals or expectations lead us to view it as significant. Even a housemate's softly spoken phone announcement will command our attention if we are anticipating an important call. Last, communication that deviates from our expectations is salient. An unexpected verbal attack will always be more salient than an expected one.

ORGANIZING THE INFORMATION YOU'VE SELECTED

Once you've selected something as the focus of your attention, you take that information and structure it into a coherent pattern inside your mind, a phase of the perception process known as **organization** (Fiske & Taylor, 1991). For example, imagine that a cousin is telling you about a recent visit to your hometown. As she shares her story with you, you select certain bits of her narrative on which to focus your attention based on salience, such as a mutual friend she saw during her visit or a favorite old hangout she saw. You then organize your own representation of her story inside your head.

During organization, you engage in **punctuation**, structuring the information you've selected into a chronological sequence that matches how you experienced the order of events (Watzlawick, Beavin, & Jackson, 1967). You determine which words and actions occurred first, second, and so on, and which comments or behaviors caused subsequent actions to occur. To illustrate punctuation, think about how you might punctuate the sequence of events in our housemate example. You hear a noise, open your eyes, see your housemate in your room, and then hear her yelling at you. But two people involved in the same interpersonal encounter may punctuate it in very different ways. Here's how your housemate might punctuate the same incident:

> I was in my room studying for finals, but my cell phone kept ringing. I
> got so irritated that I turned my phone off. But then my housemate's cell
> phone rang. I yelled for him to get it, but the phone kept ringing. I ran out

VideoCentral ▣

bedfordstmartins.com
/reflectrelate

Punctuation
*Watch this clip online
to answer the questions
below.*

How does punctuation influence each person's perception and communication in the video? How might the previous communication between two people influence how each would punctuate a situation, for example, between a parent and a child or between romantic partners?

to the kitchen and grabbed his phone. I shouted outside his door, "Your phone is ringing," but he didn't respond. I blew up, charged into his room, and found him there with his headphones on, listening to music. I said, "I've been yelling at you to pick up your phone for the last five minutes! What's going on?"

If you and another person organize and punctuate information from an encounter differently, the two of you may well feel frustrated with one another. Disagreements about punctuation, and especially disputes about who "started" unpleasant encounters, are a common source of interpersonal conflict (Watzlawick et al., 1967). For example, your housemate may contend that "you started it" because she told you to get your phone but you ignored her. You may believe that "she started it" because she barged into your room without knocking.

We can avoid perceptual misunderstandings that lead to conflict by understanding how our organization and punctuation of information differ from those of other people. For instance, if you asked your housemate why she was yelling at you and learned that she thought you were ignoring her, you might realize that she wasn't interrupting your study break just to be annoying. And if she asked why you didn't get your phone and learned that you didn't hear her, her frustration might dissipate as well. One helpful way to forestall such conflicts is to practice asking others to share their views of encounters. You might say, "Here's what I saw, but that's just my perspective. What do *you* think happened?"

INTERPRETING THE INFORMATION

As we organize information we have selected into a coherent mental model, we also engage in **interpretation**, assigning meaning to that information. We call to mind familiar information that's relevant to the current encounter, and we use that information to make sense of what we're hearing and seeing. We also create explanations for why things are happening as they are.

Using Familiar Information   We make sense of others' communication in part by comparing what we currently perceive with knowledge that we already possess. For example, I proposed to my wife by surprising her after class. I had decorated her apartment with several dozen roses and carnations, was dressed in my best (and only!) suit, and was spinning "our song" on her turntable—the Spinners' "Could It Be I'm Falling in Love." When she opened the door, and I asked her to marry me, she immediately interpreted my communication correctly. But how, given that she never had been proposed to before? Because she knew from friends, family members, movies, and television shows what a marriage proposal looks and sounds like. Drawing on this familiar information, she correctly figured out what I was up to and (thank goodness!) accepted my proposal.

The knowledge we draw on when interpreting interpersonal communication resides in **schemata**, mental structures that contain information defining

self-reflection

Recall a conflict in which you and a friend disagreed about "who started it." How did you punctuate the encounter? How did your friend punctuate it? If each of you punctuated differently, how did those differences contribute to the conflict? If you could revisit the situation, what might you say or do differently to resolve the dispute?

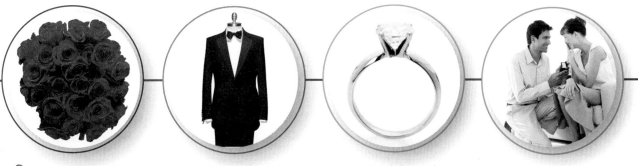

⬤ Schemata are mental structures that help us understand a concept's characteristics, and we use them to interpret communication. Together, a bunch of roses, a nice suit, and a diamond ring are schemata that suggest a marriage proposal.

the characteristics of various concepts, as well as how those characteristics are related to each other (Macrae & Bodenhausen, 2001). Each of us develops schemata for individual people, groups of people, places, events, objects, and relationships. In the example above, my wife had a schemata for "marriage proposal," and that enabled her to correctly interpret my actions.

Because we use familiar information to make sense of current interactions, our interpretations reflect what we presume to be true. For example, suppose you're interviewing for a job with a manager who has been at the company for 18 years. You'll likely interpret everything she says in light of your knowledge about "long-term employees." This knowledge includes your assumption that "company veterans generally know insider information." So, when your interviewer talks in glowing terms about the company's future, you'll probably interpret her comments as credible. Now imagine that you're interviewing with someone who has been with the company only a few weeks. Although he may present the exact same message to you about the company's future, you'll probably interpret his comments differently. Based on your perception of him as "new employee," and on the information you have in your "new employee" schema, you may interpret his message as naïve speculation rather than "expert commentary"—even if his statements are accurate.

Creating Explanations   In addition to drawing on our schemata to interpret information from interpersonal encounters, we create explanations for others' comments or behaviors, known as **attributions**. Attributions are our answers to the "why" questions we ask every day. "Why didn't my partner return my text message?" "Why did my best friend post that horrible, embarrassing photo of me on Facebook?"

Consider an example shared with me by a friend of mine, Sarah. She had finished teaching for the semester and was visiting her mother, who lived out-of-state. A student of hers, whom we'll call "Janet," had failed her course. During the time Sarah was out of town, Janet e-mailed to ask if there was anything she could do to change her grade. However, Sarah was offline for the week and missed Janet's e-mail. Checking her messages upon her return, she discovered Janet's original e-mail, along with a second, follow-up message:

> **From:** Janet [mailto:janet@school.edu]
> **Sent:** Tuesday, May 15, 2012 10:46 AM
> **To:** Professor Sarah
> **Subject:** FW: Grade
>
> Maybe my situation isn't a priority to you, and that's fine, but a response e-mail would've been appreciated! Even if all you had to say was "there's nothing I can do." I came to you seeking help, not a hand-out!—Janet.[2]

Put yourself in Janet's shoes for a moment. What attributions did Janet make about Sarah's failure to respond? How did these attributions shape Janet's communication in her second e-mail? Now consider this situation from Sarah's perspective. If you were in her shoes, what attributions would you make about Janet, and how would they shape how you interpreted her e-mail?

Attributions take two forms, internal and external (see Table 3.1). *Internal attributions* presume that a person's communication or behavior stems from internal causes, such as character or personality. For example, "My professor didn't respond to my e-mail because she doesn't care about students," or "Janet sent this message because she's rude." *External attributions* hold that a person's communication is caused by factors unrelated to personal qualities: "My professor didn't respond to my e-mail because she hasn't checked her messages yet," or "Janet sent this message because I didn't respond to her first message."

Like schemata, the attributions we make influence powerfully how we interpret and respond to others' communication. For example, if you think Janet's

table 3.1 **Internal versus External Attributions**

Communication Event	Internal Attribution	External Attribution
Your romantic partner doesn't reply after you send a flirtatious text message.	"My partner doesn't care about me."	"My partner is probably too busy to respond."
Your unfriendly coworker greets you warmly.	"My coworker is friendlier than I thought."	"Something unusual must have happened to make my coworker act so friendly."
Your friend ridicules your taste in music.	"My friend has an unpredictable mean streak."	"My friend must be having a really bad day."

---

[2]This is an example e-mail contributed to the author by a professional colleague, with all identifying information removed to protect the identity of the student in question.

e-mail was caused by her having a terrible day, you'll likely interpret her message as an understandable venting of frustration. If you think her message was caused by her personal rudeness, you'll probably interpret the e-mail as inappropriate and offensive.

Given the dozens of people with whom we communicate each day, it's not surprising that we often form invalid attributions. One common mistake is the **fundamental attribution error**, the tendency to attribute others' behaviors solely to internal causes (the kind of person they are) rather than the social or environmental forces affecting them (Heider, 1958). For example, communication scholar Alan Sillars and his colleagues found that during conflicts between parents and teens, both parties fall prey to the fundamental attribution error, making internal attributions about each other's messages that contribute to escalating the conflict (Sillars, Smith, & Koerner, 2010). Parents commonly attribute teens' communication to "lack of responsibility" and "desire to avoid the issue" whereas teens attribute parents' communication to "desire to control my life." All these assumptions are internal causes. These errors make it harder for teens and parents to constructively resolve their conflicts, something we discuss more in Chapter 8.

The fundamental attribution error is so named because it is the most prevalent of all perceptual biases and each of us falls prey to it (Langdridge & Butt, 2004). Why does this error occur? Because when we communicate with others, they dominate our perception. They—not the surrounding factors that may be causing their behavior—are most salient for us. Consequently, when we make judgments about why someone is acting in a certain way, we overestimate the influence of the person and underestimate the significance of his or her immediate environment (Heider, 1958; Langdridge & Butt, 2004).

The fundamental attribution error is especially common during online interactions (Shedletsky & Aitken, 2004). Because we aren't privy to the rich array of environmental factors that may be shaping our communication partners' messages—all we perceive is words on a screen—we're more likely than ever to interpret others' communication as stemming solely from internal causes (Wallace, 1999). As a consequence, when a text message, Facebook wall post, e-mail, or instant message is even slightly negative in tone, we're very likely to blame that negativity on bad character or personality flaws. Such was the case when Sarah presumed that Janet was a "rude person" based on her e-mail.

A related error is the **actor-observer effect**, the tendency of people to make external attributions regarding their own behaviors (Fiske & Taylor, 1991). Because our mental focus during interpersonal encounters is on factors external to us—especially the person with whom we're interacting—we tend to credit these factors as causing our own communication. This is particularly prevalent during unpleasant interactions. Our own impolite remarks during family conflicts are viewed as "reactions to their hurtful communication" rather than "messages caused by our own insensitivity." Our terseness toward coworkers is seen as "a natural response to incessant work interruptions" rather than "communication resulting from our own prickly personality."

However, we don't always make external attributions regarding our own behaviors. In cases where our actions result in noteworthy success, either personal

self-reflection

Recall a fight you've had with parents or other family members. Why did they behave as they did? What presumptions did they make about you and your behavior? When you assess both your and their attributions, are they internal or external? What does this tell you about the power and prevalence of the fundamental attribution error?

skills practice

Improving Online Attributions

Improving your attributions while communicating online

❶ Identify a negative text, e-mail, IM, or Web posting you've received.

❷ Consider why the person sent the message.

❸ Write a response based on this attribution, and save it as a draft.

❹ Think of and list other possible, external causes for the person's message.

❺ Keeping these alternative attributions in mind, revisit and reevaluate your message draft, editing it as necessary to ensure competence before you send or post it.

○ People are especially susceptible to the fundamental attribution error when communicating electronically—such as texting.

or professional, we typically take credit for the success by making an internal attribution, a tendency known as the **self-serving bias** (Fiske & Taylor, 1991). Suppose, for example, you've successfully persuaded a friend to lend you her car for the weekend—something you've never pulled off before. In this case, you will probably attribute this success to your charm and persuasive skill rather than to luck or your friend's generosity. The self-serving bias is driven by *ego protection*: by crediting ourselves for our life successes, we can feel happier about who we are.

Clearly, attributions play a powerful role in how we interpret communication. For this reason, it's important to consider the attributions you make while you're interacting with others. Check your attributions frequently, watching for the fundamental attribution error, the actor-observer effect, and the self-serving bias. If you think someone has spoken to you in an offensive way, ask yourself if it's possible that outside forces—including *your own behavior*—could have caused the problem. Also keep in mind that communication (like other forms of human behavior) rarely stems from *only* external *or* internal causes. It's caused by a combination of both (Langdridge & Butt, 2004).

Finally, when you can, check the accuracy of your attributions by asking people for the reasons behind their behavior. When you've made attribution errors that lead you to criticize or lose your patience with someone else, apologize and explain your mistake to the person. After Janet learned that Sarah hadn't responded because she had been out-of-state—as opposed to intentionally blowing her off—Janet apologized. She also explained why her message was so terse: she thought Sarah was intentionally ignoring her. Upon receiving Janet's apology, Sarah apologized also. She realized that she, too, had succumbed to the fundamental attribution error: she had wrongly presumed that Janet was rude, when in fact Janet's frustration over not getting a response was what had caused her to communicate as she did.

REDUCING UNCERTAINTY

When intercultural communication scholar Patricia Covarrubias (2000) was a young girl, she and her family immigrated to the United States from Mexico. On her first day of school in her adoptive country, Patricia's third-grade teacher, Mrs. Williams, led her to the front of the classroom to introduce her to her new classmates. As Patricia stood excitedly before them, she waited for Mrs. Williams to introduce her as "Patricia Covarrubias," or perhaps "Patricia." Of course, when Patricia was growing up in Mexico, her friends and family members rarely used either of these names. Instead, they called her *la chiquita* (the little one) or *mi Rosita de Jerico* (my rose of Jericho). But in the more formal setting of the classroom, Patricia expected her teacher to introduce her using her first and last name. Instead, Mrs. Williams, her hand gently resting on Patricia's shoulder, turned to the class and said, "Class, this is *Pat.*"

Patricia was dumbfounded. In her entire life, she had never been "Pat," nor could she understand why someone would call her "Pat." As she explains, "In one unexpected moment, all that I was and had been was abridged into three-letter, bottom-line efficiency" (Covarrubias, 2000, pp. 10–11). And although Mrs. Williams was simply trying to be friendly—using an abbreviation most Euro-Americans would consider "informal"—Patricia was mortified. The encounter bolstered her feeling that she was an outsider in an uncertain environment.

In most interpersonal interactions, the perception process unfolds in a rapid, straightforward manner. But sometimes we find ourselves in situations where people communicate in perplexing ways. In such contexts, we experience *uncertainty*, the anxious feeling that comes when we can't predict or explain someone else's communication.

Uncertainty is common during first encounters with new acquaintances, when we don't know much about the people with whom we're communicating. According to **Uncertainty Reduction Theory**, our primary compulsion during initial interactions is to reduce uncertainty about our communication partners by gathering enough information about them so their communication becomes predictable and explainable (Berger & Calabrese, 1975). When we reduce uncertainty, we're inclined to perceive people as attractive and likable, talk further, and consider forming relationships with them (Burgoon & Hoobler, 2002). When we can't predict or explain people's communication or behavior, our uncertainty escalates, and we're inclined to not communicate further, to form negative impressions, and to avoid developing relationships.

Uncertainty can be reduced in several ways, each of which has advantages and disadvantages (Berger & Bradac, 1982). First, you can observe how someone interacts with others. Known as *passive strategies*, these approaches can help you predict how he or she may behave when interacting with you, reducing your uncertainty. Examples include observing someone hanging out with friends at a party or checking out someone's Facebook page. Second, you can try *active strategies* by asking other people questions about someone you're interested in. You might find someone who knows the person you're assessing and then get him or her to disclose as much information as possible about that individual. Be aware, though, that this poses risks: the target person may find out that you've been asking questions. That could embarrass you—and upset the target. In addition, third-party information may not be accurate. Third, and perhaps most effective, are

◯ When we are uncertain about other people's behavior, we can learn more about them by observing them, by asking their friends about them, or even by interacting with them directly. This helps us make decisions about our future communication with them.

self-reflection

When do you use passive strategies to reduce your uncertainty? Active strategies? Interactive? Which do you prefer and why? What ethical concerns influence your own use of passive and active strategies?

interactive strategies: starting a direct interaction with the person you're interested in. Inquire where the person is from, what he or she does for a living, and what interests he or she has. You should also disclose personal information about yourself. This enables you to test the other person's reactions to you. Is the person intrigued or bored? That information can help you reduce your uncertainty about how to communicate further.

Influences on Perception

Culture, gender, and personality affect perception

A sense of directness dominates the perceptual process. Someone says something to us, and with lightning speed we focus our attention, organize information, and interpret its meaning. Although this process seems unmediated, powerful forces outside of our conscious awareness shape our perception during every encounter, whether we're communicating with colleagues, friends, family members, or lovers. Three of the most powerful influences on perception are culture, gender, and personality.

PERCEPTION AND CULTURE

Your cultural background influences your perception in at least two ways. Recall from Chapter 1 that *culture* is an established, coherent set of beliefs, attitudes, values, and practices shared by a large group of people. Whenever you interact with others, you interpret their communication in part by drawing on information from your schemata. But your schemata are filled with the beliefs, attitudes, and values you learned in your own culture (Gudykunst & Kim, 2003). Consequently, people raised in different cultures have different knowledge in their schemata, so they interpret one another's communication in very different ways. Competent interpersonal communicators recognize this fact. When necessary and appropriate, they check the accuracy of their interpretation by asking questions such as "I'm sorry, could you clarify what you just said?"

Second, culture affects whether you perceive others as similar to or different from yourself. When you grow up valuing certain cultural beliefs, attitudes, and values as your own, you naturally perceive those who share these with you as fundamentally similar to yourself—people you consider **ingroupers** (Allport, 1954). You may consider individuals from many different groups as your ingroupers as long as they share substantial points of cultural commonality with you, such as nationality, religious beliefs, ethnicity, socioeconomic class, or political views (Turner, Hogg, Oakes, Reicher, & Wetherell, 1987). In contrast, you may perceive people who aren't similar to yourself as **outgroupers**.

Perceiving others as ingroupers or outgroupers is one of the most important perceptual distinctions we make. We often feel passionately connected to our ingroups, especially when they are tied to central aspects of our self-concept such as sexual orientation, religious beliefs, or ethnic heritage. Consequently, we are more likely to give valued resources such as money, time, and effort to

⊙ Ingroupers on outgroupers? It depends on your point of view. As psychologist Marilynn Brewer (1999) describes, "The very factors that make ingroup attachment and allegiance important to individuals also provide a fertile ground for antagonism and distrust of those outside the ingroup boundaries" (p. 442).

those who are perceived as ingroupers versus those who are outgroupers (Castelli, Tomelleri, & Zogmaister, 2008). Basically, we like people who are "like" us. Think about it. If two different volunteers show up at your door asking you to donate money and time to a fund-raising effort, which one are you more likely to support: the volunteer working for a group you feel connected to, or the person acting on behalf of a group you feel no link to whatsoever? The answer is simple: the ingrouper.

We also are more likely to form positive interpersonal impressions of people we perceive as ingroupers (Giannakakis & Fritsche, 2011). One study of 30 different ethnic groups in East Africa found that members of each group perceived ingroupers' communication as substantially more trustworthy, friendly, and honest than outgroupers' communication (Brewer & Campbell, 1976). And in cases where people communicate in rude or inappropriate ways, you're substantially more inclined to form negative, internal attributions if you perceive them as outgroupers (Brewer, 1999). So, for example, if a cashier chides you for breaking a large bill but he's wearing a T-shirt emblazoned with a message advocating your beliefs and values, you're likely to make an external attribution: "He's just having a bad day." The same communication coming from someone who is proudly displaying chestwide messages attacking your beliefs likely will provoke a negative, internal attribution: "What a jerk! He's just like all those other people who believe that stuff!"

While categorizing people as ingroupers or outgroupers, it's easy to make mistakes. For example, even if people dress differently than you do, they may hold beliefs, attitudes, and values similar to your own. If you assume they're outgroupers based on surface-level differences, you may communicate with them in ways that prevent the two of you from getting to know each other better. You may never discover that you share other important qualities, and you lose an opportunity to make a friend, gain a new colleague, or forge a romantic bond.

self-reflection

Consider people in your life who you view as outgroupers. What points of difference lead you to see them that way? How does their outgrouper status shape your communication toward them? Is there anything you could learn about them that would lead you to judge them as ingroupers?

PERCEPTION AND GENDER

Get your family or friends talking about gender differences, and chances are you'll hear most of them claim that men and women perceive interpersonal communication differently. They may insist that "men are cool and logical" while "women see everything emotionally." But the relationship between gender and perception is much more complex. For example, through magnetic resonance imaging and positron emission tomography, we have learned that the structure of the brain's cerebral cortex differs in men and women (Frederikse, Lu, Aylward, Barta, & Pearlson, 1999). Researchers maintain that this difference enables men to perceive time and speed more accurately than women and to mentally rotate three-dimensional figures more easily. The difference in cerebral cortex structure allows women to understand and manipulate spatial relationships between objects more skillfully than men do and to more accurately identify others' emotions. Women also have a greater ability to process information related to language simultaneously in both of the brain's frontal lobes, resulting in higher scores on tests of language comprehension and vocabulary (Schlaepfer et al., 1995).

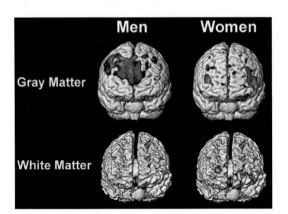

◐ Professor Richard Haier of the University of California, Irvine, led a study that showed men use the gray matter part of the brain more while women use more white matter. However, the study points out that just because men and women think differently, this has no effect on intelligence (i.e., one is not better than the other, just different).

But whether variation in brain structure actually translates into differences in interpersonal communication is hotly debated among scholars. Linguist Deborah Tannen (1990) argues that men and women perceive and produce communication in vastly different ways. For example, Tannen suggests that when problems arise, men focus on solutions, and women offer emotional support.

Perceiving Race

Race is a way we classify people based on common ancestry or descent and is almost entirely judged by physical features (Lustig & Koester, 2006). Once we perceive race, other perceptual judgments follow, most notably the assignment of people to ingrouper versus outgrouper status (Brewer, 1999). People we perceive as being the "same race" we see as being ingroupers. Their communication is perceived more positively than the communication of people of "other races," and we're more likely to make positive attributions about their behavior.

Not surprisingly, the perception of racial categories is more salient for people who suffer racial discrimination than for those who don't. Consider the experience of Canadian professor Tara Goldstein (2001). She asked students in her teacher education class to sort themselves into "same race" groups for a discussion exercise. Four black women immediately grouped together; several East Asian students did the same. But the white students were perplexed. One shouted, "All Italians—over here!" while another inquired, "Any other students of Celtic ancestry?" One white female approached Dr. Goldstein and said, "I'm not white, I'm Jewish." Following the exercise, the white students commented that they had never been sorted by their whiteness and didn't perceive themselves or one another as white.

The concept of whiteness has been investigated only recently. Whiteness can often seem "natural" or "normal" to individuals who are white, but for scholars interested in whiteness and for people of color, it means privilege. In her book *White Privilege,* Peggy McIntosh (1999) lists 26 privileges that she largely takes for granted and that result from her skin color. For example, as a white person, McIntosh is able to swear, dress in secondhand clothes, or not answer e-mail without having members of her race or other races attribute these behaviors to bad morals, poverty, or computer illiteracy. This perception of verbal and nonverbal communication may seem mundane, but as McIntosh says, it is part of white privilege, "an invisible package of unearned assets which I can count on cashing in each day, but about which I was meant to remain oblivious" (p. 79).

discussion questions

● What race do you identify with? How does your race affect your perception of ingrouper versus outgrouper communication? How does your race affect other people's perception of your communication?

● Is race an ethical way to perceive how others communicate? Do you think some races have more or less privilege in their interpersonal communication? If so, why?

Consequently, women perceive men's solutions as unsympathetic, and men perceive women's needs for emotional support as unreasonable. In contrast, researchers from communication and psychology argue that men and women are actually more similar than different in how they interpersonally communicate (Hall, Carter, & Horgan, 2000). Researchers Dan Canary, Tara Emmers-Sommer, and Sandra Faulkner (1997) reviewed data from over 1,000 gender studies and found that if you consider all of the factors that influence our communication and compare their impact, only about 1 percent of people's communication behavior is caused by gender. They concluded that when it comes to interpersonal communication, "men and women respond in a similar manner 99% of the time" (p. 9).

Despite the debate over differences, we know one thing about gender and perception for certain: people are socialized to *believe* that men and women communicate differently. Within Western culture, a long tradition exists of emphasizing communication differences between men and women. People believe that women talk more about their feelings than men, talk about "less important" issues than men (women "gossip," whereas men "discuss"), and generally talk more than men (Spender, 1984). But in one of the best-known studies of this phenomenon, researchers found that this was more a matter of perception than real difference (Mulac, Incontro, & James, 1985). Two groups of participants were given the same speech. One group was told that a man had authored and presented the speech, while the other was told that a woman

⚲ Despite popular beliefs, most researchers from communication and psychology argue that men and women are more similar than different in how they interpersonally communicate.

had written and given it. Participants who thought the speech was a woman's perceived it as having more "artistic quality." Those who believed it was a man's saw the speech as having more "dynamism." Participants also described the "man's" language as strong, active, and aggressive, and the "woman's" language as pleasing, sweet, and beautiful, despite the fact that the speeches were identical.

Given our tendency to presume broad gender differences in communication, can we improve the accuracy of our perception? Yes—if we challenge the assumptions we make about gender and if we remind ourselves that both genders' approaches to communication are more similar than different. The next time you find yourself thinking, "Oh, she said that because she's a woman," or "He sees things that way because he is a man," question your perception. Are these people really communicating differently because of their gender, or are you simply perceiving them as different based on *your* beliefs about their gender?

PERSONALITY

When you think about the star of a hit television show, a cartoon aardvark isn't usually the first thing to come to mind. But, as any one of the 10 million weekly viewers of PBS's *Arthur* will tell you, the appeal of the show is more than just the title character. It is the breadth of personalities displayed across the entire cast, allowing us to link each of them to people in our own lives. Sue Ellen loves art, music, and world culture, while the Brain is studious, meticulous, and responsible. Francine loves interacting with people, especially while playing sports, and Buster is laid-back, warm, and friendly to just about everyone.

◖ Characters from the television show *Arthur* exhibit a range of personality traits that influence how they perceive the world around them as well as how we perceive them.

table 3.2 **The Big Five Personality Traits (OCEAN)**

Personality Trait	Description
Openness	The degree to which a person is willing to consider new ideas and take an interest in culture. People high in openness are more imaginative, creative, and interested in seeking out new experiences than those low in openness.
Conscientiousness	The degree to which a person is organized and persistent in pursuing goals. People high in conscientiousness are methodical, well organized, and dutiful; those low in conscientiousness are less careful, less focused, and more easily distracted. Also known as *dependability*.
Extraversion	The degree to which a person is interested in interacting regularly with others and actively seeks out interpersonal encounters. People high in extraversion are outgoing and sociable; those low in extraversion are quiet and reserved.
Agreeableness	The degree to which a person is trusting, friendly, and cooperative. People low in agreeableness are aggressive, suspicious, and uncooperative. Also known as *friendliness*.
Neuroticism	The degree to which a person experiences negative thoughts about oneself. People high in neuroticism are prone to insecurity and emotional distress; people low in neuroticism are relaxed, less emotional, and less prone to distress. Also known as *emotional stability*.

D.W. drives Arthur crazy with her moods, obsessions, and tantrums; while Arthur—at the center of it all—combines all of these traits into one appealing, complicated package.

In the show *Arthur*, we see embodied in animated form the various dispositions that populate our real-world interpersonal lives. And when we think of these people and their personalities, visceral reactions are commonly evoked. We like, loathe, or even love people based on our perception of their personalities and how their personalities mesh with our own.

Clearly, personality shapes how we perceive others, but what exactly is it? **Personality** is an individual's characteristic way of thinking, feeling, and acting, based on the traits—enduring motives and impulses—that he or she possesses (McCrae & Costa, 2001). Contemporary psychologists argue that although thousands of different personalities exist, each is comprised of only five primary traits, referred to as the "Big Five" (John, 1990). These are openness, conscientiousness, extraversion, agreeableness, and neuroticism (see Table 3.2 above). A simple way to remember them is the acronym *OCEAN*. Alternatively, you can think Sue Ellen, the Brain, Francine, Buster, and D.W.! The degree to which a person possesses each of the Big Five traits determines his or her personality (McCrae, 2001).

Prioritizing Our Own Traits When Perceiving Others   Our perception of others is strongly guided by the personality traits we see in ourselves and how we evaluate these traits. If you're an extravert, for example, another person's

What Kind of Personality Do You Have?

For each of the five personality traits, check the descriptions that accurately describe your personality. Then total up the number of check marks for each category. Use the Scoring key below to determine whether you're low, moderate, or high in each category.

I see myself as someone who . . .

Extraversion

_____ is talkative

_____ is full of energy

_____ generates a lot of enthusiasm

_____ has an assertive personality

_____ is outgoing, sociable

Conscientiousness

_____ does a thorough job

_____ is a reliable worker

_____ perseveres until the task is finished

_____ does things efficiently

_____ makes plans and follows through with them

Openness

_____ is curious about many different things

_____ has an active imagination

_____ values artistic, aesthetic experiences

_____ is sophisticated in art, music, or literature

_____ likes to reflect, play with ideas

Agreeableness

_____ is helpful and unselfish with others

_____ has a forgiving nature

_____ is generally trusting

_____ is considerate and kind to almost everyone

_____ likes to cooperate with others

Neuroticism

_____ is depressed, blue

_____ can be tense

_____ worries a lot

_____ can be moody

_____ gets nervous easily

Note: This *Self-Quiz* is adapted from John, Donahue, and Kentle (1991).

Scoring: 0–1, low; 2–3, moderate; 4–5, high

extraversion becomes salient to you when you're communicating with him or her. Likewise, if you pride yourself on being friendly, other people's friendliness becomes your perceptual focus.

But it's not just a matter of focusing on certain traits to the exclusion of others. We evaluate people positively or negatively in accordance with how we feel about our own traits. We typically like in others the same traits we like in ourselves, and we dislike in others the traits that we dislike in ourselves.

To avoid this preoccupation with your own traits, carefully observe how you focus on other people's traits and how your evaluation of these traits reflects your own feelings about yourself. Strive to perceive people broadly, taking into consideration all of their traits and not just the positive or negative ones that you share. Then evaluate them and communicate with them independently of your own positive and negative self-evaluations.

self-reflection

What personality traits do you like in yourself? When you see these traits in others, how does that impact your communication toward them? How do you perceive people who possess traits you don't like in yourself? How do these perceptions affect your relationships with them?

Generalizing from the Traits We Know   Another effect that personality has on perception is the presumption that because a person is high or low in a certain trait, he or she must be high or low in other traits. For example, say that I introduce you to a friend of mine, Shoshanna. Within the first minute of interaction you perceive her as highly friendly. Based on your perception of her high friendliness, you'll likely also presume that she is highly extraverted, simply because high friendliness and high extraversion intuitively seem to "go together." If people you've known in the past who were highly friendly and extraverted also were highly open, you may go further, perceiving Shoshanna as highly open as well.

Your perception of Shoshanna was created using **implicit personality theories**, personal beliefs about different types of personalities and the ways in which traits cluster together (Bruner & Taguiri, 1954). When we meet people for the first time, we use implicit personality theories to perceive just a little about an individual's personality and then presume a great deal more, making us feel that we know the person and helping to reduce uncertainty. At the same time, making presumptions about people's personalities is risky. Presuming that someone is high or low in one trait because he or she is high or low in others can lead you to communicate incompetently. For example, if you presume that Shoshanna is high in openness, you might mistakenly presume she has certain political or cultural beliefs, leading you to say things to her that cut directly against her actual values such as "Don't you just hate when people mix religion and politics?" However, Shoshanna might respond with "No, actually I think that government should be based on scriptural principles."

Forming Impressions of Others

> Perception creates impressions that may evolve over time

When we use perception to size up other people, we form **interpersonal impressions**—mental pictures of who people are and how we feel about them. All aspects of the perception process shape our interpersonal impressions: the information we select as the focus of our attention, the way we organize this information, the interpretations we make based on knowledge in our schemata and our attributions, and even our uncertainty.

Given the complexity of the perception process, it's not surprising that impressions vary widely. Some impressions come quickly into focus. We meet a person and take an immediate dislike to him. Or we quickly decide that someone's a "fun person" after chatting with her briefly. Other impressions form slowly, over a series of encounters. Some impressions are intensely positive, others neutral, and still others negative. But regardless of their form, interpersonal impressions exert a profound impact on our communication and relationship choices. To illustrate this impact, imagine yourself in the following situation.

It's summer, and you're at a lake, hanging out with friends. As you lie on the beach, the man pictured in the photo on page 93 approaches you. He introduces himself as "Ted" and tells you that he's waiting for some friends who were supposed to help him load his sailboat onto his car. He's easy to talk to, friendly, and has a nice smile. His left arm is in a sling, and he casually mentions that he injured it playing racquetball. Because his arm is hurting, and his friends are missing, he asks if you would help him with his boat. You say, "Sure." You walk with him to the parking lot, but when you get to Ted's car, you don't see a boat. When you ask him where his boat is, he says, "Oh! It's at my folks' house, just up the hill. Do you mind going with me? It'll just take a couple of minutes." You tell him you can't go with him because your friends will wonder where you are. "That's OK," Ted says cheerily, "I should have told you it wasn't in the parking lot. Thanks for bothering anyways." As the two of you walk back to the beach, Ted repeats his apology and expresses gratitude for your willingness to help him. He's polite and strikes you as sincere.

Think about your encounter with Ted, and all that you've perceived. What's your impression of him? What traits besides the ones you've observed would you expect him to have? What do you predict would have happened if you had gone with him to his folks' house to help load the boat? Would you want to play racquetball with him? Would he make a good friend? Does he interest you as a possible romantic partner?

The scenario you've read actually happened. The above description is drawn from the police testimony of Janice Graham, who was approached by Ted at Lake Sammamish Park, near Seattle, Washington, in 1974 (Michaud & Aynesworth, 1989). Graham's decision not to accompany Ted saved her life. Two other women—Janice Ott and Denise Naslund—were not so fortunate. Each of them went with Ted, who raped and murdered them. Friendly, handsome, and polite Ted was none other than Ted Bundy, one of the most notorious serial killers in U.S. history.

Thankfully, most of the interpersonal impressions we form don't have life-or-death consequences. But all impressions do exert a powerful impact on how we communicate with others and whether we pursue relationships with them. For this reason, it's important to understand how we can flexibly adapt our impressions to create more accurate and reliable conceptions of others.

CONSTRUCTING GESTALTS

One way we form impressions of others is to construct a **Gestalt**, a general sense of a person that's either positive or negative. We discern a few traits and, drawing upon information in our schemata, we arrive at a judgment based on these traits. (As discussed earlier in this chapter, *schemata* are the mental structures we use to interpret information during the perception process.) The result is an impression of the person as a whole rather than as the sum of individual parts (Asch, 1946). For example, suppose you strike up a conversation with the person sitting next to you at lunch. The person is funny, friendly, and attractive—characteristics associated with positive information in your schemata. You immediately construct an overall positive impression ("I like this person!") rather than spending additional time weighing the significance of his or her separate traits.

Gestalts form rapidly. This is one reason why people consider "first impressions" so consequential. Gestalts require relatively little mental or communicative effort. Thus, they're useful for encounters in which we must render quick judgments about others with only limited information—an interview at a job fair in which you have only a few minutes to size up the interviewer, for instance. Gestalts also are useful for interactions involving casual relationships (contacts with acquaintances or service providers) and contexts in which we are meeting and talking with a large number of people in a small amount of time (business conferences or parties). During such exchanges, it isn't possible to carefully scrutinize every piece of information we perceive about others. Instead, we quickly form broad impressions and then mentally walk away from them. But this also means that Gestalts have significant shortcomings.

The Positivity Bias   In 1913, author E. H. Porter published a novel titled *Pollyanna*, about a young child who was happy nearly all of the time. Even when faced with horrible tragedies, Pollyanna saw the positive side of things. Research on human perception suggests that some Pollyanna exists inside each of us (Matlin & Stang, 1978). Examples of *Pollyanna effects* include people believing pleasant events as more likely to happen than unpleasant ones, most people deeming their lives "happy" and describing themselves as "optimists," and most people viewing themselves as "better than average" in terms of physical attractiveness and intellect (Matlin & Stang, 1978; Silvera, Krull, & Sassler, 2002).

Pollyanna effects come into play when we form Gestalts. When Gestalts are formed, they are more likely to be positive than negative, an effect known as the **positivity bias**. Let's say you're at a party for the company where you just started working. During the party, you meet six new coworkers for the first time and talk with each of them for a few minutes. You form a Gestalt for each. Owing to the positivity bias, most or all of your Gestalts are likely to be positive. Although the positivity bias is helpful in initiating relationships, it also can lead us to make bad interpersonal decisions, such as when we pursue relationships with people who turn out to be unethical or even abusive.

The Negativity Effect   When we create Gestalts, we don't treat all information that we learn about people as equally important. Instead, we place emphasis on the negative information we learn about others, a pattern known as the **negativity effect**. Across cultures, people perceive negative information as more informative about someone's "true" character than positive information (Kellermann, 1989). Though you may be wondering whether the negativity effect contradicts Pollyanna effects, it actually derives from them. People tend to believe that positive events, information, and personal characteristics are more commonplace than negative events, information, and characteristics. So when we learn something negative about another person, we see it as "unusual." Consequently, that information becomes more salient, and we judge it as more truly representative of a person's character than positive information (Kellermann, 1989).

Sometimes the negativity effect leads us to accurate perceptions of people. One of the women who rejected Ted Bundy's request for assistance at Lake Sammamish Park reported that she had seen him "stalking" other women before he approached her. This information led her to form a negative Gestalt before he even talked with her—an impression that saved her life. But just as often, the negativity effect leads us away from accurate perception. Accurate perception is rooted in carefully and critically assessing everything we learn about people, then flexibly adapting our impressions to match these data. When we weight negative information more heavily than positive, we perceive only a small part of people, aspects that may or may not represent who they are and how they normally communicate.

Halos and Horns   Once we form a Gestalt about a person, it influences how we interpret that person's subsequent communication and the attributions we make regarding that individual. For example, think about someone for whom you've formed a strongly positive Gestalt. Now imagine that this person discloses a dark secret: he or she lied to a lover, cheated on exams, or stole from the office. Because of your positive Gestalt, you may dismiss the significance of this behavior, telling yourself instead that the person "had no choice" or "wasn't acting normally." This tendency to positively interpret what someone says or does because we have a positive Gestalt of them is known as the **halo effect** (see Table 3.3).

The counterpart of the halo effect is the **horn effect**, the tendency to negatively interpret the communication and behavior of people for whom we have negative Gestalts (see Table 3.3). Call to mind someone you can't stand. Imagine that this person discloses the same secret as the individual described above. Although the information in both cases is the same, you would likely chalk up this individual's unethical behavior to bad character or lack of values.

CALCULATING ALGEBRAIC IMPRESSIONS

A second way we form interpersonal impressions is to develop **algebraic impressions** by carefully evaluating each new thing we learn about a person (Anderson,

table 3.3   The Halo and Horn Effects

The Halo Effect		
Impression	**Behavior**	**Attribution**
Person we like :)	Positive behavior	Internal
Person we like :)	Negative behavior	External
The Horn Effect		
Person we dislike :(	Positive behavior	External
Person we dislike :(	Negative behavior	Internal

Note: Information in this table is adapted from Guerin (1999).

self-reflection

Think of someone for whom you have a negative Gestalt. How did the negativity effect shape your impression? Now call to mind personal flaws or embarrassing events from your past. If someone learned of this information and formed a negative Gestalt of you, would his or her impression be accurate? Fair?

VideoCentral

bedfordstmartins.com /reflectrelate

Halo Effect
Watch this clip online to answer the questions below.

When have you made a perceptual error based on the halo effect? How would you suggest reducing the halo effect in hiring practices?

Want to see more? Check out VideoCentral for clips on **horn effect** and **algebraic impressions**.

When Annie first meets Helen in the movie *Bridesmaids*, she is intimidated by Helen's looks, money, and close relationship with their mutual friend Lillian. Over the course of the film, the two women's perceptions of each other evolve from animosity and distrust to something akin to friendship. How have you used algebraic impressions to get closer to or distance yourself from a friend?

skills practice

Algebraic Impressions
Strengthen your ability to use algebraic impressions.

❶ When you next meet a new acquaintance, resist forming a general positive or negative Gestalt.

❷ Instead, observe and learn everything you can about the person.

❸ Then make a list of his or her positive and negative traits and weigh each trait's importance.

❹ Form an algebraic impression based on your assessment, keeping in mind that this impression may change over time.

❺ Across future interactions, flexibly adapt your impression as you learn new information.

1981). Algebraic impressions involve comparing and assessing the positive and negative things we learn about a person in order to calculate an overall impression, then modifying this impression as we learn new information. It's similar to solving an algebra equation, in which we add and subtract different values from each side to compute a final result.

Consider how you might form an algebraic impression of Ted Bundy from our earlier example. At the outset, his warmth, humor, and ability to chat easily with you strike you as "friendly" and "extraverted." These traits, when added together, lead you to calculate a positive impression: friendly + extraverted = positive impression. But when you accompany Bundy to the parking lot and realize his boat isn't there, you perceive this information as deceptive. This new information—Ted is a liar—immediately causes you to revise your computation: friendly + extraverted + potential liar = negative impression.

When we form algebraic impressions, we don't place an equal value on every piece of information in the equation. Instead, we weight some pieces of information more heavily than others, depending on the information's *importance* and its *positivity* or *negativity*. For example, your perception of potential romantic partners' physical attractiveness, intelligence, and personal values likely will carry more weight when calculating your impression than their favorite color or breakfast cereal—unless you view colors and cereals as important.

As this discussion illustrates, algebraic impressions are more flexible and accurate than Gestalts. For encounters in which we have the time and energy to ponder someone's traits and how they add up, algebraic impressions offer us the opportunity to form refined impressions of people. We can also flexibly change them every time we receive new information about people. But since algebraic impressions require a fair amount of mental effort, they aren't as efficient as Gestalts. In unexpected encounters or casual conversations, such mental calculations are unnecessary and may even work to our disadvantage, especially if we need to render rapid judgments and act on them.

USING STEREOTYPES

A final way we form impressions is to categorize people into social groups and then evaluate them based on information we have in our schemata related to these groups (Bodenhausen, Macrae, & Sherman, 1999). This is known as **stereotyping**, a term first coined by journalist Walter Lippmann (1922) to describe overly simplistic interpersonal impressions. When we stereotype others, we replace the subtle complexities that make people unique with blanket assumptions about their character and worth based solely on their social group affiliation.

We stereotype because doing so streamlines the perception process. Once we've categorized a person as a member of a particular group, we can apply all of the information we have about that group to form a quick impression (Bodenhausen et al., 1999). For example, suppose a friend introduces you to Conor, an Irish transfer student. Once you perceive Conor as "Irish," beliefs that you might hold about Irish people could come to mind: they love to tell exaggerated stories (the blarney), have bad tempers, like to drink, and are passionate about soccer. Mind you, none of these assumptions may be accurate about Irish people or relevant to Conor. But if this is what you *believe* about the Irish, you'll keep it in mind during your conversation with Conor and look for ways to confirm your beliefs. So when he tells you about "seeing a great match" last weekend, you might assume he's talking about soccer rather than tennis or chess. If he discloses that he went to a party last night, you might picture him with a pint of Guinness in his hand rather than a root beer.

As this example suggests, stereotyping frequently leads us to form flawed impressions of others. One study of workplace perception found that male supervisors who stereotyped women as "the weaker sex" perceived female employees' work performance as deficient and gave women low job evaluations—regardless of the women's actual job performances (Cleveland, Stockdale, & Murphy, 2000). A separate study examining college students' perceptions of professors found a similar biasing effect for ethnic stereotypes. Euro-American students who stereotyped Hispanics as "laid-back" and "relaxed" perceived Hispanic professors who set high expectations for classroom performance as "colder" and "more unprofessional" than Euro-American professors who set identical standards (Smith & Anderson, 2005).

However, stereotyping doesn't automatically lead to negative outcomes. Communication scholars Valerie Manusov and Radha Hegde (1993) found that during encounters between American and Indian students, the Americans who held positive or negative stereotypes about Indians were more inquisitive and actively engaged during the interaction than those who lacked stereotypes. As this study suggests, stereotyping can create an opportunity for communication, but the quality of the communication will depend on the nature of the stereotype.

Stereotyping is almost impossible to avoid. Researchers have documented that categorizing people in terms of their social group affiliation is the most common way we form impressions, more common than either Gestalts or algebraic impressions (Bodenhausen et al., 1999). Why? Social group categories such as race and gender are among the first things we notice about others upon meeting them. As a consequence, we often perceive people in terms of their social group membership before any other impression is even possible

⬤ Whom do you see in this photograph of Tupac Shakur? A tattooed African American male? A famous rapper? A gangster who died young in a hail of gunfire? Or perhaps a man who was named after an Inca chief, who studied ballet and acting, and whose mother required him as a young boy to read *The New York Times*?

(Devine, 1989). The Internet provides no escape from this tendency. Without many of the nonverbal cues and additional information that can distinguish a person as a unique individual, people communicating online are even more likely than those communicating face-to-face to form stereotypical impressions when meeting others for the first time (Spears, Postmes, Lea, & Watt, 2001).

Most of us presume that our beliefs about groups are valid. As a consequence, we have a high degree of confidence in the legitimacy of our stereotypical impressions, despite the fact that such impressions are frequently flawed (Brewer, 1993). We also continue to believe in stereotypes even when members of a stereotyped group repeatedly behave in ways that contradict the stereotype. In fact, contradictory behavior may actually *strengthen* stereotypes. For example, if you think of Buddhists as quiet and contemplative and meet a talkative and funny Buddhist, you may dismiss his or her behavior as atypical and not worthy of your attention (Seta & Seta, 1993). You'll then actively seek examples of behavior that confirm the stereotype to compensate for the uncertainty that the unexpected behavior aroused (Seta & Seta, 1993). As a result, the stereotype is reinforced.

You can overcome stereotypes by critically assessing your beliefs about various groups, especially those you dislike. Is the information in your schemata related to these groups accurate or flawed? Then educate yourself about these groups. Pick several groups you feel positively or negatively about. Read a variety of materials about these groups' histories, beliefs, attitudes, values, and behaviors. Look for similarities and differences between people affiliated with these groups and yourself. Finally, when interacting with members of these groups, keep in mind that just because someone belongs to a certain group, it doesn't necessarily mean that all of the defining characteristics of that group apply to that person. Since each of us simultaneously belongs to multiple social groups, don't form a narrow and biased impression of someone by slotting him or her into just one group.

Improving Your Perception of Others

Explore empathy, world-mindedness, and perception-checking

Malcolm X is most remembered for his fiery rhetoric denouncing white racism and his rejection of nonviolent protest as a means for dealing with oppression. Less well known is the marked change in his perception and communication that occurred following his visit to Saudi Arabia. Malcolm traveled to Mecca for a traditional Muslim hajj, or pilgrimage. During his visit, he worshipped, ate, socialized, and slept in the same room with white Muslims. In doing so, he was shocked to discover that despite their differences in skin color, they all shared similar degrees of religious devotion. The experience was a revelation, and led him to reassess his long-standing belief in an unbridgeable racial divide between whites and blacks. As he explained in a letter home: ". . . on this pilgrimage, what I have seen and expe-

Malcolm X's perception changed after 1964 as shown in this quote: "I believe in recognizing every human being as a human being, neither white, black, brown, nor red—when you are dealing with humanity as one family, it's just one human being marrying another human being, or one human being living around or with another human being."

rienced has forced me to rearrange my thought-patterns and toss aside some of my previous conclusions" (Malcolm X, 1964).

Malcolm's transformation suggests important lessons for everyone interested in improving his or her own perception and communication. He came to appreciate others' perspectives and feel a strong emotional kinship with those he previously disparaged based on skin color. He accepted others' beliefs as legitimate and deserving of respect. He also freely called into question his own perceptual accuracy by critically assessing his prior judgments and correcting those found to deviate from "the reality of life." These changes reveal three ways we can improve our perception and interpersonal communication: offering empathy, embracing world-mindedness, and checking our perception.

OFFERING EMPATHY

Empathy is one of our most valuable tools for communicating competently with others (Campbell & Babrow, 2004). The word *empathy* comes from the Greek word *empatheia*, meaning "feeling into." When we experience **empathy**, we "feel into" others' thoughts and emotions, making an attempt to understand their perspectives and be aware of their feelings in order to identify with them (Kuhn, 2001).

Empathy consists of two components. The first is *perspective-taking*—the ability to see things from someone else's vantage point without necessarily experiencing that person's emotions (Duan & Hill, 1996). The second is *empathic concern*—becoming aware of how the other person is feeling, experiencing a sense of compassion regarding the other person's emotional state, and perhaps even experiencing some of his or her emotions yourself (Stiff, Dillard, Somera, Kim, & Sleight, 1988).

But experiencing empathy isn't sufficient in itself to improve your interpersonal communication and relationships. You also must convey your empathy to others. To competently communicate the perspective-taking part of empathy, let others know that you're genuinely interested in hearing their viewpoints ("I'd love to get your impression"), and tell them that you think their views are important and understandable ("Seeing it from your side makes a lot of sense"). To communicate empathic concern, disclose to others that you

self-QUIZ

Test Your Empathy

Read these statements, marking the ones with which you agree. Total up your check marks and interpret your score below.

Perspective-Taking

_____ Before I criticize a person, I try to imagine how I would view the situation in his or her place.

_____ I believe there are two sides to every question, and I try to look at both sides.

_____ I find it easy to see things from another person's point of view.

_____ I try to look at everybody's side of a disagreement before I make a decision.

_____ When I am upset with someone, I usually try to put myself in his or her "shoes" for a while.

Empathic Concern

_____ When I see a person being taken advantage of, I feel protective toward him or her.

_____ I often have tender, concerned feelings for people who seem less fortunate than I.

_____ I would describe myself as a pretty softhearted person.

_____ Other people's misfortunes disturb me a great deal.

_____ I am often touched by the things that I see happen to people around me.

Note: This *Self-Quiz* is adapted from Stiff et al. (1988).

Scoring: For each section, a score of 0–1 indicates that you have low empathy, 2–3 indicates moderate empathy, and 4–5 indicates high empathy.

skills practice

Enhancing Empathy
Improving your ability to experience and express empathy

❶ Identify a challenging interpersonal encounter.

❷ As the encounter unfolds, consider how the other person is viewing you and the interaction.

❸ Think about the emotions he or she is feeling.

❹ Communicate perspective-taking, avoiding "I know" messages.

❺ Express empathic concern, letting the person know you value his or her feelings.

❻ Disclose your own feelings.

care about them and their feelings ("I hope you're doing OK"). Share with them your own emotions regarding their situation ("I feel terrible that you're going through this").

Importantly, avoid using "I know" messages ("I know just how you feel" or "I know just what you're going through"). Even if you make such comments with kind intentions, others will likely view you as presumptuous and perhaps even patronizing, especially if they suspect that you don't or can't feel as they do. For example, when people suffer a great loss—such as the death of a loved one—many don't believe that anyone else could feel the depth of anguish they're experiencing. Saying "I know how you feel" isn't helpful under these conditions.

EMBRACING WORLD-MINDEDNESS

The second way to improve your perception is to embrace **world-mindedness**: acceptance of and respect toward other cultures' beliefs, values, and customs (Hammer, Bennett, & Wiseman, 2003). This is done in three ways (Shah, King, & Patel, 2004). First, accept others' cultural expressions as natural elements in their interpersonal communication, in the same way that your interpersonal communication is a reflection of your cultural background. Second, avoid the temptation to evaluate others' cultures as "better" or "worse" than your own. Third, consistently treat people from different cultures with respect.

One way to embrace world-mindedness is to experience other cultures firsthand. Groups like the Peace Corps provide volunteering opportunities around the world (shown), while some college students choose to study abroad for a semester or more. No matter the situation, when you communicate with people from other cultures, be sure to do so in respectful ways that increase your world-mindedness.

This can be especially challenging when differences in race, nationality, religion, or sexual orientation seem unbridgeable or when others' cultural ways conflict with your own beliefs, attitudes, and values. But practicing world-mindedness means more than just coldly "tolerating" cultural differences you find perplexing or problematic. Treating people with respect means communicating in a consistently kind and courteous fashion, and endeavoring to preserve others' personal dignity by respecting their rights to possess viewpoints that differ from yours.

World-mindedness is the opposite of **ethnocentrism**, the belief that one's own cultural beliefs, attitudes, values, and practices are superior to those of others. Highly ethnocentric people view their own culture as the center of everything and the standard against which all other cultures should be judged (Neuliep & McCroskey, 1997). Ethnocentric people tend to presume that their own communication is competent, while that of people from other cultures is incompetent. Ironically, this leads them to be more incompetent communicators, especially when interacting with people from other cultures (Massengill & Nash, 2009).

CHECKING YOUR PERCEPTION

The final way to improve your perception is, as Malcolm X put it, to "rearrange your thought-patterns" and "toss aside previous conclusions" when they prove to be wrong. This is accomplished through **perception-checking**, a five-step process in which you apply all that you've learned in this chapter to your perception of others.

1. *Check your punctuation.* People punctuate encounters in different ways, often disagreeing on "who/what started it" or "who/what ended it." This kind of disagreement is common during interpersonal conflicts. When you experience a conflict, be aware of your own punctuation and keep in mind that other people may see things differently. Remember to ask others to share their punctuation with you.

Balancing Impressions and Empathy

BACKGROUND

One relationship challenge we face is forging constructive, collaborative work relationships with people whom we judge to be "outgroupers." This can be even more challenging when we've formed negative impressions of them and they begin to behave in questionable ways. To understand how you might competently manage such a relationship challenge, read the case study and work through the five steps under Your Turn.

CASE STUDY

Your professor assigns a group project that will count for a significant portion of your final course grade.[3] Each group member gets two grades for the project: one for the group presentation and one for individual contribution. The professor selects you as a group leader. Your responsibilities include making sure that each group member gets his or her work done and telling the professor what grade you think each person deserves. The professor will evaluate you in part based upon your skill as group leader.

At your first group meeting, everyone is on time except Dylan. He apologizes and says that "something came up." As everyone introduces themselves, it becomes clear that Dylan's tardiness isn't his only difference from you and the others. He's wearing a shirt emblazoned with extreme political slogans, viewpoints opposed to yours. It quickly becomes clear that his religious beliefs are dissimilar as well. The more you talk with him, the more you dislike him.

Despite your distaste for Dylan, the meeting goes well. The project you all decide on is interesting and provocative. A ton of research needs to be done, but split several ways you *might* get it done—if everyone does his or her fair share. If even one person fails to follow through, however, it will be a disaster. You exit the meeting excited but anxious.

As the project progresses, Dylan seldom makes it to meetings on time and skips one meeting entirely. At that meeting, two members petition you to remove him from the group, but others argue for keeping him. You decide to give Dylan another chance. A few hours later, Dylan e-mails you an apology, saying he's been "dealing with family problems." He offers to do extra research to make amends, and you gladly accept his offer, as you're stressed about getting the project done.

It's Thursday afternoon. The group's in-class presentation is next Tuesday. The plan is to rehearse tomorrow afternoon, then use the weekend to do any final tweaking that needs to be done. Your phone rings, and it's Dylan. He says, "I am so sorry, but I don't have my research done yet, and can't get it done by tomorrow. My family situation has been holding me back. Can I have more time?"

---

[3]Situation adapted from the "Ron" situation developed by O'Keefe (1988).

3 YOUR TURN

Think about the interpersonal communication concepts, skills, and insights you have learned while reading this book, especially in this chapter. Try to keep all of this in mind while working through the following five steps, which will help you become aware of how you can make better interpersonal communication choices in your relationships. Remember, there are no right answers, so think hard about what choice you will make! (P.S. Need help? See the *Helpful Concepts* listed below.)

● step 1

Reflect on yourself. What are your thoughts and feelings in this situation? What attributions are you making about Dylan and his behavior? Are your attributions accurate, or are they being shaded by your impression of him?

● step 2

Reflect on your partner. Using perspective-taking and empathic concern, put yourself in Dylan's shoes. What is he thinking and feeling in this situation?

● step 3

Identify the optimal outcome. Think about all the information you have about Dylan, his communication with you, your relationship with him, and the situation surrounding the group project (including your responsibilities as group leader). Consider your own feelings as well as Dylan's. Given all these factors, what's the best, most constructive outcome possible here? Be sure to consider not just what's best for *you*, but what's best for Dylan as well.

● step 4

Locate the roadblocks. Taking into consideration your own thoughts and feelings, Dylan's, and all that has happened in this situation, what's preventing you from achieving the optimal outcome you identified in Step 3?

● step 5

Chart your course. What can you say and do to overcome the roadblocks you've identified and achieve your optimal outcome?

HELPFUL CONCEPTS

Attribution errors, **81**

Uncertainty-reducing strategies, **82**

Ingroupers and outgroupers, **84**

Negativity effect, **94**

Algebraic impressions, **95**

Perception-checking, **101**

2. *Check your knowledge.* Your perception of others is only as accurate as the information you have in your schemata. Never presume that you know the "truth" about what others "really" mean or what they're "really" like. When in doubt, ask others to explain their meaning to you.

3. *Check your attributions.* Avoid the common temptation to attribute others' communication and behavior exclusively to internal causes such as character or personality. Question any internal attributions you make. Remember that all behavior—including interpersonal communication—stems from a complex combination of internal and external forces.

4. *Check perceptual influences.* Reflect on how culture, gender, and personality are shaping your perception of others. Are you perceiving others as ingroupers or outgroupers? If so, on what basis? How is this perception affecting your communication? Your relationships?

5. *Check your impressions.* Reflect on your impressions as you're forming them. If you find yourself making Gestalts, realize that your Gestalts may bias your perception of subsequent information you learn about a person. Resist stereotyping but also realize that it's difficult to avoid, given the natural human tendency to categorize people into groups upon first meeting. Strive to create flexible impressions, thoughtfully weighing new information you learn about a person and reshaping your overall impression based on new data.

Perception-checking is an intense mental exercise. Mastering it takes time and effort, but the ability to critically check your own perception goes, as Malcolm X wrote, "hand in hand with every form of intelligent search for truth," whether the truth is personal, interpersonal, or universal. When you routinely perception-check, errors are corrected and perception becomes more accurate, balanced, and objective. As a result, you will make fewer communication blunders, and you will be able to tailor your communication to people as they really are, making your messages more sensitive and effective. The ultimate result will also be perceptual: *others* seeing *you* as a competent communicator.

Practicing Responsible Perception

> Perception affects every interpersonal encounter

We experience our interpersonal reality—the people around us, our communication with them, and the relationships that result—through the lens of perception. But perception is a product of our own creation, metaphorical clay we can shape in whatever ways we want. At each stage of the perception process we make choices that empower us to mold our perception in constructive or destructive ways. What do I select as the focus of my attention? What attributions do I make? Do I form initial impressions and cling to them in the face of contradictory evidence? Or do I strive to adapt my impressions of others as I learn new information about them? The choices we make at each of these decision points feed directly into how we communicate with and relate to others. When we negatively stereotype people, for example, or refuse to empathize with someone because he or she is an outgrouper, we immediately destine ourselves to incompetent communication.

To improve our interpersonal communication and relationship decisions, we must practice responsible perception. This means routinely perception-checking and correcting errors. It means striving to adjust our impressions of people as we get to know them better. It means seeing those who populate our interpersonal world through eyes of empathy, honoring their cultural perspectives as equal to our own, emotionally reaching out to them, and communicating this perspective-taking and empathic concern in open, appropriate ways. Practicing responsible perception means not just mastering the knowledge of perception presented in these pages, but translating this intellectual mastery into active practice during every interpersonal encounter. We all use perception as the basis for our communication and relationship decisions. But when we practice *responsible* perception, the natural result is more competent communication and wiser relationship choices.

We began this chapter with an account of a football game marked by brutality and accusations of unfair play and an examination of its perceptual aftermath. Following the Dartmouth-Princeton game, fans from both sides felt the opposition had played dirty and that their own team had behaved honorably. Although there was only one game, fans perceived two radically different contests.

When you observe the "game film" of your own life, how often do you perceive others as instigating all of the rough play and penalties you've suffered while seeing yourself as blameless? Do you widen the perceptual gulf between yourself and those who see things differently? Or do you seek to bridge that divide by practicing and communicating empathy?

More than 60 years ago, two teams met on a field of play. Decades later, that game—and people's reactions to it—remind us of our own perceptual limitations and the importance of overcoming them. Although we'll never agree with everyone about everything that goes on around us, we can strive to understand one another's viewpoints much of the time. In doing so, we build lives that connect us to others rather than divide us from them.

POSTSCRIPT

key terms

▶ You can watch brief, illustrative videos of these terms and test your understanding of the concepts online in *VideoCentral: Interpersonal Communication* at bedfordstmartins .com/reflectrelate.

key concepts

Perception as a Process

- We make sense of our interpersonal world through **perception**, a process during which we engage in **selection**, **organization**, and **interpretation** of information received from our senses. This process begins when we focus our attention on certain things, a decision guided by **salience**.

- When we mentally organize information related to interpersonal encounters, we order this information into a chronological sequence that reflects how we experienced the event. When people disagree on **punctuation**, conflicts can arise.

- We interpret the meaning of communication in part by drawing on known information stored in our mental **schemata**. We also make **attributions** regarding why people said and did certain things. Sometimes we fall prey to the **fundamental attribution error**, the **actor-observer effect**, and the **self-serving bias**, all of which draw us away from interpreting communication accurately.

- According to **Uncertainty Reduction Theory**, we commonly experience uncertainty during first encounters with new acquaintances. A number of strategies are available for reducing uncertainty, each of which has advantages and disadvantages.

Influences on Perception

- Culture plays a major role in shaping our perception of communication. When we perceive people as **ingroupers**, we typically view them and their communication more positively than if we perceive them as **outgroupers**.

- Although few gender differences actually exist in how people communicate, people perceive the communication of men and women in very different ways.

- **Personality** influences our perception of the traits we possess and how we perceive the traits of others. **Implicit personality theories** help guide our perceptions of others' personalities. Sometimes they lead us to presume in others traits that they actually don't possess, resulting in ineffective and inappropriate communication.

Forming Impressions of Others

- When we perceive others, we form **interpersonal impressions**. Sometimes we create general **Gestalts**, which quite often are positive, thanks to the **positivity bias**.

- The **negativity effect** plays an important role in shaping how we perceive information that we learn about others.

- When we form strong positive or negative Gestalts, this sometimes leads to a **halo effect** or a **horn effect**. Both of these cause us to perceive subsequent information we learn about people in distorted ways.

- The most accurate and refined impressions of others are **algebraic impressions**. When we carefully calculate our impressions based on each individual trait, we're more likely to see people as they really are and be able to adapt our communication accordingly.

- The most common form of interpersonal impression is **stereotyping** because the first thing we perceive about people is often their social group membership.

Improving Your Perception of Others

- You can improve your perception and communication by feeling and expressing **empathy**. When you can take the perspective of others and experience empathic concern toward them, your communication naturally becomes more sensitive and adaptive.

- Embracing **world-mindedness** by accepting others' cultural expressions without judgment is the opposite of **ethnocentrism**.

- Responsible perception is rooted in **perception-checking**, routinely questioning your own perceptions and correcting errors that may lead to ineffective communication.

key skills

- Ever experience disputes regarding "who started it"? See pages 77–78 to find out why, as well as how such conflicts can be avoided.

- Want to improve your attribution accuracy when online? Check out the *Skills Practice* on page 81.

- How can you reduce uncertainty during first encounters? Learn the different strategies and their advantages and disadvantages on pages 82–84.

- Curious about personality and how it shapes perception? Take the *Self-Quiz* on page 91, and read about the effects of personality on perception on pages 89–92.

- Why do people think first impressions are so important? Review the importance of first impressions and negative information in shaping impressions on pages 92–95, as well as the risks associated with placing too much emphasis on this information.

- Want to form more accurate, balanced, and flexible impressions of others? Learn how by reading pages 95–96 and completing the *Skills Practice* on page 96.

- Not sure how to effectively express empathy toward others? Try the *Skills Practice* on page 100 for suggestions on how to experience and express empathy.

- Are you an empathic person? Take the *Self-Quiz* on page 100 to discover your level of perspective-taking and empathic concern.

- Want to master a straightforward process for checking your perceptual accuracy? Consult the steps of perception-checking on pages 101 and 104.

- How would you communicate with a difficult group member you perceive as an outgrouper? Work through *Making Relationship Choices* on pages 102–103 to find out.

4

Experiencing and Expressing Emotions

Emotion fills our lives with meaning

When radio personality and producer Vy Higginsen created the nonprofit Gospel for Teens program, her mission was to teach teens gospel music.[1] Higginsen and a group of volunteer instructors met weekly with kids ages 13 to 19, honing their vocal skills and sharing with them the history of gospel. As Higginsen notes, "The lyrics of gospel songs provide courage, inner strength, and hope for a better life in the future." But she quickly found that her program wouldn't only be about introducing gospel to a generation more versed in rap and hip-hop. Instead, Gospel for Teens would become a powerful vehicle for helping teens manage intense and challenging emotions.

Higginsen originally instituted a simple rule governing emotions and program participation: *leave the baggage at the door*. As she describes, "The teen years are a vulnerable time in kids' lives, and they are dealing with shyness, anxiety, trauma, and family dysfunction. Many students are uncomfortable about their physical appearance and self-esteem based on the peers around them. Some are overcome with anxiety from their home life, school, and thoughts of their futures." To keep difficult emotions from hindering performances, Higginsen started each singing session by having participants stand up and shake their hands, arms, legs, and

---

[1]The information that follows is adapted from a personal interview with the author, October 2011, and www.mamafoundation.org, retrieved October 12, 2011. Interview content published with permission from Vy Higginsen.

4 / Experiencing and Expressing Emotions

feet, physically purging themselves of emotional constraints. As she instructed, "Any worry, any pain, any problem with your mother, your father, your sister, your brother, the boyfriend, the girlfriend, I want that out now of your consciousness. That's your baggage; leave the bags outside because *this* time is for you!"

But Higginsen's "no baggage" policy was abandoned when the cousin of one of her most talented students was shot and killed. Higginsen realized that many program participants had suffered similar tragedies, and that her class could provide a forum within which students could safely share their stories, their pain, and their grief with one another—working together to begin healing. As she describes, "Our teens are living a very adult life—their friends and family are getting murdered, dying from diseases and drugs—and it's leaving emotional scars on them. They

need something uplifting in their lives. So I decided to allow the students to bring their baggage in. I invited the students to share what was happening in their worlds. I wasn't trying to fix their situations because I couldn't—but their being heard was a profound step in their being healed. It made our choir realize we are not alone in our experience. We made a connection, emotionally, personally, and interpersonally."

Whereas Higginsen once encouraged students to leave their emotions at the door, she now realizes that the experience of singing—and sharing the experience of singing with others—provides students with a powerful vehicle for managing negative emotions in positive ways. "I would like the teens to take away the idea that we have emotions yet we are not our emotions. We can recover and thrive by changing our mind and rechanneling our energy through music, art, service, acceptance, meditation, and practice. In simple terms, we can rechannel the negative to the positive and use this as an opportunity for excellence. Gospel music has the power to empower and transform. More than anything, I want my students to know that joy, hope, faith, and goodness are possible."

Emotion fills our lives with meaning (Berscheid & Peplau, 2002). To experience emotion is to feel "alive," and to lack emotion is to view life itself as colorless and meaningless (Frijda, 2005). Because emotion is so important, we feel compelled to express our emotional experiences to others through communication. And when we share our emotions with others, they transition from private and personal to profoundly interpersonal. It's at this point that choice becomes relevant. We may not be able to select our emotions before they arise, but we can choose how to handle and convey them after they occur. When we intelligently manage and competently communicate emotional experiences, our relationship satisfaction and overall life happiness increase. When we don't, our relationships suffer, and these lapses are reflected in relationships and lives torn by anger and sadness.

In this chapter, we examine the most personal and interpersonal of human experiences—emotion. You'll learn:

- The important differences between emotions, feelings, and moods, as well as the best approaches to managing negative moods
- Ways in which gender, personality, and culture influence emotion
- Why improving your emotional intelligence can help you more competently manage your experience and expression of emotion
- How to deal with emotional challenges such as communicating empathy online, fading romantic passion, managing anger, and suffering grief.

The Nature of Emotion

Distinguishing between emotions, feelings, and moods

Take a moment and recall the most recent "emotion" you felt. What comes to mind? For most people, it's a "hot" emotion—that is, a physically and mentally intense experience like joy, anger, or grief, during which your palms sweated, your mouth felt dry, and your heart pounded (Berscheid & Regan, 2005). When we are asked to translate these emotions into words, we use vivid physical metaphors. Joy makes "our hearts leap" while anger makes "our blood boil." Grief is "a living hell" (Frijda, 2005). Understanding what emotions are and how they differ from feelings and moods are the first steps in better managing our emotions.

DEFINING EMOTION

Scholarly definitions of emotion mirror our everyday experiences. **Emotion** is an intense reaction to an event that involves interpreting event meaning, becoming physiologically aroused, labeling the experience as emotional, managing reactions, and communicating through emotional displays and disclosures (Gross, Richards, & John, 2006). This definition highlights the five key features of emotion. First, emotion is reactive, triggered by our perception of outside events

▶ Emotions are not just internally felt but are also expressed through body language, gestures, facial expressions, and other physical behaviors.

(Cacioppo, Klein, Berntson, & Hatfield, 1993). A friend telling you that her cancer is in remission leads you to experience joy. Receiving a scolding text message from a parent triggers both your surprise and your anger. When an emotion-inducing event occurs, we engage in the same perceptual process as we do with other types of interpersonal events—selecting, organizing, and interpreting information related to that event. As we interpret the event's meaning, we decide whether the incident is positive, neutral, negative, or somewhere in-between, triggering corresponding emotions (Smith & Kirby, 2004).

A second feature of emotion is that it involves physiological arousal in the form of increased heart rate, blood pressure, and adrenaline release. Many researchers consider arousal *the* defining feature of emotion, a belief mirrored in most people's descriptions of emotion as "intense" and "hot" (Berscheid, 2002).

Third, to experience emotion, you must become aware of your interpretation and arousal as "an emotion"—that is, you must consciously label them as such (Berscheid, 2002). For example, imagine that you and a good friend have struck a bargain not to discuss with anyone else an event that embarrassed you. One evening while checking Facebook, you see that he has posted your tale of humiliation in his status update. Within seconds, you interpret his behavior as negative—a betrayal of your trust. Your face grows hot, your breathing quickens, and you become consciously aware of these physical sensations. This awareness, combined with your assessment of the situation, causes you to label your experience as the emotion "anger."

Fourth, how we each experience and express our emotions is constrained by historical, cultural, relational, and situational norms governing what is and isn't appropriate (Metts & Planalp, 2002). As a consequence, once we become aware that we're experiencing an emotion, we try to manage that experience and express that emotion in ways we consider acceptable. We may allow our emotion

self-reflection

Recall an emotional event in a close relationship. What specific action triggered your emotion? How did you interpret the triggering event? What physical sensations resulted? What does this tell you about the link between events, mind, and body that is the basis of emotional experience?

to dominate our thoughts and communication, try to channel it in constructive ways, or suppress our emotion completely. Emotion management results from the recognition that the totally unrestrained experience and expression of emotion will lead to negative consequences.

Finally, when emotion occurs, the choices you make regarding emotion management are reflected outward in your verbal and nonverbal displays, in the form of word choices, exclamations or expletives, facial expressions, body posture, and gestures (Mauss, Levenson, McCarter, Wilhelm, & Gross, 2005). The communicative nature of emotion is so fundamental that emoticons have been developed to represent emotional expressions in mediated communication like text messages and e-mail. Emoticons enable people to convey happiness, sadness, anger, and other emotions (see Table 4.1).

Another way in which emotion is communicative is that we talk about our emotional experiences with others, a form of communication known as **emotion-sharing**. Much of interpersonal communication consists of emotion-sharing—disclosing emotions, talking about them, and pondering them. Studies on emotion-sharing suggest that people share between 75 and 95 percent of their emotional experiences with at least one other person, usually a spouse, parent, or friend (Frijda, 2005). The people with whom we share our emotions generally enjoy being confided in. Often, they share the incident with others, weaving a socially intimate network of emotion-sharing. The teens in the Gospel for Teens program (described in our chapter opener) use emotion-sharing to connect with one another and collaboratively work together to heal their individual experiences of grief and anger.

Sometimes emotion-sharing leads to **emotional contagion**, when the experience of the same emotion rapidly spreads from one person to others. Emotional contagion can be positive, such as when the joy you experience over an unexpected job promotion spreads to your family members as you tell them about it. At other times, emotional contagion can be negative, such as when fear moves quickly from person to person in a large crowd. Such was the case in the 1903 stampede in Chicago's Iroquois Theater, one of the deadliest disasters in American history. A small fire broke out, and although it was quickly extinguished, people's fear of the fire swept through the crowd, causing a panicked stampede that killed more than 500 people (Brown, 1965).

FEELINGS AND MOODS

We often talk about emotions, feelings, and moods as if they are the same thing. But they're not. **Feelings** are short-term emotional reactions to events that generate only limited arousal; they typically do not trigger attempts to manage their experience or expression (Berscheid, 2002). We experience dozens, if not hundreds, of feelings daily—most of them lasting only a few seconds or minutes. An attractive stranger casts you an approving smile, causing you to feel momentarily flattered. A friend texts you unexpectedly when you're trying to study, making you feel briefly annoyed. Feelings are like "small emotions." Common feelings include gratitude, concern, pleasure, relief, and resentment.

table 4.1
Common Emoticons

:o	Surprised
:D	Joyous
:(	Sad
:)	Happy
8O	Astonished
>:(	Annoyed
>:<	Angry

self-reflection

With whom do you share your emotional experiences? Does such sharing always have a positive impact on your relationships, or does it cause problems at times? What ethical boundaries govern emotion-sharing?

⬤ It can be tempting to improve bad moods by drinking alcohol or caffeinated beverages, taking recreational drugs, or eating. However, studies show that one of the best ways to feel better is through physical exercise.

Whereas emotions occur occasionally in response to substantial events and feelings arise frequently in response to everyday incidents, moods are different. **Moods** are low-intensity states—such as boredom, contentment, grouchiness, or serenity—that are not caused by particular events and typically last longer than feelings or emotions (Parkinson, Totterdell, Briner, & Reynolds, 1996). Positive or negative, moods are the slow-flowing emotional currents in our everyday lives. We can think of our frequent, fleeting feelings and occasional intense emotions as riding on top of these currents, as displayed in Figure 4.1.

Moods powerfully influence our perception and interpersonal communication. People who describe their moods as "good" are more likely to form positive impressions of others than those who report being in "bad" moods (Forgas & Bower, 1987). Similarly, people in good moods are more likely than those in bad moods to perceive new acquaintances as sociable, honest, giving, and creative (Fiedler, Pampe, & Scherf, 1986). Our moods also influence how we talk with partners in close relationships (Cunningham, 1988). People in good moods are significantly more likely to disclose relationship thoughts and concerns to close

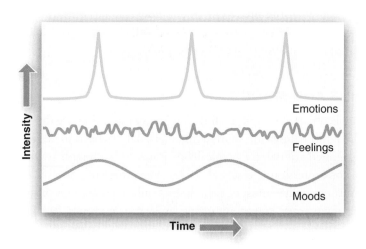

figure 4.1 **The Flow of Emotions, Feelings, and Moods**

friends, family members, and romantic partners. People in bad moods typically prefer to sit and think, to be left alone, and to avoid social and leisure activities (Cunningham, 1988).

Your mood's profound effect on your perception and interpersonal communication suggests that it's important to learn how to shake yourself out of a bad mood (Thayer, Newman, & McClain, 1994). Unfortunately, some of the most commonly practiced strategies for improving bad moods—drinking alcohol or caffeinated beverages, taking recreational drugs, and eating—are also the least effective and may actually worsen your mood (Thayer et al., 1994). More effective strategies for improving bad moods are ones that involve active expenditures of energy, especially strategies that combine relaxation, stress management, mental focus and energy, and exercise. The most effective strategy of all appears to be rigorous physical exercise (Thayer et al., 1994). Sexual activity does not seem to consistently elevate mood.

self-reflection

How do you behave toward others when you're in a bad mood? What strategies do you use to better your mood? Are these practices effective in elevating your mood and improving your communication in the long run, or do they merely provide a temporary escape or distraction?

TYPES OF EMOTIONS

Take a moment and look at the emotions communicated by the people in the photos on pages 116–117. How can you discern the emotion expressed in each picture? One way to distinguish between different types of emotions is to examine consistent patterns of facial expressions, hand gestures, and body postures that characterize specific emotions. By considering these patterns, scholars have identified six emotions they consider **primary emotions**—emotions that involve unique and consistent behavioral displays across cultures (Ekman, 1972). The six primary emotions are surprise, joy, disgust, anger, fear, and sadness.

Some situations, like receiving an unexpected gift from a romantic partner or experiencing the death of a close relative, provoke especially intense primary emotions. In such cases, we often use different words to describe the emotion, even though what we're experiencing is simply a more intense version of the same primary emotion (Plutchik, 1980). For instance, receiving a gift from a romantic partner may cause intense joy that we think of as "ecstasy," just as the passing of a close relative likely will trigger intense sadness that we label as "grief" (see Table 4.2).

table 4.2 Intense Primary Emotions

Primary Emotion	High-Intensity Counterpart
Surprise	Amazement
Joy	Ecstasy
Disgust	Loathing
Anger	Rage
Fear	Terror
Sadness	Grief

In other situations, an event may trigger two or more primary emotions simultaneously, resulting in an experience known as **blended emotions** (Plutchik, 1993). For example, imagine that you're borrowing your romantic partner's computer when a "new message" e-mail alert pops up. Giving in to temptation, you click to the message, only to read, "Thinking of you constantly since our

Happiness across Cultures

A Chinese proverb warns, "We are never happy for a thousand days, a flower never blooms for a hundred" (Myers, 2002, p. 47). Although most of us understand that our positive emotions may be more passing than permanent, we tend to presume that greater joy lies on the other side of various cultural fences. If only we made more money, lived in a better place, or even were a different age or gender, *then* we truly would be happy. But the science of human happiness has torn down these fences, suggesting instead that happiness is interpersonally based.

Consider class, the most common cultural fence believed to divide the happy from the unhappy. Studies suggest that wealth actually has little effect on happiness. Across countries and cultures, happiness is unaffected by the gain of additional money once people have basic human rights, safe and secure shelter, sufficient food and water, meaningful activity with which to occupy their time, and worthwhile relationships.

What about age? The largest cross-cultural study of happiness and age ever conducted, which examined 170,000 people in 16 countries, found no difference in reported happiness and life satisfaction based on age (Myers, 2002). And gender? Differences in gender account for less than 1 percent in reported life happiness (Michalos, 1991; Wood, Rhodes, & Whelan, 1989). Men

and women around the globe all report roughly similar levels of happiness. Even population density drops as a predictor of joy: people in rural areas, towns, suburbs, and big cities report similar levels of happiness (Crider, Willits, & Kanagy, 1991).

When asked, "What is necessary for your happiness?" people overwhelmingly cite satisfying close relationships with family, friends, and romantic partners at the top of their lists (Berscheid & Peplau, 2002). Faith also matters. Studies over the past 20 years in both Europe and the United States repeatedly have documented that people who are religious are more likely to report being happy and satisfied with life than those who are nonreligious (Myers, 2002). Finally, living a healthy life breeds joy. The positive effect of exercise on mood extends to broader life satisfaction: people who routinely exercise report substantially higher levels of happiness and well-being than those who don't (Myers, 2002).

discussion questions

- What are your own sources of happiness and life satisfaction?
- Do you agree that interpersonal relationships, spiritual beliefs, and healthy living are the most essential ingredients for happiness?

According to studies performed by psychologist Paul Ekman (1972), people around the world associate the same facial expressions with particular feelings. Part of improving your interpersonal communication is to recognize others' emotions. Can you identify the ones displayed in each of these photographs? (From left to right, the emotions shown are joy, surprise, anger, disgust, fear, and sadness.)

night together. Can't wait to see you this weekend!" What emotion do you experience at that moment? Many people in this situation would experience jealousy, a blended emotion because it combines the primary emotions anger, fear, and sadness (Guerrero & Andersen, 1998): in this case, *anger* at your partner, *fear* that your relationship may be threatened, and *sadness* at the thought of potentially losing your partner to a rival. Other examples of blended emotions include contempt (anger and disgust), remorse (disgust and sadness), and awe (surprise and fear) (Plutchik, 1993).

While North Americans often identify six primary emotions—surprise, joy, love, anger, fear, and sadness (Shaver, Wu, & Schwartz, 1992)—some cultural variation exists. For example, in traditional Chinese culture, shame and sad love (an emotion concerning attachment to former lovers) are primary emotions. Traditional Hindu philosophy suggests nine primary emotions: sexual passion, amusement, sorrow, anger, fear, perseverance, disgust, wonder, and serenity (Shweder, 1993).

Forces Shaping Emotion

Culture, gender, and personality affect emotion

What I remember most about that Tuesday morning, besides its absolute normalcy, was the beauty of the day. It was gorgeous outside, with a deep ocean-blue sky and a bite in the air that seemed to say, "Autumn is coming!" Driving my boys to school before heading to the university, I was listening to my favorite radio station when the DJ joked about how "some idiot has apparently managed to fly his plane into the Twin Towers." Within minutes, however, the truth of that day filled the television and radio airwaves. As rage and grief surged within me, I felt an almost primal compulsion to communicate with my closest intimates. I rushed home to talk with my wife, phoned my friends in New York to make sure they were OK, and called my parents and my brother.

Arriving in the lecture hall an hour later, I found a classroom full of students equally eager to share their emotions. But although we all felt intense negative emotions, the specific nature of our experiences and expressions cut along lines carved by culture, gender, and personality. Visiting students from other countries displayed widely varying reactions. Some remained sad and silent; others offered quiet condolences or openly vented their anger. Whereas most of the women in my class expressed grief over the loss of life, the men felt blindingly angry.

VideoCentral ▣

bedfordstmartins.com
/reflectrelate

Blended Emotions
Watch this clip online to answer the questions below.

What blended emotions is the woman in the video experiencing? What type of situation could cause this? What types of communication situations make you experience blended emotions? Why?

Want to see more? Check out VideoCentral for a clip on **emotional contagion**.

Personality also seemed to make a difference. For example, my less agreeable students vocalized their anger and insisted that the attacks confirmed "the innate evil of human nature."

After September 11, 2001, people around the globe were united by emotional pain. But the faces and voices I saw and heard in my classroom on the morning of 9/11 were both united and divided. We were united in a newly forged bond of anger and sadness over the loss of so many innocent lives, but divided along lines of culture, gender, and personality in how we each experienced this bitter bond.

CULTURE

In all cultures, children are taught guidelines for where, when, and how to manage and communicate emotions (Saarni, 1993). When people in a given culture agree about which forms of emotion management and communication are socially desirable and appropriate, these norms are called **display rules**. Display rules powerfully shape how we each communicate our emotional experiences to others. For example, on the morning of 9/11, when individuals from disparate cultures experienced the same negative emotions, the manner in which they communicated these emotions differed widely depending on the students' cultural display rules. Some openly wept or angrily shouted; others silently mourned.

Because of differences in socialization, traditions, and ideals, display rules show considerable variation across cultures (Soto, Levenson, & Ebling, 2005). Consider the two fastest-growing ethnic groups in the United States—Mexican Americans and Chinese Americans (Buriel & De Ment, 1997). In traditional Chinese culture, emotional control and moderation are emphasized above all else; intense emotions are considered dangerous and are even thought to cause illness (Wu & Tseng, 1985). This belief shapes communication in close relationships as well; Chinese American couples discussing their relationships display fewer periods of openly expressed positive emotion toward one another than do Euro-American couples (Tsai & Levenson, 1997). In contrast, traditional Mexican culture encourages openly expressing emotion, even more so than in Euro-American culture (Soto et al., 2005). For people of Mexican descent, the experience, open expression, and deep discussion of emotions and feelings provide some of life's greatest rewards and satisfactions.

When families emigrate to a new society, the move often provokes tension over which set of display rules should be honored. People more closely oriented to their cultures of origin continue to communicate their emotions in traditional ways. Others—usually the first generation of children born in the new society—may move away from traditional forms of expression (Soto et al., 2005). For example, Chinese Americans who adhere strongly to traditional Chinese culture openly display fewer negative emotions than those who are Americanized (Soto

VideoCentral ◉

bedfordstmartins.com /reflectrelate

Display Rules
Watch this clip online to answer the questions below.

Is the couple in the video breaking or conforming to display rules? How? What experiences have you had with cultural differences in display rules, for example, governing how people show affection in public, express grief, or celebrate joy?

◖ A father who lost his son on 9/11 has an emotional response to seeing his son's name at the North Pool of the 9/11 Memorial in New York City.

What display rules did you learn growing up? How have these rules shaped your communication? Have you ever caused offense by expressing emotion in a way that violates these rules? If so, what lesson did you learn about the relationship between display rules and competent interpersonal communication?

et al., 2005). Similarly, Mexican Americans with strong ties to traditional Mexican culture express intense negative emotion more openly than "Americanized" Mexican Americans.

Competent interpersonal communicators adjust their expression of emotion according to the cultural background of the people with whom they're interacting. Keep in mind that the exact same emotional expression—for example, an open and vivid venting of intense joy—might be considered an enormous breach of social etiquette in some cultures but a healthy and normal behavior in others.

GENDER

Across cultures, women report experiencing more sadness, fear, shame, and guilt than men, while men report feeling more anger and other hostile emotions (Fischer, Rodriguez Mosquera, van Vianen, & Manstead, 2004). In Western cultures, gender differences in emotion derive in part from differences in how men and women orient to interpersonal relationships (Brody & Hall, 2000). Women are more likely than men to express emotions that support relationships and suppress emotions that assert their own interests over another's (Zahn-Waxler, 2001). As a consequence, women may feel sadness more often than men, because sadness, unlike anger, isn't directed outward at another person; thus, it doesn't threaten relationships. Sadness communicates personal vulnerability and signals the need for comforting from others. It therefore reflects a willingness to submit oneself to the care of another. By contrast, anger conveys a motivation to achieve one's own goals or to take satisfaction in one's success over another's (Chaplin, Cole, & Zahn-Waxler, 2005).

Though men and women may experience emotions with different frequency and express these emotions differently, when they experience the same emotions, there is no difference in the intensity of the emotion experienced (Fischer et al., 2004). Whether it's anger, sadness, joy, or disgust, men *and* women experience these emotions with equal intensity.

PERSONALITY

Like culture and gender, personality exerts a pronounced impact on our emotions. Recall the Big Five personality traits described in Chapter 3—openness, conscientiousness, extraversion, agreeableness, and neuroticism (or OCEAN). Of these five, three strongly influence our experience and communication of emotion (Pervin, 1993). The first is *extraversion*, the degree to which one is outgoing and sociable versus quiet and reserved. High-extraversion people experience positive emotions more frequently than low-extraversion people. The greater occurrence of positive emotions appears to be due to enhanced sensitivity to positive events. Put simply, high-extraversion people "look for happiness" in their everyday lives, focusing their attention more on positive events than on negative (Larsen & Ketelaar, 1991). High-extraversion people also rate themselves as better able to cope with stress and more skilled at managing their emotional communication than do low-extraversion people (Lopes, Salovey, Cote, & Beers, 2005).

Another personality trait that influences emotion is *agreeableness*. People high in agreeableness—those who are trusting, friendly, and cooperative—report being happier in general, better able to manage stress, and more skilled at managing their emotional communication than low-agreeable people. High-agreeable people also score substantially higher on measures of emotion management and are rated by their peers as having superior emotion management skills (Lopes et al., 2005).

The tendency to think negative thoughts about oneself, known as *neuroticism*, also affects emotional experience and expression. High-neurotic people focus their attention primarily on negative events (Larsen & Ketelaar, 1991). Consequently, they report more frequent negative emotions than do low-neurotic people and rate themselves as less happy overall. They also describe themselves as less skilled at emotional communication, and they test lower on scientific measures of emotion management than do low-neurotic people (Lopes et al., 2005).

Although these findings seem to suggest that highly neurotic people are doomed to lives of negative emotion, this isn't necessarily the case. Psychologist Albert Ellis (1913–2007) dedicated much of his professional life to helping neurotics change their self-defeating beliefs. Ellis believed that much of neurosis—and its accompanying emotional states such as sadness, anger, and anxiety—is tied to three extreme, irrational beliefs: "I must be outstandingly competent or I am worthless," "Others must treat me considerately or they are absolutely rotten," and "The world should always give me happiness or I will die" (Ellis & Dryden, 1997). Ellis developed **Rational Emotive Behavior Therapy (REBT)** as a way for therapists to help neurotic patients systematically purge themselves of such beliefs.

If you find yourself habitually plagued by negative thoughts similar to those mentioned above, you can use Ellis's five steps on your own to change your thoughts and the negative emotions that flow from them. First, call to mind common situations that lead you to be upset. Second, identify irrational beliefs about your self and others that are tied to these situations. Third, consider the emotional, behavioral, and relational consequences that you suffer as a result of these beliefs—negative outcomes that you would like to change. Fourth, critically challenge these beliefs—disputing their validity. Is there really any support for these beliefs? What evidence contradicts them? What is the worst thing that can happen if you abandon these beliefs? The best thing that can happen? Finally, identify more accurate and realistic beliefs about yourself, others, and the world at large that cause more positive emotional, behavioral, and relational outcomes, and embrace these beliefs fully.

Clearly, your degree of extraversion, agreeableness, and especially neuroticism influences how often you experience positive and negative emotions and how effectively you manage and communicate these emotions. At the same time, keep in mind that personality is merely one of many pieces that make up the complex puzzle that is emotion. Part of becoming a competent emotional communicator is learning how your personality traits shade your emotional experience and expression, and treating personality-based emotion differences in others with sensitivity and understanding.

Managing Your Emotional Experience and Expression

Dealing with emotions before, while, and after they occur

It's arguably the most well-known psychology experiment.[2] Over a six-year period, Stanford psychologist Walter Mischel brought 653 young children from the university's Bing Nursery School into a room and offered them a tasty treat of their choice: marshmallow, Oreo cookie, or pretzel stick. But he also presented them with a dilemma. If they could resist eating the treat while he stepped out for several minutes, they would get a second treat as a reward. The children were then left alone. The experiment was a simple test of impulse control: the ability to manage one's emotional arousal, excitement, and desire. Most of the kids gave in and ate the treat, usually in less than three minutes. But about 30 percent held out. Years later, Mischel gathered more data from the same children—who were then in high school. He was stunned to learn that their choices in the experiment predicted a broad range of outcomes. Children who had waited were more socially skilled, better able to cope with stress, less likely to have emotional outbursts when frustrated, and better able to deal with temptations, and had closer, more stable friendships than those who hadn't waited. They also had substantially higher SAT scores. Why was "the marshmallow test" such a powerful predictor of long-term personal and interpersonal outcomes? Because it taps a critical skill: the ability to constructively manage emotions. As Mischel notes, "If you can deal with hot emotions in the face of temptation, then you can study for the SAT instead of watching television. It's not just about marshmallows."

⬆ Can you recall a time when you had to resist an emotional impulse or desire, like in the marshmallow study? What was the outcome of this event?

---

[2]The information that follows is adapted from Goleman (2007b); Lehrer (2009); and Shoda, Mischel, and Peake (1990).

EMOTIONAL INTELLIGENCE

Managing your emotions is part of **emotional intelligence**: the ability to interpret emotions accurately and to use this information to manage emotions, communicate them competently, and solve relationship problems (Gross & John, 2002). People with high degrees of emotional intelligence typically possess four skills:

1. Acute understanding of their own emotions

2. Ability to see things from other's perspectives and have a sense of compassion regarding others' emotional states—that is, *empathy*

3. Aptitude for constructively managing their own emotions

4. Capacity for harnessing their emotional states in ways that create competent decision making, communication, and relationship problem solving (Kotzé & Venter, 2011)

To check your own level of emotional intelligence, take the *Self-Quiz* "Assessing Your Emotional Intelligence" on page 124.

Given that emotional intelligence (EI) involves understanding emotions coupled with the ability to manage them in ways that optimize interpersonal competence, it's not surprising that people with high EI experience a broad range of positive outcomes. For example, within leadership positions, people with high EI are more likely than low EI people to garner trust, inspire followers, and be perceived as having integrity (Kotzé & Venter, 2011). High EI individuals are less likely than low EI people to bully people, or use violence to get what they want (Mayer, Salovey, & Caruso, 2004). High EI people even find it easier to forgive relational partners who have wronged them, because of their strong empathy and skill at emotion management (Hodgson & Wertheim, 2007).

Of the skills comprising emotional intelligence, emotion management is arguably the most important one to improve, because—as demonstrated by Mischel's research—it directly influences your communication choices and the outcomes that result (Lopes et al., 2005). How? Put bluntly, *if you can't manage your emotions, you can't communicate competently.* **Emotion management** involves attempts to influence which emotions you have, when you have them, and how you experience and express them (Gross et al., 2006). Emotions naturally trigger attempts to manage them. Consequently, the practical issue is not whether you will manage your emotions but how you can do so in ways that improve your interpersonal communication and relationships.

MANAGING YOUR EMOTIONS AFTER THEY OCCUR

One strategy for managing emotions is to try to modify or control them after we become aware of them (Gross et al., 2006). An event triggers arousal, interpretation, and awareness of an emotion. We then consciously try to modify our internal experience and outward communication of that emotion.

The two most common ways people manage emotions after they have been triggered are suppression and venting. **Suppression** involves inhibiting

self-QUIZ

Assessing Your Emotional Intelligence

Consider your emotional experience and communication in your daily life. Then look at the statements listed under each of the four emotional intelligence dimensions, placing a check mark next to each statement that describes your abilities. Follow the directions below to interpret your score.

Perceiving Emotions

Accurately perceiving and interpreting emotional messages as they are communicated by others' facial expressions, vocal tones, and gestures; accurately perceiving your own emotions based on your physiological and mental experiences

_____ I can accurately identify emotions experienced by other people.

_____ I can accurately identify my own emotions by interpreting my physical and psychological states.

_____ I can communicate my emotions accurately to others.

_____ I can discriminate between accurate/honest feelings and inaccurate/dishonest feelings in myself and others.

Understanding Emotions

Accurately labeling emotions and learning how they blend together and change over time

_____ I understand the similarities and differences between various emotions.

_____ I understand the causes and consequences of emotions.

_____ I understand the differences between feelings, moods, emotions, and blended emotions.

_____ I understand how the experience of emotion changes as time passes.

Using Emotions to Facilitate Thinking

Recognizing how emotions and moods influence perception and learning to harness emotional states for more effective problem solving, reasoning, decision making, and creative endeavors

_____ I can redirect and reorganize my thoughts based on emotions I am experiencing.

_____ I can use my emotions to help improve my relationship choices.

_____ I can use my mood changes to help appreciate different points of view.

_____ I can use my emotions to facilitate problem solving and creativity.

Managing Emotional Experience and Communication

Learning how to manage the experience and communication of emotions to avoid negative or destructive consequences

_____ I am open to experiencing both pleasant and unpleasant emotions.

_____ I monitor and reflect on my emotions.

_____ I can engage in, prolong, or detach from an emotional state, depending on whether I perceive it as constructive or destructive.

_____ I effectively manage my own emotions.

Note: Information in this _Self-Quiz_ is adapted from Mayer and Salovey (1997).

Scoring: Count the number of check marks you made in each dimension. Scores of 0–2 for a particular dimension represent an area of emotional intelligence that needs strengthening; scores of 3–4 represent an area of strength.

thoughts, arousal, and outward behavioral displays of emotion (Richards, Butler, & Gross, 2003). For example, one participant in an emotion management study describes suppressing his communication of happiness and surprise after scoring well on a college paper in which he had invested little effort (Gross et al., 2006):

> I didn't work very hard on this paper so I was surprised. My roommate actually did some work and didn't get a good grade, so he was very down about it. I was very happy inside, but at the same time, I didn't want to show up my roommate because he's my friend. Instead of acting happy and surprised, I kind of put on my academic sad face and said, "Oh, I didn't do well either." (p. 11)

The desire to suppress stems from the recognition that feeling, thinking, and openly communicating certain emotions would be relationally, socially, or culturally inappropriate. Although people sometimes suppress positive emotion, suppression occurs most commonly with negative emotions, especially anger and sadness (Gross et al., 2006). This is because displays of pleasant emotions elicit favorable responses from others, whereas the expression of negative emotions often drives other people away (Argyle & Lu, 1990; Furr & Funder, 1998).

Suppression is the most widely practiced strategy for managing unavoidable and unwanted emotions. But its effectiveness is marginal, because you are trying to modify intense arousal you are already experiencing, the thoughts you are already thinking, and the body's natural inclination to display this arousal and these thoughts in the form of expressions (Lopes et al., 2005).

The inverse of suppression is **venting**: allowing emotions to dominate our thoughts and explosively expressing them (Fuendeling, 1998; Kostiuk & Fouts, 2002). Venting may be positive, such as when we jump up and shout for joy after learning we got the job we wanted. At other times, we vent negative emotions, such as when we "blow up" at a spouse or other family member who has been pestering us repeatedly.

PREVENTING EMOTIONS

An alternative to managing emotions after they occur is to prevent unwanted emotions from happening in the first place. Four strategies are commonly used for preventing emotions (Gross et al., 2006), the first of which is **encounter avoidance**: staying away from people, places, or activities that you know will provoke emotions you don't want to experience. For example, suppose that seeing

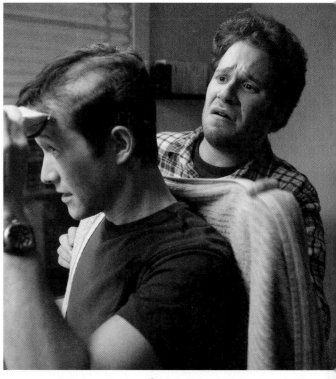

⬤ When Adam Lerner is diagnosed with cancer in the movie *50/50*, he finds it difficult to manage the multiple emotions he experiences. At times, his diagnosis triggers emotions that lead him to behave fearlessly, like when he shaves off his hair.

self-reflection

Consider your own use of suppression and venting. What leads you to choose one or the other strategy? Are there limits to how often you vent or how long you suppress? What ethical considerations arise related to each strategy?

a former romantic partner always provokes intense and unpleasant emotions within you. To use encounter avoidance, you might find out your ex's work or class schedule and then adjust your own schedule so that you systematically avoid running into him or her.

A second preventive strategy is **encounter structuring**: intentionally avoiding specific topics that you know will provoke unwanted emotion during encounters with others. For example, I love my in-laws (honestly!), but my political attitudes are very different from theirs. Early in our acquaintanceship, my father-in-law and I would both get angry whenever we discussed politics. After a few such battles, we agreed to avoid this topic and now structure our encounters so politics isn't discussed.

A third preventive strategy is **attention focus**: intentionally devoting your attention only to aspects of an event or encounter that you know will not provoke an undesired emotion. Imagine that you're at a family get-together. As your dad is showing everyone footage from your family's recent vacation, two of your cousins sitting in the back of the room are quietly making fun of your father's new haircut. To use attention focus, you would actively keep watching and listening to your dad so that your cousins' rudeness doesn't set you off.

A fourth way people preventively manage emotion is **deactivation**: systematically desensitizing yourself to emotional experience (Fuendeling, 1998). Some people, especially after experiencing a traumatic emotional event, decide that they no longer want to feel anything. The result is an overall deadening of emotion. Though the desire to use this strategy is understandable, deactivation can trigger deep depression.

REAPPRAISING YOUR EMOTIONS

Imagine that you (like me) occasionally receive friendly e-mails or Facebook messages from former romantic partners. You feel ethically obligated to share these messages with your current partner, but you also know that when you do, he or she will respond by popping off nasty remarks about your ex that anger you. Knowing this will happen, how can you best manage the emotions that will arise?

The most fruitful strategy for engaging difficult and unavoidable emotions is **reappraisal**: actively changing how you think about the meaning of emotion-eliciting situations so that their emotional impact is changed (Jackson, Malmstadt, Larson, & Davidson, 2000). To use reappraisal in the previous example, you might think vividly about your partner's positive aspects, your mutual love for one another, and your future together (Richards et al., 2003). As a result, you'll be more likely to communicate positively—"I know you don't like my ex, and I can totally understand why; I would feel the same if I was in your shoes"—rather than negatively—"Why do you always feel the need to criticize my ex?!"

Reappraisal is effective because you employ it *before* a full-blown emotional reaction commences. This strategy requires little effort compared to trying to suppress or control your emotions after they've occurred. In addition, reappraisal produces interpersonal communication that is partner-focused and perceived as engaged and emotionally responsive (Gross et al., 2006). Across studies, people who are most effective at managing their emotional communication report reappraisal as their primary strategy (John & Gross, 2004).

Reappraisal is accomplished in two steps. First, before or during an encounter that you suspect will trigger an undesired emotion in yourself, *call to mind the positive aspects of the encounter*. If you truly can't think of anything positive about the other person, your relationship, or the situation, focus on seeing yourself as the kind of person who can constructively communicate even during unpleasant encounters with people you ardently dislike. Second, *consider the short- and long-term consequences of your actions*. Think about how communicating positively in the here-and-now will shape future outcomes in constructive ways.

You can use reappraisal to effectively manage problematic positive emotions as well. Imagine you've spent much of your morning pondering a new romance. Although you're uncertain of your partner's feelings, you realize that you are falling in love. Just then, your partner calls, saying, "I just wanted to say 'Hi.'" Your adrenaline surges, your heart leaps into your throat, and you feel joy. But you also realize that you must manage your emotional communication, lest you overwhelm your partner with your intensity.

To use reappraisal in this case, you would focus your thoughts on your partner's perspective, recalling that you don't yet know whether he or she feels the same way you do. You would remind yourself why your partner has called (to say "Hi"), and assess your relationship (just beginning). Finally, you would consider the potential consequences of this encounter—such as frightening your partner away. With the situation reappraised and your emotions managed, you might say something like, "What a nice surprise—I was just thinking about you!" This may be a far more appropriate response than what might have come out of your mouth had you not reappraised: "I've been thinking about you nonstop all morning and just realized I'm completely in love with you!"

Emotional Challenges

Intense emotions are the most difficult to handle

Each day we face personal trials that trigger difficult-to-manage emotions affecting our communication, relationships, and the quality of our lives. For example, romantic jealousy—which we discuss in Chapter 9—is toxic to interpersonal communication and must be managed effectively for relationships to survive (Guerrero & Andersen, 1998). Likewise, fear—of emotional investment, vulnerability, or long-term commitment—can prevent us from forming intimate connections with others (Mickelson, Kessler, & Shaver, 1997). In the remainder of this chapter, we focus on four such challenges that occur all too frequently in our daily lives: lack of empathy online, anger, passion, and grief.

ONLINE COMMUNICATION AND EMPATHY DEFICITS

After giving a lecture about stereotypes, I received an e-mail from a student: "Stereotypes are DEMEANING!! People should DENOUNCE them, not TEACH them!!! WHY LECTURE ABOUT STEREOTYPES???" Noting

skills practice

Using Reappraisal
Managing difficult emotions through reappraisal

❶ Identify a recurring behavior or event that triggers emotions you'd like to manage more effectively.

❷ When the behavior or event happens, focus your thoughts on positive aspects of yourself, the other person, your relationship, and the situation.

❸ Consider ways to communicate that will foster positive outcomes.

❹ Communicate in those ways.

❺ Observe how your positive thoughts and constructive communication affect the relationship.

the lack of greeting, capped letters, and excessive punctuation, I interpreted the message as angry. Irritated, I popped back a flippant response, "Uhhhh . . . because people often wrongly believe that stereotypes are true?" Hours later, I received a caustic reply: "I think it's really disrespectful of you to treat my question so rudely!! I'M PAYING YOU TO TEACH, NOT MOCK!!!"

You have probably had similar experiences—online encounters in which anger or other emotions were expressed inappropriately, triggering a destructive exchange. In most of these interactions, the messages traded back and forth would never have been expressed face-to-face.

Why are we more likely to inappropriately express our emotions online? Two features of online interaction—asynchronicity and invisibility—help explain this phenomenon (Suler, 2004). Much of our online communication is *asynchronous*. That is, we don't interact with others in real time but instead exchange messages (such as text, e-mail, or Facebook postings) that are read and responded to at later points. When communicating asynchronously, it's almost as if time is magically suspended (Suler, 2004). We know that there likely *will* be responses to our messages, but we choose when (and if) we view those responses. This predisposes us to openly express emotions that we might otherwise conceal if we knew the response would be immediate.

Online communication also provides us with a sense of *invisibility*. Without sharing a physical context with the people with whom we're communicating, we feel as if we're "not really there"—that is, people can't really see or hear us. Consequently, we feel distant from the consequences of our messages.

Recent brain research suggests that our sense of invisibility when communicating online may have a neurological basis. Recall from Chapter 1 that *feedback* consists of the verbal and nonverbal messages recipients convey to indicate their reaction to communication. Now remember our definition of *empathy* from Chapter 3: the ability to experience others' thoughts and emotions. Research documents that the same part of the brain that controls empathy—the orbitofrontal cortex—also monitors feedback (Goleman, 2006). This means that our ability to experience

◉ When we communicate face-to-face, we have the advantage of communicating in real time and having feedback from the person with whom we are interacting. Online communication can cause empathy deficits that we may need to compensate for.

empathy is neurologically tied to our ability to perceive feedback (Beer, John, Scabini, & Knight, 2006). During face-to-face and phone encounters, we constantly track the feedback of others, watching their facial expressions, eye contact, and gestures, and listening to their tone of voice. This enables us to feel empathy for them, to consider what they're thinking and feeling about our communication. When we see or hear people react negatively to something we're saying, we can instantly modify our messages in ways that avoid negative consequences.

Now consider what happens when we lack feedback—such as when we're communicating online. Without the ability to perceive others' immediate responses to our communication, it's difficult for us to experience empathy and to adjust our communication in ways that maintain appropriateness (Goleman, 2007a). We're less able to *perspective-take* (see the situation and our communication from our partner's point of view) and to feel *empathic concern* (experience his or her emotions and feelings). Consequently, we're more likely to express negative emotions—especially anger—in blunt, tactless, and inappropriate ways. We may "shout" at others by using capped letters and exclamation points or we may "say" things we'd never say over the phone or face-to-face. Complicating matters further, people on the receiving end of our communication have the same deficit. Their online messages are less sensitive, less tactful, and maybe even more offensive than their offline messages. *Without feedback, we have difficulty experiencing empathy and gauging the appropriateness of our emotional expression.*

What can you do to experience and express emotions more competently online? First, keep in mind that we do not experience as much empathy online as when we're communicating face-to-face. Compensate for this deficit by investing intense effort into perspective-taking and empathic concern.

Second, communicate these aspects of empathy directly to your online partners, following suggestions from Chapter 3. Integrate into your online messages questions that seek the other person's perspectives, such as "What's your view on this situation?" Validate their views when they provide them: "You make a lot of sense." Communicate empathic concern by saying things like, "I hope you're doing OK." If you receive what looks like an angry message, convey that you recognize the other person is angry and that you feel bad about it: "I feel really terrible that you're so upset."

Third, expect and be tolerant of any aggressive messages you receive, accepting that such behavior is a natural outcome of the online environment, rather than evidence that other people are "mean" or "rude." Finally, avoid crafting and sending angry online messages in the heat of the moment. For instance, my wife has given me a 24-hour rule in such situations: When I get upset during an online encounter, I create a message, and then I store it as a draft (as discussed in Chapter 1). I wait 24 hours, revisit it, assess it in terms of empathy, and then modify or even delete it if it's inappropriate.

ANGER

Anger is a negative primary emotion that occurs when you are blocked or interrupted from attaining an important goal by what you see as the improper action

self-reflection

Recall an online encounter in which you inappropriately expressed emotion. How did lack of empathy shape your behavior? Would you have communicated the same way face-to-face? What does this tell you about the relationship between feedback, empathy, and emotional expression?

skills practice

Managing Anger Online
Responding competently during an online encounter in which you're angry

❶ Identify a message or post that triggers anger.

❷ Before responding, manage your anger.

❸ Practice perspective-taking and empathic concern toward the message source.

❹ Craft a response that expresses empathy, and save it as a draft.

❺ Later, review your message, revise it as necessary, and then send it.

of an external agent (Berkowitz & Harmon-Jones, 2004). As this definition suggests, anger is almost always triggered by someone or something external to us, and is driven by our perception that the interruption is "unfair" (Scherer, 2001). So, for example, when your roommate who is always offering to lend you money refuses to give you a much-needed loan, you're more likely to feel angry if you think he or she can afford to give you the loan but is simply choosing not to (you decide that your roommate's behavior is "unjust" given his or her past offers and your current financial standing). By contrast, if you think your roommate is willing but unable to help you (he or she wants to lend you money but has none to give), you'll be less likely to feel anger toward him or her.

Anger is commonplace: the average person is mildly to moderately angry anywhere from several times a day to several times a week (Berkowitz & Harmon-Jones, 2004). Perhaps because of its frequency, we commonly underestimate anger's destructive potential. We wrongly presume that we can either suppress it or openly express it and that the damage will be minimal. But anger is our most intense and potentially destructive emotion. For example, anger causes perceptual errors that enhance the likelihood we will respond with verbal or physical violence toward others (Lemerise & Dodge, 1993). Both men and women report the desire to punch, smash, kick, bite, or take similar violent actions toward others when they are angry (Carlson & Hatfield, 1992). The impact of anger on interpersonal communication is also devastating. Angry people are more likely to argue, make accusations, yell, swear, and make hurtful and abusive remarks (Knobloch, 2005). Additionally, passive-aggressive communication such as ignoring others, pulling away, giving people dirty looks, and using the "silent treatment" are all more likely to happen when you're angry (Knobloch, 2005).

⚫ Anger is our most intense and potentially destructive emotion. Both men and women report the desire to react to anger in similar ways through verbal or physical violence.

The most frequently used strategy for managing anger is suppression. You "bottle it up" inside rather than let it out. You might pretend that you're not really feeling angry, blocking your angry thoughts and attempting to control

communication of your anger. Occasional suppression can be constructive, such as when open communication of anger would be unprofessional, or when anger has been triggered by mistaken perceptions or attributions. But *always* suppressing anger can cause physical and mental problems: you put yourself in a near-constant state of arousal and negative thinking known as **chronic hostility**. People suffering from chronic hostility spend most of their waking hours simmering in a thinly veiled state of suppressed rage. Their thoughts and perceptions are dominated by the negative. They are more likely than others to believe that human nature is innately evil and that most people are immoral, selfish, exploitative, and manipulative. Ironically, because chronically hostile people believe the worst about others, they tend to be difficult, self-involved, demanding, and ungenerous (Tavris, 1989).

A second common anger management strategy is *venting*: explosively disclosing all of your angry thoughts to whoever triggered them. Many people view venting as helpful and healthy; it "gets the anger out." The assumption that venting will rid you of anger is rooted in the concept of **catharsis**, which holds that openly expressing your emotions enables you to purge them. But in contrast to popular beliefs about the benefits of venting, research suggests that while venting may provide a temporary sense of pleasure, it actually *boosts* anger. One field study of engineers and technicians who were fired from their jobs found that the more individuals vented their anger about the company, the angrier they became (Ebbeson, Duncan, & Konecni, 1975).

To manage your anger, it's better to use strategies such as encounter avoidance, encounter structuring, and reappraisal. In cases where something or someone has already triggered anger within you, consider using the **Jefferson strategy**, named after the third president of the United States. When a person says or does

Test Your Chronic Hostility

Place a check mark next to the statements with which you agree. Count up all your check marks, and then use the Scoring key below to interpret your score.

_____ People are always trying to use me for their own selfish purposes.

_____ It's human nature to be immoral and exploitative.

_____ I can't help but feel angry when I consider the rudeness of others.

_____ People seem to enjoy behaving in ways that annoy and provoke me.

_____ It's hard to not blow up at people, given how they're always screwing up.

_____ I get furious just thinking about how inconsiderate most people are.

_____ Most people are manipulative and they truly sicken me.

Scoring: A score of 0–2 means low hostility. If you've scored in this range, you likely experience anger on an occasional basis, triggered in the normal way by events that you perceive negatively. A score of 3–4 means moderate hostility. If you fall into this range, anger may be an issue of concern in your interpersonal relationships. A score of 5–7 means high hostility. You likely experience anger frequently, and your interpersonal relationships are probably strongly and detrimentally affected by your anger.

something that makes you angry, count slowly to 10 before you speak or act (Tavris, 1989). If you are very angry, count slowly to 100; then speak or act. Thomas Jefferson adopted this simple strategy for reducing his own anger during interpersonal encounters.

Although the Jefferson strategy may seem silly, it's effective because it creates a delay between the event that triggered your anger, the accompanying arousal and awareness, and your communication response. The delay between your internal physical and mental reactions and your outward communication allows your arousal to diminish somewhat, including lowering your adrenaline, blood pressure, and heart rate. Therefore, you communicate in a less extreme (and possibly less inappropriate) way than if you had not "counted to 10." A delay also gives you time for critical self-reflection, perception-checking, and empathy. These three skills can help you identify errors in your assessment of the event or person and plan a competent response. The Jefferson strategy is especially easy to use when you're communicating by e-mail or text-messaging, two media that naturally allow for a delay between receiving a message and responding.

PASSION

When Bella first meets Edward in the book *Twilight*, she is confused, bewildered, and even angered by him and his unpredictable behavior. Over time, however, his ability to surprise her in pleasing ways, and his stunningly handsome appearance, feed a deepening attraction. Eventually, she learns that the passion she feels is mutually shared:

> "Isabella." He pronounced my full name carefully, then playfully ruffled my hair with his free hand. A shock ran through my body at his casual touch. "Bella, I couldn't live with myself if I ever hurt you." He lifted his glorious, agonized eyes to mine. "You are the most important thing to me now. The most important thing to me ever." He raised his free hand and placed it gently on the side of my neck. I sat very still, the chill of his touch a natural warning—a warning telling me to be terrified. But there was no feeling of fear in me. There were, however, other feelings. My blood was racing, and I wished I could slow it, sensing that this must make everything so much more difficult—the thudding of my pulse in my veins. Surely he could hear it. (Meyer, 2005, p. 273)

As illustrated by the incredible success of the *Twilight* book and movie series, few emotions fascinate us more than passion. Thousands of Web sites, infomercials, books, and magazine articles focus on how to create, maintain, or recapture passion. Feeling passion toward romantic partners seems almost obligatory in Western culture, and we often decide to discard relationships when passion fades (Berscheid & Regan, 2005). At the same time, most of us recognize that passion is fleeting and distressingly fragile (Berscheid, 2002).

Passion is a blended emotion, a combination of surprise and joy coupled with a number of positive feelings such as excitement, amazement, and sexual attraction. Akin to Bella's response to Edward, people who elicit passion in us are those

◁ The passion between *Twilight* characters Bella and Edward is mirrored by the offscreen romance of Kristen Stewart and Robert Pattinson—the actors who play the lovers in the film versions.

who communicate in ways that deviate from what we expect (triggering surprise and amazement), whom we interpret positively (generating joy and excitement), and whom we perceive as physically pleasing (leading to sexual attraction).

Because passion stems in large part from surprise, the longer and better you know someone, the less passion you will experience toward that person on a daily basis (Berscheid, 2002). In the early stages of romantic involvements, our partners communicate in ways that are novel and positive. The first time our lovers invite us on a date, kiss us, or disclose their love all are surprising events and intensely passionate. But as partners become increasingly familiar with each other, their communication and behavior do too. Things that once were perceived as unique become predictable. Partners who have known each other intimately for years may be familiar with almost all of the communication behaviors in each other's repertoires (Berscheid, 2002). Consequently, the capacity to surprise partners in dramatic, positive, and unanticipated ways is diminished (Hatfield, Traupmann, & Sprecher, 1984).

Because passion derives from what we perceive as surprising, you can't engineer a passionate evening by carefully negotiating a dinner or romantic rendezvous. You or your partner might experience passion if an event is truly unexpected, but jointly planning and then acting out a romantic candlelight dinner together or spending a weekend in seclusion cannot recapture passion for both you and your partner. When it comes to passion, the best you can hope for in long-term romantic relationships is a warm afterglow (Berscheid, 2002). However, this is not to say that you can't maintain a happy *and* long-term romance; maintaining this kind of relationship requires strategies that we discuss in Chapter 9.

self-reflection

How has passion changed over time in your romantic relationships? What have you and your partners done to deal with these changes? Is passion a necessary component of romance, or is it possible to be in love without passion?

GRIEF

Stop all the clocks, cut off the telephone,
Prevent the dog from barking with a juicy bone,
Silence the pianos and with muffled drum
Bring out the coffin, let the mourners come.
Let aeroplanes circle moaning overhead
Scribbling on the sky the message He Is Dead,
Put crepe bows round the white necks of the public doves,
Let the traffic policemen wear black cotton gloves.
He was my North, my South, my East and West,
My working week and my Sunday rest,
My noon, my midnight, my talk, my song;
I thought that love would last for ever: I was wrong.
The stars are not wanted now: put out every one;
Pack up the moon and dismantle the sun;
Pour away the ocean and sweep up the wood.
For nothing now can ever come to any good.

— W. H. Auden,
"Stop All the Clocks, Cut Off the Telephone"

The intense sadness that follows a substantial loss, known as **grief**, is something each of us will experience. We cannot maintain long-term, intimate involvements with other mortal beings without at some point losing loved ones to death. But grief isn't only about mortality. You're likely to experience grief in response to *any* type of major loss. This may include parental (or personal) divorce, physical disability due to injury, romantic relationship breakup, loss of a much-loved job, or even the destruction or misplacing of a valued object such as an engagement ring or treasured family heirloom.

Managing grief is enormously and uniquely taxing. Unlike other negative emotions such as anger, which is typically triggered by a onetime, short-lived event, grief stays with us for a long time—triggered repeatedly by experiences linked with the loss.

Managing Your Grief   No magic pill can erase the suffering associated with a grievous loss. It seems ludicrous to think of applying strategies such as reappraisal, encounter structuring, or the Jefferson strategy to such pain. Can you systematically change your thoughts about your loss so that the pain goes away? Avoid all mention of your suffering so you feel better? Count to 10 or 100 and find the pain gone? No. Grief is a unique emotional experience, and none of the emotion management strategies discussed in this chapter so far can help you.

Instead, you must use *emotion-sharing*: talking about your grief with others who are experiencing or have experienced similar pain, or people who are skilled at providing you with much-needed emotional support and comfort. Participating in a support group for people who have suffered similar losses can encourage you to

This photograph taken by Arko Datta shows a woman mourning a relative who was killed in the 2004 tsunami in South Asia. It won the World Press Photo Foundation Spot News award in 2005.

share your emotions. When you share your grief, you feel powerfully connected with others—and this sense of connection can be a source of comfort. You also gain affirmation that the grief process you're experiencing is normal. For example, a fellow support-group participant who also lost his mother to cancer might tell you that he, too, finds Mother's Day a particularly painful time or that he, too, finds himself weeping suddenly at inopportune moments. Finally, other participants in a support group can help you remember that grief does get gradually more bearable over time.

For those of us without ready access to face-to-face support groups, online support offers a viable alternative. Besides not requiring transportation and allowing access to written records of any "missed" meetings, online support groups also provide a certain degree of anonymity for people who feel shy or uncomfortable within traditional group settings (Weinberg, Schmale, Uken, & Wessel, 1995). You can interact in a way that preserves some degree of privacy. This is an important advantage, as many people find it easier to "discuss" sensitive topics online than face-to-face, where they'd run the risk of embarrassment (Furger, 1996).

Comforting Others The challenges you face in helping others manage their grief are compounded by the popular tendency to use suppression for managing sadness. The decision to use suppression derives from the widespread belief that it's important to maintain a stoic bearing, a "stiff upper lip," during personal tragedies (Beach, 2002). However, a person who uses suppression to manage

135

⊙ A candlelight vigil can be a powerful source of comfort and connection for those grieving similar losses.

VideoCentral ▶

bedfordstmartins.com /reflectrelate

Supportive Communication

Watch this clip online to answer the questions below.

What supportive messages are given in this video? How successful are they? If you had to comfort someone grieving, how would you convey supportive communication?

grief can end up experiencing stress-related disorders such as chronic anxiety or depression. Also, the decision to suppress can lead even normally open and communicative people to stop talking about their feelings. This places you in the awkward position of trying to help others manage emotions that they themselves are unwilling to admit they are experiencing.

The best way you can help others manage their grief is to engage in **supportive communication**—sharing messages that express emotional support and that offer personal assistance (Burleson & MacGeorge, 2002). Competent support messages convey sincere expressions of sympathy and condolence, concern for the other person, and encouragement to express emotions. Incompetent support messages tell a person how he or she *should* feel or indicate that the individual is somehow inadequate or blameworthy. Communication scholar and social support expert Amanda Holmstrom offers seven suggestions for improving your supportive communication.[3]

1. *Make sure the person is ready to talk.* You may have amazing support skills, but if the person is too upset to talk, don't push it. Instead, make it clear that you care and want to help, and that you'll be there to listen when he or she needs you.

---

[3]Content that follows was provided to the author by Dr. Amanda Holmstrom, and published with permission. The author thanks Dr. Holmstrom for her contribution.

136

2. *Find the right place and time.* Once a person *is* ready, find a place and a time conducive to quiet conversation. Avoid distracting settings such as parties where you won't be able to focus, and find a time of the day where neither of you has other pressing obligations.

3. *Ask good questions.* Start with open-ended queries such as "How are you feeling?" or "What's on your mind?" Then follow up with more targeted questions based on the response, such as "Are you eating and sleeping OK?" (if not, a potential indicator of depression), or "Have you connected with a support group?" (essential to emotion-sharing). Don't assume that because you've been in a similar situation, you know what someone is going through. Refrain from saying, "I know just how you feel." Importantly, *if you suspect a person is contemplating suicide, ask him or her directly about it.* Say, "Have you been thinking about killing yourself?" or "Has suicide crossed your mind?" People often mistakenly think that direct questions such as these will "push someone over the edge," but in fact it's the opposite. Research suggests that someone considering suicide *wants* to talk about it, but believes that no one cares. If you ask direct questions, a suicidal person typically *won't* be offended or lie, but instead will open up to you. Then you can encourage the person to seek counseling. Someone *not* considering suicide will express surprise at the question, often laughing it off with a "What? No way!"

4. *Legitimize, don't minimize.* Don't dismiss the problem or the significance of the person's feelings by saying things such as "It could have been worse," "Why are you so upset?!" or "You can always find another lover!" Research shows these comments are unhelpful. Instead, let the person know that it's normal and OK to feel as they do.

5. *Listen actively.* Show the person that you are interested in what is being said. Engage in good eye contact, lean toward him or her, and say "Uh-huh" and "Yeah" when appropriate.

6. *Offer advice cautiously.* We want to help someone who is suffering. So we often jump right in and offer advice. But many times that's not helpful or even wanted. Advice is best when it's asked for, when the advice giver has relevant expertise or experience (e.g., a relationship counselor), or when it advocates actions the person can actually do. Advice is hurtful when it implies that the person is to blame or can't solve his or her own problems. When in doubt, ask if advice would be appreciated—or just hold back.

7. *Show concern and give praise.* Let the person know you genuinely care and are concerned about his or her well-being ("I am *so* sorry for your loss; you're really important to me"). Build the person up by praising his or her strength in handling this challenge. Showing care and concern helps connect you to someone while praise will help a person feel better.

skills
practice

Supportive Communication
Skillfully providing emotional support

❶ Let the person know you're available to talk, but don't force an encounter.

❷ Find a quiet, private space.

❸ Start with general questions, and work toward more specific. If you think he or she might be suicidal, ask directly.

❹ Assure the person that his or her feelings are normal.

❺ Show that you're attending closely to what is being said.

❻ Ask before offering advice.

❼ Let the person know you care!

Managing Anger and Providing Support

1 BACKGROUND

Managing your anger and providing supportive communication are two skills that can clash when you're trying to support someone who is making you angry. Read the case study, and work through the five steps under Your Turn to learn how you might competently deal with this situation.

2 CASE STUDY

You're the oldest sibling in a close family in which everyone freely expresses their emotions and often talks about daily events. Of all your siblings, you seem to share an especially close bond with John, the youngest. When John accepts a job offer out of state, you're sad to see him go, but you're excited for his future and take comfort in the daily texts and e-mails you exchange.

Shortly after John moves away, your grandmother has a heart attack. Doctors initially think she will make a full recovery, so you e-mail John and tell him not to worry. However, her condition suddenly worsens, and she passes away. Everyone is grief-stricken, but John is devastated. He is the only one in your immediate family who didn't see her before she died. John was very close to her because she took care of him during much of his childhood when your mom went back to school.

When John arrives for the funeral, he seems sullen and bitter. But so much is going on that you don't get a chance to talk with him at length. Before you know it, he has left. Following the funeral, John rebuffs your attempts to communicate with him. He doesn't return your texts, and after several messages he finally e-mails you, "leave me alone!" You become increasingly worried about how he is dealing with his grief. You leave John a voice mail telling him that you're coming to visit. Despite receiving no response, you opt to go anyway.

Arriving after several hours of grueling travel, you are shocked to find John unwelcoming. Scowling, he says, "What are you *doing* here? I thought I told you to leave me alone." You start getting angry. After all, you spent a good portion of your savings to get here, and you made the trip out of love and concern for John. As you try to manage your anger by using the Jefferson strategy, John attacks: "Oh, I get it. This is the big 'ease your conscience' trip. You figure that if you comfort me, I'll feel better about you lying to me about Grandma's condition. Well, it's not going to work. I didn't get to see her before she died and it's your fault, so why don't you take your self-serving concern and go home!" He slams the door in your face.

You're left standing on the porch, furious. Do you make the several-hour trip home, heeding John's request even though you know he said it out of anger? Or do you pursue your original plan of trying to help John deal with his grief?

3 YOUR TURN

While working through the following steps, keep in mind the interpersonal communication concepts, skills, and insights you've learned so far in this book, especially this chapter. Also remember: there are no right answers, so think hard about the choice you make! (P.S. Need help? Review the *Helpful Concepts* listed below.)

● step 1

Reflect on yourself. What are your thoughts and feelings in this situation? Are your impressions accurate, or could you be mistaken in some way?

● step 2

Reflect on your partner. Put yourself in John's shoes. What is he thinking and feeling? Is his perspective legitimate?

● step 3

Identify the optimal outcome. When you think about this situation, as well as your feelings, John's feelings, and your relationship with him, what's the best, most constructive relationship outcome possible? Be sure to consider not just what's best for you, but what's best for all those who are involved.

● step 4

Locate the roadblocks. Taking into consideration your own thoughts and feelings, those of John, and all that has happened in this situation, what obstacles are keeping you from achieving the optimal outcome?

● step 5

Chart your course. What can you say and do to overcome the roadblocks you've identified and achieve your optimal relationship outcome?

HELPFUL CONCEPTS

Gender and emotion, **120**

Emotion management strategies, **122–127**

Anger, **129–132**

Grief, **134–137**

Supportive communication, **135–137**

We create joy—through every decision we make and every thought, word, and deed

Living a Happy Emotional Life

Interpersonal connections determine our joy

We all live lives rich in relationships and punctuated with emotion. Lovers arrive, bringing gifts of passion and tenderness, and then exit, marking their passage with anger and sadness. Children flash into being, evoking previously unimaginable exhilaration and exhaustion. Friends and family members tread parallel paths, sharing our emotions, and then pass on, leaving grief and memories in their wake.

Across all of our relationship experiences, what balances out our anger and grief is our joy. All human beings share the capacity to relish intense joy and the desire to maintain such happiness in an impermanent and ever-changing world. Also universal is the fact that our personal joy is determined by the quality of our interpersonal connections. When our relationships with family, friends, coworkers, and romantic partners are happy, we are happy, and when they're not, we're not.

Yet joy doesn't drop magically from the sky into our hearts and minds and stay there. *We* create joy—through every decision we make and every thought, word, and deed. When we manage our emotional experiences and communication poorly, the interpersonal sorrows we wreak on others reflect back on us in the form of personal unhappiness. When we steadfastly and skillfully manage our emotions, the positive relationship outcomes we create multiply, and with them, our happiness and the joy of those who surround us.

We began this chapter with the story of a woman committed to transforming the lives of teenagers. Vy Higginsen founded Gospel for Teens in part to create a musical refuge for young people to escape their emotional turmoil. But she quickly learned that her students' emotions couldn't be suppressed, and that through sharing their emotions with one another they could more quickly heal their wounds of anger and grief.

How do you manage the emotional challenges of your life? Do you leave your baggage at the door, burying your emotions? Or do you let your baggage in, sharing your emotions with others?

The story of Vy Higginsen and her students reminds us that although we have emotions, we are not our emotions. It's our capacity to constructively manage the emotions we experience, and communicate them in positive ways, that makes hope and goodness in our lives possible.

POSTSCRIPT

key terms

○ You can watch brief, illustrative videos of these terms and test your understanding of the concepts online in *VideoCentral: Interpersonal Communication* at bedfordstmartins .com/reflectrelate.

key concepts

The Nature of Emotion

- **Emotion** is the most powerful of human experiences and typically involves thoughts, physiological arousal, and communication. Emotions are such significant life events that we feel compelled to engage in **emotion-sharing** with our relationship partners. Sometimes communicating about our emotions leads to **emotional contagion**.

- Emotions are relatively rare compared to **feelings**, which occur numerous times daily, and typically arise and decay with little conscious awareness. **Moods** endure much longer than either feelings or emotions and have pronounced effects on our perception and communication. The most effective strategy for improving bad moods appears to be rigorous physical exercise.

- Six **primary emotions** appear to exist, based on consistent patterns of nonverbal behavior: surprise, joy, disgust, anger, fear, and sadness. Sometimes we experience more than one of these primary emotions simultaneously; the result is **blended emotions**.

Forces Shaping Emotion

- Culture and gender play powerful roles in shaping our experience and expression of emotion. As just one example, we each learn cultural **display rules** growing up that influence what we believe to be socially acceptable and desirable emotional communication.

- Personality also influences our emotional experience. In extreme cases, **Rational Emotive Behavior Therapy** may be used to help neurotics stop negative beliefs about themselves.

Managing Your Emotional Experience and Expression

- Effective **emotion management** is a critical part of **emotional intelligence**. Two of the most common ways people manage their emotions after they have occurred are **suppression** and **venting**. Strategies people use for preventing emotions before they occur include **encounter avoidance**, **encounter structuring**, **attention focus**, and **deactivation**.

- Of all the strategies available to people for managing emotions, by far the most effective is **reappraisal**. Reappraisal can be used to effectively manage both positive and negative emotions, and it results in dramatically improved emotional communication.

Emotional Challenges

- Asynchronicity and invisibility are two key reasons why we inappropriately express emotions online. The lack of *feedback* makes it difficult for us to experience and express empathy.

- **Anger** is extremely difficult to manage, given its intensity. People who routinely manage anger through suppression sometimes develop **chronic hostility**. Others mistakenly think that openly venting anger will purge them of it because of their belief in **catharsis**.

- When anger has already been triggered, an additional approach for managing it is the **Jefferson strategy**. Providing a time delay between the onset of anger and your communicative response can be especially effective during online communication.

- Although an entire industry exists offering advice for how to permanently maintain **passion** in romantic relationships, most people experience intense passion in the early stages of their involvements and then a steady decline the longer the relationship endures.

- **Grief** is intensely demanding. Managing one's own grief is best accomplished through emotion-sharing, whereas providing **supportive communication** is the best approach for aiding others in overcoming their grief.

key skills

- Want to improve a bad mood and enhance the effectiveness of your perception and communication as a result? Check out the strategies for improving bad moods on pages 113–115.

- If you experience constant self-defeating thoughts and beliefs, try the Rational Emotive Behavior Therapy process on pages 121–122.

- Curious about your emotional intelligence? Take the *Self-Quiz* on page 124.

- Interested in preventing unwanted emotions before they occur? Find out how on pages 125–126.

- Why is reappraisal the most effective strategy for managing emotion? Learn the answer on pages 126–127. Then complete the *Skills Practice* on page 127 to bolster your reappraisal skills.

- Want to improve your responses during online encounters? Try the *Skills Practice* on page 129.

- Do you use suppression to deal with unwanted anger? You may be putting yourself at risk for chronic hostility. Test your chronic hostility by taking the *Self-Quiz* on page 131.

- Interested in an alternative approach for managing anger? Try the Jefferson Strategy described on pages 131–132.

- Want to improve your skill at comforting others when they are suffering grief? Learn how on pages 135–137. Then check out the *Skills Practice* on page 137.

- Could you communicate in a supportive fashion toward someone who is grieving but is also making you angry? Find out by completing the *Making Relationship Choices* exercise on pages 138–139.

5 Listening Actively

Listening is our most primal and primary communication skill

red McFeely Rogers began each day by swimming laps in a local pool.[1] A nonsmoking, nondrinking vegetarian, he was happily married for close to 50 years and helped raise two sons. He also was the most awarded person in television history: he received two Peabody Awards, numerous Emmys, the Presidential Medal of Freedom, and a star on the Hollywood Walk of Fame. But Rogers saw himself primarily as a minister who believed in the power of listening. From his perspective, the greatest communicative gift people could give was attentive silence that encouraged others to openly express their deepest emotions.

Although he eventually would receive honorary degrees from more than 40 different institutions—including Yale, Carnegie Mellon, and Boston University—Rogers's first degree was in music composition from Rollins College in Florida. Rogers planned on entering the seminary after graduation but was sidetracked by the chance to help establish the first public television station, WQED in Pittsburgh. As he later explained, "I got into television because I hated it so, and I thought there's some way of using this fabulous instrument to nurture those who would watch and listen" (Stimson, 1998). While working at the station, Rogers attended classes at Pittsburgh Theological Seminary. Ordained in 1963, he decided to

---

[1] All information regarding Fred Rogers was obtained from Millman (1999), Stimson (1998), and Mister Rogers (n.d.).

minister to children and their families by creating *Mister Rogers' Neighborhood*, a TV program emphasizing affirmation, acceptance, and, most of all, listening. In Rogers's words, "being a good listener is a vital part of ministry, especially ministry with children. . . . I cultivated my own listening skills in part by integrating silence into my life as a part of my daily spiritual discipline." By providing children with an adult who would listen to their concerns, Rogers's show helped youngsters express their emotions in healthy ways. During the Gulf War, for example, Rogers dedicated a series of episodes to parents and children with close relatives fighting in Desert Storm. He encouraged parents to discuss life and death openly with their children rather than lying to them or avoiding their questions.

Rogers's renowned listening ability matched a talent for speaking powerfully in ways that made *others* listen. In the late 1960s, a congressional committee headed by notoriously gruff Senator John Pastore was considering halving public broadcasting's funding. Rogers testified before the committee, describing the importance of providing children with a compassionate adult listener on television. After hearing Rogers's testimony, Pastore remarked, "I'm supposed to be a pretty tough guy, but this is the first time I've had goose bumps in the last two days." The committee then voted to approve full funding for public broadcasting.

Mister Rogers' Neighborhood became the longest-running show in television history. During a 33-year span, Rogers welcomed guests as diverse as the Harlem Boys Choir, chef Julia Child, and cellist Yo-Yo Ma. The show became so well known that it remains a cultural icon—many people still remember the opening song, the gentle lilt of Rogers's voice, and his famous cardigan sweaters. Rogers was lampooned by everyone from comedian Eddie Murphy to the writers of the animated series *Family Guy*. But through it all, he remained committed to the central message of his subtle, nondenominational television ministry: listen to others and offer them love, respect, and kindness. Even after his death in 2003, the words he shared at the end of each episode still linger: "I'll be back when the day is new, and I'll have more ideas for you. And you'll have things you'll want to talk about. I will too."

We often take listening for granted. It's a natural but otherwise unremarkable part of our interpersonal communication. Compared with the knowledge, motivation, and skill that competent speaking requires, listening seems to just happen. But if we view listening as secondary to speaking, we miss two truths about it. First, listening is our most primal and primary communication skill. As children, we develop the ability to listen long before we learn how to speak, read, or write. As adults, we spend more time listening than we do in any other type of communication activity (Wolvin & Coakley, 1996). Second, we each have the potential to develop our listening into something far more profound than passive action. When we practice *active listening*, we transcend our own thoughts, ideas, and beliefs, and begin to directly experience the words and worlds of other people (McNaughton, Hamlin, McCarthy, Head-Reeves, & Schreiner, 2007). By focusing our attention, tailoring our listening to the situation, and letting others know we understand them, we move beyond the personal and create the *interpersonal*. The result is improved relationships (Bunkers, 2010).

In this chapter, we discuss how to build your active listening skills. You'll learn:

- The five stages of the listening process and strategies for improving your listening skills
- The many functions of listening
- The advantages and disadvantages of different listening styles
- Ways to avoid common forms of incompetent listening

Listening: A Five-Step Process

Listening draws on auditory and visual cues

The scares in horror movies almost always begin with sounds. Long before we ever see the demon that haunts the family in the movie *Insidious* (2010), for example, the young boy Dalton hears mysterious noises from the attic. While investigating, he hears a threatening rustling coming at him from the darkness. Later, his mother hears whispering voices in the baby monitor. When she goes to check, she hears a loud and angry voice—even though no one is there. Similar sounds haunt such films as *Paranormal Activity*, *The Haunting*, and *The Amityville Horror*. As we sit in the comfort of movie theaters or living rooms—feeling our blood pressure rising—we too listen intently to these voices and sounds, trying to understand them, and imagining how we would respond if we were in similar situations.

Horror screenwriters use sounds to trigger fear because they know the powerful role that listening plays in our lives. But what the writers, and we, often don't think about is that listening isn't just one isolated experience. Instead, it's a complex process. Specifically, **listening** involves receiving, attending to, understanding, responding to, and recalling sounds and visual images (Wolvin & Coakley,

self-reflection

Think of the most recent instance in which you were truly frightened. What triggered your fear? Was it a noise you heard, or something someone told you? Or was it something you only saw? What does this tell you about the primacy of listening in shaping intense emotions?

147

▶ In *Insidious*, Dalton's mother listens intently to the strange whispers coming from her son's baby monitor, causing an emotional response of fear but also prompting her to investigate. Whenever we hear sounds or listen to others, we go through a process to help us figure out what we heard and how to respond.

1996). When you're listening to someone, you draw on both auditory and visual cues. In addition to spoken messages, behaviors such as head nodding, smiling, gestures, and eye contact affect how you listen to others and interpret their communication. The process of listening also unfolds over time, rather than instantaneously, through the five steps discussed here.

RECEIVING

While walking to class, you unexpectedly run into a good friend and stop to chat with her. As she talks, you listen to her words as well as observe her behavior. But how does this process happen? As you observe your friend, light reflects off her skin, clothes, and hair and travels through the lens of your eye to your retina, which contains optic nerves. These nerves become stimulated, sending information to your brain, which translates the information into visual images such as your friend smiling or shaking her head, an effect called *seeing*. At the same time, sound waves generated by her voice enter your inner ear, causing your eardrum to vibrate. These vibrations travel along acoustic nerves to your brain, which interprets them as your friend's words and voice tone, an effect known as **hearing**.

Together, seeing and hearing constitute **receiving**, the first step in the listening process. Receiving is critical to listening—you can't listen if you don't "see" or hear the other person. Unfortunately, our ability to receive is often hampered by *noise pollution*, sound in the surrounding environment that obscures or distracts our attention from auditory input. Sources of noise pollution include crowds, road and air traffic, construction equipment, and music.

Although noise pollution is inescapable, especially in large cities, some people intentionally expose themselves to intense levels of noise pollution. This can result in *hearing impairment*, the restricted ability to receive sound input across the humanly audible frequency range. For example, research suggests that more than 40 percent of college students have measurable hearing impairment due to loud music in bars, home stereos, head-phones, and concerts, but only 8 percent believe that it is a "big problem" compared with other health issues (Chung, Des Roches, Meunier, & Eavey, 2005). One study of rock and jazz musicians found that 75 percent suffered substantial hearing loss from exposure to chronic noise pollution (Kaharit, Zachau, Eklof, Sandsjo, & Moller, 2003).

You can enhance your ability to receive—and improve your listening as a result—by becoming aware of noise pollution and adjusting your interactions accordingly. Practice monitoring the noise level in your environment during your interpersonal encounters, and notice how it impedes your listening. When possible, avoid interactions in loud and noisy environments, or move to quieter locations when you wish to exchange important information with others. If you enjoy loud music or live concerts, always use ear protection to ensure your auditory safety. As a lifelong musician, I myself never practice, play a gig, or attend a concert without earplugs.

⬤ Repeated exposure to intense levels of noise pollution can result in hearing impairment. Guitarist Pete Townshend of the Who, after years of exposure to his own noise pollution, can no longer hear spoken words during normal conversations.

ATTENDING

When Cleveland rapper Colson Baker (aka "Machine Gun Kelly") tweeted his fans: "Today we flash mob NO MATTER WHAT! 5pm at SouthPark mall in the food court," hundreds of fans showed up (as did police who had heard about the tweet). What makes such flash mobs possible? The fact that we pay attention to the messages that interest us the most.

Attending, the second step in the listening process, involves devoting attention to the information you've received. If you don't attend to information, you can't go on to interpret and understand it, or respond to it (Kahneman, 1973). The extent to which you attend to received information is determined largely by its *salience*—the degree to which it seems especially noticeable and significant. As discussed in Chapter 3, we view information as salient when it's *visually or audibly stimulating*, *unexpected*, or *personally important* (Fiske & Taylor, 1991). In the Colson Baker case, fans attended to his Twitter post in part because he used caps (visually stimulating), and because it was unexpected (Baker hadn't made any public appearances in Ohio since he had signed a major record deal). But the main reason they attended to his invite—and showed up at the mall—was because he was important to them: he was a local boy who had made it big. As he noted in a YouTube video after the incident, "It was kind of a chance to show all the kids that we really care about them, and that we're still here, and we're still grounded, and we're gonna be Ohio boys and Cleveland boys until we're six feet under."

We have only limited control over salience; whether people communicate in stimulating, unexpected, or important ways is largely determined by them, not us. However, we do control our attention level. To improve your attention, consider trying two things: limiting your multitasking and elevating your attention.

Limiting Multitasking Online   One way to improve attention is to limit the amount of time you spend each day *multitasking online*—that is, using multiple forms of technology at once, each of which feeds you unrelated streams of information (Ophir, Nass, & Wagner, 2012). An example of such multitasking is writing a class paper on your computer while also Facebook chatting with several friends, watching TV, playing an online computer game, and texting family members. Stanford psychologist Clifford Nass has found that habitual multitaskers are extremely confident in their ability to perform at peak levels on the tasks they simultaneously juggle (Glenn, 2010). However, their confidence is misplaced. Multitaskers perform substantially worse on tasks compared with individuals who focus their attention on only one task at a time (Ophir et al., 2012).

Why is limiting multitasking online important for improving attention? Because multitasking erodes your capacity for sustaining focused attention (Jackson, 2008). Cognitive scientists have discovered that our brains adapt to the tasks we regularly perform during our waking hours, an effect known as *brain plasticity* (Carr, 2010). In simple terms, we "train our brains" to be able to do certain things, through how we live our daily lives. People who spend much of their time, day after day, shifting attention rapidly between multiple

self-QUIZ

Multitasking and Attention

This quiz gauges how multitasking between various forms of technology can divide your attention and how your ability to focus may suffer as a result. Read each statement below and mark the ones with which you agree. Use your score to assess the degree to which your attention is divided.

_____ 1. At any one time, I typically have multiple forms of technology turned on, including my phone and computer.

_____ 2. If I focus my attention on just one task, I find that my mind quickly starts drifting to other stuff, such as who is messaging me, or what is happening online.

_____ 3. Even during class or while I'm at work, I stay connected to and communicate with others through text, e-mail, cell phone, or the Internet.

_____ 4. When I spend too much time doing any one thing, I get bored.

_____ 5. Text messages, cell-phone calls, e-mail, and online posts frequently interrupt activities I am trying to focus upon and perform.

_____ 6. I spend much of my day switching rapidly between multiple activities and apps, including Facebook, text, e-mail, games, schoolwork, and Web surfing.

_____ 7. I feel that I am more easily distracted now than I was just a few years ago.

Note: Adapted from Bane (2010).

Scoring: Total up the number of items with which you agree. If you agree with 0–2 of these, your attention is not divided by multitasking, and you likely find it easy to concentrate on one thing for extended periods of time. If you agree with 3–4 of these, you have moderately divided attention and may be experiencing challenges with focusing attention. If you agree with 5–7 of these items, you spend much of your time multitasking and likely find it challenging to focus your attention on just one thing.

forms of technology train their brains to *only* be able to focus attention in brief bursts. The consequence is that they lose ability to focus attention for long periods of time on just one task (Jackson, 2008). Not surprisingly, habitual multitaskers have grave difficulty listening, as listening requires extended attention (Carr, 2010). Limiting your multitasking, and spending at least some time each day focused on just one task (such as reading, listening to music, or engaged in prayer or meditation), without technological distractions, helps train your brain to be able to sustain attention. To gauge the degree to which multitasking has impacted your attention, take the *Self-Quiz* "Multitasking and Attention" on page 150.

Elevating Attention   The second thing you can try to improve your attention is to elevate it, by following these steps (Marzano & Arredondo, 1996). First, develop awareness of your attention level. During interpersonal interactions, monitor how your attention naturally waxes and wanes. Notice how various factors such as fatigue, stress, or hunger influence your attention. Second, take note of encounters in which you *should* listen carefully, but that seem to trigger low levels of attention. These might include interactions with parents, teachers, or work managers, or situations such as family get-togethers, classrooms, or work meetings. Third, consider the optimal level of attention required for adequate listening during these encounters. Fourth, compare the level of attention you observed in yourself versus the level of attention that is required, identifying the "attention gap" that needs to be bridged for you to improve your attention.

Finally, and most important, elevate your level of attention to the point necessary to take in the auditory and visual information you're receiving. You can do this in several ways. Before and during an encounter, boost the salience of the exchange by reminding yourself of how it will impact your life and relationships. Take active control of the factors that may diminish your attention. When possible, avoid important encounters when you are overly stressed, hungry, ill, fatigued, or under the influence of alcohol—such factors substantially impair attention. If you have higher energy levels in the morning or early in the week, try to schedule attention-demanding activities and encounters during those times. If you find your attention wandering, practice **mental bracketing**, systematically putting aside thoughts that aren't relevant to the interaction at hand. When irrelevant thoughts arise, let them pass through your conscious awareness and drift away without allowing them to occupy your attention fully.

UNDERSTANDING

While serving with her National Guard unit in Iraq, Army Specialist Claudia Carreon suffered a traumatic brain injury (TBI).[2] The injury wiped her memory clean. She could no longer remember major events or people from her past, including her husband and her 2-year-old daughter. However, because she seemed

---

[2]The information that follows is adapted from http://www.braininjurymn.org/library/NewWarsHallmarkInjury.pdf, retrieved October 12, 2011.

---

skills practice

Elevating Attention
Focusing your attention during interpersonal encounters

❶ Identify an important person to whom you find it difficult to listen.

❷ List factors—fatigue, time pressure—that impede your attention when you're interacting with this person.

❸ Before your next encounter with the individual, address factors you can control.

❹ During the encounter, increase the person's salience by reminding yourself of his or her importance to you.

❺ As the encounter unfolds, practice mental bracketing to stay focused on your partner's communication.

physically "normal," her TBI went unnoticed and she returned to duty. A few weeks later, Carreon received an order from a commanding officer, but she couldn't understand it and shortly afterward forgot it. She subsequently was demoted for "failure to follow an order." When Army doctors realized that she wasn't being willfully disobedient—but instead simply couldn't understand or remember orders—her rank was restored, and Carreon was rushed to the Army's Polytrauma Center in Palo Alto, California. Now Carreon, like many other veterans who have suffered TBIs, carries with her captioned photos of loved ones and a special hand-held personal computer, to help her remember people and make sense of everyday conversations.

The challenges faced by Claudia Carreon illustrate the essential role that memory plays in shaping the third stage of listening. **Understanding** involves interpreting the meaning of another person's communication by comparing newly received information against our past knowledge (Macrae & Bodenhausen, 2001). Whenever you receive and attend to new information you place it in your **short-term memory**, the part of your mind that temporarily houses the information while you seek to understand its meaning. While the new information sits in your short-term memory, you call up relevant knowledge from your **long-term memory**, the part of your mind devoted to permanent information storage. You then compare relevant prior knowledge from your long-term memory with the new information in your short-term memory to create understanding. In Claudia Carreon's case, her long-term memory was largely erased by her injury. Consequently, whenever she hears new information, she has no foundation from which to make sense of it.

▶ Claudia Carreon now relies on captioned photos to supplement her damaged long-term memory. Without this help, she can't compare new information with previous knowledge, prohibiting her from fully understanding any message she may receive.

RESPONDING

You're spending the afternoon at your apartment discussing your wedding plans with two friends, John and Sarah. You want them to help you with ideas for your rehearsal dinner, ceremony, and reception. As you talk, John looks directly at you, smiles, nods his head, and leans forward. He also asks questions and makes comments periodically during the discussion. Sarah, in contrast, seems completely uninterested. She alternates between looking at the people strolling by your living-room window and texting on her phone. She also sits with her body half-turned away from you and leans back in her chair. You become frustrated because it's obvious that John is listening closely and Sarah isn't listening at all.

What leads you to conclude that John is listening and Sarah isn't? It's the way your friends are **responding**—communicating their attention and understanding to you. Responding is the fourth stage of the listening process. When you actively listen, you do more than simply attend and understand. You also convey your attention and understanding to others by clearly and constructively responding through positive feedback, paraphrasing, and clarifying (McNaughton et al., 2007).

Feedback   Critical to active listening is using verbal and nonverbal behaviors known as **feedback** to communicate attention and understanding *while* others are talking. Scholars distinguish between two kinds of feedback, positive and negative (Wolvin & Coakley, 1996). When you use positive feedback, like John in our earlier example, you look directly at the person speaking, smile, position your body so that you're facing him or her, and lean forward. You may also offer **back-channel cues**, verbal and nonverbal behaviors such as nodding and making comments—like "Uh-huh," "Yes," and "That makes sense"—that signal you've paid attention to and understood specific comments (Duncan & Fiske, 1977). All of these behaviors combine to show speakers that you're actively listening. In contrast, people who use negative feedback, like Sarah in our example, send a very different message to speakers: "I'm not interested in paying attention to you or understanding what you're saying." Behaviors that convey negative feedback include avoiding eye contact, turning your body away, looking bored or distracted, and not using back-channel cues.

The type of feedback we provide while we're listening has a dramatic effect on speakers (Wolvin & Coakley, 1996). Receiving positive feedback from listeners can enhance a speaker's confidence and generate positive emotions.

self-reflection

Recall an encounter in which you were saying something important but the other person gave you negative feedback. How did the feedback affect your communication? Your relationship? Is negative feedback ever appropriate? If so, under which circumstances?

FRANK & ERNEST © 1998 Thaves. Reprinted by permission of UNIVERSAL UCLICK for UFS. All right reserved.

⬥ In many Protestant churches, it is perfectly acceptable for audience members to express their feedback loudly during the minister's sermon by shouting "Amen!" or "Hallelujah!" The same type of positive feedback would be radically inappropriate in a traditional Catholic church.

Negative feedback can cause speakers to hesitate, make speech errors, or stop altogether to see what's wrong and why we're not listening.

To effectively display positive feedback during interpersonal encounters, try four simple suggestions (Barker, 1971; Daly, 1975). First, make your feedback obvious. As communication scholar John Daly notes, no matter how actively you listen, unless others perceive your feedback, they won't view you as actively listening. Second, make your feedback appropriate. Different situations, speakers, and messages require more or less intensity of positive feedback. Third, make your feedback clear by avoiding behaviors that might be mistaken as negative feedback. For example, something as simple as innocently stealing a glance at your phone to see what time it is might unintentionally suggest that you're bored or wish the person would stop speaking. Finally, always provide feedback quickly in response to what the speaker has just said.

Paraphrasing and Clarifying   Active listeners also communicate attention and understanding through saying things *after* their conversational partners have finished their turns—things that make it clear they were listening. One way to do this is by **paraphrasing**, summarizing others' comments after they have finished ("My read on your message is that . . ." or "You seem to be saying that . . ."). This practice can help you check the accuracy of your understanding during both face-to-face and online encounters. Paraphrasing should be used judiciously, however. Some conversational partners may find paraphrasing annoying if you use it a lot or they view it as contrived. Paraphrasing can also lead to conversational lapses, silences of three seconds or longer that participants perceive as awkward (McLaughlin & Cody, 1982).

Paraphrasing can cause lapses because when you paraphrase, you do nothing to usefully advance the conversational topic forward in new and interesting ways (Heritage & Watson, 1979). Instead, you simply rehash what has already been said. Consequently, the only relevant response your conversational partner can provide is a simple acknowledgment, such as "Yeah" or "Uh-huh." In such cases, a lapse is likely to ensue immediately after, unless one of you has a new topic ready to introduce to advance the conversation. This is an important practical concern for anyone interested in being perceived as interpersonally competent because the more lapses that occur, the more likely your conversational partner is to perceive you as incompetent (McLaughlin & Cody, 1982). To avoid this perception, always couple your paraphrasing with additional comments or questions that usefully build on the previous topic or take the conversation in new directions.

Of course, on some occasions, we simply don't understand what others have said. In such instances, it's perfectly appropriate to respond by seeking clarification rather than paraphrasing, saying, "I'm sorry, but could you explain that again? I want to make sure I understood you correctly." This technique not only helps you clarify the meaning of what you're hearing, it also enables you to communicate your desire to understand the other person.

RECALLING

The fifth stage of listening is **recalling**, remembering information after you've received, attended to, understood, and responded to it. As researchers L. Todd Thomas and Timothy Levine (1994) note, recalling is a crucial part of the listening process because we judge the effectiveness of listening based on our ability to accurately recall information after we've listened to it. Think about it: when a romantic partner asks, "Were you listening to me?" how do you demonstrate that you really were actively listening? By recalling everything that was said and reciting it back to your partner. Indeed, practically every scientific measure of listening uses recall accuracy as evidence of listening effectiveness (Janusik, 2007).

Your recall accuracy varies depending on the situation. When people have no task other than simple memorization, recall accuracy is high. For example, laboratory studies examining facial recall have found that when people are asked to memorize others' faces, they can subsequently recall which faces they've seen with close to 100 percent accuracy (Freides, 1974). But when people are engaged in activities more complicated than straight memorization, recall accuracy plummets. That's because in such cases, we're receiving a lot of information, which increases the likelihood of perceptual and recall errors. Research on the recall accuracy of criminal eyewitnesses, for instance, has found that people frequently err in their recall of crimes, something most jurors and even the eyewitnesses themselves don't realize (Wells, Lindsay, & Tousignant, 1980). Our recall of interpersonal and relational encounters is not exempt from error. Especially for negative and unpleasant interactions, such as conflicts, we tend to recall our own behavior as positive and constructive and the behavior of others as comparatively negative, regardless of what actually happened (Sillars, Smith, & Koerner, 2010).

skills practice

Responding Online
Responding effectively during online encounters

❶ Identify an online interaction that's important.

❷ During the exchange, provide your conversational partner with immediate, positive feedback to his or her messages, sending short responses like "I agree!" and attaching positive emoticons.

❸ Check your understanding by paraphrasing your partner's longer messages ("My read on your last message is . . .").

❹ Seek clarification regarding messages you don't understand ("I'm having trouble understanding—would you mind explaining that a bit more?").

When Nobody Will Listen

On March 6, 1988, the board of trustees at the nation's oldest university for the deaf, Gallaudet University, announced that Elizabeth A. Zinser was selected as the university's president. Zinser was a hearing person with little knowledge of the deaf community. The decision shocked Gallaudet faculty, staff, and students, who had hoped the board (most of whom were hearing) would for the first time hire a deaf president.

A large crowd of student protesters gathered. Board chair Jane Spilman, a hearing person, refused to listen to the students' concerns and defended the board's decision, saying, "Deaf people are not able to function in a hearing world." The protest escalated, and the demonstrators made four demands: Zinser must resign and be replaced by a deaf president, Spilman must resign from the board, deaf representation on the board must be at least 51 percent, and there must be no reprisals toward any of the protesters.

The board refused to listen and the students responded by refusing to meet with Zinser and blocking campus gates (Mercer, 1998). Zinser realized her candidacy was doomed by administrators' and students' refusal to listen to each other. As she notes, "We had found no reasonable means to establish contact or communication on campus. So I resigned." The board then met the remaining demands.

Ten years later, former protesters, board members, and Zinser returned to Gallaudet to remember and honor the protest. Zinser was asked, if she could go back in time, knowing what she now knows, would she change her decision to resign? She responded, "Gallaudet looms large in my life, in the deeper awareness that I gained for what people who have been oppressed feel. I've had fantasies of getting through those gates, talking with all the students and listening to their concerns. But had I found a way to actually sit down and talk to them, in fairly short order I would have concluded the same thing" (Mercer, 1998).

discussion questions

- Have you experienced an encounter in which you and another person refused to listen to each other because of perceived differences?
- What happened to your relationship with that person? What could you have done differently to facilitate better mutual listening?

Note: All information was obtained from "Deaf President Now Protest" (n.d.), "Deaf President Now" (n.d.), and Mercer (1998).

How can you enhance your recall ability? One way is to use **mnemonics**, devices that aid memory. For example, when I was an undergraduate at the University of Washington, I delivered pizzas. Many of my deliveries went to the Wallingford neighborhood, a residential area west of campus. Wallingford was different from other neighborhoods because the streets had names instead of numbers: Eastern, Sunnyside, Corliss, Bagley, Meridian, Burke, Wallingford, Densmore, Woodlawn, and Ashworth. No matter how many times my supervisor told me, "No, Woodlawn is *between* Densmore and Ashworth!" I couldn't recall the street order when I was out on a run. So I created a mnemonic. I took the first syllable of each street name, in order from east to west, and created a simple phrase, "Eas-Sun Cor-Bag Mer-Bur Wal-Den Wood-Ash." The phrase was so distinct that it stuck in my mind, and from then on I had no problem locating the streets. The mnemonic was so powerful that even now, nearly 30 years later, I can recall it, even though I live thousands of miles from Seattle and the pizza restaurant for which I delivered no longer exists.

self-reflection

What's an example of a mnemonic you've created? How did you go about constructing it? Has it helped you more effectively recall important information? If not, what could be done to improve its usefulness?

My experience creating a pizza-delivery mnemonic supports one of the most common findings in mnemonic research, the **bizarreness effect**, which causes us to remember unusual information more readily than commonplace information (Worthen, Garcia-Rivas, Green, & Vidos, 2000). The bizarreness effect occurs because unusual information and events trigger heightened levels of our attention and require us to work harder to make sense of them; thus, we remember the information better. The bizarreness effect can be used to enhance your recall of information by creating links between information you are listening to and unusual images or information that you can link with what you're trying to remember. You can create unique phrases or acronyms based on the information you're trying to remember, and use these as memory prompts. For example, the phrase "Cor-Bag" for me was so strange sounding that it was the most memorable part of my mnemonic, and I could remember the entire mnemonic by calling to mind "Cor-Bag."

Several other practices can also help you boost your recall ability. Because listening is rooted in both visual and auditory information and memory is enhanced by using all five senses, try bolstering your memory of an interpersonal communication encounter by linking information you've listened to with pleasant or even silly visuals, scents, or sounds. To create visual images of an interpersonal encounter, you could write detailed notes or draw diagrams documenting the contents of a conversation. You could also link a new acquaintance's name with a unique physical feature characterizing him or her. Finally, when you develop mnemonics or notes, review them repeatedly, including reciting them out loud, because repetition helps aid memory.

⬢ The bizarreness effect occurs because something unusual triggers heightened levels of our attention and requires us to work harder to make sense of it.

The Five Functions of Listening

Adapting our listening purposes

When style gurus Stacy London and Clinton Kelly give a makeover to a hapless fashion victim on their hit TLC show, *What Not to Wear*, they don't just dole out advice. Instead, they spend a lot of time listening. Upon first meeting a new participant, they listen carefully to her story, so they can better comprehend where she is coming from. When they think someone is lying to them, or hiding important fears or feelings, they listen carefully to her tone of voice and wording, trying to discern her inner states. When a participant argumentatively defends fashion faux pas, Stacy and Clinton listen analytically, looking for ways to attack her reasoning and move her in a different direction. When a guest joyously describes her experience, they listen appreciatively—sharing in her happiness. Finally, given the emotional intensity of deconstructing one's appearance, Stacy and Clinton often listen supportively when a participant breaks down and cries.

The different reasons for listening displayed on *What Not to Wear* mirror the **listening functions**, or purposes for listening, we experience daily. Akin to Stacy and Clinton, our interpersonal encounters are characterized by five common listening functions: to comprehend, to discern, to analyze, to appreciate, and to support.

LISTENING TO COMPREHEND

Think for a minute about your interpersonal communication class—the course for which this text was assigned. When you're attending class, *why* do you listen to your professor? The answer is so obvious it's silly: you listen so that you can comprehend the information he or she is presenting to you. When you listen for this purpose, you work to accurately interpret and store the information you

▶ Fashion gurus Stacy London and Clinton Kelly use a variety of listening styles on their show *What Not to Wear*. While it may seem like they listen only to analyze, one of their strengths is their ability to adjust their listening styles depending on the situation.

receive, so you can correctly recall it later. Additional examples of this type of listening include listening to a coworker explain how to use a software application at work and listening to a prospective landlord explain your contractual obligations if you sign a lease on an apartment.

LISTENING TO DISCERN

When you listen to discern, you focus on distinguishing specific sounds from each other. The most common form is to listen carefully to someone's vocal tone to assess mood and stress level. For example, if you're concerned that your romantic partner is angry with you, you might listen carefully to the sound of his or her voice rather than the actual words to gauge how upset he or she is.

LISTENING TO ANALYZE

When you listen to analyze, you carefully evaluate the message you're receiving, and you judge it. For instance, you might analyze your father's neutral comments about his recent medical checkup, listening for signs of worry so you can determine whether he's hiding serious health problems.

LISTENING TO APPRECIATE

When you listen to appreciate, your goal is simply to enjoy the sounds and sights you're experiencing and then to respond by expressing your appreciation. Common examples include listening to your child excitedly share the story of his Little League home run or listening while a close friend tells a funny story.

LISTENING TO SUPPORT

You're making lunch in your apartment one afternoon, when your best friend calls you. You answer only to hear him sobbing uncontrollably. He tells you that he and his girlfriend just broke up because she cheated on him. He says he needs someone to talk to.

Providing comfort to a conversational partner is another common purpose for listening. To provide support through listening, you must suspend judgment—taking in what someone else says without evaluating it, and openly expressing empathy. Examples include comforting a relative after the death of a spouse or responding with a kind e-mail to a coworker who sends you a message complaining that her boss just criticized her at a team meeting.

ADAPTING YOUR LISTENING PURPOSE

The five functions that listening commonly serves are not mutually exclusive. We change between them frequently and fluidly. You might change your purpose for listening even within the same encounter. For example, you're listening with appreciation at a concert when suddenly you realize one of the musicians is out of tune. You might shift to discerning listening (trying to isolate that particular instrument from the others) and ultimately to listening to analyze (trying to assess whether you are in fact correct about its being out of tune). If the musician happens to be a friend of yours, you might even switch to supportive listening following the event, as she openly laments her disastrous performance!

An essential part of active listening is skillfully and flexibly adapting your listening purposes to the changing demands of interpersonal encounters (Bunkers, 2010). To strengthen your ability to adapt your listening purpose, heighten your awareness of the various possible listening functions during your interpersonal encounters. Routinely ask yourself, "What is my primary purpose for listening at this moment, in this situation? Do I want to comprehend, discern, analyze, appreciate, or support?" Then adjust your listening accordingly. As you do this, keep in mind that for some situations, certain approaches to listening may be inappropriate or even unethical, like listening to analyze when a relational partner is seeking emotional support.

self-reflection

Recall a situation in which you listened the wrong way. For instance, a friend needed you to listen supportively, but you listened to analyze. What led you to make this error? What consequences ensued from your mistake? What can you do in the future to avoid such listening mishaps?

Understanding Listening Styles

Culture and gender affect listening styles

When Fred Rogers first began hosting his children's show, he intentionally adopted a nonthreatening listening style that put children at ease and helped them feel safe. His listening style reflected his religious practice of contemplative silence, which emphasizes responding empathically to others. While Rogers's trademark listening style has earned ridicule from some quarters of our popular culture, it proved extremely effective in the context of his show and with his chosen audience.

FOUR LISTENING STYLES

Your **listening style** is your habitual pattern of listening behaviors, which reflects your attitudes, beliefs, and predispositions regarding the listening process (Watson, Barker, & Weaver, 1995). Four different primary listening styles exist (Bodie & Worthington, 2010). **Action-oriented listeners** want brief, to-the-point, and accurate messages from others—information they can then use to make decisions or initiate courses of action. Action-oriented listeners can grow

⬇ Active listeners understand that different situations require different listening styles. For example, what type(s) of listening style(s) would be appropriate in the images below? Why?

impatient when communicating with people they perceive as disorganized, long-winded, or imprecise in their talk. For example, when faced with an upset spouse, an action-oriented listener would want information about what caused the problem, so a solution could be generated. He or she would be less interested in hearing elaborate details of the spouse's feelings.

Time-oriented listeners prefer brief and concise encounters. They tend to let others know in advance exactly how much time they have available for each conversation. Time-oriented listeners want to stick to their allotted schedules, and often look at clocks, watches, or phones to ensure this is the case (Bodie & Worthington, 2010).

In contrast, **people-oriented listeners** view listening as an opportunity to establish commonalities between themselves and others. When asked to identify the most important part of effective listening, people-oriented listeners cite concern for other people's emotions. Like Fred Rogers, they strive to demonstrate empathy when listening by using positive feedback and offering supportive responses. People-oriented listeners tend to score high on measures of extraversion and overall communication competence (Villaume & Bodie, 2007).

Content-oriented listeners prefer to be intellectually challenged by the messages they receive during interpersonal encounters. They enjoy receiving complex and provocative information. Content-oriented listeners often take time to carefully evaluate facts and details before forming an opinion about information they've heard. Of the four listening styles, content-oriented listeners are the most likely to ask speakers clarifying or challenging questions (Bodie & Worthington, 2010).

Most of us use only one or two listening styles in all of our interpersonal interactions (Chesebro, 1999). One study found that 36.1 percent of people reported exclusively using a single listening style across all of their interpersonal encounters; an additional 24.8 percent reported that they never use more than

VideoCentral ◉

bedfordstmartins.com
/reflectrelate

**Action-Oriented
Listeners**
*Watch this clip online
to answer the questions
below.*

How does the boss in this video signal his listening style? Be specific. When have you been an action-oriented listener? Why did you choose that approach?

Want to see more? Check out VideoCentral for clips on **time-oriented listeners** and **content-oriented listeners**.

◁ In this photo from the filming of the movie *Black Swan*, actress Natalie Portman talks with director Darren Aronofsky. Using a content-oriented listening style can be very effective in work situations where your primary goal is to comprehend.

self-QUIZ

Discover Your Listening Styles

Place a check mark next to each of the items you agree with. Then determine how many listening styles you use by seeing which categories have three or more checked statements. Don't be surprised if you have more than one listening style!

People-Oriented Listeners

_____ I focus my attention on others' feelings when listening to them.

_____ When listening to others, I quickly notice whether they are pleased or disappointed.

_____ I become emotionally involved when listening to others' problems.

_____ I nod my head and use good eye contact to show interest in what others are saying when I listen.

Content-Oriented Listeners

_____ I enjoy listening to technical information.

_____ I prefer to listen to facts and evidence so I can personally evaluate them.

_____ I like the challenge of listening to complex information.

_____ I enjoy asking probing questions to gather additional information.

Action-Oriented Listeners

_____ I become frustrated when others don't present their ideas in an orderly, efficient way.

_____ When listening to others, I focus on inconsistencies or errors in what they're saying.

_____ I often jump ahead and finish others' thoughts in my own mind while listening.

_____ I get impatient with people who ramble on during conversations.

Time-Oriented Listeners

_____ When hurried, I let others know that I have only a limited amount of time to listen.

_____ I often begin discussions by telling others how long I can meet with them.

_____ I interrupt others when I feel pressure to move on to another task.

_____ I look at my watch or at a clock when I have limited time to listen to others.

two different styles (Watson et al., 1995). We also resist attempts to switch from our dominant styles, even when those styles are ill-suited to the situation at hand. This can cause others to perceive us as insensitive, inflexible, and even incompetent communicators.

To be an active listener, you have to use all four styles, so you can strategically deploy each of them as needed. For example, in situations where your primary listening function is to provide emotional support—when friends, family members, or romantic partners obviously want to discuss feelings or turn to you for comfort—you should quickly adopt a people-oriented listening style (Barker & Watson, 2000). Studies document that use of a people-oriented listening style substantially boosts others' perceptions of your interpersonal sensitivity (Chesebro, 1999). In such encounters, use of a content-, time-, or action-oriented style would likely be perceived as incompetent.

table 5.1 **Active Listening**

To be a more active listener, try these strategies:
1. Concentrate on important aspects of encounters and control factors that impede your attention.
2. Communicate your understanding to others in competent and timely ways by providing polite, obvious, appropriate, clear, and quick feedback.
3. Improve your recall abilities by using mnemonics or linking new information to other senses, visuals, or features.
4. Develop an awareness of your primary listening functions in various situations.
5. Practice shifting your listening style quickly, depending on the demands of the encounter.

By contrast, if your dominant listening function is to comprehend—for instance, during a training session at work—you'll need to use a content-oriented listening style. Similarly, if you're talking with someone who is running late for an appointment or who has to make a decision quickly, you should use a more time- or action-oriented style. For additional tips on how to improve your active listening, see Table 5.1.

GENDER DIFFERENCES IN LISTENING STYLES

Studies have found that women and men differ in their listening-style preferences and practices (Watson et al., 1995). Women are more likely than men to use people-oriented and content-oriented listening styles, and men are more likely to use time-oriented and action-oriented styles. These findings have led researchers to conclude that men (in general) tend to have a task-oriented and hurried approach to listening whereas women perceive listening as an intellectual, emotional, and ultimately relational activity.

Keeping these differences in mind during interpersonal encounters is an important part of active listening. When interacting with men, observe the listening styles they display and adapt your style to match theirs. Don't be surprised if time- or action-oriented styles emerge the most. When conversing with women, follow the same pattern, carefully watching their listening styles and adjusting your style accordingly. Be prepared to quickly shift to more people- or content-oriented styles if needed. But don't automatically assume that just because a person is female or male means that she or he will always listen—or expect you to listen—in certain ways. Take your cue from the actual person you are talking with.

CULTURE AND LISTENING STYLES

Culture powerfully shapes the use and perception of listening styles. What's considered effective listening by one culture is often perceived as ineffective by others, something you should always keep in mind when communicating with

self-reflection

Do your preferred listening styles match research on male–female differences? How have your listening styles affected your communication with people of the same gender? The opposite gender?

people from other cultures. For example, in individualistic cultures such as the United States and Canada (and particularly in the American workplace), time-oriented and action-oriented listening styles dominate. People often approach conversations with an emphasis on time limits ("I have only 10 minutes to talk"). Many people also feel and express frustration if others don't communicate their ideas efficiently ("Just say it!").

The value that people from individualistic cultures put on time and efficiency—something we'll discuss more in Chapter 7—frequently places them at odds with people from other cultures. In collectivistic cultures, people- and content-oriented listening is emphasized. In many East Asian countries, for example, Confucian teachings admonish followers to pay close attention when listening, display sensitivity to others' feelings, and be prepared to assimilate complex information—hallmarks of people- and content-oriented listening styles (Chen & Chung, 1997). Studies have found that students from outside of the United States view Americans as less willing and patient listeners than individuals who come from Africa, Asia, South America, and southern Europe—regions that emphasize people-oriented listening (Wolvin, 1987).

Preventing Incompetent Listening

Avoiding the most common listening pitfalls

No one is a perfect active listener all the time. At one time or another we all make errors during the listening process, fail to identify the right purpose for listening during an interpersonal encounter, or neglect to use the appropriate listening style. In previous sections of this chapter, we discussed ways to avoid such errors. But being an active listener also means systematically avoiding five notoriously incompetent types of listening.

SELECTIVE LISTENING

A colleague stops by your office to chat and shares exciting news: a coworker to whom you're romantically attracted is similarly interested in you. As your thoughts become riveted upon this revelation, the remainder of what he says fades from your awareness, including important information he shares with you about an upcoming project deadline.

Perhaps the greatest challenge to active listening is overcoming **selective listening**, taking in only those bits and pieces of information that are immediately salient during an interpersonal encounter and dismissing the rest. When we selectively listen, we rob ourselves of the opportunity to learn information from others that may affect important personal or professional outcomes, such as a missed project deadline.

Selective listening is difficult to avoid because it is the natural result of fluctuating attention and salience. To overcome selective listening, you shouldn't strive to learn how to listen to everything all at once. Instead, seek to slowly and steadily broaden the range of information you can actively attend to during your encounters with others. The best way to do this is by improving your overall level

On the television show *30 Rock*, ineffective listening styles are often the cause of frustration for the characters and laughter for the audience. Network executive Jack Donaghy, for example, occasionally becomes so preoccupied with his own ideas that he only selectively listens to his coworkers like Liz Lemon and misses important details.

of attention, through practicing the techniques for enhancing attention discussed earlier in this chapter. Through these means, you boost your chances of noticing information that has important short- and long-term consequences for your personal and professional relationships.

EAVESDROPPING

In *Wuthering Heights*, Emily Brontë's classic tale of romance and vengeance, a major turning point occurs when Heathcliff eavesdrops on a conversation between his lover Catherine and Nelly, the story's narrator. Heathcliff's interpretation of Catherine's comments cause him to abandon her, setting in motion a tragic series of events that lead to Catherine's death (Brontë, 1995):

> "It would degrade me to marry Heathcliff, now; so he shall never know how I love him; and that, not because he's handsome, Nelly, but because he's more myself than I am. Whatever our souls are made of, his and mine are the same." Ere this speech ended I became sensible of Heathcliff's presence. Having noticed a slight movement, I turned my head, and saw him rise from the bench, and steal out, noiselessly. He had listened till he heard Catherine say it would degrade her to marry him, and then he staid to hear no farther. (p. 80)

We often assume that our conversations occur in isolation and that the people standing, sitting, or walking around the participants can't hear the exchange. But they can. As sociologist Erving Goffman (1979) noted, the presence of other individuals within the auditory and visual range of a conversation should be considered the rule and not the exception. This is the case even with phone conversations, e-mail, and texting. Most cell-phone conversations occur with others in the immediate proximity, and e-mail and texting are no more secure than a postcard.

When people intentionally and systematically set up situations so they can listen to private conversations, they are **eavesdropping** (Goffman, 1979). People eavesdrop for a host of reasons: desire to find out if someone is sharing personally, professionally, or legally incriminating information; suspicion that others are talking behind their backs; or even simple curiosity. Eavesdropping is both inappropriate and unethical (hence, incompetent) because it robs others of their right to privacy and it disrespects their decision to not share certain information with you. Perhaps not surprisingly, the social norms governing this behavior are powerful. If people believe that you eavesdropped on a conversation, they typically will be upset and angry, and they may threaten reprisals.

Eavesdropping can be personally damaging as well. People occasionally say spiteful or hurtful things that they don't really mean, simply to impress others, fit in, or draw attention to themselves. As the *Wuthering Heights* example illustrates,

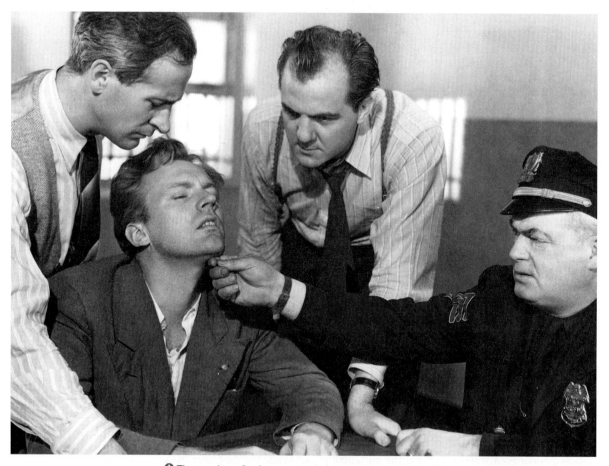

⬡ The good cop/bad cop scenario is something we have all seen on television and in movies. The "bad cop" succeeds only if the "good cop" listens well enough to draw information out of the intimidated person both are interrogating. The bad cop's aggressive listening style is unlikely to work on its own.

The Gift of Active Listening

Active listening creates interpersonal opportunities

When we are newborns struggling to make sense of a world filled with mysterious noises, we quickly learn to listen. Long before we recognize written words as having meaning, and long before we can produce our own words, we come to understand the words of others. Our lives as interpersonal communicators begin at that point.

It is ironic, then, that this first communicative gift shared by human beings—the gift of listening—poses so many challenges for us when we reach adulthood. We struggle with listening in part because it is exceptionally demanding. Active listening requires dedication to mastering knowledge, hard work in practicing skills, and the motivation to continually improve.

Yet when we surmount the challenges of active listening by focusing our attention, training our memories, adapting our listening styles, and avoiding incompetent listening, an amazing thing happens. The activity that we originally mistook as passive begins to crackle with the energy of opportunity. For when we actively listen, the words and worlds of others wash over us, providing us with rich and unanticipated opportunities to move beyond the constraints of our own thoughts and beliefs and to forge interpersonal connections with others.

We began this chapter with the story of a man who dedicated his life to active listening. Fred Rogers brought his ministerial values of compassion and kindness to the small screen, and through television he touched the lives of millions of children. In addition to establishing the longest-running show in history, he created a safe space in which children felt simultaneously entertained, educated, and affirmed by an adult who genuinely listened to them.

How do you use listening in *your* life? What values underlie your listening? Do you create metaphorical "neighborhoods" through your listening—places in which people feel welcomed and valued? Or, as Eddie Murphy once quipped, do you create places where whenever you "move in, everyone else moves away"?

The PBS soundstage Fred Rogers once strolled through lies abandoned now, just as his famous cardigan hangs empty in a Smithsonian display case. He'll never again "be back when the day is new." Yet the values he espoused will endure as long as people actively, compassionately, and respectfully listen to one another.

POSTSCRIPT

key terms

▶ You can watch brief, illustrative videos of these terms and test your understanding of the concepts online in *VideoCentral: Interpersonal Communication* at **bedfordstmartins .com/reflectrelate**.

key concepts

Listening: A Five-Step Process

- Although we often think of **listening** as an isolated experience, it's actually a complex process. The first step of listening is **receiving**, which involves seeing and **hearing** the communication of others.

- A critical part of active listening is **attending** to information in an alert and energized fashion. To improve your attention skills, you should limit multitasking, control factors that impede attention (such as fatigue, stress, and consumption of drugs or alcohol), and practice **mental bracketing**.

- **Understanding** the meaning of others' communication requires us to compare information in our **short-term memory** and **long-term memory**, using prior knowledge to evaluate the meaning of new information.

- Active listening requires **responding** to the communication of others in clear and constructive ways. Indications of effective responding include positive **feedback** and the use of **back-channel cues**. **Paraphrasing** can also help you convey understanding, but if you use it extensively during face-to-face encounters, your partners may find it annoying, and you run the risk of conversational lapses.

- Listening effectiveness is often measured in terms of our **recalling** ability, something you can improve through the use of **mnemonics**. In creating effective mnemonics, reduce complex information to simpler forms, employ visual images (as well as information from other senses), and use the **bizarreness effect**.

The Five Functions of Listening

- Even during a single interpersonal encounter, you will likely have multiple purposes for listening, known as **listening functions**. Active listeners recognize the importance of quickly switching from function to function as circumstances dictate.

Understanding Listening Styles

- Although different situations require different approaches to listening, most people have one or two dominant **listening styles** that they use across situations. The four most common listening styles are **people-**, **action-**, **content-**, and **time-oriented** listening. Both gender and culture impact perceptions of which styles are most effective, as well as preferences for using particular styles.

Preventing Incompetent Listening

- To listen effectively, you must learn to recognize and avoid incompetent forms of listening. One of the greatest challenges to active listening is **selective listening**, which is a natural result of fluctuating attention.
- **Eavesdropping** is an especially destructive form of listening and can have serious consequences, such as legal action against you.
- If you use **pseudo-listening** deliberately to deceive others, you're behaving unethically.
- Some people use **aggressive listening** to attack others. People who do so during online encounters are known as provocateurs.
- People who engage in **narcissistic listening** constantly seek to turn the focus of the conversation back to themselves and may pout or whine if the talk strays from their interests.

key skills

- What can you do to deal with noise pollution and its negative effects on your ability to accurately receive information? Look at pages 148–149 for the answer.
- Interested in improving your attention in ways that enhance your listening? Review the suggestions on pages 149–151. Then try the *Self-Quiz* on your multitasking habits on page 150 and the *Skills Practice* on page 151.
- What two things can you do to effectively communicate your attention and understanding to others when responding? Find out on pages 153–155.
- How can you enhance your positive feedback skills to improve your interpersonal communication? Follow the four rules detailed on page 154.
- Do you want to improve your ability to understand and respond to messages online? Try the *Skills Practice* on page 155.
- Want to improve your recall ability? Apply the practical tips for improving recall skills offered on pages 155–157.
- Interested in effectively adapting your listening purpose during interpersonal encounters? Review the discussion on pages 159–160.
- Curious about your dominant listening style? Complete the *Self-Quiz* on page 162 to find out. Then review the discussion of listening styles on pages 160–163 to discover how listening styles influence your interpersonal effectiveness.
- What are the best listening styles to use when you're engaged in cross-gender or cross-cultural encounters? Find the answers on pages 163–164.
- Want to more effectively communicate with someone who employs an aggressive listening style? Complete the *Skills Practice* on page 170 to discover how.
- Interested in putting your active listening skills to the test? Complete the *Making Relationship Choices* exercise on pages 168–169.

6
Communicating Verbally

"The game is pretty near up," George Washington wrote his cousin in 1776.[1] His army had suffered several devastating defeats, and the British had taken New York City. With only 3,000 of his original 20,000 troops remaining, Washington retreated to the Delaware River. There, his troops hunkered down in the snow, sick and fatigued. Ten miles upstream, on the opposing shore, lay the city of Trenton—and a British garrison filled with German "Hessian" mercenaries.

The morning of Christmas Eve, Congressman Benjamin Rush paid Washington a visit, hoping to lift his spirits. During their conversation, Washington furiously scribbled on scraps of paper. Seeing one fall to the floor—and thinking perhaps they were notes to loved ones—Rush picked it up. He was surprised to see only three words: "Victory or Death." It was Washington's password to his officers for an assault on Trenton.

Washington's plan was audacious and unprecedented: he would launch a surprise attack on Christmas Day. The risks were enormous. With so few men left, if the ploy failed, the war would be lost, and with it, the dream of a free and independent "United States." The odds of success were minimal. Washington's troops would have to navigate the turbulent, ice-packed river with horses, equipment, and weapons, at night, then hike 10 miles through the snow to attack a heavily

> Verbal communication opens doorways to shared understanding, intimacy, and enduring relationships

[1]All information in this section is adapted from Randall (1998) and Rothbard (1999).

fortified encampment filled with highly trained troops.

But Washington had a secret motivational weapon. Five days earlier, intellectual and revolutionary Thomas Paine had penned "The American Crisis," an essay that opened with the following words:

> These are the times that try men's souls. The summer soldier and the sunshine patriot will, in this crisis, shrink from the service of their country; but he that stands it now, deserves the love and thanks of man and woman. Tyranny, like hell, is not easily conquered; yet we have this consolation with us: the harder the conflict, the more glorious the triumph!

Sensing his soldiers' low morale, and realizing the power of the spoken word to inspire, Washington ordered officers along the riverbank to read Paine's passage out loud to their troops before they embarked. It worked. Uplifted by the impassioned words, the troops braved the crossing without incurring any losses, despite the giant chunks of ice that surged down the river and rammed their boats.

By 4 a.m. the crossing was complete, and the troops began their cold, treacherous journey to Trenton. It took four hours to march the 10 miles. But when they arrived, they immediately attacked—and caught the sleeping Hessians and their British officers unawares. As they stormed the town, Washington's sleet- and mud-covered troops shouted, "These are the times that try men's souls!"

The battle ended quickly. The Americans suffered only four casualties, whereas 100 Hessians were killed or wounded, over 900 were taken prisoner, and the garrison and all of its weapons and supplies were confiscated. More importantly, a stunning psychological blow had been landed against the British: the "upstart colonists" could fight—and win—after all. In the months that followed, Washington prevailed in a series of similar clashes, ultimately winning the war itself and ensuring the survival of the fledgling nation.

On Christmas Day 1776, a beleaguered general put his faith in the power of verbal communication to motivate forlorn troops to cross an impassable river and attack an impregnable fortress. Centuries later, millions of people live, learn, and love in a country that exists because of those words.

In a life filled with firsts—first kiss, first job, first car—it's a first we don't even remember. But it's celebrated by the people around us, who recognize in that fleeting moment the dawning of a life filled with language. Our first word drops from our mouths as the simplest of monosyllables: "cup," "dog," "ball." But once the sound has left our lips, the path has been irrevocably forged. By age 6, we learn more than 15 new words a day, and our vocabularies have grown to anywhere between 8,000 and 14,000 words (Cole & Cole, 1989). As we master our native tongues, we discover the power of verbal communication. Through exchanging words with others via text, online, over the phone, and face-to-face, we share ideas, influence others, and make relationship choices. We also learn that language can serve both constructive and destructive ends. Used constructively, verbal communication opens doorways to shared understanding, intimacy, and enduring relationships. Used destructively, verbal communication can mislead and injure others and damage our relationships.

In this chapter, we examine the nature and role of verbal communication in our lives. You'll learn:

- The defining characteristics of language
- The important functions that verbal communication serves in our interpersonal encounters and relationships
- Principles you can apply to use verbal communication more cooperatively
- The behaviors and actions that undermine cooperative verbal communication—and what can be done about them

Characteristics of Verbal Communication

Understanding how language works

When we think of what it means to communicate, what often leaps to mind is the exchange of spoken or written language with others during interactions, known as **verbal communication**. Across any given day, we use words to communicate with romantic partners, family members, friends, and coworkers. Our verbal communication bridges multiple media; we exchange language through Facebook posts, via e-mail, on the phone, and face-to-face. During each of these encounters, we tailor our language in creative ways, depending on whom we're speaking with. We shift grammar, word choices, and sometimes even the entire language itself—for example, firing off a Spanish text message to one friend and an English text to another.

Because verbal communication is defined by our use of language, the first step toward improving our verbal communication is to deepen our understanding of language.

self-reflection

How is the language that you use different when talking with professors, versus when talking to your best friend or romantic partner? Which type of language makes you feel more comfortable or close? What does this tell you about the relationship between language and intimacy?

177

 Whether face-to-face or online, we exchange verbal communication daily in our interactions with others.

LANGUAGE IS SYMBOLIC

Take a quick look around you. You'll likely see a wealth of images: this book, the surface on which it (or your computer) rests, and perhaps your roommate or romantic partner. You might experience thoughts and emotions related to what you're seeing—memories of your roommate asking to borrow your car or feelings of love toward your partner. Now imagine communicating all of this to others. To do so, you need words to represent these things: "roommate," "lover," "borrow," "car," "love," and so forth. Whenever we use items to represent other things, they are considered **symbols**. In verbal communication, words are the primary symbols that we use to represent people, objects, events, and ideas (Foss, Foss, & Trapp, 1991).

All languages are basically giant collections of symbols in the form of words that allow us to communicate with one another. When we agree with others on the meanings of words, we communicate easily. Your friend probably knows exactly what you mean by the word *roommate*, so when you use it, misunderstanding is unlikely. But some words have several possible meanings, making confusion possible. For instance, in English, the word *table* might mean a piece of furniture, an element in a textbook, or a verb referring to the need to end talk ("Let's table this discussion until our next meeting"). For words that have mul-

tiple meanings, we rely on the surrounding context to help clarify meaning. If you're in a classroom and the professor says, "Turn to Table 3 on page 47," you aren't likely to search the room for furniture.

LANGUAGE IS GOVERNED BY RULES

When we use language, we follow rules. Rules govern the meaning of words, the way we arrange words into phrases and sentences, and the order in which we exchange words with others during conversations. **Constitutive rules** define word meaning: they tell us which words represent which objects (Searle, 1965). For example, a constitutive rule in the English language is: "The word *dog* refers to a domestic canine." Whenever you learn the vocabulary of a language—words and their corresponding meanings—you're learning the constitutive rules for that language.

    Regulative rules govern how we use language when we verbally communicate. They're the traffic laws controlling language use—the dos and don'ts. Regulative rules guide everything from spelling ("*i* before *e* except after *c*") to sentence structure ("The article *the* or *a* must come before the noun *dog*") to conversation ("If someone asks you a question, you should answer").

    To communicate competently, you must understand and follow the constitutive and regulative rules governing the language you're using. If you don't know which words represent which meanings (constitutive rules), you can't send clear messages to others or understand messages delivered by others. Likewise, without knowing how to form a grammatically correct sentence and when to say particular things (regulative rules), you can't communicate clearly with others or accurately interpret their messages to you.

LANGUAGE IS FLEXIBLE

Although all languages have constitutive and regulative rules, people often bend those rules. Partners in close relationships, for example, often create **personal idioms**—words and phrases that have unique meanings to them (Bell, Buerkel-Rothfuss, & Gore, 1987). One study found that the average romantic couple had created more than a half dozen idioms, the most common being nicknames such as "Honeybear" or "Pookie." When large groups of people share creative variations on language rules, those variations are called **dialects** (Gleason,

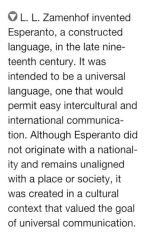

○ L. L. Zamenhof invented Esperanto, a constructed language, in the late nineteenth century. It was intended to be a universal language, one that would permit easy intercultural and international communication. Although Esperanto did not originate with a nationality and remains unaligned with a place or society, it was created in a cultural context that valued the goal of universal communication.

○ We use words as symbols to represent objects, actions, people, places, and ideas.

self-QUIZ

Test Your Knowledge of American Dialects

Each of the following phrases is common to a specific U.S. dialect. See if you know what each one means and where it is from.

1. "Are you packing a card?"
2. "Check out the second growth."
3. "Mind if I use your commode?"
4. "Hey, that guy just budged!"
5. "Is there a bubbler nearby?"

6. "You're blocking my dooryard."
7. "He's just a leafer."
8. "Let's sit in the parlor."
9. "It's in the locker."

Note: Information in this *Self-Quiz* was obtained from "Regional vocabularies of American English" (n.d.).

Answers: (1) Union membership, Pacific Northwest. (2) Timber that has grown back on a previously harvested area, Pacific Northwest. (3) Bathroom, Deep South. (4) Cut in line, eastern Wisconsin and Minnesota. (5) Drinking fountain, eastern Wisconsin. (6) Driveway, Maine and northern New England. (7) Tourist traveling to see the seasonal foliage, northern New England. (8) Living room, Delaware Valley. (9) Closet, New Orleans.

1989). A dialect may include unique phrases, words, and pronunciations (what we call "accents"). Dialects can be shared by people living in a certain region (midwestern, southern, or northeastern United States), people with a common socioeconomic status (upper-middle-class suburban, working class urban), or people of similar ethnic or religious ancestry (Yiddish English, Irish English, Amish English) (Chen & Starosta, 2005).

Most people prefer their own dialect. Communication scholar Jesse Delia (1972) conducted a study that asked people to form impressions of others based solely on voice recordings of dialects. Listeners formed positive impressions of persons who used dialects similar to their own, and more negative impressions of those with dissimilar dialects. Since dialects powerfully influence our perceptions of others, you should be aware of how they may affect your own communication. Resist making negative or stereotypical judgments about others who speak with dialects different from your own.

LANGUAGE IS CULTURAL

self-reflection

What language do you consider your native tongue? In what ways does this language connect you culturally to those who share it? How does it distance you from those who don't speak it?

Languages and cultures are fused in fundamental ways. Language is the set of symbols that members of a culture create to communicate their thoughts, beliefs, attitudes, and values with one another. Once created, a language is used to bolster a sense of cultural identity and connectedness (Whorf, 1952). Thus, languages both reflect the cultures that created them and enable people to perpetuate those cultures, while also sustaining a sense of collective identity—for example, "We are Japanese" or "We are Kenyans."

Moreover, people use language differently depending on the extent to which they assume that others share their cultural beliefs, attitudes, and values. Consider the challenges that a friend of mine, communication professor Naomi

Kagawa, faced when she first arrived in the United States. In her home country of Japan, elaborate social norms govern how requests are expressed, accepted, and rejected. People presume this knowledge is shared by others. So, for example, when undesirable requests are received, respondents often reject them using language that in the United States would signal consent (words equivalent to "OK" or "sure"). Japanese reject in this way because it maintains the harmony of the encounter; requesters aren't blatantly denied, and thus they don't lose face. These words and phrases, however, are accompanied by subtle vocal tones that *imply* "no." Requesters and rejecters—informed by their knowledge of Japanese customs—recognize that such seeming assents are actually rejections. In the United States, people typically don't presume that others share similar knowledge and beliefs, so they "spell things out" much more explicitly. When people reject requests, for instance, they may come right out and say "no," then provide an explanation of why they can't grant the request. Needless to say, Naomi—and those with whom she interacted upon first arriving in the States—experienced much confusion. She rejected unwanted requests by saying "OK," only to find that people thought she was consenting rather than refusing!

The struggle Naomi faced reflects the difference between *high-* and *low-context cultures* (Hall & Hall, 1987). Within **high-context cultures**, such as in China, Korea, and Japan, people presume that listeners share extensive knowledge in common with them. As a result, they don't feel a need to provide a lot of explicit information to gain listeners' understanding. People can hint, imply, or suggest meanings and feel confident that they will be understood. Consequently, communicators in high-context cultures rely more on indirect and ambiguous language and even silence to convey important meanings. They also often "talk around" points rather than addressing them directly.

In contrast, in **low-context cultures**, people tend *not* to presume that listeners share their beliefs, attitudes, and values, so they tailor their verbal communication to be informative, clear, and direct (Hall & Hall, 1987). They openly express their own viewpoints and attempt to persuade others to accept them (Hall, 1976, 1997a). Within such cultures, which include Germany, Scandinavia, Canada, and the United States, people tend not to rely as much on implying or hinting. Instead, they strive to make important information obvious in the words themselves ("Here are my thoughts on this situation . . .").

LANGUAGE EVOLVES

Each year, the American Dialect Society selects a "Word of the Year." Recent winners include *tweet*, a "short, timely message sent via the Twitter.com service," and *app*, "an abbreviated form of application, a software program for a computer or phone operating system." Even the *Oxford English Dictionary*—the resource that defines the English language—annually announces what new terms have officially been added to the English vocabulary. In 2011, this included *cyberbullying* ("the use of electronic communication to bully a person, typically by sending messages of an intimidating or threatening nature") and *sexting* ("the sending of sexually explicit photographs or messages via mobile phone").

⬤ As technology changes, we add new words to our vocabulary, such as *iPad* and *app*. Meanwhile, other words may become associated with new meanings, such as *tablet* and *tweet*.

Many people view language as fixed. But in fact, language constantly changes. A particular language's constitutive rules—which define the meanings of words—may shift. As time passes and technology changes, people add new words to their language (*tweet*, *app*, *cyberbullying*, *sexting*) and discard old ones. Sometimes people create new phrases, such as *helicopter parent*, that eventually see wide use. Other times, speakers of a language borrow words and phrases from other languages and incorporate them into their own.

Consider how English-speakers have borrowed from other languages: If you tell friends that you want to *take* a *whirl* around the United States, you're using Norse (Viking) words, and if your trip takes you to *Wisconsin*, *Oregon*, and *Wyoming*, you're visiting places with Native American names.[2] If you stop at a café and request a cup of *tea* along the way, you're speaking Amoy (eastern China), but if you ask the waiter to spike your coffee with *alcohol*, you're using Arabic. If, at the end of the trip, you express an eagerness to return to your *job*, you're employing Breton (western France), but if you call in sick and tell your *manager* that you have *influenza*, you're speaking Italian.

A language's regulative rules also change. When you learned to speak and write English, for example, you probably were taught that *they* is inappropriate as a singular pronoun. But before the 1850s, people commonly used *they* as the singular pronoun for individuals whose gender was unknown—for example, "the owner went out to the stables, where they fed the horses" (Spender, 1990). In 1850, male grammarians petitioned the British Parliament to pass a law declaring that all gender-indeterminate references be labeled *he* instead of *they* (Spender, 1990). Since that time, teachers of English worldwide have taught their students that *they* used as a singular pronoun is "not proper."

Functions of Verbal Communication

Language guides our interactions

He was crowned "Sportsman of the Century" by *Sports Illustrated*, and "Sports Personality of the Century" by the BBC.[3] He is considered by many to be the greatest boxer of all time, a fact reflected in his nickname, "The Greatest." He certainly was the most verbal. Muhammad Ali made a name for himself early in his career by poetically boasting about his abilities ("Your hands can't hit what your eyes can't

---

[2]The information regarding the origins of these words was obtained from "The English language: Words borrowed from other languages" (n.d.).

[3]The information that follows is adapted from Hauser (2006).

◀ Muhammad Ali's verbal communication skills served important functions throughout his life, whether intimidating opponents or attracting supporters to his causes.

see!") and trash-talking his opponents. "I'm going to float like a butterfly, and sting like a bee," he told then-champion Sonny Liston—who Ali dubbed "the big ugly bear"—before defeating him to claim the World Heavyweight title. Ali was just as verbal outside of the boxing ring. Early in his professional career, he embraced Islam, and subsequently abandoned his birth name of Cassius Clay because the surname came from his ancestors' slave owners. Years before public sentiment joined him, Ali spoke out repeatedly against the Vietnam War. His refusal to participate in the military draft cost him both his world title and his boxing license (both of which were eventually reinstated). Years later, he continues to be outspoken—on behalf of humanitarian causes. His work with U.N. hunger relief organizations has helped feed tens of millions of people ("Service to others is the rent you pay for your room here on earth"), and he was a United Nations Messenger of Peace and a recipient of the Presidential Medal of Freedom. Whether in the boxing ring or on a charity mission, he has used his prowess with verbal communication to achieve his goals and dreams.

Similar to Muhammad Ali, we all use verbal communication to serve many different functions in our daily lives. Let's examine six of the most important of these, all of which strongly influence our interpersonal communication and relationships.

SHARING MEANING

The most obvious function verbal communication serves is enabling us to share meanings with others during interpersonal encounters. When you use language to verbally communicate, you share two kinds of meanings. The first is the literal meaning of your words, as agreed on by members of your culture, known as **denotative meaning**. Denotative meaning is what you find in dictionaries—for example, the word *bear* means "any of a family (Ursidae of the order Carnivora) of large heavy mammals of America and Eurasia that have long shaggy hair" (*Merriam-Webster Dictionary*, 2011). When Ali called Sonny Liston a "big ugly bear," he knew Liston would understand the denotative meanings of his words, and interpret them as an insult.

But when we verbally communicate, we also exchange **connotative meaning**: additional understandings of a word's meaning based on the situation and the knowledge we and our communication partners share. Connotative meaning is implied, suggested, or hinted at by the words you choose while communicating with others. Say, for example, that your romantic partner has a large stuffed teddy bear that, despite its weathered and worn appearance, is your partner's most prized childhood possession. To convey your love and adoration for your partner, and how valued he or she is in your eyes, you might say, "You're *my* big ugly bear." In doing so, you certainly don't mean that your lover is big, ugly, or bearlike in appearance! Instead, you rely on your partner understanding your implied link to his or her treasured object (the connotative meaning). Relationship intimacy plays a major role in shaping how we use and interpret connotative meanings while communicating with others (Hall, 1997a): people who know each other extremely well can convey connotative meanings accurately to one another.

SHAPING THOUGHT

In addition to enabling us to share meaning during interpersonal encounters, verbal communication also shapes our thoughts and perceptions of reality. Feminist

We see the world through the lens of our language.

scholar Dale Spender (1990) describes the relationship between words and our inner world in this way:

> To speak metaphorically, the brain is blind and deaf; it has no direct contact with light or sound. The brain has to interpret: it only deals in symbols and never knows the real thing. And the program for encoding and decoding is set up by the language which we possess. What we *see* in the world around us depends in large part on our language. (pp. 139–140)

Consider an encounter I had at a family gathering. My 6-year-old niece told me that a female neighbor of hers had helped several children escape a house fire. When I commended the neighbor's heroism, my niece corrected me. "Girls can't be *heroes*," she scolded. "Only boys can be *heroes*!" In talking with her further, I discovered she knew of no word representing "brave woman." Her only exposure to *heroine* was through her mother's romantic novels. Not knowing a word for "female bravery," she considered the concept unfathomable: "The neighbor lady wasn't a hero, she just saved the kids."

The idea that language shapes how we think about things was first suggested by researcher Edward Sapir, who conducted an intensive study of Native American languages in the early 1900s. Sapir argued that because language is our primary means of sharing meaning with others, it powerfully affects how we perceive others and our relationships with them (Gumperz & Levinson, 1996). Almost 50 years later, Benjamin Lee Whorf expanded on Sapir's ideas in what has become known as the Sapir-Whorf Hypothesis. Whorf argued that we

Yet different people from different cultures use different languages.

cannot conceive of that for which we lack a vocabulary—that language quite literally defines the boundaries of our thinking. This view is known as **linguistic determinism**. As contemporary scholars note, linguistic determinism suggests that our ability to think is "at the mercy" of language (Gumperz & Levinson, 1996). We are mentally "constrained" by language to only think certain thoughts, and we cannot interpret the world in neutral ways, because we always see the world through the lens of our languages.

Both Sapir and Whorf also recognized the dramatic impact that culture has on language. Because language determines our thoughts, and different people from different cultures use different languages, Sapir and Whorf agreed that people from different cultures would perceive and think about the world in very different ways, an effect known as **linguistic relativity**.

self-reflection

Think about the vocabulary you inherited from your culture for thinking and talking about relationships. What terms exist for describing serious romantic involvements, casual relationships that are sexual, and relationships that are purely platonic? How do these various terms shape your thinking about these relationships?

NAMING

A third important function of verbal communication is **naming**—that is, creating linguistic symbols for objects. The process of naming is one of humankind's most profound and unique abilities (Spender, 1984). When we name people, places, objects, and ideas, we create symbols that represent them. We then use these symbols during our interactions with others to communicate meaning about these things. Because of the powerful impact language exerts on our thoughts, the decisions we make about what to name things ultimately determine not just the meanings we exchange but also our perceptions of the people, places, and objects we communicate about. This was why Muhammad Ali decided to abandon his birth name of Cassius Clay. He recognized that our names are *the* most powerful symbols that define who we are throughout our lives, and he wanted a name that represented his Islamic faith while also renouncing the surname of someone who had, years earlier, enslaved his forebears.

As the Ali example suggests, the issue of naming is especially potent for people who face historical and cultural prejudice, given that others outside the group often label them with derogatory names. Consider the case of gays and lesbians. For many years, gays and lesbians were referred to as "homosexual." But, as scholar Julia Wood (1998) notes, many people shortened "homosexual" to "homo" and used the new term as an insult. In response, lesbian and gay activists in the 1960s renamed themselves "gay." This move also triggered disputes, however. Antigay activists protested the use of a term that traditionally meant "joyous and lively." Some lesbian activists argued that "gay" meant only men and was therefore exclusionary to women. Many straight people began using "gay" as an insult in the same manner as earlier epithets. In the 2000s, the inclusive label of "LGBTQ" (lesbian, gay, bisexual, transgendered, queer) was created to embrace the entire community. But this name still doesn't adequately represent many people's self-impressions. One study identified over a dozen different names that individuals chose for their sexual orientation and gender identity, including "pansexual," "omnisexual," and "same-gender loving/SGL" (Morrison & McCornack, 2011). Given the way positive names have been turned to negative in the past, some people reject names for nonstraight sexual orienta-

Challenging Traditional Gender Labels

In September 2011, Australia changed its passport policy to allow three gender options on travel documents instead of two: male, female, and indeterminate.[4] The goal was to remove discrimination against transgendered persons. As Australian Senator Louise Pratt described, "It's an important recognition of people's human rights." The same month, Pomona College in California revised its student constitution to remove gendered pronouns. "A lot of students do not identify as 'male' or 'female' and aren't using the pronouns 'he' or 'she,' so we are trying to better represent the student body," said Student Commissioner Sarah Applebaum. "Ideally, this will help promote a more supportive campus for gender-nonconforming, queer, and transgender students."

These changes are part of a larger cultural trend toward challenging traditional language labels for gender and replacing them with "preferred gender pronouns" or PGPs—gender names of a person's own choosing. As Eliza Byard, executive director of the Gay, Lesbian, and Straight Education Network, describes, "More students today than ever are thinking about what gender means and are using language to get away from masculine and feminine gender assumptions." Some of the more creative PGPs currently in use include "ze," "hir," and "hirs."

Although the use of PGPs is global, the motivation for embracing them is deeply personal. PGPs are a way of using language to authentically capture one's true gender identity. "This has nothing to do with your sexuality and everything to do with who you feel like inside," notes Ann Arbor teen Katy Butler. "My PGPs are 'she,' 'her' and 'hers' and sometimes 'they,' 'them' and 'theirs.'"

discussion questions

● What language label do you most commonly use in reference to your gender? Why do you use this label?

● Does this label authentically and comprehensively capture how you think of yourself in terms of gender?

---

[4]The information that follows is adapted from Conlin (2011), McGuirk (2011), and Wu (2011).

---

tions altogether. As one study respondent put it, "I don't use labels—I'm not a can of soup!" (Morrison & McCornack, 2011).

PERFORMING ACTIONS

A fourth function of verbal communication is that it enables us to take action. We make requests, issue invitations, deliver commands, or even taunt—as Ali did to his competitors. We also try to influence others' behaviors. We want our listeners to grant our requests, accept our invitations, obey our commands, or suffer from our curses. The actions that we perform with language are called **speech acts** (Searle, 1969). (See Table 6.1 on page 188 for types of speech acts.)

During interpersonal encounters, the structure of our back-and-forth exchange is based on the speech acts we perform (Jacobs, 1994; Levinson, 1985). When your professor asks you a question, how do you know what to do next? You recognize that the words she has spoken constitute a "question," and you realize that an "answer" is expected as the relevant response. Similarly, when your best

table 6.1 **Types of Speech Acts**

Act	Function	Forms	Example
Representative	Commits the speaker to the truth of what has been said	Assertions, Conclusions	"It sure is a beautiful day."
Directive	Attempts to get listeners to do things	Questions, Requests, Commands	"Can you loan me five dollars?"
Commissive	Commits speakers to future action	Promises, Threats	"I will always love you, no matter what happens."
Expressive	Conveys a psychological or emotional state that the speaker is experiencing	Thanks, Apologies, Congratulations	"Thank you so much for the wonderful gift!"
Declarative	Produces dramatic, observable effects	Marriage Pronouncements, Firing Declarations	"From this point onward, you are no longer an employee of this organization."

Note: The information in this table is adapted from Searle (1976).

friend text-messages you and inquires, "Can I borrow your car tonight?" you immediately recognize his message as a "request." You also understand that two speech acts are possible as relevant responses: "granting" his request ("no problem") or "rejecting" it ("I don't think so").

CRAFTING CONVERSATIONS

A fifth function served by language is that it allows us to craft conversations. Language meanings, thoughts, names, and acts don't happen in the abstract; they occur within conversations. Although each of us intuitively knows what a conversation is, scholars suggest four characteristics fundamental to conversation (Nofsinger, 1999). First, conversations are *interactive*. At least two people must participate in the exchange for it to count as a conversation, and participants must take turns exchanging messages.

Second, conversations are locally managed. *Local management* means that we make decisions regarding who gets to speak when, and for how long, each time we exchange turns. This makes conversation different from other verbal exchanges such as debate, in which the order and length of turns are decided before the event begins, and drama, in which people speak words that have been written down in advance.

Third, conversation is *universal*. Conversation forms the foundation for most forms of interpersonal communication and for social organization generally. Our relationships and our places in society are created and maintained through conversations.

Fourth, conversations often adhere to *scripts*—rigidly structured patterns of talk. This is especially true in first encounters, when you are trying to reduce other people's uncertainty. For example, the topics that college students discuss when they first meet often follows a set script. Communication researcher Kathy

Kellermann (1991) conducted several studies looking at the first conversations of college students and found that 95 percent of the topic changes followed the same pattern regardless of gender, age, race, or geographic region. (See Figure 6.1.) This suggests that a critical aspect of appropriately constructing conversations is grasping and following relevant conversational scripts.

Does the fact that we frequently use scripts to guide our conversations mean this type of communication is inauthentic? If you expect more from an exchange than a prepackaged response, scripted communication may strike you as such. However, communication scripts allow us to relevantly *and* efficiently exchange greetings, respond to simple questions and answers, trade pleasantries, and get to know people in a preliminary fashion without putting much active thought into our communication. This saves us from mental exertion and allows us to focus our energy on more involved or important interpersonal encounters.

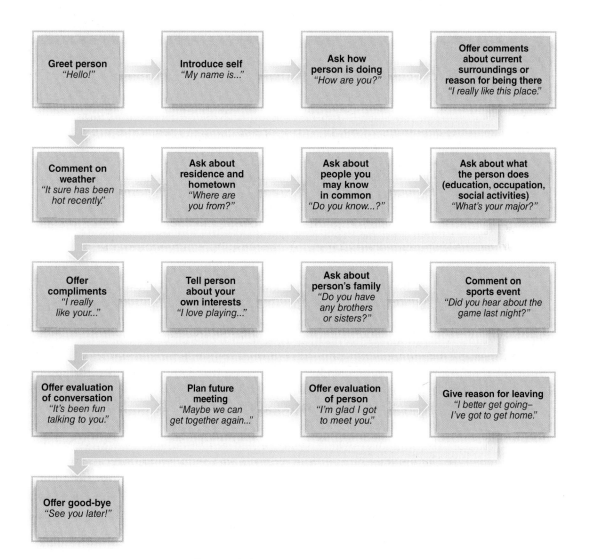

figure 6.1 **Conversational Pattern**

◗ Ray creates a deeper, more intimate relationship with Susie when he communicates his love for her in *The Lovely Bones*.

MANAGING RELATIONSHIPS

In Alice Sebold's (2002) award-winning novel *The Lovely Bones*, Indian high school student Ray Singh is desperately in love with the central character, Susie Salmon. Seeing her sneaking into school late one morning (while he himself is cutting class and hiding out in the school theater), he decides to declare his feelings.

> "You are beautiful, Susie Salmon!" I heard the voice but could not place it immediately. I looked around me. "Here," the voice said. I looked up and saw the head and torso of Ray Singh leaning out over the top of the scaffold above me. "Hello," he said. I knew Ray had a crush on me. He had moved from England the year before, but was born in India. That someone could have the face of one country and the voice of another and then move to a third was too incredible for me to fathom. It made him immediately cool. Plus, he seemed eight hundred times smarter than the rest of us, and he had a crush on me. That morning, when he spoke to me from above, my heart plunged to the floor. (p. 82)

self-reflection

Consider a recent instance in which a relationship of yours suddenly changed direction, either for better or worse. What was said that triggered this turning point? How did the words that were exchanged impact intimacy? What does this tell you about the role that language plays in managing relationships?

Verbal communication's final, and arguably most profound, function in our lives is to help us manage our relationships. We use language to create relationships by declaring powerful, intimate feelings to others, "You are beautiful!" Verbal communication is the principal means through which we maintain our ongoing relationships with lovers, family members, friends, and coworkers (Stafford, 2011). For example, romantic partners who verbally communicate frequently with each other, and with their partners' friends and families, experience less uncertainty in their relationships and are not as likely to break up as those who verbally communicate less often (Parks, 2007). Finally, most of the heartbreaks we'll experience in our lives are preceded by verbal messages that state, in one form or another, "It's over." We'll discuss more about how we forge, maintain, and end our relationships in Chapters 9 through 12.

Cooperative Verbal Communication

Creating understandable messages

Eager to connect with your teenage son, you ask him how his day was when he arrives home from school. But you get only a grunted "Fine" in return, as he quickly disappears into his room to play computer games. You invite your romantic partner over for dinner, excited to demonstrate a new recipe. But when you query your partner's opinion of the dish, the response is "It's interesting." You text your best friend, asking for her feedback on an in-class presentation you gave earlier that day. She responds, "You talked way too fast!"

Although these examples seem widely disparate, they share an underlying commonality: people failing to verbally communicate in a fully cooperative fashion. To understand how these messages are uncooperative, consider their cooperative counterparts. Your son tells you, "It was all right—I didn't do as well on my chem test as I wanted, but I got an A on my history report." Your partner says, "It's good, but I think it'd be even better with a little more salt." Your friend's text message reads, "It went well, but I thought it could have been presented a little slower."

When you use **cooperative verbal communication**, you produce messages that have three characteristics. First, you speak in ways that others can easily understand, using language that is informative, honest, relevant, and clear. Second, you take active ownership for what you're saying by using "I" language. Third, you make others feel included rather than excluded—for example, through the use of "we."

UNDERSTANDABLE MESSAGES

In his exploration of language and meaning, philosopher Paul Grice noted that cooperative interactions rest on our ability to tailor our verbal communication so

◖ Oral storytelling is an ancient art, one that creates and passes histories and mythologies down from generation to generation. Through blogs and pod-casts, this tradition continues to take on new forms.

▶ Practicing the Cooperative Principle is important in your relationships with coworkers, with whom information often needs to be shared in a timely and professional manner. This is especially relevant when communicating via e-mail, where nonverbal cues, such as vocal tone and gestures, are not possible.

others can understand us. To produce understandable messages, we have to abide by the **Cooperative Principle**: making our conversational contributions as *informative, honest, relevant,* and *clear* as is required, given the purposes of the encounters in which we're involved (Grice, 1989).

Being aware of situational characteristics is critical to applying the Cooperative Principle. For example, while we're ethically bound to share important information with others, this doesn't mean we *always* should. Suppose a friend discloses a confidential secret to you and your sibling later asks you to reveal it. In this case, it would be unethical to share this information without your friend's permission.

Being Informative   According to Grice (1989), being informative during interpersonal encounters means two things. First, you should present all of the information that is relevant and appropriate to share, given the situation. When a coworker passes you in the hallway and greets you with a quick "How's it going?" the situation requires that you provide little information in return—"Great! How are you?" The same question asked by a concerned friend during a personal crisis creates very different demands; your friend likely wants a detailed accounting of your thoughts and feelings.

Second, you want to avoid being *too* informative—that is, disclosing information that isn't appropriate or important in a particular situation. A detailed description of your personal woes ("I haven't been sleeping well lately, and my cat is sick . . .") in response to your colleague's quick "How's it going?" query would likely be perceived as inappropriate and even strange.

The responsibility to be informative overlaps with the responsibility to be ethical. To be a cooperative verbal communicator, you must share information with others that has important personal and relational implications for them. To illustrate, if you discover that your friend's spouse is having an affair, you're ethically obligated to disclose this information if your friend asks you about it.

Being Honest   **Honesty** is the single most important characteristic of cooperative verbal communication because other people count on the fact that the information you share with them is truthful (Grice, 1989). Honesty means not sharing information that you're uncertain about and not disclosing information that you know is false. When you are dishonest in your verbal communication, you violate standards for ethical behavior, and you lead others to believe false things (Jacobs, Dawson, & Brashers, 1996). For example, if you assure your romantic partner that your feelings haven't changed when in fact they have, you give your partner false hope about your future together. You also lay the groundwork for your partner to make continued investments in a relationship that you know is already doomed.

Being Relevant   Relevance means making your conversational contributions responsive to what others have said. When people ask you questions, you provide answers. When they make requests, you grant or reject their requests. When certain topics arise in the conversation, you tie your contributions to that topic. During conversations, you stick with relevant topics and avoid those that aren't. Dodging questions or abruptly changing topics is uncooperative, and in some instances, others may see it as an attempt at deception—especially if you change topics to avoid discussing something you want to keep hidden (McCornack, 2008).

Being Clear   Using clear language means presenting information in a straightforward fashion rather than framing it in obscure or ambiguous terms. For example, telling a partner that you like a recipe but that it needs more salt is easier to understand than veiling your meaning by vaguely saying, "It's interesting." But note that using clear language doesn't mean being brutally frank or dumping offensive and hurtful information on others. Competent interpersonal communicators always consider others' feelings when designing their messages. When information is important and relevant to disclose, choose your words carefully to be both respectful *and* clear, so that others won't misconstrue your intended meaning.

Dealing with Misunderstanding   Of course, just because you use informative, honest, relevant, and clear language doesn't guarantee that you will be understood by others. When one person misperceives another's thoughts, feelings, or beliefs as expressed in the other individual's verbal communication, **misunderstanding** occurs. Misunderstanding most commonly results from a failure to actively listen. Recall, for example, our discussion of action-oriented listeners in Chapter 5. Action-oriented listeners often become impatient with others while listening and frequently jump ahead to finish other people's

self-reflection

Recall an encounter where you possessed important information but knew that disclosing it would be personally or relationally problematic. What did you do? How did your decision impact your relationship? Was your choice ethical? Based on your experience, is it always cooperative to disclose important information?

○ One downside of our frequent online communication is that it is easy to misunderstand others' messages, often mistaking them as ruder or less clear than intended. If you need a message to be error-free, consider delivering it in person or over the phone.

self-reflection

Recall an online encounter in which you thought you understood someone's e-mail, text message, or post, then later found out you were wrong. How did you discover that your impression was mistaken? What could you have done differently to avoid the misunderstanding?

(presumed) points (Watson, Barker, & Weaver, 1995). This listening style can lead them to misunderstand others' messages. To overcome this source of misunderstanding, practice the active listening skills described in Chapter 5.

Misunderstanding occurs frequently online, owing to the lack of nonverbal cues to help clarify one another's meaning. One study found that 27.2 percent of respondents agreed that e-mail is likely to result in miscommunication of intent and 53.6 percent agreed that it is relatively easy to misinterpret an e-mail message (Rainey, 2000). The tendency to misunderstand communication online is so prevalent that scholars suggest the following practices: *If a particular message absolutely must be error-free or if its content is controversial, don't use e-mail or text messaging to communicate it.* Whenever possible, conduct high-stakes encounters, such as important attempts at persuasion, face-to-face. Finally, never use e-mails, posts, or texts for sensitive actions such as professional reprimands or dismissals, or relationship breakups (Rainey, 2000).

USING "I" LANGUAGE

It's the biggest intramural basketball game of the year, and your team is down by a point with five seconds left when your teammate is fouled. Stepping to the line for two free throws and a chance to win the game, she misses both, and your team loses. As you leave the court, you angrily snap at her, "You really let us down!"

The second key to cooperative verbal communication is taking ownership of the things you say to others, especially in situations where you're expressing negative feelings or criticism. You can do this by avoiding **"you" language**, phrases that place the focus of attention and blame on other people, such as *"You let us down."* Instead, rearrange your statements so that you use **"I" language**, phrases that emphasize ownership of your feelings, opinions, and beliefs (see Table 6.2). The difference between "I" and "you" may strike you as minor, but it actually has powerful effects: "I" language is less likely to trigger defensiveness on the part of your listeners than "you" language (Kubany, Richard, Bauer, & Muraoka, 1992). "I" language creates a clearer impression on listeners that you're responsible for what you're saying and that you're expressing your own perceptions rather than stating unquestionable truths.

VideoCentral ▣

bedfordstmartins.com /reflectrelate

"You" Language
Watch this clip online to answer the questions below.

In this video, how did the boss's "you" language affect the interaction? How did the employee respond? How would you recommend both the boss and the employee change their communication? Please give specific examples.

Want to see more? Check out VideoCentral for clips on **"I" language** and **"we" language**.

table 6.2 "You" Language versus "I" Language

"You" Language	"I" Language
You make me so angry!	I'm feeling so angry!
You totally messed things up.	I feel like things are totally messed up.
You need to do a better job.	I think this job needs to be done better.
You really hurt my feelings.	I'm feeling really hurt.
You never pay any attention to me.	I feel like I never get any attention.

USING "WE" LANGUAGE

It's Thursday night, and you're standing in line waiting to get into a club. In front of you are two couples, and you can't help but overhear their conversations. As you listen, you notice an interesting difference in their verbal communication. One couple expresses everything in terms of "I" and "you"—"What do you want to do later tonight?" "I don't know, but I'm hungry, so I'll probably get something to eat. Do you want to come?" The other couple consistently uses "we"—"What should we do later?" "Why don't we get something to eat?"

What effect does this simple difference in pronoun usage—"we" rather than "I" or "you"—have on your impressions of the two couples? If you perceive the couple using "we" as being closer than the couple using "I" and "you," you would be right. "We" is a common way people signal their closeness (Dreyer, Dreyer, & Davis, 1987). Couples who use **"we" language**—wordings that emphasize inclusion—tend to be more satisfied with their relationships than those who routinely rely on "I" and "you" messages (Honeycutt, 1999).

An important part of cooperative verbal communication is using "we" language to express your connection to others. In a sense, "we" language is the inverse of "I" language. We use "I" language when we want to show others that our feelings, thoughts, and opinions are separate from theirs and that we take sole responsibility for our feelings, thoughts, and opinions. But "we" language helps us bolster feelings of connection and similarity with not only romantic partners but also anyone to whom we want to signal a collaborative relationship. When I went through my training to become a certified Yoga instructor, part of the instruction was to replace the use of "you" with "we" and "let's" during in-class verbal cueing of moves. Rather than saying, "You should lunge forward with your left leg" or "I want you to step forward left," we were taught to say, "*Let's* step forward with *our* left legs." After I implemented "we" language in my Yoga classes, my students repeatedly commented on how they liked the "more personal" and "inclusive" nature of my verbal cueing.

GENDER AND COOPERATIVE VERBAL COMMUNICATION

Powerful stereotypes exist regarding what men and women value in verbal communication. These stereotypes suggest that men appreciate informative, honest, relevant, and clear language more than women do. In Western cultures, many people believe that men communicate in a clear and straightforward fashion and that women are more indirect and wordy (Tannen, 1990). These stereotypes are reinforced powerfully through television, in programs in which female characters often use more polite language than men ("I'm *sorry* to bother you . . ."), more uncertain phrases ("I *suppose* . . ."), and more flowery adjectives ("that's *silly*," "oh, how *beautiful*"), and male characters fill their language with action verbs ("let's *get a move on!*") (Mulac, Bradac, & Mann, 1985).

But research suggests that when it comes to language, men and women are more similar than different. For example, data from 165 studies involving nearly a million and a half subjects found that women do not use more vague and wordy verbal communication than men (Canary & Hause, 1993). The primary

skills
practice

**Cooperative
Language Online**
*Using cooperative language
during an important online
interaction*

❶ Identify an important
online encounter.

❷ Create a rough draft of
the message you wish to
send.

❸ Check that the language
you've used is fully informative, honest, relevant, and
clear.

❹ Use "I" language for all
comments that are negative
or critical.

❺ Use "we" language
throughout the message,
where appropriate.

❻ Send the message.

On the television show *Bones*, Dr. Temperance Brennan (Emily Deschanel) is so direct and concise, she often accidentally offends those around her. Dr. Lance Sweets (John Francis Daley), in contrast, uses more indirect language and questions so that people must infer his actual meaning. How do these differences compare to common stereotypes about the ways in which men and women communicate?

determinant of whether people's language is clear and concise or vague and wordy is not gender but whether the encounter is competitive or collaborative (Fisher, 1983). Both women and men use clear and concise language in competitive interpersonal encounters, such as when arguing with a family member or debating a project proposal in a work meeting. Additionally, they use comparatively vaguer and wordier language during collaborative encounters, such as eating lunch with a friend or relaxing in the evening with a spouse.

CULTURE AND COOPERATIVE VERBAL COMMUNICATION

Culture exerts a significant impact on verbal communication. As we noted earlier in this chapter, language is cultural, and each culture has its own idea of what constitutes cooperative verbal communication. So how can you tailor your use of language when communicating with people from other cultures? For starters, you can study a particular culture's guidelines for verbal expression before communicating with members of that culture and then adapt your own use of language according to those guidelines (Chen & Starosta, 2005).

But also consider **communication accommodation theory**, which holds that people are especially motivated to adapt their language when they seek social approval, when they wish to establish relationships with others, and when they view others' language usage as appropriate (Giles, Coupland, & Coupland, 1991). In contrast, people tend to accentuate differences between their language and others' when they wish to convey emotional distance and disassociate themselves from others.

Research on accommodation suggests that when you moderately adjust your language use to match that of others from different cultures, you will be perceived as having high communication skills (Coupland, Giles, & Wiemann, 1991; Giles

 Moderately adjusting our language when communicating with people from other cultures can help establish new friendships.

et al., 1991). The key to such adjustments is adapting to others' speech rate, clarity of language, and desired balance of turn-taking (Bianconi, 2002). This means attuning yourself early in the conversation to how long the other person takes with his or her turns, how rapidly the individual speaks, how direct he or she is, and how much the person appears to want to talk compared to you. You then fine-tune your verbal communication accordingly: matching the person's speech rate, employing appropriately direct or more ambiguous language, using turn lengths you believe will please the person, and monitoring the other's feedback while you are speaking to see whether he or she wants you to continue or stop. At the same time, avoid matching the other person's dialect or word choices. He or she will likely perceive your behavior as inappropriate and insulting.

Barriers to Cooperative Verbal Communication

Destructive language can damage relationships

In the Coen brothers' Oscar-winning film *No Country for Old Men* (2007), Javier Bardem plays Anton Chigurh, a psychopathic hit man who enjoys making potential victims flip coins for their lives. Chigurh also savors elaborate and philosophical verbal banter: in one scene he queries fellow hit man Carson Wells (played by Woody Harrelson), "If the rule you followed brought you to this, of what use was the rule?" But more than anything else, Chigurh uses language for aggression. When a gas station owner innocently asks, "Ya'll getting any rain up your way? I've seen you was from Dallas . . . ," Chigurh responds with the chilling, "What business is it of yours where I'm from, *friendo*?" When the owner apologizes, Chigurh mocks his drawling accent, and then proceeds to insult him, "You don't know what you're talking about, do you?"

When used cooperatively, language can clarify understandings, build relationships, and bring us closer to others. But language also has the capacity to

skills practice

Intercultural Interaction
Bolstering your communication accommodation skills

❶ Recognize when you're interacting with someone from another culture.

❷ Observe the person's speech rate and turn lengths.

❸ Adjust your speech rate to match the pace of his or her language.

❹ Adapt your turn lengths to mesh with the individual's desired distribution of talk time.

❺ Evaluate his or her language clarity and directness.

❻ Modify your language to be similarly direct or indirect.

⬤ In *No Country for Old Men*, hit man Anton Chigurh uses verbal aggression to intimidate and taunt everyone he comes across.

skills practice

Overcoming Apprehension

Creating communication plans to overcome communication apprehension

❶ Think of a situation or person that triggers communication apprehension.

❷ Envision yourself interacting in this situation or with this person.

❸ List plan actions: topics you will discuss and messages you will present.

❹ List plan contingencies: events that might happen during the encounter, things the other person will likely say and do, and your responses.

❺ Implement your plan the next time you communicate in that situation or with that person.

create divisions and damage relationships. Some people use verbal communication to defensively lash out at others, or intentionally deceive them. Others are filled with fear and anxiety about interacting and therefore do not speak at all. In *No Country for Old Men*, Anton Chigurh uses language as a weapon in his arsenal, aggressively challenging and taunting people. In this section, we explore the darker side of verbal communication by looking at four common barriers to cooperative verbal communication: communication apprehension, defensive communication, verbal aggression, and deception.

COMMUNICATION APPREHENSION

Some people experience **communication apprehension**, fear or anxiety associated with interaction that keeps them from being able to communicate cooperatively (Daly, McCroskey, Ayres, Hopf, & Ayres, 2004). People with high levels of communication apprehension experience intense discomfort while talking with others, and therefore have difficulty forging productive relationships. Such individuals also commonly experience physical symptoms such as nervous stomach, dry mouth, sweating, increased blood pressure and heart rate, mental disorganization, and shakiness (McCroskey & Richmond, 1987).

Most of us experience communication apprehension at some points in our lives. The key to overcoming it is to develop **communication plans**—mental maps that describe exactly how communication encounters will unfold—*prior* to interacting in the situations or with the people or types of people that cause your apprehension. Communication plans have two elements. The first is *plan actions*, the "moves" you think you'll perform in an encounter that causes you anxiety. Here, you map out in advance the topics you will talk about, the messages you will say in relation to these topics, and the physical behaviors you'll demonstrate.

The second part of a communication plan is *plan contingencies*, the messages you think your communication partner or partners will say during the encounter and how you will respond. To develop plan contingencies, think about the topics your partner will likely talk about, the messages he or she will likely present, his or her reaction to your communication, and your response to your partner's messages and behaviors.

When you implement your communication plan during an encounter that causes you apprehension, the experience is akin to playing chess. While you're communicating, envision your next two, three, or four possible moves—your plan actions. Try to anticipate how the other person will respond to those moves and how you will respond in turn. The goal of this process is to interact with enough confidence and certainty to reduce the anxiety and fear you normally feel during such encounters.

DEFENSIVE COMMUNICATION

A second barrier to cooperative verbal communication is **defensive communication** (or *defensiveness*), impolite messages delivered in response to suggestions, criticism, or perceived slights. For example, at work, you suggest an alternative approach to a coworker, but she snaps, "We've *always* done it this way." You broach the topic of relationship concerns with your romantic partner, but he or she shuts you down, telling you to "Just drop it!" People who communicate defensively dismiss the validity of what another person has said. They also refuse to make internal attributions about their own behavior, especially when they are at fault. Instead, they focus their responses away from themselves and on the other person.

Four types of defensive communication are common (Waldron, Turner, Alexander, & Barton, 1993). Through *dogmatic messages*, a person dismisses suggestions for improvement or constructive criticism, refuses to consider other views, and continues to believe that his or her behaviors are acceptable. With *superiority messages*, the speaker suggests that he or she possesses special knowledge, ability, or status far beyond that of the other individual. In using *indifference messages*, a person implies that the suggestion or criticism being offered is irrelevant, uninteresting, or unimportant. Through *control messages*, a person seeks to squelch criticism by controlling the other individual or the encounter (see Table 6.3).

Defensive communication is *interpersonally incompetent*, because it violates norms for appropriate behavior, rarely succeeds in effectively achieving interpersonal goals, and treats others with disrespect (Waldron et al., 1993). People who communicate in a chronically defensive fashion suffer a host of negative consequences, including high rates of conflict and lower satisfaction in their personal and professional relationships (Infante, Myers, & Burkel, 1994). Yet even highly competent communicators behave defensively on occasion. Defensiveness is an almost instinctive reaction to behavior that makes us angry—communication we perceive as inappropriate, unfair, or unduly harsh. Consequently, the key to overcoming it is to control its triggering factors. For example, if a certain person or situation invariably provokes defensiveness in you, practice preventive anger management strategies such as encounter avoidance or encounter restructuring (see Chapter 4). If you can't avoid the person or situation, use techniques such as reappraisal and the Jefferson Strategy (also in Chapter 4). Given that defensiveness frequently stems from attributional errors—thinking the other person is "absolutely wrong" and you're "absolutely right"—perception-checking (Chapter 3) can also help you reduce your defensiveness.

To prevent others from communicating defensively with you, use "I" and "we" language appropriately, and offer empathy and support when communicating suggestions, advice, or criticism. At the same time, realize that using cooperative language is not a panacea for curing chronic defensiveness in another person. Some people are so deeply entrenched in their defensiveness that any language you use, no matter how cooperative, will still trigger a defensive response. In such situations,

self-reflection

Recall a situation in which you were offered a suggestion, advice, or criticism, and you reacted defensively. What caused your reaction? What were the outcomes of your defensive communication? How could you have prevented a defensive response?

table 6.3 **Examples of Defensive Communication**

Message Type	Example
Dogmatic message	"Why would I change? I've always done it like this!"
Superiority message	"I have more experience and have been doing this longer than you."
Indifference message	"*This* is supposed to interest me?"
Control message	"There's no point to further discussion; I consider this matter closed."

the best you can do is strive to maintain ethical communication by treating the person with respect. You might also consider removing yourself from the encounter before it can escalate into intense conflict.

VERBAL AGGRESSION

The most notable aspect of Anton Chigurh's communication in *No Country for Old Men* was his **verbal aggression**, the tendency to attack others' self-concepts rather than their positions on topics of conversation (Infante & Wigley, 1986). Verbally aggressive people denigrate others' character, abilities, or physical appearance rather than constructively discussing different points of view—for example, Chigurh telling the gas station owner, "You don't know what you're talking about, do you?" Verbal aggression can be expressed not only through speech but also through behaviors, such as physically mocking another's appearance, displaying rude gestures, or assaulting others (Sabourin, Infante, & Rudd, 1993). When such aggression occurs over an extended period of time and is directed toward a particular target, it can evolve into *bullying*, something we discuss more in Chapter 12.

When dealing with a verbally aggressive person, sometimes it is better to leave the encounter than to allow it to escalate into a conflict.

Why are some people verbally aggressive? At times, such aggression stems from a temporary mental state. Most of us have found ourselves in situations at one time or another where various factors—stress, exhaustion, frustration or anger, relationship difficulties—converge. As a result, we "lose our heads" and spontaneously "go off" on another person. Some people who are verbally aggressive suffer from chronic hostility (see Chapter 4). Others are frequently aggressive because it helps them achieve short-term interpersonal goals (Infante & Wigley, 1986). For example, people who want to cut in front of you in line, win an argument, or steal your parking spot may believe that they stand a better chance of achieving these objectives if they use insults, profanity, and threats. Unfortunately, their past experiences may bolster this belief because many people give in to verbal aggression, which encourages the aggressor to use the technique again.

If you find yourself consistently communicating in a verbally aggressive fashion, identify and address the root causes behind your aggression. Has external stress (job pressure, a troubled relationship, a family conflict) triggered your aggression? Do you suffer from chronic hostility? If you find that anger management strategies don't help you reduce your aggression, seek professional assistance.

Communicating with others who are verbally aggressive is also a daunting challenge. Dominic Infante (1995), a leading aggression researcher, offers three tips. First, avoid communication behaviors such as teasing, baiting, or insulting that may trigger verbal aggression in others. Second, if you know someone who is chronically verbally aggressive, avoid or minimize contact with that person. For better or worse, the most practical solution for dealing with such individuals is to not interact with them at all. Third, if you can't avoid interacting with a verbally aggressive person, remain polite and respectful during your encounters with him or her. Allow the individual to speak without interruption. Stay calm, and express empathy (when possible). Avoid retaliating with personal attacks of your own; they will only further escalate the aggression. Finally, end interactions when someone becomes aggressive, explaining gently but firmly, "I'm sorry, but I don't feel comfortable continuing this conversation."

DECEPTION

A student of mine, Taryn, had finished her junior year and was doing a summer internship. One night at a club, a handsome but obviously underage boy approached her and introduced himself as "Paul." After exchanging pleasantries, he told her, "I'm a pilot with United Airlines." *So that's how you want to play it!* Taryn thought. She returned the lie, saying, "I'm an account exec with Chase." Banter completed, their conversation progressed, and—somewhat to Taryn's surprise—attraction kindled. Before parting ways, she gave Paul her number. The next day he called, and once again they felt a passionate connection. He asked her to dinner, and when he picked her up, she was dumbfounded to see him driving a Porsche.

Paul was a 27-year-old pilot. At dinner, Taryn joked about his "baby face" and told him how she thought he had lied about his job. She was setting the stage for confessing her own lie about being an account executive at Chase. But when he replied, "I wouldn't lie—I value honesty above all else," she held off.

In the weeks that followed, they fell in love. Taryn kept looking for chances to tell him the truth but couldn't find them. By August, she was an emotional wreck. The week before she had to leave for school, she came clean: "You know how we always joke about our first meeting? Well, because I thought *you* were lying, *I* lied. I'm actually a senior in college." It was Paul's turn to be dumbfounded. He said, "All summer you've kept this from me? I have no idea who you are, or what kind of game you're playing. But I want no part of it—or you." And he left. He ignored her texts, e-mails, and calls. It was over. Taryn returned to school, devastated.

When most of us think of deception, we think of situations like Taryn's, in which one person communicates false information to another ("I'm an account exec"). But people deceive in any number of ways, only some of which involve saying untruthful things. **Deception** occurs when people deliberately use uninformative, untruthful, irrelevant, or vague language for the purpose of misleading others. The most common form of deception doesn't involve saying anything false at all: studies document that *concealment*—leaving important and relevant information out of messages—is practiced more frequently than all other forms of deception combined (McCornack, 2008).

As noted in previous chapters, deception is commonplace during online encounters. People communicating on online dating sites, posting on social networking sites, and sending messages via e-mail and text distort and hide whatever information they want, providing little opportunity for the recipients of their messages to check accuracy. Some people provide false information about their backgrounds, professions, appearances, and gender online to amuse themselves, to form alternative relationships unavailable to them offline, or to take advantage of others through online scams (Rainey, 2000).

Deception is uncooperative, unethical, impractical, and destructive. It exploits the belief on the part of listeners that speakers are communicating cooperatively—"tricking" them into thinking that the messages received are informative, honest,

Dealing with Difficult Truths

1 BACKGROUND

Cooperative verbal communicators constantly strive to use language that is appropriately informative, honest, relevant, and clear. But sometimes information that is relevant to share with others can be damaging. In such situations, deception becomes a tempting alternative. To find out how you would cope with such a situation, read this case study and work through the five steps under Your Turn.

2 CASE STUDY

Since her early youth, your cousin Britney has always gotten her way. Whenever she wanted something, she would throw a tantrum, and your aunt and uncle would give in. Now she's an adult version of the same child: spoiled and manipulative. Thankfully, you see Britney only during the holidays, and she usually ignores you.

Over the past year, Britney has had troubles. She dropped out of college, and lost her license after totaling the new car her parents bought her. Her drug abuse worsened to the point where her folks forced her into rehab. Despite your dislike, you felt sorry for her when this happened, because you've struggled with your own substance abuse challenges over the years. Now she apparently has recovered and reenrolled in school.

At your annual family reunion, Britney greets you with a big hug and smile. "How's my favorite cousin?" she gushes. As she talks, your surprise turns to suspicion. She's acting *too* friendly, and you think she may be high. Sure enough, when the two of you are alone, she pulls a bag of Vicodin tablets from her purse. "Do you want some?" she offers, and when you refuse, says, "Oh, that's right— You're *in recovery*," in a mocking tone. When you ask about rehab, she laughs, "It may have been right for you, but I did it just to shut my parents up." When you point out the stress she has caused them, Britney snaps, "When I want your worthless opinion, I'll ask!"

Afterward, you corner your folks and disclose what happened. They counsel silence. If you tell Britney's parents, Britney will just lie, and they will believe her over you. What's more, everyone in the family will have to take sides, and it will ruin the reunion.

Over dinner, while Britney smirks, your aunt and uncle praise her recovery. Your aunt then announces that she is rewarding Britney by buying her another car. Your blood boils. Although your aunt and uncle are well-intentioned, Britney is deceiving and exploiting them! Noticing your sullen expression, your uncle says, "I'm not sure what's bothering you, but I think it might be envy. Not everyone has Britney's strength of character in dealing with adversity. You could learn a lot from her, don't you think?"

3 YOUR TURN

Think about the interpersonal communication concepts, skills, and insights you have learned while reading this book, especially this chapter. Try to keep all of this in mind while working through the following five steps, which will help you become aware of how you can make better interpersonal communication choices in your relationships. Remember, there are no right answers, so think hard about what choice you will make! (P.S. Need help? See the *Helpful Concepts* listed below.)

• step 1

Reflect on yourself. What are your thoughts and feelings in this situation? What attributions are you making about Britney? Her parents? Are your attributions accurate, or are they being shaded by your impressions of her and them?

• step 2

Reflect on your partners. Using perspective-taking and empathic concern, put yourself in Britney's shoes. What is she thinking and feeling in this situation? Now do the same for her parents, and your parents. What are they thinking and feeling?

• step 3

Identify the optimal outcome. Think about all the information you have about Britney, her communication with you, your relationship with her, and your other family members—including your parents, your aunt and uncle, and your other relatives. Consider your own feelings as well as those of everyone else. Given these factors, what's the best, most constructive outcome possible

here? Be sure to consider not just what's best for *you*, but what's best for Britney, and your family as well.

• step 4

Locate the roadblocks. Taking into consideration your own thoughts and feelings, Britney's, and all that has happened in this situation, what's preventing you from achieving the optimal outcome you identified in Step 3?

• step 5

Chart your course. What can you say and do to overcome the roadblocks you've identified and achieve your optimal outcome?

HELPFUL CONCEPTS

Being informative, **192–193**

Being honest, **193**

Using "I" and "we" language, **194–195**

Defensive communication, **198–200**

Deception, **201, 204**

self-QUIZ Test Your Deception Acceptance

People vary widely in the degree to which they think deception is an acceptable and appropriate form of verbal communication. To test your deception acceptance, check each statement that you agree with. Then total your checks and compare the result to the scoring key.

———— 1. You should never tell anyone the real reason you did something unless it is useful to do so.

———— 2. It is okay to lie to achieve your goals.

———— 3. What people don't know can't hurt them.

———— 4. The best way to handle people is to tell them what they want to hear.

———— 5. It is often better to lie than to hurt someone's feelings.

———— 6. There is nothing wrong with lying as long as you don't get caught.

———— 7. In some situations, lying can be the most ethical thing to do.

———— 8. Honesty isn't always the best policy.

———— 9. There are many instances in which lying is justified.

————10. Lying can sometimes solve problems more effectively than telling the truth.

Note: This *Self-Quiz* is adapted from the lie acceptability scale developed by Levine, McCornack, and Baldwin Avery (1992).

Scoring: 0–3: Low deception acceptance. You believe that deception is unacceptable no matter the circumstance, and you likely react extremely negatively when you find out people have lied to you. 4–6: Moderate deception acceptance. You believe that deception is acceptable under certain circumstances, and you probably are more accepting when others lie to you. 7–10: High deception acceptance. You believe that deception is an acceptable form of behavior, and you likely use it regularly to deal with difficult communication and relationship situations.

relevant, and clear when they're *not* (McCornack, 2008). Deception is unethical, because when you deceive others, you deny them information that may be relevant to their continued participation in a relationship, and in so doing, you fail to treat them with respect (LaFollette & Graham, 1986). Deception is also impractical. Although at times it may seem easier to deceive than to tell the truth (McCornack, 2008), deception typically calls for additional deception. In Taryn's case, she had to conceal her internship from Paul throughout the summer. Finally, deception is destructive: it creates intensely unpleasant personal, interpersonal, and relational consequences. As occurred with Taryn and Paul, the discovery of deception typically causes intense disappointment, anger, and other negative emotions, and frequently leads to relationship breakups (McCornack & Levine, 1990).

At the same time, keep in mind that people who mislead you may not be doing so out of malicious intent. As noted earlier, many cultures view ambiguous and indirect language as hallmarks of cooperative verbal communication. In addition, sometimes people intentionally veil information out of kindness and desire to maintain the relationship, such as when you tell a close friend that her awful new hairstyle looks great because you know she'd be agonizingly self-conscious if she knew how bad it really looked (McCornack, 1997; Metts & Chronis, 1986). For me, this was the most haunting aspect of Taryn's story: she sincerely loved Paul and wanted to build a life with him, but she was doomed by a seemingly small lie told during playful bar banter.

The Power of Verbal Communication

Language creates our most important moments

We can't help but marvel at the power of verbal communication. Words are our symbolic vehicle for creating and exchanging meanings, performing actions, and forging relationships. We use language to name all that surrounds us, and, in turn, the names we have created shape how we think and feel about these things.

But for most of us, the power of language is intensely personal. Call to mind the most important relationship events in your life. When you do, you'll likely find they were not merely accompanied by verbal communication but were defined and created through it. Perhaps it was the first time you said "I love you" to a partner or posed the heart-stopping query "Will you marry me?" Maybe it was a doctor declaring, "It's a boy!" "It's a girl!" "It's twins!" Or perhaps the relational events that float upward into memory are sadder in nature, the words bitter remnants you wish you could forget: "I don't love you anymore." "I never want to see you again." "I'm sorry, but the prognosis is grim."

"With great power comes great responsibility," as the saying goes, and our power to shape and use verbal communication is no different. The words we exchange profoundly affect not only our interpersonal communication and relationships but also others'. The responsibility we bear because of this power is to communicate cooperatively.

At the time that General George Washington ordered his officers to read aloud the words of Thomas Paine to their troops, the war to create the United States appeared lost. Washington, along with his officers and soldiers, seemed doomed to certain death. But as they stood on the icy shore of the Delaware River, this simple act of verbal communication—"These are the times that try men's souls . . ."—transformed the mood of the moment. Fatigued men's spirits were uplifted, and the soldiers set out across a seemingly impassable river to triumph in a mission that just a few hours earlier had seemed hopeless.

What words have helped you to ford the raging rivers of your life? How have you used verbal communication to inspire others to face their own daunting personal and interpersonal challenges?

More than 200 years ago, a disheartened general borrowed the words of a patriot to raise his soldiers' spirits. In so doing, he created the first link in a chain of events that led to the creation of a country. Now, centuries later, the power of verbal communication to inspire, uplift, embolden, and create is still available to each of us.

POSTSCRIPT

chapter review

key terms

▶ You can watch brief, illustrative videos of these terms and test your understanding of the concepts online in *VideoCentral: Interpersonal Communication* at **bedfordstmartins .com/reflectrelate**.

key concepts

Characteristics of Verbal Communication

- We use **verbal communication** when interacting with coworkers, friends, family members, and romantic partners. In doing so, we employ words as **symbols** to represent people, objects, and ideas.

- Verbal communication is governed by both **constitutive rules** and **regulative rules**. These rules define meanings and clarify appropriate spelling, grammar, and even conversational structure.

- Partners in close relationships often develop **personal idioms** for each other that convey intimacy and uniqueness. Large groups develop common **dialects** that include distinct pronunciations and word choices. People often judge those with dissimilar dialects more negatively than they judge those with similar dialects.

- Culture has an enormous impact on language perception and usage. People within **low-context cultures** tend not to presume commonly shared knowledge with others, and consequently use direct, informative language. Because individuals in **high-context cultures** assume a high degree of shared knowledge in others, they tend to rely more on implied meanings and indirect expression.

- Language constantly changes and evolves. New words are created or are incorporated from other languages while grammar and usage rules also evolve over time.

Functions of Verbal Communication

- When we speak, we convey both **denotative meaning** and **connotative meaning** to others. People in intimate relationships often communicate to each other connotative meanings that others are incapable of interpreting.

- Proponents of **linguistic determinism** suggest that our capacity for thought is defined by the limits of our language. Because language is defined by culture, people from different cultures perceive and experience different realities, due to **linguistic relativity**.

- Although language shapes our thoughts, we control language through the power of **naming**. Members of groups who face prejudice often seek out names for themselves that are more positive to offset the social stigma they face in daily life.

- Words don't merely express meanings, they also perform actions. Whenever we interact with others, we use language to perform **speech acts**, and our conversations are in large part structured in accordance with the types of speech acts we perform.
- We use language to manage our relationships by sharing our thoughts, feelings, ideas, and experiences, whether positive or negative, with others.

Cooperative Verbal Communication

- Using **cooperative verbal communication** requires that you abide by the **Cooperative Principle**. This suggests using language that is informative, **honest**, relevant, and clear, to help avoid **misunderstandings**.
- You also should avoid expressing negative evaluations and opinions through **"you" language**; instead, replace it with **"I" language**. **"We" language** is a good means of fostering the sense of inclusiveness characteristic of cooperative communication.
- Although men and women perceive cooperative communication in largely similar ways, substantial cultural differences exist. A good approach for communicating cooperatively across cultures is to follow the guidelines of **communication accommodation theory**, adapting your language use in appropriate ways to match those of your conversational partners.

Barriers to Cooperative Verbal Communication

- Some people experience **communication apprehension** that inhibits them from communicating competently. One way to overcome such apprehension is to develop **communication plans**.
- People who use **defensive communication** dismiss the validity of what another person says. Expressed through a variety of message types, it is often a reaction to behavior that makes us angry.
- A close cousin of defensive communication is **verbal aggression**, a form of communication that is best prevented in oneself through anger management. When others display verbal aggression, it's best to remain polite and respectful or to remove yourself from the encounter.
- **Deception** can occur through a variety of means, but the most common form is concealment.

key skills

- How do dialects shape your perception, and how might you best communicate verbally with people who use different dialects? Review the answers on pages 179–180, then complete the *Self-Quiz* on page 180 to test your knowledge of American dialects.
- What topics should you discuss when communicating with a fellow college student for the first time? Review Figure 6.1 on page 189 to refresh your memory.
- How can you learn to create understandable messages? Check out the advice on pages 191–194.
- What can you do to prevent misunderstandings during online encounters? Discover the answer on page 194.
- How can you take better ownership over your negative opinions and evaluations of others? Find out on page 194.
- Want to learn how to use cooperative language during online encounters? Try the *Skills Practice* on page 195.
- What is the key to cooperative verbal communication across cultures, and the one thing you never want to do in a cross-cultural encounter? Find out on pages 196–197; then do the *Skills Practice* on page 197.
- Do you suffer from communication apprehension? If so, revisit the discussion of communication plans on page 198, then complete the *Skills Practice* on page 198.
- Interested in overcoming your own defensiveness or in dealing more competently with people who communicate defensively? Review the recommendations on pages 198–200.
- What's the best way to communicate with verbally aggressive people? Learn the answer on pages 200–201.
- Are you inclined to conceal information or give misleading information? Discover your level of deception acceptance by taking the *Self-Quiz* on page 204.
- Interested in finding out how to be appropriately honest in difficult situations? Complete the *Making Relationship Choices* exercise on pages 202–203.

7 Communicating Nonverbally

Nonverbal communication powerfully shapes others' perceptions of you

Closely examine this photograph. As you do, try to recall other images of Native Americans from the late 1800s or early 1900s that you've seen. What is different, unique, or interesting about this photo? How does the picture make you feel? What's your impression of the people in it?

I first came upon this image in poster form in my son's preschool classroom, and I was stunned. Intuitively, I found the picture perplexing and provocative, but I couldn't put my finger on precisely why. Seeing me staring at it, the teacher approached me. "Pretty neat, isn't it?" she said. "Yes," I said, "but something about it strikes me as unusual. Do you know what it is?" "Of course," she replied. "They're *smiling*."

By the late 1800s, stereotypical images of Native Americans were being sold as tourist postcards and magazine illustrations (Silversides, 1994). These images depicted Native peoples in full ceremonial dress, astride their horses or posed in front of teepees, scowling fearsomely.

As Cambridge University professor Maria Tippett (1994) notes, "The image one gets throughout this seventy year period is of a blank-faced, stiff, and unengaged people" (p. 2). When I surveyed more than 5,000 photos from this era, I found not a single image portraying Native Americans with smiles— except for this family photo.[1]

---

[1]Author review of 5,000 photos in the Curtis Archives, http://curtis.library.northwestern.edu/toc.cgi

7 / Communicating Nonverbally

In contrast, this rare portrait, taken by amateur photographer Mary Schaffer (1861–1939), shows people who, rather than staring blankly into the camera, "communicate with the eyes behind it" (Tippett, 1994). The image has an intriguing history. Schaffer, with her friend Mollie Adams and two guides, were exploring the headwaters of the Saskatchewan and Athabasca Rivers in Canada in late 1907, where they met a band of Stoney Indians who befriended them. Among them were Samson Beaver, his wife Leah, and their young daughter Frances, who invited Mary to dinner. After the meal, Mary asked them if she could take their picture, and they agreed.

The Beaver family photo provides a literal and metaphorical snapshot of an interpersonal encounter: the postures, faces, dress, and use of space during a family meeting with a new friend late one sunny afternoon. You can almost feel the fellowship that must have infused the conversation, communicated through Samson's smile, his forward lean, and his direct gaze—all cues conveying intimacy and closeness. If you feel an immediate connection and empathy with Samson, you're not alone. This is a typical human reaction to the sight of a smiling person. A scowling face has quite the opposite effect.

The Beaver family photo reminds us of the universal and transcendent nature of human nonverbal expression and of its powerful role in shaping our impressions of others. A hundred years ago, a family joined new friends to share a meal and something of themselves with one another. Although they're all long since dead, the image of their encounter serves as an enduring reminder of the power of human nonverbal expression to shape our interpersonal communication and relationships.

Learning to manage your nonverbal communication is both important and challenging. It's important because most of the meaning we exchange during interpersonal encounters comes from our nonverbal expressions (Burgoon & Hoobler, 2002). What's more, nonverbal skill is associated with a host of positive outcomes, including high self-esteem, perceptions of attractiveness and popularity by others, and relationship satisfaction (Hodgins & Belch, 2000). It's challenging because nonverbal communication involves many different aspects of behavior, all of which must be considered and controlled simultaneously. When you communicate nonverbally, you manipulate your bodily movements, your voice, and the way you touch others. You also decide how to occupy space, craft your appearance, and use time. To do so competently requires knowledge of the various means of nonverbal communication, the ability to shape and adapt nonverbal expression, and the motivation to do so.

In this chapter, we discuss nonverbal communication and offer guidelines for strengthening your skills. You'll learn:

- How nonverbal communication differs from verbal communication

- How culture and gender affect our nonverbal communication

- What the eight codes of nonverbal communication are, and how you can more skillfully use them when interacting with others

- What purposes nonverbal communication serves in our everyday lives

- How to competently manage your nonverbal communication

Principles of Nonverbal Communication

How nonverbal expression differs from verbal communication

In this book, we define **nonverbal communication** as the intentional or unintentional transmission of meaning through an individual's nonspoken physical and behavioral cues (Patterson, 1995). This definition embraces both intentional and unintentional nonverbal behaviors as communication. Sometimes we do things like yawn, sigh, or grimace and mean nothing by them. But others may interpret these behaviors as acts of communication, and this perception may lead others to respond in ways that affect us, our interpersonal communication, and our relationships. A boss who catches you yawning may express concern that you're "not paying attention," even though you're closely attending to your work. At other times, we intentionally craft nonverbal behaviors to communicate information to others. We add frowning emoticons ☹ to texts and e-mails to show family members we're sad, or we look at coworkers to signal we're ready for meetings. We touch other people to signal sympathy or affection, and move closer or farther away from them to indicate intimacy or emotional distance. We arrange and light our offices and homes to convey power or peacefulness, dress and groom ourselves to communicate casualness or formality, and don artifacts such as jewelry and watches to display status and wealth.

⬤ What comes to mind when you think about nonverbal communication? Is it as subtle as the look in your partner's eyes when you've said something funny? Is it as dramatic as an image from a movie that sticks in your memory?

As you might have gathered, nonverbal communication differs greatly from verbal communication. Let's take a closer look at the key distinctions between nonverbal and verbal forms of expression.

NONVERBAL COMMUNICATION USES MULTIPLE CHANNELS

In contrast with verbal communication, which we transmit through a single channel at a time (the human voice when speaking; written text when online), our nonverbal messages are expressed through multiple channels simultaneously—such as auditory, visual, and tactile. When you talk with a good friend, for example, you simultaneously listen to your friend's tone of voice (auditory); watch your friend's facial expressions, use of eye contact, and hand gestures (visual); and perhaps even touch and receive touch from your friend (tactile). What's more, you do this while also listening to and making sense of your friend's verbal communication.

NONVERBAL COMMUNICATION IS MORE AMBIGUOUS

Nonverbal meanings are more flexible and ambiguous than verbal meanings. A smile can express comfort or contempt, just as a shared glance can convey intimacy or warning—depending on the situation. The ambiguity of nonverbal messages can pose difficulties for interpersonal communication and relationships. For instance, suppose a friend you suspect of harboring romantic feelings for you gives you an extra-long hug. Is he or she just being friendly or signaling romantic interest?

NONVERBAL COMMUNICATION HAS FEWER RULES

Nonverbal communication is more ambiguous than verbal communication because it is governed by fewer rules. As you saw in Chapter 6, you learn literally thousands of constitutive and regulative rules regarding grammar, spelling, pronunciation, and meaning as you master your first and any additional languages. But consider how rarely you've been instructed in the use of nonverbal communication. To be sure, nonverbal rules do exist, such as "Raise your hand if you want to be called on." However, most of these rules are informal norms—for instance, "It's not polite to stare at people," and "You shouldn't stand too close to another person in an elevator, if only two of you are riding."

NONVERBAL COMMUNICATION HAS MORE MEANING

When we interact with others, we often deduce more meaning from people's nonverbal communication than from their verbal, and we convey more meaning to them through our nonverbal than through our verbal. Suppose you meet someone new at a party and find yourself intrigued. To assess the person's attractiveness, you probably gather a lot more information from his or her facial expressions, eye contact, posture, gestures, vocal tone, clothing, and other nonverbal signals than you do from the person's words. This is because during first encounters, nonverbal communication has a greater impact on our overall impressions of attractiveness than does verbal communication (Zuckerman, Miyake, & Hodgins, 1991).

Our reliance on nonverbal communication escalates even higher when people display **mixed messages**, verbal and nonverbal behaviors that convey contradictory meanings (Burgoon & Hoobler, 2002). A friend says she "isn't sad," but her slumped shoulders and downturned mouth suggest otherwise. In such cases, we almost always trust the nonverbal messages over the verbal ones. In contrast, when verbal and nonverbal messages align ("Yes, I'm sad" coupled with slumped shoulders and frown), the amount of attention we pay to verbal communication rises (Burgoon & Hoobler, 2002).

NONVERBAL COMMUNICATION IS INFLUENCED BY CULTURE

You're at a dinner party, and an Iranian student named Amid introduces himself. Amid approaches you very closely—standing so close that his face is only about 12 inches from yours. You think, "Close talker," and you back up, but he closes the distance again. The two of you end up repeating this little "distance dance" throughout your conversation—him closing the distance, you expanding it again, and both of you feeling uncertain and uncomfortable.

This "hypothetical" example happened to me when I was in college. Although Amid and I went on to become close friends, our initial conversation was awkward because of our competing views regarding the appropriate amount of distance that should exist during first encounters. As I learned later, Amid perceived my moves to establish greater distance as communicating "aloofness," whereas I viewed his desire for close distance as intrusive.

As my encounter with Amid illustrates, nonverbal communication and culture are inextricably linked, in ways we will discuss throughout this chapter. You can wrinkle your brow, use a hand gesture, or speak loudly to make a point, but if people in the culture surrounding you don't understand your behavior, you

◒ Whether you intend it or not, your nonverbal communication will transmit meaning to others.

self-reflection

When you receive mixed messages from someone, which do you put more faith in, the verbal or the nonverbal communication? Why? Is it ethical to deliberately send mixed messages to someone?

haven't communicated your message. Consider cultural differences in the meaning of eye contact, for example (Chen & Starosta, 2005). In the United States and Canada, it's considered impolite or even offensive for men to gaze openly at women, but in Italy, people view it as perfectly appropriate. Middle Easterners view gazing as a sign of respect during conversation, but Cambodians see direct eye contact as insulting and an invasion of privacy. Euro-Americans use more eye contact when they're listening than when they're talking, but for African Americans, the opposite often is true.

Or consider the difference that sparked the discomfort between me and Amid—cultural variation in the use of personal space. North Americans feel most comfortable an arm's-length distance apart while conversing. Latin Americans tend to keep a closer distance, while Japanese and Chinese tend to keep a longer distance. North Americans may feel that people from North Africa and the northern and western Middle East intrude on their personal space—as I did with Amid. Likewise, people from those cultures (such as Amid) may judge North Americans' desire for larger distance as off-putting (Chen & Starosta, 2005).

The tight link between culture and nonverbal communication makes cross-cultural communication difficult to master. Sure, the nonverbal symbols used in different cultures are easy enough to learn. But familiarity with the full tapestry of cues—use of personal space, attitudes toward time, perception of touch, appropriateness of gaze, facial expressions—takes much longer. Most people need many years of immersion in a culture before they fully understand the meanings of that culture's nonverbal communication (Chen & Starosta, 2005).

NONVERBAL COMMUNICATION IS INFLUENCED BY GENDER

Try Googling "men and women's body language," and see what pops up.[2] You'll receive *millions* of results. Most are self-help or advice sites that focus on how to tell whether men and women are romantically attracted to you. If you skim through these, you'll see a theme about gender repeatedly expressed: women are better at nonverbal communication than men. For example, AskMen.com declares, "Women are MUCH better at reading body language than men!" Allstardatingtips.com claims that women are "up to *twenty times* better than men at reading body language cues."

Although online content regarding interpersonal communication and relationships often is inaccurate and stereotypical (like the examples above), in the case of gender and nonverbal communication some posts on popular Web sites are derived from research. Psychologist Judith Hall has examined data from hundreds of gender studies (Hall, Carter, & Horgan, 2000). Her findings suggest four consistent patterns, the first of which matches common wisdom: women *are* better than men at both sending and receiving nonverbal messages (although there's no evidence to suggest that they're "twenty times" better!).

self-reflection

Consider content you've read online regarding gender differences in nonverbal communication. Is this information based on reliable research, or stereotypes? Does it match or deviate from your own experiences communicating with men and women? What does this tell you about the trustworthiness of this information?

---

[2]The information that follows is adapted from DeAngelo (2011) and Talbot (2008).

We often deduce more meaning from people's nonverbal communication than from their verbal

Women surpass men at nonverbally communicating in ways receivers can correctly interpret, and women are more accurate than men in their interpretations of others' nonverbal expressions.

Second, women show greater facial expressiveness than men, and they smile more. The difference in smiling stems in part from cultural expectations that women should exhibit only positive and pleasant nonverbal expressions (Spender, 1990). Third, women gaze more at others during interpersonal interactions. This is especially apparent within same-gender conversations, where mutual gaze occurs much more often between females than between males.

Finally, men are more territorial than women. Men maintain more physical space between themselves and others during encounters. Women tolerate more intrusion into their personal space, give way to others more frequently if space is scarce, and try to take up less space than do men. Women also adopt closer conversational distances during same-gender encounters than do men, prefer side-by-side seating more than men, and perceive crowded situations more favorably.

You can use your knowledge of these differences to improve your nonverbal skills. When interacting with men, be aware that they may prefer greater conversational distance and a less direct gaze than women, and take pains to convey nonverbal messages as clearly as possible. During encounters with women, don't be surprised if they adopt a closer conversational distance, and be sensitive to their likely preference for a more direct gaze and more frequent eye contact. Failing to recognize these differences may result in frustration or misunderstandings. For example, a friend of mine celebrated her first anniversary with her husband by returning to the spot where their wedding had occurred: underneath a large tree overlooking beautiful fields. She expected that they would sit down facing each other, open up their picnic basket, and gaze lovingly into each other's eyes while eating and reviewing their first year of married life. Instead, he sat next to her and gazed off into the distance for a good part of the time. She felt that he was ignoring her and got angry. He later explained to her that he felt very intimate sitting next to her and looking out over the fields surrounding their wedding spot. She told me later that if she had known ahead of time that men often prefer less direct gaze, she might have interpreted the incident differently and experienced not only far less pain but possibly a greater feeling of intimacy by knowing that *he* felt intimate.

NONVERBAL COMMUNICATION IS LIBERATED THROUGH TECHNOLOGY

When I walked into the kitchen and found my two youngest sons giggling, I knew they'd been up to something. "What were you doing?" I asked. "Come see!" they gleefully invited. Walking over, I found them watching themselves on YouTube. They had posted a music video of their own creation. The clip was almost entirely nonverbal: it showed them dancing wildly, waving their hands in the air, making funny faces, and pretending (badly) to sing. When I asked them why they had created the video, they said, "Because we want our friends who are gone for the summer to be able to see us!" Sure enough, the rest of the evening was spent checking the number of "views" they had received, and texting their vacationing friends regarding the video.

⬤ When you text or post photos for your friends and loved ones, you're engaging in nonverbal communication. How else do you communicate nonverbally via technology?

As recently as 20 years ago, our ability to communicate nonverbally was radically restricted by technology. Phone calls limited us to vocal cues, and communicating on the computer meant seeing words on a screen—nothing else. Only one option existed for experiencing the full tapestry of nonverbal communication: face-to-face interaction. But now, nonverbal communication has been liberated through technology. We can upload and download photos and video clips on our smartphones, iPads, and laptops. We can podcast, stream videos, and post clips of ourselves—then alert all our friends via e-mail, Twitter, texts, and Facebook that our content is available for viewing. As of 2012, over 4 billion videos are viewed *daily* on YouTube ("YouTube Statistics," n.d.).

This shift from technological restriction to liberation has created two notable outcomes. First, whereas we used to have just two communication modes—face-to-face interaction or methods with limited nonverbal content (such as phone calls or text-only online messages)—now we can choose various media that let us hear *and* see others when interacting. Second, we can use these media to better maintain intimate, long-distance relationships. A generation ago, soldiers stationed overseas waited a week (or more) to receive written letters from loved ones back home. Now, they can exchange messages rich with verbal and nonverbal expressions in real time via the Web. Like my sons and their YouTube video, friends separated by distance—through summer vacations or unanticipated relocations—can also maintain intimate connections through frequent sharing of video clips and photos.

NONVERBAL AND VERBAL COMBINE TO CREATE COMMUNICATION

Despite the differences between verbal and nonverbal forms of expression, and the weight we give nonverbal communication when sending and receiving information, both forms are essential. When we interact with others, our verbal and nonverbal behaviors combine to create meaning (Jones & LeBaron, 2002). In everyday encounters, verbal and nonverbal communication are not experienced or expressed separately, but are used jointly to create interpersonal communication (Birdwhistell, 1970). Keep this in mind: your skill as a nonverbal communicator goes hand in hand with your skill as a verbal communicator, so you need *both* to communicate competently.

Nonverbal Communication Codes

Explore the variety of nonverbal channels

One reason nonverbal communication contains such rich information is that, during interpersonal encounters, we use many different aspects of our behavior, appearance, and surrounding environment simultaneously to communicate meaning. You can greatly strengthen your nonverbal communication skills by understanding **nonverbal communication codes**, the different means used for transmitting information nonverbally (Burgoon & Hoobler, 2002). Scholars distinguish eight different nonverbal communication codes, summarized in Table 7.1 on the next page.

skills practice

Maintaining Online Friendship
Using nonverbal communication online to maintain a friendship

❶ Identify a long-distance friend with whom you haven't communicated recently.

❷ Think of a story or an update that you want to share with that friend.

❸ Compose a message explaining your story that uses nonverbal cues such as photos or video of yourself.

❹ Before sending, review your facial expressions, eye contact, body movement, voice, and appearance; make sure they communicate positively what you want to express.

❺ E-mail or post the footage, and see how your friend responds.

table 7.1   **The Eight Codes of Nonverbal Communication**

Code	Description
Kinesics	Visible body movements, including facial expressions, eye contact, gestures, and body postures
Vocalics	Vocal characteristics such as loudness, pitch, speech rate, and tone
Haptics	Duration, placement, and strength of touch
Proxemics	Use of physical distance
Chronemics	Organization and use of time
Physical appearance	Appearance of hair, clothing, body type, and other physical features
Artifacts	Personal possessions displayed to others
Environment	Structure of physical surroundings

COMMUNICATING THROUGH BODY MOVEMENTS

She's one of the most memorable movie villains in years, and the most loyal of Lord Voldemort's "Death Eaters." Across the various *Harry Potter* films in which she has appeared, Bellatrix Lestrange (played by Helena Bonham Carter) is almost always a flurry of motion. Her facial expression is soft and mocking one moment, hard and vicious the next. Her eyes are constantly watchful, and she stares intensely with hostility at any who oppose her. Her gestures are large and vivid, even as her body shifts quickly from one posture to the next, rarely remaining still. All of these movements combine to accentuate the anger, loathsomeness, and evil associated with her character.

As depicted in the movies, Bellatrix exemplifies the power of **kinesics** (from the Greek *kinesis*, meaning "movement")—visible body movements. Kinesics is the richest nonverbal code in terms of its power to communicate meaning, and it includes most of the behaviors we associate with nonverbal communication: facial expression, eye contact, gestures, and body postures.

Facial Expression   "A person's character is clearly written on the face." As this traditional Chinese saying suggests, the face plays a pivotal role in shaping our perception of others. In fact, some scholars argue that facial cues rank first among all forms of communication in their influence on our interpersonal impressions (Knapp & Hall, 2002). We use facial expression to communicate an endless stream of emotions, and we make judgments about what others are feeling by assessing their facial expressions. Our use of emoticons (such as ☹ and ☺) to communicate attitudes and emotions online testifies to our reliance on this type of kinesics, and the primacy of the face even influences our labeling of interpersonal encounters ("face-to-face") and Web sites devoted to social networking ("Facebook").

○ In the *Harry Potter* movies, Bellatrix Lestrange's body movements—from her vicious facial expressions to her vivid, unpredictable gestures—combine to make her one of the series's most unforgettable villains. What experiences have you had with people who use body movements to communicate traits such as strength, power, or even kindness?

Eye Contact   Eye contact serves many purposes during interpersonal communication. We use our eyes to express emotions, signal when it's someone else's turn to talk, and show others that we're listening to them. We also demonstrate our interest in a conversation by increasing our eye contact, or signal relationship intimacy by locking eyes with a close friend or romantic partner.

Eye contact can convey hostility as well. One of the most aggressive forms of nonverbal expression is *prolonged staring*—fixed and unwavering eye contact of several seconds' duration (typically accompanied by a hostile facial expression)—like that used by Bellatrix in the *Harry Potter* films. Although in the real world women seldom stare, men use this behavior to threaten others, invite aggression ("staring someone down" to provoke a fight), and assert their status (Burgoon, Buller, & Woodall, 1996).

Gestures   Imagine that you're driving to an appointment and someone is riding right on your bumper. Scowling at the offender in your rearview mirror, you're tempted to raise your middle finger and show it to the other driver, but you restrain yourself. The raised finger is an example of a *gesture*, a hand motion used to communicate messages (Streek, 1993). "Flipping" someone "the bird" falls into a category of gestures known as **emblems**, which represent specific verbal meanings (Ekman, 1976). With emblems, the gesture and its verbal meaning are interchangeable. You can say the words or use the gesture, and you'll send the same message.

Unlike emblems, **illustrators** accent or illustrate verbal messages. You tell your spouse about a rough road you recently biked, and as you describe the bumpy road you bounce your hand up and down to illustrate the ride.

❯

> Within a few days of birth, infants can communicate with caregivers through eye contact

Regulators control the exchange of conversational turns during interpersonal encounters (Rosenfeld, 1987). Listeners use regulators to tell speakers to keep talking, repeat something, hurry up, or let another person talk (Ekman & Friesen, 1969). Speakers use them to tell listeners to pay attention or to wait longer for their turn. Common examples include pointing a finger while trying to interrupt and holding a palm straight up to keep a person from interrupting. During online communication, abbreviations such as *BRB* ("be right back") and *JAS* ("just a second") serve as textual substitutes for gestural regulators.

Adaptors are touching gestures that serve a psychological or physical purpose (Ekman & Friesen, 1969). For example, you smooth your hair to make a better impression while meeting a potential new romantic partner.

Posture The fourth kinesic is your bodily posture, which includes straightness of back (erect or slouched), body lean (forward, backward, or vertical), straightness of shoulders (firm and broad or slumped), and head position (tilted or straight up). Your posture communicates two primary messages to others: immediacy and power (Mehrabian, 1972). **Immediacy** is the degree to which you find someone interesting and attractive. Want to nonverbally communicate that you like someone? Lean forward, keep your back straight and your arms open, and hold your head up and facing toward the person when talking. Want to convey dislike? Lean back, close your arms, and look away.

Power is the ability to influence or control other people or events (discussed in detail in Chapter 8). Imagine attending two job interviews in the same afternoon. The first interviewer sits upright, with a tense, rigid body posture. The second

◁ Our postures are determined by conditions and tools. In Western cultures, where many people work in offices, the chair greatly influences body posture. In agrarian and pastoral societies, where people spend most of their lives working outside, body postures are shaped accordingly. In Asia and Africa, for example, a common posture is the deep squat.

interviewer leans back in his chair, with his feet up on his desk and his hands behind his head. Which interviewer has more power? Most Americans would say the second. In the United States, high-status communicators typically use relaxed postures (Burgoon et al., 1996), but in Japan, the opposite is true. Japanese display power through erect posture and feet planted firmly on the floor.

COMMUNICATING THROUGH VOICE

Grammy winner T-Pain has collaborated with an enviable who's who list of rap, hip-hop, and R&B stars: Ludacris, Lil Wayne, Chris Brown, Kanye West, and a host of others. But what makes T-Pain unique, and his songs so instantly recognizable, is his pioneering work with the pitch-correction program Auto-Tune. He was one of the first musicians to realize that Auto-Tune could be used not only to subtly correct singing errors, but to alter one's voice entirely. Running his vocals through the program, his normally full, rich voice becomes thin and reedy sounding, jumping in pitch precisely from note to note without error. The result is a sound that is at once musical yet robotic. The style is so popular that he even released an iPhone app called "I Am T-Pain," allowing fans to record and modify their own voices so they could sound like him.

The popularity of T-Pain's vocal manipulations illustrates the impact that **vocalics**—vocal characteristics we use to communicate nonverbal messages—has upon our impressions. Indeed, vocalics rival kinesics in their communicative power (Burgoon et al., 1996) because our voices communicate our social, ethnic, and individual identities to others. Consider a study that recorded people from diverse backgrounds answering a series of "small talk" questions such as "How are you?" (Harms, 1961). People who listened to these recordings were able to accurately judge participants' ethnicity, gender, and social class, often within only 10 to 15 seconds, based solely on their voices. Vocalics strongly shape our perception of others when we first meet them. If we perceive a person's voice as calm and smooth (not nasal or shrill), we are more likely to view him or her as

skills practice

Communicating Immediacy

Using kinesics to communicate immediacy during interpersonal encounters

❶ Initiate an encounter with someone whom you want to impress as an attentive and involved communicator (such as a new friend or a potential romantic partner).

❷ While talking, keep your facial expression pleasant. Don't be afraid to smile!

❸ Make eye contact, especially while listening, but avoid prolonged staring.

❹ Directly face the person, keep your back straight, lean forward, and keep your arms open and relaxed (rather than crossing them over your chest).

❺ Use illustrators to enhance important descriptions, and regulators to control your exchange of turns.

◉ Rapper T-Pain regularly uses the pitch-correction program Auto-Tune to dramatically alter his voice, giving it an unnatural, "computerized" tone. What impressions do you think he is trying to convey by changing his voice? Have you ever consciously modified or "corrected" your natural voice?

attractive, form a positive impression, and judge the person as extraverted, open, and conscientious (Zuckerman, Hodgins, & Miyake, 1990).

When we interact with others, we typically experience their voices as a totality—they "talk in certain ways" or "have a particular kind of voice." But people's voices are actually complex combinations of four characteristics: tone, pitch, loudness, and speech rate.

Tone   The most noticeable aspect of T-Pain's vocals is their unnatural, "computerized" tone. Tone is the most complex of human vocalic characteristics, and involves a combination of richness and breathiness. You can control your vocal tone by allowing your voice to resonate deep in your chest and throat—achieving a full, rich tone that conveys an authoritative quality while giving a formal talk, for example. By contrast, letting your voice resonate through your sinus cavity creates a more whiny and nasal tone—often unpleasant to others. Your use of breath also affects tone. If you expel a great deal of air when speaking, you convey sexiness. If you constrict the airflow when speaking, you create a "thin" and "hard" tone that may communicate nervousness or anxiety.

English-speakers use vocal tone to emphasize and alter the meanings of verbal messages. Regardless of the words you use, your tone can make your statements serious, silly, or even sarcastic, and you can shift tone extremely rapidly to convey different emphases. For example, when talking with your friends, you can suddenly switch from your normal tone to a much more deeply chest-resonant tone to mimic a pompous politician, then nearly instantly constrict your airflow and make your voice sound more like SpongeBob SquarePants. In online communication, we use italics to convey tone change ("I can't *believe* you did that").

Pitch   You're introduced to two new coworkers, Rashad and Paul. Both are tall and muscular. Rashad has a deep, low-pitched voice; Paul, an unusually high-pitched one. How do their voices shape your impressions of them? If you're like most people, you'll conclude that Rashad is strong and competent, while Paul is weak (Spender, 1990). Not coincidentally, people believe that women have higher-pitched voices than men and that women's voices are more "shrill" and "whining" (Spender, 1990). But although women across cultures do use higher pitch than men, most men are capable of using a higher pitch than they normally do but *choose* to intentionally limit their range to lower pitch levels to convey strength (Brend, 1975).

self-reflection

Think about someone you know whose voice you find funny, strange, or irritating. What is it about this person's voice that fosters your negative impression? Is it ethical to judge someone solely from his or her voice? Why or why not?

Loudness   Consider the following sentence: "Will John leave the room" (Searle, 1965). Say the sentence aloud, each time emphasizing a different word. Notice that emphasizing one word over another can alter the meaning from statement to question to command, depending on which word is emphasized ("WILL John leave the room" versus "Will JOHN leave the room").

Loudness affects meaning so powerfully that people mimic it online by USING CAPITAL LETTERS TO EMPHASIZE CERTAIN POINTS. Indeed, people who extensively cap are punished for being "too loud." For example, a member of a music Web site I routinely visit accidentally left his "cap lock" key on while posting, and all of his messages were capped. Several other members immediately pounced, scolding him, "Stop shouting!"

Speech Rate   The final vocal characteristic is the speed at which you speak. Talking at a moderate and steady rate is often considered a critical technique for effective speaking. Public-speaking educators urge students to "slow down," and people in conversations often reduce their speech rate if they believe that their listeners don't understand them. But MIT computer science researcher Jean Krause found that speech rate is not the primary determinant of intelligibility (Krause, 2001). Instead, it's pronunciation and articulation of words. People who speak quickly but enunciate clearly are just as competent communicators as those who speak moderately or slowly.

COMMUNICATING THROUGH TOUCH

Using touch up to communicate nonverbally is known as **haptics**, from the ancient Greek word *haptein*. Touch is likely the first sense we develop in the womb, and receiving touch is a critical part of infant development (Knapp & Hall, 2002). Infants deprived of affectionate touch walk and talk later than others and suffer impaired emotional development in adulthood (Montagu, 1971).

Touch can vary based on its duration, the part of the body being touched, and the strength of contact, and these varieties influence how we interpret the physical contact (Floyd, 1999). Scholars distinguish between six types of touch. We use **functional-professional touch** to accomplish some type of task. Examples include touch between physicians and patients, between teachers and students, and between coaches and athletes. **Social-polite touch** derives from social norms and expectations. The most common form of social-polite touch is the handshake, which has been practiced as a greeting in one form or another for over 2,000 years

Touch and Distance

Cultures vary in their norms regarding appropriate touch and distance, some with lots of touching and close distance during interpersonal encounters and others with less (Hall, 1966). Often, these differences correlate with latitude and climate. People living in cooler climes tend to be low contact and people living in warmer areas tend to be high contact (Andersen, 1997). The effect of climate on touch and distance is even present in countries that have both colder and hotter regions. Below, Cindy, a former student, describes her experience juggling norms for touch and distance.*

I'm a Mexican American from El Paso, Texas, which is predominantly Latino. There, most everyone hugs hello and good-bye. And I'm not talking about a short slap on the back—I mean a nice encompassing *abrazo* (hug). While I can't say that strangers greet each other this way, I do recall times where I've done it. Growing up, it just seemed like touching is natural, and I never knew how much I expected it, maybe even relied on it, until I moved.

I came to Michigan as a grad student. My transition here was relatively smooth, but it was odd to me the first time I hung out with friends and didn't hug them

hello and good-bye. A couple of times on instinct I did greet them this way, and I'll never forget the strange tension that was created. Some people readily hugged me back, but most were uneasy. Quickly I learned that touching was unacceptable.

Now I find that I hold back from engaging people in this manner. I feel like I'm hiding a part of myself, and it is frustrating. Nonetheless, this is the way things are done here, and I've had to adjust. Fortunately, I now have a few friends who recognize my need to express myself in this way and have opened themselves up to it. I'm grateful for that, and through these people a piece of me and my identity is saved.

discussion questions

- What has your culture taught you about the use of touch and distance? Are you a high- or low-contact person?
- When communicating with people from other cultures, how do you adapt your use of touch and distance?

*Cindy's narrative was provided voluntarily to the author with full permission for publication.

(Heslin, 1974). Other examples include light hugging between friends or relatives, and the light cheek kiss. We rely on **friendship-warmth touch**—for example, gently grasping a friend's arm and giving it a squeeze—to express liking for another person. **Love-intimacy touch**—cupping a romantic partner's face tenderly in your hands, giving him or her a big, lingering hug—lets you convey deep emotional feelings. **Sexual-arousal touch**, as the name implies, is intended to physically stimulate another person. Finally, **aggressive-hostile touch** involves forms of physical violence like grabbing, slapping, and hitting—behaviors designed to hurt and humiliate others.

Cultural upbringing has a strong impact on how people use and perceive touching. For example, many Hispanics use friendship-warmth touch more frequently than do Europeans and Euro-Americans. Researchers in one study monitored casual conversations occurring in outdoor cafés in two different locales: San Juan, Puerto Rico, and London, England. They then averaged the number of touches between conversational partners. The Puerto Ricans touched each other an average of 180 times per hour. The British average? Zero (Environmental Protection Agency, 2002).

Because people differ in the degree to which they feel comfortable giving and receiving touch, consider adapting your use of touch to others' preferences, employing more or less touch depending on your conversational partner's behavior responses to your touching. If you are talking with a "touchy" person, who repeatedly touches your arm gently while talking (a form of social-polite touch), you can probably presume that such a mild form of touch would be acceptable to reciprocate. But if a person offers you no touch at all, not even a greeting handshake, you would be wise to inhibit your touching.

COMMUNICATING THROUGH PERSONAL SPACE

The fourth nonverbal communication code, **proxemics** (from the Latin *proximus*, meaning "near"), is communication through the use of physical distance. Edward T. Hall, one of the first scholars to study proxemics, identified four communication distances: intimate, personal, social, and public (Hall, 1966). **Intimate space** ranges from 0 to 18 inches. Sharing intimate space with someone counts among the defining nonverbal features of close relationships (see Figure 7.1). **Personal space** ranges between 18 inches and 4 feet and is the distance we occupy during encounters with friends. For most Americans and Canadians, personal space is about your "wingspan"—that is, the distance from fingertip to fingertip when you extend your arms. **Social space** ranges from about 4 to 12 feet. Many people use it when communicating in the workplace or with acquaintances and strangers. In **public space**, the distance between persons ranges upward from 12 feet, including great distances; this span occurs most often during formal occasions such as public speeches or college lectures.

VideoCentral ◉

bedfordstmartins.com /reflectrelate

Proxemics
Watch this clip online to answer the questions below.

When first meeting someone you are romantically interested in, which proxemics zones do you use? Why? In the video, what prompts the woman to place her coat on the empty chair next to her? What message is the man sending as he changes chairs?

Want to see more? Check out VideoCentral for a clip on **haptics**.

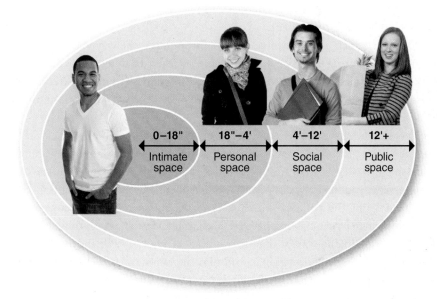

| 0–18" | 18"–4' | 4'–12' | 12'+ |
| Intimate space | Personal space | Social space | Public space |

figure 7.1 **Physical Distance in Communication**

self-
reflection

Which locations in your
physical spaces at home
and work do you consider
your most valued territories?
How do you communicate
this territoriality to others?
What do you do when peo-
ple trespass? Have your
reactions to such trespasses
caused negative personal or
professional consequences?

In addition to the distance we each claim for ourselves during interpersonal encounters, we also have certain physical areas or spaces in our lives that we consider our turf. **Territoriality** is the tendency to claim physical spaces as our own and to define certain locations as areas we don't want others to invade without permission (Chen & Starosta, 2005). Human beings react negatively to others who invade their perceived territory, and we respond positively to those who respect it (King, 2001). Imagine coming home to your apartment after school. Walking into your bedroom, you find your housemate sitting at your desk, watching a movie on your computer. How would you respond? If you're like most people, you would feel angry and upset. Even though your housemate is not violating your personal space (distance from your body), he or she is inappropriately encroaching on physical space that you consider your territory.

What can you do to become more sensitive to differences in the use of personal space? Keep in mind that, as noted earlier in this chapter, North Americans' notions of personal space tend to be larger than those in most other cultures, especially people from Latin America or the Middle East. When interacting with people from other cultures, adjust your use of space in accordance with your conversational partner's preferences. Realize, also, that if you're from a culture that values large personal space, others will feel most comfortable interacting at a closer distance than you're used to. If you insist on maintaining a large personal space bubble around yourself when interacting with people from other cultures, they may think you're aloof or distant or that you don't want to talk with them.

COMMUNICATING THROUGH TIME

It's the middle of a busy workday. Looming over you is a 3 p.m. deadline for a report and a 3:30 appointment with the dentist. Suddenly your father calls. He wants to talk to you about plans for an upcoming surprise party for your mother. Should you disrupt your work schedule and talk or tell your father that another time would be more convenient?

Dilemmas such as this revolve around **chronemics**, the way you use time to communicate during interpersonal encounters. Edward Hall, who pioneered work on proxemics, also wrote extensively on chronemics (from the Greek word *khronos*, meaning "time"). Hall distinguished between two time orientations: *M-time* and *P-time* (Hall, 1997b).

People who have an **M-time** (or monochronic) orientation value careful scheduling and time management. They view time as a precious resource: it can be saved, spent, wasted, lost, or made up, and it can even run out. So, if you have an M-time view, you likely would perceive your father's call as an interruption, and time taken during the workday to discuss a party as "misspent." Many people living in cultures where M-time is emphasized (such as the United States) think M-time is the only reasonable way of organizing life. As Hall (1997b) notes, time for M-time people "is so thoroughly woven into the fabric of our existence that we hardly are aware of the degree to which it determines and coordinates everything we do, including our relationships with others—social and business life, even one's sex life, is commonly schedule-dominated" (pp. 278–279).

If you're an M-time person, "spending time" with someone, or "making time" in your schedule to share activities with him or her, sends the message that you consider that person and your relationship important (Hall, 1983). You may view time as a gift you give to others to show love or caring, or a tool with which you can punish ("I no longer have time for you").

In contrast to M-time, people who have a **P-time** (or polychronic) orientation don't view time as a resource to be spent, saved, or guarded. And they rarely think of time as "wasted." If you're a P-time person, you might view your father's phone call as a welcome reprieve from the stress of work and an opportunity for an enjoyable and lengthy conversation.

Differences in time orientation can create problems when people from different cultures make appointments with each other (Hall, 1983). For example, those with an M-time orientation, such as many Americans, often become impatient if P-time people show up "late" for a meeting. In cultures with a heavy P-time emphasis, such as those in Middle Eastern, African, Caribbean, and Latin American countries,

Are You an M-Time or a P-Time Person?

self-QUIZ

Read the questions below and choose the answer that most closely reflects your view of time. When you're done, review your answers and see what they suggest about your personal time orientation: Are you an M-time person or a P-time person?

1. Do you have a personal planner or smartphone in which you carefully keep track of your daily schedule and appointments?

   (a) _____ Of course! How could I survive without one?

   (b) _____ What exactly do I need to plan?

2. Do you often check the time during the day to see if you're "on schedule"?

   (a) _____ All the time. I also make sure that my watch is synchronized with my cell phone, and I program my cell to issue alarm reminders for key appointments.

   (b) _____ Never. I don't even own a watch.

3. Do you get stressed out about not having enough time to do the things you're supposed to?

   (a) _____ Not having enough time to do what I'm supposed to do is the number-one source of stress in my life.

   (b) _____ What exactly are "the things we're supposed to do," other than share life with those we love and be happy?

4. Your best friend calls you at work, says that she has been dumped by her romantic partner, and badly needs to talk with you. You

   (a) _____ check your schedule to see if there's an opening at some point later in the day.

   (b) _____ arrange to leave work to go comfort your friend.

5. You have to renew your driver's license because it expires tomorrow. You use your lunch hour to do so, but there are only two people working the counter at the registry of motor vehicles, and the line is long. You

   (a) _____ check your watch and feel your stress increase as the hour passes and you're still not at the head of the line. Finally, you cut to the front and ask, "Is there any way I can go next? I've been waiting for an hour!"

   (b) _____ take the opportunity to chat with other people who are waiting, making new acquaintances.

Note: Examples in this *Self-Quiz* were gathered by the author from undergraduate volunteers.

self-reflection

Think about people you know who have different time orientations from your own. How has the disparity in view of time affected your interpersonal communication? Your relationships? What might you do to resolve tensions deriving from differences in time orientation?

arriving 30 minutes or more after a meeting's scheduled start is considered "on time," and changing important plans at the last minute is viewed as acceptable.

How can you become more sensitive to other people's time frames and, as a result, improve your nonverbal communication? Learn about the time orientation of a destination or country before traveling there. Also, respect others' time orientation. If you're an M-time person interacting with a P-time individual, don't abruptly end the encounter because you feel you have to stick to your schedule. Your communication partner will likely view you as rude. If you're a P-time person interacting with an M-time partner, realize that he or she likely views the interaction as time-bounded. This individual may view a lengthy, leisurely conversation or late arrival to an appointment as inconsiderate. In addition, avoid criticizing or complaining about behaviors that stem from others' alternative time orientations. Instead, accept the unavoidable fact that others may have views of time markedly different from yours, and be willing to adapt your own use of time when interacting with them.

COMMUNICATING THROUGH PHYSICAL APPEARANCE

On the hit TLC show *Say Yes to the Dress*, Randy Fenoli and other sales associates at Kleinfeld Bridal in New York City help prospective brides find the ideal wedding dresses for what is (for many people) "the most important day of their lives." The show involves not just finding a dress, but finding the dress that fits a bride's ideal image for how she should look. However, the show is not just about superficial allure. Instead, the choice of dress and accessories conveys a powerful communicative message to others about the bride's self-identity. As Randy notes, "One of the most important things I tell brides is that you should always choose a gown that really represents *who you are*, because what you're doing at a wedding is telling a story about who you are as a person, and as a couple" (Herweddingplanner.com, 2011).

▶ On *Say Yes to the Dress*, a bride's dress choice is not merely a fashion statement, but a statement about who she is as a person. Similarly, your daily physical appearance is a form of nonverbal communication that expresses how you want others to see you.

Although weddings are an extreme example in terms of the emphasis placed on how we look, our **physical appearance**—visible attributes such as hair, clothing, body type, and other physical features—profoundly influences all of our interpersonal encounters. In simple terms, how you look conveys as much about you as what you say. And beauty counts. Across cultures, people credit individuals they find physically attractive with higher levels of intelligence, persuasiveness, poise, sociability, warmth, power, and employment success than they credit to unattractive individuals (Hatfield & Sprecher, 1986).

This effect holds in online environments as well. For example, the physical attractiveness of friends who post their photos on your Facebook page has noteworthy effects on people's perceptions of *your* attractiveness (Walther, Van Der Heide, Kim, Westerman, & Tong, 2008). That is, if you have attractive friends' photos on your page, people will perceive you as more physically and socially attractive; if you have unattractive friends, you'll seem less attractive to others.

What physical appearance characteristics does it take to be judged attractive? Standards of beauty are highly variable, both across cultures and across time periods. But one factor that's related to attractiveness across cultures is *facial symmetry*—the degree to which each side of your face precisely matches the other. For example, this can include whether someone's eyes are the same shape or whether someone's ears are at the exact same height. People with symmetrical faces are judged as more attractive than people with asymmetrical faces (Grammer & Thornhill, 1994), although perfect facial symmetry may be seen as artificial and unattractive (Kowner, 1996).

Your clothing also has a profound impact on others' perceptions of you. More than 40 years of research suggests that clothing strongly influences people's judgments about profession, level of education, socioeconomic status, and even personality and personal values (Burgoon et al., 1996). The effect that clothing has on perception makes it essential that you consider the appropriateness of your dress, the context for which you are dressing, and the image of self you wish to nonverbally communicate. When I worked for a Seattle trucking company, I was expected to wear clothes that could withstand rough treatment. On my first day, I "dressed to impress" and was teased by coworkers and management for dressing as if I was an executive at a large corporation. But expectations like this can change in other situations. During job interviews, for example, dress as nicely as you can. Being even moderately formally dressed is one of the strongest predictors of whether an interviewer will perceive you as socially skilled and highly motivated (Gifford, Ng, & Wilkinson, 1985).

self-reflection

Consider your physical appearance, as shown in photos on your Facebook page or other personal Web sites. What do your face, hair, clothing, and body communicate to others about who you are and what you're like? Now examine friends' photos on your pages. How might their appearances affect others' perceptions of you?

COMMUNICATING THROUGH OBJECTS

Take a moment to examine the objects that you're wearing and that surround you: jewelry, watch, cell phone, computer, art or posters on the wall, and so forth. These **artifacts**—the things we possess that influence how we see ourselves and that we use to express our identity to others—constitute another code of nonverbal communication. As with our use of posture and of personal space, we use artifacts to communicate power and status. For example, by displaying expensive watches, cars, or living spaces, people "tell" others that they're wealthy and influential (Burgoon et al., 1996).

COMMUNICATING THROUGH THE ENVIRONMENT

A final way in which we communicate nonverbally is through our **environment**, the physical features of our surroundings. As the photo of the Google office (below) illustrates, our environment envelops us, shapes our communication, and implies certain things about us, often without our realizing it.

Two types of environmental factors play a role in shaping interpersonal communication: fixed features and semifixed features (Hall, 1981). *Fixed features* are stable and unchanging environmental elements such as walls, ceilings, floors, and doors. Fixed features define the size of a particular environment, and size has an enormous emotional and communicative impact on people. For example, the size of structures communicates power, with bigger often being better. In corporations, it's often assumed that larger offices equal greater power for their occupants, and historically, the square footage of homes has communicated the occupant's degree of wealth.

Semifixed features are impermanent and usually easy to change; they include furniture, lighting, and color. We associate bright lighting with environments that are very active and soft lighting with environments that are calmer and more intimate. Color also exerts a powerful effect on our mood and communication: we experience blues and greens as relaxing, yellows and oranges as arousing and energizing, reds and blacks as sensuous, and grays and browns as depressing (Burgoon et al., 1996).

self-reflection

Look around the room you're in right now. How does this room make you feel? How do the size of the space, furniture, lighting, and color contribute to your impression? What kind of interpersonal communication would be most appropriate for this space—personal or professional? Why?

▶ Examine how these Google employees have set up their shared office space. What do their choices in semifixed features like personal decorations, wall art, furniture, and lighting communicate about them?

Functions of Nonverbal Communication

How we use nonverbal behaviors in communication

It was 4th and 24 with 4 minutes to go in the 4th quarter and the Chicago Bears were down by 17 points to the New Orleans Saints.[3] As Bears quarterback Jay Cutler dropped back to pass, Saints defenders Roman Harper and Malcolm Jenkins converged from opposite sides, and pounded him to the turf—turning the ball back to the Saints, and ensuring victory. Leaping up, the two defensive backs began to move about in a bizarre fashion. They leaned back, looked skyward, let their arms dangle loosely, and began shuffling and flailing about. What were they doing? Why were they doing it? Harper and Jenkins were doing the "Bernie Dance," from the ISA song "Movin' Like Berney" and the film *Weekend at Bernie's*. In the movie (and its sequel), two hapless insurance agents try to convince people that their dead boss Bernie is actually alive, even to the point of making his corpse dance. Hence, the "Bernie Dance." Of course, Harper and Jenkins weren't "moving like Bernie" just to honor a dance fad. Instead, they were using their nonverbal communication to serve several different functions, including rousing their hometown crowd in celebration and expressing their joy at having sacked Cutler and (in effect) ending the game.

⬤ This photo was taken immediately after New Orleans Saints defenders Roman Harper and Malcolm Jenkins made a game-winning tackle during their 2011 season. Their eye-catching victory dance communicated their joy and excitement with no words at all.

Like Harper and Jenkins, we use nonverbal communication for many different purposes in our daily lives. Within interpersonal encounters, nonverbal communication serves five functions: it conveys meanings, expresses emotion, presents ourselves to others, helps manage interactions, and defines relationships (Argyle, 1969).

CONVEYING MEANINGS

Just as we use words to signify unique meanings, we often use nonverbal communication to directly convey meanings. Your boss flips you a thumbs-up gesture following a presentation, and you know she means "Good job!" A friend makes a two-finger "V" at a campus rally, and you recognize it as an emblem for peace.

At other times we use nonverbal communication more indirectly, as a means for accenting or augmenting verbal communication meanings (Malandro & Barker, 1983). We do this in five ways, the first of which is by *reiterating*. Nonverbal communication is used to reiterate or repeat verbal messages, as when you say "Up!" and then point upward. Second, we *contradict* our verbal messages with our nonverbal communication. For example, a friend may ask if you're angry, but you respond by scowling and angrily shouting "No, I'm not angry!" Third, we use nonverbal communication to *enhance* the meaning of verbal messages, such as when you tell an intimate "I love you" while smiling and offering a gentle touch to emphasize the

---

[3]The information that follows is adapted from 1079ishot.com, "New Orleans Saints' Roman Harper & Malcolm Jenkins Move It Like Bernie," retrieved October 25, 2011.

point. Fourth, we sometimes use nonverbal communication to *replace* verbal expressions—such as when you shake your head instead of saying "no." Finally, we use nonverbal communication to *spotlight* certain parts of verbal messages, such as when you increase the loudness of just one word: "STOP hitting your brother with that light saber!"

EXPRESSING EMOTION

VideoCentral ⊙

bedfordstmartins.com /reflectrelate

Affect Display
Watch this clip online to answer the questions below.

What emotions do you think the woman in this video is displaying through her facial expressions? How well are you able to identify the emotions in the facial expressions of a close friend? How about a casual acquaintance? How important is it to know someone in order to accurately read that person's affect displays?

We communicate emotion nonverbally through **affect displays**—intentional or unintentional nonverbal behaviors that display actual or feigned emotions (Burgoon et al., 1996). This was the primary purpose behind Harper and Jenkins's "Bernie Dance"—the players wanted to physically convey their joy and excitement at having won the game. In everyday interactions, however, affect displays are presented primarily through the face and voice. Intentional use of the face to communicate emotion begins during late infancy, when babies learn to facially communicate anger and happiness to get what they want (Burgoon et al., 1996). Unintentional affect displays begin even earlier. Infants in the first few weeks of life instinctively and reflexively display facial expressions of distress, disgust, and interest. As adults, we communicate hundreds, if not thousands, of real and faked emotional states with our faces.

People also use vocalics to convey emotions. Consider how you communicate love through your voice. What changes do you make in pitch, tone, volume, and speech rate? How does your "loving" voice differ from your "angry" voice? Most people express emotions such as grief and love through lowered vocal pitch, and hostile emotions such as anger and contempt through loudness (Costanzo, Markel, & Costanzo, 1969). Pitch conveys emotion so powerfully that the source of the sound (human voice or other) is irrelevant, and words aren't necessary. Researcher Klaus Scherer (1974) mimicked voice patterns on a music synthesizer and had listeners judge the emotion conveyed. Participants strongly associated high pitch with emotions such as anger, fear, and surprise, and they linked low pitch with pleasantness, boredom, and sadness.

PRESENTING SELF

Think about your interactions with your manager at work. How do you let him or her know—without words—that you're a dedicated and hardworking employee? Chances are, you employ almost all the nonverbal codes discussed above, simultaneously. You convey attentiveness through focused eye contact and pleasant facial expression, and you communicate seriousness through moderate speech rate and pitch. You likely avoid crowding your boss and touching him or her. You strive to show up at meetings on time if you sense that your manager is M-time oriented. You also dress appropriately for the office and try to obey workplace norms regarding how you decorate your work space.

Now imagine that your manager confides to you a recent diagnosis of terminal illness. How would you use nonverbal communication to convey a different self—one who's compassionate and supportive? You'd likely adopt a facial expression conveying sadness and concern. You'd slow your speech rate and lower the pitch of your voice to convey empathy. You'd decrease your interpersonal distance to communicate support. And you might touch your boss lightly on the elbow or gently clasp his or her shoulder to signify caring.

As these examples suggest, nonverbal communication can help us present different aspects of our self to others. We all use nonverbal communication codes to create our identities during interpersonal encounters. An important part of being a competent nonverbal communicator is recognizing the need to shift our nonverbal communication quickly to present ourselves in different ways when the situation demands—for example, dedicated employee one moment, concerned fellow human being another.

MANAGING INTERACTIONS

Nonverbal communication also helps us to manage interpersonal interactions. For example, during conversations, we use regulators, eye contact, touch, smiling, head nods, and posture shifts to signal who gets to speak and for how long (Patterson, 1988). While chatting with a friend, you probably look at him or her anywhere from 30 to 50 percent of your talk time. Then, when you're approaching the end of your conversational turn, you invite your friend to talk by decreasing your pitch and loudness, stopping any gestures, and focusing your gaze on the other person. As your friend begins speaking, you now look at your partner almost 100 percent of his or her talk time, nodding your head to show you're listening (Goodwin, 1981).

During conversations, we also read our partners' nonverbal communication to check their level of interest in what we're saying—watching for signals like eye contact, smiles, and head nods. Yet we're usually unaware that we're doing this until people behave in unexpected ways. For example, if a partner *fails* to react to something we've said that we consider provocative or funny, we may shoot them a glance or frown to express our displeasure nonverbally.

Nonverbal communication also helps us regulate others' attention and behavior. For example, a sudden glance and stern facial expression from a parent or babysitter can stop a child from reaching for the forbidden cookie jar. In my sons' school, the principal gains students' attention by clapping loudly three times—Clap! Clap! Clap!—a pattern that students then repeat back to him, falling silent afterward to listen for an important announcement.

DEFINING RELATIONSHIPS

You're sitting at a local diner, eating lunch and people-watching. Two couples are sitting in nearby booths. One couple sits with one partner very close to the other. They cuddle, touch, and occasionally kiss. When they're not touching, they're smiling and gazing at each other. The couple sitting at the next booth over is behaving very differently. The man sits up tall and straight, his arms extended on both sides of the table. He glares at his partner, interrupts her, and doesn't look at her when she's talking. Her eyes are downcast, her hands are folded in her lap, and she speaks softly. What does the nonverbal communication of each of these couples tell you about the degree of intimacy in their relationship? The partners'

skills practice

Professional Self-Presentation
Presenting yourself in a professional fashion in the workplace

❶ Display a pleasant facial expression, make good eye contact, lean forward, and exhibit upright posture.

❷ Use a moderately resonant and breathy vocal tone, medium pitch and volume, and moderate speech rate.

❸ Adapt your use of proxemics to others' needs for personal space, and respect their territory.

❹ Adjust your touching to match others' preferences.

❺ Keep appointments or allow flexibility regarding punctuality.

❻ Ensure that your physical appearance and artifacts are appropriate, asking your coworkers' and manager's opinions if you're uncertain.

▶ Think about the functions nonverbal communication is playing in this photo. Can you tell what emotions are being expressed? What about the relationships and interactions between the women? What does this tell you about the influence of nonverbal communication in our daily experiences?

relative dominance? A final function of nonverbal communication is to define the nature of our interpersonal relationships. In particular, we use our nonverbal communication to create intimacy and define dominance or submissiveness in our relationships (Burgoon & Hoobler, 2002).

Intimacy   One crucial function nonverbal communication serves is to create **intimacy**, the feeling of closeness and "union" that exists between us and our partners (Mashek & Aron, 2004). For example, in her novel *Written on the Body*, acclaimed British author Jeanette Winterson (1993) offers a vivid and poignant description of how the nonverbal code of touch defines intimacy:

> Articulacy of fingers, the language of the deaf. Who taught you to write on my back? Who taught you to use your hands as branding irons? You have scored your name into my shoulders, referenced me with your mark. The pads of your fingers have become printing blocks, you tap a message on to my skin, tap meaning into my body. Your Morse code interferes with my heart beat. I had a steady heart before I met you, I relied upon it, it had seen active service and grown strong. Now you alter its pace with your rhythm, you play upon me, drumming me taut. (p. 89)

But intimacy isn't defined solely through touch. Physical closeness, shared gaze, soft voices, relaxed postures, sharing of personal objects, and, of course, spending time together—each of these nonverbal behaviors highlights and enhances intimacy. Consider just a few specifics. Smiling and gazing are associated with intimacy (Floyd & Burgoon, 1999), something vividly illustrated in the Beaver family photo in our chapter opening. Individuals share more personal space with intimates and liked others than with strangers, and use proximity to convey affection (Floyd & Morman, 1999). Studies that have instructed people to communicate liking to others have found that the primary way people do so is through increasing gaze, smiling, and leaning forward (Palmer & Simmons,

③ YOUR TURN

While working through the following steps, keep in mind the interpersonal communication concepts, skills, and insights you've learned so far in this book, especially this chapter. Also remember: there are no right answers, so think hard about the choice you make! (P.S. Need help? Review the *Helpful Concepts* listed below.)

• step 1

Reflect on yourself. What are your thoughts and feelings in this situation? What attributions are you making about Dakota based on your friend's interpersonal communication? Are your attributions accurate? Why or why not?

• step 2

Reflect on your partner. Using perspective-taking and empathic concern, put yourself in Dakota's shoes. Consider how your friend is thinking and feeling, especially how Dakota likely feels about you and your relationship.

• step 3

Identify the optimal outcome. Think about all the information you have regarding Dakota and this relationship. Consider your own feelings as well as your friend's. Given all these factors, what's the best, most constructive relationship outcome possible here? Be sure to consider not just what's best for you, but what's best for Dakota as well.

• step 4

Locate the roadblocks. Taking into consideration your own thoughts and feelings, Dakota's, and all that has happened, what's preventing you from achieving the optimal outcome you identified in Step 3?

• step 5

Chart your course. How will you communicate with Dakota to overcome the roadblocks you've identified and achieve your optimal relationship outcome?

HELPFUL CONCEPTS

The ambiguity of nonverbal communication, **212**

Mixed messages, **213**

Immediacy, **220**

Friendship-warmth touch, **224**

The importance of spending time in M-time cultures, **226–228**

Intimacy, **234–235**

In contrast, **submissiveness** is the willingness to allow others to exert power over us. We communicate submissiveness to others nonverbally by engaging in behaviors that are opposite to those that express dominance, such as taking up less space; letting others control our time, space, and possessions; smiling more; and permitting others to interrupt us.

Competently Managing Your Nonverbal Communication

Ways to improve your nonverbal expression

As you interact with others, you use various nonverbal communication codes naturally and simultaneously. Similarly, you take in and interpret others' nonverbal communication instinctively. Look again at the Beaver family photo (on the next page). While viewing this image, you probably don't think, "What's Samson's mouth doing?" or "Gee, Frances's arm is touching Samson's shoulder." When it comes to nonverbal communication, although all the parts are important, it's the overall package that delivers the message.

Given the nature of nonverbal communication, we think it's important to highlight some general guidelines for how you can competently manage your nonverbal communication. In this chapter, we've offered very specific advice for improving your use of particular nonverbal codes. But we conclude with four principles for competent nonverbal conduct, which reflect the three aspects of competence first introduced in Chapter 1: effectiveness, appropriateness, and ethics.

First, when interacting with others, remember that people view your nonverbal communication as at least as important as what you say, if not more so. Although you should endeavor to build your active listening skills (Chapter 5), and use of cooperative language (Chapter 6), bear in mind that people will often assign the greatest weight to what you do nonverbally.

For romantic couples, the level of nonverbal involvement is a direct indicator of the relationship's health.

Second, nonverbal communication competence is inextricably tied to culture. In our discussion, you've repeatedly seen the vast cultural differences as to what is appropriate in body movements (kinesics), space (proxemics), touch (haptics), and time (chronemics), to mention just four. Part of competently managing your nonverbal communication is knowing the cultural display rules for appropriate nonverbal expression prior to interpersonally interacting within a culture, and then adapting your nonverbal communication to match those rules. In addition, competent managers of nonverbal communication are respectful of cultural differences. When someone from another culture uses more or less touch than you, has a different orientation toward time, or adjusts personal distance in ways at odds with your own practice, your ethical obligation

is to be tolerant and accepting of this difference, rather than dismissive or disparaging, and to adapt your own nonverbal communication in ways sensitive to the validity of this difference.

Third, be sensitive to the demands of interpersonal situations. For example, if an interaction seems to call for more formal or more casual behavior, adapt your nonverbal communication accordingly. Remind yourself, if necessary, that being interviewed for a job, sharing a relaxed evening with your roommate, and deepening the level of intimacy in a love relationship all call for different nonverbal messages. You can craft those messages through careful use of the many different nonverbal codes available to you.

Finally, remember that verbal communication and nonverbal communication flow with one another. Your experience of nonverbal communication from others and your nonverbal expression to others are fundamentally fused with the words you and they choose to use. As a consequence, you cannot become a skilled interpersonal communicator by focusing time, effort, and energy only on verbal or only on nonverbal elements. Instead, you must devote yourself to both, because it is only when both are joined as a union of skills that more competent interpersonal communication ability is achieved.

Reflect on the postures, dress, use of space, eye contact, and facial expressions depicted in the Beaver family photo. Then think about how nonverbal communication shapes your life. What judgments do you make about others, based on their scowls and smiles? Their postures? Their appearance and voice? Do you draw accurate conclusions about certain groups of people based on their nonverbal communication? How do others see you? As you communicate with others throughout a typical day, what do your facial expressions, posture, dress, use of space, and eye contact convey?

POSTSCRIPT

We began this chapter with a family of smiles. The smile is one of the simplest, most commonplace expressions. Yet like so many nonverbal expressions, the smile has the power to fundamentally shift interpersonal perceptions. In the case of the Beaver family, seeing the smiles that talking with a friend evoked 100 years ago helps erase more than a century of Native American stereotypes. But the power of the Beaver family's smiles goes beyond simply remedying a historical distortion. It highlights the power that even your simplest nonverbal communication has in shaping and shifting others' perceptions of you.

key terms

⊚ You can watch brief, illustrative videos of these terms and test your understanding of the concepts online in *VideoCentral: Interpersonal Communication* at **bedfordstmartins .com/reflectrelate**.

key concepts

Principles of Nonverbal Communication

- **Nonverbal communication** includes all unspoken behavioral displays.

- Nonverbal communication generally carries more meaning than verbal, especially when we send or receive **mixed messages**.

- Both culture and gender shape people's perceptions and use of nonverbal communication.

Nonverbal Communication Codes

- Although eight different **nonverbal communication codes** exist, the behaviors that most people associate with nonverbal communication, such as facial expressions, gestures, and body posture, are **kinesics**. Four different forms of gestures are commonly used during our interpersonal encounters: **emblems**, **illustrators**, **regulators**, and **adaptors**.

- Something as seemingly simple as body posture—how we lean, position our shoulders, and hold our heads—can communicate substantial information regarding **immediacy** and **power** to others.

- Although we often think of the voice as one thing, many different specific features (such as tone, pitch, loudness, and speech rate) contribute to the complex nonverbal code of **vocalics**.

- People vary their duration, placement, and strength of touch (known as **haptics**) to communicate a broad range of meanings, including **functional-professional touch**, **social-polite touch**, **friendship-warmth touch**, **love-intimacy touch**, **sexual-arousal touch**, and **aggressive-hostile touch**. People's impressions of these various forms of touch are strongly influenced by culture.

- Culture also influences **proxemics**, or use of space and interpersonal distance during encounters with others. Forms of distance include **intimate**, **personal**, **social**, and **public space**. All human beings experience **territoriality** and resent perceived invasions of personal domains.

- We send powerful messages about intimacy and caring through **chronemics**, or our use of time. People differ in their perceptions of the significance of time. Some have an **M-time** orientation, others a **P-time** view.

- Like it or not, our **physical appearance** strongly molds others' impressions of us. Many people favor those they perceive as attractive over those they perceive as unattractive.

- We use personal **artifacts** to portray who we are to others and to communicate information regarding our worth, status, and power.

- Features of our physical **environment**—such as size, furnishings, and materials used in our home or office—also send distinct messages about status and mood.

Functions of Nonverbal Communication

- Our nonverbal communication serves many purposes in our interpersonal encounters and relationships. One of the most common is **affect displays**, which function to show others how we are feeling.

- We can harness all of the nonverbal communication codes to send powerful messages of **intimacy**, **dominance**, and **submissiveness** to others.

key skills

- How might you use your knowledge of gender differences to improve your nonverbal communication skills? Review the practical tips on pages 214 and 216.

- How can you use online communication to better maintain long-distance relationships? Try the *Skills Practice* on page 217.

- Want to nonverbally communicate that you like someone? Follow the suggestions on page 220 for how to effectively convey immediacy; then do the *Skills Practice* on page 221.

- What should you do to effectively use touch during interpersonal encounters? Find out on pages 223–225.

- What can you do to enhance your use of personal space during encounters with people from other cultures? Review the suggestions on pages 225–226.

- Do you understand the differences between M-time and P-time orientations? Take the *Self-Quiz* on page 227, and review the rules for increasing sensitivity to others with different time orientations on page 228.

- Why is it important to dress appropriately for the situations and encounters you're going to face? Find out on pages 228–229.

- Want to improve your nonverbal communication in the workplace? See the tips for effective nonverbal self-presentation in the workplace on pages 232–233; then do the *Skills Practice* on page 233.

- Do you know which nonverbal cues are most likely to be perceived by others as communicating dominance? Test your dominance knowledge by taking the *Self-Quiz* on page 235.

- What are mixed messages, and how can you most effectively deal with them if you receive them from others? Review *Making Relationship* Choices on pages 236–237 to find out.

- What general guidelines can help you responsibly manage your nonverbal communication? Refresh your memory by consulting pages 238–239.

8 Managing Conflict and Power

When Amy Chua's *Battle Hymn of the Tiger Mother* hit bookstores, a firestorm of controversy erupted regarding her parenting.[1] Chua boasts of never letting daughters Sophia and Lulu watch TV or play computer games, drilling them in piano and violin for hours daily, and demanding that they never get a grade below an A. Although Chua intended *Tiger Mother* to be humorous and satirical, critics decried her behavior as abusive. Blogger Betty Ming Liu even declared, "Parents like Amy Chua are the reason Asian-Americans like me are in therapy." But Chua's book is about more than just parenting rules; it's a tale of power, conflict, and the negative outcomes of approaching disagreements destructively (Cullen, 2011).

Throughout her book, Chua describes her need to wield power over others. While on vacation in Greece, Chua demands that the entire family (including husband Jed and her parents) delay sightseeing of local ruins until after Lulu rehearses her violin. The marathon practice session that follows results in everyone missing their planned activities. "I wouldn't wish the misery that followed on anyone," Chua laments, not seeming to realize it was an outcome of her decision making (pp. 90–91).

Chua's approach to conflict involves demanding that others do what she wants, then verbally abusing them if they don't do so. When

Conflict is a normal part of all relationships

---

[1] All content that follows is adapted from Chua (2011), Choi (2011), Cullen (2011), and Liu (2011).

8 / Managing Conflict and Power

Lulu refuses to practice piano, Chua insults her for "being lazy, cowardly, self-indulgent, and pathetic!" When Jed intervenes— reminding her that Lulu has a different musical skill set than her prodigy sister Sophia—Chua sarcastically snipes, "Even losers are special in their own special way" (pp. 60–61).

The conflicts escalate for years, culminating in a public blowup at a restaurant. When Lulu refuses to try caviar, Chua taunts her: "There is nothing more common and low than an American teenager who won't try things— You're boring, Lulu." Lulu explodes, "I HATE YOU! You don't love me. You make me feel bad about myself every second. You've wrecked my life. I can't stand to be around you. You're a terrible mother. You're selfish. You don't care about anyone but yourself!" Chua retaliates in kind, "You're a terrible daughter!" (pp. 204–206).

Although Chua attributes her behavior to her Chinese heritage, research suggests otherwise. Temple University psychologist Laurence Steinberg studied thousands of Latino, Euro-, African, and Asian American families and found that authoritarian parents occur in *all* ethnic groups. Chinese caregivers are *not* more likely than others to aggressively abuse power or manage conflict by insulting others (Choi, 2011). Steinberg concludes, "One can't talk about Chinese households as if there isn't variability there . . . that can be misleading" (as quoted in Choi, 2011, para. 13).

Importantly, managing conflict and power in Chua's fashion leads to decidedly negative outcomes. Such behaviors within family settings elevate anxiety, depression, and psychosomatic problems, and children whose parents bully them are less self-assured and socially poised as a result. Late in her book, Chua seems to realize this as she reflects on the destructive legacy of her communication choices: "I don't know how my daughters will look back on all this twenty years from now. Will they tell their own children, 'My mother was a controlling fanatic who even in India made us practice before we could see Bombay and New Delhi?' Or will they have softer memories?" (p. 91).

It's easy to read Amy Chua's book, or watch videos of her appearance on *The Colbert Report*, and laugh at the extremity of her conflict style. Even she makes fun of the things she said and did while fighting with her daughters. But when we face a bullying parent, find ourselves locked in battle with a lover, or get trapped in an intractable disagreement with a friend, the pain becomes personal. The words people most commonly associate with interpersonal conflict are *destruction*, *heartache*, and *hopelessness* (Wilmot & Hocker, 2001).

Yet conflicts don't have to be hopeless, because we're not helpless. Each of us has the ability to choose constructive approaches to managing conflicts that will help create positive outcomes for everyone involved. In this chapter, we explore interpersonal conflict and how best to manage it. You'll learn:

- The nature of conflict
- The role power plays in conflict
- Different approaches for handling interpersonal conflict
- The impact of gender, culture, and technology on conflict
- Resolutions and long-term outcomes of conflict
- The challenges to resolving conflict in close relationships, and how to overcome them

Conflict and Interpersonal Communication

> Most conflicts occur between people who know each other

We like to think of conflict as unusual, an unpleasant exception to the normal routine of our relationships. Each conflict seems freshly painful and unprecedented. "I can't believe it!" we text or post on Facebook, "We had a *terrible* fight last night!" Friends immediately fire back messages echoing our shock: "OMG, really?!" Observing other couples, we judge their relationships by how much they fight: couples who argue too much are "doomed to fail," whereas those who rarely disagree must be "blissfully happy."

But such beliefs are mistaken. Conflict is a normal part of *all* relationships (Canary, 2003). Dealing with other human beings (and their unique goals, preferences, and opinions) means regularly having your wants and needs run up against theirs, triggering disputes (Malis & Roloff, 2006). On average, people report seven conflicts a week, mostly with relatives, friends, and lovers with whom they've argued before (Benoit & Benoit, 1990). Thus, the challenge you face is not how to avoid conflict, or how to live a conflict-free life, but instead how to constructively manage the conflicts that *will* arise in your interpersonal relationships.

WHAT IS CONFLICT?

Almost any issue can spark conflict—money, time, sex, religion, politics, love, chores, and so on—and almost anyone can get into a conflict: family members, friends, lovers, coworkers, or casual acquaintances. Despite such variations, all

▶ Conflict is fueled by the perception of opposition. As long as people perceive their goals to be incompatible, conflict will endure.

conflicts share similar attributes. **Conflict** is the process that occurs when people perceive that they have incompatible goals or that someone is interfering in their ability to achieve their objectives (Wilmot & Hocker, 2010). Four features characterize most conflicts: they begin with perception, they involve clashes in goals or behaviors, they unfold over time as a process, and they are dynamic.

Conflict Begins with Perception   Conflict occurs when people perceive incompatible goals or actions (Roloff & Soule, 2002). Because conflict begins with perception, perceptual errors (see Chapter 3) shape how our conflicts unfold. As we'll discuss later in this chapter, during conflicts we blame others more than ourselves, and perceive them as uncooperative and ourselves as helpful. These self-enhancing errors can lead us to manage conflict in ways that create unsatisfying outcomes.

Conflict Involves Clashes in Goals or Behaviors   At the heart of conflicts are clashes in goals or behaviors (Zacchilli, Hendrick, & Hendrick, 2009). Some conflicts revolve around incompatible goals, ranging from everyday leisure activity disputes ("I want to go out dancing!" vs. "I want to stay home and play video games!") to serious arguments regarding personal values ("I want our children to be raised Jewish!" vs. "I want them to be Catholic!"). Other disputes break out when one person's actions clash with another's. A friend texts you repeatedly while you're studying, and you fire back a nasty message, or your manager demands that you work over a holiday weekend, and you refuse.

Conflict Is a Process   Although people often describe conflict as a series of unrelated events ("I sent her this carefully worded e-mail, and for no reason, she blasted me in response!"), conflict is a process that unfolds over time. Its course is determined by the communication choices we make—everything we say and do during a conflict influences everything our partner says and does, and vice versa.

Moreover, most conflicts proceed through several stages, each involving decisions and actions that affect the conflict's direction and consequences for the individuals involved. In its most basic form, the process of conflict involves people perceiving that a conflict exists, choosing an approach for how to handle the conflict, and then dealing with the conflict resolutions and outcomes that follow. Conflict is not a one-time-only event: how you handle a conflict with someone will have consequences for your future interactions and relationship with that person.

Conflict Is Dynamic   Because conflict typically unfolds over a series of exchanged messages, it is ever-changing and unpredictable. Research looking at the dynamic nature of conflict finds that in 66.4 percent of disputes, the focus shifts substantially as the conflict progresses (Keck & Samp, 2007). A fight over your father's snide remark regarding your job quickly becomes a battle about his chronic disapproval of you. Or, a dispute regarding your roommate eating your leftovers becomes an argument about her failure to be a supportive friend. When a conflict shifts topic, it can devolve into **kitchen-sinking** (from the expression, "throwing everything at them but the kitchen sink"), in which combatants hurl insults and accusations at each other that have little to do with the original disagreement. For example, a couple fighting over whether one of them was flirting with their server at dinner may say things like: "What about the time when you completely forgot our anniversary?!" and "Oh yeah?! Well, your family sucks!"

Since conflict often dynamically branches out into other troublesome topics, managing conflict is extremely challenging—you can never fully anticipate the twists and turns that will occur. But remember: you have total control over what *you* say and do—and that can influence how someone responds. If you think a conflict is getting completely off-track, choose your communication carefully to help bring it back on topic.

CONFLICT IN RELATIONSHIPS

Most conflicts occur between people who know each other and are involved in close relationships, such as romantic partners, friends, family members, and co-workers (Benoit & Benoit, 1990). Unlike people who don't know each other well, people in close relationships experience prolonged contact and frequent interaction, which set the stage for disagreements over goals and behaviors.

In close relationships, conflicts typically arise from one of three issues (Peterson, 2002): *irritating partner behaviors* (e.g., a family member has an annoying personal habit, or your partner interrupts you while you're working), *disagreements regarding relationship rules* (e.g., you and your partner disagree about texting with ex-partners, or family members disagree about inviting friends on family vacations), and *personality clashes* (e.g., you have a sunny disposition but your friend is a complainer, or you're organized and ambitious but your partner is carefree and lazy).

self-
reflection

Think of a relational partner
with whom you have the
same conflict over and over
again. What effect does this
conflict have on your relationship? In what ways do
you contribute to its con-
tinuance? How might you
change your communication
to end this repetitive cycle?

Relationship partners often develop consistent patterns of communication for dealing with conflict that either promote or undermine their happiness. For example, happily married couples are more likely than unhappily married couples to avoid personal attacks during conflicts and instead focus their discussion on the differences at hand (Peterson, 2002). Such patterns are self-perpetuating: happy couples remain motivated to behave in ways guaranteed to keep them happy, and because they believe they can solve their problems, they are more likely to work together to resolve conflict (Caughlin & Vangelisti, 2000). In contrast, dissatisfied couples often choose to avoid important conflicts. Their failure to deal directly with their problems further fuels their unhappiness (Afifi, McManus, Steuber, & Coho, 2009).

Managing conflicts in close relationships presents unique challenges. We feel connected to our intimate partners, and disputes threaten that sense of connection (Berscheid, 2002). *Your conflicts with loved ones are guaranteed to be intense and emotionally draining experiences.* Conflicts also powerfully affect your *future* encounters and relationships. For example, if you and a sibling fight via text messages, this conflict will shape not only how the two of you will communicate when you are next face-to-face, but how you'll feel about your relationship moving forward. As scholar Donald Peterson (2002) notes, "Every conflict and every resolution, as well as every failure at resolution, becomes a part of your overall relationship history" (p. 363).

Power and Conflict

Power influences who will prevail in conflicts

In Suzanne Collins's futuristic novel *The Hunger Games* (2008), North America has become Panem, consisting of a wealthy Capitol city surrounded by twelve outlying districts.[2] Following suppression of a mass rebellion by the districts, the Capitol creates the annual "Hunger Games." Children from each district are selected and pitted against each other in a fight to the death that is televised live. Child participants are chosen lottery-style, and for district residents there is no choice: to not participate in the lottery means death for all. As Katniss Everdeen, the story's central character, describes it:

> Taking kids from our districts, forcing them to kill one another while we watch—this is the Capitol's way of reminding us how totally we are at their mercy. Whatever words they use, the real message is clear: look how we take your children and sacrifice them and there's nothing you can do. If you lift a finger, we will destroy every last one of you." (p. 18)

The dominant theme of *The Hunger Games* is **power**: the ability to influence or control people and events (Donohue & Kolt, 1992). Understanding power is critical for constructively managing conflict, because people in conflict often wield whatever power they have to overcome the opposition and achieve their

---

[2]All material that follows is adapted from Collins (2008).

In *The Hunger Games*, Effie Trinket wields the Capitol's power by escorting children to the Hunger Games, a televised competition in which youth are forced to fight to the death. When main character Katniss Everdeen volunteers to take her younger sister's place in the Games, she exercises her own power and influences the sequence of events that follow.

goals. In conflicts where one party has more power than the other—like the Capitol has over the districts—the more powerful tend to get what they want.

POWER'S DEFINING CHARACTERISTICS

Most of us won't ever experience power wielded as brutally as in *The Hunger Games*. But power does permeate our everyday lives and is an integral part of interpersonal communication and relationships. Power determines how partners relate to one another, who controls relationship decisions, and whose goals will prevail during conflicts (Dunbar, 2004). Let's consider power's defining characteristics, as suggested by scholars William Wilmot and Joyce Hocker (2010).

Power Is Always Present   Whether you're talking on the phone with a parent, texting your best friend, or spending time with your lover, power is present in all your interpersonal encounters and relationships. Power may be balanced (e.g., friend to friend) or imbalanced (e.g., manager to employee, parent to young child). When power is balanced, **symmetrical relationships** result. When power is imbalanced, **complementary relationships** are the outcome.

Although power is always present, we're typically not aware of it until people violate our expectations for power balance in the relationship, such as giving orders or "talking down" to us. Your dorm-floor resident advisor tells you (rather than asks you) to pick him up after class. Your work supervisor grabs inventory you were stocking and says, "No—do it *this* way!" even though you were doing it properly. According to **Dyadic Power Theory** (Dunbar, 2004), people with only moderate power are most likely to use controlling communication. Because their power is limited, they can't always be sure they're going to get their way. Hence, they feel more of a need to wield power in noticeable ways (Dunbar, 2004). In contrast, people with high power feel little need to display it; they *know* that their words will be listened to and their wishes granted. This means that you're most likely to run into controlling communication and power-based bullying when dealing with people who have moderate amounts of power over you, such as mid-level managers, team captains, and class-project group leaders as opposed to people with high power (in such contexts) like vice presidents, coaches, or faculty advisors.

Power Can Be Used Ethically or Unethically   Power itself isn't good or bad—it's the way people use it that matters. Many happy marriages, family relationships, and long-term friendships are complementary. One person controls more resources and has more decision-making influence than the other. Yet the person in charge uses his or her power only to benefit both people and the relationship. In other relationships, the powerful partner wields his or her power unethically or recklessly. For example, a boss threatens to fire her employee unless he sleeps with her, or an abusive husband tells his unhappy wife that she'll never see their kids again if she leaves him.

Power Is Granted   Power doesn't reside within people. Instead, it is granted by individuals or groups who allow another person or group to exert influence over them. For example, a friend of mine invited his parents to stay with him and his wife for the weekend. His parents had planned on leaving Monday, but come Monday morning, they announced that they had decided to stay through the end of the week. My friend accepted their decision even though he could have insisted that they leave at the originally agreed-upon time. In doing so, he granted his parents the power to decide their departure date without his input or consent.

self-reflection

Think of a complementary personal relationship of yours, in which you have more power than the other person. How does the imbalance affect how you communicate during conflicts? Is it ethical for you to wield power over the other person during a conflict to get what you want? Why or why not?

Power Influences Conflicts   If you strip away the particulars of what's said and done during most conflicts, you'll find power struggles underneath. Who has more influence? Who controls the resources, decisions, and feelings involved? People struggle to see whose goals will prevail, and they wield whatever power they have to pursue their own goals. But power struggles rarely lead to mutually beneficial solutions. As we'll see, the more constructive approach is to set aside your power and work collaboratively to resolve the conflict.

POWER CURRENCIES

Given that power is not innate but something that some people grant to others, how do you get power? To acquire power, you must possess or control some form of **power currency**, a resource that other people value (Wilmot & Hocker, 2010). Possessing or controlling a valued resource gives you influence over individuals who value that resource. Likewise, if individuals have resources you view as valuable, you will grant power to them.

Five power currencies are common in interpersonal relationships. **Resource currency** includes material things such as money, property, and food. If you possess material things that someone else needs or wants, you have resource power over them. Parents have nearly total resource power over young children because they control all the money, food, shelter, clothing, and other items their children need and want. Managers have high levels of resource power over employees, as they control employees' continued employment and salaries.

Expertise currency comprises special skills or knowledge. The more highly specialized and unique the skill or knowledge you have, the more expertise power you possess. A Stuttgart-trained Porsche mechanic commands a substantially higher wage and choicer selection of clients than a minimally trained Quick Lube oil change attendant.

A person who is linked with a network of friends, family, and acquaintances with substantial influence has **social network currency**. Others may value his or her ability to introduce them to people who can land them jobs, "talk them up" to potential romantic partners, or get them invitations to exclusive parties.

Personal characteristics—beauty, intelligence, charisma, communication skill, sense of humor—that people consider desirable constitute **personal currency**. Even if you lack resource, expertise, and social network currency, you can still achieve a certain degree of influence and stature by being beautiful, funny, or smart.

Finally, you acquire **intimacy currency** when you share a close bond with someone that no one else shares. If you have a unique intimate bond with someone—a lover, friend, or family member—you possess intimacy power over him or her, and he or she may do you a favor "only because you are my best friend."

POWER AND CULTURE

Views of power differ substantially across cultures. Power derives from the perception of power currencies, so people are granted power not only according to which power currencies they possess, but also according to the degree to which those power currencies are valued in a given culture. In Asian and Latino

VideoCentral ◉

bedfordstmartins.com
/reflectrelate

Expertise Currency
*Watch this clip online
to answer the questions
below.*

What types of expertise currency do you have? When are they beneficial to you? Have there been any times when your expertise worked to your disadvantage? If so, how?

Want to see more? Check out VideoCentral for clips illustrating all the power currencies, including **resource**, **social network**, **personal**, and **intimacy**.

◖ Power expresses itself in the form of different power currencies. As shown here, these include resource currency, expertise currency, social network currency, personal currency, and intimacy currency.

cultures, high value is placed on resource currency; consequently, people without wealth, property, or other such material resources are likely to grant power to those who possess them (Gudykunst & Kim, 2003). In contrast, in northern European countries, Canada, and the United States, people with wealth may be admired or even envied, but they are not granted unusual power. If your rich neighbor builds a huge mansion, you might be impressed. But if her new fence crosses onto your property, you'll confront her about it ("Sorry to bother you, but your new fence is one foot over the property line"). Members of other cultures would be less likely to say anything, given her wealth and corresponding power.

Cultures also differ widely in the degree to which people view the unequal distribution of power as acceptable, known as **power-distance** (Hofstede, 1991, 2001). In *high power-distance cultures*, it's considered normal and even desirable for people of different social and professional status to be widely separated in terms of their power. Within such cultures, people give privileged treatment and extreme respect to those in high-status positions (Ting-Toomey, 1999). People of lesser status are expected to behave humbly, especially when they're around people of higher status, while high-status people are expected to act superior. In *low power-distance cultures*, people in high-status positions strive to minimize the differences between themselves and lower-status persons, often interacting with lower-status persons in an informal and equal fashion (see Table 8.1).

Power-distance influences how people deal with conflict. In low power-distance cultures, people who possess few power currencies may still choose to engage in conflict with high-power people. Employees may question management decisions, or people may attend a town meeting and argue with the mayor. These behaviors are much less likely to occur in high power-distance cultures (Bochner & Hesketh, 1994).

Power-distance also plays a role in shaping close relationship communication, especially in families. In traditional Mexican culture, for instance, the value of *respeto* emphasizes power-distance between those who are younger and their elders (Delgado-Gaitan, 1993). As part of *respeto*, children are expected

table 8.1 Power-Distance across Countries

High Power-Distance Countries	Moderate Power-Distance Countries	Low Power-Distance Countries
Malaysia	Spain	Norway
Panama	Pakistan	Sweden
Guatemala	Italy	Ireland
Philippines	South Africa	New Zealand
Mexico	Hungary	Denmark
Venezuela	Jamaica	Israel
China	United States	Austria

Source: Hofstede (2009).

Are You a High or a Low Power-Distance Person?

Read each statement. Place a check mark next to the statements with which you agree. Then follow the instructions for interpreting your score.

_____ Obedience and respect for authority are the most important values children should learn.

_____ What young people need most is strict discipline, rugged determination, and the willingness to sacrifice for family and country.

_____ Every person should have complete faith in some supernatural power whose decisions he or she obeys without question.

_____ Young people sometimes get rebellious ideas, but as they grow up they ought to get over these ideas and settle down.

_____ There are few things worse than a person who doesn't feel gratitude and respect for his or her parents.

_____ What this country needs most is a few courageous, tireless, and devoted leaders in whom the people can put their faith.

_____ In times of doubt, people should trust our country's leaders to do what's right.

Note: Information in this _Self-Quiz_ is adapted from Ray (1972).

Scoring: If your total score is 5–7, you're likely high power-distance; a score of 3–4 suggests you're moderate power-distance; 0–2 indicates you're low power-distance.

to defer to elders' authority and to avoid openly disagreeing with them. In contrast, many Euro-Americans believe that once children reach the age of adulthood, power in family relationships should be balanced—children and their elders treating one another in a symmetrical fashion as friends (Kagawa & McCornack, 2004).

POWER AND GENDER

To say that power and gender are intertwined is an understatement. Throughout history and across cultures, _the_ defining distinction between the genders has been men's power over women. Through patriarchy, which means "the rule of fathers," men have used cultural practices to maintain their societal, political, and economic power (Mies, 1991). Men have built and sustained patriarchy by denying women access to power currencies.

Although many North Americans presume that the gender gap in power has narrowed, the truth is more complicated. The World Economic Forum's 2010 report examined four "pillars" of gender equality: economic opportunity, educational access, political representation, and physical health (Hausmann, Tyson, & Zahidi, 2010). Across 134 nations representing over 90 percent of the world's population, the gaps between women and men in terms of education and health _have_ largely been closed. Women now have 93 percent of the educational opportunities of men, and 96 percent of the health and medical support. But they still dramatically lack both economic and political power.

When Cristina Fernández became Argentina's 55th president in 2007, she was one of only a handful of women currently serving as an elected head of state. How does this disparity reflect the wider difference between men's and women's political influence in the world?

Women have only 59 percent of the economic opportunities and resources that men share, and a paltry 18 percent of the political representation. Iceland, Norway, Finland, and Sweden top the list of the most gender-equal nations on the planet. Where do the United States and Canada rank? Nineteenth and twentieth overall; but in terms of political empowerment, the United States ranks 40th and Canada, 36th.

How does lack of power affect women's interpersonal communication? As gender scholar Cheris Kramarae (1981) notes, women with little or no power "are not as free or as able as men are to say what they wish, when and where they wish. . . . Their talk is often not considered of much value by men" (p. 1). By contrast, what men say and do is counted as important, and women's voices are muted. In interpersonal relationships, this power difference manifests itself in men's tendency to expect women to listen attentively to everything they say while men select the topics they wish to attend to when women are speaking (Fishman, 1983). Whereas men may feel satisfied that their voices are being heard in their relationships, women often feel as though their viewpoints are being ignored or minimized, both at home and in the workplace (Spender, 1990).

Handling Conflict

How you approach conflict affects the outcomes

I was flying home after spending spring break with my folks. The jet provided so little space between seats that if someone in front of you leaned back, you couldn't have your tray table out. Across the aisle was "Mike," a large-bellied businessman writing furiously on his laptop. An hour into the flight, the man sitting in front of him, "Tom," suddenly leaned his seat back and began reading a book. Of course, the moment he did so, the tray table on the back of his seat jammed into Mike's belly and the seat back forced his laptop closed.

"*Excuse* me!" snapped Mike, "I'm using my computer—can you lean your seat forward?"

"But I want to lean back," said Tom, staying where he was.

"But I'm trying to use my computer, and I can't if you're leaning back!" snarled Mike.

"Your computer isn't my problem! I have the right to lean back if I want!" exclaimed Tom. Mike then buzzed the flight attendant, who approached Tom.

"Sir, if you could just move your seat forward a little, he can use his computer." Tom went berserk. "WHY DOES IT HAVE TO BE ME WHO COMPROMISES? I'M NOT MOVING!" he shouted. The attendant then offered a different seat to Mike, who proceeded to shove Tom's seat back when exiting so that it hit him in the head.

What would you have done in this situation? Would you have avoided the conflict by pretending that you weren't being inconvenienced? Would you have demanded that your desires be met? Would you have "freaked out"? Or would you have attempted to work collaboratively, seeking an agreeable compromise or a solution that met both of your needs?

In situations where others are interrupting your goals or actions, your most important decision is how to handle the conflict (Sillars & Wilmot, 1994). *Your choice about what you'll say and do will shape everything that follows—whether the situation will go unresolved, escalate, or be resolved.* Your communication choices also influence whether your relationship with the other person (if one exists) will be damaged or grow stronger.

In this section, we examine the approaches people use for handling conflict. In addition, we look at the impact that gender, culture, and technology have upon selection of these approaches.

APPROACHES TO HANDLING CONFLICT

People generally handle conflict in one of five ways: avoidance, accommodation, competition, reactivity, or collaboration (Lulofs & Cahn, 2000; Zacchilli et al., 2009). Before reading about each approach, take the *Self-Quiz* on page 256 to find out how you typically approach conflict.

Avoidance   One way to handle conflict is **avoidance**: ignoring the conflict, pretending it isn't really happening, or communicating indirectly about the situation. One common form of avoidance is **skirting**, in which a person avoids a conflict by changing the topic or joking about it. You think your lover is having an affair and raise the issue, but he or she just laughs and says (in a Southern accent), "Don't you know we'll always be together, like Noah and Allie from *The Notebook*?" Another form of avoidance is **sniping**—communicating in a negative fashion and then abandoning the encounter by physically leaving the scene or refusing to interact further. You're fighting with your brother through Skype, when he pops off a nasty comment ("I see you're still a spoiled brat!") and signs off before you have a chance to reply.

Avoidance is the most frequently used approach to handling conflict (Sillars, 1980). People opt for avoidance because it seems easier, less emotionally draining, and lower risk than direct confrontation (Afifi & Olson, 2005). But avoidance poses substantial risks (Afifi et al., 2009). One of the biggest is **cumulative annoyance**, in which repressed irritation grows as the mental list of grievances we have against our partners builds (Peterson, 2002). Eventually, cumulative annoyance overwhelms our capacity to suppress it and we suddenly explode in anger. For example, you constantly remind your teenage son about his homework, chores, personal hygiene, and room cleanliness. This bothers you immensely because you feel these matters are his responsibility, but you swallow your anger because you don't want to make a fuss or be seen by him as "nagging." One evening, after reminding him twice to hang up his expensive new leather jacket, you walk into his bedroom to find the coat crumpled in a ball on the floor. You go on a tirade, listing all of the things he has done to upset you in the past month.

self-reflection

Recall a conflict in which you chose avoidance. Why did you make this choice? What consequences ensued? Were there any positive outcomes? If you could relive the encounter, what, if anything, would you say and do differently to obtain more positive results?

self-QUIZ   How Do You Approach Conflict?

Read through the statements, placing a check mark next to each statement with which you agree.

During conflicts, I typically . . .

Avoidance

_____ keep my feelings about the disagreement to myself.

_____ avoid open discussion of the dispute.

_____ stay away from the topic of disagreement.

_____ avoid any type of unpleasant exchange.

Accommodation

_____ accommodate the other person's wishes.

_____ give in to the other person's desires.

_____ go along with the other person's suggestions.

_____ pretend to agree just to satisfy the other person's expectations.

Competition

_____ try to convince the other person that I'm right.

_____ take control so that the decision goes in my favor.

_____ pursue my side of the issue.

_____ use my power to win.

Reactivity

_____ explode violently with anger.

_____ say things that I know will hurt the other person.

_____ scream or yell loudly and throw things.

_____ accuse the other person of wrongdoing.

Collaboration

_____ investigate the issue of dispute to find a solution acceptable to both parties.

_____ try to work with the other person to find solutions that satisfy both our expectations.

_____ exchange information with the other person so we can solve the problem together.

_____ bring all of our concerns out in the open so the issue can be resolved.

Note: Adapted from Rahim and Mager (1995); Zacchilli, Hendrick, and Hendrick (2009).

Scoring: The category with the most check marks indicates how you primarily manage conflict. If you score equally high on two or more different approaches, you use more than one approach.

A second risk posed by avoidance is **pseudo-conflict**, the perception that a conflict exists when in fact it doesn't. For example, you mistakenly think your romantic partner is about to break up with you because you see tagged photos of him or her arm in arm with someone else on Facebook. So you decide to preemptively end your relationship even though your partner actually has no desire to leave you (the photos were of your partner and a cousin).

Despite the risks, avoidance can be a wise choice for managing conflict in situations where emotions run high (Berscheid, 2002). If everyone involved is angry, and yet you choose to continue the interaction, you run the risk of saying things that will damage your relationship. It may be better to avoid through leaving, hanging up, or not responding to texts or messages until tempers have cooled.

Accommodation   Through **accommodation**, one person abandons his or her own goals and acquiesces to the desires of the other person. For example, your supervisor at work asks you to stay an extra hour tonight because a coworker is showing up late. Although you had plans for the evening, you cancel them and act as if it's not a problem.

If you're like most people, you probably accommodate people who have more power than you. Why? If you don't, they might use their power to control or punish you. This suggests an important lesson regarding the relationship between power and conflict: people who are more powerful than you probably won't accommodate your goals during conflicts.

Another factor that influences people's decision to accommodate is love. Accommodation reflects a high concern for others and a low concern for self; you want to please those you love (Frisby & Westerman, 2010). Hence, accommodation is likely to occur in healthy, satisfied close relationships where selflessness is characteristic (Hendrick & Hendrick, 1992). For example, your romantic partner is accepted into a summer study-abroad program in Europe. Even though you had planned on spending the summer together, you encourage him or her to accept the offer.

Competition   Think back to the airline conflict. Each of the men involved aggressively challenged the other and expressed little concern for the other's perspective or goals. This approach is known as **competition**: an open and clear discussion of the goal clash that exists and the pursuit of one's own goals without regard for others' goals (Sillars, 1980).

The choice to use competition is motivated in part by negative thoughts and beliefs, including a desire to control, a willingness to hurt others in order to gain, and a lack of respect for others (Bevan, Finan, & Kaminsky, 2008; Zacchilli et al., 2009). Consequently, you'll be less likely to opt for competition when you are

bedfordstmartins.com
/reflectrelate

Accommodation
Watch this clip online to answer the questions below.

In this video, how does one partner accommodate the other? When have you found it most wise to accommodate in a conflict situation?

Want to see more? Check out VideoCentral for clips illustrating **avoidance**, **sniping**, **competition**, and **collaboration**.

◐ The day after Thanksgiving is traditionally the first day of the winter holiday shopping season. Black Friday, as it's known, often causes situations where shoppers compete for limited-supply products or deals. What have you experienced or heard about how conflicts are handled in these potentially tense situations?

in a conflict with someone whose needs you are interested in and whom you admire. Conversely, if people routinely approach conflict by making demands to the exclusion of your desires, they likely do not respect you (Hendrick & Hendrick, 2006).

At a minimum, competitive approaches can trigger *defensive communication* (described in Chapter 6)—someone refusing to consider your goals or dismissing them as unimportant, acting superior to you, or attempting to squelch your disagreement by wielding power over you (Waldron, Turner, Alexander, & Barton, 1993). But the primary risk of choosing a competitive approach is **escalation**, a dramatic rise in emotional intensity and increasingly negative and aggressive communication—just like in the airline dispute. If people in conflict both choose competition, and neither is willing to back down, escalation is guaranteed. Even initially trivial conflicts can quickly explode into intense exchanges.

Reactivity   A fourth way people handle conflict is by not pursuing any conflict-related goals at all; instead, they communicate in an emotionally explosive and negative fashion. This is known as **reactivity**, and is characterized by accusations of mistrust, yelling, crying, and becoming verbally or physically abusive. Reactivity is decidedly nonstrategic. Instead of avoiding, accommodating, or competing, people simply "flip out." For example, one of my college dating partners was intensely reactive. When I noted that we weren't getting along, and suggested taking a break, she screamed "I *knew* it! You've been cheating on me!" and hurled a vase of roses I had given her at my head. Thankfully I ducked out of the way, but it took the campus police to calm her down. Her behavior had nothing to do with "managing our conflict." She simply *reacted*.

Similar to competition, reactivity is strongly related to a lack of respect (Bevan et al., 2008; Zacchilli et al., 2009). People prone to reactivity have little interest in others as individuals, and do not recognize others' desires as relevant (Zacchilli et al., 2009).

Collaboration   The most constructive approach to managing conflict is **collaboration**: treating conflict as a mutual problem-solving challenge rather than something that must be avoided, accommodated, competed over, or reacted to. Often the result of using a collaborative approach is *compromise*, where everyone involved modifies their individual goals to come up with a solution to the conflict. (We'll discuss compromise more on page 265.) You're most likely to use collaboration when you respect the other person and are concerned about his or her desires as well as your own (Keck & Samp, 2007; Zacchilli et al., 2009). People who regularly use collaboration feel more trust, commitment, and overall satisfaction with their relationships than those who don't (Smith, Heaven, & Ciarrochi, 2008). Whenever possible, opt for collaboration.

To use a collaborative approach, try these suggestions from Wilmot and Hocker (2010). First, *attack problems not people*. Talk about the conflict as something separate from the people involved, saying, for instance, "This issue has really come between us." This frames the conflict as the source of trouble and unites the people trying to handle it. At the same time, avoid personal attacks

self-reflection

Call to mind someone you know who consistently approaches conflict with reactivity. How has this shaped your willingness to broach issues of disagreement? Impacted your feelings? Given the relationship between reactivity and respect, is it possible to sustain a healthy, close relationship with a reactive person? Why or why not?

table 8.2 **Competitive versus Collaborative Conflict Approaches**

Situation	Competitive Approach	Collaborative Approach
Roommate hasn't been doing his or her share of the housework.	"I'm sick and tired of you never doing anything around here! From now on, you are doing all the chores!"	"We've both been really busy, but I'm concerned that things are not getting done. Let's make a list of all the chores and figure out how to fairly divide them up."
Coworker is draining large blocks of your work time by socializing with you.	"It's obvious that you don't care about your job or whether you get fired. But I need this job, so stop bugging me all the time and let me get my work done!"	"I enjoy spending time with you, but I'm finding I don't have enough time left to get my work done. Let's figure out how we can better balance hanging out and working."
Romantic partner wants you to abandon a beloved pastime because it seems too dangerous.	"I've been racing dirt bikes long before I met you, and there's no way I'm giving them up. If you really loved me, you'd accept that instead of pestering me to quit!"	"Sorry my racing worries you; I know the reason you're concerned is because you care about me. Let's talk about what we can both do so I don't worry you so much."

while being courteous and respectful, regardless of how angry you may be. This is perhaps the hardest part of collaboration, because you likely *will* be angry during conflicts (Berscheid, 2002). Just don't let your anger cause you to say and do things you shouldn't. If someone attacks you and not the problem, don't get sucked into trading insults. Simply say "I can see you're very upset; let's talk about this when we've both had a chance to cool off," and end the encounter before things escalate further.

Second, *focus on common interests and long-term goals.* Keep the emphasis on the desires you share in common, not the issue that's driving you apart. Use "we" language (see Chapter 6) to bolster this impression: "I know we both want what's best for the company." Arguing over positions ("I want this!" versus "I want that!") endangers relationships because the conflict quickly becomes a destructive contest of wills.

Third, *create options before arriving at decisions.* Be willing to negotiate a solution, rather than insist on one. To do this, start by asking questions that will elicit options: "How do you think we can best resolve this?" or "What ideas for solutions do you have?" Then propose ideas of your own. Be flexible. Most collaborative solutions involve some form of compromise, so be willing to adapt your original desires, even if it means not getting everything you want. Then combine the best parts of the various suggestions to come up with an agreeable solution. Don't get bogged down searching for a "perfect" solution—it may not exist.

skills practice

Collaboration

Using collaboration to manage a conflict

❶ During your next significant conflict, openly discuss the situation, emphasizing that it's an understandable clash between goals rather than people.

❷ Highlight common interests and long-term goals.

❸ Create several solutions for resolving the conflict that are satisfactory to both of you.

❹ Combine the best elements of these ideas into a single, workable solution.

❺ Evaluate the solution you've collaboratively created, ensuring that it's fair and ethical.

⬤ Popular television shows depict a variety of conflict management styles among married couples. How do these depictions match or contradict your own experiences?

Finally, *critically evaluate your solution.* Ask for an assessment: "Is this equally fair for both of us?" The critical issue is livability: Can everyone live with the resolution in the long run? Or, is it so unfair or short of original desires that resentments are likely to emerge? If anyone can answer "yes" to the latter question, go back to creating options (Step 3) until you find a solution that is satisfactory to everyone.

GENDER AND HANDLING CONFLICT

Traditional gender socialization creates challenges for men and women as they seek to constructively resolve conflicts. Women are encouraged to avoid and suppress conflict and to sacrifice their own goals to accommodate others (Wood, 1998). Consequently, many women have little experience in constructively pursuing their goals during a dispute. Men, in contrast, learn to adopt competitive or even violent approaches to interpersonal clashes, as such approaches suggest strength and manliness (Wood, 1998). At the same time, they're taught not to harm women. Thus, during a contentious exchange with a woman, men face a dilemma: compete or avoid? Many men handle the dilemma by downplaying conflicts or simply leaving the scene instead of seeking constructive resolution.

Given that gender can sometimes interfere with constructive conflict management, reconsider how you approach conflict with men and women. When experiencing conflicts with women, encourage the open expression of goals to allow for a collaborative solution. Above all, avoid assuming that no conflict exists just because the other person hasn't voiced any concerns. When managing conflicts with men, be aware of the male emphasis on competitive approaches. Stress collaboration, and as you communicate, steadfastly avoid forms of communication such as personal criticism, insults, or threats that may escalate the conflict.

CULTURE AND HANDLING CONFLICT

The strongest cultural factor that influences your conflict approach is whether you belong to an individualistic or a collectivistic culture (Ting-Toomey, 1997). People raised in collectivistic cultures often view direct messages regarding conflict as personal attacks (Nishiyama, 1971) and consequently are more likely to manage conflict through avoidance or accommodation. People from individualistic cultures feel comfortable agreeing to disagree and don't necessarily see such clashes as personal affronts (Ting-Toomey, 1985). They are more likely to compete, react, or collaborate.

Given these differences, how might you manage conflict effectively across cultures? If you're an individualist embroiled in a dispute with someone from a collectivistic culture, consider the following practices (Gudykunst & Kim, 2003):

- Recognize that collectivists may prefer to have a third person mediate the conflict (Kozan & Ergin, 1998). Mediators allow those in conflict to manage their disagreement without direct confrontation, thereby helping to maintain harmony in the relationship—which is especially important to collectivists.

- Use more indirect verbal messages. For example, sprinkle your comments with "maybe" and "possibly," and avoid blunt responses such as "no."

- Let go of the situation if the other person does not recognize that the conflict exists or does not want to deal with it.

self-reflection

Consider a conflict you've had that was complicated because of cultural differences. What specific differences amplified the conflict? How might knowledge of cultural difference have helped you better understand what was happening and resolve the conflict more effectively?

focus on CULTURE

Accommodation and Radical Pacifism

You're walking down the street, and a man approaches you and demands your wallet. You immediately give it and then ask him whether he also wants your coat. Or suppose you badly want an open position at work. When you find out that a coworker also wants it, you inform your supervisor that you no longer want the job and encourage her to give it to your colleague instead.

As the biblical verse "When a man takes your coat, offer him your shirt as well" (Luke 6:29) suggests, one way to deal with conflict is an extreme form of accommodation known as *radical pacifism.* Although it is often associated with antiwar movements (Bennett, 2003), radical pacifism embodies a broader philosophy about the nature of interpersonal connections between human beings and how conflict is best resolved. Those practicing radical pacifism believe in a moral obligation to behave in selfless and self-sacrificial ways that quickly end conflicts and that assist others. During interpersonal conflict, this means discovering what someone else wants and needs, then aiding that person in attaining these goals, even if it means sacrificing your own.

The practice of radical pacifism cuts across countries, ethnicities, and social classes; it is primarily rooted in the religion of cultures. For example, in the Buddhist text *Punnovada Sutta* (Bodhi & Nanamoli translation, 1995), the Buddha asks his disciple Punna what he would do if someone attacked him with a knife. "I would think they were truly kind, for not taking my life." "What if they kill you?" asks the Buddha. "I would be happy, because many disciples, disgusted by the body, sought to have their lives ended with a knife, but I was fortunate enough to have it happen without even seeking it!" Amish church elders embracing radical pacifism share a similar view: "Even if the result of our pacifism is death at the hands of an attacker during a violent conflict, so be it; death is not threatening to us as Christians. Hopefully the attacker will have at least had a glimpse of the love of Christ in our nonviolent response" (Pennsylvania Dutch Country Welcome Center, n.d.).

discussion questions

- What are your beliefs regarding radical pacifism?
- Do you have an ethical obligation to accommodate others when their interests clash with yours? At what point, if any, does this obligation end?

If you're a collectivist in contention with someone from an individualistic culture, the following guidelines may help:

- Recognize that individualists often separate conflicts from people. Just because you're in conflict doesn't mean that the situation is personal.

- Use an assertive style and be direct. For example, use "I" messages and candidly state your opinions and feelings.

- Manage conflicts when they arise, even if you'd much rather avoid them.

TECHNOLOGY AND HANDLING CONFLICT

Evenings at my house are filled with the musical chiming of text-message alerts, as my sons chat with friends and girlfriends. But I can always tell when a fight is brewing. The messaging suddenly accelerates, then there's an actual phone call, followed by a quick scurry up the stairs for privacy. Asking if everything's OK, I always get the same response, "Yes—we're just *fighting*!"

Given how much of our daily communication occurs via technology, it's no surprise that conflicts occur through text- or instant-messaging, e-mail, and Web posts. Nearly two-thirds of college students (61.2 percent) report using mediated channels to engage in conflicts, the most popular form being text-messaging (Frisby & Westerman, 2010). When asked why they choose mediated channels rather than face-to-face contact, respondents report "geographical distance" as the most common reason. Without the means for immediately seeing someone, texting becomes a tempting alternative for handling conflict.

Unfortunately, such media are not well suited for resolving conflicts. The inability to see nonverbal reactions to messages makes people less aware of the consequences of their communication choices (Joinson, 2001). As a result, people are more likely to prioritize their own goals, minimize a partner's goals, and use hostile personal attacks in pursuit of their goals online than face-to-face (Shedletsky & Aitken, 2004).

Thus, the first and most important step in managing conflict constructively is to *take the encounter offline*. Doing so can dramatically reduce the likelihood of attributional errors and substantially boost empathy. When college students were asked which channel should be used for handling conflict, they noted that "face-to-face is so much better" because it allows you "to know how the other person feels with their facial expressions" (Frisby & Westerman, 2010, p. 975). If meeting face-to-face isn't an option at the time, you can try to stall the encounter by saying, "I think this is best handled in person. When can we get together and talk?" If you can't (or don't want to) meet, then switch to a phone call. That way, you'll at least have vocal cues to gauge a partner's reaction and enhance your empathy.

If, however, you're in a situation in which you must deal with the conflict online, try these suggestions (Munro, 2002):

1. *Wait and reread.* All conflict—whether it's online or off—begins with a triggering event: something said or done that elicits anger, challenges goals, or blocks desired actions. When you receive a message that provokes you,

YOU HAVE HATE MAIL.

don't respond right away. Instead, wait for a while, engage in other activities, and then reread it. This helps you to avoid communicating when your anger is at its peak. It also provides the opportunity for reassessment: often, in rereading a message later, you'll find that your initial interpretation was mistaken.

2. *Assume the best and watch out for the worst.* When you receive messages that provoke you, presume that the sender meant well, but didn't express him- or herself competently. Give people the benefit of the doubt. Keep in mind all you know about the challenges of online communication: anonymity and online disinhibition, empathy deficits, and people's tendency to express themselves inappropriately. At the same time, realize that some people enjoy conflict. Firing back a nasty message may be exactly what they want.

3. *Seek outside counsel.* Before responding to online conflict messages, discuss the situation *offline* (ideally, face-to-face) with someone who knows you well, and whose opinion you trust and respect. Having an additional viewpoint will enhance your ability to perspective-take and will help you make wise communication decisions.

4. *Weigh your options carefully.* Choose cautiously between engaging or avoiding the conflict. Consider the consequences associated with each option, and which is most likely to net you the long-term personal and relationship outcomes you desire. Ask yourself: will responding at this time help to resolve the conflict, or escalate things further?

5. *Communicate competently.* When crafting your response, draw upon all you know about competent interpersonal communication. That is, use "I" language, incorporate appropriate emoticons, express empathy and perspective-taking, encourage the other person to share relevant thoughts and feelings, and make clear your willingness to negotiate mutually agreeable solutions. Perhaps most important, start and end your message with positive statements that support rather than attack the other person's viewpoints.

skills practice

Online Conflict
Effectively working through conflict online

❶ Wait before responding to a message or post that provokes you.

❷ Reread and reassess the message.

❸ Consider all of the factors that may have caused the other person to communicate this way.

❹ Discuss the situation offline with someone you trust.

❺ Craft a competent response that begins and ends with supportive statements, uses "I" language, expresses empathy, and emphasizes mutuality rather than just your own perspective and goals.

Conflict Endings

Learn about short-term and long-term conflict outcomes

It's one of the most epic action films ever made, so noteworthy, in fact, that it is included in the U.S. Library of Congress National Film Registry. It even features a line so iconic, people who've never seen the movie know it: "I'll be back!" But what is often overlooked is that this line was said to end a conflict. In *The Terminator* (1984), Arnold Schwarzenegger plays an android programmed to kill Sarah Connor. When he discovers that Sarah is at a police station, he enters, tells the front desk officer that he's her friend, and demands to see her. But the officer says, "No." Prevented from attaining his goal, Schwarzenegger

In *The Terminator*, Arnold Schwarzenegger plays an android whose notorious declaration "I'll be back" signals the end of a conflict. Are there particular words or phrases you use to end conflicts in your relationships?

leans forward and says, "I'll be back!" Moments later, he crashes his car through the entrance of the station, and launches a devastating assault.

In the real world, conflicts are rarely resolved as dramatically as killer androids forcing their will by driving cars through police stations. But conflicts *do* end. Think about the most recent serious conflict you experienced, and consider the way it ended. Did one of you "win" and the other "lose"? Were you both left dissatisfied, or were you each pleased with the resolution? More important, were you able to resolve the underlying issue that triggered the disagreement in the first place, or did you merely create a short-term fix?

Given their emotional intensity and the fact that they typically occur in relationships, conflicts conclude more gradually than many people would like. You may arrive at a short-term resolution leading to the immediate end of the conflict. But afterward, you'll experience long-term outcomes as you remember, ponder, and possibly regret the incident. These outcomes will influence your relationship health and happiness long into the future.

SHORT-TERM CONFLICT RESOLUTIONS

The approach you and your partner choose to handle the conflict usually results in one of five short-term conflict resolutions (Peterson, 2002). First, some conflicts end through **separation**, the sudden withdrawal of one person from the encounter. This resolution is characteristic of approaching conflict through avoidance. For example, you may be having a disagreement with your mother, when she suddenly hangs up on you. Or you're discussing a concern with your roommate, when he unexpectedly gets up, walks into his bedroom, and shuts the door behind him. Separation ends the immediate encounter, but it does nothing to solve the underlying incompatibility of goals or the interference that triggered the dispute in the first place.

However, separation isn't always negative. In some cases, short-term separation may help bring about long-term resolution. For example, if you and your partner have both used competitive or reactive approaches, your conflict may have escalated so much that any further contact may result in irreparable relationship damage. In such cases, temporary separation may help you both to cool off, regroup, and consider how to collaborate. You can then come back and work together to better resolve the situation.

Second, **domination**—akin to Schwarzenegger's "Terminator" crashing into the police station—occurs when one person gets his or her way by influencing the other to engage in accommodation and abandon goals. Conflicts that end with domination are often called *win-lose solutions*. The strongest predictor of domination is the power balance in the relationship. In cases where one person has substantial power over the other, that person will likely prevail.

In some cases, domination may be acceptable. For example, when one person doesn't feel strongly about achieving his or her goals, being dominated may

Conflict resolutions depend on the balance of power in a relationship. For example, many parents end conflict with their children through domination.

have few costs. However, domination is destructive when it becomes a chronic pattern and one individual always sacrifices his or her goals to keep the peace. Over time, the consistent abandonment of goals can spawn resentment and hostility. While the accommodating "losers" are silently suffering, the dominating "victors" may think everything is fine because they are used to achieving their goals.

Third, during **compromise**, both parties change their goals to make them compatible. Often, both people abandon part of their original desires, and neither feels completely happy about it. Compromise typically results from people using a collaborative approach and is most effective in situations where both people treat each other with respect, have relatively equal power, and don't consider their clashing goals especially important (Zacchilli et al., 2009). In cases where the two parties do consider their goals important, however, compromise can foster mutual resentment and regret (Peterson, 2002). Say that you and your spouse want to spend a weekend away. You planned this getaway for months, but your spouse now wants to attend a two-day workshop that same weekend. A compromise might involve you cutting the trip short by a night, and your spouse missing a day of his or her workshop, leaving both of you with substantially less than you originally desired.

Fourth, through **integrative agreements**, the two sides preserve and attain their goals by developing a creative solution to their problem. This creates a

skills practice

Resolving Conflict
Creating better conflict resolutions

❶ When a conflict arises in a close relationship, manage your negative emotions.

❷ Before communicating with your partner, call to mind the consequences of your communication choices.

❸ Employ a collaborative approach, and avoid kitchen-sinking.

❹ As you negotiate solutions, keep your original goals in mind but remain flexible about how they can be attained.

❺ Revisit relationship rules or agreements that triggered the conflict, and consider redefining them in ways that prevent future disputes.

more positively than their partners', and blame partners for failure to resolve the conflict (Sillars, Roberts, Leonard, & Dun, 2000).

Sillars and his colleagues also found little evidence of complex thought. While conflicts are unfolding, people typically do *not* consider long-term outcomes ("How is this going to impact our relationship?") and do *not* perspective-take ("How is she feeling?"). Instead, their thoughts are locked into simple, unqualified, and negative views: "He's lying!" or "She's blaming me!" (Sillars et al., 2000, p. 491). In only 2 percent of cases did respondents attribute cooperativeness to their partners and uncooperativeness to themselves. This means that in 98 percent of fights, you'll likely think, "I'm trying to be helpful, and my partner is being unreasonable!" However, your partner will be thinking the exact same thing about you.

Self-enhancing thoughts dominate conflict encounters, stifling the likelihood of collaboration. Consequently, *the most important thing you can do to improve your conflict-management skills is to routinely practice critical self-reflection during disputes.* Although you might not ever achieve objectivity or neutrality in your thoughts, you can work toward this goal by regularly going through this mental checklist:

- Is my partner *really* being uncooperative, or am *I* making a faulty attribution?
- Is my partner *really* solely to blame, or have *I* also done something to cause the conflict?
- Is the conflict *really* due to ongoing differences between us, or is it *actually* due to temporary factors such as stress or fatigue?

DESTRUCTIVE MESSAGES

Think back to the chapter opener when Amy Chua had a fight with Lulu in a restaurant. They both were so irate that they said horrible and unforgivable things to one another. When conflicts escalate and anger peaks, our minds are filled with negative thoughts of all the grievances and resentments we feel toward others (Sillars et al., 2000). These thoughts often leap out of our mouths, in the form of messages that permanently damage our relationships (McCornack & Husband, 1986).

Sudden-death statements occur when people get so angry that they suddenly declare the end of the relationship, even though breaking up wasn't a possibility before the conflict. When my wife Kelly and I had been married for two years, we had a major argument while visiting her parents. A small dispute over family differences quickly escalated into a full-blown conflict. After flinging a number of kitchen-sink messages at each other, we both shouted, "Why are we even together?! We're so different!" Fortunately, this sudden-death statement caused us to calm down. But many couples who blurt out such things during escalation follow through on them.

Perhaps the most destructive messages are **dirty secrets**: statements that are honest in content but have been kept hidden to protect a partner's feelings. Dirty secrets can include acts of infidelity ("I cheated, and it was great!"). They can also include intense criticism of a partner's appearance ("You know how I've always said I like your nose? Well, I hate it!"), and even a lack of feelings ("I haven't been in love with you for years!"). Dirty secrets are designed to hurt, and because the content is true, they can irreparably damage the recipient and the relationship.

Needless to say, destructive messages can destroy relationships. Couples who exchange critical and contemptuous messages during the first seven years of marriage are substantially more likely to divorce than couples who refrain from such negativity (Gottman & Levenson, 2000). Thus, no matter your level of anger, or the caustic thoughts that fill your head, it's essential to always communicate toward your partner in a civil, respectful fashion.

SERIAL ARGUMENTS

Another conflict challenge we face in close relationships is **serial arguments**: a series of unresolved disputes, all having to do with the same issue (Bevan, Finan, & Kaminsky, 2008). Serial arguments typically stem from deep disagreements, such as differing relationship expectations or clashes in values and beliefs. By definition, serial arguments occur over time, and consist of cycles in which things "heat up" and then lapse back into a temporary state of truce (Malis & Roloff, 2006). During these "quiet" periods, individuals are likely to think about the conflict, attempt to repair the relationship, and cope with the stress resulting from the most recent fight (Malis & Roloff, 2006).

Serial arguments are most likely to occur in romantic and family involvements, where the frequency of interaction provides ample opportunity for repetitive disagreements (Bevan et al., 2008). They are also strongly predictive

self-reflection

Recall a conflict in which you and the other person exchanged destructive messages such as sudden-death statements or dirty secrets. What led to them being said? What impact did these messages have on the conflict? How did they affect your relationship?

◖ In the movie *Blue Valentine*, main characters Dean and Cindy struggle with serial arguments and are unable to resolve the conflicts that ultimately destroy their marriage.

of relationship failure: couples who suffer serial arguments experience higher stress levels and are more likely to have their relationships end than those who don't (Malis & Roloff, 2006).

Although many serial arguments involve heated verbal battles, others take the form of **demand-withdraw patterns**, in which one partner in a relationship demands that his or her goals be met, and the other partner responds by withdrawing from the encounter (Caughlin, 2002). Demand-withdraw patterns typically are triggered when a person is bothered by a repeated source of irritation, but doesn't confront the issue until his or her anger can no longer be suppressed. At that point, the person explodes in a demanding fashion (Malis & Roloff, 2006).

If you find yourself in a close relationship in which a demand-withdraw pattern has emerged, discuss this situation with your partner. Using a collaborative approach, critically examine the forces that trigger the pattern, and work to generate solutions that will enable you to avoid the pattern in the future.

PHYSICAL VIOLENCE

The most destructive conflict challenge is physical violence, a strategy to which people may resort if they cannot think of a better way to deal with conflict or if they believe no other options are available (Klein, 1998). In the National Violence Against Women Survey (Tjaden & Thoennes, 2000), 52 percent of women and 66 percent of men reported that at some time in their lives they had been physically assaulted during conflicts. Both men and women *use* violence as a strategy for dealing with conflicts. Approximately 12 percent of women and 11 percent of men surveyed reported having committed a violent act during conflict with their spouse in the preceding year (Barnett, Miller-Perrin, & Perrin, 1997). Moreover, in an analysis of data from 82 violence studies, researcher John Archer found no substantial difference between men and women in their propensity toward violence as a conflict strategy (2000). At the same time, however, women are substantially more likely to be injured or killed, owing to their lesser physical size and strength (Archer, 2000; O'Leary & Vivian, 1990). Physical violence doesn't restrict itself to heterosexual relationships; nearly 50 percent of lesbian and 30 to 40 percent of gay respondents have been victims of violence during interpersonal conflicts at some time in their lives (Peplau & Spalding, 2000).

One outcome of physical violence in close relationships is the **chilling effect**, whereby individuals stop discussing relationship issues out of fear of their partners' negative reactions (Solomon & Samp, 1998). In these relationships, individuals who are "chilled" constrain their communication and actions to a very narrow margin, avoiding all topics and behaviors they believe may provoke a partner (Afifi et al., 2009). The result is an overarching relationship climate of fear, suppression, anxiety, and unhappiness.

If you find yourself in a relationship in which your partner behaves violently toward you, seek help from family members, friends, and, if necessary, law enforcement officials. Realize that your best option might be to end the relationship and avoid all contact with the person. We discuss tactics for dealing with relational violence in more detail in Chapter 9.

If you find that you are inclined to violence in relationships, revisit the anger management techniques described in Chapter 4 as well as the suggestions for constructively handling conflict described previously. Most aggression during conflicts stems from people's perception that they have no other options. Although situations may exist where there truly are no other options—for example, self-defense during a violent assault or robbery—within most encounters more constructive alternatives are available. If you are unable to control your impulses toward violence, seek professional counseling.

UNSOLVABLE DISPUTES

A final conflict challenge is that some disputes are unsolvable. In the climactic scene of Margaret Mitchell's Civil War classic *Gone with the Wind*, the principal character, Scarlett O'Hara, declares her love for Rhett Butler, only to find that he no longer feels the same about her (Mitchell, 1936).

> "Stop," she said suddenly. She knew she could no longer endure with any fortitude the sound of his voice when there was no love in it. He paused and looked at her quizzically. "Well, you get my meaning, don't you?" he

Some conflicts are impossible to solve

Dealing with Family Conflict

1 BACKGROUND

Conflict poses complex challenges for your interpersonal communication and relationships. But when you throw in parental expectations, power differences between generations, and the emotional connections within families, effectively managing conflict becomes even more difficult. To see how you would deal with family conflict, read the case study and work through the five steps under Your Turn.

2 CASE STUDY

Your parents are "old school" in their views of parental power: they believe that children should show deference to elders without exception. Although you're still in college, your brother Sanjay is much older and has a family of his own, including a teenage son, Devdas. You love your brother dearly, and get along well with Devdas, but Devdas is going through a rebellious phase in which he shows little respect for authority figures.

Your parents decide to spend a week with Sanjay and his family. You're nervous, because your father delights in picking on Devdas about his hair, clothing, and music, and given Devdas's recent attitude, you're afraid he may lash back. Sure enough, toward the end of the week, you get a phone call. It's your father, and he tells you that he and your mother ended their visit early, and that he wishes no further contact with your brother or his family. He says that Devdas "swore at him for no reason at all." He tells you, "I have no interest in associating with people who raise children to behave like that." When you ask whether he provoked Devdas, your father angrily responds, "*I did nothing wrong! Are you taking his side?*"

Shortly after, you get an e-mail from your brother. He says that your father is delusional and "made the whole thing up." Chatting online, you ask Sanjay whether Devdas might have cussed at your dad. "Absolutely not," your brother fires back, "Devdas doesn't even *know* such words; how can you ask that?!"

As the weeks go by, the rift deepens. Your brother refuses to talk with your father until he apologizes. Your father refuses contact with your brother until "he admits his son's wrong-doing!" Poisoning the relationship further, Devdas's birthday comes and goes, without a call or gift from the grandparents. Now, with the holidays approaching, both parties are pressuring you to choose sides. Sanjay demands that you "stand with him" against your father and says that "you're no longer family if you don't." Your father tells you, "If you continue to support Sanjay in this shameful matter, I will be forced to rethink my financial support for your education."

3 YOUR TURN

While working through the following steps, keep in mind the concepts, skills, and insights you've learned so far in this book, especially in this chapter. Also remember: there are no right answers, so think hard about the choice you make! (P.S. Need help? Review the *Helpful Concepts* listed below.)

step 1

Reflect on yourself. What are your thoughts and feelings in this situation? What attributions are you making about your father? About Sanjay? About Devdas? Are your attributions accurate? Why or why not?

step 2

Reflect on your father and brother. Using perspective-taking and empathic concern, put yourself in your father's shoes. Consider how he is thinking and feeling. Then do the same for your brother. How do they likely perceive you?

step 3

Identify the optimal outcome. Think about all the information you have regarding your family (your father, Sanjay, and Devdas), and your relationships with them. Consider your own feelings as well as theirs. Given all these factors, what's the best, most constructive outcome possible here? Be sure to consider not just what's best for *you*, but what's best for your family as well.

step 4

Locate the roadblocks. Taking into consideration your own thoughts and feelings, those of your father, Sanjay, and Devdas, and recent events in this situation, what's preventing you from achieving the optimal outcome you identified in Step 3?

step 5

Chart your course. What will you say to your father, Sanjay, and Devdas to overcome the roadblocks you've identified and achieve your optimal outcome?

HELPFUL CONCEPTS

Power principles, **249–250**

Collaboratively managing conflict, **258–260**

Critiquing your perceptions and attributions, **268**

Conflict resolutions and outcomes, **263–267**

Unsolvable conflicts, **271, 274**

questioned, rising to his feet. "No," she cried. "All I know is that you do not love me and you are going away! Oh, my darling, if you go, what shall I do?" For a moment he hesitated as if debating whether a kind lie were kinder in the long run than the truth. Then he shrugged. "Scarlett, I was never one to patiently pick up broken fragments and glue them together and tell myself that the mended whole was as good as new. What is broken is broken—and I'd rather remember it as it was at its best than mend it and see the broken places as long as I lived. I wish I could care what you do or where you go, but I can't." He drew a short breath, and said lightly but softly: "My dear, I don't give a damn." (p. 732)

As this famous fictional scene illustrates, if one person loves another but the feeling isn't reciprocated, no amount of collaborating will fix things. Part of effectively managing conflict is accepting that some conflicts are impossible to resolve. How can you recognize such disputes? Clues include: you and the other person aren't willing to change your negative opinions of one another; your goals are irreconcilable and strongly held; and at least one partner is uncooperative, chronically defensive, or violent. In these cases, the only options are to avoid the conflict, hope that your attitudes or goals will change over time, or abandon the relationship, as Rhett Butler did.

self-reflection

Think of an unsolvable conflict you've had. What made it unsolvable? How did the dispute affect your relationship? Looking back on the situation, could you have done anything differently to prevent the conflict from becoming unsolvable? If so, what?

⬤ Conflicts do not need to destroy your closest interpersonal relationships. When navigating a challenging conflict with a loved one, remember that renewed intimacy and happiness may be just around the corner.

Managing Conflict and Power

Conflicts can be opportunities for positive change	Whether it's big or small, when a dispute arises, you may feel that no one else has ever had the same thoughts and emotions. The anger, fear of escalation, pain of hurtful

comments that should have been left unsaid, and uncertainty associated with not knowing the long-term relationship outcomes combine to make the experience intense and draining.

But conflicts and struggles over power needn't be destructive. Though they carry risk, they also provide the opportunity to engineer positive change in the way you communicate with others and manage your relationships. Through conflict, you can resolve problems that, left untouched, would have eroded your relationship or deprived you of greater happiness in the future. The key distinguishing feature between conflict and power struggles that destroy and those that create opportunities for improvement is how you interpersonally communicate.

We've discussed a broad range of communication skills that can help you manage conflict and power more effectively. Whether it's using collaborative approaches, critiquing your perceptions and attributions, knowing when to take a conflict offline, or being sensitive to gender and cultural differences, you now know the skills necessary for successfully managing the disagreements, disputes, and contests that will erupt in your life. It is up to you now to take these skills and put them into practice.

This chapter began with a woman determined to dominate her children.

Amy Chua made headlines and best-seller lists when she boasted of her dictatorial parenting style. Her book, *Battle Hymn of the Tiger Mother*, describes her dysfunctional approaches to managing conflict and power in painful detail, including taunts, tantrums, insults, and accusations.

What messages did you learn growing up about how conflict and power should best be managed? Did the way in which your parents or caregivers dealt with conflicts leave you feeling better about yourself and your relationship with them? Or did it leave a wake of interpersonal destruction and heartache behind?

Satirical or not, Chua's book provides a powerful lesson for us all regarding the relationship between choices, communication, and outcomes. When you consistently choose to manage disputes in unyielding, aggressive ways, the relationship outcomes will be as unsatisfying and unpleasant as the conflict itself.

POSTSCRIPT

key terms

▣ You can watch brief, illustrative videos of these terms and test your understanding of the concepts online in *VideoCentral: Interpersonal Communication* at **bedfordstmartins .com/reflectrelate**.

key concepts

Conflict and Interpersonal Communication

- **Conflict** arises whenever people's goals clash or they compete for valued resources. Because everyone is pursuing important goals at any point in time, conflict is inevitable.

- Conflict in close relationships poses unique challenges. Avoid **kitchen-sinking**, hurling insults and accusations that have little to do with the original dispute.

Power and Conflict

- Conflict and **power** go hand in hand because whenever people perceive their goals as clashing, they often wield whatever influence they have to achieve their goals.

- Power is present in all interpersonal communication. Friendships and romantic involvements are typically **symmetrical relationships**, whereas parent-child, manager-employee, and teacher-student are **complementary relationships**.

- **Dyadic Power Theory** proposes that people with only moderate power are the most likely to use controlling communication.

- Power isn't innate. It's something granted to you by others, depending on the **power currency** you possess. Types of power currencies include **resource**, **expertise**, **social network**, **personal**, and **intimacy**.

- Different cultures have very different beliefs about **power-distance**. High power-distance cultures emphasize disparities. Low power-distance cultures typically encourage power equality across all people.

- Across cultures and time, men have consolidated power over women by strategically depriving women of access to power currencies.

Handling Conflict

- The most commonly used approach to managing conflict is **avoidance**. However, avoidance can lead to damaging behaviors, including **skirting**, **sniping**, **cumulative annoyance**, and the inability to overcome **pseudo-conflict**.

- **Accommodation**, another approach to managing conflict, often is motivated by the desire to please the people we love or to acquiesce to those who have power over us.

- **Competition** involves the aggressive pursuit of one's own goals at the expense of others' goals.

Competition can trigger defensive communication and also creates severe risk of **escalation**.

- Some people respond to conflict through **reactivity**, communicating in an emotionally explosive and negative fashion.

- The most constructive approach to conflict is **collaboration**. This is your best bet for reinforcing trust and commitment in your relationships and building relational satisfaction.

- Whether a culture is individualistic or collectivistic determines how people manage conflict: individualistic cultures are inclined to approach conflicts more competitively and directly than collectivistic cultures.

- The restrictive nature of online communication can make it challenging to deal productively with conflict. If possible, take the encounter offline.

Conflict Endings

- In the short term, conflicts resolve through **separation**, **domination**, **compromise**, **integrative agreements**, or **structural improvements**.

- Then partners involved in the conflict ponder whether they've resolved the underlying goal clash that triggered the conflict, and consider the long-term impact on their relationship.

Challenges to Handling Conflict

- During conflicts we engage in self-enhancing thoughts through which we selectively remember information that supports ourselves and contradicts those with whom we are in conflict.

- **Sudden-death statements** occur when people get so angry that they suddenly declare the end of the relationship. The most destructive form is **dirty secrets**.

- In close relationships, there is a risk of engaging in **serial arguments**, which may lead to **demand-withdraw patterns**.

- When people believe that no other option exists, they may commit acts of violence. One outcome is **the chilling effect**, when partners stop discussing certain issues in an attempt to stop any negative reactions in advance.

- Some conflicts are impossible to resolve. In this case, try to avoid the conflict, hope goals will change over time, or abandon the relationship.

key skills

- Why does power make managing conflict constructively difficult? Find out on pages 248–250.

- Are you inclined to competitively challenge authority during a conflict? Try the *Self-Quiz* on page 253 to find out.

- What is your approach for managing conflict? Find out by taking the *Self-Quiz* on page 256.

- Do you manage conflicts through avoidance? If so, you may want to revisit the risks associated with this approach, described on pages 255–256.

- Do you use a competitive approach to deal with conflict? Review the consequences associated with competitiveness on pages 257–258 to see why this might not be the wisest choice.

- Want to improve your ability to use collaboration to constructively manage conflicts? Review the suggestions on pages 258–260, then do the *Skills Practice* on page 259.

- How might you use your knowledge of gender differences to improve your conflict skills? Revisit the suggestions on page 260.

- What can people do to constructively manage conflict with individuals from other cultures? See the recommendations on pages 260–262.

- Do you want to resolve online conflicts effectively? If so, review the suggestions on pages 262–263, and then do the *Skills Practice* on page 263.

- Learn about five short-term conflict resolutions on pages 264–266, and then try the *Skills Practice* on page 265.

- Want the best possible outcome for your conflicts? Check out the long-term effects of the various conflict approaches on pages 266–267.

- To work toward minimizing self-enhancing thoughts, review the checklist on page 268.

- How might you reduce the likelihood of violence during intense disagreements? Follow the guidelines on pages 270–271.

- How would you approach a seemingly unresolvable family conflict? Find out by completing the *Making Relationship Choices* exercise on pages 272–273.

9 Relationships with Romantic Partners

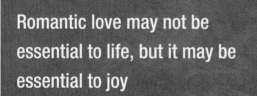

Romantic love may not be essential to life, but it may be essential to joy

T he temperature was −70°.[1] Although he was only a few miles from his supply depot—and salvation in the form of food and gear—the weather was impassable. Suffering from frostbite and malnutrition, Antarctic explorer Sir Robert Falcon Scott knew two things for certain: he would soon die, and a recovery team would eventually find his body. So he penned a letter to his wife, Kathleen. *"To my widow,"* he began. What followed is one of the most moving testimonials to romantic love ever written.

Scott had led a British team trying to be the first to reach the South Pole. Arriving at their goal on January 17, 1912, they were stunned to find a tent erected on the site. Inside was a note left by Norwegian explorer Roald Amundsen: he had beaten Scott's team by a month. Defeated, Scott and his comrades began the 800-mile return trip, beset by snow blindness, hunger, and exhaustion. The weather worsened, and one by one his team members perished.

Huddled inside his shelter, Scott crafted a note to Kathleen that was at once passionate, practical, upbeat, and astonishingly selfless. Longing and sentiment poured from his pen: "You know I have loved you, you know my thoughts must have constantly dwelt on you . . . the worst aspect of this situation is the thought that I shall not see you again. . . .

[1]All information and quotes that follow are adapted from the Scott Polar Institute. Retrieved from http://news.admin.cam.ac.uk/news/2007/01/09/captainscott146sfinallettershomegoondisplay/.

9 / Relationships with Romantic Partners

Oh what a price to pay—to forfeit the sight of your dear dear face!" He grieved the lost chance to see his son mature, " . . . what dreams I have had of his future." But he praised Kathleen's practicality, and entreated her "to take the whole thing very sensibly as I am sure you will. . . . Make the boy interested in natural history, if you can, it is better than games."

Though suffering from frostbite, he remained relentlessly upbeat. "There is a painless end, so don't worry—How much better it has been than lounging in comfort at home." In the most striking passage of all, Scott granted Kathleen romantic liberty: "Cherish no sentimental rubbish about remarriage—when the right man comes to help you in life you ought to be your happy self again. I hope I shall be a good memory."

Eight months later a recovery team reached Scott's encampment. Searching the remnants of his tent, they found Scott's personal journal and his letter to Kathleen. They then built a tomb of ice and snow over the bodies of Scott and his companions, and placed a cross on top to mark the site.

In the years that followed, Scott would be honored across Britain as a tragic hero. Dozens of monuments were raised, and memorial funds created to support the families of the fallen. In January of 2007, Scott's letters and journal were donated for display at the University of Cambridge. But in the dim light of his tent in March 1912, with storms raging and death approaching, Sir Robert Falcon Scott was just another human being trying to capture in writing the multifaceted complexity of romantic love. To read his words is to be reminded that *love is not singular, but plural*: it is many things at once, including passion, practicality, commitment, respect, sentiment, and selflessness.

Throughout time and across cultures, people have fallen in love with one another. When each of us discovers love for ourselves, we honor that legacy, sharing in an experience that is both uniquely and universally human. We also find that romantic love is a multiplicity of elements, some of which seem contradictory. Our affairs may be all about passion, but they also bring with them the rewards (and costs) of companionship. Our love for others may be self-less and giving, yet we're driven to build and sustain only those relationships that benefit us the most, and end those that don't. Although romance may be senti-mental and otherworldly, the maintenance of love is decidedly practical. Romantic *relationships* are hard work, entailing constant upkeep to survive the innumerable and unforeseen challenges that threaten them.

In this chapter, the first of four on relationships, you'll learn:

- The defining characteristics of romantic love and relationships
- What drives you to feel attracted to some people and not to others
- How communication changes as your romantic relationships come together . . . and fall apart
- How to communicate in ways that keep your love alive
- The dark side of romantic relationships and how to deal effectively with these challenges

Defining Romantic Relationships

People experience different types of love

Romantic love may not be essential to life, but it may be essential to joy. Life without love would be for many people like a black-and-white movie—full of events and activities but without the color that gives vibrancy and provides a sense of celebration. Beyond the theories, beyond the research, romantic love is one of life's compensations for drudgery, illness, and, perhaps in some small way, for mortality.[2]
—love researchers Clyde and Susan Hendrick

We often think of romantic relationships as exciting and filled with promise—a joyful fusion of closeness, communication, and sexual connection. When re-searchers Pamela Regan, Elizabeth Kocan, and Teresa Whitlock (1998) asked several hundred people to list the things they associated most with "being in love," the most frequent responses were trust, honesty, happiness, bondedness, companionship, communication, caring, intimacy, shared laughter, and sexual desire. But apart from such associations, what exactly *is* romantic love? How does it differ from liking? How does interpersonal communication shape love relationships? The answers to these questions can help you build more satisfying romantic partnerships.

---

[2]The quote is excerpted from Hendrick and Hendrick (1992, p. 117).

LIKING AND LOVING

Most scholars agree that liking and loving are separate emotional states, with different causes and outcomes (Berscheid & Regan, 2005). **Liking** is a feeling of affection and respect that we typically have for our friends (Rubin, 1973). *Affection* is a sense of warmth and fondness toward another person, while *respect* is admiration for another person apart from how he or she treats you and communicates with you. **Loving**, in contrast, is a vastly deeper and more intense emotional experience and consists of three components: intimacy, caring, and attachment (Rubin, 1973).

- *Intimacy* is a feeling of closeness and "union" between you and your partner (Mashek & Aron, 2004).

- *Caring* is the concern you have for your partner's welfare and the desire to keep him or her happy.

- *Attachment* is a longing to be in your partner's presence as much as possible.

The ideal combination for long-term success in romantic relationships occurs when partners both like and love each other.

DIFFERENT TYPES OF ROMANTIC LOVE

Though most people recognize that loving differs from liking, many also believe that to be *in* love, one must feel constant and consuming sexual attraction toward a partner. In fact, many different types of romantic love exist, covering a broad range of emotions and relationship forms. At one end of the spectrum is **passionate love**, a state of intense emotional and physical longing for union with another (Hendrick & Hendrick, 1992). For example, in Helen Simonson's bestselling novel *Major Pettigrew's Last Stand* (2011), Ernest and Jasmina are lovers

People who are passionately in love experience an intense longing to be physically near one another. What other traits or experiences do you associate with passionate love?

facing bitter opposition from friends and family because of their interethnic romance (he is English, she Pakistani). After sharing the night together at a secluded lodge, they awake and celebrate their passion.[3]

> In the early morning he stood by the empty lake and watched a lone bird, falcon or eagle, gliding high on the faintest of thermals. He raised his arms to the air, stretching with his fingertips, and wondered whether the bird's heart was as full as his own. As he gazed, the French door was pushed open and she came out, carrying two mugs of tea, which steamed in the air. "You should have woken me," she said, "I hope you weren't fleeing the scene?" "I needed to do a little capering about," he said. "Some beating of the chest and cheering—manly stuff." "Oh, do show me," she said, laughing, while he executed a few half-remembered dance steps, and kicked a large stone into the lake. "Do I get a turn?" she asked. She handed him a mug for each hand and then spun herself in wild pirouettes to the shore where she stomped her feet in the freezing waters. Then she came running back and kissed him while he spread his arms wide and tried to keep his balance. "Careful," he said, feeling a splash of scalding tea on his wrist. "Passion is all very well, but it wouldn't do to spill the tea."

If you've been passionately in love before, these feelings likely are familiar: the desire to stretch for the sky, dance, laugh, and splash about, coupled with a strong desire to touch, hold, and kiss your partner. Studies of passionate love support the universality of these sentiments, and suggest that five things are true about the experience and expression of passion. First, people in the throes of passionate love often view their loved ones and relationships in an excessively idealistic light. For instance, many partners in passionate love relationships talk about how "perfect" they are for each other and how their relationship is the "best ever."

Second, people from all cultures feel passionate love. Studies comparing members of individualistic versus collectivistic cultures have found no differences in the amount of passionate love experienced (Hatfield & Rapson, 1987). Although certain ethnicities, especially Latinos, often are stereotyped as more "passionate," studies comparing Latino and non-Latino experiences of romantic love suggest no differences in intensity (Cerpas, 2002).

Third, no gender or age differences exist in people's experience of passionate love. Men and women report experiencing this type of love with equal frequency and intensity, and studies using a "Juvenile Love Scale" (which excludes references to sexual feelings) have found that children as young as age 4 report passionate love toward others (Hatfield & Rapson, 1987). The latter finding is important to consider when talking with children about their romantic feelings. Although they lack the emotional maturity to fully understand the consequences of their relationship decisions, their feelings toward romantic interests are every bit as intense and turbulent as our adult emotions. So if your 6- or 7-year-old child or sibling reveals a crush on a schoolmate, treat the disclosure with respect and empathy, rather than teasing him or her.

---

[3]Adapted from Simonson (2011).

self-reflection

Is passion the critical defining feature of being in love? Or can you fall in love without ever feeling passion? Given that passion typically fades, is romantic love always doomed to fail, or can you still be in love after passion leaves?

Fourth, for adults, passionate love is integrally linked with sexuality and sexual desire (Berscheid & Regan, 2005). In one study, undergraduates were asked whether they thought there was a difference between "being in love" and "loving" another person (Ridge & Berscheid, 1989). Eighty-seven percent of respondents said that there was a difference and that sexual attraction was the critical distinguishing feature of being in love.

Finally, passionate love is *negatively* related to relationship duration. Like it or not, the longer you're with a romantic partner, the less intense your passionate love will feel (Berscheid, 2002).

Although the "fire" of passionate love dominates media depictions of romance, not all people view being in love this way. At the other end of the romantic spectrum is **companionate love**: an intense form of liking defined by emotional investment and deeply intertwined lives (Berscheid & Walster, 1978). Many long-term romantic relationships evolve into companionate love. As Clyde and Susan Hendrick (1992) explain, "Sexual attraction, intense communication, and emotional turbulence early in a relationship give way to quiet intimacy, predictability, and shared attitudes, values, and life experiences later in the relationship" (p. 48).

Between the poles of passionate and companionate love lies a range of other types of romantic love. Sociologist John Alan Lee (1973) suggested six different forms that range from friendly to obsessive and gave them each a traditional Greek name: *storge, agape, mania, pragma, ludus,* and *eros* (see Table 9.1 for an explanation of each). As Lee noted, there is no "right" type of romantic love—different forms appeal to different people.

Despite similarities between men and women in their experiences of passionate love, substantial gender differences exist related to one of Lee's love types—*pragma*, or "practical love." Across numerous studies, women score higher than men on *pragma* (Hendrick & Hendrick, 1988, 1992), refuting the common stereotype that women are "starry-eyed" and "sentimental" about romantic love (Hill, Rubin, & Peplau, 1976). What's more, although men are often stereotyped as being "cool" and "logical" about love (Hill et al., 1976), they are much more likely than women to perceive their romantic partners as "perfect" and believe that "love at first sight is possible," that "true love can overcome any obstacles," and that "there's only one true love for each person" (Sprecher & Metts, 1999).

table 9.1 Romantic Love Types

Type	Description	Attributes of Love
Storge	Friendly lovers	Stable, predictable, and rooted in friendship
Agape	Forgiving lovers	Patient, selfless, giving, and unconditional
Mania	Obsessive lovers	Intense, tumultuous, extreme, and all-consuming
Pragma	Practical lovers	Logical, rational, and founded in common sense
Ludus	Game-playing lovers	Uncommitted, fun, and played like a game
Eros	Romantic lovers	Sentimental, romantic, idealistic, and committed

Test Your Love Attitudes

Call to mind your current or most recent romantic partner. If you haven't yet had a "romantic" relationship, think about how you would feel if you *were* in such a relationship. Then read the statements below, and place a check mark next to the ones with which you agree.

Storge

_____ It is hard to say exactly where friendship ends and love begins.

_____ Love is really a deep friendship, not a mysterious, mystical emotion.

Agape

_____ When my lover gets angry with me, I still love him/her fully and unconditionally.

_____ I would rather suffer myself than let my lover suffer.

Mania

_____ Sometimes I get so excited about being in love that I can't sleep.

_____ When my lover doesn't pay attention to me, I feel sick all over.

Pragma

_____ I try to plan my life carefully before choosing a lover.

_____ I consider what a person is going to become in life before I commit myself to him/her.

Ludus

_____ I try to keep my lover a little uncertain about my commitment to him/her.

_____ I enjoy playing the "game of love" with a number of different partners.

Eros

_____ My lover and I have the right physical "chemistry" between us.

_____ I feel that my lover and I were meant for each other.

Scoring: Count the number of statements with which you agree for each love attitude. 0 = low on that attitude, 1 = moderate, 2 = high.

KEY ELEMENTS OF ROMANTIC RELATIONSHIPS

We know that loving differs from liking and that people experience different types of love. But what exactly does it mean to have a romantic relationship? A **romantic relationship** is a chosen interpersonal involvement forged through communication in which the participants perceive the bond as romantic. Six elements of romantic relationships underlie this definition.

Perception   A romantic relationship exists whenever the two partners perceive that it does. As perceptions change, so too does the relationship. For example, a couple may consider their relationship "casual dating" but still define it as "romantic" (rather than friendly). Or, a long-term couple may feel more companionate than passionate but still consider themselves "in love." If two partners' perceptions of their relationship differ—for example, one person feels romantic and the other does not—they do not have a romantic relationship (Miller & Steinberg, 1975).

Diversity   Romantic relationships exhibit remarkable diversity in the ages and genders of the partners, as well as in their ethnic and religious backgrounds and

▶ Depictions of romantic love are often found in art, movies, literature, poetry, music, and other media, but they rarely detail the everyday interpersonal communication that makes successful relationships work.

sexual orientations. Yet despite this diversity, most relationships function in a similar manner. For example, whether a romantic relationship is between lesbian, gay, or straight partners, the individuals involved place the same degree of importance on their relationship, devote similar amounts of time and energy to maintaining their bond, and demonstrate similar openness in their communication (Haas & Stafford, 2005). The exact same factors that determine marital success between men and women (such as honesty, loyalty, commitment, and dedication to maintenance) also predict stability and satisfaction within same-sex couples (Kurdek, 2005). As relationship scholar Sharon Brehm sums up, gay and lesbian couples "fall in love in the same way, feel the same passions, experience the same doubts, and feel the same commitments as straights" (Brehm, Miller, Perlman, & Campbell, 2002, p. 27).

Choice   We enter into romantic relationships through choice, selecting not only with whom we initiate involvements but also whether and how we maintain these bonds. Thus, contrary to widespread belief, love doesn't "strike us out of the blue" or "sweep us away." Choice plays a role even in arranged marriages: the spouses' families and social networks select an appropriate partner, and in many cases the betrothed retain at least some control over whether the choice is acceptable (Hendrick & Hendrick, 1992).

Commitment   Romantic relationships often involve **commitment**: a strong psychological attachment to a partner and an intention to continue the relationship long into the future (Arriaga & Agnew, 2001). When you forge a commitment with a partner, positive outcomes often result. Commitment leads couples to work harder on maintaining their relationships, resulting in greater satisfaction (Rusbult, Arriaga, & Agnew, 2001). Commitment also reduces the likelihood that partners will cheat sexually when separated by geographic distance (Le, Korn, Crockett, & Loving, 2010).

Although men are stereotyped in the media as "commitment-phobic," this stereotype is false. *Both* men and women view commitment as an important part of romantic relationships (Miller, Perlman, & Brehm, 2007). Several studies even suggest that men often place a higher value on commitment than do women. For example, when asked which they would choose, if forced to decide between a committed romance or an important job opportunity, more men than women chose the relationship (Mosher & Danoff-Burg, 2007). Men also score higher than women on measures of commitment in college dating relationships (Kurdek, 2008). These trends aren't new. Throughout fifty years of research, men have consistently reported more of a desire for marriage than have women, and described "desire for a committed relationship" as more of a motivation for dating (Rubin, Peplau, & Hill, 1981).

Tensions   When we're involved in intimate relationships, we often experience competing impulses, or tensions, between our selves and our feelings toward others, known as **relational dialectics** (Baxter, 1990). Relational dialectics take three common forms. The first is *openness versus protection*. As relationships become more intimate, we naturally exchange more personal information with our partners. Most of us enjoy the feeling of unity and mutual insight created through such sharing. But while we want to be open with our partners, we also want to keep certain aspects of our selves—such as our most private thoughts and feelings—protected. Too much openness provokes an uncomfortable sense that we've lost our privacy and must share *everything* with our lovers.

The second dialectic is *autonomy versus connection*. We elect to form romantic relationships largely out of a desire to bond with other human beings. Yet if we come to feel so connected to our partners that our individual identity seems to dissolve, we may choose to pull back and reclaim some of our autonomy.

The final dialectic is the clash between our need for stability and our need for excitement and change—known as *novelty versus predictability*. We all like the security that comes with knowing how our partners will behave, how we'll behave, and how our relationships will unfold. Romances are more successful when the partners behave in predictable ways that reduce uncertainty (Berger & Bradac, 1982). However, predictability often spawns boredom. As we get to know our partners, the novelty and excitement of the relationship wears off, and things seem increasingly monotonous. Reconciling the desire for predictability with the need for novelty is one of the most profound emotional challenges facing partners in romantic relationships.

self-reflection

How much do you desire or fear commitment? Are your feelings based on your gender, or other factors? Consider your male and female friends and acquaintances. Do all the men you know dread commitment, and all the women crave it? What does this tell you about the legitimacy of commitment stereotypes?

VideoCentral ◎

bedfordstmartins.com /reflectrelate

Relational Dialectics
Watch this clip online to answer the questions below.

When have you experienced the tension between being completely open and wishing to keep something private from someone? How did you deal with this tension? Is it ever ethical to keep something private in order to not hurt someone's feelings? Why or why not?

Communication   Romantic involvements, like all interpersonal relationships, are forged through interpersonal communication. By interacting with others online, over the phone, and face-to-face, we build a variety of relationships—some of which blossom into romantic love. And once love is born, we use interpersonal communication to foster and maintain it.

Romantic Attraction

Why we are attracted to some people and not others

On the hit TV show *Glee*, Artie excitedly wheels his chair to the sign-up sheet for the new school song-and-dance club.[4] When he struggles to reach the list, Tina intervenes and helps him. An instant attraction is sparked. As they spend time together, they quickly learn that they share much more in common than music. Both are intensely intellectual and somewhat "off-beat" in their views. Both struggle with disabilities—Artie is paralyzed from the waist down, and Tina wrestles with a speech impediment. The degree to which they rise above their respective limitations spawns a strong foundation of shared respect. Their mutual attraction deepens and eventually culminates in a kiss—Artie's first. But when Tina reveals that she was faking her disability, Artie is shattered, and he angrily breaks off their relationship.

Every day, you meet and interact with new people while in class, standing in line at the local coffee shop, or participating in clubs like the one depicted on *Glee*. Yet few of these individuals make a lasting impression on you, and even

▶ On *Glee*, Artie and Tina's instant attraction is disrupted when it is revealed that Tina isn't as similar to Artie as it first seemed. Have you ever misled a romantic interest into thinking you shared a common concern or value? If so, did you eventually confess? What was the outcome?

---

[4]All information that follows is from www.fox.com/glee.

fewer strike a chord of romantic attraction. What draws you to those special few? Many of the same factors that drew Artie and Tina together: proximity, physical attractiveness, similarity, reciprocal liking, and resources (Aron et al., 2008). These factors influence attraction for both men and women, in both same- and opposite-sex romances (Felmlee, Orzechowicz, & Fortes, 2010; Hyde, 2005).

PROXIMITY

The simple fact of physical proximity—being in one another's presence frequently—exerts far more impact on romantic attraction than many people think. In general, you'll feel more attracted to those with whom you have frequent contact and less attracted to those with whom you interact rarely, a phenomenon known as the **mere exposure effect** (Bornstein, 1989).

Proximity's pronounced effect on attraction is one reason that mixed-race romantic relationships are much rarer than same-race pairings in the United States. Despite this nation's enormous ethnic diversity, most Americans cluster into ethnically homogeneous groups, communities, and neighborhoods. This clustering reduces the likelihood that they will meet, regularly interact with, and eventually become attracted to individuals outside their own cultural group (Gaines, Chalfin, Kim, & Taing, 1998). Those who do form interethnic romances typically have living arrangements, work situations, or educational interests that place them in close proximity with diverse others, fostering attraction (Gaines et al., 1998).

self-reflection

How much daily contact do you have with people of other ethnicities, based on where you live, work, and go to school? Do you date outside of your own ethnic group? How has the frequency with which you've had contact with diverse others shaped your dating decision?

◗ You're more likely to be attracted to people you're around a lot, but the effect of proximity on attraction depends on your experience with the people. At least one study has found that people feel most negatively toward those whom they find bothersome and those whom they live nearest to.

⚫ Although people lust after gorgeous others, most of us end up in long-term relationships with those we perceive to be our equals in physical attractiveness.

PHYSICAL ATTRACTIVENESS

It's no secret that many people feel drawn to those they perceive as physically attractive. In part this is because we view beautiful people as competent communicators, intelligent, and well-adjusted, a phenomenon known as the **beautiful-is-good effect** (Eagly, Ashmore, Makhijani, & Longo, 1991). But although most of us find physical beauty attractive, we tend to form long-term romantic relationships with people we judge as similar to ourselves in physical attractiveness. This is known as **matching** (Feingold, 1988). Research documents that people don't want to be paired with those they think are substantially "below" or "above" themselves in looks (White, 1980).

SIMILARITY

No doubt you've heard the contradictory clichés regarding similarity and attraction: "Opposites attract" versus "Birds of a feather flock together." Which is correct? Scientific evidence suggests that we are attracted to those we perceive as similar to ourselves (Miller et al., 2007). This is known as the **birds-of-a-feather effect**. One explanation for this phenomenon is that people we view as similar to us are less likely to provoke uncertainty. In first encounters, they seem easier to predict and explain than people we perceive as dissimilar (Berger & Calabrese, 1975). Thus, we feel more comfortable with them.

Similarity means more than physical attractiveness; it means sharing parallel personalities, values, and likes and dislikes (Markey & Markey, 2007). Having fundamentally different personalities or widely disparate values erodes attraction between partners in the long run. At the same time, differences in mere tastes and preferences have no long-term negative impact on relationship health, as long as you and your partner are similar in other, more important ways. For example, I like heavier music (Motörhead, Mastodon, Pantera), and my wife hates it. But we have very similar personalities and values, so our attraction and our relationship endure.

Because differences in tastes and preferences don't predict relationship success, you shouldn't dismiss potential romantic partners because of their minor likes and dislikes. For example, imagine that you meet someone new who interests you. But in exploring his or her Facebook profile, you find that you have radically different tastes in music, TV, and movies. It would be premature to dismiss the possibility of a romance without first seeing whether you share similarities in personality and values.

RECIPROCAL LIKING

A fourth determinant of romantic attraction is one of the most obvious and often overlooked: whether the person we're attracted to makes it clear, through communication and other actions, that the attraction is mutual, known as **reciprocal liking** (Aron et al., 2008). Reciprocal liking is a potent predictor of attraction; we tend to be attracted to people who are attracted to us. Studies examining people's narrative descriptions of "falling in love" have found that reciprocal liking is *the* most commonly mentioned factor leading to love (Riela, Rodriguez, Aron, Xu, & Acevedo, 2010).

RESOURCES

A final spark that kindles romantic attraction is the unique resources that another person offers. Resources include qualities such as sense of humor, intelligence, kindness, supportiveness, and whether the person seems fun, and these attributes are viewed as valuable by both straight persons and gays and lesbians (Felmlee et al., 2010). But what leads *you* to view a person's resources as desirable?

Social exchange theory proposes that you'll feel drawn to those you see as offering substantial benefits (things you like and want) with few associated costs (things demanded of you in return). Two factors drive whether you find someone initially attractive: whether you perceive them as offering the kind of rewards you think you deserve in a romantic relationship (affection, emotional support, money, sex, etc.), and whether you think that the rewards they can offer you are superior to those you can get elsewhere (Kelley & Thibaut, 1978). In simple terms, you're attracted to people who can give you what you want, and who offer better rewards than others.

Once you've experienced attraction because of perceived rewards, the balance of benefits and costs exchanged by you and the other person, known as **equity**, determines whether a relationship will take root (Stafford, 2003). Romantic partners are happiest when the balance of giving and getting in their relationship is equal for both, and they're least happy when inequity exists (Hatfield, Traupmann, Sprecher, Utne, & Hay, 1985).

What is *inequity*? People in relationships have a strong sense of proportional justice: the balance between benefits gained from the relationship versus contributions made to the relationship (Hatfield, 1983). Inequity occurs when the benefits or contributions provided by one person are greater than those provided by the other. People who get more rewards from their relationships for fewer costs than their partners are *overbenefited*; those who get fewer rewards from their relationships for more costs than their partners are *underbenefited*. Overbenefited individuals experience negative emotions such as guilt, while underbenefited partners experience emotions such as sadness and anger (Sprecher, 2001).

⬥ Approximately 50 percent of students surveyed think interracial dating is acceptable, but this masks substantial race and gender differences. While 81 percent of European American and 75 percent of African American men express willingness to date outside their ethnicity, the majority of European American and African American women report negative attitudes toward interracial dating.

Equity strongly determines the short- and long-term success of romantic relationships. One study found that only 23 percent of equitable romances broke up during a several-month period, whereas 54 percent of inequitable romantic relationships broke up (Sprecher, 2001).

TECHNOLOGY AND ROMANTIC ATTRACTION

I pick my son Colin up from a school "activity night." "How'd it go?" I ask. "Great!" he exclaims. "I met this really cool girl, and got her number." "Are you going to call her?" I ask. Colin rolls his eyes at me. "I'm going to *text* her," he says. Sure enough, the exchange of text messages begins during the ride home, and as soon as we get through the door, he sprints for the computer and begins exchanging IMs with her.

Today, the enormous range of communication technologies available has refined and enhanced the attraction process. You can establish virtual proximity to attractive others by befriending them on social networking sites (Facebook, Tumblr) and then exchanging daily (or even hourly) updates and posts. Similar to my son Colin, you can assess a prospective partner's similarity to you and the rewards he or she could offer you by interacting with the person through text-messaging or simply by checking their personal Web pages and online profiles. You can assess physical attractiveness by viewing online photo albums and video clips. On dating sites such as Match.com, eHarmony, or even free sites such as Craigslist, you can enter a set of search parameters—desired age, profession, appearance, interests, sexual orientation—and immediately see a broad range of potential partners.

⬇ A challenge of online dating is transferring the romance from online to offline. Newer online dating services like HowAboutWe.com focus on just that by encouraging users to plan specific activities with one another. What challenges, if any, have you faced in this transition?

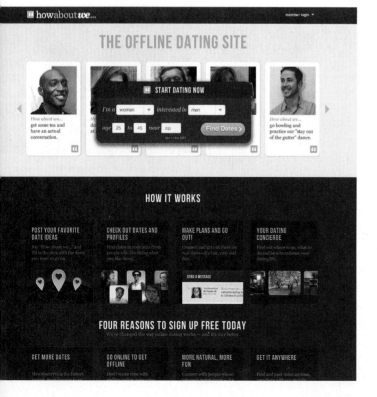

But despite the conveniences they offer, these technologies also evoke tensions. For one thing, you have to decide how honest to be in your online self-presentations (Ellison, Heino, & Gibbs, 2006). Because so many people now use online communication to gauge each other, you may feel great pressure to present yourself as highly attractive—even if that means providing a distorted self-description. In a survey of more than 5,000 online dating service users, misrepresentation of self was commonplace (Hall, Park, Song, & Cody, 2010). Men were more likely than women to exaggerate their education level and income, and women were more likely to lie about their weight. And both men and women over 50 routinely distorted their ages to appear younger. Correspondingly, people view others' online dating profiles skeptically. Users liken profiles to "résumés"; that is, they are vehicles for marketing one's "best self," rather than accurate glimpses into one's authentic identity (Heino, Ellison, & Gibbs, 2006). Just as people lie on their résumés, so too do online daters presume that others will lie in their profiles. As one online dating service user describes, "Everyone is so wonderful over the Internet. What the Internet doesn't tell you is that, 'I'm defensive, I talk about my problems all the time, I can't manage my money'" (Heino et al., 2006, p. 435).

If your goal is to forge an offline romantic relationship, distorting your online self-description is ultimately self-defeating (Ellison et al., 2006). When you mislead someone online about your appearance or other personal attributes and then take your romance offline, your partner *will* discover the truth. Such unpleasant revelations are commonplace: one study found that 86 percent of people using online dating sites report having met others who they felt had misrepresented their physical attractiveness (Gibbs, Ellison, & Heino, 2006). When people feel misled, the outcome is often a damaged impression, negative emotion (such as resentment or anger), and an injured or even ruined relationship (McCornack & Levine, 1990). Clearly, the most ethical and practical thing you can do in your online self-descriptions is to accentuate your attractive attributes without resorting to distortion or dishonesty. If you feel you may be "crossing the line" into deception, have a trustworthy friend check your online description or personal profile and assess its authenticity.

Relationship Development and Deterioration

How couples come together and separate

Romantic relationships come together and apart in as many different ways and at as many different speeds as there are partners who fall for each other (Surra & Hughes, 1997). Many relationships are of the "casual dating" variety—they flare quickly, sputter, and then fade. Others endure and evolve with deepening levels of commitment. But all romantic relationships undergo stages marked by distinctive patterns in partners' communication, thoughts, and feelings. We know these transitions intuitively: "taking things to the next level," "kicking it up a notch," "taking a step back," or "taking a break." Communication scholar Mark Knapp (1984) modeled these patterns as ten stages: five of "coming together" and five of "coming apart."

COMING TOGETHER

Knapp's stages of coming together illustrate one possible flow of relationship development (see Figure 9.1). As you read through the stages, keep in mind that these suggest turning points in relationships and are not fixed rules for how involvements should or do progress. Your relationships may go through some, none, or all of these stages. They may skip stages, jump back or forward in order, or follow a completely different and unique trajectory.

figure 9.1 Stages of Coming Together

Initiating   During the **initiating** stage, you size up a person you've just met or noticed. You draw on all available visual information (physical attractiveness, body type, age, ethnicity, gender, clothing, posture) to determine whether you find him or her attractive. Your primary concern at this stage is to portray yourself in a positive light. You also ponder and present a greeting you deem appropriate. This greeting might be in person or online—more than 16 million people in the United States have used online dating sites to meet new partners (Heino, Ellison, & Gibbs, 2010).

Experimenting   Once you've initiated an encounter with someone else (online or face-to-face), you enter the **experimenting** stage, during which you exchange demographic information (names, majors, where you grew up). You also engage in *small talk*—disclosing facts you and the other person consider relatively unimportant but that enable you to introduce yourselves in a safe and controlled fashion. As you share these details, you look for points of commonality on which you can base further interaction. Relationships at this stage are generally pleasant and "light." This is the "casual dating" phase of romance. For better or worse, *most involvements never progress beyond this stage.* We go through life experimenting with many people but forming deeper connections with very few.

Intensifying   Occasionally, you'll progress beyond casual dating and find yourself experiencing strong feelings of attraction toward another person. When this happens, your verbal and nonverbal communication becomes increasingly intimate. During this **intensifying** stage, you and your partner begin to reveal previously withheld information, such as secrets about your past or important life dreams and goals. You may begin using informal forms of address or terms of endearment ("honey" versus "Joe") and saying "we" more frequently. One particularly

"Conversation? I thought we were just meeting for coffee."

strong sign that your relationship is intensifying is the direct expression of commitment. You might do this verbally ("I think I'm falling for you") or online by marking your profile as "in a relationship" rather than "single." You may also spend more time in each other's personal spaces, as well as begin physical expressions of affection, such as hand-holding, cuddling, or sexual activity.

Integrating   During the **integrating** stage, your and your partner's personalities seem to become one. This integration is reinforced through sexual activity and the exchange of belongings (items of clothing, music, photos, etc.). When you've integrated with a romantic partner, you cultivate attitudes, activities, and interests that clearly join you together as a couple—"*our* favorite movie," "*our* song," and "*our* favorite restaurant." Friends, colleagues, and family members begin to treat you as a couple—for example, always inviting the two of you to parties or dinners. Not surprisingly, many people begin to struggle with the dialectical tension of *connectedness versus autonomy* at this stage. As a student of mine once told his partner when describing this stage, "I'm not me anymore, I'm *us*."

Bonding   The ultimate stage of coming together is **bonding**, a public ritual that announces to the world that you and your partner have made a commitment to one another. Bonding is something you'll share with very few people—perhaps only one—during your lifetime. The most obvious example of bonding is marriage.

Bonding institutionalizes your relationship. Before this stage, the ground rules for your relationship and your communication within it remain a private matter, to be negotiated between you and your partner. In the bonding stage, you import into your relationship a set of laws and customs determined by governmental authorities and perhaps religious institutions. Although these laws and customs help to solidify your relationship, they can also make your relationship feel more rigid and structured.

VideoCentral ▣

bedfordstmartins.com
/reflectrelate

Integrating
*Watch this clip online
to answer the questions
below.*

How many of your relationships have progressed to the integrating stage? How did you know when they reached that stage? What verbal and nonverbal behaviors do two people in the integrating stage of their relationship use?

Want to see more? Check out VideoCentral for clips illustrating **experimenting** and **bonding**.

◖ There are many ways for couples to bond, but the key is that both partners agree and make a deep commitment to each other.

COMING APART

Coming together is often followed by coming apart. One study of college dating couples found that across a three-month period, 30 percent broke up (Parks & Adelman, 1983). Similar trends occur in the married adult population: the divorce rate has remained stable at around 40 percent since the early 1980s (Hurley, 2005; Kreider, 2005). This latter number may surprise you, because the news media, politicians, and even academics commonly quote the divorce rate as "50 percent."[5] But studies that have tracked couples across time have found that 6 out of 10 North American marriages survive until "death does them part" (Hurley, 2005). Nevertheless, the 40 percent figure translates into a million divorces each year.

In some relationships, breaking up is the right thing to do. Partners have grown apart, they've lost interest in one another, or perhaps one person has been abusive. In other relationships, coming apart is unfortunate. Perhaps the partners could have resolved their differences but didn't make the effort. Thus, they needlessly suffer the pain of breaking up.

Like coming together, coming apart unfolds over stages marked by changes in thoughts, feelings, and communication (see Figure 9.2). But unlike coming together, these stages often entail emotional turmoil that makes them difficult to negotiate skillfully. Learning how to communicate supportively while a romantic relationship is dissolving is a challenging but important part of being a skilled interpersonal communicator.

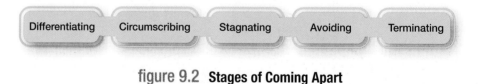

Differentiating   Circumscribing   Stagnating   Avoiding   Terminating

figure 9.2   **Stages of Coming Apart**

---

[5]The "50 percent" claim came from a U.S. Census Bureau calculation that computed the divorce rate by dividing the number of marriages in a given year by the number of divorces. But this calculation is obviously flawed, because the people marrying that year are not usually the same people who are getting divorced.

Differentiating   In all romantic relationships, partners share differences as well as similarities. But during the first stage of coming apart, **differentiating**, the beliefs, attitudes, and values that distinguish you from your partner come to dominate your thoughts and communication ("I can't *believe* you think that!" or "We are *so* different!").

Most healthy romances experience occasional periods of differentiating. These moments can involve unpleasant clashes and bickering over contrasting viewpoints, tastes, or goals. But you can move your relationship through this difficulty—and thus halt the coming-apart process—by openly discussing your points of difference and working together to resolve them. To do this, review the constructive conflict skills discussed in Chapter 8.

Circumscribing   If one or both of you respond to problematic differences by ignoring them and spending less time talking, you enter the **circumscribing** stage. You actively begin to restrict the quantity and quality of information you exchange with your partner. Instead of sharing information, you create "safe zones" in which you discuss only topics that won't provoke conflict. Common remarks made during circumscribing include, "Don't ask me about that" and "Let's not talk about that anymore."

Stagnating   When circumscribing becomes so severe that almost no safe conversational topics remain, communication slows to a standstill, and your relationship enters the **stagnating** stage. You both presume that communicating is pointless because it will only lead to further problems. People in stagnant relationships often experience a sense of resignation; they feel "stuck" or "trapped." However, they can remain in the relationship for months or even years. Why? Some believe that it's better to leave things as they are rather than expend the effort necessary to break up or rebuild the relationship. Others simply don't know how to repair the damage and revive their earlier bond.

Avoiding   During the **avoiding** stage, one or both of you decide that you no longer can be around each other, and you begin distancing yourself physically. Some people communicate avoidance directly to their partner ("I don't want to see you anymore"). Others do so indirectly—for example, by going out when the partner's at home, screening cell-phone calls, ignoring texts, and changing their Facebook status from "in a relationship" to "single."

Terminating   In ending a relationship, some people want to come together for a final encounter that gives a sense of closure and resolution. During the **terminating** stage, couples might discuss the past, present, and future of the relationship. They often exchange summary statements about the past—comments on "how our relationship was" that are either accusations ("No one has ever treated me so badly!") or laments ("I'll never be able to find someone as perfect as you"). Verbal and nonverbal behaviors indicating a lack of intimacy are readily apparent—including physical distance between the two individuals and reluctance to make eye contact. The partners may also discuss the future status of their relationship. Some couples may agree to end all contact going forward. Others may choose to

skills practice

Differentiating
Overcoming the challenge of differentiating

❶ Identify when you and your romantic partner are differentiating.

❷ Check your perception of the relationship, especially how you've punctuated encounters and the attributions you've made.

❸ Call to mind the similarities that originally brought you and your partner together.

❹ Discuss your concerns with your partner, emphasizing these similarities and your desire to continue the relationship.

❺ Mutually explore solutions to the differences that have been troubling you.

self-reflection

Have most of your romantic relationships ended by avoiding? Or have you sought the closure provided by terminating? In what situations is one approach to ending relationships better than the other? Is one more ethical?

▶ Gender stereotypes dominate our thinking about men and women in romantic relationships, but research discredits many of these damaging presumptions. For example, although women in Western cultures are depicted as sentimental and men as rational, women actually are more likely than men to base their romantic relationship decisions on practical considerations.

maintain some level of physical intimacy even though the emotional side of the relationship is officially over. Still others may express interest in "being friends."

Many people find terminating a relationship painful or awkward. It's hard to tell someone else that you no longer want to be involved, and it is equally painful to hear it. Draw on your interpersonal communication skills to best negotiate your way through this dreaded moment. In particular, infuse your communication with empathy—offering empathic concern and perspective-taking (see Chapter 3). Realize that romantic breakups are a kind of death and that it's normal to experience grief, even when breaking up is the right thing to do. Consequently, offer supportive communication ("I'm sorry things had to end this way" or "I know this is going to be painful for both of us") and use grief management tactics (see Chapter 4). Conversations to terminate a relationship are never pleasant or easy. But the communication skills you've learned can help you minimize the pain and damage, enabling you and your former partner to move on to other relationships.

Maintaining Romantic Relationships

Strategies to sustain romances, even long-distance ones

In the movie *Eternal Sunshine of the Spotless Mind*, Joel (Jim Carrey) and Clementine (Kate Winslet) are lovers struggling to maintain a bittersweet romance (Bregman, Golin, Gondry, & Kaufman, 2004). Clementine, an outgoing, self-described "high-maintenance girl," is the opposite of quiet, book-ish Joel, who communicates more with his private journal than with her. Following a fight, Clementine impetuously visits a clinic that specializes in memory erasure and has Joel expunged from her mind. Despondent, Joel follows suit. But the two meet again and find themselves attracted. Eventually discovering the truth—that they aren't strangers at all but longtime lovers—they face a momentous decision. Do they invest the time and energy necessary to maintain their romance a second time, knowing that they failed so terribly before that they chose to destroy their memories? Or do they end it before their history of relational disaster can repeat itself? They discuss their dilemma:

> **CLEMENTINE:** I'm not a concept, Joel, I'm just a messed-up girl who's looking for my own peace of mind. I'm not perfect.
>
> **JOEL:** I can't see anything that I don't like about you.
>
> **CLEMENTINE:** But you will!
>
> **JOEL:** I can't.
>
> **CLEMENTINE:** But you *will*! You know, you *will* think of things, and I'll get bored with you and feel trapped because that's what happens with me!
>
> **JOEL:** OK.
>
> **CLEMENTINE:** OK?
>
> **JOEL:** OK.

◀ In *Eternal Sunshine of the Spotless Mind*, Joel and Clementine decide to take another shot at their relationship despite the risks.

Romantic relationships aren't always about happiness and celebration. No matter how much you love your partner, you will still experience unpleasant moments such as feeling irked, bored, or trapped. In fact, on any given day, 44 percent of us are likely to be seriously annoyed by a close relationship partner (Kowalski, Walker, Wilkinson, Queen, & Sharpe, 2003). Though such experiences are normal, many people find them disturbing and wonder whether they should end the relationship. But Clementine's and Joel's choice in the conclusion of *Eternal Sunshine*—to accept the inevitable negatives as natural and move forward regardless—offers a message of hope. Wiping our mental slates clean and leaving our partners behind is not the only solution to romantic relationship challenges. Instead, we can choose to harness our interpersonal communication skills and invest the effort necessary to maintain our love.

To this point we've talked a good deal about the nature of love, and we've traced the stages through which many romances progress. Now let's shift focus to a more practical concern: how can you use interpersonal communication to maintain a satisfying, healthy romantic relationship?

MAINTENANCE STRATEGIES

Many people believe that love just happens—that once it strikes, it endures. But a basic rule of romantic love is that maintenance is necessary to keep relationships from deteriorating (Stafford, 2003). **Relational maintenance** refers to using communication and supportive behaviors to sustain a desired relationship status and level of satisfaction (Stafford, Dainton, & Haas, 2000). Across several studies, communication scholar Laura Stafford has observed seven strategies that satisfied couples—no matter their ethnicity or sexual orientation—routinely use to maintain their romances (Stafford, 2010). (See Table 9.2 for an overview of these categories.)

Positivity   Positivity includes communicating in a cheerful and optimistic fashion, doing unsolicited favors, and giving unexpected gifts. Partners involved in romantic relationships cite positivity as *the* most important maintenance tactic for ensuring happiness (Dainton & Stafford, 1993). This holds true for men and women in straight relationships (Stafford, 2010), and for same-sex partners in gay and lesbian romances (Haas & Stafford, 2005). You use positivity when:[6]

- You try to make each interaction with your partner enjoyable.
- You try to build your partner up by giving him or her compliments.
- You try to be fun, upbeat, and romantic with your partner.

You undermine positivity when:

- You constantly look for and complain about problems in your relationship without offering solutions.

VideoCentral ⊙

bedfordstmartins.com /reflectrelate

Relational Maintenance
Watch this clip online to answer the questions below.

Maintaining a relationship after a conflict can be a challenging situation. How is the couple in the video handling the situation? What maintenance strategies are they using? What maintenance strategies do you think are especially important after a fight? How about on a daily basis?

---

[6]All bulleted items that follow are adapted from the revised relationship maintenance behavior scale of Stafford (2010).

- You whine, pout, and sulk when you don't get your way.
- You criticize favors and gifts from your partner.

Assurances The second-most-powerful maintenance tactic in boosting relationship satisfaction is assurances: messages that emphasize how much a partner means to you, how important the relationship is, and that describe a secure future together. Assurances may be expressed directly, such as saying, "I love you" or "I can't see myself ever being with anyone else but you." You may also communicate assurances more indirectly, by emphasizing the value you place on your time together—for example, sending a text message saying, "I can't wait to see you again" or "I'm really looking forward to tonight" (Rabby, 1997). You use assurances when:

- You regularly tell your partner how devoted you are to your relationship.
- You talk about future plans and events to be shared together (e.g., anniversaries, vacations, marriage, children).
- You do and say things to demonstrate the depth of your feelings for your partner.

You undermine assurances when:

- You flirt with others and talk about how attractive they are in front of your partner.
- You tell your partner not to count on anything long-term.
- You systematically avoid pledging love or fidelity to your partner.

Sharing Tasks The most *frequently* practiced form of maintenance is sharing tasks. This involves taking mutual responsibility for chores and negotiating an equitable division of labor. Although this may sound like something that only serious, cohabiting, or married couples face, sharing tasks is relevant for all couples, and includes responsibilities like providing transportation to work or campus, running errands, and making reservations for dinner. You share tasks when:

- You try to pitch in equally on everyday responsibilities.
- You ask your partner how you can help out.
- You make an effort to handle tasks before your partner asks you to do them.

You undermine task sharing when:

- You strategically avoid having to do your share of the work.
- You never ask your partner how you can help out.
- You expect your partner to run errands and do chores for you, without reciprocating.

Acceptance Part of what builds a strong sense of intimacy between romantic partners is the feeling that lovers accept us for who we really are, fully and

▶ Constant, daily maintenance is needed to keep romantic relationships alive and healthy.

completely, and forgive us our flaws. Acceptance involves communicating this affirmation and support. You convey acceptance when:

- You forgive your partner when he or she makes mistakes.
- You support your partner in his or her decisions.
- You are patient with your partner when he or she is irritable or in a bad mood.

You undermine acceptance when:

- You hold grievances and grudges against your partner.
- You tell your partner that you wish he or she were different.
- You critique your partner's appearance, personality, beliefs, and values.

Self-Disclosure   An essential part of maintaining intimacy is creating a climate of security and trust within your relationship. This allows both partners to feel that they can disclose fears and feelings without repercussion. To foster self-disclosure, each person must behave in ways that are predictable, trustworthy, and ethical. Over time, consistency in behavior evokes mutual respect and the perception that self-disclosure will be welcomed. You use self-disclosure when:

- You tell your partner about your fears and vulnerabilities.
- You share your feelings and emotions with your partner.
- You encourage your partner to disclose his or her thoughts and feelings, and offer empathy in return.

You undermine self-disclosure when:

- You disparage your partner's perspective.
- You routinely keep important information hidden from your partner.

◗ When romantic partners take an interest in each other's favorite activities, they support each other and deepen the level of intimacy in their relationship. How do you support your partner when you're in a romantic relationship?

table 9.2 Romantic Relationship Maintenance Strategies

Maintenance Strategy	Suggested Actions
Positivity	Be cheerful and optimistic in your communication.
Assurances	Remind your partner of your devotion.
Sharing Tasks	Help out with daily responsibilities.
Acceptance	Be supportive and forgiving.
Self-Disclosure	Share your thoughts, feelings, and fears.
Relationship Talks	Make time to discuss your relationship and really listen.
Social Networks	Involve yourself with your partner's friends and family.

- You betray your partner by sharing confidential information about him or her with others.

Relationship Talks   Romantic maintenance includes occasionally sitting down and discussing the status of your relationship, how you each feel about it, and where you both see it going. Relationship talks allow you to gauge how invested you each are and whether you agree on future plans and goals. They also provide a convenient forum for expressing and resolving concerns, forestalling future conflict. You encourage relationship talks when you:

- Set aside time in your schedule to chat about your relationship.
- Openly and respectfully share your relationship concerns with your partner.
- Encourage your partner to share his or her feelings about the relationship with you.

You undermine relationship talks when you:

- React defensively and egocentrically whenever your partner shares relationship concerns.
- Avoid or refuse to have relationship talks with your partner.
- Actively ridicule the need to discuss the relationship.

Social Networks   Romances are more likely to survive if important members of the couples' social networks approve of the relationship (Felmlee, 2001). For example, communication scholars Malcolm Parks and Mara Adelman (1983) measured how much support romantically involved individuals received from their partners' friends and family, what percentage of their partners' network they had met, and how often they communicated with these people. Using these factors and others, Parks and Adelman were able to predict with 88 percent accuracy which relationships would survive. What were the strongest determinants of whether couples stayed together? Support from family and friends and regular communication with one's partner.

Fostering healthy relationships with surrounding friends and family appears especially crucial for those involved in interethnic relationships (Baptiste, 1990), and for gay and lesbian couples. Approximately 67 percent of interethnic marriages end in divorce, compared with an overall divorce rate of 40 percent, the largest reasons being lack of network support and cultural disapproval (Gaines & Agnew, 2003). Gay and lesbian couples report having supportive environments such as churches or clubs and being treated "the same" as straight couples by their friends and family as especially important for their relationship stability and satisfaction (Haas & Stafford, 1998). You foster supportive social networks when you:

- Tell your partner how much you like his or her friends and family.
- Invite your partner's friends or family members to share activities with the two of you.
- Willingly turn to family members of both partners for help and advice when needed.

You undermine social networks when you:

- Make critical and disparaging remarks regarding your partner's friends and family.
- Intentionally avoid encounters with your partner's friends and family.
- Demand that your partner choose between spending time with you and spending it with friends and family.

MAINTAINING ROMANCE ACROSS DISTANCE

A common challenge to maintaining romantic relationships is geographic separation. At any one time, nearly half of college students are involved in romances separated by geography, and 75 percent will experience a long-distance dating relationship while in school (Aylor, 2003).

People often think that long-distance relationships are doomed to fail. However, long-distance romantic relationships have actually been found to be *more* satisfying and stable than those that are geographically close (Stafford, 2010). On measures of love, positivity, agreement, and overall communication quality, geographically distant couples score *higher* than local partners (Stafford & Merolla, 2007). Why? Stafford (2010) offers several reasons. Couples separated by distance often constrain their communication to only that which is positive, steadfastly shying away from troublesome topics that provoke conflict. Geographically distant couples also idealize their partners more. When you're not around your partner every day, it's easy to cherish misconceptions about his or her "perfection." And visits between partners are typically occasional, brief in duration, and passionate. This amplifies the feeling that all their time together is intense and positive—an unsustainable illusion when people see each other regularly (Sahlstein, 2004).

The most difficult maintenance challenge long-distance couples face is not the separation, but their eventual reunion. Almost all couples separated by distance express a desire to be near each other again, and they anticipate that being together will result in dramatic relationship improvements (Stafford, Merolla, & Castle, 2006). But the reality is more complicated. Couples who are reunited following

◁ In the movie *Like Crazy*, college students Jacob and Anna fall in love during their senior year. When immigration laws force Anna to return to her native England, they begin a long-distance relationship. Despite texting, e-mails, and phone calls, the relationship becomes strained. If you have ever been in a long-distance relationship, how did you use communication to ease the distance?

separation are twice as likely to break up, compared with those who remain long-distance (Stafford & Merolla, 2007). Rather than being "all bliss, all the time," living locally presents a blend of rewards and costs (Stafford, Merolla, & Castle, 2006). On the plus side, couples get to spend more time together, savoring each other's company and sharing in the "little" things they missed when apart. On the minus side, partners' cherished illusions about each other are shattered. Reunited couples report realizing for the first time their lovers' negative characteristics, such as laziness, sloppiness, immaturity, or failure to invest effort in the relationship. They describe a substantial reduction in autonomy, experienced as a loss of time and space for themselves, loss of interaction with friends and family, and irritation with having to be accountable to partners. Reunited couples also report increased conflict, as formerly "taboo" topics become regularly discussed and fought over.

Despite the challenges, you can have a happy and enduring long-distance romance. Here are some suggestions to help maintain such relationships:

1. While separated, use technology to regularly communicate with your partner. Using text, e-mail, IM, Facebook, and Skype has a significant impact on improving relationship health (Dainton & Aylor, 2002a).

2. When communicating with your distant partner, follow the maintenance tactics discussed in the previous section. In particular, focus on the two most important for maintaining satisfaction—positivity and assurances—and keep your interactions upbeat, positive, and filled with discussions of shared future plans and dreams.

3. When you permanently reunite, expect a significant period of adjustment, one that is marked by tension (as you rebalance autonomy versus connection), disappointment (as idealistic illusions of your partner are replaced by the reality), and conflict (as you begin talking about topics you shelved during the separation). Avoid expecting everything to be perfect, and use the strategies you've learned in our discussion of conflict (Chapter 8) to manage difficult dilemmas when they arise.

skills practice

Technology and Maintenance
Using technology to maintain romance

❶ Send your partner a text or e-mail that has no purpose other than to compliment him or her.

❷ Post a message on your partner's Web page, saying how excited you are about seeing her or him soon.

❸ During a high-stress day for your partner, send an e-mail or text that says, "Just thinking of you."

❹ Recall a friend or family member whom your partner has been concerned about, and send an e-mail or text to your partner inquiring about how the person is doing.

❺ Think of a task your partner has been wanting you to do, complete it, then text-message your partner to let her or him know you took care of it.

DECIDING WHETHER TO MAINTAIN

Of course, not all romantic involvements are worth the effort to maintain. In some cases, it may be healthier to end the involvement rather than communicate in ways designed to foster its survival. The decision of whether to maintain or dissolve a struggling romance is one of the most challenging interpersonal decisions we face.

As one way to work through this decision, familiarize yourself with the characteristics of couples whose relationships survive. Four factors—each of which we've discussed—appear to be most important in predicting survival of a romantic relationship. First is *the degree to which the partners consider themselves "in love."* Couples are more likely to stay together if they think of themselves as in love, are considering marriage or a lifelong commitment, rate their relationship as high in closeness, or date each other exclusively (Hill et al., 1976). Second is *equity.* Romantic relationships are happiest and most stable when the balance of giving and getting is equal for both partners (Hatfield et al., 1985). Third is *similarity.* Highly similar couples are more likely to stay together than couples who are dissimilar (Hill et al., 1976). Fourth is *network support.* A romance is more likely to endure when the couple's social networks approve of the relationship (Felmlee, 2001; Parks & Adelman, 1983). To determine how well your relationship meets these criteria, ask yourself the following questions:

1. Are you still in love with your partner?
2. Is your relationship equitable?
3. Do you and your partner share values and personality traits?
4. Do your family and friends support your relationship?

If you answer "yes" to these questions, your relationship may warrant investment in maintenance. But remember: *deciding whether to maintain a struggling relationship or to let it go is a choice only you can make.* Friends, family members, pop-culture relationship experts, and even textbooks can't tell you when to keep or when to leave a romantic involvement. That being said, romantic relationships are in many ways practical endeavors. Your decision to maintain or end a struggling romance should be based on a long-term forecast of your relationship. Stacking your relationship up against those four criteria can give you insight into whether your relationship has a solid foundation on which to invest further effort.

The Dark Side of Romantic Relationships

Addressing issues related to romance

Think about the Robert Falcon Scott story that began this chapter. His letter to Kathleen reminds us of the high ideals that love can inspire: compassion, caring, generosity, selflessness. But romance has a dark side as well. As scholar Robin Kowalski pointedly puts it, "people in romantic relationships do a lot of mean and nasty things to one another" (Kowalski et al., 2003, p. 472). And when they do, the result is often unparalleled pain and despair. In this section, we explore some of the most troubling issues related to romance—betrayal, jealousy, intrusion, and violence—and discuss communication strategies for addressing them.

BETRAYAL

Betrayal is one of the most devastating experiences that can occur in a close involvement (Haden & Hojjat, 2006). **Romantic betrayal** is defined as an act that goes against expectations of a romantic relationship and, as a result, causes pain to a partner (Jones, Moore, Scratter, & Negel, 2001). Common examples include *sexual infidelity* (engaging in sexual activity with someone else), *emotional infidelity* (developing a strong romantic attachment to someone else), *deception* (intentional manipulation of information), and *disloyalty* (hurting your partner to benefit yourself). But any behavior that violates norms of loyalty and trustworthiness can be considered betrayal.

In romantic relationships, partners inevitably behave in ways that defy one another's expectations and cause disappointment. But betrayal is different. Betrayal is *intentional*. As a result, it typically evokes two intense, negative reactions in betrayed partners. The first is an overwhelming sense of relational devaluation—the realization that our partners do not love and respect us as much as we thought they did (Leary, 2001). This sense of devaluation, which is triggered most by sexual infidelity and deception, is difficult to overcome and often leads us to abandon our relationships. The second is a profound sense of loss. In the wake of betrayal, we may feel that all the time and effort we invested in our partner and the relationship were a waste, and that intimacy, commitment, and trust have been permanently destroyed (Haden & Hojjat, 2006). Consequently, when you are betrayed by a lover, expect to feel *grief* over the loss of the relationship that was. (See Chapter 4 for more on grief management.)

Sexual Infidelity   The most destructive form of romantic betrayal is sexual infidelity. A partner who cheats on you has broken a fundamental sacrament—the spoken or unspoken pledge to remain faithful. Not surprisingly, many people react to infidelity with a strong urge to leave their partner. One study found that more than 20 percent of American women and men would consider

How Often Do You Betray Romantic Partners?

self-QUIZ

Read each statement and rate how often you have done the activity: 1 (never), 2 (once), 3 (a few times), 4 (several times), 5 (many times). Get your score by adding up your answers.

_____ Snubbing a romantic partner when you are with a group you want to impress

_____ Gossiping about a romantic partner behind his or her back

_____ Making a promise to a romantic partner with no intention of keeping it

_____ Telling others information given to you in confidence by a romantic partner

_____ Lying to a romantic partner

_____ Failing to stand up for a romantic partner when he or she is being criticized or belittled by others

Note: Information in this *Self-Quiz* adapted for romantic relationships is from Jones and Burdette (1994).

Scoring: 6–14 = You're an infrequent betrayer; 15–23 = You're a moderate betrayer; 24–30 = You're a frequent betrayer.

Regardless of which approach you take, the hard truth is that, after a betrayal, your relationship will never be the same, and it will never be "better" than it previously was in terms of trust, intimacy, and satisfaction. You certainly can rebuild a strong and enduring relationship, but it will always be scarred. As my therapist friend Joe says, "You will *never* get over it. You just learn to live with it."

JEALOUSY

A second problem for romantic relationships is **jealousy**—a protective reaction to a perceived threat to a valued relationship (Hansen, 1985). Most scholars agree that jealousy isn't a singular emotion but rather a combination of negative emotions—primarily anger, fear, and sadness (Guerrero & Andersen, 1998).

Jealousy especially plagues users of online social networking sites like Facebook. Such sites open the possibility for people other than your romantic partner to post provocative photos, write enticing posts on your wall, and send alluring messages—all of which can trigger your partner's jealousy. Imagine how you'd

focus on CULTURE

Infidelity Internationally

In Japan it's called "going off the path" and in Israel it's "eating to the side" (Druckerman, 2007). But regardless of differences in lingo, the suffering that ensues from sexual betrayal is similar around the globe.

Wall Street Journal reporter Pamela Druckerman interviewed people in 10 different countries, gauging their infidelity attitudes and behaviors. She discovered vast cultural differences, and some similarities. For example, in Japan, intricate rules of discretion guide how one cheats, whereas in Finland, people are more open in discussing and engaging in adultery. In Russia, Druckerman was struck by its sheer prevalence. One marital therapist told her, "Affairs should be obligatory, because they make for stronger marriages," and an issue of Russian *Cosmopolitan* provided instructional tips to women for how to hide their betrayals from their partners.

Druckerman's observations mirror scientific research. A study of nonmarital sex involving 24 nations and 33,000 respondents found that the top three countries in infidelity acceptance were Russia, Bulgaria, and the Czech Republic (Widmer, Treas, & Newcomb, 1998). What countries were the most infidelity *intolerant*? The Philippines, Ireland, and the United States.

Despite cultural differences, however, Druckerman notes at least three betrayal universals (as cited in Corner, 2007). First, across cultures, people who cheat prefer partners who also are seriously involved, making the risks "evenly shared." Second, cheaters typically describe themselves as "not the cheating type." Third, regardless of cultural attitudes or prevalence, sexual betrayal almost always causes intense emotional pain and relationship distress. When asked the lessons learned from her study, Druckerman described, "I still very much believe in monogamy as the ideal, but I have become more realistic—or fatalistic—about it. I now think it could easily happen to me. And, if it does, I won't automatically assume my relationship is over."

discussion questions

- What lessons have you learned from your culture regarding the ethics of infidelity? How have these lessons shaped your beliefs? Your relationship behaviors?
- If a partner cheated on you, would you assume that your involvement was over, or would you try to repair and rebuild your relationship? What impact would your cultural values have upon your decision?

 Jealousy can easily form if you see flirty wall posts or suggestive photos on your lover's social networking pages. If you feel threatened, it's important to communicate in a cooperative and constructive manner when discussing your feelings with your partner. What experiences have you had with jealousy of this kind?

feel if you saw such communication on your partner's page. Studies of Facebook have found that jealousy is one of the most frequent problems reported by users (Morrison, Lee, Wiedmaier, & Dibble, 2008). Jealousy can intensify even further if site users engage in what communication scholar Kelly Morrison calls **wedging.** Through wedging, a person deliberately uses messages, photos, and posts to try and "wedge" him- or herself between partners in a romantic couple because he or she is interested in one of the partners (Morrison et al., 2008).

The most effective way to deal with jealousy is *self-reliance*: allowing yourself to feel jealous but not letting whatever sparked your jealousy to interrupt you. You should continue your current activities and give yourself time to cool off (Salovey & Rodin, 1988). Avoid communicating with your partner until you're able to do so in a cooperative and constructive fashion. When you *are* ready to talk, don't be afraid to candidly acknowledge your own jealousy, and discuss your perception of threat with your partner: "I saw that post from your old girlfriend, and I'm worried that she wants to get back together with you. Am I reading too much into this, or should I really feel threatened?"

RELATIONAL INTRUSION

Sometimes romantic partners try to control you or behave in ways that invade your privacy. In mild cases, they might check up on you—talking with your friends or family to verify your whereabouts. In more extreme instances, they might search your phone or read your e-mail without permission. Such behaviors are known as **relational intrusion**: the violation of one's independence and privacy by a person who desires an intimate relationship (Cupach & Spitzberg, 1998). Intrusion happens in all cultures, is equally likely to be perpetrated by

skills practice

Dealing with Jealousy
Communicating more competently when jealousy strikes

❶ Identify a situation in which your jealousy is sparked.

❷ Continue your current activities, not letting the jealousy-evoking event distract you from completing what you were doing.

❸ Avoid immediate communication with your partner.

❹ While you're finishing what you were doing, practice the Jefferson Strategy, counting to 10 or 100 until you cool off.

❺ Initiate communication with your partner, using your cooperative language skills and explaining to him or her why the event caused you to feel jealous. Solicit your partner's perspective.

men or women, and occurs both in current relationships and in those in which the partners have broken up (Lavy, Mikulincer, Shaver, & Gillath, 2009).

Within intact romances, two forms of intrusion are common (Lavy et al., 2009). The first is *monitoring and controlling*. A partner may text you constantly to ensure that you are always accounted for and instruct you to be home by a certain time. He or she may follow you or hire a private investigator to conduct surveillance. People who have experienced this behavior describe it as: "My partner wants to know where I am and what I'm doing all the time," and "My partner does not let me meet my family or friends without him being present" (Lavy et al., 2009, p. 995). The second form of intrusion is *invasion of privacy*. This includes nosing or snooping through your belongings, computer, and phone and asking overly personal and suspicious questions designed to "interrogate" you.

For romances that have ended, intrusion is symptomatic of a person's inability to let go. Of people who report difficulty in dealing with breakups, 79 percent admit behaving intrusively (Dutton & Winstead, 2006). The most common forms of postrelationship intrusion are leaving gifts and messages for the ex-partner, expressing exaggerated levels of affection (such as public serenades or posting love poems), physically following the ex-partner around, and showing up uninvited at the ex-partner's home or work. If done repeatedly, these latter behaviors may turn into stalking, which is a criminal offense.

For its recipients, relational intrusion is decidedly negative and threatening. If the relationship is intact, intrusion generates strong negative impressions, uncertainty, and relational turmoil (Lavy et al., 2009). As one victim describes, "He was acting so unfair; I no longer was sure about our relationship" (Lavy et al., 2009, p. 999). For people dealing with postrelationship intrusion, anger and fear are common responses, and the intrusion may spark a desire to seek revenge against or act violently toward the intruding partner (Lavy et al., 2009).

What makes intrusion tricky, however, is that perpetrators typically perceive their behaviors *positively*, as reflecting love, loyalty, or just the desire to stay in touch (Cupach & Spitzberg, 2004). Consequently, they tend to minimize or deny the harms created by their undesirable actions.

How can you best deal with intrusion? Realize first that intrusion is absolutely unacceptable and unethical. No one has the right to impose themselves on another in an unwanted fashion. If you're on the receiving end of intrusion, talk with your partner or ex directly about his or her behavior, and firmly express your discontent and discomfort. Use "I" language, avoid "you" language, and make it clear that your privacy is being violated and that the intrusive behavior is unacceptable ("I feel really uncomfortable receiving this gift" or "I am really upset by this, and I feel that my privacy is being invaded"). Importantly, keep your language respectful and polite. Avoid lashing out verbally, especially if you're angry, as it will only escalate the situation. If the person's behavior persists, contact local authorities to see what can be done. If you find yourself engaging in intrusive behaviors, desist immediately. The fact that *you* view your actions as well-intentioned is irrelevant. If you are making a partner or ex feel uncomfortable, you are behaving unethically. If you don't know how to stop, seek counseling from a licensed therapist.

DATING VIOLENCE

Scott and I became friends in grad school, when we both served as instructors with a campus karate club. Scott was originally from Southern California, where he was a kickboxing champion.[7] He was 6 foot 3, all muscle, and had a very long reach—something I learned the hard way when he caught me with an unexpected back-fist on my nose while sparring!

Soon after our friendship began, Scott met Pam, and the two fell for each other hard and fast. But within a few weeks, Scott confessed to me several concerns: Pam was extremely jealous and constantly accused him of cheating. She called him names, swore at him, and ridiculed his sexual performance. She demanded that he no longer go out with his friends, and when he refused, she threatened to leave him. Visiting him one afternoon, I was stunned to see the glass frame of his black-belt certificate shattered. "Yeah," he admitted, "Pam threw it at me the other night." When she learned that Scott was confiding in me, Pam told him a series of lies to alienate him from me: I had "stolen money from him," I had "hit on her," I was "gay and wanted him to myself" (never mind that the last two were contradictory). But Scott stayed with her until she put him in the hospital with a broken nose and third-degree burns across his face. She had demanded that he quit karate, and when he refused, she had hit him in the face with a heated clothes iron. When I asked why he didn't fight back, or at least defend himself (given his abundant skills), he looked at me in disbelief. "I can't hit *a girl*, man. I'm not that kind of guy!"

Dating violence affects millions of people, and as Scott's story shows, despite common beliefs, dating violence knows no demographic boundaries: men and women of all ages, sexual orientations, social classes, ethnicities, and religions experience violence in romantic relationships. According to the Centers for Disease Control, by the time students graduate from high school, 10 percent have experienced dating violence, defined as "being hit, slapped, or physically hurt, on purpose, by a boyfriend or girlfriend in the preceding 12 months" (Centers for Disease Control, 2008). Twenty-one percent of college students report having experienced such violence (National Center for Victims of Crimes, 2008). In addition to physical injuries (and in extreme cases, death), victims of dating violence are more likely than others to suffer from substance abuse, low self-esteem, suicidal thoughts, and eating disorders (Ackard & Neumark-Sztainer, 2002).

It's easy, if you haven't experienced a violent relationship, to think, "Well, the person should have seen it coming!" But this is false, for at least two reasons (Eisikovits & Buchbinder, 2000). First, violence doesn't happen all at once—it typically escalates slowly over time. Also, it often doesn't evolve into full-blown physical violence until relationships are firmly established—making victims all that much more vulnerable, because of their love and commitment. Second, potential abusers often mask their jealousy, violent anger, and excessive need for control in the early stages of a relationship, making it difficult to discern "warning

---

[7]Although the facts of this story are true, the names and demographic information have been changed to protect the identities of the parties involved.

Dealing with a Jealous Partner

1 BACKGROUND

All romantic relationships face challenges. But when a partner whom you love, and who is adored by friends and family, begins behaving erratically because of jealousy, your communication skills and relationship decision making are put to the test. To consider how you might deal with such a dilemma, read the case study and work through the five steps under Your Turn.

2 CASE STUDY

Your relationship with Taegan is the most passionate you've yet experienced, and you consider yourself "head-over-heels in love." Taegan is extremely attractive, and you two share a powerful sexual connection. But sense of humor, intelligence, and charisma are Taegan's most alluring qualities. Your family adores Taegan, and your best friend thinks Taegan is "a hottie." Although your feelings developed quickly, you were surprised by how rapidly Taegan invested: within days of first meeting you, Taegan was insisting, "You and I are meant to be!"

Last week, however, a troubling incident occurred at a party. Taegan and you were having a great time until you decided to spend a few minutes catching up with your friend Chris, whom you hadn't seen in a while. Although you're not romantically interested in Chris, Chris is very attractive. Seeing you hug Chris good-bye, Taegan blew up, "Don't think I don't know what's going on here!" It was so weird and unexpected that you actually thought Taegan was joking. But when you downplayed it with a teasing response, Taegan hissed, "Do you think I'm a fool? I know you're cheating on me!" and stormed off. You were incredibly embarrassed, and apologized to Chris before leaving to find Taegan. Taegan refused to return your text messages for several hours, but when you two finally talked, Taegan offered a tearful apology: "I'm so sorry—it's just that I love you so much; seeing you with Chris made me crazy."

Today you get a call from Chris, asking, "Why did you de-friend me on Facebook?" "I didn't," you respond. "Well, you better check your account, because I've been removed from your friends list!" Puzzled, you sign on, only to find that several of your friends have been deleted, photos of you with your ex have been removed from your albums, and wall postings from Chris and others have been purged. Suspecting Taegan, you call, and Taegan says, "Yes, I changed your page. I watched you type in your password the other day, and used it to gain access. You know what a jealous person I am! You shouldn't have had those photos and messages on your page in the first place!"

3 YOUR TURN

While working through the following steps, keep in mind the concepts, skills, and insights you've learned so far in this book, especially in this chapter. Also remember: there are no right answers, so think hard about the choice you make! (P.S. Need help? Review the *Helpful Concepts* listed below.)

● step 1

Reflect on yourself. What are your thoughts and feelings in this situation? What attributions are you making about Taegan? Are your attributions accurate? Why or why not?

● step 2

Reflect on your partner. Using perspective-taking and empathic concern, put yourself in Taegan's shoes. Consider how your romantic partner is thinking and feeling. How does Taegan likely perceive this situation? How does Taegan feel about you and your relationship?

● step 3

Identify the optimal outcome. Think about all the information you have about Taegan and about this relationship. Consider your own feelings as well as your partner's. Given all these factors, what's the best, most constructive relationship outcome possible here? Be sure to consider not just what's best for you, but what's best for Taegan as well.

● step 4

Locate the roadblocks. Taking into consideration your own thoughts and feelings, Taegan's, and the situation, what's preventing you from achieving the optimal outcome you identified in Step 3?

● step 5

Chart your course. What will you say to Taegan to overcome the roadblocks you've identified and achieve your optimal relationship outcome?

HELPFUL CONCEPTS

Romantic love types, **282–284**

Deciding whether to maintain or end, **306**

Jealousy, **310–311**

Relational intrusion, **311–312**

Dating violence, **313, 316**

table 9.3   Five Common Warning Signs of an Abusive Partner

An abusive partner will . . .

(1) isolate you from others.
Examples: restricting your contact with friends and family, showing extreme paranoid jealousy regarding perceived romantic rivals, or telling you lies about friends and family

(2) use power to control you.
Examples: insisting they make all decisions about leisure activities, including sex; exploding into anger when you "disobey" them; demanding knowledge of your whereabouts; or displaying violence such as throwing or breaking objects

(3) frequently threaten you in various ways.
Examples: threatening to leave you or hurt themselves if you leave, threatening violence against past lovers or perceived romantic rivals, threatening to lie about you to others or file false charges against you, or threatening violence

(4) use emotionally abusive language.
Examples: criticizing your weight, appearance, intelligence, career, or sexual skill; calling you names; swearing at you; or ridiculing your pain when they've hurt you

(5) shift the blame to you.
Examples: blaming you for their jealousy, violence, and destructiveness, or tricking you into behaving badly so they can exploit your guilt

Source: Adapted from "Indicators of Abusive Relationships," An Abuse, Rape, Domestic Violence, Aid and Resource Collection (AARDVARC). Retrieved from http://www.aardvarc.org/dv/symptoms.shtml.

signs" (see Table 9.3 for a detailed list). In Scott's case, both of these reasons played a role in making him vulnerable. Pam seemed perfectly "normal" in the first few weeks of their relationship. She was funny, attractive, smart, and outgoing. By the time the first incidents occurred, he was already in love. And the destructiveness of her behaviors escalated slowly—starting with minor jealous tantrums, and only evolving into violence after many months. As a consequence, Scott didn't perceive Pam's abusiveness as particularly "severe," until she put him in the hospital.

What should *you* do if you find yourself in a relationship with a violent partner? First and foremost, let go of the belief that you can "heal" your partner through love, or "save" him or her by providing emotional support. Relationship repair strategies will not prevent or cure dating violence. Your only option is to extricate yourself from the relationship. As you move toward ending the involvement, keep in mind that the most dangerous time comes immediately after you end the relationship, when the abuser is most angry. So, make sure you cut all ties to the abuser, change your phone numbers, and have ready a *safety plan*: a road map of action for departing the relationship that provides you with the utmost protection. For information on how to develop such a plan, or for help in dealing with an abusive relationship, call the National Domestic Violence Hotline, 1-800-799-SAFE, or visit www.thehotline.org.

The Hard Work of Successful Love

Love is not singular, but plural

Romantic relationships are most satisfying and stand a greater chance of surviving when you and your partner view your bond without illusions and embellishments. When you do this, when you look love square in the face, you'll find that it isn't one simple, clear, obvious thing. Instead, love is complex. Love is triumph *and* heartache. It is passion *and* peaceful companionship. It is joy *and* grief. And keeping love alive is hard work. Some days, your love for your partner will take your breath away. On others, everything they do will annoy you. Most days, it will fall somewhere in between.

Romantic relationships endure because *partners choose to communicate in ways that maintain their relationship*. It's the everyday communication and effort that you and your partner invest that will most enable you to build a satisfying, intimate bond—and sustain it if that's what you choose to do. Enduring couples succeed at love by working at it day in and day out—helping each other with studying or the dishes, cheering each other with kind words following disheartening days at school or work, nursing each other through illness, and even holding each other close as one partner lets go of life.

○ The positive communication decisions you make with your partner have a profound effect on the overall happiness and health of your bond. While successful, satisfying love is something you must consciously work at, it is also one of life's greatest joys.

POSTSCRIPT

We began this chapter with the dying words of a doomed explorer. As Sir Robert Falcon Scott huddled inside his tent, awaiting death, he penned a last letter to his "widow." Of all the possible things he could say during those final moments—the limitless selection of topics and words available to sum up his life—what did he choose to focus upon? *Love.*

When the impassable storms of your life rage around you, what shelter does love provide? If you had but a few hours to live, and were going to craft a final statement, what view of love would you elaborate?

Scott's letter reminds us that love is not one thing, but many. To experience romantic love means to feel passion, practicality, commitment, respect, sentiment, and selflessness—all at the same time. Although no two people ever experience love in exactly the same way, we do share this in common: romantic love may not be essential to life, but it may be essential to joy.

key terms

▶ You can watch brief, illustrative videos of these terms and test your understanding of the concepts online in *VideoCentral: Interpersonal Communication* at bedfordstmartins .com/reflectrelate.

key concepts

Defining Romantic Relationships

- Although **loving** is sometimes thought of as an intense form of **liking**, the two are very different. You can like someone without loving him or her, and love someone without liking the person.

- When people consider what it means to be in love, they frequently think of **passionate love**. Passionate love is experienced across cultures and ages and is distinct from **companionate love**, although many romantic relationships evolve from passionate to companionate love.

- Between the poles of passionate and companionate love are six different love types, although there is not one "right" type of romantic love.

- When both partners in a relationship perceive it as romantic, a **romantic relationship** exists. This relationship often involves **commitment** and **relational dialectics**.

Romantic Attraction

- Attraction is strongly influenced by proximity: how frequently you see others and interact with them. This **mere exposure effect** is one reason for the comparative rarity of interethnic romances.

- Most of us find physically appealing people more attractive than physically unappealing people, and we often attribute a host of positive characteristics to them—the **beautiful-is-good effect**. At the same time, we tend to engage in **matching** when it comes to forming long-term romantic relationships.

- Perceived similarity (in interests, beliefs, and values) plays a powerful role in driving attraction, and in general, the **birds-of-a-feather effect** holds true.

- We tend to be attracted to those we know are attracted to us, a concept known as **reciprocal liking**.

- **Social exchange theory** suggests that attraction to others is driven in part by the resources they can offer you. People perceived as offering many benefits and few costs are seen as desirable. For relationships to survive, however, **equity** must exist in the balance of rewards and costs exchanged between partners.

Relationship Development and Deterioration

- Romantic relationships develop in stages. When coming together, couples commonly go through **initiating** and **experimenting**.

- Some couples move beyond experimenting to **intensifying** and **integrating**. Few relationships progress to **bonding**.
- As relationships come apart, **differentiating** leads partners to believe that their differences are insurmountable. If they fail to constructively deal with differentiating, they may begin **circumscribing** or even **stagnating**.
- Many relationships end by **avoiding**, although couples who feel they need more "closure" may conduct a **terminating** discussion.

Maintaining Romantic Relationships

- Couples who endure typically use several **relational maintenance** tactics. The most common strategies include treating each other in a positive fashion, providing frequent assurances regarding relationship commitment, and sharing tasks.
- Long-distance romantic relationships can create unique maintenance issues. To help maintain long-distance relationships, use multiple forms of technology to communicate, follow the same maintenance tactics as couples who are geographically close, and allow for an adjustment period when both partners are permanently reunited.

The Dark Side of Romantic Relationships

- Perhaps the gravest threat to relationship survival is **romantic betrayal**. Two of the most damaging forms of betrayal are sexual infidelity and deception. These cause profound damage because they create a sense of relational devaluation and a sense of loss.
- Some relationships are challenged by **jealousy**. Online, jealousy can be caused by **wedging**, when someone deliberately interferes in a relationship.
- If a romantic partner uses behaviors that try to control you or invade your privacy, it is called **relational intrusion**. This can create turmoil if the relationship is still intact and anger or fear if the relationship is over.
- Despite common beliefs, dating violence affects both men and women of all ages and ethnicities. If you experience such abuse, reach out for professional help.

key skills

- Want to know which type of love characterizes your relationship? Check out the *Self-Quiz* on page 285.
- Why does similarity generate attraction? Discover the answer on pages 290–291.
- Curious about how your online profile will influence an offline relationship? Learn about the tensions technology can create on pages 292–293.
- How can you communicate in ways that will overcome differentiating? Find the answers on pages 296–297; then complete the *Skills Practice* on page 297.
- What can you do to best deal with a terminating encounter? Review the material on pages 297–298.
- Trying to maintain your romance? Review the tips for using positivity, assurances, sharing tasks, acceptance, self-disclosure, relationship talks, and social networks described on pages 300–304. Then do the *Skills Practice* on page 305 to discover how to integrate these strategies into your online communication with your partner.
- Dealing with a long-distance relationship? See the suggestions for maintenance on pages 304–305.
- Trying to figure out whether your relationship has a bright enough future to invest further effort in maintaining it? Answer the four questions on page 306 to help you decide.
- Wondering if you tend to betray your romantic partners? Take the *Self-Quiz* on page 307 to determine your betrayal potential.
- Need to control or reduce your jealousy? Check out the strategies on pages 310–311; then complete the *Skills Practice* on page 311.
- How can you best deal with relational intrusion? Review the discussion on pages 311–312.
- Not sure how to communicate with a partner displaying jealous tendencies? Try the *Making Relationship Choices* exercise on pages 314–315.

and bad. "They know when I need a kick in the butt and when I need someone to listen. Recently I was feeling sorry for myself after missing a penalty shot at a tournament. My mother found out from my boyfriend, and the next thing you know I get a comforting text message from my dad and a phone call from my mom. She reminded me that it's my choice to continue to play and if I'm going to dwell on mistakes that I shouldn't play anymore. She wants me to be the champion I am—no fear. Gotta love her!"

The Villa family is always willing to sacrifice for one another. For example, Brenda's training camps for the U.S. Team were in Chula Vista—a two-hour commute from Commerce. Her parents drove her, without debate or resentment. As Brenda describes,

"I don't remember asking my parents to do this—they just did it. And I never realized how hard it was for them. My mother would accompany my dad because she was afraid he would fall asleep on the drive home. I didn't appreciate the depth of their sacrifice at the time, as a kid, but now that I'm older, I'm so thankful that they put me first." The willingness to sacrifice communicated a powerful message of love. "Their love is unconditional. It warms my heart to think that my mom would accompany my dad just to keep him awake. *That's* love!"

Though she's one of America's most talented and celebrated female athletes, Brenda Villa remains humble about her accolades. As the Women's Sports Foundation notes, "[Brenda] seems unaware of the splash she has made as role model and hero to Latina athletes. Maybe she's just too busy and too modest by nature" (Lewellen, 2008). But the truth is, Brenda doesn't think of herself as role model—she thinks of her *parents* that way. "I look at their 30-plus years of marriage and how they still always put their kids first. I hope to be as selfless as them with my own children."

Families have a primacy that no other relationships rival. Family members are the first people we see, hear, touch, and interact with. As we grow from infancy to childhood, we learn from family the most basic of skills: how to walk, talk, feed, and clothe ourselves. As we develop further, our families teach us deeper lessons about life akin to those learned by Brenda Villa from her parents: the importance of support, honesty, sacrifice, and love. As our relationships broaden to include friendships and romances, we still use kinship as a metaphor to describe closeness: "How close are we? We're like *family*!" (Rubin, 1996). But family relationships are also compulsory. We don't *choose* our families—we are brought into them by birth, adopted into them by law, or integrated into them by remarriage. When problems arise in our family relationships, the stress is unrivaled. One survey of adults found that the greatest source of emotional strain the preceding day was "family" (Warr & Payne, 1982). When the same sample was asked to name the greatest source of pleasure from the previous day, the answer was identical: "family." Day in and day out, family relationships provide us with our greatest joys and most bitter heartaches (Myers, 2002).

In this chapter, we look at the most influential and enduring of our close involvements: family relationships. You'll learn:

- The defining features of family
- The different ways in which families communicate
- Communication strategies to maintain healthy family relationships
- Challenges that families face, and how to manage them

Defining Family

Family identity is created through communication

When many of us think of family, iconic TV images come to mind, like Chris's family in *Everybody Hates Chris* or the Dunphys from *Modern Family*. These images are simple and comforting: families consist of happily married heterosexual couples raising their biological children, bonded by love, and united in facing any challenges that confront them (Braithwaite et al., 2010).

But families today are more diverse than such depictions suggest. Between 1970 and 2010, the percentage of households composed of married couples with biological children in the United States declined from 40 percent to just 20 percent (Tavernise, 2011). In Canada, this kind of family declined from 55 percent in 1981 to 34.6 percent in 2006 (HRSDC, 2006). Instead, couples are increasingly living together rather than getting married, making marriage less common than at any prior time in history (Cherlin, 2004). Rising divorce rates over the past half century have also decreased the average size of households, as families divide into smaller units and re-form into blended arrangements featuring stepparents and stepchildren. Adding to this complexity, individual families are constantly in flux, as children move out, then lose jobs and move back in with parents;

⬤ Although every family possesses its own distinct identity, all families hold certain things in common. Whether bound together by marriage, blood, or commitment, each family has a profound, shared history made up of the small, everyday moments they spend together.

grandparents join the household to help with daycare or receive care themselves; and spouses separate geographically to pursue job opportunities (Crosnoe & Cavanagh, 2010).

DEFINING CHARACTERISTICS OF FAMILY

The enormous diversity in contemporary families requires a broad, inclusive definition. **Family** is a network of people who share their lives over long periods of time and are bound by marriage, blood, or commitment; who consider themselves as family; and who share a significant history and anticipated future of functioning in a family relationship (Galvin, Brommel, & Bylund, 2004). This definition highlights six characteristics that distinguish families from other social groups.

First, families possess a strong sense of family identity, created by how they communicate (Braithwaite et al., 2010). The way you talk with family members, the stories you exchange, and even the manner in which members of your family deal with conflict all contribute to a shared sense of what your family is like (Tovares, 2010).

Second, families use communication to define boundaries, both inside the family and to distinguish family members from outsiders (Afifi, 2003; Koerner & Fitzpatrick, 2006). As we'll discuss later, some families constrict information that flows out ("Don't talk about our family problems with anyone else"). Some also restrict physical access to the family—for example, by dictating with whom family members can become romantically involved ("No son of mine is going to marry a Protestant!"). Others set few such boundaries. For instance, a family may welcome friends and neighbors as unofficial members, such as an "uncle" or "aunt" who isn't really related to your parents (Braithwaite et al., 2010). A family may even welcome others' children, such as the neighbors across the street whom you think of as your "family away from home." If remarriage occurs and step-families form, these boundaries are renegotiated (Golish, 2003).

Third, the emotional bonds underlying family relationships are intense and complex. Family members typically hold both warm *and* antagonistic feelings toward one another (Silverstein & Giarrusso, 2010). As author Lillian Rubin (1996) notes, family relationships have "an elemental quality that touches the deepest layers of our inner life and stirs our most primitive emotional responses" (p. 256). Consider the strength of feeling that arises in you when you get into an argument with a parent or sibling, or when you celebrate an important milestone (a graduation, a wedding, a new job) with family members.

Fourth, families share a history (Galvin et al., 2004). Such histories can stretch back for generations and feature family members from a broad array of cultures. These histories often set expectations regarding how family members should behave ("We Ngatas have always been an honest bunch, and we're not about to change that now"). Families also share a common future: they expect to maintain their bonds indefinitely. For better or worse, everything you say and do becomes a part of your family history, shaping future interactions and determining whether your family relationships are healthy or destructive.

Fifth, family members may share genetic material (Crosnoe & Cavanagh, 2010). This can lead to shared physical characteristics as well as similar person-alities, outlooks on life, mental abilities, and ways of relating to others. For ex-ample, some studies suggest that interpersonal inclinations such as shyness and aggressiveness are influenced by genes (Carducci & Zimbardo, 1995).

Finally, family members constantly juggle multiple and sometimes compet-ing roles (Silverstein & Giarrusso, 2010). Within your family, you're not just a daughter or son, but perhaps a sibling, a spouse, or an aunt or uncle as well. By the time you reach middle age, you simultaneously may be a parent, spouse, grandparent, daughter or son, *and* sibling—and each of these roles carries with it varying expectations and demands. This makes communicating competently within families challenging.

TYPES OF FAMILY

No "typical" family type exists. Instead, families come in many different forms (Braithwaite et al., 2010). But even these forms are not fixed: you may experi-ence several different family structures as you progress through life and as our larger society evolves. For example, 60 years ago, the **nuclear family**—a wife, husband, and their biological or adopted children—was the most common fam-ily type in North America. Today, it is in the minority. Instead, families may include children or not; have one parent or two; be headed by heterosexual, les-bian, gay, bisexual, or transgendered people; include other relatives such as grand-parents; include stepparents and stepsiblings; or any other combination you can imagine! While we discuss the family types below, consider how your family expe-riences align with or depart from these depictions. But, perhaps most importantly, keep this in mind: *what matters most is not the "type" of family you have, but whom you consider part of your family in terms of love, respect, and communication.*

self-reflection

With whom do you share more intense emotional bonds: family members, or friends, lovers, or cowork-ers? Do you always feel pos-itively toward your family, or do some members consis-tently trigger negative emo-tions in you? What does this tell you about the intensity and complexity of emotional bonds in family relation-ships?

self-reflection

What type of family did you grow up with? What makes you collectively a family—the fact that you are biologically related, live in the same household, or share a strong emotional bond? Now think about other people's families. Are there groups that consider themselves families that you don't? If so, why?

When relatives such as aunts, uncles, parents, children, and grandparents live together in a common household, the result is an **extended family**. By the year 2050, 100 million people in the United States will be over the age of 65, and many of these individuals will be sharing a household with relatives. Numerous Italian American, African American, and Asian American families fall into this category.

Approximately half of marriages in the United States and Canada are remarriages for one or both partners (Coleman, Ganong, & Fine, 2000). This often creates a **stepfamily** in which at least one of the adults has a child or children from a previous relationship (Ganong & Coleman, 1994). Stepfamilies often are called "blended" or "remarried" families. More than 50 percent of children born throughout the twenty-first century will grow up in stepfamilies (Crosnoe & Cavanagh, 2010).

Some couples live together prior to or instead of marriage. These **cohabiting couples** consist of two unmarried, romantically involved adults living together in a household, with or without children. Cohabitation is steadily increasing in Western societies (Adams, 2004). This is partly due to an increase in cohabitation among middle-aged and older adults, many of whom were formerly married but now want the relational flexibility that cohabitation affords (Silverstein & Giarrusso, 2010). Cohabitation is far from new, however; it has long been popular in poorer, less-industrialized countries (Adams, 2004).

In a **single-parent family**, only one adult resides in the household, possessing sole responsibility as caregiver for the children. As of 2011, 27 percent of children in the United States (U.S. Census Bureau, 2011) and about 16 percent of children in Canada (HRSDC, 2006) were growing up in single-parent households.

FAMILY STORIES

Characteristics and types define families from the outside looking in. But from the inside, one of the most powerful ways we define our collective family identity is to share stories (Tovares, 2010). For example, when I was growing up, family storytelling was a nightly ritual. Some tales were from my parents' college days, like the time my dad and his buddies filled a friend's dorm room from floor to ceiling with wadded-up newspaper while the friend was away for the weekend. Others were created from shared family experiences, like when I fed

◖ No matter who is in them, families are some of the most central and formative interpersonal relationships that we have.

my scrambled eggs to my dog Lottie because I didn't want to eat them. Then Lottie regurgitated them in front of my mom, incriminating me. Now, years later, when we get together for visits, we relive and retell these stories and others like them, enjoying the sense of family history they provide.

Family stories are narrative accounts shared repeatedly within a family that retell historical events and are meant to bond the family together (Stone, 2004). Such stories help create and promote a unique family identity by teaching individuals about their role in the family and about the family's norms, values, and goals (Kellas, 2005). They also provide powerful images of family relationships. When people tell family stories, they typically lace their narratives with opinions and emotions that make clear how they feel about other family members (Vangelisti, Crumley, & Baker, 1999). Importantly, it's not just the content of the stories that bonds families together; it's the activity of storytelling. Family members often collaborate in telling stories: adding details, disagreeing, correcting discrepancies, and confirming perspectives (Kellas, 2005).

However, family stories aren't always positive; some criticize family values, condemn specific family members' actions, or discourage dissent. These stories may also involve family histories of abandonment, abuse, or parental oppression—and corresponding lessons about how *not* to parent (Goodsell, Bates, & Behnke, 2010). While families share many types of stories, three stand out as especially potent in affirming family identity: *courtship stories*, *birth stories*, and *survival stories* (Stone, 2004).

Courtship Stories   One of my family's most poignant stories tells how my dad serenaded my mom from the courtyard of her dorm at Pomona College, while she stood on her balcony listening. Forty-five years later, my parents and I visited Pomona. While driving around campus, Mom suddenly shouted "Stop!" and leapt from the car. Dad and I followed her into a well-worn building, only to find her standing in the very courtyard that I had heard described so many times. Mom stood there, gazing at the balcony where she'd listened to Dad's song more than four decades earlier. "There it is," she whispered, "the spot where your father serenaded me," and her eyes filled with tears.

Some families share *courtship stories* about how the parents fell in love. Courtship stories emphasize the solidity of the parents' relationship, which children find

self-
reflection

What are the most memorable family stories that were shared with you during your upbringing? What lessons did they teach you about your family and the values that you share? Did the stories function to bring you together as a family, or drive you apart?

⬮ Sharing old photographs can bring family stories to life by providing lasting, powerful images of family relationships. Do you associate any particular images or other mementos with your favorite family stories?

reassuring. But perhaps most important, such stories give children a framework for understanding romantic love, by suggesting what one should feel about love, and how to recognize it when it occurs (Stone, 2004).

Birth Stories Families also may share *birth stories*, which describe the latter stages of pregnancy, childbirth, and early infancy of a child. Birth stories help children understand how they fit into the family ("You'll always be the baby"), which roles they're expected to play ("Firstborns are always so independent"), and what their parents hope and dream for them ("We knew from the moment you were born that you'd accomplish great things!").

Unlike biological children, adopted children often have little knowledge of their birth or birth parents. Consequently, the stories that adoptive parents create about how and why the children entered their adoptive families—known as *entrance stories*—are important in providing the child with a sense of personal identity and self-esteem (Krusiewicz & Wood, 2001). Entrance stories also help heal the broken bond with birth parents, by giving the child an explanation of why the adoption occurred. For example, one of the most common and constructive entrance stories involves framing the birth mother's decision as altruistic: "the loving, painful decision of an amazing, caring woman" (Krusiewicz & Wood, 2001, p. 793).

Survival Stories *Survival stories* relate the coping strategies family members have used to deal with major challenges. Survival in these stories may be physical—as in the accounts that combat soldiers and famine victims tell. Or, survival may refer to a family member's ability to prevail by achieving a level of financial stability or other forms of success. Survival stories give children the sense that they come from a tough, persevering family, which prepares them to face their own difficulties. For example, the mother of water polo star Brenda Villa (featured in our chapter opener) emigrated from Mexico when she was only 18, following the death of her father.[2] She came to the United States to earn money and help support her family back home. This story of struggle and hardship inspired Brenda to work hard and achieve her own goals.

Telling Family Stories The breadth and depth of your family experiences provide a rich resource to share with family members. But not all shared experiences are ones your family members would like to relive. To ensure that family stories strengthen, rather than erode, family relationships, select experiences that cast the

---

[2]Excerpted from interview with author, July 13, 2011. Published with permission.

family and individual members in a positive light and that emphasize unity rather than discord. When sharing stories with younger family members, keep in mind that they will learn values from your story (Tovares, 2010). Ask yourself whether the story sends the message you intend about your family's values.

Stories that cast individual family members in a humorous light require special care. Although such stories may be perfectly appropriate to share, make sure that the "target" family member enjoys and agrees to the telling. For example, you might repeatedly revisit the time your brother brought home an exceptionally strange date or recount the day your father accidentally drove the car through the garage wall while miraculously avoiding injury. Avoid sharing stories that breach personal confidences ("John never told any of you what *really* happened, but here it is!") or that make sport of family members in ways they don't enjoy. When in doubt, simply (but privately) ask the family member whether he or she wants you to share the story. If the answer is "no," keep silent.

Communicating in Families

Communication patterns determine how families converse

Few literary families rival the Weasleys from the *Harry Potter* series in terms of closeness and camaraderie.[3] Their intimacy is shown through their communication: the importance they place upon sharing conversation and the diversity of topics available for discussion. When Harry first visits the Weasleys, he learns that the family is almost always together—and they actually *enjoy* each other's company! Few topics are off-limits. Mr. Weasley even talks about a subject loathsome to most magical people: the study of Muggles (nonmagical folk). "Mr. Weasley liked Harry to sit next to him at the dinner table so that he could bombard him with questions about life with the Muggles, asking him to explain how things like plugs and the postal service worked" (1999, p. 42). Harry, who has never experienced such intimacy and openness in a family, is awed: "This is the best house I've ever been in!" His life at home with the Dursleys is the complete opposite. There is little interest in sharing conversation, and they are fiercely incurious about activities or people outside of their own, narrow sphere of interests. Growing up, Harry learns "Don't ask questions—that was the first rule for a quiet life with the Dursleys" (1997, p. 20). Another rule discouraged bringing up unusual topics: "If there was one thing the Dursleys hate even more than [Harry's] asking questions, it was his talking about anything acting in a way it shouldn't, no matter if it was in a dream or even a cartoon" (p. 26).

Like the fictional Weasleys and Dursleys, our own families' communication is guided by shared beliefs about how families should converse. These beliefs, and the resulting interpersonal communication, are known as *family communication patterns* (Koerner & Fitzpatrick, 2002). Family communication patterns evolve from two communication dimensions, which we'll discuss next.

---

[3]The content that follows is adapted from Rowling (1997) and Rowling (1999).

⬡ In the *Harry Potter* series, the Weasleys are high on conversation orientation and low on conformity orientation, encouraging individual expression and appreciating one another's ideas, while the Dursleys are low on conversation orientation and high on conformity orientation, avoiding conversation with one another and valuing uniformity above all else. Where does your family fall on the conformity and conversation orientation spectrum?

COMMUNICATION DIMENSIONS

According to **Family Communication Patterns Theory** (Koerner & Fitzpatrick, 2006), two dimensions underlie the communication between family members. The first is **conversation orientation**: the degree to which family members are encouraged to participate in unrestrained interaction about a wide array of topics. Families high on conversation orientation are like the Weasleys: they believe that open and frequent communication is essential to an enjoyable and rewarding family life. Consequently, they interact often, freely, and spontaneously without many limitations placed on time spent together and topics discussed.

In contrast, families with a low conversation orientation are like the Dursleys; they view interpersonal communication as something irrelevant and unnecessary for a satisfying, successful family life. Such families interact only infrequently and limit their conversations to a few select topics—weather, daily activities, current events, and the like. Disclosure of intimate thoughts and feelings between family members is discouraged, as is debate of attitudes and perspectives.

The second dimension is **conformity orientation**, the degree to which families believe that communication should emphasize similarity or diversity in attitudes, beliefs, and values. Like the Dursleys, high conformity families use their interactions to highlight and enforce uniformity of thought. Such families are sometimes perceived as more "traditional," because children are expected to obey parents and other elders, who (in turn) are counted on to make family decisions. Members of these families tend to prioritize family relationships over outside connections such as friendships and romantic involvements. Moreover, they are expected to sacrifice their personal goals for the sake of the family.

Low conformity families like the Weasleys communicate in ways that emphasize diversity in attitudes, beliefs, and values, and that encourage members' uniqueness, individuality, and independence. These families typically view outside relationships as equally important to those within the family, and they prioritize individual over family interests and goals. In low conformity families, children contribute to family decision making, and members view the family as a vehicle for individual growth rather than a collective in which members must sacrifice their own interests for the good of the whole.

FAMILY COMMUNICATION PATTERNS

According to communication scholars Ascan Koerner and Mary Anne Fitzpatrick (2006), conversation and conformity dimensions give rise to four possible family communication patterns: consensual, pluralistic, protective, and laissez-faire.

What Communication Pattern Does Your Family Have?

self-QUIZ

Place a check mark next to each statement with which you agree. Then check your score to determine your family communication pattern.

Conversation Orientation

_____ In my family, we often talk about our plans and hopes for the future.

_____ We frequently talk as a family about the things we have done during the day.

_____ My parents tend to be very open about their emotions.

_____ I really enjoy talking with my parents, even when we disagree.

_____ My parents and I often have long, relaxed conversations about nothing in particular.

_____ In our family, we often discuss our feelings together.

_____ I can tell my parents almost anything.

_____ My parents often ask my opinion when the family is talking about something important.

_____ My parents frequently say things like, "Every member of this family should have some say in decisions."

Conformity Orientation

_____ When anything really important is involved, my parents expect me to obey without question.

_____ In our home, my parents usually have the last word.

_____ My parents feel that it is important that they be the boss.

_____ My parents sometimes become irritated when my views differ from theirs.

_____ If my parents don't approve of a particular behavior, they don't want to know about it.

_____ When I am at home, I am expected to obey my parents' rules.

_____ My parents often say things like, "My ideas are right, and you shouldn't question them."

_____ My parents often say things like, "There are some things that just shouldn't be talked about."

_____ My parents often say things like, "You'll know better when you're older."

Note: This *Self-Quiz* is adapted from the Revised Family Communication Pattern Instrument (Ritchie & Fitzpatrick, 1990).

Scoring: For each orientation, a total number of check marks of 0–4 indicates "Low," and a total of 5–9 indicates "High." High conversation/high conformity suggests that your family is consensual; high conversation/low conformity, pluralistic; low conversation/high conformity, protective; and low conversation/low conformity, laissez-faire.

▶ Sitting down and sharing a meal often gives families the opportunity to catch up on daily events, discuss issues large and small, make decisions, and even deal with conflicts. When your family has a meal together, what do you talk about? How does this align with what you perceive as your family communication pattern?

VideoCentral ◉

bedfordstmartins.com
/reflectrelate

Consensual Families
*Watch this clip online
to answer the questions
below.*

How does the family in the video exhibit both high conversation and conformity orientation? In what types of situations has your own family used a more "consensual" approach to communication? Why?

Consensual Families   Families high in both conversation and conformity are **consensual families**. In such families, members are encouraged to openly share their views with one another as well as debate these beliefs. Consensual family communication is marked by high disclosure, attentive listening, and frequent expressions of caring, concern, and support toward one another (Rueter & Koerner, 2008). At the same time, consensual family members are expected to steadfastly share a single viewpoint. Parents in such households typically exert strong control over the attitudes, behaviors, and interactions of their children (Rueter & Koerner, 2008). For example, parents may encourage their children to share their thoughts and feelings about important issues ("What do you think we should do?"), but then make clear that only one perspective (the parents') is acceptable. Because of their emphasis on conformity, consensual families perceive conflict as intensely threatening. Consequently, they address conflicts as they occur and seek to resolve them as constructively as possible to preserve family unity.

Pluralistic Families   Families high in conversation but low in conformity are **pluralistic families**. They communicate in open and unconstrained ways, discussing a broad range of topics and exploring them in depth. Pluralistic families enjoy debating the issues of the day, and judge one another's arguments on their merit rather than whether they mesh with other members' attitudes. People in pluralistic families typically don't try to control other family members' beliefs or attitudes (Rueter & Koerner, 2008). Since parents don't feel compelled to wield power over their children, children's contributions to family discussions and decision making are treated as relevant and equally valid. For example, parents in a pluralistic family might ask for their children's opinions regarding a job opportunity ("Should Mom accept the offer from TelCo?") or a family vacation ("Where should we go this year?"). Pluralistic families deal directly with conflict, seeking to resolve disputes in productive, mutually beneficial ways. They may, for instance, establish "official" times (such as mealtimes or family meetings) when members can vent their concerns and work collaboratively to settle them. For this reason, pluralistic family members report the highest rates of conflict resolution of any of the four family types.

Protective Families　　**Protective families** are low on conversation and high on conformity. Communication in these families functions to maintain obedience and enforce family norms, and little value is placed on the exchange of ideas or the development of communication skills. Parent-child power differences are firmly enforced, and children are expected to quietly obey. Sayings such as "Children should be seen and not heard" and "Children should speak when spoken to" reflect this mind-set. Parents invest little effort in creating opportunities for family discussion, and the result is low levels of disclosure amongst family members (Rueter & Koerner, 2008). Protective families avoid conflict because it threatens the conformity they value and because they often lack the skills necessary to manage conflicts constructively. Members may tell each other, "Don't make waves," or "You don't want to cause trouble."

Laissez-Faire Families　　Families low in both conversation and conformity are **laissez-faire families**. Few emotional bonds exist between their members, resulting in low levels of caring, concern, and support expressed within the family (Rueter & Koerner, 2008). Their detachment shows itself in a lack of interaction and a decided disinterest in activities that might foster communication or maintenance of the family as a unit. Similar to parents in pluralistic families, laissez-faire parents believe that children should be independent thinkers and decision makers. But this belief derives from their disinterest in their children's thoughts and decisions. Such parents tend to leave it up to their children to form their own opinions regarding sexual behavior, drug and alcohol usage, and educational achievement. Because members of such families interact infrequently, they rarely get embroiled in conflict. If a disagreement does erupt, they avoid it or (if they feel strongly invested in the issues at stake) they compete to "win" the debate.

VideoCentral ▣

bedfordstmartins.com
/reflectrelate

Protective Families
*Watch this clip online
to answer the questions
below.*

In your view, what are the potential advantages and disadvantages of protective families? Do you think family patterns might change as the children grow older?

　Want to see more? Check out VideoCentral for clips illustrating **pluralistic families** and **laissez-faire families**.

Maintaining Family Relationships

All family relationships need constant maintenance

When Arizona caseworker Heather Shew-Plummer met Steven and Roger Ham, she knew they would be ideal adoptive parents.[4] They were "patient, loving, fun and ceaseless advocates for kids." Shew-Plummer helped the Hams adopt a young Hispanic boy, Michael. But Michael worried about his four younger siblings, who were still in foster care. "These kids obviously loved one another," Steven says. "I knew they had to be together, and I was going to make that happen." Eventually, the couple adopted *all* of Michael's siblings and worked

---

[4]All information that follows is adapted from Bland (2011).

to reassure the children about the family's stability by telling them, "*This* [family] is forever." Seeing their success, caseworkers began placing children of all ethnicities, ages, and abilities with the Hams. They now have twelve.

Critical to their family success is the positive atmosphere Steven and Roger create. "They are really supportive of anything I do," says their daughter Vanessa, and their constant encouragement traverses many varied activities: basketball, karate, ROTC, and cheerleading. The Hams also emphasize open, honest communication. Some of their kids are old enough to remember their troubled previous lives, and the Hams discuss their pasts forthrightly, helping the children to grieve and move forward. "Children should be able to come to you about anything," Steven says. But more than anything else, the Ham family focuses on love. "A loving home is a loving home," Roger says. "Our kids have two parents who love them; not all of their friends do."

The story of the Ham family reminds us of a simple truth: *we create our families through how we communicate.* Although you're only one member of your family, the interpersonal choices you make—and what you say and do as a result—ripple outward. To help boost your family's closeness and happiness, use your interpersonal communication skills to maintain your family relationships and work carefully to balance ongoing family tensions.

MAINTENANCE STRATEGIES FOR FAMILIES

Many people take their family relationships for granted. Instead of communicating in ways designed to maintain these relationships, people assume that "your family is always there for you" (Vogl-Bauer, 2003). As a consequence, we often treat family members less favorably than we treat individuals who have no biological or legal connection to us. But all family relationships need constant

▶ On the sitcom *Modern Family*, Phil and Claire Dunphy encourage their family to make time for one another and to practice positive, respectful communication. By doing so, Phil and Claire uphold positive family maintenance strategies and cultivate a supportive environment for the family (even when that means getting Phil to do something he doesn't want to!).

maintenance to be sustained. As illustrated by Steven and Roger Ham, three of the most important strategies for maintaining family relationships are positivity, assurances, and self-disclosure (Vogl-Bauer, 2003).

Positivity The most powerful maintenance tactic for families is *positivity* (Stafford, 2010). In family settings, this means communicating with your family members in an upbeat and hopeful fashion. To implement positivity in your family encounters, start doing favors for other family members without being asked, and unexpectedly gift them in little ways that show you care. Invest energy into making each encounter with family members enjoyable. Avoid complaining about family problems that have no solutions; ridiculing family members; whining or sulking when you don't get your way; and demanding that caregivers, siblings, or other kin give you favored treatment.

Assurances The second way you can bolster your family relationships is by offering regular *assurances* of how much your family means to you. Let other family members know that you consider your relationship with each of them unique and valuable, and that you are committed to maintaining these bonds well into the future ("I love you," "I will always be here for you," "I miss you," or "I can't wait to be home again so I can spend time with you"). Avoid devaluing family relationships in front of others ("They're *just* my family") and commenting on how other families are superior to yours ("I'd give anything to have other parents").

Self-Disclosure *Self-disclosure* in family relationships means sharing your private thoughts and feelings with family members and allowing them to do the same without fear of betrayal. You do this by treating other family members in ways that are consistent, trustworthy, and ethical. Ways to practice self-disclosure include making time in your schedule to talk with parents, siblings, or children about how they are doing; encouraging them to share their feelings and concerns with you; and offering your perspectives in a cooperative, respectful way. It also means avoiding communication practices that undermine disclosure, such as betraying confidences, refusing to make time for family conversation, reacting defensively when family members share their feelings with you, disparaging family members' viewpoints, and hiding things from your family.

TECHNOLOGY AND FAMILY MAINTENANCE

My parents live two thousand miles away from me, in an isolated valley in southern Oregon. But we "talk" several times each week by e-mail—exchanging cartoons, photos, and articles of interest. My nephew John, a student at the University of Washington, chats with me regularly via Facebook. And my oldest son, Kyle, while doing his homework upstairs, routinely sends me music and movie clips—even as I sit in our living room below, working.

Although some lament that technology has replaced face-to-face interaction and reduced family intimacy ("Families are always on the computer and never *talk* any more!"), families typically use online and face-to-face communication in

Making You Noise
—for my mother

The day before you are deaf
completely, I will make you
noise. I will bring birds,
bracelets, chimes to hang
in the wind. We will drive
from Idaho to Washington again,
and I will read to keep you
awake, and I will tap
little poems on the backs
of your arms, your neck
to be sure you hear me.
I will play spoons on your body
in restaurants, smack
my lips, heave you
sighs, each one deeper
than the rest. We will finally
shout. And then, as quiet
slips in, settling over,
I will speak. I will keep speaking.
I will sing you nonsense songs
until you go to sleep.

By Francesca Bell

skills practice

Technology and Family Maintenance
Ways to communicate positivity and assurances to family members

❶ Send an e-mail to a family member with whom you've been out of touch, letting him or her know you care.

❷ Offer congratulations via text or e-mail to a family member who has recently achieved an important goal.

❸ Post a message on the Facebook page of a family member with whom you've had a disagreement, saying that you value his or her opinions and beliefs.

❹ Send an e-card to a long-distance family member, sharing a message of affection.

❺ Post a supportive response to a family member who has expressed concerns via Twitter or Facebook.

a complementary, rather than substitutive, fashion. Families who communicate frequently via e-mail, Facebook, and IM *also* communicate frequently face-to-face or on the phone. They typically choose synchronous modes of communication (face-to-face, phone) for personal or urgent matters, and asynchronous modes (e-mail, text, Facebook) for less important issues (Tillema, Dijst, & Schwanen, 2010). What's more, technology, especially the use of cell phones, allows families to connect, share, and coordinate their lives to a degree never before possible, resulting in boosted intimacy and satisfaction (Kennedy, Smith, Wells, & Wellman, 2008). Similarly, families whose members are geographically separated but who use online communication to stay in touch report higher satisfaction, stronger intimacy, more social support, and reduced awareness of the physical separation, compared to families who don't (McGlynn, 2007).

Despite being comparatively "old school," e-mail is the dominant electronic way families communicate. Interpersonal scholar Amy Janan Johnson and her colleagues found that more than half of college students reported interacting with family members via e-mail in the preceding week and that the primary purpose of these e-mails was relationship maintenance (Johnson, Haigh, Becker, Craig, & Wigley, 2008). Students used e-mail to maintain *positivity* ("Have a great day!"), provide *assurances* ("I love you and miss you!"), and *self-disclose* ("I'm feeling a bit scared about my stats exam tomorrow").

Of course, the biggest advantage of online communication is that, unlike face-to-face and phone, it lets you get in touch with family members at any time (Oravec, 2000). For example, my folks and I live in different time zones, making it difficult to find times we can talk. But we still share day-to-day events and interests via e-mail and text messages. Rarely a day goes by when I don't receive a message from my mom detailing their dog Teddy's latest feat of canine intelligence, or from my dad about his progress on his MG "project car." Such messages make us feel close, even though we're thousands of miles apart.

DEALING WITH FAMILY DIALECTICS

Within all families, tension exists between competing impulses, known as *relational dialectics* (see Chapter 9). Two dialectics are especially pronounced in families: *autonomy versus connection* and *openness versus protection*. As we mature, each of us must balance our desire for autonomy against the connection that we share with our families and the corresponding expectations and obligations regarding who we "should" be as family members. We also face frequent decisions regarding how openly we should communicate with other family members, as well as how much information about our families we should share with those outside the family unit. Balancing these tensions is challenging. However, you *can* strike a balance—by applying the techniques described below.

Balancing Autonomy and Connection   Even though you may feel intensely connected to your family, you probably also struggle to create your own separate identity. You may enjoy the feeling of intimacy that connectedness brings, while resenting how your family seems blind to your true abilities: "My family insists on seeing me as the family clown," or "My family doesn't think I can make mature decisions because I'm the youngest."

The tension between autonomy and connection in families is especially difficult to manage during adolescence (Crosnoe & Cavanagh, 2010). As children move through their teen years, they begin to assert their independence from parents. Their peers eventually replace parents and other family members as having the most influence on their interpersonal decisions (Golish, 2000).

How can you best manage the tension between autonomy and connection in your family? Use two additional relationship maintenance strategies discussed in Chapter 9—sharing tasks and cultivating social networks. In this case, however, it is important to strike a balance between family relationships and outside relationships. First, for sharing tasks you want to balance your dependence on family members to help you carry out everyday chores with a reliance on yourself and people outside your family. Too much dependence on family members—especially for tasks you could accomplish on your own—can erode your self-reliance, self-confidence, and independence (Strauss, 2006).

Second, examine your social networks (including your family), and assess the degree to which family members constitute the closest people in your life. As

self-reflection

Who has more influence in shaping your relationship decisions: your family or your friends? Whom do you look to for emotional support in times of need? Has the degree to which you depend on your family versus your friends changed over time? If so, why?

○ As in any relationship, conflict is an unavoidable part of family life.

Autonomy and Class: Helicopter Parents

Robyn Lewis's sons may attend college, but it doesn't mean her involvement in their lives has lessened (ABCnews.go.com, 2005). She creates daily "to do" lists for them, checks their grades and bank accounts online, proofreads their papers, and screens their e-mail. "It's nice to have someone who serves as a secretary mom," says son Brendan. Robyn's response? "I think that's great—a secretary helps keep the boss focused and organized, right?"

In the United States, people have different views of how families should balance autonomy with connection, and these differences often cut along class lines. Middle- and upper-income parents (such as Lewis) are more inclined to view their role as cultivating their children's talents in a highly orchestrated fashion (Lareau, 2003). Organized activities, created and controlled by parents, dominate these children's lives. In extreme form, these children have little or no autonomy, as parents "hover" over all aspects of their lives like helicopters. Technology facilitates such hovering: parents can check up on their kids 24/7 through Facebook, text-messaging, and e-mail.

Lower-income parents, however, tend to view their role as allowing their children to mature without adult interfer-

ence (Lareau, 2003). These children often have more independence in their leisure activities—they are free to roam their neighborhoods and play with friends, for example—as opposed to participating in arranged "playdates." And when they enter college or the work world, their parents continue to let them develop primarily on their own.

Public elementary and secondary schools in the United States strongly endorse intense connection between parents and children, and they structure their curricula and school-related activities accordingly (Lareau, 2003). But many believe that such intense connectedness does a disservice to children, especially as they mature (Strauss, 2006). For instance, Linda Walter, administrator at Seton Hall University, maintains that "many young adults entering college have the academic skills they need to succeed, but are lacking in self-reliance" (Strauss, 2006).

discussion questions

- How has your parents' or caregivers' approach to balancing autonomy and connection influenced their relationship with you? Are they "helicopters"?
- What are the advantages and disadvantages of the way your parents or caregivers balanced your connection with them and your autonomy?

with sharing tasks, a balance between family relationships and outside connections is ideal. If you have few or even no close ties with anyone outside of the family sphere, you may feel intensely dependent on your family and experience a corresponding loss of autonomy. Likewise, having no close ties to any family members can create a sense of independence so extreme that you feel little emotional bond with your family.

Balancing Openness and Protection   Families also experience tension between openness and protection. In any close relationship—family bonds included—we want both to share personal information and to protect ourselves from the possible negative consequences of such sharing (Afifi & Steuber, 2010). In families, the tension between these two needs is even more pronounced. For example, your family may be extremely close, and as a consequence almost anything that you tell one family member quickly becomes common knowledge.

◐ In the movie *The Descendants*, the family dialectics for Matt King (George Clooney) shift dramatically when he becomes a single parent to daughters Alexandra and Scottie. In his new role, Matt faces family obligations and expectations previously unknown to him, while Alexandra and Scottie are disoriented by their mother's absence and the greater autonomy it affords them.

This creates a dilemma when you want to share something with only one family member. Do you disclose the information, knowing that within a week's time your entire family will also know it, or do you withhold it?

According to **Communication Privacy Management Theory** (Petronio, 2000), individuals create informational boundaries by carefully choosing the kind of private information they reveal and the people with whom they share it. These boundaries are constantly shifting, depending on the degree of risk associated with disclosing information. The more comfortable people feel disclosing, the more likely they are to reveal sensitive information. Inversely, people are less likely to share when they expect negative reactions to the disclosure (Afifi & Steuber, 2010).

Within families, these boundaries are defined by **family privacy rules**: the conditions governing what family members can talk about, how they can discuss such topics, and who should have access to family-relevant information (Petronio & Caughlin, 2006). In some families, members feel free to talk about any topic, at any time, and in any situation. In other families, discussion of more sensitive topics such as politics and religion may be permissible only in certain settings. Your family might talk about religion immediately after attending services together or debate political issues over dinner, but you might not discuss such matters during breakfast or on the golf course. Or, some topics may be permanently excluded from your family discussion altogether: personal sexual history, assault, or abuse; severe legal or financial woes; or extreme health problems. Breaking a family privacy rule by forcing discussion of a "forbidden" topic can cause intense emotional discomfort among other family members and may prompt the family to exclude the "rule breaker" from future family interactions.

self-reflection

What topics, if any, are off-limits for discussion within your family? Why are these topics taboo? What would be the consequences of forcing a discussion on these issues? How does not being able to talk about these things with family members make you feel about your family?

Keep this in mind before you force discussion of an issue that other family members consider off-limits.

Family privacy rules govern *how* family members talk about topics as well—including what's considered an acceptable opinion and how deeply family members can explore these opinions. It may be acceptable to talk at any time about the personal lives of your various family members, for instance, but only if your comments are positive. Or it may be permissible to discuss religion after church, but only if you have a certain viewpoint.

Additionally, family privacy rules identify the people with whom family members can talk. If your family holds a particular religious or political viewpoint that is at odds with surrounding neighbors' views, you might be instructed to avoid these topics when conversing with neighborhood friends. ("This stays within the family," or "Don't talk about this at school.")

Although family privacy rules help members know how to balance openness and protection, they can also amplify tension within families as people age. When children grow up, the parent-child relationship often shifts from being authority based to friendship based (Silverstein & Giuarrusso, 2010). As this occurs, people may feel pressure to change long-standing privacy rules. For example, even if your family has never openly discussed severe illness, you may feel compelled to talk about this topic if your mother starts displaying early symptoms of Alzheimer's disease.

How can you improve your family privacy rules and, in doing so, bring about a better balance of openness and protection? First, remember that all families have approved and taboo conversational topics, certain viewpoints they promote over others, and people whom they include or exclude from receiving information about the family. Effective family privacy rules aren't "one size fits all." Instead, they should strike the balance between openness and protection that best fits your family. Second, be respectful of the varying opinions and preferences individual family members have regarding openness and protection. Keep in mind that if your family communication pattern is low on conversation orientation and high on conformity orientation, any push for a change in privacy rules may strike others as a threat to the family.

Finally, if you believe that your family privacy rules should be altered to allow greater openness or increased protection, avoid abrupt, dramatic, and demanding calls for change—"We need to learn how to talk more openly about sex!" Such pronouncements will likely offend family members and put them on the defensive. Instead, identify a single family member who you think might share your views. Discuss your desire for change with him or her by using your interpersonal competence skills and cooperative language (Chapters 1 and 6). Ask this person's opinion on the possibility of modifying your family's privacy rules, and invite him or her to suggest ideas for implementing the change. If he or she agrees that change is needed, identify an additional family member who might also concur. Then initiate a three-way discussion. Changes in long-standing family privacy rules—especially for low conversation, high conformity families—are best accomplished slowly through interactions with one family member at a time.

skills practice

Changing Family Communication Rules
Changing communication about an important issue that's being avoided

❶ Identify an important issue that your family currently avoids discussing.

❷ Select one family member who might be open to talking about this concern.

❸ Initiate a discussion with this person, using competent and cooperative language.

❹ Mutually create a plan for how the issue can be raised with other family members and what exactly you both will say.

❺ Implement your plan, one additional family member at a time.

Family Relationship Challenges

Managing stepfamily transitions and family conflicts

In the movie *Life as a House*, Hayden Christensen plays Sam Monroe, a 16-year-old struggling to deal with his fractured family life. His birth parents, George and Robin, suffered a bitter divorce a decade earlier, and now they can't have even a casual conversation without a fight erupting. Their constant arguing haunts Sam, who feels torn between them. Making matters worse, he finds no comfort at home with his stepfamily, in which all attention and affection is channeled toward Robin's new children (and Sam's half-brothers), Adam and Ryan. Mired in despair, Sam numbs his pain with pot, pharmaceuticals, and inhalants. But when his father George is diagnosed with terminal cancer, the family is transformed. George forces Sam to live with him for the summer, and they work together to build a seaside house. As they live and labor together, the bond between father and son is slowly rekindled, and the rifts between Sam and his mother, and between his mother and father, are repaired.

We like to think of family relationships as simple, straightforward, and uniformly positive. Family consists of the most supportive people in our lives—individuals whom we like, love, and depend on. For many people this is true. But as *Life as a House* reminds us, family relationships also face daunting challenges. Three of the most difficult to navigate are stepfamily transition, parental favoritism, and interparental conflict.

◯ Perhaps one of the more powerful messages from the movie *Life as a House* is that even families facing daunting challenges—like divorce, stepfamily transitions, and interparental conflict—can still work together to overcome obstacles and strengthen their relationships.

STEPFAMILY TRANSITION

Transitioning to a stepfamily is a common challenge, given that approximately half of the marriages in the United States and Canada involve a re-marriage for one or both partners (Coleman, Ganong, & Fine, 2000). While most people enter into stepfamilies with the best intentions for a new start, not all stepfamily members experience the transition equally. As illustrated by Sam in *Life as a House*, adolescents tend to have more difficulty transitioning into a stepfamily than preadolescents or young adults. Studies have found that children in stepfamilies have more frequent behavioral problems, turbulent relationships, and lower self-esteem than children in first-marriage families (Golish, 2003).

The majority of stepfamilies confront very similar challenges, including negotiating new family privacy rules, discrepancies in conflict management styles, and building solidarity as a family unit (Golish, 2003). But the most frequent and perplexing challenge is **triangulation**: loyalty conflicts that arise when a coalition is formed, uniting one family member with another against a third person (Schrodt & Afifi, 2007). Two forms of triangulation are common within stepfamilies: children feeling caught between their custodial and non-custodial parents, and stepparents feeling caught between the children in their stepfamily (Golish, 2003). Family members caught in triangulation feel "torn" between different loyalties. As one daughter described her triangulation between her birth parents, "I would carry things from her, she'd say stuff about him, and he'd do the same and talk about her. It's kind of hard to get both sides of it. So I avoided them for a while . . . I just felt that I was caught in the middle" (Golish, 2003, p. 52).

Given such challenges, how can *you* help ease the transition to a stepfamily, should you experience it? Try these suggestions:

1. *Go slow, but start early.* Except for the couple getting married, the relationships between other stepfamily members are involuntary. Yet stepfamily members often feel pressure to immediately become intimate (Ganong, Coleman, Fine, & Martin, 1999). This can cause stress and anxiety, as no one enjoys feeling forced to be close to others. To avoid this, *go slow* in building ties with your stepparents, stepchildren, or stepsiblings. Take the time to get to know one another, forging relationships in the same way you would any other interpersonal involvements—by having fun and doing things together. If possible, *start early* in creating these bonds— ideally as soon as it becomes certain that a stepfamily will form. Not doing so can lead to tension and conflict later, when the stepfamily formally becomes a family unit.

2. *Practice daily maintenance.* Research on stepfamilies emphasizes the importance of displaying affection, attending important activities and events, engaging in everyday talk, and sharing humorous stories—the behaviors fundamental to all families (Afifi, 2003). Try to express your

---

self-reflection

Call to mind an instance of triangulation within your family, stepfamily, or the family of someone you know. Who was involved? Why was the coalition formed? What impact did the triangulation have upon the relationships among the triangulated people? The family as a whole?

support for your new family members by doing at least some of these things every day.

3. *Create new family rituals.* A critical part of building a new family identity is creating *stepfamily rituals*: events or activities shared between stepfamily members that function to define the group as a family. This can be sharing a weekly dinner together or attending religious services together. Whatever form it takes, the most constructive stepfamily rituals are those that bring stepfamily members together as a family, but still recognize and value what was important from the previous families (Schrodt, 2006).

4. *Avoid triangulating family members.* You may feel it's strategic or even enjoyable to team up and triangulate against a stepparent or stepsibling. But such behavior damages your relationship with them and creates family stress (Schrodt & Afifi, 2007). If you're the one caught in the middle of triangulation, confront the perpetrators. Using your interpersonal skills (cooperative language, competent interpersonal communication), respectfully explain to them how their behavior is making you feel and the damage it is doing to the family. Remind them that stepfamilies are difficult enough to maintain without also having to deal with alliances, loyalty struggles, and power battles. Ask them to cease such behavior.

5. *Be patient.* Whenever families experience a major transition, there is always a lengthy period of adjustment. In the case of remarriage, it typically takes anywhere from three to five *years* for a stepfamily to stabilize as a family unit (Hetherington, 1993). Consequently, be patient. Expect that new relationship bonds are going to take a long time to develop, that you will feel uncertain about your new family roles, and that disputes will arise over privacy rules and personal boundaries (Golish, 2003).

PARENTAL FAVORITISM

Few things matter more to children than expressions of affection from parents (Floyd & Morman, 2005). Such displays include verbal statements ("I love you"), nonverbal contact (hugs, cuddling), gifts, favors, and other resources that make children feel adored and appreciated. But when there is more than one child in the family, competition between children for parental affection becomes a natural part of family life (Golish, 2003).

Many parents respond to this age-old dilemma by equally allocating their affection and resources. However, some parents engage in **parental favoritism**: where one or both parents allocate an unfair amount of valuable resources to one child over others. This may include intangible forms of affection, such as statements of love, praise, undue patience (letting one child "get away with anything"), and emotional support. Or it may involve tangible resources, such as cash loans, college tuition, cars, or job offers. For example, when my friend "Susan" was growing up, her father blatantly favored her sister over her. He

self-reflection

Does your family or stepfamily have rituals? Which rituals mean the most to you, and why? How does the regular practice of these rituals affect how you feel about your family or stepfamily?

to Susan to help her pay for nursing school. Although Susan and her father no longer speak, she and her sister are quite close. This is an unusual outcome only achieved through both sisters' hard work to overcome the bitter wedge driven between them in their youth.

INTERPARENTAL CONFLICT

One of the most potent family challenges is **interparental conflict**: overt, hostile interactions between parents in a household. While such constant fighting is harmful to the parents' relationship, the impact upon children in the household is worse. Interparental conflict is associated with children's social problems, including lower levels of play with peers and lower friendship quality (Rodrigues & Kitzmann, 2007). Such children are also more likely to imitate their parents' destructive interaction styles and, consequently, are more at risk for aggressive and delinquent behaviors (Krishnakumar, Buehler, & Barber, 2003).

But the most devastating effects of interparental conflict are relational. Adolescents who perceive a high frequency of interparental conflict are more likely to report feelings of jealousy and fears of abandonment in their romantic relationships (Hayashi & Strickland, 1998). Interparental conflict also negatively impacts late teen and adult perceptions of interpersonal trust, love attitudes, sexual behaviors, relationship beliefs, cohabitation, and attitudes toward marriage and divorce (Rodrigues & Kitzmann, 2007).

Why do children suffer so many profound and negative outcomes from fights between parents? One explanation is the **spillover hypothesis**: emotions, affect, and mood from the parental relationship "spill over" into the broader family, disrupting children's sense of emotional security (Krishnakumar et al., 2003). Children living in households torn by interparental conflict experience a chronic sense of instability—not knowing when the next battle will erupt and if or when their parents will break up. This gives them a deep-seeded sense of emotional insecurity related to relationships (Rodrigues & Kitzmann, 2007), which manifests in their own intimate involvements, months and even years later.

What can you do to manage interparental conflict and its outcomes? If you're the child of parents who fight, encourage them individually to approach their conflicts more constructively. Share with them all you know about conflict from Chapter 8: effective approaches for managing conflict, the negative role of self-enhancing thoughts, the dangers associated with destructive messages, and the trap of serial arguments. If you feel that you are suffering negative outcomes from having grown up in a conflict-ridden household, seek therapy from a reputable counselor. And if you're a parent with children, realize this: *everything you say and do within the family realm—including interactions you have with your spouse or partner—spills over into the emotions and feelings of your children.*

skills practice

Managing Interparental Conflict

Helping parents better manage their conflicts

❶ Following a significant conflict between parents or caregivers, reach out to each person individually, letting them know you're available to talk.

❷ Encourage them to be mindful of how negative emotions and flawed attributions shape their conflict perceptions and decisions.

❸ Remind them of the relational damage wrought by destructive messages.

❹ Help them identify the causes of the conflict.

❺ List goals and long-term interests they share in common.

❻ Use these points of commonality to collaboratively create solutions that will prevent similar conflicts in the future.

❼ Evaluate these solutions in terms of fairness for both of them.

The Primacy of Family

Family ties run so deep that we often use kinship as a metaphor to describe closeness in other relationships

As with romantic relationships, the day-to-day work of maintaining family bonds isn't especially glamorous. Birth, adoption, marriage, or remarriage may structure your family, but the quality of your family relationships is defined by whether you invest time and energy in your interpersonal communication. Such efforts don't have to be complex: a story told to your child or shared with a sibling, gratitude expressed to a parent, an affectionate e-mail sent to a grandparent—all of these simple acts of communication keep your family bonds alive and thriving.

Yet we often neglect to communicate with family members in these ways, in part because such relationships lack the sparkle, excitement, and drama of romances. When we dismiss, look past, or simply take for granted our families, we're like Dorothy in *The Wizard of Oz*—running away from Auntie Em and the farm, thinking we'll do just fine on our own.

But life is *not* a skip down the yellow brick road. When we battle metaphorical witches in the form of hardship, disappointment, and even tragedy, it's our family members who often lock arms with us. They're the ones who help us charge forward, even though we're afraid or discouraged. The truth about our family relationships stands like the wizard behind the curtain. When you step forward boldly and pull the curtain back, it's revealed. There *is* no place like home.

W e began this chapter with a world champion and the family who encouraged her to excel. Throughout her life, Brenda Villa's parents have been a source of inspiration and motivation. Through their support, honesty, sacrifice, and love, they created the foundation upon which Brenda has built the most successful water polo career in U.S. history.

To whom do you turn to listen—or to provide you with a necessary kick in the butt— when you're feeling sorry for yourself? From whom did you get the confidence and swagger to face the competitions that life presents?

The story of Brenda Villa and her parents reminds us of a simple truth regarding the primacy of family. The successes, victories, and medals we achieve in our lives may be won through our own

POSTSCRIPT

efforts, but they were made possible by the people who raised us.

chapter review

key terms

▶ You can watch brief, illustrative videos of these terms and test your understanding of the concepts online in *VideoCentral: Interpersonal Communication* at **bedfordstmartins .com/reflectrelate**.

key concepts

Defining Family

- Given the diversity in contemporary **family** structures, scholars define family in very inclusive ways. Families come in myriad forms, including **nuclear**, **extended**, **step-**, **cohabiting couples**, and **single-parent**.

- Families solidify their sense of identity by sharing **family stories**. These narrative accounts of birth, courtship, and survival bind children, parents, and other relatives together.

Communicating in Families

- Regardless of the structure of a family, **Family Communication Patterns Theory** suggests that most families' communication is determined by two dimensions: **conversation orientation** and **conformity orientation**.

- These two dimensions often lead to four family communication patterns: **consensual**, **pluralistic**, **protective**, and **laissez-faire**. Such families have very different communication beliefs and practices that shape the interpersonal relationships among family members.

Maintaining Family Relationships

- Three of the most important strategies for maintaining family relationships are positivity, assurances, and self-disclosure. Technology is making it easier for families to communicate such maintenance strategies, especially when distance separates them.

- The ways family members deal with dialectical tensions can be understood through **Communication Privacy Management Theory**. These boundaries are defined by **family privacy rules**: the conditions governing what family members can talk about, how they can discuss such topics, and who should have access to family-relevant information.

Family Relationship Challenges

- A common challenge in stepfamily transition is **triangulation**. Such loyalty conflicts can make individuals feel "torn" between family members.

- **Parental favoritism** can include both intangible and tangible forms of affection, and often drives a wedge between siblings in addition to other long-term effects.

- Dealing with **interparental conflict** is one of the hardest family communication challenges. Such fights can have long-term and devastating effects on the parents and the children as explained by the **spillover hypothesis**.

key skills

- Curious about what would make an appropriate family story? Review the suggestions for telling family stories on pages 328–329.

- Want to know your family's communication pattern? Review pages 331–333, then take the *Self-Quiz* on page 331.

- How can you integrate positivity, openness, and assurances into your face-to-face and online family communication and, in doing so, better maintain your family relationships? Check out the suggestions on pages 334–336, then do the *Skills Practice* on page 336.

- What can you do to balance the tension between autonomy and connection in your family relationships? Follow the suggestions on pages 337–338.

- How can you improve your family privacy rules? Revisit the discussion on pages 339–340, as well as the *Skills Practice* on page 340.

- Interested in easing the transition to a stepfamily? Check out the suggestions on pages 342–343.

- Want to know how to assess favoritism in a family? Try the *Self-Quiz* on page 345 and read about the best approach for dealing with parental favoritism on pages 345 and 348.

- Dealing with interparental conflict is never easy. You can try to help manage such fights by reviewing the advice on page 348 and trying the *Skills Practice* on page 348.

- Curious about how to communicate in a new stepfamily and deal with parents who are constantly fighting? Try the *Making Relationship Choices* exercise on pages 346–347.

added, "I know for sure: I will *never* sleep with [Oprah's boyfriend] Stedman!"

A common tabloid story about Oprah and Gayle is that they are actually lovers. This irks Oprah, because if she *was* a lesbian, and Gayle *was* her lover, the two would be open and honest about it. At the same time, Oprah isn't surprised. "I understand why people think we're gay. There isn't a definition in our culture for this kind of bond between women. So I get why people have to label it—how can you be this close without it being sexual? How else can you explain this level of intimacy?"

Gayle and Oprah have been best friends for more than 30 years. But despite all the public scrutiny their friendship has undergone, and all the effort they've put in to maintain it, there's still an aspect of it that defies description. "There isn't a model for something like this," offers Oprah. "Something about this relationship feels otherworldly to me, like it was designed by a power and a hand greater than my own. Whatever this friendship is, it's been a very fun ride—and we've taken it together."

anything," says Gayle. "I don't want to offend her, but I'm never afraid to be truthful with her."

Oprah and Gayle offer each other unconditional support. As Oprah describes, "We're talking about a relationship in which someone always loves you, always respects you, wants the best for you in every single situation of your life. Lifts you up. Supports you. Always!" The two women trust each other to never betray their friendship. Oprah once hosted an episode of her TV show in which she interviewed women who had slept with their best friend's husbands. This type of betrayal is inconceivable to the two. "That is not possible in this relationship," says Oprah. Gayle

Few friendships are as enduring, intimate, and famous as that of Oprah Winfrey and Gayle King. Nevertheless, the friendships that fill our lives are akin to theirs in important ways. Like Oprah and Gayle, we are drawn to our friends through the realization of shared similarities. We count on our friends to provide support. We build our friendships by disclosing our thoughts, feelings, and vulnerabilities while trusting our friends to not betray us. At the same time, our friendships can be difficult to define. They lack the permanence of family bonds and the clear constraints and expectations of romantic involvements. This makes them more delicate and mysterious than other close relationships. Friendships often leave us pondering, like Oprah, "I know this is fun, but what exactly *is* this?"

In this chapter, we look at friendship. You'll learn:

- How friendships are unique and distinct
- Varied types of friendships you'll experience
- Ways you can communicate so that your friendships survive and thrive
- Challenges to friendships and how to overcome them

The Nature of Friendship

Friendships are both delicate and deep

Like family and romantic bonds, friendship plays a crucial role in our lives. Friendship is an important source of emotional security and self-esteem (Rawlins, 1992). Friendship facilitates a sense of belonging when we're young, helps solidify our identity during adolescence, and provides satisfaction and social support when we're elderly (Miller, Hefner, & Scott, 2007). But what exactly *is* friendship?

FRIENDSHIP DEFINED

Friendship is a voluntary interpersonal relationship characterized by intimacy and liking (McEwan, Babin Gallagher, & Farinelli, 2008). Whether it's casual or close, short- or long-term, friendship has several distinguishing characteristics.

Friendship Is Voluntary We have greater liberty in choosing our friends than we do in choosing partners for any other relationship type (Sias et al., 2008). Whether a friendship forms is determined largely by the people involved, based on their mutual desire to create such a relationship. This is different from romantic, workplace, and family involvements. Consider romantic relationships. You may face substantial familial or cultural constraints in your choice of romantic partners. You may be expected (or allowed) only to date people of a certain age, gender, ethnicity, religion, or income level. You may even have a spouse chosen *for* you in an arranged marriage. In the workplace (as we'll discuss more in Chapter 12), you are required to work collaboratively with certain people, whether you like them or not. And in your family, you're bound to others

self-reflection

What constraints, if any, do you face in whom you can choose as friends? Who puts these limits on you? In your experience, do you have more, or less, freedom in choosing friends than lovers? How does this influence your choice of friends?

▶ On *The Big Bang Theory*, close friends Leonard, Sheldon, Howard, and Rajesh regularly get together and indulge their mutual passion for physics, sci-fi movies, and intricate science experiments. Their shared interests are a point of commonality that began but also sustains their friendships over time. What first drew you to your closest friends?

through birth, adoption, or the creation of a stepfamily. These ties are involuntary. As French poet Jacques Delille (1738–1813) put it, "Fate chooses your relations, you choose your friends."

Friendship Is Driven by Shared Interests   As shown by Oprah Winfrey and Gayle King, similarity is the primary force that draws us to our friends (Parks & Floyd, 1996). This is true across ages, genders, sexual orientations, and ethnicities. One practical implication of this is that when your interests and activities change, so do your friendships. If you change your political or religious beliefs or suffer an injury that prevents you from playing a beloved sport, friendships related to those things may change as well. Some friendships will endure— the focus of the relationship shifting to new points of commonality—but others will fade away. One of the most common reasons for friendships ending is a change in shared interests and beliefs (Miller et al., 2007).

Friendship Is Characterized by Self-Disclosure   We consider most people in our lives "acquaintances." Only a select few rise to the level of "friends." What distinguishes the two groups? *Self-disclosure.* Both men and women report that being able to freely and deeply disclose is *the* defining feature of friendship (Parks & Floyd, 1996). Self-disclosure between friends means sharing private thoughts and feelings, and believing (like Gayle and Oprah) that "we can tell each other anything." The relationship between friendship and self-disclosure is reciprocal as well. The more you consider someone a friend, the more you will disclose, and the more you disclose, the more you will consider that person a friend (Shelton, Trail, West, & Bergsieker, 2010).

Friendship Is Rooted in Liking   We feel affection and respect for our friends. In other words, we *like* them (Rubin, 1973). We also enjoy their company; pleasure in sharing time together is a defining feature of friendships (Hays, 1988). At the same time, because friendships are rooted in liking—rather than love— we're not as emotionally attached to our friends as we are to other intimates, and we're not as emotionally demanding of them. Correspondingly, we're expected to be more loyal to and more willing to help romantic partners and family members than friends (Davis & Todd, 1985).

Friendship Is Volatile   Friendships are less stable, more likely to change, and easier to break off than family or romantic relationships (Johnson, Wittenberg, Villagran, Mazur, & Villagran, 2003). Why? Consider the differences in depth of commitment. We're bonded to friends by choice, rooted in shared interests. But we're bonded to families by social and legal commitment, and to lovers by deep emotional and sexual attachment. These loyalties mean we may choose or forgo professional opportunities to preserve romances or stay close to family. But most of us will choose to pursue our careers over staying geographically close to friends (Patterson, 2007).

FRIENDSHIP FUNCTIONS

Friendships serve many different functions in our lives. Two of the most important are that they help us to fulfill our need for *companionship*—chances to do fun things together and receive emotional support—and they help us *achieve practical goals*—friends help us deal with problems or everyday tasks (de Vries, 1996). These functions are not mutually exclusive, as many friendships facilitate both.

Communal Friendships   One of the functions friendships serve is enabling us to share life events and activities with others. Compared to family and work relationships, friendship interactions are the least task oriented and tend to revolve around leisure activities such as talking or eating (Argyle & Furnham, 1982). Scholar William Rawlins (1992) describes friendships that focus primarily on sharing time and activities together as **communal friendships**. Communal friends try to get together as often as possible, and they provide encouragement and emotional support to one another during times of need. Importantly, because emotional support is a central aspect of communal friendship, only when both friends fulfill the expectations of support for the relationship does the friendship endure (Burleson & Samter, 1994).

Agentic Friendships   We also look to friends for help in achieving practical goals in both our personal and our professional lives. Friends help us study for exams, fix cars, set up computers, and complete professional projects. Friendships in which the parties focus primarily on helping each other achieve practical goals are known as **agentic friendships** (Rawlins, 1992). Agentic friends value sharing time together—but only if they're available and have no other priorities to handle at the moment. They also aren't interested in the emotional interdependence and mutual sharing of personal information that characterize communal friendships.

self-reflection

Call to mind your three closest friends in middle school. Then do the same for high school. Now think about your three closest friends today. Are the lists the same? How have they changed? Why? What does this tell you about the volatility of friendships?

VideoCentral ◉

bedfordstmartins.com /reflectrelate

Communal Friendships
Watch this clip online to answer the questions below.

Why are the men in this video considered communal friends? How much do factors like gender, culture, shared interests, and self-disclosure influence your communal friendships?

Want to see more? Check out VideoCentral for a clip illustrating **agentic friendships**.

◯ Although less intimate than communal friendships, people in agentic friendships can help each other with practical tasks and goals like moving. Can you recall a time when an agentic friend helped you achieve a significant goal?

self-reflection

Do you have more communal or agentic friends? How do you communicate differently with the two types of friends? Which type of friend do you depend on more, day to day? Why?

They're available when the need arises, but beyond that, they're uncomfortable with more personal demands or responsibilities. For example, an agentic friend from work may gladly help you write up a monthly sales report, but she may feel uncomfortable if you ask her for advice about your romantic problems.

FRIENDSHIP ACROSS THE LIFE SPAN

The importance we attribute to our friendships changes throughout our lives. Up through the fourth grade, most children look to their family as their sole source of emotional support (Furman & Simon, 1998). If a child suffers a disappointment at school, has a frightening dream, or just wants to share the events of the day, he or she will turn to parents or siblings. But during adolescence, children slowly transfer their emotional attachment from their family to friends (Welch & Houser, 2010). For example, by the seventh grade, young people rely just as much on same-sex friends as they do on family for support. By tenth grade, same-sex friends have become the principal providers of emotional support. This trend continues into early adulthood: for college students, friends are the primary relationship for fulfilling relational needs (McEwan et al., 2008).

By middle adulthood, many people form long-term romantic commitments and start families of their own. Consequently, their romantic partners and children become the primary providers of companionship, affection, and support. The importance of friendships begins to wane (Carbery & Buhrmester, 1998). This is especially the case for married men, who before marriage tend to spend most of their time with male friends (Cohen, 1992). Late in life, however, the pattern shifts back once more, as spouses and siblings pass on and children form their own families. For the elderly, friendships are the most important relationships for providing social support and intimacy (Patterson, 2007).

◖ In the movie *I Love You, Man*, Peter Klaven (Paul Rudd) is happily engaged to Zooey (Rashida Jones), but feels pressure to make more male friends before getting married. When Peter meets Sydney Fife (Jason Segel) and they quickly become inseparable, their open displays of affection and eagerness to spend time together cause Zooey to worry she is no longer the primary source of intimacy in Peter's life.

FRIENDSHIP, CULTURE, AND GENDER

People from different cultures have varied expectations regarding friendships. For example, most Westerners believe that friendships don't endure, that you'll naturally lose some friends and gain others over time (Berscheid & Regan, 2005). This belief contrasts sharply with attitudes in other cultures, in which people view friendships as deeply intimate and lasting. As just one example, when asked to identify the closest relationship in their lives, Euro-Americans tend to select romantic partners, whereas Japanese tend to select friendships (Gudykunst & Nishida, 1993).

Friendship beliefs and practices across cultures are also entangled with gender norms. In the United States and Canada, for instance, friendships between women are often stereotyped as communal, whereas men's friendships are thought to be agentic. But male and female same-sex friendships are more similar than they are different (Winstead, Derlaga, & Rose, 1997).[2] Men and women rate the importance of both kinds of friendships equally (Roy, Benenson, & Lilly, 2000), and studies of male friendships in North America have found that companionship is the primary need met by the relationship (Wellman, 1992).

At the same time, Euro-American men, unlike women, learn to avoid direct expressions of affection and intimacy in their friendships with other males.

---

[2]As defined in Chapter 2, *gender* is the composite of social, psychological, and cultural attributes that characterize us as male or female (Canary, Emmers-Sommer, & Faulkner, 1997). *Sex* refers to the biological sex organs with which we're born. When communicating, people orient to gender, not sex (which they typically don't see!). But usage of the terms *sex* and *gender* by scholars often is inconsistent (Parks, 2007). For example, within the friendship literature, male-female friendships are referred to as opposite-*sex* and male-male and female-female friendships as same-*sex*, rather than opposite-gender and same-gender. Consequently, in this section, we use the terms *cross-sex* and *same-sex*.

Owing to traditional masculine gender roles, a general reluctance to openly show emotion, and homophobia (among other factors), many men avoid verbal and nonverbal intimacy in their same-sex friendships, such as disclosing personal feelings and vulnerabilities, touching, and hugging (Bank & Hansford, 2000). But in many other cultures, both men and women look to same-sex friends as their primary source of intimacy. For example, in southern Spain, men and women report feeling more comfortable revealing their deepest thoughts to same-sex friends than to spouses (Brandes, 1987). Traditional Javanese (Indonesian) culture holds that marriage should not be too intimate and that a person's most intimate relationship should be with his or her same-sex friends (Williams, 1992).

FRIENDSHIP AND TECHNOLOGY

As with other interpersonal relationships, communication technologies such as social networking sites, Twitter, smartphones, e-mail, and text-messaging have reshaped the way people create friendships. In the past, people forged friendships slowly. They took time to discover the values and interests of their neighbors, coworkers, and acquaintances, and only then built friendships with those who shared their values and interests. Now, however, you can form friendships quickly and with more people—some whom you may never actually meet in person—simply by friending them on Facebook or other online communities (Stafford, 2005). This provides a valuable resource to people suffering from chronic shyness. They can interact with others and garner social and emotional support, without suffering the anxiety that direct face-to-face contact may cause (Pennington, 2009).

Of course, just because someone is your "Facebook friend" doesn't necessarily mean that they're a "real" friend. For example, 80 percent of Facebook users report that their real-world friends also are Facebook friends (Pennington,

▶ Communication technologies have reshaped the ways people create and maintain friendships. Even while socializing with friends face-to-face, it is now possible to stay connected to friends who aren't present. How do you maintain friendships using online communication?

2009). But the inverse isn't true. Most people have dozens of friends, four (or so) close friends, and one (or more) "best" friend—yet well over three *hundred* Facebook friends (Pennington, 2009). The vast bulk of these "friends" aren't friends at all, but instead, coworkers, acquaintances, neighbors, family, and the like.

Communication technologies make it possible for friends to stay constantly connected with one another. For better or worse, you now can keep your friends updated 24/7 on the latest news in your life through posts and messages. Interestingly, much like within families (see Chapter 10), technology does not replace in-person interaction. People who regularly use cell phones to call and text their friends are *more* likely to also seek face-to-face encounters (Wang & Andersen, 2007).

Despite all of this technology, people continue to recognize the superiority of offline relationships and communication. Studies comparing offline versus online friendships find that offline friendships have higher degrees of intimacy, understanding, interdependence, and commitment (Chan & Cheng, 2004). Additionally, people prefer face-to-face interactions with friends when discussing deeply personal or troubling topics (Pennington, 2009).

self-reflection

Think of friends you only know and interact with online, and compare them with the friends who populate your offline world. Which friends do you consider closer? When you're confronted with a challenging problem or personal crisis, which friends do you turn to for support? Why?

Types of Friendship

Characteristics and roles of different friends

The *Sex and the City* franchise—spanning books, TV, and movies—is known for many things, including frank discussions of sex, romantic entanglements, and fashion. But more than anything else, it's a story of friendships. At the center is the intensely bonded foursome of Carrie, Miranda, Charlotte, and Samantha. They spend almost all of their leisure time together, disclose everything to each other, and support one another through hardships—including heartbreaks, infidelity, infertility, elder care, and even cancer. Surrounding them is a broader network of associated friends, the closest of whom are two gay men, Stanford and Anthony. In addition, as various lovers come and go, the ones who stay—Big, Steve, Harry, and Smith Jerrod—forge friendships with the other women. And in the first movie, Carrie forms a close alliance with her African American assistant, Louise, as they bond over their shared love of Louis Vuitton.

Sex and the City provides us with an admittedly narrow glimpse into friendships, one that is predominantly Euro-American, affluent, and urban. But despite this limited view, it does provide an accurate reflection of the many *types* of friendship that populate our lives, regardless of sex or city. When one considers these types, two stand out from the rest as unique, challenging, and significant: best friends and cross-category friends.

BEST FRIENDS

Think of the people you consider *close friends*—that is, people with whom you exchange deeply personal information and emotional support, share many interests and activities, and around whom you feel comfortable and at ease (Parks & Floyd, 1996). How many come to mind? Chances are you can count them on one hand. A study surveying over one thousand individuals found that, on average, people

▶ During their regular brunch date, Carrie, Miranda, Samantha, and Charlotte provide one another with emotional support as they exchange deeply personal information about their lives and relationships. As the women's social identities shift and as they change partners, switch careers, and even have children, these best friends accept, respect, and support one another.

have four close friends (Galupo, 2009). While this number closely parallels the women at the center of *Sex and the City*, there's an important difference: Carrie, Miranda, Samantha, and Charlotte aren't just close friends, they're best friends.

What makes a close friend a *best friend*? Many things. First, best friends typically are same-sex rather than cross-sex (Galupo, 2009). Although we may have close cross-sex friendships, comparatively few of these relationships evolve to being a "best." Second, best friendship involves greater intimacy, more disclosure, and deeper commitment than close friendship (Weisz & Wood, 2005). People talk more frequently and more deeply with best friends about their relationships, emotions, life events, and goals (Pennington, 2009). This holds true for both women *and* men. Third, people count on their best friends to listen to their problems without judging, and to "have their back"—that is, provide unconditional support (Pennington, 2009). Fourth, best friendship is distinct from close friendship in the degree to which shared activities commit the friends to each other in substantial ways. For example, best friends are more likely to join clubs together, participate on intramural or community sports teams, move in together as roommates, and share a spring break, study abroad, or other type of vacation together (Becker et al., 2009).

Finally, the most important factor that distinguishes best friends is unqualified provision of **identity support**: behaving in ways that convey understanding, acceptance, and support for a friend's valued social identities. **Valued social identities** are the aspects of your public self that you deem the most important in defining who you are—for example, musician, athlete, poet, dancer, teacher, mother, and so on. Whomever we are—and whomever we dream of being—our best friends understand us, accept us, respect us, and support us, no matter what. Say that a close friend who is a pacifist suddenly announces that she is joining the Army because she feels strongly about defending our country. What would you say to her? Or imagine that a good friend tells you that he actually is not gay but transgendered, and henceforth will be living as a woman in accordance with his true gender. How would you respond? In each of these cases, *best* friends would distinguish themselves by supporting such identity shifts even if they found them surprising. Research following friendships across a four-year time span found that more than any other factor—including amount of communication and perceived closeness—participants who initially reported high levels of identity support from a new friend were more likely to describe that person as their *best* friend four years later (Weisz & Wood, 2005).

CROSS-CATEGORY FRIENDSHIPS

Given that friendships center on shared interests and identity support, it's no surprise that people tend to befriend those who are similar demographically (with regard to age, gender, economic status, etc.). As just one example, studies of straight, gay, lesbian, bisexual, and transgendered persons find that, regardless of sexual orientation or gender identity, people are more likely to have close

What Kind of Friend Are You?

self-QUIZ

Think about how you communicate with, relate to, and behave toward your friends. Then place a check mark next to the statements with which you agree and total the number you have marked. Check your score at the bottom.

_____ I strive to always maintain equal give-and-take in my friendships.

_____ I'm the kind of person my friends can talk with about anything and feel relaxed around.

_____ I think like my friends do and share a similar sense of humor with them.

_____ I don't hold my friends' mistakes against them.

_____ I can be trusted by my friends to keep a secret.

_____ I'm honest with my friends; I don't lie or hold things back.

_____ I can be serious with my friends, and I don't make fun of them when they want to talk about difficult issues.

_____ I'm considerate about my friends' feelings, and I don't do spiteful things.

_____ I can take care of myself, and I have my own ideals and beliefs apart from my friends'.

_____ I respect my friends' needs for privacy.

_____ I encourage my friends when they're up, and I cheer them up when they're down.

_____ I'm generous toward my friends and not self-centered.

_____ I'm fun to be around when I'm with my friends.

_____ I have an upbeat personality and stress the positive side of things when communicating with my friends.

_____ I always keep my promises to friends.

Note: This *Self-Quiz* is adapted from Maeda and Ritchie (2003).

Scoring: These statements represent the qualities people associate with close, trustworthy, and dependable friends. If you scored 11–15, you are an exceptionally trustworthy friend; 6–10, you are moderately trustworthy; 0–5, you exhibit low levels of trustworthiness.

friendships with others of the same ethnicity (Galupo, 2009). But people also regularly defy this norm, forging friendships that cross demographic lines, known as **cross-category friendships** (Galupo, 2009). Such friendships are a powerful way to break down ingrouper and outgrouper perceptions and purge people of negative stereotypes. The four most common cross-category friendships are cross-sex, cross-orientation, intercultural, and interethnic.

Cross-Sex Friendships   One of the most radical shifts in interpersonal relationship patterns over the past few decades has been the increase in platonic (nonsexual) friendships between men and women in the United States and Canada. In the nineteenth century, friendships were almost exclusively same-sex, and throughout most of the twentieth century, cross-sex friendships remained a rarity (Halatsis & Christakis, 2009). For example, a study of friendship conducted in 1974 found that, on average, men and women had few or no close cross-sex friends (Booth & Hess, 1974). However, by the mid-1980s, 40 percent of men and 30 percent of women reported having close cross-sex friendships (Rubin, 1985). By the late 1990s, 47 percent of tenth- and twelfth-graders reported having a close cross-sex friend (Kuttler, LaGreca, & Prinstein, 1999).

Most cross-sex friendships are not motivated by sexual attraction (Messman, Canary, & Hause, 1994). Instead, men and women agree that through cross-sex friendships, they gain a greater understanding of how members of the other sex think, feel, and behave (Halatsis & Christakis, 2009). For men, forming friendships with women provides the possibility of greater intimacy and emotional depth than is typically available in male-male friendships (Monsour, 1997).

Despite changing attitudes toward cross-sex friendships, men and women face several challenges in building such relationships. For one thing, they've learned from early childhood to segregate themselves by sex. In most schools, young boys and girls are placed in separate gym classes, asked to line up separately for class, and instructed to engage in competitions pitting "the boys against the girls" (Thorne, 1986). It's no surprise, then, that young children overwhelmingly prefer friends of the same sex (Reeder, 2003). As a consequence of this early-life segregation, most children enter their teens with only limited experience in building cross-sex friendships. Neither adolescence nor adulthood provides many opportunities for gaining this experience. Leisure-oriented activities such as competitive sports, community programs, and social organizations—including the Boy Scouts and Girl Scouts—typically are sex segregated (Swain, 1992).

Another challenge is that our society promotes only same-sex friendship and cross-sex coupling as the two most acceptable relationship options between men and women. So no matter how rigorously a pair of cross-sex friends insist that they're "just friends," their surrounding friends and family members will likely

◖ In addition to the benefits of friendship such as companionship and shared interests, cross-category friends are often exposed to cultural experiences they may not have otherwise.

meet these claims with skepticism or even disapproval (Monsour, 1997). Family members, if they approve of the friendship, often pester such couples to become romantically involved: "You and Jen have so much in common! Why not take things to the next level?" If families disapprove, they encourage termination of the relationship: "I don't want people thinking my daughter is hanging out casually with some guy. Why don't you hang out with other girls instead?" Romantic partners of people involved in cross-sex friendships often vehemently disapprove of such involvements (Hansen, 1985). Owing to constant disapproval from others and the pressure to justify the relationship, cross-sex friendships are far less stable than same-sex friendships (Berscheid & Regan, 2005).

Cross-Orientation Friendships   As illustrated by the friendship between Carrie and Stanford in *Sex and the City*, a second type of cross-category friendship is *cross-orientation*: friendships between lesbian, gay, bisexual, transgendered, or queer (LGBTQ) people and straight men or women. As within all friendships, cross-orientation friends are bonded by shared interests and activities, and provide each other with support and affection. But these friendships also provide unique rewards for the parties involved (Galupo, 2007). For straight men and women, forming a cross-orientation friendship can help correct negative stereotypes about persons of other sexual orientations and the LGBTQ community as a whole. For LGBTQ persons, having a straight friend can provide much-needed emotional and social support from outside of the LGBTQ community, helping to further insulate them from societal homophobia (Galupo, 2007).

Although cross-orientation friendships are commonplace on television and in the movies (e.g., *Glee*, *Degrassi*, *Sex and the City*), they are less frequent in real life. Although LGBTQ persons often have as many cross-orientation friends as same-orientation, straight men and women overwhelmingly form friendships with other straight men and women (Galupo, 2009). The principal reason is homophobia, both personal and societal. Straight persons may feel reluctant to pursue such friendships because they fear being associated with members of a marginalized group (Galupo, 2007). By far the group that has the fewest cross-orientation friendships is straight men. In fact, the average number of cross-orientation friendships for straight men is *zero*: most straight men do not have a single lesbian, gay, bisexual, or transgendered friend (Galupo, 2009). This tendency may perpetuate homophobic sentiments, because these men are never exposed to LGBTQ persons who might amend their negative attitudes. The Focus on Culture box "Cross-Orientation Male Friendships" on page 366 explores the challenges of such relationships in depth.

Intercultural Friendships   A third type of cross-category friendship is *intercultural*: friendships between people from different cultures or countries. Similar to cross-sex and cross-orientation affiliations, intercultural friendships are both challenging and rewarding (Sias et al., 2008). The challenges include overcoming differences in language and cultural beliefs and negative stereotypes. Differences in language alone present a substantial hurdle. Incorrect interpretations

Cross-Orientation Male Friendships

As *New York Times* writer Douglas Quenqua notes, the biggest stereotype regarding gay and straight male friendships is "the notion that gay men can't refrain from hitting on straight friends."[3] This is false. In a poll of men involved in gay-straight friendships, Quenqua found little evidence of sexual tension. He did find several other barriers confronting such relationships, however. The most prominent was peer pressure from friends on both sides to not socialize with someone of a different orientation.

The other barriers were perceptual and communicative. Straight men often view gay men solely in terms of their sexual orientation, making it difficult to connect with them on other levels. As Matthew Streib, a gay journalist in Baltimore, describes, "It's always about my gayness for the first two months. First they have questions, then they make fun of it, then they start seeing me as a person." In addition, many straight men feel uncomfortable talking about their gay friends' romantic involvements. Without being able to discuss this critical topic, the friends necessarily face constraints in how close they can become.

One context that *has* proven conducive of close cross-orientation friendships is the military. Sociologist Jammie Price found that the straight and gay men with the closest friendships were those who had fought side by side (1999). Having learned to depend on each other for survival built a bond that far transcended differences of sexual orientation.

But regardless of barriers or bonds, one thing *is* consistent in cross-orientation male friendships: lack of consistency. As Douglas Quenqua concludes, "For every sweeping statement one can make about such friendships, there is a real-life counter example to undermine the stereotypes. As with all friendships, no two are exactly alike."

discussion questions

● What are the biggest barriers blocking you from maintaining or forming cross-orientation friendships?

● What, if anything, could be done to overcome these barriers?

---

of messages can lead to misunderstanding, uncertainty, frustration, and conflict (Sias et al., 2008). The potential rewards of intercultural friendships, however, are great, and include gaining new cultural knowledge, broadening one's worldview, and breaking stereotypes (Sias et al., 2008).

As noted throughout this chapter, the most important factor that catapults friendships forward is similarity in interests and activities. However, the defining characteristic of intercultural interactions is *difference*, and this makes formation of intercultural friendships more challenging (Sias et al., 2008). How can you overcome this? By finding, and then bolstering, some significant type of ingroup similarity. For example, a good friend—who is Japanese—and I—of Irish descent—founded our friendship upon a shared love of techno and house music. But the strongest predictor of whether someone will have an intercultural friendship is prior intercultural friendships. People who have had close friends from different cultures in the past are substantially more likely to forge such friendships in the future (Sias et al., 2008). This is because they learn the enormous benefits that such relationships provide, and lack fear and uncertainty about "outgroupers."

---

[3]All quoted material that follows is excerpted from Quenqua (2009).

Interethnic Friendships   The final type of cross-category friendship is illustrated by Carrie and Louise in the first *Sex and the City* movie. This is an *interethnic* friendship: a bond between people who share the same cultural background (for example, "American"), but who are of different ethnic groups ("African American," "Asian American," "Euro-American," and so forth). Similar to cross-orientation and intercultural friendships, interethnic friendships boost cultural awareness and commitment to diversity (Shelton, Richeson, & Bergsieker, 2009). In addition, interethnic friends apply these outcomes broadly. People who develop a close interethnic friendship become less prejudiced toward ethnicities of *all* types as a result (Shelton et al., 2009).

The most difficult barriers people face in forming interethnic friendships are attributional and perceptual errors. Too often we let our own biases and stereotypes stop us from having open, honest, and comfortable interactions with people from other ethnic groups. We become overly concerned with the "correct" way to act and end up behaving nervously. Such nervousness may lead to awkward, uncomfortable encounters and may cause us to avoid interethnic encounters in the future, dooming ourselves to friendship networks that lack diversity (Shelton et al., 2010).

How can you overcome these challenges and improve your ability to form interethnic friendships? Review Chapter 3's discussion of attributional errors and perception-checking. Look for points of commonality during interethnic encounters that might lead to the formation of a friendship—such as a shared interest in music, fashion, sports, movies, or video games. Keep in mind that sometimes encounters *are* awkward, people *don't* get along, and friendships *won't* arise—and it has nothing to do with ethnic differences.

Maintaining Friendships

Ways to sustain enduring and happy friendships

In the movie *Zombieland*, four people known by the monikers of their former hometowns struggle to survive in a postapocalyptic world (Fleischer, Reesee, & Werrick, 2009). The central character, Columbus, is a self-described loner who never had close ties to friends or family. As he puts it, "I avoided people like they were zombies, even before they *were* zombies!" To deal with the challenge of constant flesh-eater attacks, he develops a set of rules, including Rule #1: *Cardio* (stay in shape to stay ahead of zombies); Rule #17: *Don't be a hero* (don't put yourself at risk to save others); and Rule #31: *Always check the backseat* (to avoid surprises). As time passes, he bands together with three other survivors—Tallahassee, Wichita, and Little Rock—and learns that they too have trust issues, regrets regarding their former lives, and fears about the future (above and beyond zombie attacks). As they travel across the country together, they learn to trust, support, defend, and depend upon each other. This leads to a friendship that eventually deepens to a family-like bond. Columbus even chooses to bend Rule #17 to save Wichita, by being a hero. As he narrates in the final scene, "Those smart girls in the big black truck and that big guy in that snakeskin

◉ As Columbus, Wichita, Little Rock, and Tallahassee grow to trust, defend, and depend on one another in *Zombieland*, they realize that friendship is one of the key elements to surviving a zombie attack, and to being (and staying) human.

jacket—they were the closest to something I'd always wanted, but never really had—a family. I trusted them and they trusted me. Even though life would never be simple or innocent again, we had hope—we had each other. And without other people, well, you might as well be a zombie!"

It's true. We *need* our friends. Most of us don't need them for survival, as we don't face daily zombie attacks. But our friends do provide a constant and important shield against the stresses, hardships, and threats of our everyday lives. We count on friends to be there when we need them and to provide support; in return we do the same. This is what bonds us together.

At the same time, friendships don't endure on their own. As with romantic and family involvements, friendships flourish only when you consistently communicate in ways that maintain them. Two ways that we keep friendships alive are by following friendship rules and by using maintenance strategies.

FOLLOWING FRIENDSHIP RULES

In *Zombieland*, Columbus follows a set of rules that allow him to survive. In the real world, one of the ways we can help our friendships succeed is by following **friendship rules**—general principles that prescribe appropriate communication and behavior within friendship relationships (Argyle & Henderson, 1984). In an extensive study of friendship maintenance, social psychologists Michael Argyle and Monica Henderson observed 10 friendship rules that people share across cultures. Both men and women endorse these rules, and adherence to them distinguishes happy from unhappy friendships (Schneider & Kenny, 2000). Not abiding by them may even cost you your friends: people around the globe describe failed friendships as ones that didn't follow these rules (Argyle & Henderson, 1984). The 10 rules for friendship are:

1. *Show support.* Within a friendship, you should provide emotional support and offer assistance in times of need, without having to be asked (Burleson & Samter, 1994). You also should accept and respect your friend's valued social identities. When he or she changes majors, tries out for team captain, or opts to be a stay-at-home mom or dad, support the decision—even if it's one you yourself wouldn't make.

2. *Seek support.* The flip side of the first rule is that when you're in a friendship you should not only deliver support but *seek* support and counsel when needed, disclosing your emotional burdens to your friends. Other than sharing time and activities, mutual self-disclosure serves as the glue that binds friendships together (Dainton, Zelley, & Langan, 2003).

3. *Respect privacy.* At the same time friends anticipate both support and disclosure, they also recognize that friendships have more restrictive boundaries for sharing personal information than do romantic or family relationships. Recognize this, and avoid pushing your friend to share information that he or she considers too personal. Also resist sharing information about yourself that's intensely private or irrelevant to your friendship.

4. *Keep confidences.* A critical feature of enduring friendships is trust. When friends share personal information with you, do not betray their confidence by sharing it with others.

5. *Defend your friends.* Part of successful friendships is the feeling that friends "have your back." Your friends count on you to stand up for them, so defend them online and off, in situations where they are being attacked either to their face or behind their back.

6. *Avoid public criticism.* Friends may disagree or even disapprove of each other's behavior on occasion. But airing your grievances publicly in a way that makes your friends look bad will only hurt your friendship. Avoid communication such as questioning a friend's loyalty in front of other friends or commenting on a friend's weight in front of a salesperson.

7. *Make your friends happy.* An essential ingredient to successful friendships is striving to make your friends feel good while you're in their company. You can do this by practicing positivity: communicating with them in a cheerful and optimistic fashion, doing unsolicited favors for them, and buying or making gifts for them.

8. *Manage jealousy.* Unlike long-term romantic relationships, most friendships aren't exclusive. Your close friends likely will have other close friends, perhaps even friends who are more intimate than you. Accept that each of your friends has other good friends as well, and constructively manage any jealousy that arises in you.

9. *Share humor.* Successful friends spend a good deal of their time joking with and teasing each other in affectionate ways. Enjoying a similar sense of humor is an essential aspect of most long-term friendships.

self-reflection

Consider the 10 universal rules that successful friends follow. Which of these rules do you abide by in your own friendships? Which do you neglect? How has neglecting some of these rules affected your friendships? What steps might you take to better follow rules you've previously neglected?

10. *Maintain equity.* In enduring, mutually satisfying friendships, the two people give and get in roughly equitable proportions (Canary & Zelley, 2000). Help maintain this equity by conscientiously repaying debts, returning favors, and keeping the exchange of gifts and compliments balanced.

MAINTENANCE STRATEGIES FOR FRIENDS

Most friendships are built on a foundation of shared activities and self-disclosure. To maintain your friendships, strive to keep this foundation solid by regularly doing things with your friends, and making time to talk.

Sharing Activities   Through *sharing activities*, friends structure their schedules to enjoy hobbies, interests, and leisure activities together. But even more important than the actual sharing of activities is the perception that each friend is willing to make time for the other. Scholar William Rawlins notes that even friends who don't spend much time together can still maintain a satisfying connection as long as each perceives the other as "being there" when needed (Rawlins, 1994).

Of course, most of us have several friends, but only finite amounts of time available to devote to each one. Consequently, we are often put in positions where we have to choose between time and activities shared with one friend versus another. Unfortunately, given the significance that sharing time and activities together plays in defining friendships, your decisions regarding with whom you invest your time will often be perceived by friends as communicating depth of loyalty (Baxter et al., 1997). In cases where you choose one friend over another, the friend not chosen may view your decision as disloyal. To avert this, draw on your interpersonal communication skills. Express gratitude for the friend's offer, assure him or her that you very much value the relationship, and make concrete plans for getting together another time.

Self-Disclosure   A second strategy for friendship maintenance is self-disclosure. All friendships are created and maintained through the discussion of thoughts, feelings, and daily life events (Dainton et al., 2003). To foster disclosure with your friends, routinely make time just to talk—encouraging them to share their thoughts and feelings about various issues, whether online or face-to-face. Equally important, avoid betraying friends—that is, sharing with others personal information friends have disclosed to you.

But as with romantic and family relationships, balance openness in self-disclosure with protection (Dainton et al., 2003). Over time, most friends learn that communication about certain issues, topics, or even people is best avoided to protect the relationship and preclude conflict. As a result, friends negotiate communicative boundaries that allow their time together and communication shared to remain positive. Such boundaries can be perfectly healthy as long as both friends agree on them and the issues being avoided aren't central to the survival of the friendship. For example, several years ago a male friend of mine began dating a partner who I thought treated him badly. His boyfriend, whom I'll call "Mike," had a very negative outlook, constantly complained about my friend, and belittled

---

◐ Two important ways you can maintain your friendships are sharing activities and being open in your communication with friends.

him and their relationship in public. I thought Mike's communication was unethical and borderline abusive. But whenever I expressed my concern, my buddy grew defensive. Mike just had an "edge" to his personality, my friend said, and I "didn't know the real Mike." After several such arguments, we agreed that, for the sake of our friendship, the topic of Mike was off-limits. We both respected this agreement—thereby protecting our friendship—until my friend broke up with Mike. After that, we opened the topic once more to free and detailed discussion.

Friendship Challenges

Dealing with friendship betrayal, geographic distance, and attraction

Ashlee and Rachel were best friends throughout high school.[4] As Ashlee describes, "Rachel was brilliant, confident, blunt, and outgoing. She liked to mock people, but she could make me laugh like nobody else, and she loved the same things I did." After graduation, they were parted by distance: Rachel went to Stanford, while Ashlee attended the University of Washington. Although they regularly texted and e-mailed, they grew apart. The following summer they were reunited, this time as a foursome: Rachel was dating Mike (a friend from high school), and Ashlee was dating Ahmed, a Lebanese

---

[4]All information in this example is true. The names and personal information of the people in question have been altered for confidentiality. This example is used with permission from "Ashlee."

○ Discovering that a friend has betrayed you is one of the most devastating friendship challenges you can face. After seeking any support you may need, ask yourself whether you can or even should attempt to restore the friendship, remembering that some betrayals might be harder to move past than others.

transfer student. The four hung out regularly, water-skiing, going to movies, and partying.

One day, after Mike bought a new iPhone, he offered his old one to Ashlee. Arriving home, Ashlee found that her SIM card wasn't compatible, so she started manually clearing Mike's information. When she got to his text in-box, she was stunned to see this message from Rachel: "Ashlee and Ahmed are the perfect couple: stupid sorority slut and steroided camel jockey." As Ashlee describes, "My heart just stopped. I literally sat there, shaking. I thought it was a joke, until I scrolled down and found *hundreds* of similar messages." Text after text slammed Ashlee and mocked Ahmed's ethnicity. Later that night, crying hysterically, Ashlee summoned the courage to text Rachel: "I cleared out Mike's phone and found all your texts about me and Ahmed. You two are *horrible*. I want nothing to do with either of you." Rachel immediately texted back, "How dare you read our messages! Those were private! Whatever Ashlee— I'm sorry you're angry but Mike and I were just messing around. You're completely overreacting." In the aftermath, Ashlee returned Mike's iPhone, and refused all contact with Rachel. Back at school that fall, Ashlee received an e-mail with the subject line, "please don't delete." The message read: "I don't even know where to begin. I know I messed up, but I can't lose you as a friend. We've been best friends forever, and I'd hate to lose you over something this dumb. I know I'm asking a lot of you to forgive me, but please think about it." Ashlee deleted the message.

To this point, we've talked about friendships as involvements that provide us with abundant and important rewards. Although this is true, friendships also present us with a variety of intense interpersonal challenges. Three of the most common are friendship betrayal, geographic distance, and attraction.

BETRAYAL

Given the value friends place upon mutual support and defending each other, it's no surprise that betrayal is the most commonly reported reason for ending a friendship (Miller, Hefner, & Scott, 2007). Acts of friendship betrayal include breaking confidences, backstabbing (criticizing a friend behind his or her back), spreading rumors or gossip, and lying—all of which violate the friendship rules discussed earlier. When friends violate these rules, it's difficult for friendships to survive. Similar to romantic betrayal, friends who are betrayed experience an overwhelming sense of relationship devaluation and loss (Miller et al., 2007). And—as with the Ashlee and Rachel example—betrayal often leads people to realize things about their friends' characters that simply can't be tolerated.

How can you better manage friendship betrayal, when it occurs? If it's a friendship of any closeness, expect to experience grief as you suffer the loss of trust, intimacy, and the image of your friend you once held dear. Revisit the suggestions for grief management offered in Chapter 4, especially the value of *emotion-sharing*—that is, talking about your experience directly with people who have gone through the same thing. Importantly, avoid lashing out at the betrayer, or seeking revenge—both of which will simply make matters worse.

When you're able, ponder whether you can or should repair the friendship. Ask yourself the following questions to help guide your decision. First, how serious was the betrayal? Not all betrayals are of equal standing, so think carefully about whether this incident is something you can learn to live with, or not. Second, what was the context preceding and surrounding the betrayal? Did *you* do something to provoke the betrayal? Would you have done the same thing in the same situation—or *have* you done similar things in the past? Be careful about blaming others for behaviors that you caused, holding double standards, and judging friends in ways you wouldn't wish to be judged yourself. Third, do the benefits of continuing the friendship outweigh the costs? Use the friendship rules as a guide: Does your friend follow most of these rules, most of the time? If so, he or she may actually be a desirable friend. Fourth, is this betrayal a one-time event, or part of a consistent pattern? Everyone falls from grace on occasion; what you want to avoid is a person who habitually abuses your trust. Last, and perhaps most important, does this betrayal reveal something about your friend's character that you simply can't live with? Be honest with yourself and realize that some friendships are best left broken following betrayal. In Ashlee's case, despite years of having Rachel as her best friend—and all the corresponding emotional, energy, and time investment—the betrayal revealed multiple aspects of Rachel's character that Ashlee simply couldn't tolerate, including sexism, racism, phoniness, and viciousness.

GEOGRAPHIC SEPARATION

A contributing factor to Ashlee and Rachel's falling out was their geographic separation, which led them to grow apart. Separation is one of the most common and intense challenges friends face (Wang & Andersen, 2007). Upwards of 90 percent of people report having at least one long-distance friendship, and 80 percent report having a close friend who lives far away (Rohlfing, 1995). Physical separation prevents friends from adequately satisfying the needs that form the foundation of their relationship, such as sharing activities and intimate self-disclosure.

Although most friends begin long-distance separations with the intention of seeing each other regularly, they rarely visit solely for the sake of reuniting. Instead, they tend to see each other only when there's some other reason for them to be in the same area. This is because long-distance friends often don't have the money or time to travel only to visit a friend (Rohlfing, 1995). Instead, they visit when other commitments such as professional conferences, visits with relatives, or class reunions bring them together. Such contacts often leave friends feeling empty because their time together is so limited.

Which friendships tend to survive geographic distance, and which lapse? In friendships that survive, the two people feel a particularly strong *liking*—that is,

skills practice

Managing Friendship Betrayal
If you find yourself in a situation in which a friend betrays you:

❶ Manage the intense anger and grief you experience.

❷ Avoid seeking revenge or verbal retaliation.

❸ Contact others who have experienced similar betrayals, and discuss your experience with them.

❹ Evaluate the betrayal, including how serious it is, what caused it, whether it's a one-time event or part of a behavioral pattern, and whether you would have done something similar.

❺ Assess the value of your friendship, compared against the damage of the betrayal.

❻ End or repair the friendship, based on your analysis.

"Are you multitasking me?"

affection and respect—for each other. Friendships between individuals who "enjoy knowing each other" and "have great admiration for each other" are most likely to endure.

Friends who overcome separation also accept change as a natural part of life and their relationship. If you get together with a good friend you haven't seen in a long while, you both likely will have changed in terms of profession, attitudes, and appearance. Friends who are comfortable with such changes, and offer identity support, tend to have relationships that survive. Friends who want their friends to "always stay the same," don't.

Moreover, friendships that survive separation involve friends who have a strong sense of shared history. In their conversations, they frequently celebrate the past as well as anticipate sharing events in the future. This sense of shared past, present, and future enables them to "pick up where they left off" after being out of touch for a while. Successful long-distance friendships thus involve feeling a sense of relationship continuity and perceiving the relationship as solid and ongoing.

How can you communicate in ways that foster these qualities in your own long-distance friendships? Use technology (Skype, Facebook, phone, text, etc.) to regularly communicate with your friends. Focus your communication on activities and interests that you share. Doing this alleviates the feeling of loss that comes with the inability to actually spend time together (Rabby, 1997). So, for example, if a friend who now lives far away used to be your daily workout or

Friendship Distance-Durability

This quiz helps you determine whether a friendship is durable enough to survive the challenge of geographic distance. Place a check mark next to each statement below with which you agree. Then total your check marks and use the scoring key at the bottom to determine your friendship distance-durability.

_____ My friend and I share a great deal of personal history together.

_____ I feel a strong sense of warmth and fondness toward my friend.

_____ I have great respect for my friend as a person.

_____ I don't expect my friend to be the exact same person in the future as he or she is now.

_____ Having this person as my friend makes me happy.

_____ Even if we've been out of touch for a while, my friend and I always seem to be able to pick up where we left off when we communicate again.

_____ I welcome future changes in my friend's beliefs, values, and attitudes—even if they're different than mine—as long as these changes bring him or her happiness.

_____ My friend is the kind of person I would like to be.

_____ My friend and I enjoy sharing numerous stories from our past that remind us of how close we've been.

_____ I anticipate that as my friend ages, he or she will develop new and varied interests.

Scoring: 0–3 = Low durability, friendship may have difficulty surviving geographic separation; 4–6 = Moderate durability, friendship may be able to handle separation; 7–10 = High durability, friendship has strong potential for enduring across time and distance.

jogging buddy, send her regular e-mails or texts updating her on your marathon training and inquiring about her performance in local races.

Also, remind your long-distance friends that you still think of them with affection and hold them in high regard. Look for opportunities to appropriately express your feelings for your friend, such as: "I miss our Thursday night movie watching! Have you seen any good films lately?" In addition, devote some of your communication to fondly recounting events and experiences you have shared in your past, as well as discussing plans for the future. Such exchanges bolster the sense of relational continuity critical to maintaining friendships.

Finally, when your long-distance friends go through dramatic life changes—as they inevitably will—communicate your continued support of their valued social identities. For instance, a close friend you haven't seen in a while may abandon previously shared religious beliefs, adopt new political viewpoints, or substantially alter his or her looks. In making these and other kinds of significant changes, your friend may look to you for identity support, as a friend. A good long-distance friend of mine, Vikram, occupied a job for several years that required a fair degree of professional contact with me, allowing us the opportunity (and excuse) to communicate regularly. Then he accepted a new position with a different company. This new opportunity represented a dramatic professional

skills practice

Using Technology to Overcome Distance
Maintaining long-distance friendships through online communication

❶ Think of a close friend who lives far away.

❷ In your online interactions, focus your message content on common interests, making sure to ask about your friend's continued participation in these things.

❸ Send text messages saying you're thinking of and missing her or him.

❹ Craft e-mails that fondly recap past shared experiences.

❺ Forward Web links with ideas for future activities you can share together.

❻ When your friend discloses major life changes, provide support in the quickest fashion possible, whether by text, e-mail, phone call, or all three.

advancement for him, but it also meant we would have far fewer opportunities to interact once he started the new job. When he broke the news to me, he expected a certain degree of rancor on my part. Instead, I surprised him by expressing my firm support and excitement regarding his decision, even though I knew that, owing to this change, our paths wouldn't cross nearly as often.

ATTRACTION: ROMANCE AND FWB RELATIONSHIPS

A final challenge facing friends is attraction to one another beyond friendship: romantic, sexual, or both. Men typically report more of a desire for romantic involvement with their platonic friends than do women (Schneider & Kenny, 2000). However, one study found that 87 percent of college women and 93 percent of college men reported feeling sexually attracted to a friend at some point in their lives (Asada, Morrison, Hughes, & Fitzpatrick, 2003).

Within cross-sex friendships, the issue of attraction is always a challenge, even when no such attraction exists between the friends. This is because people in their surrounding networks—and the broader culture at large—presume that such attraction *will* exist between men and women, and often pester cross-sex friends about it (Halatsis & Christakis, 2009). But when attraction does blossom between friends, same-sex or cross-sex, pursuing a sexual or romantic relationship brings its own challenges. Friends who feel attracted to one another typically report high uncertainty as a result: both regarding the nature of their relationship and whether or not their friend feels the same way (Weger & Emmett, 2009).

Friends cope with attraction by doing one of three things. Some friends simply repress the attraction, most commonly out of respect for their friendship (Messman et al., 2000). Friends who seek to repress attraction typically engage in *mental management*—they do things to actively manage how they think about each other so that the attraction is diminished (Halatsis & Christakis, 2009). These may include pacts and promises to not pursue the attraction, a strict avoidance of flirting, and the curtailing of activities (such as going out drinking) that might inadvertently lead to sexual interaction (Halatsis & Christakis, 2009). Alternatively, some friends act on their attraction by either developing a full-fledged romantic involvement, or trying to blend their friendship with sexual activity through a "friends-with-benefits" arrangement.

Romance between Friends   Many friends who develop an attraction opt to pursue a romantic relationship. The first and most powerful cue of such desire is a radical increase in the amount of time the friends spend flirting with each other (Weger & Emmett, 2009). Although people in Western cultures like to think of friendships and romantic relationships as strictly separate, many enduring and successful romances evolve from friendships. One of the strongest predictors of whether or not a friendship can successfully transition to romance is simply whether the friends already possess romantic beliefs that link friendship with love (Hendrick & Hendrick, 1992).

Although it's commonly believed that pursuing a romantic relationship will "kill the friendship" if or when the romance fizzles, the results actually are mixed. People who were friends prior to a romance are much more likely to be friends following a failed romance than those who were not friends first (Schneider & Kenny, 2000). However, postromance friendships tend to be less close than those with friends who have always been platonic. How can you successfully transition from friendship to romance, or back again? First, *expect difference*. Romantic relationships and friendships are fundamentally different in expectations, demands, commitment, and corresponding emotional intensity. Don't presume that your feelings, those of your partner, or the interplay between you two, will be the same. Second, *emphasize disclosure*. Relationship transitions tend to evoke high uncertainty, as partners worry about what the other thinks and feels, and wonder where the relationship is going. To reduce this uncertainty, share your feelings in an open and honest fashion, and encourage your partner to do the same. Finally, *offer assurances*. Let your partner know that whether you two are friends or lovers, you stand by him or her, and your relationship, regardless. This is especially important when transitioning back to friendship from romance, as your partner may believe that your relationship is now over.

Friends with Benefits   No jealousy. No flowers. No sleepovers. No cuddling. These and other rules are established by the characters Emma and Adam in the movie *No Strings Attached*, in an attempt to add sex to their friendship while avoiding romantic attachment. At first it works out great: Emma can focus on her medical career, and Adam can continue to date (and sleep with) other people. However, their deal sours as feelings arise between them that clash with the rules they've established.

Like Emma and Adam in *No Strings Attached*, some friends deal with sexual attraction by forming a "friends-with-benefits" (FWB) relationship. In **FWB relationships**, the participants engage in sexual activity, but not with the purpose of transforming the relationship into a romantic attachment (Hughes, Morrison, & Asada, 2005). FWB relationships appear to be widespread. Studies

◁ Adam attempts to follow the rules of his FWB relationship by giving Emma a bouquet of carrots instead of flowers in *No Strings Attached*. However, like many FWB relationships, Adam and Emma eventually have to deal with the romantic impulses they feel toward each other.

12 / Relationships in the Workplace

each other. Our husbands do not understand how we could have so much to say to each other after working side by side all day." Silvia adds, "We always joke about being 'sisters separated at birth.' We tell everyone that!"

The van programs that Silvia and Vivian manage are very successful and so is their enduring and intimate friendship, which has survived stress, power shifts, personal change, and time. For Silvia and Vivian, as for anyone with a close coworker friendship, the line between work and home life has been blurred. In its place, what has emerged is a union of the personal and the professional that allows these friends to meet their daily work challenges *and* share in each other's private triumphs and troubles. As Vivian describes, "I could not have become the successful manager that I am without Silvia's guidance and support. We are a team. We can work very well apart from each other, but we always come back together when it comes to big decisions. I have never felt anything but love and respect for Silvia." Discussing their relationship separately, Silvia offers a similar sentiment: "We love and respect each other and always bounce big decisions [off] each other, knowing that we can trust what the other person says. We help each other and talk about everything without feeling like we are being judged."

throughout the community and provided health care services to underserved and uninsured residents. When the health van's manager resigned, Vivian recruited Silvia for the position. In a reversal of their previous workplace roles, Silvia became Vivian's supervisor. But as Silvia describes, "It didn't make any difference to our friendship."

Silvia was an excellent manager, but at heart she remained an allergy nurse. When the Children's Hospital started a second van program—a "Breathmobile" providing asthma care for uninsured children—Silvia switched to managing the Breathmobile. She persuaded Vivian to take the reins as health van manager. Today, the two women travel to schools and community clinics in the county, giving presentations to parents, teachers, and community members. Their friendship remains steadfast. As Vivian notes, "We can talk on the phone forever. It seems we always have something to run by

3 YOUR TURN

Think about the interpersonal communication concepts, skills, and insights you have learned while reading this book, especially this chapter. Try to keep all of this in mind while working through the following five steps, which will help you become aware of how you can make better interpersonal communication choices in your relationships. Remember, there are no right answers, so think hard about what choice you will make! (P.S. Need help? See the *Helpful Concepts* listed below.)

● step 1

Reflect on yourself. What are your thoughts and feelings in this situation? What attributions are you making about Karina? John and your other friends? Are your attributions accurate?

● step 2

Reflect on your friends. Using perspective-taking and empathic concern, put yourself in John's and your other friends' shoes. What are they thinking and feeling in this situation? Then consider Karina's thoughts and feelings.

● step 3

Identify the optimal outcome. Think about all the information you have about Karina, her communication with you, your history with her, and the situation with your other friends. Consider your own feelings as well as everyone else's. Given all these factors, what's the best, most constructive outcome possible here? Be sure to consider not just what's best for *you*, but what's best for Karina and your friends as well.

● step 4

Locate the roadblocks. Taking into consideration your own thoughts and feelings, Karina's, and those of your friends, what's preventing you from achieving the optimal outcome you identified in Step 3?

● step 5

Chart your course. What can you say and do to overcome the roadblocks you've identified and achieve your optimal outcome?

HELPFUL CONCEPTS

Best friends, **361–363**

Identity support, **362–363**

Friendship rules, **368–370**

Betrayal, **372–373**

suggest that around 50 percent of college students have had such a relationship (Mongeau, Ramirez, & Vorrell, 2003).

Those who form FWB relationships do so for two reasons: they welcome the lack of commitment (and all its attendant sacrifices), and they want to satisfy sexual needs (Asada et al., 2003). Both men and women cite these same reasons, contradicting stereotypes that women seek only emotional satisfaction in relationships while men want only sex.

Most partners in FWB relationships develop rules regarding emotional attachment, communication, and sex, akin to those depicted in *No Strings Attached* (Hughes et al., 2005). For example, they commonly strike an agreement to not fall in love. And they establish rules governing the frequency of phone calling, e-mailing, and text-messaging; and sex rules regarding safer sex practices, frequency of sex, and

self-reflection

Have you had an FWB relationship? If so, what were the pros and cons? Did you and your friend establish rules for the relationship? If so, what were they? How well did you both follow those rules?

For much of our lives, friendships are *the* most important close relationships we have

sexual exclusivity. But despite these rules, the majority of FWB relationships fail eventually, costing the participants their original friendship as well as the sexual arrangement. Why? As with Emma and Adam, participants tend to develop romantic feelings despite their best efforts to avoid them, and many decide that the FWB relationship doesn't satisfy them enough emotionally (Hughes et al., 2005).

The Importance of Friends

Friends provide essential emotional security

Friendships are both delicate and deep. On the one hand, they're the most transitory of our close relationships. They come and go across our life span, depending on where we're living, going to school, and working; and how our personal interests shift and evolve. As a simple test of this, make a list of the five closest friends in your life right now, in rank order. Then make the same list based on your closest friends five years ago. Chances are, at least some of the names and rankings will have changed.

But at the same time, friendships are deep. For much of our lives, friendships are *the* most important close relationships we have. Our friends keep us grounded, and provide us with support in times of crisis. When lovers betray or abandon us, or family members drive us crazy, it's our friends we turn to for support. When everything else seems wrong with the world, and our lives seem mired in misadventure, we find solace in the simple truth shared by Clarence the Angel in the movie *It's a Wonderful Life*: No one is a failure who has friends.

We began this chapter with a snowstorm and two television employees trapped together. Huddled within the shelter of a warm apartment, Oprah Winfrey and Gail King learned that despite their different backgrounds, they shared the same sensibilities. The friendship that sparked would not only stand the test of time, but would become one of the world's most famous.

Which friends love you, respect you, and want the best for you? On whom can you count to lift you up and support you, in good times and bad?

Although the relationship between Oprah and Gayle may be iconic, it mirrors the friendships we experience in our own lives. Like us, they were drawn to each other through shared interests, viewpoints, and values. And like the bonds we forge

POSTSCRIPT

with our friends, theirs remains cemented through trust, communication, and support.

key terms

▶ You can watch brief, illustrative videos of these terms and test your understanding of the concepts online in *VideoCentral: Interpersonal Communication* at bedfordstmartins .com/reflectrelate.

key concepts

The Nature of Friendship

- Unlike family relationships, **friendships** are voluntary, and the participants generally don't expect them to be as intimate or long lasting as serious romances and family relationships.

- Depending on the functions being fulfilled, friendships may be primarily **communal** or **agentic**.

- The importance we attribute to our friendships changes throughout our lives. Age, culture, gender, and life situations all influence whether friends are our primary source of intimacy.

- While technology allows us to communicate with friends 24/7, our closest friends are often those that we spend time with online and off.

Types of Friendship

- We have many types of friends, but we often consider a smaller number our *close* and *best friends.* The latter are distinguished by providing unwavering **identity support** for our **valued social identities** over time.

- **Cross-category friendships**—like cross-sex, cross-orientation, intercultural, and interethnic— are a powerful way to break down ingrouper and outgrouper perceptions and purge people of negative stereotypes.

Maintaining Friendships

- Across cultures, people agree on **friendship rules**, the basic principles that underlie the maintenance of successful friendships. Friends who follow these rules are more likely to remain friends than those who don't.

- Two of the most important maintenance strategies for friends are sharing activities and self-disclosure.

Friendship Challenges

- As in other relationships, friendship betrayal often leads to an overwhelming sense of relationship devaluation and loss. Some friendships can be repaired after a betrayal, but some will end.

- One of the greatest challenges friends face is geographic separation. Communication technologies can help such friends overcome distance by allowing for regular interaction and maintaining a sense of shared interests.

- Some people form sexual relationships with their friends, known as friends-with-benefits, or **FWB relationships**. Both men and women enter these relationships to satisfy sexual needs. Most of these relationships fail owing to unanticipated emotional challenges.

key skills

- Interested in the different functions of friendships? Read about what needs our friendships fulfill on pages 357–358.

- What kind of friend are you? Take the *Self-Quiz* on page 363 to find out.

- How can you foster intercultural and interethnic friendships? Review pages 365–367 for advice on how to balance the similarities and differences in such friendships.

- What are the rules that can help friendships succeed? Find out on pages 368–370.

- How can you use interpersonal communication to maintain a friendship? Try the *Skills Practice* on page 370.

- What can you do to deal with friendship betrayal? Read the suggestions on pages 372–373 and try the *Skills Practice* on page 373.

- Can a friendship survive geographic separation? Review the suggestions for maintaining long-distance friendships on pages 373–374; then do the *Self-Quiz* on page 375 and try the *Skills Practice* on page 376.

- Curious about whether a friendship can survive a romantic entanglement? Learn about attraction between friends on pages 376–377 and 380–381, and then review the suggestions for transitioning from romance back to friendship on page 377.

- What would you do if you had to choose between friends? Complete the *Making Relationship Choices* exercise on pages 378–379 to find out.

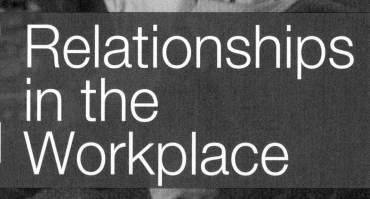

12 Relationships in the Workplace

With workplace relationships, the professional is profoundly personal

W hen Silvia Amaro and Vivian Derr first began working together at a California medical office, neither had any idea how close their relationship would become or that it would endure for more than a quarter century. Silvia was a Latina allergy nurse from south Texas; Vivian, a Euro-American pediatric nurse-practitioner from Pennsylvania. Silvia's work responsibilities included assisting physicians, meeting walk-in patients, making phone assessments, and scheduling appointments. Vivian, who was Silvia's supervisor, did all of these tasks plus oversaw the nursing staff. Working together daily, the two quickly made a deal to manage patient visitations by splitting the workload.[1]

Silvia and Vivian's workplace collaboration evolved into a close friendship as the two nurses began sharing personal information with each other. As their friendship deepened, the women's home lives and work lives became intertwined. Silvia's youngest daughter babysat Vivian's son. Vivian gave Silvia's boys sports physicals so Silvia wouldn't have to make time to bring them to a doctor.

After several years, Silvia was promoted to a management position while Vivian was recruited to work at Children's Hospital of Orange County in California. The hospital operated a health van, which traveled

---

[1]All information and quotes that follow are from V. Derr and S. Amaro (personal communications with author, March and April 2005). Published with permission.

385

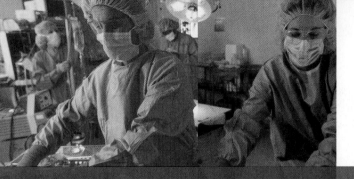

throughout the community and provided health care services to underserved and uninsured residents. When the health van's manager resigned, Vivian recruited Silvia for the position. In a reversal of their previous workplace roles, Silvia became Vivian's supervisor. But as Silvia describes, "It didn't make any difference to our friendship."

Silvia was an excellent manager, but at heart she remained an allergy nurse. When the Children's Hospital started a second van program—a "Breathmobile" providing asthma care for uninsured children—Silvia switched to managing the Breathmobile. She persuaded Vivian to take the reins as health van manager. Today, the two women travel to schools and community clinics in the county, giving presentations to parents, teachers, and community members. Their friendship remains steadfast. As Vivian notes, "We can talk on the phone forever. It seems we always have something to run by

each other. Our husbands do not understand how we could have so much to say to each other after working side by side all day." Silvia adds, "We always joke about being 'sisters separated at birth.' We tell everyone that!"

The van programs that Silvia and Vivian manage are very successful and so is their enduring and intimate friendship, which has survived stress, power shifts, personal change, and time. For Silvia and Vivian, as for anyone with a close coworker friendship, the line between work and home life has been blurred. In its place, what has emerged is a union of the personal and the professional that allows these friends to meet their daily work challenges *and* share in each other's private triumphs and troubles. As Vivian describes, "I could not have become the successful manager that I am without Silvia's guidance and support. We are a team. We can work very well apart from each other, but we always come back together when it comes to big decisions. I have never felt anything but love and respect for Silvia." Discussing their relationship separately, Silvia offers a similar sentiment: "We love and respect each other and always bounce big decisions [off] each other, knowing that we can trust what the other person says. We help each other and talk about everything without feeling like we are being judged."

We like to think of our personal and professional lives as separate. Our personal lives consist of "real" relationships: romantic partners, family members, friends. Our work lives exist in a parallel universe of less meaningful interactions. But this division is a pretense. We spend most of our adult waking hours working, and spend more time interacting with coworkers than with any other type of relationship partner (Sias & Perry, 2004). This makes our workplace relationships more important than we often care to admit. Indeed, workplace relationship health predicts both professional and personal outcomes. When our workplace communication and relationships are satisfying, we achieve more professionally and feel happier at home. When our workplace communication and relationships slip into dysfunction, on-the-job productivity and relationships outside of the workplace suffer.

In this chapter, we look at interpersonal communication and relationships in the workplace. You'll learn:

- How workplace relationships compare with other types of interpersonal relationships
- Tactics for fostering healthy relationships with peers at work
- Strategies for communicating competently with supervisors and subordinates
- Suggestions for coping with challenges to workplace relationships

The Nature of Workplace Relationships

How organizations' cultures, networks, and climates work

Whether it's a church, a branch of the military, a corporation, or a nonprofit charity, an organization exists and functions because coworkers communicate and form relationships with one another (Contractor & Grant, 1996). All of the information sharing, decision making, and emotional and practical support that occurs in the workplace does so in the context of coworker relationships (Sias, Krone, & Jablin, 2002). Consequently, interpersonal communication and relationships are an organization's lifeblood.

Any affiliation you have with a professional peer, supervisor, subordinate, or mentor can be considered a **workplace relationship**. These involvements differ along three dimensions: *status, intimacy,* and *choice* (Sias & Perry, 2004). First, most organizations are structured hierarchically in terms of status, with people ranked higher or lower than others in organizational position and power. Thus, a defining feature of workplace relationships is the equality or inequality of relationship partners. Second, workplace relationships vary in intimacy. Some remain strictly professional, with interpersonal communication restricted to work-related concerns. Others, like the relationship between Vivian Derr and Silvia Amaro, become deeply personal. Third, workplace relationships are defined by choice, the degree to which participants willingly engage in them. Although most of us don't get to handpick our coworkers, we do choose which coworkers we befriend.

Interpersonal communication and relationships are an organization's lifeblood

self-reflection

Think of the relationships you have with people at work. What makes them "good" or "bad"? When you compare the benefits and drawbacks of your close workplace relationships, how does this affect your feelings about the organization?

Like all interpersonal involvements, workplace relationships provide us with both benefits and costs. On the plus side, workplace relationships can enhance our professional skills through the insights others provide, and increase the speed with which we rise through the organizational hierarchy (Sias & Perry, 2004). They make work more enjoyable, bolster our commitment to the organization, improve morale, and decrease employee turnover (Sias & Cahill, 1998). On the negative side, workplace relationships can spawn gossip and cliques (Albrecht & Bach, 1997). They also can add additional stress to our lives by forcing us to shoulder not only our own professional burdens but the personal challenges of our workplace friends.

As we've stressed throughout this book, interpersonal relationships are forged and maintained within the broader context of social networks and surrounding ethnic, religious, and socioeconomic class cultures. Workplace relationships are no exception. However, in addition to being shaped by all of the above-mentioned forces, workplace relationships are also strongly influenced by each organization's unique culture, networks, climate, and technology.

THE CULTURE OF THE WORKPLACE

Like many teens growing up in the United States, I got my first two jobs in chain restaurants—six months at an ice cream parlor and three years at a pizza restaurant. The two workplaces couldn't have been more different. The ice cream parlor had a strict behavior code, and violations were grounds for termination. Workers had to wear buttons saying how "fun" work was, but this was far from the truth. Managers snapped orders at employees and rarely socialized with them outside of the workplace. Because employee turnover was high, few people developed close friendships with coworkers. The pizza restaurant was the opposite. Workers socialized after hours, and supervisor-subordinate relationships were friendly. A sense of camaraderie permeated the restaurant, and most employees' closest personal friends were coworkers. Employee turnover was low, and management further encouraged close friendships through outside activities, including a softball team and waterskiing parties.

In the same way that different cultures have unique traditions, each workplace possesses a distinctive set of beliefs regarding how things are done and how people should behave, known as its **organizational culture** (Katz & Kahn, 1978). Organizational culture influences everything from job satisfaction and organizational commitment to service quality and staff turnover (Glisson & James, 2002). An organization's culture derives from three sources, the first of which is *workplace values*: beliefs people share about work performance, dedication to the organization, and coworker relationships. For example, both places I worked at in my youth stressed the values of employee excellence and productivity. But the ice cream parlor discouraged friendships between coworkers, whereas the pizza restaurant encouraged such relationships. Other examples of workplace values include beliefs regarding corporate responsibility to the environment, commitment to stakeholders (customers, employees, business partners, shareholders, etc.), and worker integrity.

Workplace values create *workplace norms*—guidelines governing appropriate interpersonal communication and relationships (Eisenberg & Goodall, 2004). In each organization, expectations evolve regarding the frequency and tone of communication. In some organizations, informality is the norm. For example, you might be encouraged by your supervisor to challenge his or her ideas, regardless of your place in the hierarchy. In other organizations, people are expected to strictly observe authority.

The final influence on an organization's culture is its *workplace artifacts*—the objects and structures that define the organization (Schein, 1985). Workplace artifacts include everything from the physical layout of your workspace to dress codes and even motivational items such as hallway posters urging you to always perform at your best.

When you join an organization, you are socialized into its culture through formal and informal encounters with established coworkers (Miller, 1995). During my first day as a dishwasher at the ice cream parlor, for example, my trainer (another dishwasher) openly mocked the "it's fun to work here" buttons we were all

▶ The values, norms, and artifacts of an organization constitute its culture.

389

forced to wear, telling me instead, "People work here for one reason: the paycheck." My training at the pizza restaurant was conducted by the manager. He encouraged me to stay after work and enjoy free food and drink with my coworkers—an activity he called "new employee training."

NETWORKS IN THE WORKPLACE

Just as each of us has social networks of acquaintances, friends, and family members linked through communication, workplaces also have systems of communication linkages, known as **organizational networks** (Miller, 1995). Organizational networks are defined by three characteristics: the nature of the information that flows through them, the media or channels through which the information flows, and the frequency and number of connections among people in a network, also known as *network density*.

In each organizational network, the types of information flowing through the network are diverse (Farace, Monge, & Russell, 1977). In some parts of the network, participants exchange work-related information. For instance, people in product development may interact regularly with people in marketing to create the right advertising campaign for a new product. In other parts of the network, participants share personal information. The "rumor mill"—by which coworkers pass along gossip and speculate about one another's professional and personal lives—is an example.

The second characteristic is the media or channels through which people in workplaces exchange information. These include face-to-face encounters, cell-phone conversations, instant-messaging, and e-mail exchanges. Some networks may be **virtual networks**—groups of coworkers linked solely through e-mail, social networking sites, Skype, and other online services. Virtual networks are increasingly prevalent, as the cost of fuel for transportation skyrockets and more people opt to *telecommute* (work from home and communicate with coworkers via phone and computer). For example, 2 percent of U.S. adults in the workforce telecommute full-time, 9 percent telecommute part-time, and 48 percent of employers offer the option of telecommuting at least one day a week (Gaitonde, 2011).

Last, networks are defined by their density: how connected each member of the network is to other members. In dense networks, every worker regularly interacts with every other network member. By contrast, members of loose networks may have contact with just one or two other members. Density is influenced by a variety of factors, including job requirements (some jobs simply don't allow for much interaction between network members), physical layout of the workspace (whether network members are widely separated or clustered together), and organizational culture (some workplaces encourage frequent interaction; others discourage it). However, two of the strongest factors are familiarity and intimacy: networks in which members have known each other for a long time and are personally close tend to be denser.

Organizational networks come in many different forms. Some are formally defined by the organization—the supervisors to whom you report, the employees you oversee, the peers with whom you collaborate. Others are informal and are created by coworkers themselves. Sometimes **workplace cliques** emerge—dense networks of coworkers who share the same workplace values and broader life attitudes (Jones, 1999). Within any workplace, a number of different cliques may exist: a clique of "slackers" who do the minimum work necessary, a "fast track" clique of ambitious young workers, an "old boys" clique of longtime employees, and so forth.

Workplace cliques educate new employees about whom they can trust and which networks they should belong to, helping people to quickly assimilate into the organizational culture. They also provide information about how things work in the organization. For example, when the copier breaks down or you need to expedite a shipment, members of a workplace clique can provide you with the assistance you need. But cliques can have disadvantages. For example, they may espouse workplace values contrary to those advocated by the organization: priding themselves on being "rebels," or disparaging bosses behind their backs. Worse, they may encourage unethical workplace behavior, such as punching a friend's time card to cover up the fact that the friend is absent.

Regardless of the form that organizational networks take, they are the principal wellsprings from which people get their workplace information. As a consequence, it's vital to keep two things in mind. First, *the private is public in the workplace*. Because all workplace relationships occur within organizational networks, your communication and behavior will serve as material for discussion among network members. Presume that everything you say and do will be shared throughout your organization.

The private is public in the workplace

Second, *the organizational networks to which you belong can strongly determine the kinds of opportunities—and obstacles—you'll encounter as you advance in your career.* For this reason, it's important to build interpersonal ties with coworkers who are both respected and connected. Try to develop relationships with *organizational insiders*, workers who are reputable, knowledgeable, and connected to dense organizational networks. The coworkers you befriend will strongly determine your experiences in the organization.

ORGANIZATIONAL CLIMATES

Think about an organization with which you're currently involved, as a paid worker, volunteer, or member. How would you describe the overall emotional tone of the place—that is, the way it *feels* to be there? Is it supportive, warm, and welcoming? Detached, cool, and unfriendly? Somewhere in between? This overarching emotional quality of a workplace is known as its **organizational climate** (Kreps, 1990). Organizational climate is created primarily through interpersonal communication, specifically, the amount of trust, openness, listening, and supportiveness present in the interactions between organizational members (Mohammed & Hussein, 2008).

Two types of organizational climates exist (Kreps, 1990). In a **defensive climate** the environment is unfriendly, rigid, and unsupportive of workers' professional and personal needs. For example, supervisors may use communication as a way to strategically control others and to strictly enforce company hierarchy. Employees may resist change, be close-minded toward new ideas or outside input, and negatively perceive any dissent. In contrast, workers in a **supportive climate** describe the workplace as warm, open, and supportive. Workers communicate

VideoCentral ⊙

bedfordstmartins.com /reflectrelate

Defensive Climate
Watch this clip online to answer the questions below.

How did the coworkers in this video create a defensive climate? What influence do you think their workplace culture had on creating their organizational climate?

Want to see more? Check out VideoCentral for a clip illustrating **supportive climate**.

table 12.1   Creating a Supportive Climate

These suggestions will help you build supportiveness in the workplace. They are especially important if you are a supervisor or manager.

1. *Encourage honest communication.* Workplace climates are most supportive when people view one another as honest and open.

2. *Adopt a flexible mind-set.* Be open to others' ideas, criticisms, and suggestions. Examine your own ideas for weaknesses. Avoid using absolutes ("This is the only option").

3. *Collaborate rather than control.* Avoid trying to manipulate others. Instead, ask for their ideas and perspectives.

4. *Describe challenges rather than assign blame.* When problems arise at work, talk about them in neutral terms rather than pointing fingers.

5. *Offer concern rather than professional detachment.* When coworkers or employees seek your support on personal dilemmas, demonstrate empathy, respect, and understanding.

6. *Emphasize equality.* Avoid pulling rank on people. When you have power over others, it's vital to treat them with respect.

honestly, collaborate to solve problems, share credit, practice empathy, and encourage people to treat one another with respect, despite any imbalance in power.

Organizational climates are rarely purely defensive or supportive. Instead, most fall somewhere in between. In addition, organizations may have different climates within different units, depending on workers' personalities, job demands, and supervisor communication styles (Elci & Alpken, 2009).

As just one person in your organization, you obviously don't have sole control over the climate. Nevertheless, organizational climate is built from the ground up: it is the sum total of individuals' interpersonal behavior in the workplace. Consequently, everything you say and do in your workplace contributes to the climate. See Table 12.1 for tips on how to encourage a supportive organizational climate.

TECHNOLOGY IN THE WORKPLACE

The use of computer-based communication technologies is now standard within workplaces; everyone from executives to repairpersons uses texting, Twitter, and instant-messaging to coordinate professional activities (Berry, 2006). E-mail has largely replaced written memos and much of telephone and face-to-face interactions. In many corporate workplaces, e-mail is the *primary* communication medium; daily business could not occur without it (Waldvogel, 2007).

Computer-mediated communication in the workplace provides substantial advantages over face-to-face and phone interactions, especially when it comes to complex decision making requiring input from multiple employees, some of whom may be long-distance (Berry, 2006). For example, hosting meetings online through live chat or posting to a common site ensures more active and equal participation than face-to-face meetings. People can contribute to the interaction without

self-reflection

What is your organization's climate like? Is it supportive, defensive, or somewhere in between? What could you do differently to improve the climate?

◯ Collaboration, not only in communication, but in using teamwork to accomplish tasks and projects, is a way to create a supportive climate.

▶ Workers in the United States now spend almost two hours *a day* cyberslacking. How does such behavior influence the organizational culture and organizational climates of workplaces?

skills practice

Collaborating via Technology

Using technology to collaboratively meet organizational challenges

❶ Identify a challenge faced by your group or organization.

❷ Create an online discussion group or community related to this issue.

❸ Describe the problem in neutral terms, avoiding assignment of blame.

❹ E-mail or message everyone in your work unit, inviting them to post potential solutions.

❺ Encourage open and honest assessment of ideas.

concern for interrupting or talking over others. The conversations also are more democratic: people in authority can't "stare down" those with whom they disagree, suppressing their input; and those who suffer from shyness feel more comfortable contributing. In addition, online discussions provide participants with freedom from time and geographic constraints. People can chime in on the conversation whenever they like over a period of days or even weeks, and participants can join or leave the discussion without having to physically move—an enormous benefit to those who are geographically distant. Online discussions are often more informative, detailed, and factual than face-to-face conversations, as participants have the opportunity to fact-check the information in each of their comments before they post them. Keep these advantages in mind, if you're in a position to guide such decision-making discussions.

But the biggest advantage of communication technologies within the workplace is that they *connect* workers, in a relational fashion. Online chat has usurped gossiping in the coffee room or talking on the telephone as the leading way employees build and bolster interpersonal ties (Riedy & Wen, 2010). Technologies allow workers to form and maintain friendships with coworkers they previously would not have been able to, including workers in other divisions of the company or other parts of the country or world (Quan-Haase, Cothrel, & Wellman, 2005).

As with anything, the benefits of workplace technologies are accompanied by certain disadvantages, the most pronounced of which is the near-constant distraction provided by online games, apps, and social networking sites. Workers in the United States now spend almost two hours *a day* **cyberslacking**: using their work computers to game, web surf, update Facebook, e-mail, and IM about personal interests and activities, when they should be focused on work tasks (Garrett & Danziger, 2008). Employees higher in organizational status, male, and under the age of 30 are most likely to cyberslack (Garrett & Danziger,

2008). The lost productivity costs of cyberslacking are enormous. As just one example, companies lose an estimated one billion dollars annually each March, from people tracking results of the NCAA men's basketball tournament while at work (Garrett & Danziger, 2008).

Companies combat cyberslacking by using programs that track employee computer use—often without employees' knowledge. Tracking programs monitor what sites employees visit, screen e-mail for potentially inappropriate messages, and record images of employees' screens at periodic intervals (Riedy & Wen, 2010). Importantly, you're *not* protected by using a personal account rather than a company account while cyberslacking. Court cases in which employees have sued employers for violation of privacy have upheld the right of companies to access private employee accounts, arguing that employees do not have a reasonable expectation of privacy when using the employer's computer and Internet access (Riedy & Wen, 2010). When you're at work, remember this simple rule: *everything and anything you do on a company computer is considered company property—and you will be held accountable for it.*

Peer Relationships

Peers provide personal and practical support

What do Usher, Kanye West, and Heather Headley have in common with the Human League, Sting, and Earth, Wind, & Fire? They've all had songs written and produced by Terry Lewis and James "Jimmy Jam" Harris.[2] Lewis and Harris first began working together in the 1980s as members of Prince's opening band, the Time (featured in the movie *Purple Rain*). Jimmy Jam played keyboards and Terry played bass. They were equals, or peers, in the band, both supporting flamboyant front man Morris Day. In addition to their roles as backing musicians, they wrote songs of their own. When Prince, who managed the Time, discovered that they had penned a hit for the S.O.S. Band, he fired them. As Jimmy Jam describes, "It was really one of the worst days of our lives. We were perfectly happy being bandmembers at that point in time. But getting fired forced us to really take music production and our own songwriting seriously, and we were lucky to have lined up a couple projects at that point. All's well that ends well, I guess." The two catapulted to stardom when they wrote and produced Janet Jackson's multiplatinum album *Control*. Since then, they've collaborated to produce more than 40 Number One singles, over 100 gold and platinum albums, more than a dozen movie soundtracks, and even the music for the NBA All-Star Game. But

⬤ Music producers Terry Lewis and James "Jimmy Jam" Harris have had remarkable success in working together as professional peers. What do you think are some of the benefits and complications of working so closely with someone who is also a friend?

---

[2]The information that follows is adapted from Johnson (2004) and Kimpel (2010).

VideoCentral ▣

bedfordstmartins.com
/reflectrelate

Professional Peers
*Watch this clip online
to answer the questions
below.*

What is the difference
between being friendly with
peers at work and being
friends with coworkers?
How does your communica-
tion reflect such differences?
Do you develop the same
type of peer relationships
with face-to-face coworkers
as virtual ones? Why or
why not?

through all the fame and fortune they've achieved, the two still view each other primarily as musical coworkers and collaborators. "The number one thing is that we don't do anything alone," notes Jimmy Jam. "We approach each project as equal partners."

Our most meaningful and intimate workplace relationships are those with our **professional peers**, people holding positions of organizational status and power similar to our own. Peers are the most important source of personal and practical support for employees in any type of organization, whether it's a bank, a hospital, or a band (Rawlins, 1992). Similar to Jimmy Jam and Terry Lewis, we also develop close peer relationships in the workplace. After all, our peer relationships are not simply professional; they're often intensely personal.

TYPES OF PEER RELATIONSHIPS

Although peer relationships strongly shape the quality of our work lives, not all peer relationships are the same (Fritz & Dillard, 1994). *Information peers* are equivalent-status coworkers with whom our communication is limited to work-related content. Information peer relationships typically are created through assignment rather than choice, and as a result, they lack trust and intimacy. Although these relationships are common, especially in large corporations, many people view information peers as less open and less communicatively skilled than collegial or special peers, discussed below (Myers, Knox, Pawlowski, & Ropog, 1999).

Collegial peers are coworkers whom we consider friends. When we communicate with collegial peers, we talk about work and personal issues, and we feel moderate levels of trust and intimacy toward these individuals. Scholars sometimes describe these relationships as "blended" because they incorporate elements of both professional and personal relationships (Bridge & Baxter, 1992).

Special peers are equivalent-status coworkers with whom we share very high levels of emotional support, career-related feedback, trust, self-disclosure, and friendship (Sias et al., 2002). The rarest type of peer relationship, special peers are considered people's best friends in the workplace.

Professional peer relationships can evolve from lesser to greater levels of intimacy over time. The first and most significant relationship transition is from information peer to collegial peer (Sias & Cahill, 1998). Workers who spend extended periods of time together, are placed in proximity with each other, or socialize together outside of the workplace inevitably form stronger bonds with each other. However, sharing time and activities together is not enough to ensure that a coworker relationship will evolve from information to collegial peer. Like personal friendships, perceived similarity in interests, beliefs, and values is what decisively pushes a workplace relationship from acquaintanceship to friendship (Sias & Cahill, 1998).

The evolution of the relationship from information peer to collegial peer is similar for **virtual peers**, coworkers who communicate mainly through phone, e-mail, Skype, and other communication technologies. For virtual peers, the progression from information peer to collegial peer hinges on how much time the peers spend interacting and working on shared tasks together. Given the familiarity that many modern workers have with communication technologies and the availability of such technologies in the workplace, it's commonplace for virtual peers to become virtual friends.

The transition from collegial peer to special peer is different, however. Perceived similarity, shared time and tasks, and socializing are all important, but are not sufficient to push coworker friendships to the level of best friend (Sias & Cahill, 1998). Instead, the evolution of a coworker friendship to a higher state of intimacy is usually spurred by negative events in partners' personal lives (serious illness, marital discord) or serious work-related problems that require an exceptional level of social support. As demonstrated by the workplace relationship described at the beginning of this chapter, Silvia Amaro and Vivian Derr became special peers in response to personal life challenges each faced. The same thing happened for Jimmy Jam and Terry Lewis: their professional and personal partnership was amplified when they both were fired.

MAINTAINING PEER RELATIONSHIPS

Like other interpersonal bonds, peer relationships remain healthy through the energy and effort you and your peers invest in maintenance. One important tactic that helps maintain your peer relationships is positivity, discussed in Chapters 9 and 10. A positive perspective and upbeat communication with your peers helps offset the stress and demands everyone faces in the workplace. Practicing positivity in the workplace means communicating with your peers in a cheerful and optimistic fashion and doing unsolicited favors for them.

Openness also plays an important role. Openness means creating feelings of security and trust between you and your peers. You can create such feelings by

self-reflection

How many of your workplace peers do you consider friends rather than simply coworkers? Are there any you think of as best friends? How do your relationships with peers at work affect your feelings about your job and the organization?

⬦ No matter your workplace setting, you can maintain your peer relationships by using positivity, openness, and assurances, and by remembering that peer relationships require a blend of personal and work conversational topics.

behaving in predictable, trustworthy, and ethical ways in your relationships with peers. This means following through on your promises, respecting confidences, and demonstrating honesty and integrity in both your personal and your professional behavior.

Two additional tactics will help you maintain your collegial and special peer relationships (Sias et al., 2002). Like assurances given to a romantic partner, assurances given to collegial and special peers help demonstrate your commitment to them. Since choice is what distinguishes close peer relationships from casual ones, a critical part of maintaining these relationships is routinely stressing to your collegial and special peers that your relationships are based on choice rather than professional assignment. This can be accomplished indirectly by inviting peers to join you in activities outside of the workplace, which implies that you consider them friends and not just coworkers. More directly, you can straightforwardly tell collegial and special peers that you think of them primarily as friends.

Second, collegial and special peer relationships grow stronger when the people involved treat one another as whole human beings with unique qualities and do not strictly define each other as just coworkers. Certainly, you'll need to discuss work, but since your relationships with collegial and special peers are blended, remember to also talk about personal topics.

self-QUIZ   Test Your Maintenance of Peer Relationships

Thinking about your collegial and special peer relationships, read the following statements, and check those with which you agree. When you're finished, total up your score and interpret it below.

_____ I try to communicate in an upbeat, positive fashion toward my peers.

_____ I try to build my peers up by giving them compliments.

_____ I enjoy doing unsolicited favors for my peers, such as bringing them coffee or lunch or helping them out with work projects.

_____ I strive to communicate in consistent, reliable ways with my peers.

_____ If a peer shares something with me in confidence, I honor that confidentiality by not sharing the information with others.

_____ I try to always keep promises I've made to my peers.

_____ I regularly let my peers know that I consider them not just coworkers but friends.

_____ I do things to convey to my peers that even if we didn't work together, we'd still be friends.

_____ I strive to communicate with my peers in ways that show I value them as unique people rather than just as coworkers.

_____ I try to be there for my peers and am willing to talk with them about their personal and work-related concerns.

Note: Items in this _Self-Quiz_ are adapted by the author from the maintenance scale of Stafford and Canary (1991).

Scoring: 1–3 = you invest low effort in maintenance; 4–6 = you invest average effort in maintenance; 7–10 = you invest high effort in maintenance.

Mixed-Status Relationships

Communicating with superiors and subordinates

Following the U.S. invasion, soldier John Doe was deployed to Iraq, where he was in regular combat and subsequently received decorations for combat valor.[3] In February 2004, John Doe reenlisted as a member of the Army National Guard's Try One Program, which allows veterans to obtain military education and family medical benefits for one year. He reenlisted with the assumption that this would be his final year of service. Although he loved his military job, he wanted to spend more time with his family.

On September 4, 2004, John Doe's commanding officer ordered him and the rest of his unit to mobilize for active duty in Iraq for a period that would run at least until April 2006—more than two years after his reenlistment period. John Doe felt intensely ambivalent about his superior's order. He recognized that in the military disobeying the lawful order of a superior is a criminal act, but he had enlisted in Try One because it guaranteed him a fixed end date. John Doe felt that 12 years of exemplary military service and a combat tour in Iraq were enough. So, after much consideration, he decided to challenge the order of his superior officer. He hired an attorney and filed a lawsuit, naming the Secretary of Defense, the Secretary of the Army, and his company commander as defendants. The lawsuit was the first of its kind, and though John Doe eventually failed and was sent back to Iraq, it set off a national controversy regarding the power of military commanders to retain soldiers in their units against their will.

Although it might be tempting to characterize the relationships between military superiors and their subordinates as unusual, most organizations are

◖ In the movie *Moneyball*, Oakland Athletics general manager Billy Beane attempts to rebuild his team after a season-ending loss. In the process, he forms a partnership with his assistant manager Peter Brand, who shares Billy's vision for the team and makes equal contributions to their management strategies despite his lower status. What has been your experience with mixed-status relationships at work?

---

[3]All information regarding John Doe that follows is excerpted from Davey (2004), Philpott (2004), and Reuters (2004). John Doe's identity has been veiled in the media to protect his anonymity.

similarly hierarchical, with some people holding positions of power over others. Relationships between coworkers of different organizational status are called **mixed-status relationships**, and they provide the structural foundation on which most organizations are built (Farace et al., 1977).

Mixed-status relationships take many forms, including officer-subordinate, trainer-trainee, and mentor-protégé. But when most of us think of mixed-status relationships, what leaps to mind are *supervisory relationships*, ones in which one person outranks and supervises another (Zorn, 1995). Most of these relationships are assigned rather than chosen.

Supervisory relationships are less likely than peer relationships to evolve into friendships because of the power imbalance (Zorn, 1995). In most friendships, people downplay any difference in status and emphasize their equality. Supervisors by definition have more power. They direct their subordinates' efforts, evaluate their performance, and make decisions regarding their workers' pay and job security. They may even give orders entailing life-or-death consequences, as in the case of John Doe.

While some supervisors and subordinates can become friends, many organizations discourage or even forbid friendships between supervisors and their subordinates because it's assumed that such relationships will impair a supervisor's ability to objectively assess a subordinate's work performance (Zorn, 1995). Research on organizational decision making supports this assumption. Managers are less likely to give negative feedback to employees they like than to those they dislike (Larson, 1984). This occurs for two reasons. First, we are reluctant to give friends who work under us negative feedback because of the relationship consequences that may ensue—our friend may become angry or accuse us of unfairness. Second, as we saw in Chapter 3, our perceptions of others are substantially biased by whether we like them or not. Consequently, if we're in the supervisory position, our affection for a subordinate friend may lead us to judge his or her performance more generously than others.

MANAGING UP

When John Doe's commanding officer ordered him to deploy, he knew he had no recourse other than legal action. He couldn't just go to his superior and say, "Look, I really want to spend more time with my family, so can you please rescind your order?" Those of us in civilian jobs, however, typically have more leeway. Persuading superiors to support our work-related needs and wants is achieved through **upward communication**—communication from subordinates to superiors—and is conducted with an eye toward achieving influence. People feel more satisfied with their work lives when they believe that their supervisors listen and are responsive to their concerns (Eisenberg & Goodall, 2004).

Organizational communication scholar Eric Eisenberg argues that the most effective form of upward communication is **advocacy** (Eisenberg & Goodall, 2004). Through advocacy, you learn your superior's communication preferences and how to design messages in ways that will appeal to your superior. Advocacy is based on six principles. First, *plan before you pitch*. Most spontaneous appeals

self-reflection

If you directly supervised a collegial or special peer, could you evaluate his or her performance objectively? What might happen if the friend was doing unsatisfactory work and you gave him or her negative feedback? Could your relationship survive such an incident? If so, how?

"No, Thursday's out. How about never—is never good for you?"

to supervisors ("Can I have a raise?" "Can you sign me up for that software course?") are rejected. To avoid this, take time to craft your request before you pitch it.

Second, *know why your supervisor should agree with you.* Your supervisor has the power to make decisions, so the burden is on you to present a compelling case. In your message, connect your goals to something your supervisor thinks is important. For example, "If you sign me up for this course, I'll be able to maintain our new database."

Third, *tailor your message.* Think about successful and unsuccessful attempts to influence your supervisor. Compare the different approaches you and other people have used, and consider their efficacy. Does your supervisor respond more favorably to statistics or to an anecdote? To details or to generalities? Based on your supervisor's preferences, tailor your evidence and appeal accordingly.

Fourth, *know your supervisor's knowledge.* Many attempts at upward communication fail because subordinates present information at an inappropriate level. For example, they present their request in overly abstract terms, wrongly assuming that their supervisor is familiar with the subject. Or they present their appeal in a simplistic form, inadvertently coming across as condescending. To avoid this, know your supervisor's knowledge of the subject before you broach it. You can find this out by talking to other workers who are familiar with your supervisor.

Fifth, *create coalitions before communicating.* Most arguments made by one person are unconvincing, particularly when presented by a subordinate to a supervisor. Try to strengthen your argument with support from others in your organization. Remember to present such information as a helpful and personal observation ("Just to make sure I wasn't completely off about the situation, I checked with Joan, Denise, and Erika, and they all agreed") rather than as a threat to your supervisor's authority ("For your information, three other people feel the same way I do!"). Be sure to get approval beforehand from the people whose opinions you plan to cite. Some may not want their viewpoints referenced, and to use their sentiments as support for your arguments without their approval is highly unethical.

VideoCentral ▶

bedfordstmartins.com /reflectrelate

Advocacy
Watch this clip online to answer the questions below.

How well did the employee design his message according to the six suggested principles for advocacy? How would the employee revise his message depending on whether his superior was an "action-oriented listener," a "content-oriented listener," or a "time-oriented listener"?

Want to see more? Check out VideoCentral for clips illustrating **upward communication** and **downward communication**.

Finally, *competently articulate your message.* You can plan and tailor a message all you want, but if you're unable to articulate it, your supervisor probably won't take it seriously. Before you talk with your supervisor, revisit the information on competent interpersonal communication described in Chapters 1 and 6 to brush up on your skills.

COMMUNICATING WITH SUBORDINATES

The movie *Harold & Kumar Go to White Castle* tells the story of Harold Lee and Kumar Patel, two friends who encounter bizarre obstacles in their nightlong quest for White Castle hamburgers (Leiner, Hurwitz, Schlossberg, Kahane, & Shapiro, 2004). The film opens with a confrontation between Harold and his supervisor, Billy Carver. It's Friday afternoon, and Billy has been invited by J.D., a fellow supervisor, to a party that night. But Billy has a research report due the following morning for a Saturday meeting with German investors. J.D. encourages Billy to "just get somebody else to do your work for you," so Billy dumps the project on Harold. First, Billy attempts to get Harold to agree by suggesting that it is Harold's responsibility. When that doesn't seem to work, J.D. steps in and threatens to tell the head boss that Harold is slacking off if he doesn't do the work. Harold reluctantly agrees.

When you communicate upward, you're typically trying to influence your supervisors. But when you're the supervisor, *you* have the influence. When you present a request or demand to your subordinates—like Billy passing his report on to Harold—you don't have to worry about using advocacy. You can simply tell them what to do and use whatever language you want. Or can you?

Having formal authority in an organization gives you freedom in the messages you use when interacting with subordinates, known as **downward communication.** But with this freedom comes responsibility. Although many people in power positions exploit their freedom by bullying or harassing employees (as we'll discuss shortly), what distinguishes competent downward communication is the willingness of empowered people to communicate without relying on their power in order to appeal to subordinates in positive, empathic, respectful, and open ways.

Competent Downward Communication   A supervisor's communication sets the tone for his or her subordinates or organization. When a supervisor communicates competently, the effects radiate downward; employees are more motivated, more satisfied with their work, and more productive (Eisenberg & Goodall, 2004). But when a supervisor communicates incompetently, frustration and dissatisfaction build quickly. If you're a manager, you have not only organizational power and status but the power of your interpersonal communication to shape the morale and performance of all the workers under you, simply through how you communicate with them.

Competent downward communication can be achieved by observing five principles (Eisenberg & Goodall, 2004). First, routinely and openly emphasize the importance of communication in workplace relationships with subordinates.

The Model Minority Myth

Karen Chan had worked in the finance department of a midsize retail chain for seven years when a new supervisor was hired. Karen was shocked when he talked about her ethnicity. "My boss would make comments like, 'I can always count on you to get the budget right, because I know Asians are good with numbers.'" Her supervisor's downward communication began to influence the perception of other department heads, who sought Karen's input on complicated financial questions. "I actually majored in English, and when I chose finance as a career, it wasn't because I was a quantitative expert. I knew I had an eye for detail, and I appreciated the foundation finance would provide for a long-term career in business."

Chan decided to confront her boss. She quickly learned that her boss was behaving out of ignorance. "He didn't mean to deliberately hurt me, but I didn't want him to continue doing it. I may want to make a switch to operations or marketing, and my boss's comments were cornering me into a finance career within the firm." They both agreed to communicate about these slips as they occurred.

Note: Information regarding Karen Chan, including quotes, is excerpted from Hyun (2005).

Many Asian Americans, like Chan, are victims of the model minority myth, the belief that certain immigrant groups have overcome all the barriers to success and are self-effacing, reliable, hardworking, and technically proficient (Asian American Career Center, n.d.; Hyun, 2005). Writer Jane Hyun (2005) of the NAACP encourages workers who feel they are being stereotyped as "model minorities" to discuss the matter directly with their supervisors, much as Karen Chan did. Importantly, you should not try to combat the stereotype by acting irresponsible, loud, or wild. Most employers value workers who are reliable, hardworking, and technically proficient, so you don't want to behave in ways contrary to these attributes.

discussion questions

- How does your culture shape your supervisors' downward communication with you?
- What impact does this communication have on your work? On your workplace satisfaction?

For example, some supervisors engage in both informal and formal interactions with subordinates—hallway chats, impromptu office visits, weekly status updates, or team meetings. They also clearly and concisely explain instructions, performance expectations, and policies.

Second, listen empathically. Respond positively to your employees' attempts at upward communication rather than perceiving such attempts as a threat to power. Listen to subordinates' suggestions and complaints, and demonstrate a reasonable willingness to take fair and appropriate action in response to what they are saying.

Third, when communicating wants and needs to subordinates, frame these messages as polite requests ("Do you think you could . . .") or persuasive explanations ("Here's why we need to get this done in the next week . . ."). By contrast, incompetent downward communication involves using power to make threats ("Do this now or else") and demands ("Take care of that customer now!").

Fourth, be sensitive to your subordinates' feelings. For instance, if a reprimand is in order, try to make it in private rather than in front of other workers. Keep such exchanges focused on behaviors that need to change rather than making judgments about the subordinate's character or worth: "John, I noticed that you arrived late to the last three staff meetings. I'm worried that late arrivals disrupt the meetings and cause us to lose time. What ideas do you have for ensuring that you get to meetings on time?"

Last, share relevant information with employees whenever possible. This includes notice of impending organizational changes and explanations about why the changes are coming. For example: "Our company hasn't been meeting its forecasted revenues, so several units, including ours, are being sold to another company. We'll have an opportunity to accept jobs here or to move to the company that's acquiring us. As soon as I know more about what this change means for all of us, I'll share that information."

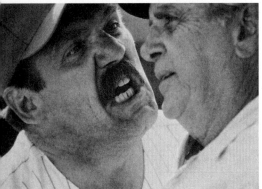

⬤ A supervisor's downward communication shapes the morale and performance of all the workers under her or him.

Compliments and Criticism Two challenges of downward communication are how to effectively praise subordinates and how to constructively criticize them. Offering subordinates praise for their workplace accomplishments fosters a healthy organizational climate. Studies repeatedly show that employees rank "appreciation" and "supervisory recognition" at the top of their lists of factors motivating them to work hard and that feeling unappreciated at work is a leading cause of employee turnover (Forni, 2002).

Complimenting your subordinates is most effectively done when the compliments are focused on a subordinate's work—his or her achievements, expertise, attitude, cooperativeness, and so forth. Avoid compliments about personal matters—like a subordinate's appearance. Regardless of your intention, something as innocuous as complimenting the stylishness of a subordinate's hairstyle or the beauty of his or her skin may make the person feel uncomfortable. In some organizations, such compliments can trigger charges of sexual harassment or discrimination.

Also, praise is best presented privately rather than publicly, except in formal contexts such as recognition dinners and award ceremonies. Many supervisors enjoy spontaneously singling out particular employees for praise in front of their coworkers ("Everyone, let's give Samantha a round of applause—she was our unit sales leader again this past month!"). These supervisors incorrectly believe that such praise improves morale, but it can do the opposite. When someone is publicly singled out in a context where such recognition is unexpected, that person's status is elevated. This might be merited, but it could foster resentment and envy among the person's peers and ultimately undermine the organization's climate.

Of course, criticizing subordinates is no easier. Especially challenging is providing constructive criticism to high-achieving employees, who often have little experience receiving criticism, and expect only praise (Field, 2005). But offering constructive criticism isn't as difficult as you might think. Instead, it requires you to draw upon the many skills you have mastered in previous chapters.

Begin by using your knowledge of emotion management from Chapter 4, remaining calm, kind, and understanding throughout the exchange. Open your interaction with positive remarks, and end your comments with similar commendations: "It was obvious you worked really hard on designing that presentation" or "This isn't the end of the world—just something I'd like you to work on for future presentations."

Second, follow the guidelines for competent interpersonal communication described in Chapter 1, and cooperative language detailed in Chapter 6. Informatively, honestly, and clearly identify the issue or behavior that concerns you, describing it neutrally rather than personalizing it or leveling accusations. For example, instead of saying, "You clearly don't realize how you came across," say, "I think the way you defended our team's work yesterday may not have been the most effective approach." Rather than "You shouldn't have gone in unprepared like that," say, "There seemed to be an expectation in the room of more precise data on projected sales."

Strive to experience and express empathy toward your subordinate through perspective-taking and empathic concern (Chapter 3), showing that you understand how he or she may feel: "The same thing has happened to me before" rather than "I would never let something like that happen." Keep in mind how you have felt when receiving criticism from your superiors, and adapt your communication accordingly.

Finally, avoid belaboring the error that has been made, and instead, focus most of your talk time on ideas for avoiding such missteps in the future. Although you have the authority to dictate corrections, subordinates respond more favorably when supervisors negotiate solutions with them. Offer your subordinate specific ideas, but frame them as suggestions, asking for their opinion. The goal of constructive criticism is not only to correct the errant behavior but to create a mutual consensus with your subordinate.

MAINTAINING MIXED-STATUS RELATIONSHIPS

As we've seen, communicating competently in mixed-status relationships presents numerous challenges—whether you're trying to influence a superior, praise a subordinate, or provide constructive criticism for an employee whose performance is inadequate. But a broader challenge is maintaining these relationships. Maintaining mixed-status relationships requires you to do two things (Albrecht & Bach, 1997). First, with your supervisor and subordinates, *develop and follow communication rules for what's appropriate to talk about as well as when and how to communicate.* For example, supervisors who think their subordinates agree with them on how they should communicate tend to rate those subordinates higher on overall performance than subordinates who hold different beliefs about communication (Albrecht & Bach, 1997). Communication rules govern matters such as how often a supervisor and subordinate meet to discuss work projects, whether communications are formal or informal, and which channels (e-mail, instant-messaging, texting, printed memos, face-to-face conversations) are the most appropriate.

Second, *communicate in consistent and reliable ways.* This means displaying a stable and professional manner with supervisors and subordinates rather than allowing personal problems or moods to influence your communication. It also means being punctual, following through on appointments and promises, and keeping confidences. Consistency builds trust, an essential component of any interpersonal relationship, and a perception that you're "trustworthy" will feed into other positive perceptions of you as well, including your integrity, openness, and competence (Albrecht & Bach, 1997).

Challenges to Workplace Relationships

Dealing with bullying, romance, and harassment

After my freshman year at the University of Washington, I dropped out of school and went to work driving for a local trucking company. My boss, Rob, delighted in tormenting me. During my initial hiring interview, I made the mistake of telling him how desperately I needed the job, so he knew from the beginning that he had substantial power over me. Several times a week he would call me into his office to verbally abuse me for his amusement—insulting me and swearing at me and then laughing because he knew I couldn't do anything about it. Rob would assign me impossible tasks, then punish me when I didn't complete them "on time." For example, he'd send me to the docks to unload a 45-foot trailer filled with sofas, but wouldn't let me use a hand truck or forklift. After I'd spent an hour struggling with enormous and weighty boxes, he'd come down and yell at me for "being slow." He assigned me to a truck that had bad brakes. Once, after parking at a delivery ramp, I came out from signing paperwork to see my truck rolling away down the alley. Like a scene from a bad comedy, I had to run after my truck, desperately trying to catch up to it so I could jump in and stop it with the emergency brake. But Rob's favorite sport was to threaten to fire me, just to make me beg him for my job (which I did). After six months of daily bullying, I decided that the financial costs of unemployment were preferable to the abuse I was suffering, and I quit.

Maintaining workplace relationships is hard. We must constantly juggle job demands, power issues, and intimacy, all while communicating in ways that are positive and professional (Sias, Heath, Perry, Silva, & Fix, 2004). Yet sometimes even more intense challenges arise. Three of the most common, and difficult to manage, are workplace bullying, the development of romantic relationships with coworkers, and sexual harassment.

WORKPLACE BULLYING

In the course of your professional lives, many of you will experience situations similar to what I went through with Rob, my trucking boss. **Workplace bullying** is the repeated unethical and unfavorable treatment of one or more persons by others in the workplace (Boddy, 2011). Bullying occurs in a variety of ways, including shouting, swearing, spreading vicious rumors, destroying the target's property or work, and excessive criticism. It is also perpetrated through "passive" means, such as the "silent treatment," exclusion from meetings and gatherings, and ignoring of requests (Tracy, Lutgen-Sandvik, & Alberts, 2006). In nearly one-fifth of cases, workplace bullying involves physical violence, including hitting, slapping, and shoving (Martin & LaVan, 2010). When bullying occurs online, it is known as *cyberbullying*. The most frequently reported forms of workplace cyberbullying are withholding or deleting important information sent via e-mail and spreading gossip or rumors through text messages, e-mails, and online posts (Privitera & Campbell, 2009). Perpetrators of workplace bullying usually combine several of these tactics to intimidate their victims. The most common forms are detailed in Table 12.2 on page 408.

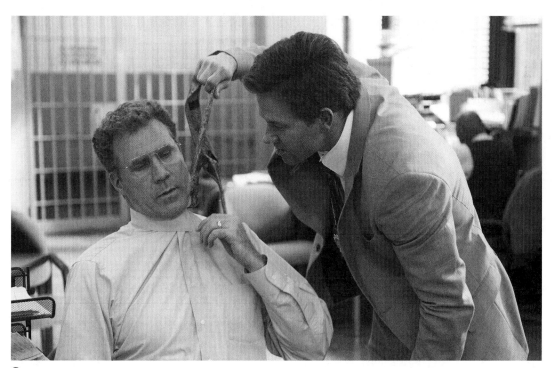

⬆ In the movie *The Other Guys*, frustrated detective Terry Hoitz (Mark Wahlberg) regularly bullies his partner, Allen Gamble (Will Ferrell), a forensic accountant in his office. Although presented for laughs in the film, workplace bullying has been shown to decrease productivity and can cause depression and other anxiety-related health problems.

table 12.2 **Common Forms of Workplace Bullying**

Form	Description
Isolation	Restrict employees' interaction with coworkers, isolate their work area away from others, exclude them from group activities and off-site social gatherings.
Control of Important Information	Prevent important information from reaching workers; provide false job-related information to them; block or delete their correspondence, e-mail, telephone calls, and work assignments.
Constraint of Professional Responsibilities	Assign workers to tasks that are useless, impossible, or absurd; intentionally leave them with nothing to do.
Creation of Dangerous Work Conditions	Distract workers during critical tasks to put them in peril; assign them tasks that endanger their health or safety; refuse to provide appropriate safety measures for their job.
Verbal Abuse	Make disdainful, ridiculing, and insulting remarks regarding workers' personal characteristics (appearance, intelligence, personality, etc.); spread rumors and lies about them.
Destruction of Professional Reputation	Attack workers' professional performance; exaggerate the importance of their work errors; ignore or distort their correct decisions and achievements.

Source: Adapted from Escartín, Rodríguez-Carballeira, Zapf, Porrúa, and Martín-Peña (2009).

Workplace bullying has devastating effects on the targets' physical and psychological health. Bullying typically generates feelings of helplessness, anger, and despair. It can even cause health problems such as sleep disorders, depression, and chronic fatigue (Tracy et al., 2006). Plus, the associated costs to companies are huge and include disability and workers' compensation claims, lawsuits, low-quality work, reduced productivity, high staff turnover, increased absenteeism, and deteriorated customer relationships (Tracy et al., 2006).

Unfortunately, workplace bullying is common: 25 percent to 30 percent of U.S. employees are bullied at some point during their work lives—10 percent at any given time (Keashly & Neuman, 2005). In one-third of cases, the bullying occurs despite existence of official antibullying workplace policies (Martin & LaVan, 2010). One reason that bullying is so widespread is that when bullied workers share their stories of abuse with others, they typically aren't believed (Tracy et al., 2006). The types of abuse that occur are often so outrageous that people simply can't accept them as true. Adding to this, workplace bullies typically put on an act for their supervisors: behaving in a supportive fashion while they are watched and then being abusive when the boss is not around (Tracy et al., 2006). Workplace bullies can be such good actors that even trial juries believe them. In 73 percent of legal cases in which bullied employees took bullying supervisors to court, juries found in favor of the supervisors (Martin & LaVan, 2010).

How can you cope with workplace bullying? Some people simply quit and find another job (Bies & Tripp, 1998). Of course, this is not an option for everyone, since most people are dependent upon their income and new job opportunities can be limited. Others give in to the bullying, choosing to ignore it or tough it out because the perceived costs of challenging the abusive supervisor are too high. For example, if you take your complaints to your supervisor's boss, that person may side with your supervisor—leading to an escalation in the bullying. Another option is to use your interpersonal communication skills and directly confront the bully (Bies & Tripp, 1998). In private, point out which actions you feel are abusive and ask the bully to stop. Some bullies may back off when they are confronted. At least one study of workplace bullying found that, although the most frequently reported strategy for dealing with workplace bullies was avoiding or ignoring them, the respondents who confronted their abusers reported improvements in their subsequent interactions (Keashly et al., 1994).

WORKPLACE ROMANCES

A second challenge to workplace relationships is the development of romantic feelings for coworkers. The workplace is a natural venue for romantic attraction to unfold, as many of the elements that foster attraction are present: a wide variety of attractive and available partners, large amounts of time spent together, physical proximity, and similarity in interests and attitudes (Appelbaum, Marinescu, Klenin, & Bytautas, 2007). Over 80 percent of North American employees have experienced a romantic relationship at work (Schaefer & Tudor, 2001), and 10 million new workplace romances are forged each year (Pierce & Aguinis, 2009), usually among peers.

Historically, companies have discouraged workplace romances, believing that they lead to favoritism, lack of worker motivation, decreased efficiency and productivity, and increased risk of sexual harassment lawsuits (Appelbaum et al., 2007). But many workplaces have begun to shift their views and policies, as research supports that romantic involvement does not hurt worker productivity (Boyd, 2010). From the worker perspective, workplace romance typically is viewed positively. Romantically involved workers are usually perceived by people in their organization as friendly and approachable (Hovick, Meyers, & Timmerman, 2003), and having romances in the workplace is seen as creating a positive work climate (Riach & Wilson, 2007). Relationship outcomes are often positive too: married couples who work in the same location have a 50 percent *lower* divorce rate than those employed at different workplaces (Boyd, 2010).

Despite these positives, workplace romances face challenges. Involvement in a romance can create the perception among coworkers that the partners are more interested in each other than in their work, leading to rumors and gossip

skills practice

Workplace Bullying
Responding more effectively to workplace bullying

❶ Consider the situation, and yourself, from the bully's perspective.

❷ List the bully's behaviors and possible motivations for them.

❸ Plan your responses. For each behavior, what would you say or do? Factor in the bully's motivations.

❹ Assess the effectiveness of your responses. Would your responses likely generate positive or negative outcomes? What are the organizational repercussions of your responses?

❺ Use your planned responses the next time the bully behaves badly.

▶ On the television show *Parks and Recreation*, colleagues Leslie Knope and Ben Wyatt violate their office policy against workplace romance when they begin secretly dating. Although initially successful at hiding their relationship from their boss and coworkers, Leslie questions their romance when she decides to run for city council and worries that there will be a scandal if their relationship is discovered during election season.

self-reflection

If you have had a workplace romance, what were the biggest challenges you faced? How did you and your partner meet these challenges? If you haven't had a workplace romance, what are your perceptions of such romances? Do you approve or disapprove of them? How could they affect your organization?

(Albrecht & Bach, 1997). As a consequence, you can't cultivate a workplace romance without expecting the relationship to become a focus of workplace gossip.

The negative outcomes associated with workplace romances are more pronounced for women than for men. Women are more likely than men to suffer unfavorable work evaluations based on romantic involvement, are judged more negatively by their colleagues following workplace romance breakups, and are more likely to be terminated by their companies for workplace affairs (Riach & Wilson, 2007). When such relationships are mixed status—in particular, if a woman is under the direct supervision of a man—others in the organization often conclude that the woman used the relationship to enhance her career. In contrast, men in workplace romances often win their coworkers' admiration (Dillard, 1987).

How can you successfully overcome the challenge of maintaining a workplace romance, should you become involved in one? First, leave your love at home, so to speak, and communicate with your partner in a strictly professional fashion during work hours. When romantic partners maintain a professional demeanor toward each other and communicate with all their coworkers in a consistent and positive fashion, the romance is usually ignored or even encouraged (Buzzanell, 1990).

Second, use e-mail, text, Facebook, and instant-messaging judiciously to maintain your relationship. When used properly, these technologies enable romantic partners to communicate frequently and in a way that maintains professional decorum (Hovick et al., 2003). However, electronic messages exchanged in the workplace should never contain overly intimate or controversial messages. Although many workers use their business accounts for personal reasons, it is wise to write messages that comply with official policies—no matter who the recipient is. Electronic messages are not secure. Anyone with the motivation and know-how can gain access to the messages you and your partner exchange. And, as noted earlier in the chapter, if the message was produced during work time, your company has a legal right to access it.

SEXUAL HARASSMENT

Sometimes sexual or romantic interest in the workplace is one-sided. Although most people are willing to abandon their attraction once they realize it's unrequited, some exploit their organizational power to pursue it. In some instances, sexual pursuit is merely a vehicle for abusively wielding power over others in the workplace. Consider the case of Leigh-Anne Goins, who took a job as an office manager before pursuing her dream of earning a graduate degree. Her job quickly became a nightmare, as she describes:[4]

> For the first few months my job was wonderful. I was in charge of the office and I was making supervisory decisions. Then my boss's true colors came out. He began coming up behind me and putting his hands on my shoulders, leaning in and talking into my ear. I thought, *no . . . I'm imagining things.* I should have bailed, but I had to pay my rent and I was trying to save money for school. The final straw came when I purchased some brownies and offered one to my boss in addition to my other coworkers. My boss said "no" because he was dieting. I offered one last time, just to be polite, and he responded by covering his mouth like he was going to tell a secret and whispering so that only I could see and hear, "You're my brownie" and licking his lips at me. That was the final straw, being called the office manager's "brownie."

Many people think the problem of sexual harassment in the workplace has been solved. It hasn't. The number of incidences of sexual harassment since the early 1990s has actually climbed, with 11,364 charges of sexual harassment made in 2011 alone (U.S. Equal Employment Opportunity Commission, 2011). These charges represent only a small portion of actual instances, since the majority of sexual harassment incidents go unreported.

Although most people condemn sexual harassment in the workplace, enormous differences exist in perceptions of what constitutes harassment. The most

---

[4]All information regarding the experience of Leigh-Anne Goins is from L.-A. Goins (personal communication with author, March 2005). Published with permission.

self-QUIZ

Test Your Perception of Sexual Harassment

Read the following statements and decide if you consider each behavior harmless, uncertain, or severe sexual harassment. Check your perceptions in the key below.

_____ 1. Your supervisor touches or pats your private parts.

_____ 2. Your supervisor requests sexual favors in exchange for rewards and perks.

_____ 3. Your supervisor repeatedly asks you out on a date, even after you make it clear you're not interested.

_____ 4. Your supervisor makes sexually suggestive remarks or gestures to you.

_____ 5. Your supervisor shows you sexually suggestive visuals.

_____ 6. Your supervisor tells you sexually oriented jokes.

_____ 7. Your supervisor tells sexually explicit jokes in your proximity.

_____ 8. Your supervisor asks you to run a personal errand.

_____ 9. Your supervisor touches or pats nonsexual parts of your body.

_____10. Your supervisor asks you for a date.

_____11. Your supervisor pays for your meal.

_____12. Your supervisor helps you with physically demanding work.

Note: Items in this *Self-Quiz* are adapted from Blakely, Blakely, and Moorman (1995).

Scoring: Most people rate statements 1–3 severe, 4–7 uncertain, and 8–12 harmless.

commonly cited definition of **sexual harassment** is one created by the U.S. Equal Employment Opportunity Commission (1980):

> Unwelcome sexual advances, requests for sexual favors, and other verbal or physical conduct of a sexual nature constitute sexual harassment when (1) submission to such conduct is made either explicitly or implicitly a term or condition of an individual's employment, (2) submission to or rejection of such conduct by an individual is used as the basis for employment decisions affecting such individual, or (3) such conduct has the intention or effect of unreasonably interfering with an individual's work performance or of creating an intimidating, hostile, or offensive working environment.

This definition suggests that two types of harassment occur in the workplace. The first is *quid pro quo harassment*—a person in a supervisory position asking for or demanding sexual favors in return for professional advancement or protection from layoffs or other undesirable events (Gerdes, 1999). Much more prevalent than quid pro quo, however, is *hostile climate harassment* (Tyner & Clinton, 2010). As Leigh-Anne Goins experienced, hostile climate harassment is sexual behavior intended to disrupt a person's work performance.

Sexual harassment has a devastating effect. Victims of sexual harassment report feeling angry, afraid, and depressed (Cochran, Frazier, & Olson, 1997). Harassment victims are more likely than others to develop substance abuse and other health problems, including weight loss and sleep and stomach disorders (Clair, 1998). Not surprisingly, they also suffer a host of professional problems, including missed work, lower productivity, and ostracism by coworkers who blame them for inviting the harassment (Hickson, Grierson, & Linder, 1991).

The most common way of coping with sexual harassment is to avoid the harasser, ignore the harassment, or interpret the harassment in ways that minimize its seriousness—"It's not a big enough deal to pursue," "He was only flirting," "That's just the way things work here," or "It was all a harmless joke" (Clair, 1993). Some workers confront the harasser, describing his or her actions as inappropriate or threatening or pursuing legal action. Confronting harassers is strongly encouraged as a matter of principle, but the practical consequences can be difficult to manage. In sexual harassment cases, people in the organization often side with the person in the position of authority (Fitzgerald, 1993).

If you are experiencing sexual harassment, remember that fewer than 5 percent of sexual-harassment victims report the problem to an authority (Fitzgerald, 1993). The decision not to report will likely perpetuate the harassment because it can teach harassers that their behavior is okay. The best long-term solution for addressing sexual harassment is to challenge it when it occurs and believe that the harassers deserve to be punished. If you're not sure what to do, contact the Equal Employment Opportunity Commission. Go to www.eeoc.gov for detailed information on how to handle such situations, or you can call 1-800-669-4000.

Workplace Relationships and Human Happiness

Happiness at work can affect other areas of our lives

In his book *The Pursuit of Happiness* (2002), psychologist David Myers comments on the role that workplace relationships play in his life:

Through our work we identify with a *community*. My sense of community is rooted in the network of supportive friends who surround me on our

◐ Workplace challenges can make already stressful places feel even more so. If you feel that you are in an unbearable (or illegal) situation, remember that you do not have to suffer silently. Reach out for the support and advice of trusted peers, and you can also use company resources (like human resources departments) to address any problems.

Dealing with Workplace Abuse

 BACKGROUND

Workplace relationships and interactions always provide unanticipated challenges. But when supervisors abuse your trust in ways that are difficult to forgive, you must choose between maintaining peer friendships or preserving your own sense of honor. To consider how you might deal with such a situation, read the case study and work through the five steps under Your Turn.

2 CASE STUDY

You take a job delivering pizzas to help pay for school. The restaurant has a supportive climate—workers are friendly and open. The delivery drivers in particular have a tight clique that they welcome you into, and you quickly become friends with several of them.

The only exception to the warmth of your new workplace is the manager, Elizabeth. She is controlling, manipulative, and dogmatic, and tries to run the restaurant "by the book." The drivers warn you to watch out for her, telling you, "She's really screwed people over before." But you get along with her pretty well because of your exemplary work performance and positive attitude.

The most important workplace rule for drivers is to never leave your money pouch unattended. The money pouch is the zippered bag into which you put all cash from sales. For safety's sake, drivers are supposed to deposit cash after every delivery run, but when things get hectic, drivers often forget—resulting in accumulated cash in the pouches.

One night you're on a run, but when a customer pays you, you discover you're missing your pouch. You hadn't deposited your money all night, and there was over $300 in it. Arriving back at the store, you tell Elizabeth, and she says, "If it's lost, company policy requires that you cover the missing money from your next paycheck!" This means you're not going to be able to afford next month's rent, much less food and gas! You tear your car and the restaurant apart looking for the pouch, and soon the other drivers are helping you search, offering their support and sympathies. But to no avail: after an hour, the pouch is still missing. Sitting in despair, you begin to cry. Just then, Elizabeth walks up, and with a smirk, hands you your pouch. "You left it unattended on the delivery table earlier, so I hid it, to teach you a lesson!" You're stunned, humiliated, and furious! After months of exemplary work performance, why would she abuse you like that? Your first instinct is to quit in protest, even though you can't afford it. But quitting would hurt the other drivers—who would have to scramble to cover your shifts—and jeopardize your friendships with them. Should you stay, but confront Elizabeth? Or just suck it up and say nothing? As you're pondering these options, Elizabeth says, "So, what lessons have you learned from this experience?"

③ YOUR TURN

While working through the following steps, keep in mind the interpersonal communication concepts, skills, and insights you've learned so far in this book, especially this chapter. Also remember: there are no right answers, so think hard about the choice you make! (P.S. Need help? Review the *Helpful Concepts* listed below.)

● step 1

Reflect on yourself. What are your thoughts and feelings in this situation? What attributions are you making about Elizabeth and her behavior? Are your attributions accurate? Why or why not?

● step 2

Reflect on your supervisor. Using perspective-taking, put yourself in Elizabeth's shoes. Consider how she is thinking and feeling. How does she likely perceive you, and your behavior, in this situation?

● step 3

Identify the optimal outcome. Think about all that has happened in this situation. Consider your feelings, those of Elizabeth, and the feelings of the other drivers. Given all these factors, what's the best, most constructive relationship outcome possible here? Be sure to consider not just what's best for *you*, but what's best for everyone else.

● step 4

Locate the roadblocks. Taking into consideration your own thoughts and feelings, those of Elizabeth, and all that has happened in this situation, what's preventing you from achieving the optimal outcome you identified in Step 3?

● step 5

Chart your course. What can you say and do to overcome the roadblocks and achieve your relationship outcome?

HELPFUL CONCEPTS

Workplace cliques, **391**

Organizational climate, **392–393**

Advocacy, **400–402**

Workplace bullying, **407–409**

415

Through our work we
identify with a community

department team, in the institution whose goals we embrace, and in the profession we call our own. (p. 130)

For many of us, our motivation to work transcends the desire to bring home a paycheck. Although we need the money our jobs provide, we also want to feel that our work is meaningful and important. When asked, "Would you continue working, even if you inherited a huge fortune that made working unnecessary?" three out of four Americans answered "yes" (Eisenberg & Goodall, 1997). This isn't just an American value: people in nearly every industrialized nation report lower satisfaction with their lives if they're unemployed, regardless of their financial standing (Myers, 2002).

But it's not the work itself that fulfills us; it's the coupling of the professional with the personal, the creation of a coworker community. Day in and day out, we endure work stress and intense demands with those who surround us—our supervisors, subordinates, and peers. These people aren't just coworkers; they can be companions, friends, and sometimes even best friends or lovers. When these relationships are healthy, the effects spread to every part of our lives. We're happier in life and more productive on the job. Those around us find us more pleasant to work with, and our organization as a whole thrives. When it comes to workplace relationships, the professional is profoundly personal.

self-reflection

Would you continue working if you didn't need to? Why or why not? If you chose not to work, what consequences can you envision for your life? How would not having a job affect your sense of purpose? Your happiness?

POSTSCRIPT

We began this chapter with the story of a deeply personal workplace relationship. Despite differences in backgrounds, personal life challenges, and changes in organizational power and status, Vivian Derr and Silvia Amaro have remained best friends in and out of the workplace for more than a quarter century.

Consider your own work life for a moment. Do you have a coworker on whom you could count to help you get through a painful divorce or surmount the challenge of new parenthood? Is there someone you get along with so well that you would recruit him or her to serve as your own supervisor?

Vivian and Silvia's friendship illustrates the primacy of interpersonal relationships in our lives. In a culture in which many of us define our worth largely through our professional accomplishments— promotions, paychecks, and portfolios—by far the most meaningful accomplishment of all is forging interpersonal relationships that thrive and endure.

chapter review

key terms

▶ You can watch brief, illustrative videos of these terms and test your understanding of the concepts online in *VideoCentral: Interpersonal Communication* at **bedfordstmartins.com /reflectrelate**.

key concepts

The Nature of Workplace Relationships

- Our **workplace relationships** are shaped by many forces. Two of the most powerful are **organizational culture** and **organizational networks**. Most workers learn their organization's culture—communication norms, artifacts, and values—during new employee socialization and from interacting with members of various networks.

- Organizational networks are the principal source of workplace information for most employees. Information in networks is exchanged through face-to-face encounters, memos, phone, and e-mail. **Virtual networks** also exist, particularly for workers who telecommute from home.

- When members of networks share common beliefs and personal values, they sometimes form **workplace cliques**. Cliques can provide useful insider information to new employees. Cliques can also be disruptive, particularly when they encourage unethical employee behavior.

- The overall emotional tone of your organization, known as the **organizational climate**, can be rigid and cold in a **defensive climate**, open and warm in a **supportive climate**, or, in most cases, somewhere in between.

- While technology in the workplace connects workers in a relational fashion, it also creates opportunities for **cyberslacking**. It is important to remember that anything you do on a company computer is considered company property.

Peer Relationships

- Our closest workplace relationships are with our **professional peers**. Friendships between peers evolve from frequent interaction and common interests. The same is true for **virtual peers**.

- We maintain peer relationships through positivity, openness, assurances, and the ability to relate to our coworkers as humans, not just colleagues.

Mixed-Status Relationships

- The primary interpersonal dynamic in **mixed-status relationships** is power. The difference in power between workers and managers makes forming friendships across status lines challenging.
- Much of **upward communication** is designed to gain influence. Although people use different tactics, the most effective is **advocacy**, designing a message that is specifically tailored to the viewpoints of your superior.
- When engaging in **downward communication**, it's important to communicate in positive, empathic, respectful, and open ways.

Challenges to Workplace Relationships

- **Workplace bullying** can occur in a variety of ways, including cyberbullying. Such bullying targets physical and psychological health.
- Even though romances in the workplace are common, they offer some positives and challenges. If you become involved in such a relationship, it is important to always maintain professional communication with your partner at work.
- Although many people think **sexual harassment** is on the wane, incidences have actually increased over the past decade.

key skills

- What are the pros and cons of workplace cliques? Find the answer on page 391.
- What are the two most important practical tips to keep in mind about organizational networks? Go to pages 391–392 to find out.
- How can you help build a supportive climate in your workplace? Review Table 12.1 on page 392.
- Interested in using technology to help you better collaborate with coworkers? Try the *Skills Practice* on page 394.
- How can you maintain healthy and happy peer relationships? Revisit the suggestions on pages 397–398. Then take the *Self-Quiz* on page 398.
- Interested in enhancing your upward communication? Practice your advocacy skills by revisiting the steps described on pages 400–402. Then do the *Skills Practice* on page 402.
- What are the five most important skills necessary for effective downward communication? Revisit pages 402–404 to find out.
- How can you more effectively praise subordinates? Review the tips for effective compliments on page 404.
- What can you do to make your criticism more constructive? Follow the suggestions on pages 404–405.
- How can you successfully maintain mixed-status relationships? Check out pages 405–406 for the answer.
- Want to enhance your understanding of workplace bullying, as well as how you can better cope with it? Complete the *Skills Practice* on page 409.
- What can you do to maintain a workplace romance? Check out the recommendations on pages 409–411.
- Think you have a firm understanding of sexual harassment? Take the *Self-Quiz* on page 412 to check your perceptions.
- What would you do if you thought your boss may have been abusive to you? Complete the *Making Relationship Choices* exercise on pages 414–415 to find out.

accommodation: (p. 257) A way of handling conflict in which one person abandons his or her goals for the goals of another. For example, Louis gives in to Martel over where they should park their cars: "You can have the driveway. I'm tired of arguing about it."

action-oriented listeners: (p. 160) Those who prefer to receive brief, to-the-point, accurate information for decision making—for example, a supervisor who requires brief summaries from department heads and does not want to bat around details in long meetings.

actor-observer effect: (p. 81) A tendency to credit external forces as causes for our behaviors instead of internal factors. For instance, Leon says he snapped at a coworker because she was slow instead of blaming his own impatience.

adaptors: (p. 220) Touching gestures, often unconsciously made, that serve a physical or psychological purpose. For example, twirling hair while reading, jingling pocket change, and fingering jewelry may be gestures that provide comfort, signal anxiety, or are simply unconscious habits.

advocacy: (p. 400) Communication from a subordinate intended to influence a superior in an organization. For example, you convince your manager to try a new product line.

affect displays: (p. 232) Intentional or unintentional nonverbal behaviors that reveal real or pretended emotions, such as a frown, a choked sob, or a smile intended to disguise fear.

agentic friendships: (p. 357) Voluntary relationships primarily focused on achieving specific practical goals, such as those among peers in a study group or colleagues at work.

aggressive-hostile touch: (p. 224) A touch designed to hurt and humiliate others, involving forms of physical violence like grabbing, slapping, and hitting.

aggressive listening: (p. 167) Listening in order to attack or collect information to use against the speaker, such as when a father encourages his son to describe his ambitions just to ridicule the son's goals. (Also known as *ambushing*.)

algebraic impressions: (p. 95) Impressions of others that continually change as we add and subtract positive or negative information that we learn about them.

anger: (p. 129) The negative primary emotion that occurs when you are blocked or interrupted from attaining an important goal by what you see as the improper action of an external agent.

appropriateness: (p. 22) A measure of communication competence that indicates the degree to which your communication matches the situational, relational, and cultural expectations regarding how people should communicate.

artifacts: (p. 229) Things we possess that influence how we see ourselves and that we use to express our identity to others. Jewelry, for instance, can indicate economic means, marital status, religious affiliation, style preferences, and taste.

attending: (p. 149) The second stage of the listening process in which a listener devotes attention to received information. For example, you may *hear* a radio but *attend* only when a favorite song comes on.

attention focus: (p. 126) Preventing unwanted emotions by intentionally devoting your attention only to aspects of an event or encounter that you know will not provoke those emotions. For example, you disregard your uncle's snide comments while forcing all your interest on your aunt's conversation.

attributions: (p. 79) Rationales we create to explain the comments or behaviors of others. For example, Ryan reasons that Jason's quietness in class means that Jason is shy.

avoidance: (p. 255) A way of handling conflict by ignoring it, pretending it isn't really happening, or communicating indirectly about the situation. For example, Martel hides behind the newspaper as Louis shouts, "Your car is blocking mine again. How many times do I have to ask you to park it to the side?" See also **skirting; sniping.**

avoiding: (p. 297) A relational stage in which one or both individuals in a couple try to distance themselves from each other physically. For example, Owen changes jobs to have an excuse to travel away from home frequently.

back-channel cues: (p. 153) Nonverbal or verbal responses that signal you've paid attention to and understood specific comments—for example, saying, "Okay, got it" after someone details extensive driving directions.

beautiful-is-good effect: (p. 290) A tendency for physical attractiveness to create the perception of competency and intelligence. For example, a witness is viewed favorably and seems credible because she is good-looking.

birds-of-a-feather effect: (p. 290) A tendency to be attracted to others if we perceive them to have similar levels of physical attractiveness, values, and interests.

bizarreness effect: (p. 157) The finding that we remember unusual or odd information more readily than commonplace information.

blended emotions: (p. 116) Two or more primary emotions experienced at the same time. For instance, Melinda feels fear and anger when her daughter is not home after curfew.

bonding: (p. 295) A relational stage in which an official, public ritual unites two people by the laws or customs of their culture. For example, Ruth marries Owen in her hometown church.

catharsis: (p. 131) Within the field of interpersonal communication, the assumption that openly expressing emotions enables you to purge them.

channel: (p. 7) The sensory dimension (sound, sight, touch, scent, or taste) used to transmit information during communication. For example, you may apologize by showing someone a sad facial expression, lightly touching his shoulder, and saying, "I'm so sorry."

chilling effect: (p. 270) An outcome of physical violence in which individuals stop discussing relationship issues out of fear of their partners' negative reactions.

chronemics: (p. 226) A nonverbal code that represents the way you use time to communicate in interpersonal encounters.

chronic hostility: (p. 131) A persistent state of simmering or barely suppressed anger and constant negative thinking.

circumscribing: (p. 297) A relational stage in which partners avoid talking about topics that produce conflict. For instance, whenever Owen mentions he's interested in moving, Ruth becomes upset and changes the subject.

cohabiting couple: (p. 326) Two unmarried adults who are involved romantically and live together with or without children.

collaboration: (p. 258) A way of handling conflict by treating it as a mutual problem-solving challenge. For example, Martel and Louis brainstorm ways to solve the problem they have with their shared parking area until they come up with an agreeable solution.

collectivistic culture: (p. 50) A culture that values the needs and goals of the community or group above an individual's. Collectivistic cultures also value the importance of belonging to groups that look after you in exchange for loyalty. Contrast **individualistic culture.**

commitment: (p. 287) A strong psychological attachment to a partner and an intention to continue the relationship long into the future.

communal friendships: (p. 357) Voluntary relationships focused on sharing time and activities together.

communication: (p. 6) The process through which people use messages to generate meanings within and across contexts, cultures, channels, and media.

communication accommodation theory: (p. 196) The idea that people are especially motivated to adapt their language when they seek social approval, wish to establish relationships with others, and view others' language use as appropriate.

communication apprehension: (p. 198) The fear or nervousness associated with communicating with others.

communication plans: (p. 198) Mental maps that describe exactly how communication encounters will unfold. For example, before calling to complain about her telephone bill, Marjorie mentally rehearses how she will explain her problem and what objections she might face.

Communication Privacy Management Theory: (p. 339) The idea that individuals create informational boundaries by choosing carefully the kind of private information they reveal and the people with whom they share it.

communication skills: (p. 22) Repeatable goal-directed behaviors and behavioral patterns that enable you to improve the quality of your interpersonal encounters and relationships. See also **appropriateness; interpersonal communication competence.**

companionate love: (p. 284) An intense form of liking defined by emotional investment and interdependent lives.

competition: (p. 257) A way of handling conflict by an open and clear discussion of the goal clash that exists and the pursuit of one's own goals without the regard for others' goals. For example, Martel and Louis yell back and forth about whose car should have the driveway parking spot and whose should be parked out front.

complementary relationships: (p. 249) Relationships characterized by an unequal balance of power, such as a marriage in which one spouse is the decision maker.

compromise: (p. 265) When, during a conflict, both parties change their goals to make them compatible. For example, though Matt wants to see the sci-fi thriller and Jane wants to see the new animated film, they agree to go to an adventure comedy.

conflict: (p. 246) The process that occurs when people perceive that they have incompatible goals or that someone is interfering in their ability to achieve their objectives.

conformity orientation: (p. 330) The degree to which family members believe communication should emphasize similarity or diversity in attitudes, beliefs, and values.

connotative meaning: (p. 184) Understanding of a word's meaning based on the situation and the shared knowledge between communication partners (i.e., not the dictionary definition). For instance, calling someone *slender* suggests something more positive than the word *skinny* or *scrawny* does, though all three words mean "underweight." Contrast **denotative meaning.**

consensual families: (p. 332) Families characterized by high levels of conformity and conversation orientation. For example, Dan's parents encourage their son to be open but also expect him to maintain family unity through agreement or obedience.

constitutive rules: (p. 179) Guidelines that define word meaning according to a particular language's vocabulary. For instance, "pencil" is *Bleistift* in German and *matita* in Italian.

content-oriented listeners: (p. 161) Those who prefer to be intellectually challenged by messages—they prefer complex, detailed information. For example, a supervisor reviews the success of a fund-raising event by requesting data analyzing the effectiveness of her team's publicity campaign instead of asking to hear about team members' experiences.

contexts: (p. 7) Situations in which communication occurs. Context includes the physical locations, backgrounds, genders, ages, moods, and relationships of the communicators, as well as the time of day.

conversation orientation: (p. 330) The degree to which family members are encouraged to participate in unrestrained interaction about a wide array of topics.

Cooperative Principle: (p. 192) The idea that we should make our verbal messages as informative, honest, relevant, and clear as is required, given what the situation requires. For example, listening closely to your friend's problem with a coworker and then responding with support would demonstrate the Cooperative Principle; interrupting your friend to brag about your new laptop would not.

cooperative verbal communication: (p. 191) Producing messages that are understandable, take ownership, and are inclusive.

cross-category friendships: (p. 364) Voluntary relationships that cross demographic lines.

culture: (pp. 27, 50) The established, coherent set of beliefs, attitudes, values, and practices shared by a large group of people.

cumulative annoyance: (p. 255) A buildup of repressed irritations that grows as the mental list of grievances we have against our partner grows. For example, Martel's anger about where Louis parks his car is a reaction to several other incidents in which Louis was inconsiderate.

cyberslacking: (p. 394) Using work computers for personal interests and activities, such as playing games, surfing the Internet, updating Facebook, sending e-mail, or instant-messaging, instead of focusing on work tasks.

deactivation: (p. 126) Preventing unwanted emotions by systematically desensitizing yourself to emotional experience. For example, Josh insulates himself with numbness after his wife's death.

deception: (p. 201) Deliberately using uninformative, untruthful, irrelevant, or vague language for the purpose of misleading others.

defensive climate: (p. 392) A workplace atmosphere that is unfriendly, rigid, or unsupportive of workers' professional and personal needs. Contrast **supportive climate.**

defensive communication: (p. 198) Impolite messages delivered in response to suggestions, criticism, or perceived slights. For instance, when Stacy asks Lena to slow down her driving, Lena snaps back, "I'm not going that fast. If you don't like the way I drive, ride with someone else."

demand-withdraw pattern: (p. 270) A way of handling conflict in which one partner in a relationship demands that his or her goals be met, and the other partner responds by withdrawing from the encounter.

denotative meaning: (p. 183) The literal, or dictionary, definition of a word. Contrast **connotative meaning.**

dialects: (p. 179) Variations on language rules shared by large groups or particular regions; this may include differences in vocabulary, grammar, and pronunciation. For example, in various regions of the United States, carbonated beverages are called *soda, pop,* or *Coke.*

differentiating: (p. 296) A relational stage in which the beliefs, attitudes, and values that distinguish you from your partner come to dominate your thoughts and communication. For example, Ruth and Owen argue over whose family they are going to visit for Thanksgiving and how little time he has spent helping her fix up the house.

dirty secrets: (p. 268) Truthful but destructive messages used deliberately to hurt someone during a conflict. For example, Judith tells her sister, "That boy you like—Craig? I heard him tell Elaine you laugh like a horse."

dismissive attachment: (p. 48) An attachment style where individuals have low anxiety but high avoidance: they view close relationships as comparatively unimportant, instead prizing self-reliance.

display rules: (p. 119) Cultural norms about which forms of emotion management and communication are socially desirable and appropriate. For example, customary ways to show grief range from stoic reserve to open weeping to exaggerated wailing.

dominance: (p. 235) The interpersonal behaviors we use to exert power or influence over others. Dominance may occur through nonverbal behavior, as in crowding threateningly into a person's intimate zone, staring someone down, or keeping another person waiting.

domination: (p. 264) When one person gets his or her way in a conflict by influencing the other to engage in accommodation and abandon his or her goals. For example, Jane wants to see the new animated film, but Matt refuses by saying that it is his choice or no movie at all.

downward communication: (p. 402) Messages from a superior to subordinates. For example, the CEO of the company calls the regional managers together for a strategy session. Contrast **upward communication.**

dyadic: (p. 11) Communication involving only two people.

Dyadic Power Theory: (p. 249) The idea that people with only moderate power are most likely to use controlling communication.

eavesdropping: (p. 166) Intentionally listening in on private conversations.

effectiveness: (p. 23) The ability to use communication to accomplish interpersonal goals.

embarrassment: (p. 53) A feeling of shame, humiliation, and sadness that comes when we lose face.

emblems: (p. 219) Gestures that symbolize a specific verbal meaning within a given culture, such as the "thumbs up" or the "V for victory" sign.

emotion: (p. 111) An intense reaction to an event that involves interpreting the meaning of the event, becoming physiologically aroused, labeling the experience as emotional, attempting to manage your reaction, and communicating this reaction in the form of emotional displays and disclosures.

emotional contagion: (p. 113) The rapid spreading of emotion from person to person, such as anger running through a mob.

emotional intelligence: (p. 123) The ability to accurately interpret your and others' emotions and use this information to manage emotions, communicate them competently, and solve relationship problems.

emotion management: (p. 123) Attempts to influence which emotions you have, when you have them, and how you experience and express them.

emotion-sharing: (p. 113) Disclosing your emotions to others.

empathy: (p. 99) Understanding of another person's perspective and awareness of his or her feelings in an attempt to identify with them. For instance, Gill doesn't agree with Mike's protest against the new policies at work, but he can see why Mike was worried and angry.

encounter avoidance: (p. 125) Preventing unwanted emotions by keeping away from people, places, and activities likely to provoke them. For example, Jessica infuriates Roxanne, so Roxanne moves out of their shared apartment.

encounter structuring: (p. 126) Preventing unwanted emotions by intentionally avoiding discussion of difficult topics in encounters with others. For instance, Natalie and Julie avoid talking about living expenses because Natalie is jealous of Julie's income.

environment: (p. 230) A nonverbal code that represents the physical features of our surroundings.

equity: (p. 291) The balance of benefits and costs exchanged by you and a romantic interest that determines whether a romantic relationship will take root (after attraction is established).

escalation: (p. 258) A dramatic rise in emotional intensity and increasingly negative communication during conflict, such as teasing that inflates to a heated exchange of insults.

ethics: (p. 23) The set of moral principles that guide our behavior toward others. Ethical communication consistently displays respect, kindness, and compassion.

ethnocentrism: (p. 101) The belief that your own culture's beliefs, attitudes, values, and practices are superior to those of all other cultures. For example, Americans, accustomed to lining up, who consider cultures that don't use waiting lines as disorganized are displaying ethnocentrism. Contrast **world-mindedness.**

experimenting: (p. 294) A relational stage in which two people become acquainted by sharing factual information about themselves and making light conversation or small talk. For instance, after Ruth is introduced to Owen, they talk about their jobs and where they went to school, and they discover they both like jazz.

expertise currency: (p. 251) Power that comes from possessing specialized skills or knowledge, such as knowing CPR if someone stops breathing.

extended family: (p. 326) A family type consisting of a group of people who are related to one another—such as aunts, uncles, cousins, or grandparents—and who live in the same household.

face: (p. 52) The self we allow others to see and know; the aspects of ourselves we choose to present publicly. For instance, you dress up and speak carefully for an important social occasion, though in private you're very casual.

family: (p. 324) A network of people who share their lives over long periods of time and are bound by marriage, blood, or commitment; who consider themselves as family; and who share a significant history and anticipated future of functioning in a family relationship.

Family Communication Patterns Theory: (p. 330) The idea that two dimensions—**conformity orientation** and **conversation orientation**—underlie the communication between family members. See also **conformity orientation; conversation orientation.**

family privacy rules: (p. 339) The conditions governing what family members can talk about, how they can discuss such topics, and who should have access to family-relevant information.

family stories: (p. 327) Narratives of family events retold to bond family members. For example, Katie's mother often recounts how Katie was born on the day of a crippling blizzard.

fearful attachment: (p. 48) An attachment style in which individuals are high in both attachment anxiety and avoidance: they fear rejection and thus shun relationships, preferring to avoid the pain they believe is an inevitable part of intimacy.

feedback: (pp. 9, 153) Verbal and nonverbal messages that receivers use to indicate their reaction to communication, such as a frown or saying, "I disagree." See also **interactive communication model.**

feelings: (p. 113) Short-term emotional reactions to events that generate only limited arousal, such as the fleeting nostalgia you experience hearing a familiar song.

fields of experience: (p. 9) Beliefs, attitudes, values, and experiences that each communicator brings to an interaction.

friendship: (p. 355) A voluntary relationship characterized by intimacy and liking.

friendship rules: (p. 368) General principles for appropriate communication and behavior within friendships, such as keeping a confidence and showing support.

friendship-warmth touch: (p. 224) A touch used to express liking for another person, such as an arm across another's shoulders, a victory slap between teammates, or playful jostling between friends.

functional-professional touch: (p. 223) A touch used to accomplish a task, such as a physical therapist positioning a client's arm or a dancer gripping his partner's waist for a lift.

fundamental attribution error: (p. 81) The tendency to attribute someone's behavior solely to his or her personality rather than to outside forces.

FWB (friends with benefits) relationships: (p. 377) Friendships negotiated to include sexual activity but not with the purpose of transforming the relationship into a romantic attachment.

gender: (pp. 28, 45) The composite of social, psychological, and cultural attributes that characterize us as male or female.

Gestalt: (p. 93) A general sense of a person that's either positive or negative. See also **halo effect; horn effect.**

grief: (p. 134) Intense sadness that follows a substantial loss (such as the death of a loved one).

halo effect: (p. 95) A tendency to interpret anything another person says or does in a favorable light because you have a positive Gestalt of that person.

haptics: (p. 223) A nonverbal code that represents messages conveyed through touch. See also **friendship-warmth touch; functional-professional touch; love-intimacy touch; sexual-arousal touch; social-polite touch.**

hearing: (p. 148) The sensory process of taking in and interpreting sound.

high-context cultures: (p. 181) Cultures that presume listeners share extensive common knowledge and therefore rely more on the context of a conversation than on the words themselves for meaning. For example, after asking to purchase two theater tickets, a Japanese person might hear, "Sorry, very difficult," and immediately understand this as a subtle, indirect response meaning, "I am embarrassed that I can't provide you with what you wish, but the performance is sold out." Contrast **low-context cultures.**

honesty: (p. 193) Truthful communication, without exaggeration or omission of relevant information. Failing to tell someone something can be as dishonest as an outright lie.

horn effect: (p. 95) A tendency to interpret anything another person says or does in a negative light because you have a negative Gestalt of that person.

identity support: (p. 362) Behaving in ways that convey understanding, acceptance, and support for a friend's valued social identities.

I-It: (p. 13) A type of perception and communication that occurs when you treat others as though they are objects that are there for your use and exploitation—for example, when you dismiss someone by saying, "I don't have time for your stupid questions. Figure it out yourself."

"I" language: (p. 194) Communication that uses the pronoun *I* in sentence construction to emphasize ownership of your feelings, opinions, and beliefs—for example, "I'm frustrated because I think I'm doing more than you are on this project" instead of "You're really underperforming on this project." See also **"we" language; "you" language.**

illustrators: (p. 219) Gestures used to accent or illustrate a verbal message. For example, a fisherman holds his hands apart to show the size of his catch, or someone points emphatically at a door while saying, "Leave!"

immediacy: (p. 220) As expressed in your posture, the degree to which you find someone interesting and attractive.

impersonal communication: (p. 13) Messages that have negligible perceived impact on your thoughts, emotions, behaviors, or relationships, such as commenting about the television schedule or passing someone and saying, "How's it going?" without looking up.

implicit personality theories: (p. 92) Personal beliefs about different types of personalities and the ways in which traits cluster together. For instance, Bradley assumes that Will is a disorganized procrastinator because of Will's casual, friendly manner.

individualistic culture: (p. 50) A culture that values individual goals over group or societal goals. Contrast **collectivistic culture.**

ingroupers: (p. 84) People you consider fundamentally similar to yourself because of their interests, affiliations, or backgrounds. Contrast **outgroupers.**

initiating: (p. 294) A relational stage in which two people meet and form their first impressions of each other. For instance, Owen introduces himself in an e-mail to Ruth after reading her profile on an online dating site, and she responds with her telephone number.

instrumental goals: (p. 19) Practical aims you want to achieve or tasks you want to accomplish through a particular interpersonal encounter.

integrating: (p. 295) A relational stage in which two people become a couple and begin to share an identity. For example, Ruth and Owen share an apartment together and spend time with each other's families.

integrative agreements: (p. 265) When, during a conflict, the two sides preserve and attain their goals by developing a creative solution to their problem. For example, because Matt and Jane can't agree on what film to see, they decide they'd both be happier going to a comedy club.

intensifying: (p. 294) A relational stage characterized by deeper self-disclosures, stronger attraction, and intimate communication. For example, Owen and Ruth have been dating for more than a year and talk with excitement about a future together.

interaction: (p. 6) A series of messages exchanged between people, whether face-to-face or online.

interactive communication model: (p. 9) A depiction of communication messages that are exchanged back and forth between a sender and a receiver and are influenced by feedback and the fields of experience of both communicators.

interparental conflict: (p. 348) Overt, hostile interactions between parents in a household.

interpersonal communication: (p. 11) A dynamic form of communication between two (or more) people in which the messages exchanged significantly influence their thoughts, emotions, behaviors, and relationships.

interpersonal communication competence: (p. 21) The ability to communicate consistently in appropriate, effective, and ethical ways.

interpersonal impressions: (p. 92) Ideas about who people are and how we feel about them. For instance, when Sarah and Georgia met, Georgia thought Sarah's quietness meant that Sarah was unfriendly and conceited.

interpersonal process model of intimacy: (p. 63) The idea that the closeness we feel toward others in our relationships is created through two things: self-disclosure and responsiveness of listeners to such disclosure.

interpretation: (p. 78) The stage of perception in which we assign meaning to the information we have selected. For instance, Randy thinks a man running down the sidewalk hurries because he is late, but Shondra infers that the man is chasing someone.

intimacy: (pp. 60, 234) A feeling of closeness and "union" that exists between us and our relationship partners.

intimacy currency: (p. 251) Power that comes from sharing a close bond with someone that no one else shares. For example, you can easily persuade a close friend to change her mind because she is fond of you.

intimate space: (p. 225) The narrowest proxemic zone—0 to 18 inches of space—between communicators.

intrapersonal communication: (p. 13) Communication involving only one person, such as talking to yourself.

I-Thou: (p. 13) A way to perceive a relationship based on embracing fundamental similarities that connect you to others, striving to see things from others' points of view, and communicating in ways that emphasize honesty and kindness.

jealousy: (p. 310) A protective reaction when a valued relationship seems threatened. For instance, Tyler is jealous when his girlfriend, Mary, flirts with Scott.

Jefferson strategy: (p. 131) A strategy to manage your anger that involves counting slowly to 10 before responding to someone who says or does something that makes you angry. (The strategy was named after the third president of the United States.)

kinesics: (p. 218) A nonverbal code that represents messages communicated in visible body movements, such as facial expressions, posture, body movements, gestures, and eye contact.

kitchen-sinking: (p. 247) A response to a conflict in which combatants hurl insults and accusations at each other that have very little to do with the original disagreement. For example, although Mary and Pat are arguing about the budget, Mary adds, "I'm sick of the mess you left in the garage and these papers all over the family room."

laissez-faire families: (p. 333) Families characterized by low levels of conformity and conversation orientation. For example, Samantha's parents prefer limited communication and encourage their daughter to make her own choices and decisions.

liking: (p. 282) A feeling of affection and respect typical of friendship.

linear communication model: (p. 8) A depiction of communication messages that flow in one direction from a starting point to an end point.

linguistic determinism: (p. 186) The view that the language we use defines the boundaries of our thinking.

linguistic relativity: (p. 186) The theory that languages create variations in the ways cultures perceive and think about the world.

listening: (p. 147) The five-stage process of receiving, attending to, understanding, responding to, and recalling sounds and visual images during interpersonal encounters.

listening functions: (p. 158) The five general purposes that listening serves: to comprehend, to discern, to analyze, to appreciate, and to support.

listening style: (p. 160) An individual's habitual pattern of listening behaviors, which reflects one's attitudes, beliefs, and predispositions regarding the listening process. See also **action-oriented listeners; content-oriented listeners; people-oriented listeners; time-oriented listeners.**

long-term memory: (p. 152) The part of your mind devoted to permanent information storage.

looking-glass self: (p. 41) Sociologist Charles Horton Cooley's idea that we define our self-concepts through thinking about how others see us. For example, a young girl who believes others consider her poor in sports formulates an image of herself as uncoordinated even though she is a good dancer.

love-intimacy touch: (p. 224) A touch indicating deep emotional feeling, such as two romantic partners holding hands or two close friends embracing.

loving: (p. 282) An intense emotional commitment based on intimacy, caring, and attachment.

low-context cultures: (p. 180) Cultures that rely on words themselves, rather than on the conversational situation, to convey meaning, resulting in direct verbal communication. In the United States, for example, we prefer directness and clarity rather than what we view as vague hints. Contrast **high-context cultures.**

mask: (p. 52) The public self designed to strategically veil your private self—for example, putting on a happy face when you are sad or pretending to be confident while inside you feel shy or anxious.

matching: (p. 290) A tendency to be attracted to others whom we perceive to be at our own level of attractiveness. For example, Michael dates Jennifer because she is pretty but not unapproachably gorgeous.

media: (p. 7) Tools used to exchange messages, including everything from newspapers, blackboards, and photographs to computers, smartphones, and television.

mental bracketing: (p. 151) Systematically putting aside thoughts that aren't relevant to the interaction at hand if your attention wanders when listening—for example, by consciously dismissing your worries about an upcoming exam in order to focus on a customer's request at work.

mere exposure effect: (p. 289) A phenomenon in which you feel more attracted to those with whom you have frequent contact and less attracted to those with whom you interact rarely. For example, the more June sees of Tom, the more attracted to him she becomes.

message: (p. 6) The package of information transported during communication.

meta-communication: (p. 16) Verbal or nonverbal communication about communication—that is, messages that have communication as their central focus.

misunderstanding: (p. 193) Confusion resulting from the misperception of another's thoughts, feelings, or beliefs as expressed in the other individual's verbal communication.

mixed messages: (p. 213) Verbal and nonverbal behaviors that convey contradictory meanings, such as saying, "I'm so happy for you," in a sarcastic tone of voice.

mixed-status relationships: (p. 400) Associations between coworkers at different levels of power and status in an organization, such as a manager and a salesclerk.

mnemonics: (p. 156) Devices that aid memory. For example, the mnemonic *Roy G. Biv* is commonly used to recall the order of the seven colors in the rainbow.

moods: (p. 114) Low-intensity states of mind that are not caused by particular events and typically last longer than emotions—for example, boredom, contentment, grouchiness, serenity.

M-time (monochronic time): (p. 226) A cultural orientation toward time that values careful scheduling and time management. In the United States, for instance, appointments are important. Contrast **P-time (polychronic time).**

naming: (p. 186) Creating linguistic symbols to represent people, objects, places, and ideas.

narcissistic listening: (p. 170) A self-absorbed approach to listening in which the listener redirects the conversation to his or her own interests. For example, Neil acts bored while Jack describes a recent ski trip, interrupting Jack and switching the topic to his own recent car purchase.

negativity effect: (p. 94) A tendency to place emphasis on the negative information we learn about others.

noise: (p. 8) Environmental factors that impede a message on the way to its destination.

nonverbal communication: (p. 211) The intentional or unintentional transmission of meaning through an individual's nonspoken physical and behavioral cues.

nonverbal communication codes: (p. 217) Different ways to transmit information nonverbally: artifacts, chronemics, environment, haptics, kinesics, physical appearance, proxemics, and vocalics.

nuclear family: (p. 325) A family type consisting of a father, a mother, and their biological or adopted children.

online communication: (p. 25) Interaction through communication technology such as social networking sites, e-mail, text- or instant-messaging, Skype, chatrooms, and even massively multiplayer online video games like *World of Warcraft.*

organization: (p. 77) The step of perception in which we mentally structure selected sensory data into a coherent pattern.

organizational climate: (p. 392) The overarching emotional quality of a workplace environment. For example, employees might say their organization feels warm, frenetic, unfriendly, or serene.

organizational culture: (p. 389) A distinct set of workplace traditions, values, and practices.

organizational networks: (p. 390) Communication links among an organization's members, such as the nature, frequency, and ways information is exchanged. For example, you have weekly face-to-face status meetings with your boss or receive daily reminder e-mails from an assistant.

outgroupers: (p. 84) People you consider fundamentally different from you because of their interests, affiliations, or backgrounds. Contrast **ingroupers.**

paraphrasing: (p. 154) An active listening response that summarizes or restates others' comments after they are finished.

parental favoritism: (p. 343) When one or both parents allocate an unfair amount of valuable resources to one child over others.

passion: (p. 132) A blended emotion of joy and surprise coupled with other positive feelings like excitement, amazement, and sexual attraction.

passionate love: (p. 282) A state of intense emotional and physical longing for union with another.

people-oriented listeners: (p. 161) Those who view listening as an opportunity to establish commonalities between themselves and others. For example, Carl enjoys Elaine's descriptions of the triumphs and difficulties she's had learning to snowboard.

perception: (p. 75) The process of selecting, organizing, and interpreting information from our senses.

perception-checking: (p. 101) A five-step process to test your impressions of others and to avoid errors in judgment. It involves checking your punctuation, knowledge, attributions, perceptual influences, and impressions.

personal currency: (p. 251) Power that comes from personal characteristics that others admire, such as intelligence, physical beauty, charm, communication skill, or humor.

personal idioms: (p. 179) Words and phrases that have unique meanings to a particular relationship, such as pet names or private phrases with special meaning. For example, Uncle Henry was known for his practical jokes; now, years after his death, family members still refer to a practical joke as "pulling a Henry."

personality: (p. 90) An individual's characteristic way of thinking, feeling, and acting based on the traits he or she possesses.

personal space: (p. 225) The proxemic zone that ranges from 18 inches to 4 feet of space between communicators. It is the spatial separation most often used in the United States for friendly conversation.

physical appearance: (p. 229) A nonverbal code that represents visual attributes such as body type, clothing, hair, and other physical features.

pluralistic families: (p. 332) Families characterized by low levels of conformity and high levels of conversation orientation. For example, Julie's parents encourage her to express herself freely, and when conflicts arise, they collaborate with her to resolve them.

positivity bias: (p. 94) A tendency for first impressions of others to be more positive than negative.

power: (pp. 220, 248) The ability to influence or control events and people.

power currency: (p. 251) Control over a resource that other people value. See also **expertise currency; intimacy currency; personal currency; resource currency; social network currency.**

power-distance: (p. 252) The degree to which people in a culture view the unequal distribution of power as acceptable. For example, in some cultures, well-defined class distinctions limit interaction across class lines, but other cultures downplay status and privilege to foster a spirit of equality.

preoccupied attachment: (p. 48) An attachment style where individuals are high in anxiety and low in avoidance; they desire closeness, but are plagued with fear of rejection.

primary emotions: (p. 115) Six emotions that involve unique and consistent behavioral displays across cultures: anger, disgust, fear, joy, sadness, and surprise.

professional peers: (p. 396) People who hold jobs at the same level of power and status as your own.

protective families: (p. 333) Families characterized by high levels of conformity and low levels of conversation orientation. For example, Brian's parents expect their son to be respectful, and they discourage family discussions.

provocateurs: (p. 167) Aggressive listeners who intentionally bait and attack others in online communication. For example, a group member stirs up trouble in a chatroom by criticizing the study group leader and then humiliates other respondents.

proxemics: (p. 225) A nonverbal code for communication through physical distance. See also **intimate space; personal space; public space; social space.**

pseudo-conflict: (p. 256) A mistaken perception that a conflict exists when it doesn't. For example, Barbara thinks Anne is angry with her because Anne hasn't spoken to her all evening, but Anne is actually worried about a report from her physician.

pseudo-listening: (p. 167) Pretending to listen while preoccupied or bored.

P-time (polychronic time): (p. 227) A cultural orientation toward time, viewing it loosely and fluidly and valuing human relationships over strict schedules and efficiency. In Mexico, for instance, punctuality may be sacrificed to savor a conversation. Contrast **M-time (monochronic time).**

public space: (p. 225) The widest proxemic zone. It ranges outward from 12 feet and is most appropriate for formal settings.

punctuation: (p. 77) A step during organization when you structure information you've selected into a chronological sequence that matches how you experienced the order of events. For example, Bobby claims his sister started the backseat argument, but she insists that he poked her first.

Rational Emotive Behavior Therapy (REBT): (p. 121) A therapy developed by psychologist Albert Ellis that helps neurotic patients systematically purge themselves of the tendency to think negative thoughts about themselves.

reactivity: (p. 258) A way of handling conflict by not pursuing conflict-related goals at all and communicating in an emotionally explosive and negative fashion instead.

reappraisal: (p. 126) Actively changing how you think about the meaning of emotion-eliciting situations so that their emotional impact is changed. For instance, though previously fearful of giving a speech, Luke reduces his anxiety by repeating positive affirmations and getting excited about the chance to share what he knows.

recalling: (p. 155) The fifth stage of the listening process in which a listener is able to remember information received.

receiver: (p. 8) The individual for whom a message is intended or to whom it is delivered.

receiving: (p. 148) The first stage of the listening process in which a listener takes in information by seeing and hearing.

reciprocal liking: (p. 291) When the person we're attracted to makes it clear, through communication and other actions, that the attraction is mutual.

regulative rules: (p. 179) Guidelines that govern how we use language when we verbally communicate—that is, spelling and grammar as well as conversational usage. For example, we know how to respond correctly to a greeting, and we know that cursing in public is inappropriate.

regulators: (p. 220) Gestures used to control the exchange of conversational turns during interpersonal encounters—for example, averting eye contact to avoid someone or zipping up book bags as a class to signal to a professor that the lecture should end.

relational dialectics: (p. 287) Opposing tensions between ourselves and our feelings toward others that exist in interpersonal relationships, such as the tension between wishing to be completely honest with a partner yet not wanting to be hurtful.

relational intrusion: (p. 311) The violation of one's independence and privacy by a person who desires an intimate relationship.

relational maintenance: (p. 300) Efforts that partners make to keep their relationship in a desired condition. They may show devotion by making time to talk, spending time together, and offering help or support to each other.

relationship goals: (p. 19) Goals of building, maintaining, or terminating relationships with others through interpersonal communication.

resource currency: (p. 251) Power that comes from controlling material items others want or need, such as money, food, or property.

responding: (p. 153) The stage of the listening process in which a listener communicates, nonverbally or verbally, their attention and understanding—for example, by nodding or murmuring agreement.

romantic betrayal: (p. 307) An act that goes against expectations of a romantic relationship and, as a result, causes pain to a partner.

romantic relationship: (p. 285) An interpersonal involvement two people choose to enter that is perceived as romantic by both. For instance, Louise is in love with Robert, and Robert returns her affections.

salience: (p. 76) The degree to which particular people or aspects of their communication attract our attention.

schemata: (p. 78) Mental structures that contain information defining the characteristics of various concepts (such as people, places, events), as well as how those characteristics are related to one another. We often use schemata when interpreting interpersonal communication. When Charlie describes his home as "retro," Amanda visualizes it before she even sees it.

secure attachment: (p. 48) An attachment style in which individuals are low on both anxiety and avoidance; they are comfortable with intimacy and seek close ties with others.

selection: (p. 76) The step of perception in which we focus our attention on specific sensory data, such as sights, sounds, tastes, touches, or smells.

selective listening: (p. 164) Listening that captures only parts of a message (those that are the most interesting to the listener) and dismisses the rest.

self: (p. 39) The evolving composite of who one is, including self-awareness, self-concept, and self-esteem.

self-awareness: (p. 39) The ability to view yourself as a unique person distinct from your surrounding environment and reflect on your thoughts, feelings, and behaviors.

self-concept: (p. 40) Your overall idea of who you are based on the beliefs, attitudes, and values you have about yourself.

self-disclosure: (p. 63) Revealing private information about yourself to others.

self-discrepancy theory: (p. 42) The idea that your self-esteem results from comparing two mental standards: your *ideal* self (the characteristics you want to possess based on your desires) and your *ought* self (the person others wish and expect you to be).

self-esteem: (p. 41) The overall value, positive or negative, you assign to yourself.

self-fulfilling prophecies: (p. 41) Predictions about future encounters that lead us to behave in ways that ensure the interaction unfolds as we predicted.

self-monitoring: (p. 22) The process of observing your own communication and the norms of the situation in order to make appropriate communication choices.

self-presentation goals: (p. 18) In interpersonal encounters, presenting yourself in certain ways so that others perceive you as being a particular type of person.

self-serving bias: (p. 82) A biased tendency to credit ourselves (internal factors) instead of external factors for our success. For instance, Ruth attributes the success of a project to her leadership qualities rather than to the dedicated efforts of her team.

sender: (p. 8) The individual who generates, packages, and delivers a message.

separation: (p. 264) A sudden withdrawal of one person from a situation during a conflict. For example, you walk away from an argument to cool off, or you angrily retreat to your room.

serial arguments: (p. 269) A series of unresolved disputes, all having to do with the same issue.

sexual-arousal touch: (p. 224) An intentional touch designed to physically stimulate another person.

sexual harassment: (p. 412) Unwelcome sexual advances, physical contact, or requests that render a workplace offensive or intimidating.

sexual orientation: (p. 29) Enduring emotional, romantic, sexual, or affectionate attraction to others that exists along a continuum ranging from exclusive heterosexuality to exclusive homosexuality and that includes various forms of bisexuality.

short-term memory: (p. 152) The part of your mind that temporarily houses information while you seek to understand its meaning.

single-parent family: (p. 326) A household in which one adult has the sole responsibility to be the children's caregiver.

skirting: (p. 255) A way of avoiding conflict by changing the topic or joking about it. For example, Martel tries to evade Louis's criticism about where Martel parked his car by teasing, "I did you a favor. You walked twenty extra steps. Exercise is good for you."

sniping: (p. 255) A way of avoiding conflict by communicating in a negative fashion and then abandoning the encounter by physically leaving the scene or refusing to interact further, such as when Martel answers Louis's criticism about where he parked his car by insulting Louis and stomping out the door.

social comparison: (p. 40) Observing and assigning meaning to others' behaviors and then comparing their behavior to ours (when judging our own actions). For example, you might subtly check out how others are dressed at a party or how they scored on an exam to see if you compare favorably.

social exchange theory: (p. 291) The idea that you will be drawn to those you see as offering substantial benefits with few associated costs. For example, Meredith thinks Leonard is perfect for her because he is much more attentive and affectionate than her previous boyfriends and seems so easy to please.

social network currency: (p. 251) Power that comes from being linked with a network of friends, family, and acquaintances with substantial influence, such as being on a first-name basis with a sports celebrity.

social penetration theory: (p. 59) Altman and Taylor's model that you reveal information about yourself to others by peeling back or penetrating layers.

social-polite touch: (p. 223) A touch, such as a handshake, used to demonstrate social norms or culturally expected behaviors.

social space: (p. 225) The proxemic zone that ranges from 4 to 12 feet of space between communicators. It is the spatial separation most often used in the United States for conversations between acquaintances and strangers.

speech acts: (p. 187) The actions we perform with language, such as the question, "Is the antique clock in your window for sale?" and the reply, "Yes, let me get it out to show you."

spillover hypothesis: (p. 348) The idea that emotions, affect, and mood from the parental relationship "spill over" into the broader family, disrupting children's sense of emotional security.

stagnating: (p. 297) A relational stage in which communication comes to a standstill. For instance, day after day, Owen and Ruth speak only to ask if a bill has been paid or what is on television, without really listening to one another's answers.

stepfamily: (p. 326) A family type where at least one of the adults has a child or children from a previous relationship.

stereotyping: (p. 96) Categorizing people into social groups and then evaluating them based on information we have in our schemata related to each group.

structural improvements: (p. 266) When people agree to change the basic rules or understandings that govern their relationship to prevent further conflict.

submissiveness: (p. 238) The willingness to allow others to exert power over you, demonstrated by gestures such as a shrinking posture or lowered eye gaze.

sudden-death statements: (p. 268) Messages, communicated at the height of a conflict, that suddenly declare the end of a relationship, even if that wasn't an option before—for example, "It's over. I never want to see you again."

supportive climate: (p. 392) A workplace atmosphere that is supportive, warm, and open. Contrast **defensive climate.**

supportive communication: (p. 136) Sharing messages that express emotional support and that offer personal assistance, such as telling a person of your sympathy or listening to someone without judging.

suppression: (p. 123) Inhibiting thoughts, arousal, and outward behavioral displays of emotion. For example, Amanda stifles her anger, knowing it will kill her chances of receiving a good tip.

symbols: (p. 178) Items used to represent other things, ideas, or events. For example, the letters of the alphabet are symbols for specific sounds in English.

symmetrical relationships: (p. 249) Relationships characterized by an equal balance of power, such as a business partnership in which the partners co-own their company.

terminating: (p. 297) A relational stage in which one or both partners end a relationship. For instance, Ruth asks Owen for a divorce once she realizes their marriage has deteriorated beyond salvation.

territoriality: (p. 226) The tendency to claim personal spaces as our own and define certain locations as areas we don't want others to invade without permission, such as spreading personal stuff to claim the entire library table.

time-oriented listeners: (p. 161) Those who prefer brief, concise messages to save time.

transactional communication model: (p. 9) A depiction of communication in which each participant equally influences the communication behavior of the other participants. For example, a salesperson who watches his customer's facial expression while describing a product is sending and receiving messages at the same time.

triangulation: (p. 342) Loyalty conflicts that arise when a coalition is formed, uniting one family member with another against a third family member.

Uncertainty Reduction Theory: (p. 83) A theory explaining that the primary compulsion during initial encounters is to reduce uncertainty about our conversational partners by gathering enough information about them so their communication becomes predictable and explainable.

understanding: (p. 152) The third stage of the listening process in which a listener interprets the meaning of another person's communication by comparing newly received information against past knowledge.

upward communication: (p. 400) Messages from a subordinate to a superior. For instance, a clerk notifies the department manager that inventory needs to be reordered. Contrast **downward communication.**

valued social identities: (p. 362) The aspects of your public self that you deem the most important in defining who you are—for example, musician, athlete, poet, dancer, teacher, mother, etc.

venting: (p. 125) Allowing emotions to dominate your thoughts and explosively expressing them, such as shrieking in happiness or storming into an office in a rage.

verbal aggression: (p. 200) The tendency to attack others' self-concepts—their appearance, behavior, or character—rather than their positions.

verbal communication: (p. 177) The exchange of spoken or written language with others during interactions.

virtual networks: (p. 390) Groups of coworkers linked solely through e-mail, social networking sites, Skype, and other Internet destinations.

virtual peers: (p. 396) Coworkers who communicate mostly through phone, e-mail, Skype, and other communication technologies.

vocalics: (p. 221) Vocal characteristics we use to communicate nonverbal messages, such as volume, pitch, rate, voice quality, vocalized sounds, and silence. For instance, a pause might signal discomfort, create tension, or be used to heighten drama.

warranting value: (p. 56) The degree to which online information is supported by other people and outside evidence.

wedging: (p. 311) When a person deliberately uses online communication—messages, photos, and posts—to try to insert him- or herself between romantic partners because he or she is interested in one of the partners.

"we" language: (p. 195) Communication that uses the pronoun *we* to emphasize inclusion—for example, "We need to decide what color to paint the living room" instead of "I need you to tell me what color paint you want for the living room." See also **"I" language; "you" language.**

workplace bullying: (p. 407) The repeated unethical and unfavorable treatment of one or more persons by others in the workplace.

workplace cliques: (p. 391) Dense networks of coworkers who share the same workplace values and broader life attitudes.

workplace relationships: (p. 387) Any affiliation you have with a professional peer, supervisor, subordinate, or mentor in a professional setting.

world-mindedness: (p. 100) The ability to practice and demonstrate acceptance and respect toward other cultures' beliefs, values, and customs. Contrast **ethnocentrism.**

"you" language: (p. 194) Communication that states or implies the pronoun *you* to place the focus of attention on blaming others—such as "You haven't done your share of the work on this project." Contrast **"I" language; "we" language.**

ABCnews.go.com. (2005, October 21). Do "helicopter moms" do more harm than good? Retrieved from http://abcnews.go.com/2020/Health/story?id=1237868&page=1

Ackard, D. M., & Neumark-Sztainer, D. (2002). Date violence and date rape among adolescents: Associations with disordered eating behaviors and psychological health. *Child Abuse and Neglect, 26,* 455–473.

Adams, B. N. (2004). Families and family study in international perspective. *Journal of Marriage and Family, 66,* 1076–1088.

Adamson, A., & Jenson, V. (Directors). (2001). *Shrek* [Motion picture]. United States: DreamWorks SKG.

Afifi, T. D. (2003). 'Feeling caught' in stepfamilies: Managing boundary turbulence through appropriate communication privacy rules. *Journal of Social and Personal Relationships, 20*(6), 729–755.

Afifi, T. D., McManus, T., Hutchinson, S., & Baker, B. (2007). Parental divorce disclosures, the factors that prompt them, and their impact on parents' and adolescents' well-being. *Communication Monographs, 74,* 78–103.

Afifi, T. D., McManus, T., Steuber, K., & Coho, A. (2009). Verbal avoidance and dissatisfaction in intimate conflict situations. *Human Communication Research, 35,* 357–383.

Afifi, T. D., & Olson, L. (2005). The chilling effect and the pressure to conceal secrets in families. *Communication Monographs, 72,* 192–216.

Afifi, T. D., & Steuber, K. (2010). The cycle of concealment model. *Journal of Social and Personal Relationships, 27*(8), 1019–1034.

Albrecht, T. L., & Bach, B. W. (1997). *Communication in complex organizations: A relational approach.* Fort Worth, TX: Harcourt Brace.

Allport, G. W. (1954). *The nature of prejudice.* Cambridge, MA: Addison-Wesley.

Altman, I., & Taylor, D. A. (1973). *Social penetration: The development of interpersonal relationships.* New York: Holt, Rinehart & Winston.

Andersen, P. A. (1997). Cues of culture: The basis of intercultural differences in nonverbal communication. In L. A. Samovar & R. E. Porter (Eds.), *Intercultural communication: A reader* (8th ed., pp. 244–255). Belmont, CA: Wadsworth.

Anderson, N. H. (1981). *Foundations of information integration theory.* Orlando, FL: Academic Press.

APA Online. (n.d.). *Just the facts about sexual orientation & youth: A primer for principals, educators, & school personnel.* Retrieved from http://www.apa.org/pi/lgbc/publications/justthefacts.html

Appelbaum, S. H., Marinescu, A., Klenin, J., & Bytautas, J. (2007). Fatal attractions: The mismanagement of workplace romance. *International Journal of Business Research, 7*(4), 31–43.

Archer, J. (2000). Sex differences in aggression between heterosexual partners: A meta-analytic review. *Psychological Bulletin, 126,* 651–680.

Argyle, M. (1969). *Social interaction.* New York: Atherton Press.

Argyle, M., & Furnham, A. (1982). The ecology of relationships: Choice of situations as a function of relationship. *British Journal of Social Psychology, 21,* 259–262.

Argyle, M., & Henderson, M. (1984). The rules of friendship. *Journal of Social and Personal Relationships, 1,* 211–237.

Argyle, M., & Lu, L. (1990). Happiness and social skills. *Personality and Individual Differences, 11,* 1255–1261.

Aron, A., Fisher, H., Strong, G., Acevedo, B., Riela, S., & Tsapelas, I. (2008). Falling in love. In S. Sprecher, A. Wenzel, & J. Harvey (Eds.), *Handbook of relationship initiation* (pp. 315–336). New York: Psychology Press.

Arriaga, X. B., & Agnew, C. R. (2001). Being committed: Affective, cognitive, and conative components of relationship commitment. *Personality and Social Psychology Bulletin, 27,* 1190–1203.

Asada, K. J. K., Morrison, K., Hughes, M., & Fitzpatrick, S. (2003, May). *Is that what friends are for? Understanding the motivations, barriers, and emotions associated with friends with benefits relationships.* Paper presented at the annual meeting of the International Communication Association, San Diego, CA.

Asch, S. E. (1946). Forming impressions of personality. *Journal of Abnormal and Social Psychology, 41,* 258–290.

Asian American Career Center. (n.d.). *Goldsea career success.* Retrieved from http://goldsea.com/Career/career.html

Aylor, B. A. (2003). Maintaining long-distance relationships. In D. J. Canary & M. Dainton (Eds.), *Maintaining relationships through communication: Relational, contextual, and cultural variations* (pp. 127–139). Mahwah, NJ: Erlbaum.

Balderrama, A. (2010, May 6). Are you paying attention to your online reputation? Employers are. *The Work Buzz.* Retrieved from http://www.theworkbuzz.com/featured/online-reputation

Bane, R. (2010, August 12). How splintered is your attention? [Blog post]. Retrieved from http://www.baneofyourresistance.com/2010/08/12/how-splintered-is-your-attention-take-the-quiz-and-find-out

Bank, B. J., & Hansford, S. L. (2000). Gender and friendship: Why are men's best same-sex friendships less intimate and supportive? *Personal Relationships, 7,* 63–78.

Baptiste, D. A., Jr. (1990). Therapeutic strategies with black-Hispanic families: Identity problems of a neglected minority. *Journal of Family Psychotherapy, 1,* 15–38.

Barker, L. L. (1971). *Listening behavior.* Englewood Cliffs, NJ: Prentice Hall.

Barker, L. L., & Watson, K. W. (2000). *Listen up.* New York: St. Martin's Press.

Barnes, S. B. (2001). *Online connections: Internet interpersonal relationships.* Cresskill, NJ: Hampton Press.

Barnett, O. W., Miller-Perrin, C. L., & Perrin, R. D. (1997). *Family violence across the life-span: An introduction.* Thousand Oaks, CA: Sage.

Barnlund, D. C. (1975). *Private and public self in Japan and the United States.* Tokyo: Simul Press.

Barry, D. (2011, May 15). A sports executive leaves the safety of his shadow life. *The New York Times*. Retrieved from http://www.nytimes.com

Bartholomew, K., & Horowitz, L. M. (1991). Attachment styles among young adults: A test of a four-category model. *Journal of Personality and Social Psychology, 61*(2), 226–244.

Baxter, L. A. (1990). Dialectical contradictions in relationship development. *Journal of Social and Personal Relationships, 7,* 69–88.

Baxter, L. A., Mazanec, M., Nicholson, J., Pittman, G., Smith, K., & West, L. (1997). Everyday loyalties and betrayals in personal relationships. *Journal of Social and Personal Relationships, 14,* 655–678.

Baxter, L. A., Wilmot, W. W., Simmons, C. A., & Swartz, A. (1993). Ways of doing conflict: A folk taxonomy of conflict events in personal relationships. In P. J. Kalbfleisch (Ed.), *Interpersonal communication: Evolving interpersonal relationships* (pp. 89–108). Hillsdale, NJ: Erlbaum.

Beach, W. A. (2002). Between dad and son: Initiating, delivering, and assimilating bad cancer news. *Health Communication, 14,* 271–298.

Becker, J. A. H., Johnson, A. J., Craig, E. A., Gilchrist, E. S., Haigh, M. M., & Lane, L. T. (2009). Friendships are flexible, not fragile: Turning points in geographically-close and long-distance friendships. *Journal of Social and Personal Relationships, 26*(4), 347–369.

Beer, J. S., John, O. P., Scabini, D., & Knight, R. T. (2006). Orbitofrontal cortex and social behavior: Integrating self-monitoring and emotion-cognition interactions. *Journal of Cognitive Neuroscience, 18,* 871–879.

Bell, R. A., Buerkel-Rothfuss, N. L., & Gore, K. E. (1987). Did you bring the yarmulke for the Cabbage Patch Kid? The idiomatic communication of young lovers. *Human Communication Research, 14,* 47–67.

Bennett, S. H. (2003). *Radical pacifism: The War Resisters League and Gandhian nonviolence in America, 1915–1963.* Syracuse, NY: Syracuse University Press.

Benoit, P. J., & Benoit, W. E. (1990). To argue or not to argue. In R. Trapp & J. Schuetz (Eds.), *Perspectives on argumentation: Essays in honor of Wayne Brockriede* (pp. 55–72). Prospect Heights, IL: Waveland Press.

Berger, C. R., & Bradac, J. J. (1982). *Language and social knowledge: Uncertainty in interpersonal relations.* London: Edward Arnold.

Berger, C. R., & Calabrese, R. J. (1975). Some explorations in initial interaction and beyond: Toward a developmental theory of interpersonal communication. *Human Communication Research, 1,* 99–112.

Berkowitz, L., & Harmon-Jones, E. (2004). Toward an understanding of the determinants of anger. *Emotion, 4,* 107–130.

Berry, G. R. (2006). Can computer-mediated asynchronous communication improve team processes and decision-making? *Journal of Business Communication, 43*(4), 344–366.

Berscheid, E. (2002). Emotion. In H. H. Kelley et al. (Eds.), *Close relationships* (2nd ed., pp. 110–168). Clinton Corners, NY: Percheron Press.

Berscheid, E., & Peplau, L. A. (2002). The emerging science of relationships. In H. H. Kelley et al. (Eds.), *Close relationships* (2nd ed., pp. 1–19). Clinton Corners, NY: Percheron Press.

Berscheid, E., & Regan, P. (2005). *The psychology of interpersonal relationships.* Upper Saddle River, NJ: Pearson Education.

Berscheid, E., & Walster, E. (1978). *Interpersonal attraction* (2nd ed.). Reading, MA: Addison-Wesley.

Bevan, J. L., Finan, A., & Kaminsky, A. (2008). Modeling serial arguments in close relationships: The serial argument process model. *Human Communication Research, 34,* 600–624.

Bianconi, L. (2002). *Culture and identity: Issues of authenticity in another value system.* Paper presented at the XII Sietar-EU Conference, Vienna.

Bies, R. J., & Tripp, T. M. (1998). Two faces of the powerless: Coping with tyranny in organizations. In R. M. Kramer & M. A. Neale (Eds.), *Power and influence in organizations* (pp. 203–219). Thousand Oaks, CA: Sage.

Birdwhistell, R. L. (1970). *Kinesics and context: Essays on body motion communication.* Philadelphia: University of Pennsylvania Press.

Blakely, G. L., Blakely, E. H., & Moorman, R. H. (1995). The relationship between gender, personal experience, and perceptions of sexual harassment in the workplace. *Employee Responsibilities and Rights Journal, 8,* 263–274.

Bland, K. (2011). Phoenix gay dads adopt, raise 12 happy kids. *The Arizona Republic.* Retrieved from http://www.azcentral.com/news/azliving/articles/2011/05/02/20110502gay-dads-ham-family-12-adopted-kids.html?page=1

Blieszner, R., & Adams, R. G. (1992). *Adult friendship.* Newbury Park, CA: Sage.

Bochner, S., & Hesketh, B. (1994). Power distance, individualism/collectivism, and job related attitudes in a culturally diverse work group. *Journal of Cross-Cultural Psychology, 25,* 233–257.

Boddy, C. R. (2011). Corporate psychopaths, bullying and unfair supervision in the workplace. *Journal of Business Ethics, 100,* 367–379.

Bodenhausen, G. V., Macrae, C. N., & Sherman, J. W. (1999). On the dialectics of discrimination: Dual processes in social stereotyping. In S. Chaiken & Y. Trope (Eds.), *Dual process theories in social psychology* (pp. 271–290). New York: Guilford Press.

Bodhi, B., & Nanamoli, B. (1995). *The middle length discourse of the Buddha: A translation of the Majjhima Nikaya.* Somerville, MA: Wisdom Publications.

Bodie, G. D., & Worthington, D. L. (2010). Revisiting the listening styles profile (LSP-16): A confirmatory factor analytic approach to scale validation and reliability estimation. *The International Journal of Listening, 24,* 69–88.

Booth, A., & Hess, E. (1974). Cross-sex friendship. *Journal of Marriage and the Family, 36,* 38–46.

Bornstein, R. F. (1989). Exposure and affect: Overview and meta-analysis of research, 1968–1987. *Psychological Bulletin, 106,* 265–289.

Bowlby, J. (1969). *Attachment and loss: Vol. 1. Attachment.* New York: Basic Books.

Boyd, C. (2010). The debate over the prohibition of romance in the workplace. *Journal of Business Ethics, 97,* 325–338.

Braithwaite, D. O., Bach, B. W., Baxter, L. A., DiVerniero, R., Hammonds, J. R., Hosek, A. M., et al. (2010). Constructing family: A typology of voluntary kin. *Journal of Social and Personal Relationships, 27*(3), 388–407.

Brandes, S. (1987). Sex roles and anthropological research in rural Andalusia. *Women's Studies, 13,* 357–372.

Bregman, A., Golin, S. (Producers), Gondry, M. (Director), & Kaufman, C. (Writer). (2004). *Eternal sunshine of the spotless mind* [Motion picture]. United States: Focus Features.

Brehm, S. S., Miller, R. S., Perlman, D., & Campbell, S. M. (2002). *Intimate relationships* (3rd ed.). Boston: McGraw-Hill.

Brend, R. (1975). Male-female intonation patterns in American English. In B. Thorne & N. Henley (Eds.), *Language and sex: Difference and dominance* (pp. 84–87). Rowley, MA: Newbury House.

Brewer, M. B. (1993). Social identity, distinctiveness, and in-group homogeneity. *Social Cognition, 11,* 150–164.

Brewer, M. B. (1999). The psychology of prejudice: Ingroup love or outgroup hate? *Journal of Social Issues, 55,* 429–444.

Brewer, M. B., & Campbell, D. T. (1976). *Ethnocentrism and intergroup attitudes: East African evidence.* Beverly Hills, CA: Sage.

Bridge, K., & Baxter, L. A. (1992). Blended relationships: Friends as work associates. *Western Journal of Communication, 56,* 200–225.

Brody, L. R., & Hall, J. A. (2000). Gender, emotion, and expression. In M. Lewis & J. M. Haviland (Eds.), *Handbook of emotions* (2nd ed., pp. 338–349). New York: Guilford Press.

Brontë, E. (1995). *Wuthering Heights.* Oxford: Oxford University Press. (Original work published 1848)

Brown, R. (1965). *Social psychology.* New York: Free Press.

Bruner, J., & Taguiri, R. (1954). The perception of people. In G. Lindzey (Ed.), *Handbook of social psychology* (Vol. 1, pp. 601–633). Cambridge, MA: Addison-Wesley.

Buber, M. (1965). *The knowledge of man: A philosophy of the interhuman.* New York: Harper & Row.

Bulfinch, T. (1985). *The golden age of myth and legend.* London: Bracken Books. (Original work published 1855)

Bunkers, S. S. (2010). The power and possibility in listening. *Nursing Science Quarterly, 23*(1), 22–27.

Burgoon, J. K., Buller, D. B., & Woodall, W. G. (1996). *Nonverbal communication: The unspoken dialogue* (2nd ed.). New York: McGraw-Hill.

Burgoon, J. K., & Dunbar, N. E. (2000). An interactionist perspective on dominance-submission: Interpersonal dominance as a dynamic, situationally contingent social skill. *Communication Monographs, 67,* 96–121.

Burgoon, J. K., & Hoobler, G. D. (2002). Nonverbal signals. In M. L. Knapp & J. A. Daly (Eds.), *Handbook of interpersonal communication* (3rd ed., pp. 240–299). Thousand Oaks, CA: Sage.

Burgoon, M. (1995). A kinder, gentler discipline: Feeling good about being mediocre. In B. R. Burleson (Ed.), *Communication yearbook 18* (pp. 464–479). Thousand Oaks, CA: Sage.

Buriel, R., & De Ment, T. (1997). Immigration and sociocultural change in Mexican, Chinese, and Vietnamese American families. In A. Booth, A. C. Crouter, & N. Landale (Eds.), *Immigration and the family: Research and policy on U.S. immigrants* (pp. 165–200). Mahwah, NJ: Erlbaum.

Burleson, B. R., & MacGeorge, E. L. (2002). Supportive communication. In M. L. Knapp & J. A. Daly (Eds.), *Handbook of interpersonal communication* (pp. 374–422). Thousand Oaks, CA: Sage.

Burleson, B. R., & Samter, W. (1994). A social skills approach to relationship maintenance: How individual differences in communication skills affect the achievement of relationship functions. In D. J. Canary & L. Stafford (Eds.), *Communication and relational maintenance* (pp. 61–90). New York: Academic Press.

Bushman, B. J., & Baumeister, R. F. (1998). Threatened egotism, narcissism, self-esteem, and direct and displaced aggression: Does self-love or self-hate lead to violence? *Journal of Personality and Social Psychology, 75,* 219–229.

Buss, D. M., Larsen, R. J., Westen, D., & Semmelroth, J. (1992). Sex differences in jealousy: Evolution, physiology, and psychology. *Psychological Science, 3,* 251–255.

Buss, D. M., Shackelford, T. K., Kirkpatrick, L. A., Choe, J. C., Lim, H. K., Hasegawa, M., et al. (1999). Jealousy and the nature of beliefs about infidelity: Tests of competing hypotheses about sex differences in the United States, Korea, and Japan. *Personal Relationships, 6,* 125–150.

Buunk, B. P., Angleitner, A., Oubaid, V., & Buss, D. M. (1996). Sex differences in jealousy in evolutionary and cultural perspective: Tests from the Netherlands, Germany, and the United States. *Psychological Science, 7,* 359–363.

Buzzanell, P. (1990, November). *Managing workplace romance.* Paper presented at the annual meeting of the Speech Communication Association, Chicago, IL.

Cacioppo, J. T., Klein, D. J., Berntson, G. G., & Hatfield, E. (1993). The psychophysiology of emotion. In M. Lewis & J. M. Haviland (Eds.), *Handbook of emotions* (pp. 119–142). New York: Guilford Press.

Campbell, R. G., & Babrow, A. S. (2004). The role of empathy in responses to persuasive risk communication: Overcoming resistance to HIV prevention messages. *Health Communication, 16,* 159–182.

Canary, D. J. (2003). Managing interpersonal conflict: A model of events related to strategic choices. In J. O. Greene & B. R. Burleson (Eds.), *Handbook of communication and social interaction skills.* Mahwah, NJ: Erlbaum.

Canary, D. J., Emmers-Sommer, T. M., & Faulkner, S. (1997). *Sex and gender differences in personal relationships.* New York: Guilford Press.

Canary, D. J., & Hause, K. S. (1993). Is there any reason to research sex differences in communication? *Communication Quarterly, 41,* 129–144.

Canary, D. J., & Zelley, E. (2000). Current research programs on relational maintenance behaviors. In M. E. Roloff (Ed.), *Communication yearbook 23* (pp. 305–339). Thousand Oaks, CA: Sage.

Carbery, J., & Buhrmester, D. (1998). Friendship and need fulfillment during three phases of young adulthood. *Journal of Social and Personal Relationships, 15,* 393–409.

Carducci, B. J., & Zimbardo, P. G. (1995, November/December). Are you shy? *Psychology Today, 28,* 34–41.

Carlson, J. G., & Hatfield, E. (1992). *Psychology of emotion.* Orlando, FL: Harcourt Brace.

Carney, D. R., Hall, J. A., & Smith LeBeau, L. S. (2005). Beliefs about the nonverbal expression of social power. *Journal of Nonverbal Behavior, 29,* 105–123.

Carr, N. (2010). *The shallows: What the Internet is doing to our brains.* New York: W. W. Norton & Co.

Castelli, L., Tomelleri, S., & Zogmaister, C. (2008). Implicit ingroup metafavoritism: Subtle preference for ingroup members displaying ingroup bias. *Personality and Social Psychology Bulletin, 34*(6), 807–818.

Caughlin, J. P. (2002). The demand/withdraw pattern of communication as a predictor of marital satisfaction over time: Unresolved issues and future directions. *Human Communication Research, 28,* 49–85.

Caughlin, J. P., & Huston, T. L. (2002). A contextual analysis of the association between demand/withdraw and marital satisfaction. *Personal Relationships, 9,* 95–119.

Caughlin, J. P., & Vangelisti, A. L. (2000). An individual difference explanation of why married couples engage in demand/

withdraw patterns of conflict. *Journal of Social and Personal Relationships, 17,* 523–551.

Centers for Disease Control and Prevention. (2008). *Youth risk behavior surveillance—United States, 2007.* Retrieved from http://www.cdc.gov/mmwr/preview/mmwrhtml/ss5704a1.htm

Cerpas, N. (2002). Variation in the display and experience of love between college Latino and non-Latino heterosexual romantic couples. *Ronald E. McNair Scholarship research report.* University of California, Berkeley.

Chaffee, S. H., & Berger, C. R. (1987). What communication scientists do. In C. R. Berger & S. H. Chaffee (Eds.), *Handbook of communication science* (pp. 99–122). Newbury Park, CA: Sage.

Chan, D. K., & Cheng, G. H. (2004). A comparison of offline and online friendship qualities at different stages of relationship development. *Journal of Social and Personal Relationships, 21*(3), 305–320.

Chaplin, T. M., Cole, P. M., & Zahn-Waxler, C. (2005). Parental socialization of emotion expression: Gender differences and relations to child adjustment. *Emotion, 5,* 80–88.

Chen, G.-M., & Chung, J. (1997). The "Five Asian Dragons": Management behaviors and organization communication. In L. A. Samovar & R. E. Porter (Eds.), *Intercultural communication: A reader* (pp. 317–328). Belmont, CA: Wadsworth.

Chen, G.-M., & Starosta, W. J. (2005). *Foundation of intercultural communication.* Boston: Allyn and Bacon.

Cherlin, A. (2004). The deinstitutionalization of American marriage. *Journal of Marriage and Family, 66,* 848–861.

Chesebro, J. L. (1999). The relationship between listening styles and conversational sensitivity. *Communication Research Reports, 16,* 233–238.

Choi, C. Q. (2011, January 18). Does science support the punitive parenting of "tiger mothering"? *Scientific American.* Retrieved from http://www.scientificamerican.com/article.cfm?id=tiger-mother-punitive-parenting

Christofides, E., Muise, A., & Desmarais, S. (2009). Information disclosure and control on Facebook: Are they two sides of the same coin or two different processes? *CyberPsychology & Behavior, 12*(3), 341–345.

Chua, A. (2011). *Battle hymn of the tiger mother.* New York: Penguin Press.

Chung, J. H., Des Roches, C. M., Meunier, J., & Eavey, R. D. (2005). Evaluation of noise-induced hearing loss in young people using a web-based survey technique. *Pediatrics, 115,* 861–867.

Clair, R. P. (1993). The use of framing devices to sequester organizational narratives: Hegemony and harassment. *Communication Monographs, 60,* 113–136.

Clair, R. P. (1998). *Organizing silence.* Albany: State University of New York Press.

Clark, R. A., & Delia, J. (1979). Topoi and rhetorical competence. *Quarterly Journal of Speech, 65,* 187–206.

Cleveland, J. N., Stockdale, M., & Murphy, K. R. (2000). *Women and men in organizations: Sex and gender issues at work.* Mahwah, NJ: Erlbaum.

Cochran, C. C., Frazier, P. A., & Olson, A. M. (1997). Predictors of responses to unwanted sexual attention. *Psychology of Women Quarterly, 21,* 207–226.

Cohen, T. F. (1992). Men's families, men's friends: A structural analysis of constraints on men's social ties. In P. M. Nardi (Ed.), *Men's friendships: Vol. 2. Research on men and masculinities* (pp. 115–131). Newbury Park, CA: Sage.

Cole, M., & Cole, S. R. (1989). *The development of children.* New York: Freeman.

Coleman, M., Ganong, L., & Fine, M. (2000). Reinvestigating remarriage: Another decade in progress. *Journal of Marriage and the Family, 62,* 1288–1307.

Collins, N. L., & Feeney, B. C. (2004). An attachment theory perspective on closeness and intimacy. In D. J. Mashek & A. Aron (Eds.), *Handbook of closeness and intimacy* (pp. 163–187). Mahwah, NJ: Erlbaum.

Collins, S. (2008). *The hunger games.* New York: Scholastic Inc.

Conlin, J. (2011, October 2). The freedom to choose your pronoun. *The New York Times.* Retrieved from http://www.nytimes.com

Contractor, N. S., & Grant, S. (1996). The emergence of shared interpretations in organizations: A self-organizing systems perspective. In J. H. Watt & C. A. VanLear (Eds.), *Dynamic patterns in communication processes* (pp. 215–230). Thousand Oaks, CA: Sage.

Cooley, C. H. (1902). *Human nature and the social order.* New York: Scribner.

Corner, L. (2007, June 3). Mrs. Infidelity: Lust in translation author Pamela Druckerman. *The Independent.* Retrieved from http://www.belfasttelegraph.co.uk/lifestyle/mrs-infidelity-lust-in-translation-author-pamela-druckerman-13448101.html

Costanzo, F. S., Markel, N. N., & Costanzo, R. R. (1969). Voice quality profile and perceived emotion. *Journal of Counseling Psychology, 16,* 267–270.

Coupland, N., Giles, H., & Wiemann, J. M. (Eds.). (1991). *Miscommunication and problematic talk.* Newbury Park, CA: Sage.

Covarrubias, P. (2000). Of endearment and other terms of address: A Mexican perspective. In M. W. Lustig & J. Koestner (Eds.), *Among us: Essays on identity, belonging, and intercultural competence* (pp. 9–17). New York: Longman.

Crider, D. M., Willits, F. K., & Kanagy, C. L. (1991). Rurality and well-being during the middle years of life. *Social Indicators, 24,* 253–268.

Crosnoe, R., & Cavanagh, S. E. (2010). Families with children and adolescents: A review, critique, and future agenda. *Journal of Marriage and Family, 72,* 594–611.

Cross, S. E., & Madson, L. (1997). Models of the self: Self-construals and gender. *Psychological Bulletin, 122,* 5–37.

Cullen, J. (2011, April 18). *Battle hymn of the tiger mother:* A remarkably bad book [Book review]. *The Cutting Edge News.* Retrieved from http://www.thecuttingedgenews.com/index.php?article=51839

Cunningham, M. (1988). Does happiness mean friendliness? Induced mood and heterosexual self-disclosure. *Personality and Social Psychology Bulletin, 14,* 283–297.

Cupach, W. R., & Spitzberg, B. H. (1998). Obsessive relational intrusion and stalking. In B. H. Spitzberg & W. R. Cupach (Eds.), *The dark side of close relationships* (pp. 233–263). Hillsdale, NJ: Erlbaum.

Cupach, W. R., & Spitzberg, B. H. (2004). *The dark side of relational pursuit: From attraction to obsession to stalking.* Mahwah, NJ: Erlbaum.

Custodio, J. (2002). The divine Ms. C.H.O.: Margaret Cho on her new stand-up movie, Lea Delaria, Joan Rivers, and the meaning of gay pride. *The Montreal Mirror.* Retrieved from www.montrealmirror.com/ARCHIVES/2002/080102/divers7.html

Dainton, M., & Aylor, B. (2002). Patterns of communication channel use in the maintenance of long-distance relationships. *Communication Research Reports, 19*, 118–129.

Dainton, M., & Stafford, L. (1993). Routine maintenance behaviors: A comparison of relationship type, partner similarity and sex differences. *Journal of Social and Personal Relationships, 10*, 255–271.

Dainton, M., Zelley, E., & Langan, E. (2003). Maintaining friendships throughout the lifespan. In D. J. Canary & M. Dainton (Eds.), *Maintaining relationships through communication: Relational, contextual, and cultural variations* (pp. 79–102). Mahwah, NJ: Erlbaum.

Daly, J. (1975). *Listening and interpersonal evaluations.* Paper presented at the annual meeting of the Central States Speech Association, Kansas City, MO.

Daly, J. A., McCroskey, J. C., Ayres, J., Hopf, T., & Ayres, D. M. (Eds.). (2004). *Avoiding communication: Shyness, reticence, and communication apprehension* (3rd ed.). Cresskill, NJ: Hampton Press.

Daniels, D. (1986). Differential experiences of siblings in the same family as predictors of adolescent sibling personality differences. *Journal of Personality and Social Psychology, 51*(2), 339–346.

Dash, J. (2001). *The world at her fingertips: The story of Helen Keller.* New York: Scholastic Press.

Davey, M. (2004, December 6). 8 soldiers sue over Army's stop-loss policy. *The New York Times.* Retrieved from http://www.nytimes.com

Davis, K. E., & Todd, M. L. (1985). Assessing friendship: Prototypes, paradigm cases, and relationship description. In S. Duck & D. Perlman (Eds.), *Understanding personal relationships: An interdisciplinary approach* (pp. 17–38). London: Sage.

Deaf President Now. (n.d.). In *Wikipedia.* Retrieved from http://en.wikipedia.org/wiki/Deaf_President_Now

Deaf President Now Protest. (n.d.). Retrieved from http://www.gallaudet.edu/gallaudet_university/about_gallaudet/dpn_home.html

Dean, J. (2011). Smartphone user survey: A glimpse into the mobile lives of college students. *Digital New Test Kitchen.* Retrieved from http://testkitchen.colorado.edu/projects/reports/smartphone/smartphone-survey

DeAngelo, D. (2011). Reading body language and more. Retrieved from http://www.askmen.com/dating/dating_advice_150/197_dating_tips.html

Deardorff, D. K. (Ed.). (2009). *The Sage handbook of intercultural competence.* Thousand Oaks, CA: Sage.

Delgado-Gaitan, C. (1993). Parenting in two generations of Mexican American families. *International Journal of Behavioral Development, 16*, 409–427.

Delia, J. G. (1972). Dialects and the effects of stereotypes on interpersonal attraction and cognitive processes in impression formation. *Quarterly Journal of Speech, 58*, 285–297.

Devine, P. G. (1989). Stereotypes and prejudice: Their automatic and controlled components. *Journal of Personality and Social Psychology, 56*, 5–18.

de Vries, B. (1996). The understanding of friendship: An adult life course perspective. In C. Magai & S. McFadden (Eds.), *Handbook of emotion, aging, and the life course* (pp. 249–268). New York: Academic Press.

Dillard, J. (1987). Close relationships at work: Perceptions of the motives and performance of relational participants. *Journal of Social and Personal Relationships, 4*, 179–193.

Dindia, K., & Allen, M. (1992). Sex differences in self-disclosure: A meta-analysis. *Psychological Bulletin, 112*, 106–124.

Domingue, R., & Mollen, D. (2009). Attachment and conflict communication in adult romantic relationships. *Journal of Social and Personal Relationships, 26*, 678–696.

Donohue, W. A., & Kolt, R. (1992). *Managing interpersonal conflict.* Newbury Park, CA: Sage.

Dreyer, A. S., Dreyer, C. A., & Davis, J. E. (1987). Individuality and mutuality in the language of families of field-dependent and field-independent children. *Journal of Genetic Psychology, 148*, 105–117.

Druckerman, P. (2007). *Lust in translation.* New York: Penguin Press.

Duan, C., & Hill, C. E. (1996). The current state of empathy research. *Journal of Counseling Psychology, 43*, 261–274.

Dunbar, N. E. (2004). Dyadic power theory: Constructing a communication-based theory of relational power. *Journal of Family Communication, 4*(3/4), 235–248.

Duncan, S., Jr., & Fiske, D. W. (1977). *Face-to-face interaction: Research, methods, and theory.* New York: Wiley.

Dutton, L. B., & Winstead, B. A. (2006). Predicting unwanted pursuit: Attachment, relationship satisfaction, relationship alternatives, and break-up distress. *Journal of Social and Personal Relationships, 23*(4), 565–586.

Eagly, A. H., Ashmore, R. D., Makhijani, M. G., & Longo, L. C. (1991). What is beautiful is good, but . . . : A meta-analytic review of research on the physical attractiveness stereotype. *Psychological Bulletin, 110*, 109–128.

Ebbeson, E., Duncan, B., & Konecni, V. (1975). Effects of content of verbal aggression on future verbal aggression: A field experiment. *Journal of Experimental Social Psychology, 11*, 192–204.

Eisenberg, E. M., & Goodall, H. L., Jr. (2004). *Organizational communication: Balancing creativity and constraint* (4th ed.). Boston: Bedford/St. Martin's.

Eisikovits, Z., & Buchbinder, E. (2000). *Locked in a violent embrace.* Thousand Oaks, CA: Sage.

Ekman, P. (1972). Universals and cultural differences in facial expressions of emotion. In J. R. Cole (Ed.), *Nebraska Symposium on Motivation, Vol. 19* (pp. 207–283). Lincoln: University of Nebraska Press.

Ekman, P. (1976). Movements with precise meanings. *Journal of Communication, 26*, 14–26.

Ekman, P., & Friesen, W. V. (1969). The repertoire of nonverbal behavior: Categories, origins, usage, and coding. *Semiotica, 1*, 49–98.

Elci, M., & Alpkan, L. (2009). The impact of perceived organizational ethical climate on work satisfaction. *Journal of Business Ethics, 84*, 297–311.

Ellis, A., & Dryden, W. (1997). *The practice of rational emotive behavior therapy.* New York: Springer.

Ellison, N. B., Steinfield, C., & Lampe, C. (2007). The benefits of Facebook "friends:" Social capital and college students' use of online social network sites. *Journal of Computer-Mediated Communication, 12*(4), article 1. Retrieved from http://jcmc.indiana.edu/vol12/issue4/ellison.html

Ellison, N., Heino, R., & Gibbs, J. (2006). Managing impressions online: Self-presentation processes in the online dating environment. *Journal of Computer-Mediated Communication, 11*(2), article 2. Retrieved from http://jcmc.indiana.edu/vol11/issue2/ellison.html

Englehardt, E. E. (2001). Introduction to ethics in interpersonal communication. In E. E. Englehardt (Ed.), *Ethical issues in interpersonal communication: Friends, intimates, sexuality, marriage, and family* (pp. 1–27). Orlando, FL: Harcourt College.

Environmental Protection Agency. (2002, September). Cross-cultural communication. Retrieved from http://www.epa.gov/superfund/community/pdfs/12ccc.pdf

Escartín, J., Rodríguez-Carballeira, A., Zapf, D., Porrúa, C., & Martín-Peña, J. (2009). Perceived severity of various bullying behaviours at work and the relevance of exposure to bullying. *Work & Stress, 23*(3), 191–205.

Farace, R. V., Monge, P. R., & Russell, H. M. (1977). *Communicating and organizing.* Reading, MA: Addison-Wesley.

Feingold, A. (1988). Matching for attractiveness in romantic partners and same-sex friends: A meta-analysis and theoretical critique. *Psychological Bulletin, 104,* 226–235.

Felmlee, D. H. (2001). No couple is an island: A social network perspective on dyadic stability. *Social Forces, 79,* 1259–1287.

Felmlee, D., Orzechowicz, D., & Fortes, C. (2010). Fairy tales: Attraction and stereotypes in same-gender relationships. *Sex Roles, 62,* 226–240.

Fenigstein, A., Scheier, M. F., & Buss, A. H. (1975). Public and private self-consciousness: Assessment and theory. *Journal of Consulting and Clinical Psychology, 43,* 522–527.

Fiedler, K., Pampe, H., & Scherf, U. (1986). Mood and memory for tightly organized social information. *European Journal of Social Psychology, 16,* 149–165.

Field, A. (2005). Block that defense! Make sure your constructive criticism works. *Harvard Management Communication Letter, 2*(4), 3–5.

Field, A. E., Cheung, L., Wolf, A. M., Herzog, D. B., Gortmaker, S. L., & Colditz, G. A. (1999). Exposure to the mass media and weight concerns among girls. *Pediatrics, 103,* 36.

Fischer, A. H., Rodriguez Mosquera, P. M., van Vianen, A. E. M., & Manstead, A. S. R. (2004). Gender and culture differences in emotion. *Emotion, 4,* 87–94.

Fisher, B. A. (1983). Differential effects of sexual composition and interactional context on interaction patterns in dyads. *Human Communication Research, 9,* 225–238.

Fishman, P. M. (1983). Interaction: The work women do. In B. Thorne, C. Kramarae, & N. Henley (Eds.), *Language, gender, and society* (pp. 89–101). Cambridge, MA: Newbury House.

Fiske, S. T., & Taylor, S. E. (1991). *Social cognition* (2nd ed.). New York: McGraw-Hill.

Fitzgerald, L. F. (1993). Sexual harassment: A research analysis and agenda for the 1990s. *Journal of Vocational Behavior, 42,* 5–27.

Fleischer, R. (Director), Reese, R., & Wernick, P. (Writers). (2009). *Zombieland* [Motion picture]. United States: Sony Pictures.

Floyd, K. (1999). All touches are not created equal: Effects of form and duration on observers' interpretations of an embrace. *Journal of Nonverbal Behavior, 23,* 283–299.

Floyd, K., & Burgoon, J. K. (1999). Reacting to nonverbal expressions of liking: A test of interaction adaptation theory. *Communication Monographs, 66,* 219–239.

Floyd, K., & Morman, M. T. (1999). The measurement of affectionate communication. *Communication Quarterly, 46,* 144–162.

Floyd, K., & Morman, M. T. (2005). Fathers' and sons' reports of fathers' affectionate communication: Implications of a naïve theory of affection. *Journal of Social and Personal Relationships, 22*(1), 99–109.

Forgas, J. P., & Bower, G. H. (1987). Mood effects on person perception judgments. *Journal of Personality and Social Psychology, 53,* 53–60.

Forni, P. M. (2002). *Choosing civility: The twenty-five rules of considerate conduct.* New York: St. Martin's Griffin.

Foss, S. K., Foss, K. A., & Trapp, R. (1991). *Contemporary perspectives in rhetoric* (2nd ed.). Prospect Heights, IL: Waveland Press.

Fox, K. R. (1992). Physical education and development of self-esteem in children. In N. Armstrong (Ed.), *New directions in physical education: II. Towards a national curriculum* (pp. 33–54). Champaign, IL: Human Kinetics.

Fox, K. R. (1997). The physical self and processes in self-esteem development. In K. Fox (Ed.), *The physical self* (pp. 111–139). Champaign, IL: Human Kinetics.

Frederikse, M. E., Lu, A., Aylward, E., Barta, P., & Pearlson, G. (1999). Sex differences in the inferior parietal lobule. *Cerebral Cortex, 9,* 896–901.

Freides, D. (1974). Human information processing and sensory modality: Cross-modal functions, information complexity, memory, and deficit. *Psychological Bulletin, 81,* 284–310.

Frijda, N. H. (2005). Emotion experience. *Cognition and Emotion, 19,* 473–497.

Frisby, B. N., & Westerman, D. (2010). Rational actors: Channel selection and rational choices in romantic conflict episodes. *Journal of Social and Personal Relationships, 27,* 970–981.

Fritz, J. H., & Dillard, J. P. (1994, November). *The importance of peer relationships in organizational socialization.* Paper presented at the annual meeting of the Speech Communication Association, New Orleans, LA.

Fuendeling, J. M. (1998). Affect regulation as a stylistic process within adult attachment. *Journal of Social and Personal Relationships, 15,* 291–322.

Furger, R. (1996). I'm okay, you're online. *PC World, 14,* 310–312.

Furman, W., & Simon, V. A. (1998). Advice from youth: Some lessons from the study of adolescent relationships. *Journal of Social and Personal Relationships, 15,* 723–739.

Furr, R. M., & Funder, D. C. (1998). A multimodal analysis of personal negativity. *Journal of Personality and Social Psychology, 74,* 1580–1591.

Gaines, S. O., Jr., & Agnew, C. R. (2003). Relationship maintenance in intercultural couples: An interdependence analysis. In D. J. Canary & M. Dainton (Eds.), *Maintaining relationships through communication: Relational, contextual, and cultural variations* (pp. 231–253). Mahwah, NJ: Erlbaum.

Gaines, S. O., Jr., Chalfin, J., Kim, M., & Taing, P. (1998). Communicating prejudice in personal relationships. In M. L. Hecht (Ed.), *Communicating prejudice* (pp. 163–186). Thousand Oaks, CA: Sage.

Gaitonde, R. (2011). When it comes to telecommuting, companies save, but the U.S. lags. Retrieved from http://broadbandbreakfast.com/2011/06/when-it-comes-to-telecommuting-companies-save-but-the-u-s-lags/

Galupo, M. P. (2007). Friendship patterns of sexual minority individuals in adulthood. *Journal of Social and Personal Relationships, 24,* 139–151.

Galupo, M. P. (2009). Cross-category friendship patterns: Comparison of heterosexual and sexual minority adults. *Journal of Social and Personal Relationships, 26*(6–7), 811–831.

Galvin, K. M., Brommel, B. J., & Bylund, C. L. (2004). *Family communication: Cohesion and change* (6th ed.). New York: Pearson.

Ganong, L. H., & Coleman, M. (1994). *Remarried family relationships.* Thousand Oaks, CA: Sage.

Ganong, L., Coleman, M., Fine, M., & Martin, P. (1999). Step-parents' affinity-seeking and affinity-maintaining strategies with stepchildren. *Journal of Family Issues, 20,* 299–327.

Garcia, P., & Geisler, J. (1988). Sex and age/grade differences in adolescents' self-disclosure. *Perceptual and Motor Skills, 67,* 427–432.

Garrett, R. K., & Danziger, J. (2008). *Gratification and disaffection: Understanding personal Internet use during work.* Paper presented at the annual meeting of the International Communication Association, Montreal, Canada.

Gerdes, L. I. (1999). *Sexual harassment: Current controversies.* San Diego, CA: Greenhaven.

Gettings, J. (2005). Civil disobedience: Black medalists raise fists for civil rights movement. Retrieved from www.infoplease.com/spot/mm-mexicocity.html

Giannakakis, A. E., & Fritsche, I. (2011). Social identities, group norms, and threat: On the malleability of ingroup bias. *Personality and Social Psychology Bulletin, 37*(1), 82–93.

Gibbs, J. L., Ellison, N. B., & Heino, R. D. (2006). Self-presentation in online personals: The role of anticipated future interaction, self-disclosure, and perceived success in Internet dating. *Communication Research, 33,* 1–26.

Gibson, B., & Sachau, D. (2000). Sandbagging as a self-presentational style: Claiming to be less than you are. *Personality and Social Psychology Bulletin, 26,* 56–70.

Gifford, R., Ng, C. F., & Wilkinson, M. (1985). Nonverbal cues in the employment interview: Links between applicant qualities and interviewer judgments. *Journal of Applied Psychology, 70,* 729–736.

Giles, H., Coupland, N., & Coupland, J. (Eds.). (1991). *Contexts of accommodation: Developments in applied linguistics.* Cambridge, UK: Cambridge University Press.

Giles, H., & Street, R. L. (1994). Communicator characteristics and behavior. In M. L. Knapp & G. R. Miller (Eds.), *Handbook of interpersonal communication* (2nd ed., pp. 103–161). Beverly Hills, CA: Sage.

Gleason, L. B. (1989). *The development of language.* Columbus, OH: Merrill.

Glenn, D. (2010, February 28). Divided attention: In an age of classroom multitasking, scholars probe the nature of learning and memory. *The Chronicle of Higher Education.* Retrieved from http://chronicle.com/article/Scholars-Turn-Their-Attention/63746/

Glisson, C., & James, L. R. (2002). The cross-level effects of culture and climate in human service teams. *Journal of Organizational Behavior, 23,* 767–794.

Goffman, E. (1955). On facework: An analysis of ritual elements in social interaction. *Psychiatry, 18,* 319–345.

Goffman, E. (1959). *The presentation of self in everyday life.* Garden City, NY: Doubleday Anchor Books.

Goffman, E. (1979). Footing. *Semiotica, 25,* 124–147.

Goldstein, T. (2001). I'm not white: Anti-racist teacher education for white early childhood educators. *Contemporary Issues in Early Childhood, 2,* 3–13.

Goleman, D. (2006). *Social intelligence: The new science of human relationships.* New York: Bantam Dell.

Goleman, D. (2007a, February 20). Flame first, think later: New clues to e-mail misbehavior. *The New York Times.* Retrieved from http://www.nytimes.com

Goleman, D. (2007b, August 24). Free won't: The marshmallow test revisited [Blog post]. Retrieved from http://danielgoleman.info/2007/free-wont-the-marshmallow-test-revisited/

Golish, T. D. (2000). Changes in closeness between adult children and their parents: A turning point analysis. *Communication Reports, 13,* 79–97.

Golish, T. D. (2003). Stepfamily communication strengths: Understanding the ties that bind. *Human Communication Research, 29*(1), 41–80.

Goodsell, T. L., Bates, J. S., & Behnke, A. O. (2010). Fatherhood stories: Grandparents, grandchildren, and gender differences. *Journal of Social and Personal Relationships, 28*(1), 134–154.

Goodwin, C. (1981). *Conversational organization: Interaction between speakers and hearers.* New York: Academic Press.

Gosling, S. D., Gaddis, S., & Vazire, S. (2007, March). *Personality impressions based on Facebook profiles.* Paper presented at the International Conference on Weblogs and Social Media (ICWSM), Boulder, CO.

Gottman, J. M., & Levenson, R. W. (2000). The timing of divorce: Predicting when a couple will divorce over a 14-year period. *Journal of Marriage and Family, 62,* 737–745.

Grammer, K., & Thornhill, R. (1994). Human facial attractiveness and sexual selection: The role of averageness and symmetry. *Journal of Comparative Psychology, 108,* 233–242.

Grice, H. P. (1989). *Studies in the way of words.* Cambridge, MA: Harvard University Press.

Gross, J. J., & John, O. P. (2002). Wise emotion regulation. In L. Feldman Barrett & P. Salovey (Eds.), *The wisdom in feeling: Psychological processes in emotional intelligence* (pp. 297–319). New York: Guilford Press.

Gross, J. J., Richards, J. M., & John, O. P. (2006). Emotion regulation in everyday life. In D. K. Snyder, J. A. Simpson, & J. N. Hughes (Eds.), *Emotion regulation in couples and families: Pathways to dysfunction and health.* Washington, DC: American Psychological Association.

Gudykunst, W. B., & Kim, Y. Y. (2003). *Communicating with strangers: An approach to intercultural communication* (4th ed.). New York: McGraw-Hill.

Gudykunst, W. B., & Nishida, T. (1993). Closeness in interpersonal relationships in Japan and the United States. *Research in Social Psychology, 8,* 85–97.

Guerin, B. (1999). Children's intergroup attribution bias for liked and disliked peers. *Journal of Social Psychology, 139,* 583–589.

Guerrero, L. K., & Andersen, P. A. (1998). Jealousy experience and expression in romantic relationships. In P. A. Andersen & L. K. Guerrero (Eds.), *Handbook of communication and emotion* (pp. 155–188). San Diego, CA: Academic Press.

Gumperz, J. J., & Levinson, S. C. (Eds.). (1996). *Rethinking linguistic relativity.* New York: Cambridge University Press.

Haas, S. M., & Stafford, L. (1998). An initial examination of maintenance behaviors in gay and lesbian relationships. *Journal of Social and Personal Relationships, 15,* 846–855.

Haas, S. M., & Stafford, L. (2005). Maintenance behaviors in same-sex and marital relationships: A matched sample comparison. *Journal of Family Communication, 5,* 43–60.

Haden, S. C., & Hojjat, M. (2006). Aggressive responses to betrayal: Type of relationship, victim's sex, and nature of aggression. *Journal of Social and Personal Relationships, 23*(1), 101–116.

Halatsis, P., & Christakis, N. (2009). The challenge of sexual attraction within heterosexuals' cross-sex friendship. *Journal of Social and Personal Relationships, 26*(6–7), 919–937.

Hall, E. T. (1966). A system of the notation of proxemics behavior. *American Anthropologist, 65,* 1003–1026.

Hall, E. T. (1976). *Beyond culture.* Garden City, NY: Anchor.

Hall, E. T. (1981). *The silent language*. New York: Anchor/Doubleday.

Hall, E. T. (1983). *The dance of life: The other dimension of time*. New York: Doubleday.

Hall, E. T. (1997a). Context and meaning. In L. A. Samovar & R. E. Porter (Eds.), *Intercultural communication: A reader* (pp. 45–53). Belmont, CA: Wadsworth.

Hall, E. T. (1997b). Monochronic and polychronic time. In L. A. Samovar & R. E. Porter (Eds.), *Intercultural communication: A reader* (8th ed., pp. 277–284). Belmont, CA: Wadsworth.

Hall, E. T., & Hall, M. R. (1987). *Understanding cultural differences*. Yarmouth, ME: Intercultural Press.

Hall, J. A., Carter, J. D., & Horgan, T. G. (2000). Gender differences in nonverbal communication of emotion. In A. H. Fischer (Ed.), *Gender and emotion: Social psychological perspectives* (pp. 97–117). Cambridge, UK: Cambridge University Press.

Hall, J. A., Park, N., Song, H., & Cody, M. J. (2010). Strategic misrepresentation in online dating: The effects of gender, self-monitoring, and personality traits. *Journal of Social and Personal Relationships, 27*(1), 117–135.

Hammer, M. R., Bennett, M. J., & Wiseman, R. (2003). Measuring intercultural sensitivity: The intercultural development inventory. *International Journal of Intercultural Relations, 27*, 421–443.

Hansen, G. L. (1985). Dating jealousy among college students. *Sex Roles, 12*, 713–721.

Harms, L. S. (1961). Listener judgments of status cues in speech. *Quarterly Journal of Speech, 47*, 164–168.

Harrison, K. (2001). Ourselves, our bodies: Thin-ideal media, self-discrepancies, and eating disorder symptoms in adolescents. *Journal of Social and Clinical Psychology, 20*, 289–323.

Hastorf, A. H., & Cantril, H. (1954). They saw a game: A case study. *Journal of Abnormal and Social Psychology, 49*, 129–134.

Hatfield, E. (1983). Equity theory and research: An overview. In H. H. Blumberg, A. P. Hare, V. Kent, & M. Davies (Eds.), *Small groups and social interaction* (Vol. 2, pp. 401–412). Chichester, UK: Wiley.

Hatfield, E., & Rapson, R. L. (1987). Passionate love: New directions in research. In W. H. Jones & D. Perlman (Eds.), *Advances in personal relationships* (Vol. 1, pp. 109–139). London: Jessica Kingsley.

Hatfield, E. E., & Sprecher, S. (1986). *Mirror, mirror . . . the importance of looks in everyday life*. Albany: State University of New York Press.

Hatfield, E., Traupmann, J., & Sprecher, S. (1984). Older women's perceptions of their intimate relationships. *Journal of Social and Clinical Psychology, 2*, 108–124.

Hatfield, E., Traupmann, J., Sprecher, S., Utne, M., & Hay, M. (1985). Equity in close relationships. In W. Ickes (Ed.), *Compatible and incompatible relationships* (pp. 91–171). New York: Springer-Verlag.

Hauser, T. (2006). *Muhammad Ali: His life and times*. New York: Simon & Schuster.

Hausmann, R., Tyson, L. D., & Zahidi, S. (2010). *The global gender gap: Report 2010*. World Economic Forum Report, Geneva, Switzerland.

Hayashi, G. M., & Strickland, B. R. (1998). Long-term effects of parental divorce on love relationships: Divorce as attachment disruption. *Journal of Social and Personal Relationships, 15*, 23–38.

Hays, R. B. (1988). Friendship. In S. Duck (Ed.), *Handbook of personal relationships: Theory, research, and interventions* (pp. 391–408). Chichester, UK: Wiley.

Heider, F. (1958). *The psychology of interpersonal relations*. New York: Wiley.

Heino, R. D., Ellison, N. B., & Gibbs, J. L. (2010). Relationshopping: Investigating the market metaphor in online dating. *Journal of Social and Personal Relationships, 27*(4), 427–447.

Hendrick, C., & Hendrick, S. S. (1988). Lovers wear rose colored glasses. *Journal of Social and Personal Relationships, 5*, 161–183.

Hendrick, S. S., & Hendrick, C. (1992). *Romantic love*. Thousand Oaks, CA: Sage.

Hendrick, S. S., & Hendrick, C. (2006). Measuring respect in close relationships. *Journal of Social and Personal Relationships, 23*, 881–899.

Heritage, J. C., & Watson, D. R. (1979). Formulations as conversational objectives. In G. Pathas (Ed.), *Everyday language: Studies in ethnomethodology*. New York: Irvington.

Hertwig, R., Davis, J. N., & Sulloway, F. J. (2002). Parental investment: How an equity motive can produce inequality. *Psychological Bulletin, 128*, 728–745.

Herweddingplanner.com (2011, April 29). *Randy Fenoli 'Say Yes to the Dress' wedding gown tips with Chantal Patton of www .herweddingplanner.com*. Retrieved from http://www.youtube .com/watch?v=9T-R3LeFjLU

Heslin, R. (1974, May). *Steps toward a taxonomy of touching*. Paper presented at the annual meeting of the Midwestern Psychological Association, Chicago.

Hetherington, E. M. (1993). An overview of the Virginia longitudinal study of divorce and remarriage with a focus on early adolescence. *Journal of Family Psychology, 7*, 39–56.

Hickson, M., III, Grierson, R. D., & Linder, B. C. (1991). A communication perspective on sexual harassment: Affiliative nonverbal behaviors in asynchronous relationships. *Communication Quarterly, 39*, 111–118.

Higgins, E. T. (1987). Self-discrepancy: A theory relating self and affect. *Psychological Review, 94*, 319–340.

Hill, C. T., Rubin, Z., & Peplau, L. A. (1976). Breakups before marriage: The end of 103 affairs. *Journal of Social Issues, 32*, 147–168.

Hodgins, H. S., & Belch, C. (2000). Interparental violence and nonverbal abilities. *Journal of Nonverbal Behavior, 24*, 3–24.

Hodgson, L. K., & Wertheim, E. H. (2007). Does good emotion management aid forgiving? Multiple dimensions of empathy, emotion management and forgiveness of self and others. *Journal of Social and Personal Relationships, 24*(6), 931–949.

Hofstede, G. (1991). *Cultures and organizations*. London: McGraw-Hill.

Hofstede, G. (1998). I, we, they. In J. N. Martin, T. K. Nakayama, & L. A. Flores (Eds.), *Readings in cultural contexts* (pp. 345–357). Mountain View, CA: Mayfield.

Hofstede, G. (2001). *Culture's consequences* (2nd ed.). Thousand Oaks, CA: Sage.

Hofstede, G. (2009). National cultural dimensions. Retrieved from http://www.geert-hofstede.com/national-culture.html

Honeycutt, J. M. (1999). Typological differences in predicting marital happiness from oral history behaviors and imagined interactions. *Communication Monographs, 66*, 276–291.

Horne, C. F. (1917). *The sacred books and early literature of the East: Vol. II. Egypt*. New York: Parke, Austin, & Lipscomb.

Hovick, S. R. A., Meyers, R. A., & Timmerman, C. E. (2003). E-mail communication in workplace romantic relationships. *Communication Studies, 54*, 468–480.

Howard, P. E. N., Rainie, L., & Jones, S. (2001, November). Days and nights on the Internet: The impact of a diffusing technology. *American Behavioral Scientist, 45*, 383–405.

HRSDC (Human Resources and Skills Development Canada). (2006). Canadians in context—households and families. Retrieved from http://www4.hrsdc.gc.ca/.3ndic.1t.4r@-eng .jsp?iid=37

Hughes, M., Morrison, K., & Asada, K. J. K. (2005). What's love got to do with it? Exploring the impact of maintenance rules, love attitudes, and network support on friends with benefits relationships. *Western Journal of Speech Communication, 69*, 49–66.

Hurley, D. (2005, April 19). Divorce rate: It's not as high as you think. *The New York Times*, p. F7.

Hyde, J. S. (2005). The gender similarities hypothesis. *American Psychologist, 60*, 581–592.

Hyun, J. (2005). *Breaking the bamboo ceiling: Career strategies for Asians*. New York: HarperCollins.

Infante, D. A. (1995). Teaching students to understand and control verbal aggression. *Communication Education, 44*, 51–63.

Infante, D. A., Chandler, T. A., & Rudd, J. E. (1989). Test of an argumentative skill deficiency model of interspousal violence. *Communication Monographs, 56*, 163–177.

Infante, D. A., Myers, S. A., & Burkel, R. A. (1994). Argument and verbal aggression in constructive and destructive family and organizational disagreements. *Western Journal of Communication, 58*, 73–84.

Infante, D. A., & Wigley, C. J. (1986). Verbal aggressiveness: An interpersonal model and measure. *Communication Monographs, 53*, 61–69.

Jackson, D. C., Malmstadt, J. R., Larson, C. L., & Davidson, R. J. (2000). Suppression and enhancement of emotional responses to unpleasant pictures. *Psychophysiology, 37*, 515–522.

Jackson, M. (2008). *Distracted: The erosion of attention and the coming dark age*. Amherst, NY: Prometheus Books.

Jacobs, S. (1994). Language and interpersonal communication. In M. L. Knapp & G. R. Miller (Eds.), *Handbook of interpersonal communication* (2nd ed., pp. 199–228). Thousand Oaks, CA: Sage.

Jacobs, S., Dawson, E. J., & Brashers, D. (1996). Information manipulation theory: A replication and assessment. *Communication Monographs, 63*, 70–82.

Janusik, L. A. (2007). Building listening theory: The validation of the conversational listening span. *Communication Studies, 58*(2), 139–156.

John, O. P. (1990). The "Big Five" factor taxonomy: Dimensions of personality in the natural language and in questionnaires. In L. A. Pervin (Ed.), *Handbook of personality: Theory and research* (pp. 66–100). New York: Guilford Press.

John, O. P., Donahue, E. M., & Kentle, R. L. (1991). *The Big Five Inventory: Versions 4a and 54*. Berkeley, CA: University of California, Berkeley, Institute of Personality and Social Research.

John, O. P., & Gross, J. J. (2004). Healthy and unhealthy emotion regulation: Personality processes, individual differences, and lifespan development. *Journal of Personality, 72*, 1301–1334.

Johnson, A. J., Haigh, M. M., Becker, J. A. H., Craig, E. A., & Wigley, S. (2008). College students' use of relational management strategies in email in long-distance and geographically close relationships. *Journal of Computer-Mediated Communication, 13*, 381–404.

Johnson, A. J., Wittenberg, E., Villagran, M. M., Mazur, M., & Villagran, P. (2003). Relational progression as a dialectic: Examining turning points in communication among friends. *Communication Monographs, 70*(3), 230–249.

Johnson, H. (2004, April 1). Jimmy Jam: Three decades of hits; one seamless partnership. Retrieved from http://mixonline.com /mag/audio_jimmy_jam

Joinson, A. N. (2001, March/April). Self-disclosure in computer-mediated communication: The role of self-awareness and visual anonymity. *European Journal of Social Psychology, 31*, 177–192.

Jones, D. C., Vigfusdottir, T. H., & Lee, Y. (2004). Body image and the appearance culture among adolescent girls and boys: An examination of friends' conversations, peer criticism, appearance magazines, and the internalization of appearance ideals. *Journal of Adolescent Research, 19*, 323–339.

Jones, S. E., & LeBaron, C. D. (2002). Research on the relationship between verbal and nonverbal communication: Emerging integrations. *Journal of Communication, 52*, 499–521.

Jones, T. E. (1999). *If it's broken, you can fix it: Overcoming dysfunction in the workplace*. New York: AMACOM Books.

Jones, W. H., & Burdette, M. P. (1994). Betrayal in relationships. In A. L. Weber & J. H. Harvey (Eds.), *Perspectives on close relationships* (pp. 243–262). Boston: Allyn and Bacon.

Jones, W., Moore, D., Scratter, A., & Negel, L. (2001). Interpersonal transgression and betrayals. In R. M. Kowalski (Ed.), *Behaving badly: Aversive behavior in interpersonal relationships* (pp. 233–256). Washington, DC: American Psychological Association.

Jourard, S. M. (1964). *The transparent self*. New York: Van Nostrand Reinhold.

Kagawa, N., & McCornack, S. A. (2004, November). *Collectivistic Americans and individualistic Japanese: A cross-cultural comparison of parental understanding*. Paper presented at the annual meeting of the National Communication Association, Chicago.

Kaharit, K., Zachau, G., Eklof, M., Sandsjo, L., & Moller, C. (2003). Assessment of hearing and hearing disorders in rock/ jazz musicians. *International Journal of Audiology, 42*, 279–288.

Kahneman, D. (1973). *Attention and effort*. Englewood Cliffs, NJ: Prentice Hall.

Kassing, J. W. (2008). Consider this: A comparison of factors contributing to employees' expressions of dissent. *Communication Quarterly, 56*(3), 342–355.

Katz, D., & Kahn, R. (1978). *The social psychology of organizations* (2nd ed.). New York: Wiley.

Katz, J. (1983). A theory of qualitative methodology. In R. M. Emerson (Ed.), *Contemporary field research: A collection of readings* (pp. 127–148). Prospect Heights, IL: Waveland Press.

Katz, J., & Farrow, S. (2000). Discrepant self-views and young women's sexual and emotional adjustment. *Sex Roles, 42*, 781–805.

Keashly, L., & Neuman, J. H. (2005). Bullying in the workplace: Its impact and management. *Employee Rights and Employment Policy Journal, 8*, 335–373.

Keashly, L., Trott, V., & MacLean, L. M. (1994). Abusive behavior in the workplace: A preliminary investigation. *Violence and Victims, 9*, 341–357.

Keck, K. L., & Samp, J. A. (2007). The dynamic nature of goals and message production as revealed in a sequential analysis of conflict interactions. *Human Communication Research, 33*, 27–47.

Keesing, R. M. (1974). Theories of culture. *Annual Review of Anthropology, 3*, 73–97.

Kellas, J. K. (2005). Family ties: Communicating identity through jointly told family stories. *Communication Monographs, 72*(4), 365–389.

Kellermann, K. (1989). The negativity effect in interaction: It's all in your point of view. *Human Communication Research, 16*, 147–183.

Kellermann, K. (1991). The conversation MOP: Progression through scenes in discourse. *Human Communication Research, 17*, 385–414.

Kelley, H. H., & Thibaut, J. W. (1978). *Interpersonal relations: A theory of interdependence.* New York: Wiley.

Kelly, A. E., & McKillop, K. J. (1996). Consequences of revealing personal secrets. *Psychological Bulletin, 120*, 450–465.

Kennedy, D. (2008). *Rock on.* Chapel Hill, NC: Algonquin Books.

Kennedy, T. L. M., Smith, A., Wells, A. T., & Wellman, B. (2008, October 19). Networked families: Parents and spouses are using the Internet and cell phones to create a "new connectedness" that builds on remote connections and shared Internet experiences. *Pew Internet & American Life Project.* Retrieved from http://www.pewinternet.org/

Kimpel, D. (2010). ASCAP Rhythm and Soul Heritage Award Jimmy Jam & Terry Lewis. Retrieved from http://www.ascap.com/eventsawards/awards/rsawards/2005/heritage.aspx

King, S. K. (2001). Territoriality. Retrieved from http://www.huna.org/html/territor.html

Klein, R. C. A. (1998). Conflict and violence in the family: Cross-disciplinary issues. In R. C. A. Klein (Ed.), *Multidisciplinary perspectives on family violence* (pp. 1–13). New York: Routledge.

Klopf, D. W. (2001*). Intercultural encounters: The fundamentals of intercultural communication* (5th ed.). Englewood, CO: Morton.

Kluger, J. (2011, October 3). Playing favorites. *Time.* Retrieved from http://www.time.com/time/magazine/article/0,9171,2094371,00.html

Knapp, M. (1984). *Interpersonal communication and human relationships.* Boston: Allyn & Bacon.

Knapp, M. L., & Hall, J. A. (2002). *Nonverbal communication in human interaction* (5th ed.). Belmont, CA: Wadsworth/Thomson Learning.

Knobloch, L. K. (2005). Evaluating a contextual model of responses to relational uncertainty increasing events: The role of intimacy, appraisals, and emotions. *Human Communication Research, 31*(1), 60–101.

Koerner, A. F., & Fitzpatrick, M. A. (2002). Toward a theory of family communication. *Communication Theory, 12*, 70–91.

Koerner, A. F., & Fitzpatrick, M. A. (2006). Family communication patterns theory: A social cognitive approach. In D. O. Braithwaite & L. A. Baxter (Eds.), *Engaging theories in family communication: Multiple perspectives* (pp. 50–65). Thousand Oaks, CA: Sage.

Koerner, S. S., Wallace, S., Lehman, S. J., & Raymond, M. (2002). Mother-to-daughter disclosure after divorce: A double-edged sword? *Journal of Child and Family Studies, 11*, 469–483.

Kogan, L. (2006, August). The O interview: Gayle and Oprah, uncensored. *O, the Oprah Magazine.* Retrieved from http://www.oprah.com/omagazine/Gayle-King-and-Oprah-Uncensored-The-O-Magazine-Interview/1

Kostiuk, L. M., & Fouts, G. T. (2002). Understanding of emotions and emotion regulation in adolescent females with conduct problems: A qualitative analysis. *The Qualitative Report, 7*, 1–10.

Kotzé, M., & Venter, I. (2011). Differences in emotional intelligence between effective and ineffective leaders in the public sector: An empirical study. *International Review of Administrative Sciences, 77*(2), 397–427.

Kowalski, R. M., Walker, S., Wilkinson, R., Queen, A., & Sharpe, B. (2003). Lying, cheating, complaining, and other aversive interpersonal behaviors: A narrative examination of the darker side of relationships. *Journal of Social and Personal Relationships, 20*, 471–490.

Kowner, R. (1996). Facial asymmetry and attractiveness judgments in developmental perspective. *Journal of Experimental Psychology: Human Perception and Performance, 22*, 662–675.

Kozan, M., & Ergin, C. (1998). Preference for third-party help in conflict management in the United States and Turkey. *Journal of Cross-Cultural Psychology, 29*, 525–539.

Kramarae, C. (1981). *Women and men speaking: Frameworks for analysis.* Rowley, MA: Newbury House.

Krause, J. (2001). *Properties of naturally produced clear speech at normal rates and implications for intelligibility enhancement.* Unpublished doctoral dissertation, Massachusetts Institute of Technology, Cambridge, MA.

Kreider, R. M. (2005). *Number, timing, and duration of marriages and divorces: 2001.* Washington, DC: U.S. Census Bureau.

Kreps, G. L. (1990). *Organizational communication.* New York: Longman.

Krishnakumar, A., Buehler, C., & Barber, B. K. (2003). Youth perceptions of interparental conflict, ineffective parenting, and youth problem behaviors in European-American and African-American families. *Journal of Social and Personal Relationships, 20*(2), 239–260.

Krusiewicz, E. S., & Wood, J. T. (2001). He was our child from the moment we walked in that room: Entrance stories of adoptive parents. *Journal of Social and Personal Relationships, 18*(6), 785–803.

Kubany, E. S., Richard, D. C., Bauer, G. B., & Muraoka, M. Y. (1992). Impact of assertive and accusatory communication of distress and anger: A verbal component analysis. *Aggressive Behavior, 18*, 337–347.

Kuhn, J. L. (2001). Toward an ecological humanistic psychology. *Journal of Humanistic Psychology, 41*, 9–24.

Kurdek, L. A. (2005). What do we know about gay and lesbian couples? *Current Directions in Psychological Science, 14*, 251–254.

Kurdek, L. A. (2008). Differences between partners from Black and White heterosexual dating couples in a path model of relational commitment. *Journal of Social and Personal Relationships, 25*, 51–70.

Kuttler, A. F., LaGreca, A. M., & Prinstein, M. J. (1999). Friendship qualities and social-emotional functioning of adolescents with close, cross-sex friends. *Journal of Research on Adolescence, 9*, 339–366.

LaFollette, H., & Graham, G. (1986). Honesty and intimacy. *Journal of Social and Personal Relationships, 3*, 3–18.

Langridge, D., & Butt, T. (2004). The fundamental attribution error: A phenomenological critique. *British Journal of Social Psychology, 43,* 357–369.

Lareau, A. (2003). *Unequal childhoods: Class, race, and family life.* Berkeley: University of California Press.

Larsen, R. J., & Ketelaar, T. (1991). Personality and susceptibility to positive and negative emotional states. *Journal of Personality and Social Psychology, 61,* 132–140.

Larson, J. R. (1984). The performance feedback process: A preliminary model. *Organizational Behavior and Human Performance, 33,* 42–76.

Lasswell, H. D. (1948). The structure and function of communication in society. In L. Bryson (Ed.), *The communication of ideas* (pp. 32–51). New York: Harper & Row.

Lavy, S., Mikulincer, M., Shaver, P. R., & Gillath, O. (2009). Intrusiveness in romantic relationships: A cross-cultural perspective on imbalances between proximity and autonomy. *Journal of Social and Personal Relationships, 26*(6–7), 989–1008.

Le, B., Korn, M. S., Crockett, E. E., & Loving, T. J. (2010). Missing you maintains us: Missing a romantic partner, commitment, relationship maintenance, and physical infidelity. *Journal of Social and Personal Relationships, 28,* 653–667.

Leary, M. R. (2001). Toward a conceptualization of interpersonal rejection. In M. R. Leary (Ed.), *Interpersonal rejection* (pp. 3–20). New York: Oxford University Press.

Lee, J. A. (1973). *The colors of love: An exploration of the ways of loving.* Don Mills, Ontario: New Press.

Lehrer, J. (2009, May 18). Don't!: The secret of self-control. *The New Yorker.* Retrieved from http://www.newyorker.com /reporting/2009/05/18/090518fa_fact_lehrer

Leiner, D. (Director), Hurwitz, J. (Writer), Schlossberg, H. (Writer), Kahane, N. (Producer), & Shapiro, G. (Producer). (2004). *Harold and Kumar go to White Castle* [Motion picture]. United States: New Line Cinema.

Lemerise, E. A., & Dodge, K. A. (1993). The development of anger and hostile interactions. In M. Lewis and J. M. Haviland (Eds.), *Handbook of emotions* (pp. 537–546). New York: Guilford Press.

Lenard, D. M. (2006). Through the wall: A cross-cultural guide to doing business in China. *Asia Times Online.* Retrieved from www.atimes.com

Lenhart, A., Purcell, K., Smith, A., & Zickuhr, K. (2010). Social media & young adults. *Pew Internet & American Life Project.* Retrieved from http://www.pewinternet.org/Reports/2010/ Social-Media-and-Young-Adults.aspx

Levine, T. R., McCornack, S. A., & Baldwin Avery, P. (1992). Sex differences in emotional reactions to discovered deception. *Communication Quarterly, 40,* 289–296.

Levinson, S. C. (1985). *Pragmatics.* Cambridge, UK: Cambridge University Press.

Lewellen, W. (2008, July 7). Brenda Villa: The American saint of water polo. *Women's Sports Foundation.* Retrieved from http://66.40.5.5/Content/Articles/Athletes/About -Athletes/B/Brenda-Villa-saint-of-Water-Polo.aspx

Lippa, R. A. (2002). *Gender, nature, and nurture.* Mahwah, NJ: Erlbaum.

Lippmann, W. (1922). *Public opinion.* New York: Harcourt Brace.

Liu, B. M. (2011, January 8). Parents like Amy Chua are the reason why Asian-Americans like me are in therapy [Blog post]. Retrieved from http://bettymingliu.com

Lopes, P. N., Salovey, P., Cote, S., & Beers, M. (2005). Emotion regulation abilities and the quality of social interaction. *Emotion, 5,* 113–118.

Luft, J. (1970). *Group processes: An introduction to group dynamics* (2nd ed.). Palo Alto, CA: National Press Books.

Lulofs, R. S., & Cahn, D. D. (2000). *Conflict: From theory to action* (2nd ed.). Needham Heights, MA: Allyn & Bacon.

Luscombe, B. (2010, November 18). Who needs marriage? A changing institution. *Time.* Retrieved from http://www.time.com/time /magazine/article/0,9171,2032116,00.html

Lustig, M. W., & Koester, J. (2006). *Intercultural competence: Interpersonal communication across cultures* (5th ed.). Boston: Allyn and Bacon.

Macrae, C. N., & Bodenhausen, G. V. (2001). Social cognition: Categorical person perception. *British Journal of Psychology, 92,* 239–255.

Maeda, E., & Ritchie, L. D. (2003). The concept of Shinyuu in Japan: A replication of and comparison to Cole and Bradac's study on U.S. friendship. *Journal of Social and Personal Relationships, 20,* 579–598.

Malandro, L. A., & Barker, L. L. (1983). *Nonverbal communication.* Reading, MA: Addison-Wesley.

Malcolm X. (1964). Personal letter. Retrieved from http:// en.wikisource.org/wiki/Letter_from_Malcolm_X

Malis, R. S., & Roloff, M. E. (2006). Demand/withdraw patterns in serial arguments: Implications for well-being. *Human Communication Research, 32,* 198–216.

Manusov, V., & Hegde, R. (1993). Communicative outcomes of stereotype-based expectancies: An observational study of cross-cultural dyads. *Communication Quarterly, 41,* 338–354.

Markey, P. M., & Markey, C. N. (2007). Romantic ideals, romantic obtainment, and relationship experiences: The complementarity of interpersonal traits among romantic partners. *Journal of Social and Personal Relationships, 24*(4), 517–533.

Martin, J. N., & Nakayama, T. K. (1997). *Intercultural communication in contexts.* Mountain View, CA: Mayfield.

Martin, W., & LaVan, H. (2010). Workplace bullying: A review of litigated cases. *Employee Responsibilities and Rights Journal, 22*(3), 175–194.

Marzano, R. J., & Arredondo, D. E. (1996). *Tactics for thinking.* Aurora, CO: Mid Continent Regional Educational Laboratory.

Mashek, D. J., & Aron, A. (2004). *Handbook of closeness and intimacy.* Mahwah, NJ: Erlbaum.

Maslow, A. H. (1970). *Motivation and personality* (2nd ed.). New York: Harper & Row.

Massengill, J., & Nash, M. (2009). *Ethnocentrism, intercultural willingness to communicate, and international interaction amongst U.S. college students.* Paper presented at the annual meeting of the International Communication Association, Chicago, IL.

Matlin, M., & Stang, D. (1978). *The Pollyanna principle: Selectivity in language, memory, and thought.* Cambridge, MA: Schenkman.

Mauss, I. B., Levenson, R. W., McCarter, L., Wilhelm, F. H., & Gross, J. J. (2005). The tie that binds: Coherence among emotion experience, behavior, and physiology. *Emotion, 5,* 175–190.

Mayer, J. D., & Salovey, P. (1997). What is emotional intelligence? In P. Salovey & J. D. Sluyter (Eds.), *Emotional development and emotional intelligence* (pp. 3–31). New York: Basic Books.

Mayer, J. D., Salovey, P., & Caruso, D. R. (2004). Emotional intelligence: Theory, findings and implications. *Psychological Inquiry, 15*(3), 197–215.

McCornack, S. A. (1997). The generation of deceptive messages: Laying the groundwork for a viable theory of interpersonal deception. In J. O. Greene (Ed.), *Message production: Advances in communication theory* (pp. 91–126). Mahwah, NJ: Erlbaum.

McCornack, S. A. (2008). Information manipulation theory: Explaining how deception works. In L. A. Baxter & D. O. Braithwaite (Eds.), *Engaging theories in interpersonal communication: Multiple perspectives* (pp. 215–226). Thousand Oaks, CA: Sage.

McCornack, S. A., & Husband, R. (1986, May). *The evolution of a long-term organizational conflict: A design logic approach.* Paper presented at the annual meeting of the International Communication Association, Chicago, IL.

McCornack, S. A., & Levine, T. R. (1990). When lies are uncovered: Emotional and relational outcomes of discovered deception. *Communication Monographs, 57,* 119–138.

McCrae, R. R. (2001). Trait psychology and culture. *Journal of Personality, 69,* 819–846.

McCrae, R. R., & Costa, P. T., Jr. (2001). A five-factor theory of personality. In L. A. Pervin and O. P. John (Eds.), *Handbook of personality: Theory and research* (2nd ed., pp. 139–153). New York: Guilford Press.

McCroskey, J. C., & Richmond, V. P. (1987). Willingness to communicate. In J. C. McCroskey & J. A. Daly (Eds.), *Personality and interpersonal communication* (pp. 129–156). Beverly Hills, CA: Sage.

McEwan, B., Babin Gallagher, B., & Farinelli, L. (2008, November). *The end of a friendship: Friendship dissolution reasons and methods.* Paper presented at the annual meeting of the National Communication Association, San Diego, CA.

McGlynn, J. (2007, November). *More connections, less connection: An examination of computer-mediated communication as relationship maintenance.* Paper presented at the annual meeting of the National Communication Association, Chicago, IL.

McGuirk, R. (2011, September 14). Australian passport gender options: 'Transgender' will be included. *Associated Press.* Retrieved from http://www.huffingtonpost.com/2011/09/14/australia-passport-gender_n_963386.html

McIntosh, P. (1999). White privilege: Unpacking the invisible knapsack. In E. Lee, D. Menkart, & M. Okazawa-Rey (Eds.), *Beyond heroes and holidays: A practical guide to K–12 anti-racist, multicultural education and staff development* (pp. 79–82). Washington, DC: Network of Educators on the Americas.

McLaughlin, M. L., & Cody, M. J. (1982). Awkward silences: Behavioral antecedents and consequences of the conversational lapse. *Human Communication Research, 8,* 299–316.

McNaughton, D., Hamlin, D., McCarthy, J., Head-Reeves, D., & Schreiner, M. (2007). Learning to listen: Teaching an active listening strategy to preservice education professionals. *Topics in Early Childhood Special Education, 27*(4), 223–231.

Mead, G. H. (1934). *Mind, self, and society.* Chicago: University of Chicago Press.

Mehrabian, A. (1972). *Nonverbal communication.* Chicago: Aldine.

Mercer, J. (1998, March 20). An unusual reunion at Gallaudet: 10 years after push for "Deaf President Now." *The Chronicle of Higher Education.* Retrieved from http://www.chronicle.com/article/An-Unusual-Reunion-at/99078/

Merriam-Webster dictionary online (2011). Definition of bear. Retrieved from http://www.merriam-webster.com/dictionary/bear

Messman, S. J., Canary, D. J., & Hause, K. S. (1994, February). *Motives, strategies, and equity in the maintenance of opposite-sex friendships.* Paper presented at the Western States Communication Association convention, San Jose, CA.

Messman, S. J., Canary, D. J., & Hause, K. S. (2000). Motives to remain platonic, equity, and the use of maintenance strategies in opposite-sex friendships. *Journal of Social and Personal Relationships, 17,* 67–94.

Metts, S., & Chronis, H. (1986, May). *Relational deception: An exploratory analysis.* Paper presented at the annual meeting of the International Communication Association, Chicago, IL.

Metts, S., & Planalp, S. (2002). Emotional communication. In M. L. Knapp & J. A. Daly (Eds.), *Handbook of interpersonal communication* (pp. 339–373). Thousand Oaks, CA: Sage.

Meyer, S. (2005). *Twilight.* New York: Little, Brown.

Michalos, A. C. (1991). *Global report on student well-being: Vol. 1. Life satisfaction and happiness.* New York: Springer-Verlag.

Michaud, S. G., & Aynesworth, H. (1989). *The only living witness: A true account of homicidal insanity.* New York: Signet.

Mickelson, K. D., Kessler, R. C., & Shaver, P. R. (1997). Adult attachment in a nationally representative sample. *Journal of Personality and Social Psychology, 73,* 1092–1106.

Mies, M. (1991). *Patriarchy and accumulation on a world scale: Women in the international division of labor.* London: Zed Books.

Miller, G. R., & Steinberg, M. (1975). *Between people: A new analysis of interpersonal communication.* Chicago: Science Research Associates.

Miller, H., & Arnold, J. (2001). Breaking away from grounded identity: Women academics on the Web. *CyberPsychology and Behavior, 4,* 95–108.

Miller, K. (1995). *Organizational communication: Approaches and processes.* Belmont, CA: Wadsworth.

Miller, L., Hefner, V., & Scott, A. (2007, May). *Turning points in dyadic friendship development and termination.* Paper presented at the annual meeting of the International Communication Association, San Francisco, CA.

Miller, R. S., Perlman, D., & Brehm, S. S. (2007). Love: Chapter 8. In R. S. Miller, D. Perlman, & S. S. Brehm (Eds.), *Intimate relationships* (pp. 244–275). New York: McGraw-Hill.

Millman, J. (1999, August 10). Brilliant careers: Fred Rogers. *Salon.com.* Retrieved from http://www.salon.com/1999/08/10/rogers_2/singleton/

Mister Rogers. (n.d.). *TVAcres.* Retrieved from http://www.tvacres.com/child_mrrogers.htm

Mitchell, M. (1936). *Gone with the wind.* New York: Macmillan.

Mohammed, R., & Hussein, A. (2008, August). *Communication climate and organizational performance.* Paper presented to the Eighth International Conference on Knowledge, Culture & Changes in Organizations, Cambridge University (UK).

Mongeau, P. A., Hale, J. L., & Alles, M. (1994). An experimental investigation of accounts and attributions following sexual infidelity. *Communication Monographs, 61,* 326–344.

Mongeau, P. A., Ramirez, A., & Vorrell, M. (2003, February). *Friends with benefits: Initial explorations of sexual, nonromantic relationships.* Paper presented at the annual meeting of the Western Communication Association, Salt Lake City, UT.

Monsour, M. (1997). Communication and cross-sex friendships across the life cycle: A review of the literature. In B. Burleson (Ed.), *Communication Yearbook 20* (pp. 375–414). Thousand Oaks, CA: Sage.

Montagu, M. F. A. (1971). *Touching: The human significance of the skin.* New York: Columbia University Press.

Morrison, K., Lee, C. M., Wiedmaier, B., & Dibble, J. L. (2008, November). *The influence of MySpace and Facebook events on interpersonal relationships.* Paper presented at the annual meeting of the National Communication Association, San Diego, CA.

Morrison, K., & McCornack, S. A. (2011). *Studying attitudes toward LGBT persons in mid-Michigan: Challenges and goals.* Technical report presented at the annual meeting of the Michigan Fairness Forum, Lansing, MI.

Mosher, C., & Danoff-Burg, S. (2007). College students' life priorities: The influence of gender and gender-linked personality traits. *Gender Issues, 24*(2). doi:10.1007/s12147-007-9002-z

Mulac, A., Bradac, J. J., & Mann, S. K. (1985). Male/female language differences and attributional consequences in children's television. *Human Communication Research, 11,* 481–506.

Mulac, A., Incontro, C. R., & James, M. R. (1985). Comparison of the gender-linked language effect and sex role stereotypes. *Journal of Personality and Social Psychology, 49,* 1098–1109.

Munro, K. (2002). Conflict in cyberspace: How to resolve conflict online. In J. Suler (Ed.), *The psychology of cyberspace.* Retrieved from http://www-usr.rider.edu/~suler/psycyber/conflict.html

Myers, D. G. (2002). *The pursuit of happiness: Discovering the pathway to fulfillment, well-being, and enduring personal joy.* New York: HarperCollins.

Myers, S. A., Knox, R. L., Pawlowski, D. R., & Ropog, B. L. (1999). Perceived communication openness and functional communication skills among organizational peers. *Communication Reports, 12,* 71–83.

National Communication Association (NCA). (1999). *NCA credo for ethical communication.* Retrieved from http://www.natcom.org

National Communication Association (NCA). (n.d.). *The field of communication.* Retrieved from http://www.natcom.org/Tertiary.aspx?id=236

Neuliep, J. W., & McCroskey, J. C. (1997). The development of a U.S. and generalized ethnocentrism scale. *Communication Research Reports, 14,* 385–398.

Nishiyama, K. (1971). Interpersonal persuasion in a vertical society. *Speech Monographs, 38,* 148–154.

Nofsinger, R. E. (1999). *Everyday conversation.* Prospect Heights, IL: Waveland Press.

Nutt, A. (2011). How to communicate in a global world. Woodridge Cross-Cultural Management Articles. Retrieved from http://cross-cultural-management.bestmanagementarticles.com/a-5711-how-to-communicate-in-a-global-world.aspx

Ohbuchi, K., & Sato, K. (1994). Children's reactions to mitigating accounts: Apologies, excuses, and intentionality of harm. *Journal of Social Psychology, 134,* 5–17.

O'Keefe, B. J. (1988). The logic of message design. *Communication Monographs, 55,* 80–103.

O'Leary, K. D., & Vivian, D. (1990). Physical aggression in marriage. In F. D. Fincham & T. N. Bradbury (Eds.), *The psychology of marriage: Basic issues and applications* (pp. 323–348). New York: Guilford Press.

Ophir, E., Nass, C. I., & Wagner, A. D. (2012, in press). Cognitive control in media multitaskers. *Proceedings of the National Academy of Sciences.* Retrieved from http://www.pnas.org/content/106/37/15583

Oravec, J. (2000). Internet and computer technology hazards: Perspectives for family counseling. *British Journal of Guidance and Counselling, 28,* 309–324.

Palmer, M. T., & Simmons, K. B. (1995). Communicating intentions through nonverbal behaviors: Conscious and nonconscious encoding of liking. *Human Communication Research, 22,* 128–160.

Palmer Stadium. (n.d.). Retrieved from http://football.ballparks.com/NCAA/Ivy/Princeton/index.htm

Park, H. S., Levine, T. R., McCornack, S. A., Morrison, K., & Ferrara, M. (2002). How people really detect lies. *Communication Monographs, 69,* 144–157.

Parkinson, B., Totterdell, P., Briner, R. B., & Reynolds, S. (1996). *Changing moods: The psychology of mood and mood regulation.* London: Longman.

Parks, M. R. (1994). Communicative competence and interpersonal control. In M. L. Knapp & G. R. Miller (Eds.), *Handbook of interpersonal communication* (2nd ed., pp. 589–620). Beverly Hills, CA: Sage.

Parks, M. R. (2007). *Personal relationships and personal networks.* Hillsdale, NJ: Erlbaum.

Parks, M. R., & Adelman, M. B. (1983). Communication networks and the development of romantic relationships: An expansion of uncertainty reduction theory. *Human Communication Research, 10,* 55–79.

Parks, M. R., & Floyd, K. (1996). Making friends in cyberspace. *Journal of Communication, 46,* 80–97.

Patterson, B. R. (2007). Relationship development revisited: A preliminary look at communication in friendship over the lifespan. *Communication Research Reports, 24*(1), 29–37.

Patterson, M. L. (1988). Functions of nonverbal behavior in close relationships. In S. W. Duck (Ed.), *Handbook of personal relationships* (pp. 41–56). New York: Wiley.

Patterson, M. L. (1995). A parallel process model of nonverbal communication. *Journal of Nonverbal Behavior, 19,* 3–29.

Payne, M. J., & Sabourin, T. C. (1990). Argumentative skill deficiency and its relationship to quality of marriage. *Communication Research Reports, 7,* 121–124.

Pennebaker, J. W. (1997). *Opening up: The healing power of expressing emotions.* New York: Guilford Press.

Pennington, N. (2009, November). *What it means to be a (Facebook) friend: Navigating friendship on social network sites.* Paper presented at the annual meeting of the National Communication Association, Chicago, IL.

Pennsylvania Dutch Country Welcome Center (n.d.). *The Amish: FAQs.* Retrieved from http://www.padutch.com/atafaq.shtml

Peplau, L. A., & Spalding, L. R. (2000). The close relationships of lesbians, gay men and bisexuals. In C. Hendrick & S. S. Hendrick (Eds.), *Close relationships: A sourcebook* (pp. 111–123). Thousand Oaks, CA: Sage.

Pervin, L. A. (1993). Affect and personality. In M. Lewis & J. M. Haviland (Eds.), *Handbook of emotions* (pp. 301–311). New York: Guilford Press.

Peterson, D. R. (2002). Conflict. In H. H. Kelley et al. (Eds.), *Close relationships* (2nd ed., pp. 360–396). Clinton Corners, NY: Percheron Press.

Petronio, S. (2000). The boundaries of privacy: Praxis of everyday life. In S. Petronio (Ed.), *Balancing the secrets of private disclosures* (pp. 37–49). Mahwah, NJ: Erlbaum.

Petronio, S., & Caughlin, J. P. (2006). Communication privacy management theory: Understanding families. In D. O. Braithwaite & L. A. Baxter (Eds.), *Engaging theories in family communication: Multiple perspectives* (pp. 35–49). Thousand Oaks, CA: Sage.

Philpott, T. (2004, October). Stop stop-loss. Retrieved from http://www.moaa.org/todaysofficer/columnists/Philpott/Stop.asp

Pierce, C. A., & Aguinis, H. (2009). Moving beyond a legal-centric approach to managing workplace romances: Organizationally sensible recommendations for HR leaders. *Human Resource Management, 48*(3), 447–464.

Planalp, S., & Honeycutt, J. M. (1985). Events that increase uncertainty in personal relationships. *Human Communication Research, 11,* 593–604.

Plutchik, R. (1980). *Emotions: A psycho-evolutionary synthesis.* New York: Harper & Row.

Plutchik, R. (1993). Emotions and their vicissitudes: Emotions and psychopathology. In M. Lewis & J. M. Haviland (Eds.), *Handbook of emotions* (pp. 53–66). New York: Guilford Press.

Pomerantz, A. (1990). On the validity and generalizability of conversation analytic methods: Conversation analytic claims. *Communication Monographs, 57,* 231–235.

Price, J. (1999). *Navigating differences: Friendships between gay and straight men.* Binghamton, NY: The Haworth Press.

Privitera, C., & Campbell, M. A. (2009). Cyberbullying: The new face of workplace bullying? *Cyberpsychology & Behavior, 12*(4), 395–400.

Pruitt, D. G., & Carnevale, P. J. (1993). *Negotiation in social conflict.* Monterey, CA: Brooks-Cole.

Pyszczynski, T., Greenberg, J., Solomon, S., Arndt, J., & Schimel, J. (2004). Why do people need self-esteem? A theoretical and empirical review. *Psychological Bulletin, 130*(3), 435–468.

Quan-Haase, A., Cothrel, J., & Wellman, B. (2005). Instant messaging for collaboration: A case study of a high-tech firm. *Journal of Computer-Mediated Communication, 10.* Retrieved from http://jcmc.indiana.edu/vol10/issue4/quan-haase.html

Quenqua, D. (2009). I love you, man (as a friend). *The New York Times.* Retrieved from http://www.nytimes.com

Rabby, M. K. (1997, November). *Maintaining relationships via electronic mail.* Paper presented at the annual meeting of the National Communication Association, Chicago, IL.

Rahim, M. A., & Mager, N. R. (1995). Confirmatory factor analysis of the styles of handling interpersonal conflict: First-order factor model and its invariance across groups. *Journal of Applied Psychology, 80,* 122–132.

Rainey, V. P. (2000, December). The potential for miscommunication using email as a source of communications. *Transactions of the Society for Design and Process Science, 4,* 21–43.

Randall, W. S. (1998). *George Washington: A life.* New York: Owl Books, Henry Holt.

Rawlins, W. K. (1992). *Friendship matters: Communication, dialectics, and the life course.* New York: Aldine de Gruyter.

Rawlins, W. K. (1994). Being there and growing apart: Sustaining friendships during adulthood. In D. J. Canary & L. Stafford (Eds.), *Communication and relational maintenance* (pp. 275–294). New York: Academic Press.

Ray, J. J. (1972). A new balanced F scale, and its relation to social class. *Australian Psychologist, 7,* 155–166.

Reeder, H. M. (2003). The effect of gender role orientation on same- and cross-sex friendship formation. *Sex Roles, 49,* 143–152.

Regan, P. C., Kocan, E. R., & Whitlock, T. (1998). Ain't love grand: A prototype analysis of the concept of romantic love. *Journal of Social and Personal Relationships, 15,* 411–420.

Regional vocabularies of American English. (n.d.). In *Wikipedia.* Retrieved from http://en.wikipedia.org/wiki/Regional_vocabularies_of_American_English

Reis, H. T., & Patrick, B. C. (1996). Attachment and intimacy: Component processes. In E. T. Higgins, & A. W. Kruglanski (Eds.), *Social psychology: Handbook of basic principles* (pp. 523–563). New York: Guilford Press.

Reis, H. T., & Shaver, P. (1988). Intimacy as an interpersonal process. In S. W. Duck (Ed.), *Handbook of personal relationships* (pp. 367–389). New York: Wiley.

Reuters. (2004, August 18). Army guardsman sues to get out. *The Washington Post.* Retrieved from http://www.washingtonpost.com/wp-dyn/articles/A9535-2004Aug17.html

Riach, K., & Wilson, F. (2007). Don't screw the crew: Exploring the rules of engagement in organizational romance. *British Journal of Management, 18,* 79–92.

Richards, J. M., Butler, E. A., & Gross, J. J. (2003). Emotion regulation in romantic relationships: The cognitive consequences of concealing feelings. *Journal of Social and Personal Relationships, 20,* 599–620.

Ridge, R. D., & Berscheid, E. (1989, May). *On loving and being in love: A necessary distinction.* Paper presented at the annual convention of the Midwestern Psychological Association, Chicago, IL.

Riedy, M. K., & Wen, J. H. (2010). Electronic surveillance of Internet access in the American workplace: Implications for management. *Information & Communications Technology Law, 19*(1), 87–99.

Riela, S., Rodriguez, G., Aron, A., Xu, X., & Acevedo, B. P. (2010). Experiences of falling in love: Investigating culture, ethnicity, gender, and speed. *Journal of Social and Personal Relationships, 27,* 473–493.

Rintel, E. S., & Pittam, J. (1997). Strangers in a strange land: Interaction management on Internet relay chat. *Human Communication Research, 23,* 507–534.

Ritchie, L. D., & Fitzpatrick, M. A. (1990). Family communication patterns: Measuring interpersonal perceptions of interpersonal relationships. *Communication Research, 17,* 523–544.

Rodrigues, L. N., & Kitzmann, K. M. (2007). Coping as a mediator between interparental conflict and adolescents' romantic attachment. *Journal of Social and Personal Relationships, 24*(3), 423–439.

Rohlfing, M. E. (1995). Doesn't anybody stay in one place anymore? An exploration of the under-studied phenomenon of long-distance relationships. In J. T. Wood & S. Duck (Eds.), *Under-studied relationships: Off the beaten track* (pp. 173–196). Thousand Oaks, CA: Sage.

Roloff, M. E., & Soule, K. P. (2002). Interpersonal conflict: A review. In M. L. Knapp & J. A. Daly (Eds.), *Handbook of interpersonal communication* (3rd ed., pp. 475–528). Thousand Oaks, CA: Sage.

Rosenburg, M. (1965). *Society and the adolescent self-image.* Princeton, NJ: Princeton University Press.

Rosenfeld, H. M. (1987). Conversational control functions of nonverbal behavior. In A.W. Siegman & S. Feldstein (Eds.), *Nonverbal behavior and communication* (2nd ed., pp. 563–602). Hillsdale, NJ: Erlbaum.

Rosenfeld, L. B., & Welsh, S. M. (1985). Differences in self-disclosure in dual-career and single-career marriages. *Communication Monographs, 52,* 253–263.

Rothbard, M. N. (1999). *Conceived in liberty* (Vol. 4). Auburn, AL: Mises Institute.

Rothbart, M. K., Ahadi, S. A., & Evans, D. E. (2000). Temperament and personality: Origins and outcomes. *Journal of Personality and Social Psychology, 78,* 122–135.

Rowatt, W. D., Cunningham, M. R., & Druen, P. B. (1998). Deception to get a date. *Personality and Social Psychology Bulletin, 24,* 1228–1242.

Rowling, J. K. (1997). *Harry Potter and the sorcerer's stone.* New York: Scholastic Inc.

Rowling, J. K. (1999). *Harry Potter and the chamber of secrets.* New York: Scholastic Inc.

Roy, R., Benenson, J. F., & Lilly, F. (2000). Beyond intimacy: Conceptualizing sex differences in same-sex friendships. *Journal of Psychology, 134,* 93–101.

Rubin, L. (1985). *Just friends.* New York: Harper & Row.

Rubin, L. B. (1996). Reflections on friendship. In K. M. Galvin & P. J. Cooper (Eds.), *Making connections: Readings in relational communication* (pp. 254–257). Los Angeles: Roxbury.

Rubin, Z. (1973). *Liking and loving: An invitation to social psychology.* New York: Holt, Rinehart & Winston.

Rubin, Z., Peplau, L. A., & Hill, C. T. (1981). Loving and leaving: Sex differences in romantic attachments. *Sex Roles, 7,* 821–835.

Rueter, M. A., & Koerner, A. F. (2008). The effect of family communication patterns on adopted adolescent adjustment. *Journal of Marriage and Family, 70,* 715–727.

Rusbult, C. E. (1987). Responses to dissatisfaction in close relationships: The exit-voice-loyalty-neglect model. In D. Perlman & S. Duck (Eds.), *Intimate relationships: Development, dynamics, and deterioration* (pp. 209–237). Newbury Park, CA: Sage.

Rusbult, C. E., Arriaga, X. B., & Agnew, C. R. (2001). Interdependence in close relationships. In G. J. O. Fletcher & M. S. Clark (Eds.), *Blackwell handbook of social psychology, vol. 2: Interpersonal processes* (pp. 359–387). Oxford: Blackwell.

Saarni, C. (1993). Socialization of emotion. In M. Lewis & J. M. Haviland (Eds.), *Handbook of emotions* (pp. 435–446). New York: Guilford Press.

Sabourin, T. C., Infante, D. A., & Rudd, J. E. (1993). Verbal aggression in marriages: A comparison of violent, distressed but nonviolent, and nondistressed couples. *Human Communication Research, 20,* 245–267.

Sahlstein, E. (2004). Relating at a distance: Negotiating being together and being apart in long-distance relationships. *Journal of Social and Personal Relationships, 21,* 689–702.

Salovey, P., & Rodin, J. (1988). Coping with envy and jealousy. *Journal of Social and Clinical Psychology, 7,* 15–33.

Savicki, V., Kelley, M., & Oesterreich, E. (1999). Judgments of gender in computer-mediated communication. *Computers in Human Behavior, 15,* 185–194.

Schaefer, C. M., & Tudor, T. R. (2001). Managing workplace romances. *SAM Advanced Management Journal, 66*(3), 4–10.

Schein, E. H. (1985). *Organizational culture and leadership.* San Francisco: Jossey-Bass.

Scherer, K. R. (1974). Acoustic concomitants of emotional dimensions: Judging affect from synthesized tone sequences. In S. Weitz (Ed.), *Nonverbal communication: Readings with commentary* (pp. 105–111). New York: Oxford University Press.

Scherer, K. R. (2001). Appraisal considered as a process of multi-level sequential checking. In K. R. Scherer, A. Schorr, & T. Johnstone (Eds.), *Appraisal processes in emotion* (pp. 92–120). Oxford, UK: Oxford University Press.

Schlaepfer, T. E., Harris, G. J., Tien, A. Y., Peng, L., Lee, S., & Pearlson, G. D. (1995). Structural differences in the cerebral cortex of healthy female and male subjects: A magnetic resonance imaging study. *Psychiatry Research, 61,* 129–135.

Schneider, C. S., & Kenny, D. A. (2000). Cross-sex friends who were once romantic partners: Are they platonic friends now? *Journal of Social and Personal Relationships, 17*(3), 451–466.

Schramm, W. (Ed.). (1954). *The process and effects of mass communication.* Urbana: University of Illinois Press.

Schrodt, P. (2006). Development and validation of the Stepfamily Life Index. *Journal of Social and Personal Relationships, 23*(3), 427–444.

Schrodt, P., & Afifi, T. D. (2007). Communication processes that predict young adults' feelings of being caught and their associations with mental health and family satisfaction. *Communication Monographs, 74*(2), 200–228.

Searle, J. (1965). What is a speech act? In M. Black (Ed.), *Philosophy in America* (pp. 221–239). Ithaca, NY: Cornell University Press.

Searle, J. A. (1969). *Speech acts.* Cambridge, UK: Cambridge University Press.

Searle, J. A. (1976). The classification of illocutionary acts. *Language in Society, 5,* 1–24.

Sebold, A. (2002). *The lovely bones.* New York: Little, Brown.

Seta, J. J., & Seta, C. E. (1993). Stereotypes and the generation of compensatory and noncompensatory expectancies of group members. *Personality and Social Psychology Bulletin, 19,* 722–731.

SFGate.com. (2005, February 6). Ad campaigns that go wrong. Retrieved from http://articles.sfgate.com/2005-02-06/opinion/17360611_1_parker-pens-latin-america-clairol

Shackelford, T. K., & Buss, D. M. (1997). Anticipation of marital dissolution as a consequence of spousal infidelity. *Journal of Social and Personal Relationships, 14,* 793–808.

Shah, M. B., King, S., & Patel, A. S. (2004). Intercultural disposition and communication competence of future pharmacists. *American Journal of Pharmaceutical Education, 69,* 1–11.

Shannon, C. E., & Weaver, W. (1949). *The mathematical theory of communication.* Urbana: University of Illinois Press.

Shaver, P. R., Wu, S., & Schwartz, J. C. (1992). Cross-cultural similarities and differences in emotion and its representation. In M. S. Clark (Ed.), *Emotion* (pp. 175–212). Newbury Park, CA: Sage.

Shedletsky, L. J., & Aitken, J. E. (2004). *Human communication on the Internet.* Boston: Pearson Education/Allyn and Bacon.

Shelton, J. N., Richeson, J. A., & Bergsieker, H. B. (2009). Interracial friendship development and attributional biases. *Journal of Social and Personal Relationships, 26*(2–3), 179–193.

Shelton, J. N., Trail, T. E., West, T. V., & Bergsieker, H. B. (2010). From strangers to friends: The interpersonal process model of intimacy in developing interracial friendships. *Journal of Social and Personal Relationships, 27*(1), 71–90.

Shoda, Y., Mischel, W., & Peake, P. K. (1990). Predicting adolescent cognitive and self-regulatory competencies from preschool delay of gratification: Identifying diagnostic conditions. *Developmental Psychology, 26*(6), 978–986.

Shweder, R. A. (1993). The cultural psychology of the emotions. In M. Lewis & J. M. Haviland (Eds.), *Handbook of emotions* (pp. 417–431). New York: Guilford Press.

Sias, P. M., & Cahill, D. J. (1998). From co-workers to friends: The development of peer friendships in the workplace. *Western Journal of Communication, 62,* 273–300.

Sias, P. M., Drzewiecka, J. A., Meares, M., Bent, R., Konomi, Y., Ortega, M., & White, C. (2008). Intercultural friendship development. *Communication Reports, 21*(1), 1–13.

Sias, P. M., Heath, R. G., Perry, T., Silva, D., & Fix, B. (2004). Narratives of workplace friendship deterioration. *Journal of Social and Personal Relationships, 21*(3), 321–340.

Sias, P. M., Krone, K. J., & Jablin, F. M. (2002). An ecological systems perspective on workplace relationships. In M. L. Knapp & J. A. Daly (Eds.), *Handbook of interpersonal communication* (pp. 615–642). Thousand Oaks, CA: Sage.

Sias, P. M., & Perry, T. (2004). Disengaging from workplace relationships: A research note. *Human Communication Research, 30,* 589–602.

Sillars, A. L. (1980). Attributions and communication in roommate conflicts. *Communication Monographs, 47,* 180–200.

Sillars, A., Roberts, L. J., Leonard, K. E., & Dun, T. (2000). Cognition during marital conflict: The relationship of thought and talk. *Journal of Social and Personal Relationships, 17,* 479–502.

Sillars, A., Smith, T., & Koerner, A. (2010). Misattributions contributing to empathic (in)accuracy during parent–adolescent conflict discussions. *Journal of Social and Personal Relationships, 27*(6), 727–747.

Sillars, A. L., & Wilmot, W. W. (1994). Communication strategies in conflict and mediation. In J. Wiemann & J. Daly (Eds.), *Communicating strategically: Strategies in interpersonal communication* (pp. 163–190). Hillsdale, NJ: Erlbaum.

Silvera, D. H., Krull, D. S., & Sassler, M. A. (2002). Typhoid Pollyanna: The effect of category valence on retrieval order of positive and negative category members. *European Journal of Cognitive Psychology, 14,* 227–236.

Silversides, B. V. (1994). *The face pullers: Photographing native Canadians, 1871–1939.* Saskatoon, Saskatchewan, Canada: Fifth House.

Silverstein, M., & Giarrusso, R. (2010). Aging and family life: A decade review. *Journal of Marriage and Family, 72,* 1039–1058.

Simonson, H. (2011). *Major Pettigrew's last stand.* New York: Random House.

Smith, C. A., & Kirby, L. D. (2004). Appraisal as a pervasive determinant of anger. *Emotion, 4,* 133–138.

Smith, G., & Anderson, K. J. (2005). Students' ratings of professors: The teaching style contingency for Latino/a professors. *Journal of Latinos and Education, 4,* 115–136.

Smith, L., Heaven, P. C. L., & Ciarrochi, J. (2008). Trait emotional intelligence, conflict communication patterns, and relationship satisfaction. *Personality and Individual Differences, 44,* 1314–1325.

Snyder, M. (1974). Self-monitoring of expressive behavior. *Journal of Personality and Social Psychology, 30,* 526–537.

Solomon, D. H., & Samp, J. A. (1998). Power and problem appraisal: Perceptual foundations of the chilling effect in dating relationships. *Journal of Social and Personal Relationships, 15,* 191–209.

Soto, J. A., Levenson, R. W., & Ebling, R. (2005). Cultures of moderation and expression: Emotional experience, behavior, and physiology in Chinese Americans and Mexican Americans. *Emotion, 5,* 154–165.

Spears, R., Postmes, T., Lea, M., & Watt, S. E. (2001). A SIDE view of social influence. In J. P. Forgas & K. D. Williams (Eds.), *Social influence: Direct and indirect processes* (pp. 331–350). Philadelphia: Psychology Press–Taylor and Francis Group.

Spender, D. (1984). Defining reality: A powerful tool. In C. Kramarae, M. Schultz, & W. O'Barr (Eds.), *Language and power* (pp. 195–205). Beverly Hills, CA: Sage.

Spender, D. (1990). *Man made language.* London: Pandora Press.

Spitzberg, B. (1997). A model of intercultural communication competence. In L. A. Samovar & R. E. Porter (Eds.), *Intercultural communication: A reader* (pp. 379–391). Belmont, CA: Wadsworth.

Spitzberg, B. H., & Cupach, W. R. (1984). *Interpersonal communication competence.* Beverly Hills, CA: Sage.

Spitzberg, B. H., & Cupach, W. R. (2002). Interpersonal skills. In M. L. Knapp & J. A. Daly (Eds.), *Handbook of interpersonal communication* (3rd ed., pp. 564–611). Thousand Oaks, CA: Sage.

Sprecher, S. (2001). A comparison of emotional consequences of and changes in equity over time using global and domain-specific measures of equity. *Journal of Social and Personal Relationships, 18,* 477–501.

Sprecher, S., & Metts, S. (1989). Development of the romantic beliefs scale and examination of the effects of gender and gender-role orientation. *Journal of Social and Personal Relationships, 6,* 387–411.

Sprecher, S., & Metts, S. (1999). Romantic beliefs: Their influence on relationships and patterns of change over time. *Journal of Social and Personal Relationships, 16*(6), 834–851.

Stafford, L. (2003). Maintaining romantic relationships: A summary and analysis of one research program. In D. J. Canary & M. Dainton (Eds.), *Maintaining relationships through communication: Relational, contextual, and cultural variations* (pp. 51–77). Mahwah, NJ: Erlbaum.

Stafford, L. (2005). *Maintaining long-distance and cross-residential relationships.* Mahwah, NJ: Erlbaum.

Stafford, L. (2010). Measuring relationship maintenance behaviors: Critique and development of the revised relationship maintenance behavior scale. *Journal of Social and Personal Relationships, 28,* 278–303.

Stafford, L., & Canary, D. J. (1991). Maintenance strategies and romantic relationship type, gender, and relational characteristics. *Journal of Social and Personal Relationships, 8,* 217–242.

Stafford, L., Dainton, M., & Haas, S. (2000). Measuring routine and strategic relational maintenance: Scale revision, sex versus gender roles, and the prediction of relational characteristics. *Communication Monographs, 67,* 306–323.

Stafford, L., & Merolla, A. J. (2007). Idealization, reunions, and stability in long-distance dating relationships. *Journal of Social and Personal Relationships, 24,* 37–54.

Stafford, L., Merolla, A. J., and Castle, J. (2006). When long-distance dating partners become geographically close. *Journal of Social and Personal Relationships, 23,* 901–919.

Stiff, J. B., Dillard, J. P., Somera, L., Kim, H., & Sleight, C. (1988). Empathy, communication, and prosocial behavior. *Communication Monographs, 55,* 198–213.

Stimson, E. (1998, March). The real Mister Rogers: This Presbyterian minister is as genuinely nice in person as he is on TV.

Retrieved from http://www.adventistreview.org/thisweek/story5.htm

Stone, E. (2004). *Black sheep and kissing cousins: How our family stories shape us*. New Brunswick, NJ: Transaction.

Strauss, V. (2006, March 21). Putting parents in their place: Outside class. *The Washington Post*, p. A08.

Streek, J. (1980). Speech acts in interaction: A critique of Searle. *Discourse Processes, 3*, 133–154.

Streek, J. (1993). Gesture as communication I: Its coordination with gaze and speech. *Communication Monographs, 60*, 275–299.

Suitor, J. J., Sechrist, J., Plikuhn, M., Pardo, S. T., Gilligan, M., & Pillemer, K. (2009). The role of perceived maternal favoritism in sibling relations in midlife. *Journal of Marriage and Family, 71*, 1026–1038.

Suler, J. R. (2004). The online disinhibition effect. *CyberPsychology and Behavior, 7*, 321–326.

Surra, C., & Hughes, D. (1997). Commitment processes in accounts of the development of premarital relationships. *Journal of Marriage and the Family, 59*, 5–21.

Swain, S. O. (1992). Men's friendships with women: Intimacy, sexual boundaries, and the informant role. In P. M. Nardi (Ed.), *Men's friendships: Vol. 2. Research on men and masculinities* (pp. 153–172). Newbury Park, CA: Sage.

Talbot, N. (2008). Using body language to attract. Retrieved from http://www.allstardatingtips.com/body-language.html

Tannen, D. (1990). *You just don't understand: Women and men in conversation*. New York: Morrow.

Tardy, C. H. (2000). Self-disclosure and health: Revising Sidney Jourard's hypothesis. In S. Petronio (Ed.), *Balancing the secrets of private disclosures* (pp. 111–122). Mahwah, NJ: Erlbaum.

Tardy, C., & Dindia, K. (1997). Self-disclosure. In O. Hargie (Ed.), *The handbook of communication skills*. London: Routledge.

Tavernise, S. (2011, May 26). Married couples are no longer a majority, census finds. *The New York Times*. Retrieved from http://www.nytimes.com

Tavris, C. (1989). *Anger: The misunderstood emotion*. New York: Touchstone Press.

Thayer, R. E., Newman, J. R., & McClain, T. M. (1994). Self-regulation of mood: Strategies for changing a bad mood, raising energy, and reducing tension. *Journal of Personality and Social Psychology, 67*, 910–925.

The English language: Words borrowed from other languages. (n.d.). Retrieved from http://www.krysstal.com/borrow.html

The Global Development Research Center, www.gdrc.org, retrieved November 6, 2011.

The National Center for Victims of Crimes. (2008). *Dating violence fact sheet*. Retrieved from http://www.ncvc.org

Thomas, L. T., & Levine, T. R. (1994). Disentangling listening and verbal recall: Related but separate constructs? *Human Communication Research, 21*, 103–127.

Thompson, J. K., Heinberg, L. J., Altabe, M., & Tantleff-Dunn, S. (1999). *Exacting beauty: Theory, assessment, and treatment of body image disturbances*. Washington, DC: American Psychological Association.

Thorne, B. (1986). Boys and girls together . . . but mostly apart: Gender arrangements in elementary schools. In W. Hartup & Z. Rubin (Eds.), *Relationships and development* (pp. 167–184). Hillsdale, NJ: Erlbaum.

Tillema, T., Dijst, M., & Schwanen, T. (2010). Face-to-face and electronic communications in maintaining social networks: The influence of geographical and relational distance and of information content. *New Media & Society, 12*(6), 965–983.

Ting-Toomey, S. (1985). Toward a theory of conflict and culture. In W. B. Gudykunst, L. P. Stewart, & S. Ting-Toomey (Eds.), *Communication, culture, and organizational processes* (pp. 71–86). Beverly Hills, CA: Sage.

Ting-Toomey, S. (1997). Managing intercultural conflicts effectively. In L. A. Samovar & R. E. Porter (Eds.), *Intercultural communication: A reader* (pp. 392–403). Belmont, CA: Wadsworth.

Ting-Toomey, S. (1999). *Communicating across cultures*. New York: Guilford Press.

Tippett, M. (1994). The face pullers [Review of the book *The face pullers*, by B. V. Silversides]. *Canadian Historical Review, 75*, 1–4.

Tjaden, P., & Thoennes, N. (2000). Full report of the prevalence, incidence, and consequences of violence against women: Findings from the national violence against women survey. *Research Report*. Washington, DC, and Atlanta, GA: U.S. Department of Justice, National Institute of Justice, and U.S. Department of Health and Human Services, Centers for Disease Control and Prevention.

Tovares, A. V. (2010). All in the family: Small stories and narrative construction of a shared family identity that includes pets. *Narrative Inquiry, 20*(1), 1–19.

Tracy, S. J., Lutgen-Sandvik, P., & Alberts, J. K. (2006). Nightmares, demons, and slaves: Exploring the painful metaphors of workplace bullying. *Management Communication Quarterly, 20*(2), 148–185.

Tsai, J. L., & Levenson, R. W. (1997). Cultural influences of emotional responding: Chinese American and European American dating couples during interpersonal conflict. *Journal of Cross-Cultural Psychology, 28*, 600–625.

Turkle, S. (1995). *Life on the screen: Identity in the age of the Internet*. New York: Simon & Schuster.

Turner, J. C., Hogg, M. A., Oakes, P. J., Reicher, S. D., & Wetherell, M. S. (1987). *Rediscovering the social group: A self-categorization theory*. Cambridge, MA: Basil Blackwell.

Tyner, L. J., & Clinton, M. S. (2010). Sexual harassment in the workplace: Are human resource professionals victims? *Journal of Organizational Culture, Communications and Conflict, 14*(1), 33–49.

U.S. Equal Employment Opportunity Commission. (1980). Guidelines on discrimination because of sex. *Federal Register, 45*, 74676–74677.

U.S. Equal Employment Opportunity Commission. (2011). *Sexual harassment charges: 1997–2011*. Retrieved from http://www.eeoc.gov/statistics/enforcement/sexual_harassment.cfm

Vallacher, R. R., Nowak, A., Froehlich, M., & Rockloff, M. (2002). The dynamics of self-evaluation. *Personality and Social Psychology Review, 6*, 370–379.

Vangelisti, A. L., Crumley, L. P., & Baker, J. L. (1999). Family portraits: Stories as standards for family relationships. *Journal of Social and Personal Relationships, 16*(3), 335–368.

Vazire, S., & Gosling, S. D. (2004). E-Perceptions: Personality impressions based on personal websites. *Journal of Personality and Social Psychology, 87*, 123–132.

Veale, D., Kinderman, P., Riley, S., & Lambrou, C. (2003). Self-discrepancy in body dysmorphic disorder. *British Journal of Clinical Psychology, 42*, 157–169.

Villaume, W. A., & Bodie, G. D. (2007). Discovering the listener within us: The impact of trait-like personality variables and communicator styles on preferences for listening style. *International Journal of Listening, 21*, 102–123.

Vogl-Bauer, S. (2003). Maintaining family relationships. In D. J. Canary & M. Dainton (Eds.), *Maintaining relationships through communication: Relational, contextual, and cultural variations* (pp. 31–50). Mahwah, NJ: Erlbaum.

Waldron, H. B., Turner, C. W., Alexander, J. F., & Barton, C. (1993). Coding defensive and supportive communications: Discriminant validity and subcategory convergence. *Journal of Family Psychology, 7*, 197–203.

Waldvogel, J. (2007). Greetings and closings in workplace email. *Journal of Computer-Mediated Communication, 12*, 122–143.

Wallace, P. (1999). *The psychology of the Internet.* Cambridge, UK: Cambridge University Press.

Wallack, T. (2005, 24 January). Blogs: Beware if your blog is related to work. *The San Francisco Chronicle.* Retrieved from http://www.sfgate.com

Walther, J. B., & Parks, M. R. (2002). Cues filtered out, cues filtered in: Computer-mediated communication and relationships. In M. L. Knapp & J. A. Daly (Eds.), *Handbook of interpersonal communication* (3rd ed., pp. 529–563). Thousand Oaks, CA: Sage.

Walther, J. B., Van Der Heide, B., Hamel, L., & Schulman, H. (2008, May). *Self-generated versus other-generated statements and impressions in computer-mediated communication: A test of warranting theory using Facebook.* Paper presented at the annual meeting of the International Communication Association, Montreal, Canada.

Walther, J. B., Van Der Heide, B., Kim, S. Y., Westerman, D., & Tong, S. T. (2008). The role of friends' appearance and behavior on evaluations of individuals on Facebook: Are we known by the company we keep? *Human Communication Research, 34*, 28–49.

Wang, H., & Andersen, P. A. (2007, May). *Computer-mediated communication in relationship maintenance: An examination of self-disclosure in long-distance friendships.* Paper presented at the annual meeting of the International Communication Association, San Francisco, CA.

Warr, P. B., and Payne, R. (1982). Experiences of strain and pleasure among British adults. *Social Science & Medicine, 16*(19), 1691–1697.

Waterman, A. (1984). *The psychology of individualism.* New York: Praeger.

Watson, K. W., Barker, L. L., & Weaver, J. B., III. (1995). The listening styles profile (LSP-16): Development and validation of an instrument to assess four listening styles. *International Journal of Listening, 9*, 1–13.

Watzlawick, P., Beavin, J. H., & Jackson, D. D. (1967). *Pragmatics of human communication: A study of interactional patterns, pathologies, and paradoxes.* New York: Norton.

Weger, H., & Emmett, M. C. (2009). Romantic intent, relationship uncertainty, and relationship maintenance in young adults' cross-sex friendships. *Journal of Social and Personal Relationships, 26*(6–7), 964–988.

Weinberg, N., Schmale, J. D., Uken, J., & Wessel, K. (1995). Computer-mediated support groups. *Social Work with Groups, 17*, 43–55.

Weisz, C., & Wood, L. F. (2005). Social identity support and friendship outcomes: A longitudinal study predicting who will be friends and best friends 4 years later. *Journal of Social and Personal Relationships, 22*(3), 416–432.

Welch, R. D., & Houser, M. E. (2010). Extending the four-category model of adult attachment: An interpersonal model of friendship attachment. *Journal of Social and Personal Relationships, 27*(3), 351–366.

Wellman, B. (1992). Men in networks: Private communities, domestic friendships. In P. M. Nardi (Ed.), *Men's friendships: Vol. 2. Research on men and masculinities* (pp. 74–114). Newbury Park, CA: Sage.

Wells, G. L., Lindsay, R. C. L., & Tousignant, J. P. (1980). Effects of expert psychological advice on human performance in judging the validity of eyewitness testimony. *Law and Human Behavior, 4*, 275–285.

Wheeless, L. R. (1978). A follow-up study of the relationships among trust, disclosure, and interpersonal solidarity. *Human Communication Research, 4*, 143–145.

White, G. L. (1980). Physical attractiveness and courtship progress. *Journal of Personality and Social Psychology, 39*, 660–668.

Whorf, B. L. (1952). *Collected papers on metalinguistics.* Washington, DC: Department of State, Foreign Service Institute.

Widmer, E., Treas, J., & Newcomb, R. (1998). Attitudes toward nonmarital sex in 24 countries. *Journal of Sex Research, 35*, 349–358.

Wiederman, M. W., & Kendall, E. (1999). Evolution, sex, and jealousy: Investigation with a sample from Sweden. *Evolution and Human Behavior, 20*, 121–128.

Wiemann, J. M. (1977). Explication and test of a model of communicative competence. *Human Communication Research, 3*, 195–213.

Williams, W. L. (1992). The relationship between male-male friendship and male-female marriage: American Indian and Asian comparisons. In P. M. Nardi (Ed.), *Men's friendships: Vol. 2. Research on men and masculinities* (pp. 186–200). Newbury Park, CA: Sage.

Wilmot, W. W., & Hocker, J. L. (2010). *Interpersonal conflict* (8th ed.). Boston: McGraw-Hill.

Winstead, B. A., Derlaga, V. J., & Rose, S. (1997). *Gender and close relationships.* Thousand Oaks, CA: Sage.

Winterson, J. (1993). *Written on the body.* New York: Knopf.

Wolvin, A. D. (1987). *Culture as a listening variable.* Paper presented at the summer conference of the International Listening Association, Toronto, Canada.

Wolvin, A., & Coakley, C. G. (1996). *Listening.* Madison, WI: Brown & Benchmark.

Wood, J. T. (1998). *But I thought you meant . . . : Misunderstandings in human communication.* Mountain View, CA: Mayfield.

Wood, W., Rhodes, N., & Whelan, M. (1989). Sex differences in positive well-being: A consideration of emotional style and marital status. *Psychological Bulletin, 106*, 249–264.

Worthen, J. B., Garcia-Rivas, G., Green, C. R., & Vidos, R. A. (2000). Tests of a cognitive-resource-allocation account of the bizarreness effect. *Journal of General Psychology, 127*, 117–144.

Wu, C. (2011, September 21). Students vote to adopt gender-neutral constitution. *The Student Life.* Retrieved from http://tsl.pomona.edu/articles/2011/9/22/news/356-students-vote-to-adopt-gender-neutral-constitution

Wu, D. Y. H., & Tseng, W. (1985). Introduction: The characteristics of Chinese culture. In W. Tseng & D. Y. H. Wu (Eds.), *Chinese culture and mental health* (pp. 3–13). Orlando, FL: Academic Press.

YouTube Statistics. (n.d.). Retrieved from http://www.youtube .com/t/press_statistics

Zacchilli, T. L., Hendrick, C., & Hendrick, S. S. (2009). The romantic partner conflict scale: A new scale to measure relationship conflict. *Journal of Social and Personal Relationships, 26,* 1073–1096.

Zahn-Waxler, C. (2001). The development of empathy, guilt, and internalization of distress: Implications for gender differences in internalizing and externalizing problems. In R. Davidson (Ed.), *Anxiety, depression, and emotion: Wisconsin symposium on emotion, Vol. 1* (pp. 222–265). New York: Oxford University Press.

Znaniecki, F. (1934). *The method of sociology.* New York: Farrar & Rinehart.

Zorn, T. E. (1995). Bosses and buddies: Constructing and performing simultaneously hierarchical and close friendship relationships. In J. T. Wood & S. Duck (Eds.), *Under-studied relationships: Off the beaten track* (pp. 122–147). Thousand Oaks, CA: Sage.

Zuckerman, M., Hodgins, H., & Miyake, K. (1990). The vocal attractiveness paradigm: Replication and elaboration. *Journal of Nonverbal Behavior, 14,* 97–112.

Zuckerman, M., Miyake, K., & Hodgins, H. S. (1991). Crosschannel effects of vocal and physical attractiveness and their implications for interpersonal perception. *Journal of Personality and Social Psychology, 60,* 545–554.

Credits

Text Credits

23, Snyder, M., adapted from "Self-Monitoring of Expressive Behavior," *Journal of Personality and Social Psychology*, 1974, Volume 30, Issue 4 (Oct). Copyright © 1974 by the American Psychological Association. Adapted with permission of the American Psychological Association and Mark Snyder; **24,** *The Credo of the National Communication Association.* Reprinted with permission of the National Communication Association; **91,** John, O. P., & Srivastava, S., "What Kind of Personality Do You Have?" from *The Big-Five Trait Taxonomy: History, Measurement, and Theoretical Perspectives.* Used by permission of the author; **100,** Stiff, J. B., Dillard, J. P., Somera, L., Kim, H., & Sleight, C. Quiz adapted from "Empathy, Communication, and Pro-Social Behavior." Copyright © 1988 *Communication Monographs.* Reprinted by permission of Taylor & Francis, www.informa.com; **134,** Auden, W. H. "Stop All the Clocks" from *The Collected Poems* by W. H. Auden. Copyright © 1940 and renewed 1968 by W. H. Auden. Used by permission of Random House and Curtis Brown, Ltd; **252,** Table 8.1., "Power Distance across Countries." Based on Geert Hofstede, Gert Jan Hofstede, and Michael Minkov, *Cultures and Organizations: Software of the Mind*, 3rd revised edition. McGraw-Hill, 2010. Used by permission of Geert Hofstede BV; **300–304,** Stafford, L., & Canary, D. J. From "Maintenance Strategies and Romantic Relationship Type, Gender, and Relational Characteristics." *Journal of Social and Personal Relationships*, Vol. 8, No. 2, 217–242. Copyright © 1991 by *Journal of Social and Personal Relationships.* Reprinted by permission of Sage Publications via Copyright Clearance Center; **316,** Five Common Signs of an Abusive Partner. Adapted from "Indicators of Abusive Relationships," An Abuse, Rape, Domestic Violence, Aid, and Resource Collection (AARDVARC). Copyright © 2009 by AARDVARC.org, Inc. http://www.aardvarc.org/legal.shtml; **335,** Francesca Bell, "Making You Noise." First appeared in *Nimrod.* Copyright © Francesca Bell. Used with permission of the author.

Art Credits

Key: CO = Corbis, EC = courtesy, The Everett Collection, GI = Getty Images, PF = Photofest

Inside front cover, (top to bottom) David M. Grossman/ The Image Works; Nick David/GI; (left) © Peter Coombs/ Alamy; (right) Bedford/St. Martin's; GI; **xxiii,** Virginia Hagin; **xxiv,** Photo by Scott Rosenfeld; AP Photo/Wide World; **xxv,** Photo by G. N. Miller/MaMa Foundation, Gospel for Teens; **xxvi,** Michael Krasowitz/GI; **xxvii,** Washington Crossing the Delaware River, 25th December 1776, 1851 (oil on canvas) (copy of an original painted in 1848), Leutze, Emanuel Gottlieb (1816–68)/Metropolitan Museum of Art, New York, USA/The Bridgeman Art Library; **xviii,** The Beaver Family, 1907. Whyte Museum of the Canadian Rockies, #V527, by Mary Schaffer, Photographer; **xix,** Erin Patrice O'Brien; **xxx,** GI (large snowy landscape image); © TopFoto/The Image Works (portraits); **xxxi,** MCT/Newscom; **xxxii,** Frazer Harrison/GI for AFI; David Joel/GI; **2–4,** Virginia Hagin; **6,** © Fox Searchlight/EC; **7,** © Kelly-Mooney Photography/CO; **12,** Katja Heinemann/Aurora; **14,** AP Photo/Mark Lennihan; **15,** Ben Glass/© Warner Bros. Pictures/EC; **17,** Kris Timken/GI; **18,** © Bettmann/CO; **21,** © Comedy Central/EC; **22,** Arthur Schatz/Time Life Pictures/GI; **28,** (top left) Danny Lehman/CO; (top right) Heiko Meyer/laif/ Redux Pictures; (bottom left) Carl De Keyzer/Magnum Photos; (bottom right) Kelvin Murray/GI; **31,** © Kristin Gerbert/zefa/CO; **33,** Virginia Hagin; **36–38,** Photo by Scott Rosenfeld; **40,** Cornell Capa © International Center of Photography/Magnum Photos; **43,** (t.) © Randy Faris/CO; (b.) GI; **46,** (l.) Nancy Honey/GI; (center) Caroline Penn/Panos Pictures; (r.) Digital Vision/Punchstock; **47,** Allan Grant/Time & Life Pictures/GI; **49,** John Dominis/Time & Life Pictures/GI; **50,** (l.–r.) West Rock/GI; © Image Source/ Alamy; © John Elk III/Alamy; © Exotica.im 15/Alamy; **51,** (l.) © Paul A. Souders/CO; (r.) © David R. Frazier Photolibrary, Inc./ Alamy; **52,** Photo AP/The Arizona Republic, Michael Chow; **54,** Courtesy of Facebook Inc; **55,** Brendan McDermid/Reuters/ Landov; **58,** Dreamworks LLC/The Kobal Collection; **60,** Cathy Yeulet/123RF.com; **64,** Cliff Lipson/CBS/Landov; **67,** © Lawrence Manning/CO; **68,** Time & Life Pictures/GI; **69,** Photo by Scott Rosenfeld; **72–74,** AP Photo/Wide World; **75,** Stephen Vaughan/© Warner Bros./EC; **79,** (l.–r.) © Royalty-Free/CO; Tom Schierlitz/GI; © Royalty-Free/CO; © Royalty-Free/CO; **82,** © David Grossman/The Image Works; **83,** (t.) © Cindy Charles/PhotoEdit; (c.) Jonas Ingerstedt/GI; (b.) David R. Frazier/The Image Works; **85,** AP Photo/Evan Vucci; **86,** www.livescience.com; **88,** Fox Photos/GI; **89,** Marc Brown; **93,** © Bettmann/CO; **96,** Suzanne Hanover/© Universal Pictures/EC; **97,** Photo by Chi Modu/diverseimages/GI; **99,** (l.) AP/Wide World Photos; (r.) © Bettmann/CO; **101,** Courtesy of the Peace Corps; **103,** Michael Krasowitz/GI; **105,** AP Photo/Wide World; **108–110,** Photo by G. N. Miller/MaMa Foundation, Gospel for Teens; **112,** Raul Arboleda/AFP/GI; **114,** (l.) Blasius Erlinger/GI; (r.) AP Photo/Pat Sullivan; **115,** Ferdinando Scianna/Magnum Photos; **116,** (l.–r.) © Lisa B./CO; Ferdinando Scianna/Magnum Photos; Digital Vision/ GI; Randy Faris/CO; **117,** (l.) Richard Kalvar/Magnum Photos; (r.) © David Leeson/Dallas Morning News/Sygma/CO; **118,** Justin Lane/AFP/GI; **122,** © Quinn Kirk/Terry Wild Stock; **125,** Chris Helcermanas-Benge/© Summit Entertainment/EC; **128,** (l.) © Steve Hix/Somos Images/CO; (r.) © Michael Doolittle/Alamy; **130,** (l.) © Richard Schulman/CO; (c.) Phil Schermeister/GI; (r.) Justin Guariglia/NGS/GI; **133,** Max Nash/AFP/GI; **135,** © Arko Datta/Reuters/CO; **136,** AP Photo/Jessica Hill; **139,** Michael Krasowitz/GI; **140,** Damon Winter; **141,** Photo by G. N. Miller/ MaMa Foundation, Gospel for Teens; **144–145,** Michael Krasowitz/GI; **148,** © FilmDistrict/EC; **149,** © Neal Preston/CO; **152,** Disabled American Veterans (DAV) www.dav.org; **154,** (l.) © Philip Gould/CO; (r.) © Jason Lee/Reuters/CO; **157,** (l.) Zeng Yi/ Xinhua/Landov; (r.) Stephen Dunn/GI; **158,** Scott Gries/© The Learning Channel/EC; **160,** (l.) Scott Olson/GI; (r.) Creatas/ Newscom; **161,** Niko Tavernise/TM and copyright © Fox Searchlight Pictures. All rights reserved/EC; **165,** NBC/PF; **167,** 20th Century Fox/The Kobal Collection/Art Resource; **169,** Rafal Olechowski/Shutterstock; **170,** (l.–r.) Bernd Opitz/Getty Images; © Lucidio Studio Inc./CO; Somos/Punchstock; Photodisc/Alamy; **171,** Michael Krasowitz/GI; **174–175,** Washington Crossing the Delaware River, 25th December 1776, 1851 (oil on canvas) (copy of an original painted in 1848), Leutze, Emanuel Gottlieb (1816–68)/ Metropolitan Museum of Art, New York, USA/The Bridgeman Art Library; **178,** (t.) Bloomberg via GI; (b. l.–r.) © Royalty-Free/CO; White Packert/GI; Photodisc/GI; **179,** (t. r.) © Mary Evans

▶ *VideoCentral: Interpersonal Communication*

bedfordstmartins.com/reflectrelate

Check out all that *VideoCentral: Interpersonal Communication* has to offer. Below is a complete list (by chapter) of every video available in the collection. An asterisk notes which videos also appear in the VideoCentral book feature, while the page number will help you locate each term in the text quickly. For directions on how to access these videos online, please see the instructions to the right.